Laplace Transform Theory and Electrical Transients

(formerly titled *Transformation Calculus and Electrical Transients*)

BY

STANFORD GOLDMAN, Ph.D.

Professor of Electrical Engineering
Syracuse University

DOVER PUBLICATIONS, INC.

NEW YORK

Published in Canada by General Publishing Company, Ltd., 30 Lesmill Road, Don Mills, Toronto, Ontario.
Published in the United Kingdom by Constable and Company, Ltd., 10 Orange Street, London WC 2.

This Dover edition, first published in 1966, is an unabridged and unaltered republication of the fifth printing (1955) of the work originally published by Prentice-Hall, Inc., in 1949 under the title *Transformation Calculus and Electrical Transients.*

Standard Book Number: 486-61741-6
Library of Congress Catalog Card Number: 66-29558

Manufactured in the United States of America
Dover Publications, Inc.
180 Varick Street
New York, N.Y. 10014

To Dorothy

Preface

This book deals with certain branches of mathematics that should be standard working tools for development and research workers in electrical engineering. The principal aim of the book is to develop the methods of the Laplace transformation and its inverse for the solution of problems in electrical circuit transients.

The book emphasizes questions of physical interpretation and gives the solution of many important examples. Almost all the mathematical results obtained have appeared previously, but it is believed that many have been arrived at in the present book by considerably simpler means. The book attempts to give a comprehensive and systematic treatment of the subject of transients in linear networks. Non-linear networks are not treated.

A word is in order concerning the name "transformation calculus." Many of the problems treated in this book are similar to those treated by Heaviside's operational calculus. The emphasis, however, has shifted from the question of an operational point of view to the question of transformations between the t axis and the s plane. Thus, for example, the derivation of the relation between attenuation and phase characteristics is certainly not an operational problem. Accordingly, the author has taken the liberty to coin the term "transformation calculus."

It is assumed that as a prerequisite for reading the present book the student has a knowledge of calculus and some general engineering background, and that he has an elementary knowledge of complex quantities and differential equations.

The book is written at the level of seniors or graduate students in electrical engineering or applied mathematics. It can be used as the text of either a one-semester or full year's course of three lectures per week, depending upon how much of the material is to be covered.

Like the author's *Frequency Analysis, Modulation and Noise*, the book had its origin in out-of-hours courses taught to the engineers of the Electronics Receiver Division of the General Electric Company.

The book was completed during the period of the author's residence at the Massachusetts Institute of Technology.

The author has received assistance from many friends and colleagues in the preparation of the book. He wishes particularly to mention A. W. Sear, R. B. Dome, Max Scherberg, J. F. McAllister, Jr., Jorgan Jensen, B. F. Mills, W. E. Vivian, W. H. Kautz, G. C. Newton, Jr., and S. J. Mason. He also wishes to thank I. J. Kaar and C. G. Fick, who arranged for the General Electric Company's sponsorship of the early work. Finally, he wishes to express his appreciation to George Allen for his skillful preparation of the illustrations.

Stanford Goldman

Massachusetts Institute of Technology
Cambridge, Massachusetts

Contents

CHAPTER 3

Transient Solutions of Circuit Problems by Means of the Laplace Transformation

CHAPTER 4

Some Fundamental Concepts and Relations in Circuit Theory

CHAPTER 5

Theory of Functions of a Complex Variable

CHAPTER 6

LOCI OF COMPLEX FUNCTIONS

CHAPTER 7

THE INVERSION THEOREM AND RELATED TOPICS

CHAPTER 8

Gamma and Error Functions

CHAPTER 9

Bessel Functions

CHAPTER 10

Transients in Transmission Lines—Solution of Partial Differential Equations

CHAPTER 11

Solutions in Series

CHAPTER 12

Some Additional Applications to Electrical Engineering

Laplace Transform Theory
and
Electrical Transients

Introduction

In the author's *Frequency Analysis, Modulation and Noise,* it was pointed out that the salient features of mathematics, among them those features which allow mathematics to give an insight into the physical world, are what may be called the *phenomena of mathematics.* Taylor series expansions and Fourier series expansions are examples of mathematical phenomena with which the reader is no doubt familiar. The development of mathematics consists to a large extent of the discovery and application of various phenomena of mathematics. These phenomena, like those of the natural sciences, are of interest not only because they are useful, but often even more so because they have an intrinsic appeal to the human intellect.

This is a book about a branch of applied mathematics, and as such it also is a book about phenomena of mathematics. Foremost among those we shall meet are the properties of analytic functions of a complex variable. The simplicity which the use of these functions introduces into the study of a wide variety of physical phenomena, especially transients, is astonishing. Difficult problems in the time domain can be reduced to relative simplicity by transformation of these problems into the plane of the complex variable, s. The poles in the s plane of the admittance functions of a network determine the properties of its transient response as the genes of the chromosomes determine the characteristics of living things. The relation between the poles and the transients, however, is mathematically exact and we shall learn how to calculate one from the other.

Transformation calculus adds many new points of view to those of elementary calculus. Thus, in elementary calculus, the value of a function at an arbitrary point—its life history, as it were—is studied in terms of its properties at a given point, namely the value of the function and its derivatives of all orders at the given point. In transformation calculus, on the other hand, the life history is expressed as a superposition integral of elementary functions.

These elementary functions may be step functions or impulse functions, or, as in the case of Fourier integrals, they may be sine waves. When, however, the elementary functions are the exponential functions of a Bromwich integral, they are especially useful, for they can reduce the solution of the differential equations of networks to simple algebraic manipulations.

It will be our purpose in this book to develop the tools of transformation calculus, starting from a level at which we hope that any electrical engineer will be prepared to begin. We will try to keep the discussion as elementary as is consistent with a thorough understanding of what we are doing. We will also try to arrive at useful and practical results as early as possible so that the reader will not have to read the entire book before he has acquired useful tools.

CHAPTER 1
Determinants

1.1. Introduction

Suppose we have two simultaneous equations

$$a_{11}x + a_{12}y = k_1 \tag{1}$$
$$a_{21}x + a_{22}y = k_2 \tag{2}$$

and we wish to solve for x and y. To do this, we eliminate one variable, say y. Thus we multiply Eq. (1) by a_{22} and Eq. (2) by a_{12}, and subtract Eq. (2) from Eq. (1). Accordingly, we get

$$(a_{11}a_{22} - a_{21}a_{12})x = k_1a_{22} - k_2a_{12} \qquad \text{or} \qquad x = \frac{k_1a_{22} - k_2a_{12}}{a_{11}a_{22} - a_{21}a_{12}} \tag{3}$$

If we had eliminated x instead, we would have obtained

$$(a_{11}a_{22} - a_{21}a_{12})y = k_2a_{11} - k_1a_{21} \qquad \text{or} \qquad y = \frac{k_2a_{11} - k_1a_{21}}{a_{11}a_{22} - a_{21}a_{12}} \tag{4}$$

Since the solution of simultaneous equations of the form of Eqs. (1) and (2) proceeds in a perfectly standard manner, it is convenient for us to write it down immediately from the original equations without the intermediate steps. We can do so with the aid of some mathematical symbols known as determinants. Accordingly, Eqs. (3) and (4) may be written

$$x = \frac{\begin{vmatrix} k_1 & a_{12} \\ k_2 & a_{22} \end{vmatrix}}{\begin{vmatrix} a_{11} & a_{12} \\ a_{21} & a_{22} \end{vmatrix}} \tag{5}$$

$$y = \frac{\begin{vmatrix} a_{11} & k_1 \\ a_{21} & k_2 \end{vmatrix}}{\begin{vmatrix} a_{11} & a_{12} \\ a_{21} & a_{22} \end{vmatrix}} \tag{6}$$

The quantities $\begin{vmatrix} k_1 & a_{12} \\ k_2 & a_{22} \end{vmatrix}$, $\begin{vmatrix} a_{11} & k_1 \\ a_{21} & k_2 \end{vmatrix}$, and $\begin{vmatrix} a_{11} & a_{12} \\ a_{21} & a_{22} \end{vmatrix}$

are called determinants—in particular, determinants of the second order. The value of the determinant

$$\begin{vmatrix} A & B \\ C & D \end{vmatrix}$$

is $AD - BC$.

As can be seen in Eqs. (5) and (6), the value of either of the variables, x or y, is the quotient of two determinants. The components of the determinant in the denominator are the coefficients of x and y. The determinant in the numerator is obtained from the one in the denominator by substituting the constants on the right side of the equation for the coefficients of the variable whose value is wanted.

The method of Eqs. (5) and (6) for solving simultaneous linear equations can be extended to any number of variables. Before proving this, however, we wish to consider some general properties of determinants in the following sections.

Exercise

From the equations

$$\begin{aligned} 4x - 2y &= 2 \\ 2x + y &= 7 \end{aligned}$$

find x and y by using Eqs. (5) and (6).

1.2. Definitions

Analogous to the definition of a determinant of the second order, we define a determinant of the third order.

$$\begin{vmatrix} a_{11} & a_{12} & a_{13} \\ a_{21} & a_{22} & a_{23} \\ a_{31} & a_{32} & a_{33} \end{vmatrix} = a_{11}a_{22}a_{33} - a_{11}a_{32}a_{23} + a_{31}a_{12}a_{23} - a_{21}a_{12}a_{33} + a_{21}a_{32}a_{13} - a_{31}a_{22}a_{13} \quad (7)$$

For convenience, we shall now define a few terms commonly used in connection with determinants.

An *element* of a determinant is any one of the individual quantities in the determinant a_{11}, a_{21}, a_{22} --- etc.

A *column* of a determinant is a vertical group of the elements, such as

$$\begin{matrix} a_{11} \\ a_{21} \\ a_{31} \end{matrix}$$

A *row* of a determinant is a horizontal group of the elements, such as

$$a_{21}\ a_{22}\ a_{23}$$

The group of elements

$$\begin{matrix} a_{11} & & \\ & a_{22} & \\ & & a_{33} \end{matrix}$$

is called the *main diagonal* of a determinant.

Returning now to the consideration of Eq. (7), we see that on the right side we have terms consisting of every possible combination of the elements of the determinant in which each term has only one element from each column and one from each row. We shall show that the sign of each term is determined from the order of the first subscripts of the elements in it after the elements are arranged so that their second subscripts are in numerical order. The first subscript tells from which row each element came, and the second subscript tells from which column. Thus the order of row subscripts of the first term is 1 2 3. This term, incidentally, is obtained from the main diagonal. The order of row subscripts of any other term can be made the same as that of the main diagonal term by an interchange of numbers. Thus the order of row subscripts of the term $a_{21}a_{32}a_{13}$ is 2 3 1. This order can be made the same as the diagonal order (1 2 3) by interchanging first 1 and 3 to give (2 1 3) and then 2 and 1 to give (1 2 3). We note that two interchanges were required, altogether.

Having thus pointed out the meaning of interchanges, we state the following rules for determining the sign of a term. *First arrange the elements of a term in the numerical order of their columns in the determinant.* Then

Rule I: *If an odd number of interchanges is necessary to make the order of row subscripts of a term the same as that of the main diagonal, the sign of the term is* (−).

Rule II: *If an even number of interchanges is necessary to make the order of row subscripts of a term the same as that of the main diagonal, the sign of the term is* (+).

The student may now verify this rule for all the terms in Eq. (7).

It should be pointed out that an order of *row* subscripts can be brought to the diagonal order by interchanges in a variety of ways. Thus, consider the order (3 2 1). By interchanging 1 and 2, we get (3 1 2). Then interchanging 1 and 3, we get (1 3 2). Finally, interchanging 2 and 3, we get (1 2 3). Three interchanges were made, altogether. However, if in the original order (3 2 1) we had interchanged 3 and 1, we would have obtained the order (1 2 3) in one interchange. The sign of the term, however, is unaffected by the method of interchanging used, since both one and three are odd numbers, both making the sign of the term $(-)$. The student will find that the particular method of interchanging used will never affect the sign of the terms. The reason is that the number of interchanges for a given term is either always even or always odd, no matter in what order the interchanging is performed. This can be proved, but the proof is lengthy and will not be given here.

Continuing our definitions, we define a *determinant of the fourth order* as the sum of 24 terms, each term being the product of four elements of the determinant, but no term containing more than one element from each column and one from each row.[1] Thus

$$\begin{vmatrix} a_{11} & a_{12} & a_{13} & a_{14} \\ a_{21} & a_{22} & a_{23} & a_{24} \\ a_{31} & a_{32} & a_{33} & a_{34} \\ a_{41} & a_{42} & a_{43} & a_{44} \end{vmatrix} = \sum_{24 \text{ terms}} \pm\, a_{q1}a_{r2}a_{s3}a_{t4} \tag{8}$$

where q, r, s, and t are any one of the 24 possible arrangements of (1,2,3,4). The sign of each term is determined by Rules I and II. The definitions of determinants of higher order can be made by appropriate generalizations.

Exercise

Show that

$$\begin{vmatrix} 2 & 1 & 6 & 4 \\ 4 & 9 & 4 & 2 \\ 5 & 0 & 6 & 2 \\ 4 & 9 & 4 & 2 \end{vmatrix} = 0$$

by expanding the determinant in accordance with Eq. (8).

1.3. A convenient method for determining the sign of a term

Suppose we have the order of row subscripts q, r, s, t. If this is the diagonal order, then each row subscript is less than all the

[1] The symbol Σ (capital sigma) is generally used to indicate a summation. Thus the right side of Eq. (8) consists of the sum of the 24 terms obtained by substituting 1, 2, 3, and 4 in all possible combinations for q, r, s, and t, with the sign of each term determined by Rules I and II.

following row subscripts. If the order is not diagonal, then we can record for each row subscript the number of following row subscripts which it exceeds. We shall then find the following convenient rule for determining the sign of a term in a determinant.

Rule III: *To find the sign of a term, first arrange the elements of the term in the numerical order of their columns in the determinant. Then write down the row subscripts in the order in which they occur in the term. Record for each row subscript the number of following row subscripts which it exceeds, and add all these recorded numbers. If the sum is an even number, the sign of the term is* (+). *If the sum is an odd number, the sign of the term is* (−).

The student can show as an exercise that Rule III will always give the same answer as Rules I and II.

Rule III is ordinarily the most convenient method for finding the signs of terms. Suppose we apply it to a few terms in Eq. (7). Take the term $a_{31}a_{22}a_{13}$. Here the order of row subscripts is (3 2 1). Now 3 exceeds two following numbers, namely 2 and 1. Therefore, let us record 2. Furthermore, 2 exceeds one following number, namely 1. Therefore record 1. Adding the recorded numbers, we obtain 3. Since 3 is odd, the sign of $a_{31}a_{22}a_{13}$ is (−).

As another example, take the term $a_{21}a_{32}a_{13}$. Here 2 exceeds 1, and we record 1. Furthermore, 3 exceeds 1, and we record another 1. Adding the recorded numbers, we get 2, which is even. Therefore the sign of $a_{21}a_{32}a_{13}$ is (+).

1.4. Some important properties of determinants

Theorem I: *Any determinant is not altered in value if in its symbol we replace the elements of the first, second --- nth rows by the elements which formerly appeared in the same order in the first, second, --- nth columns.* Or briefly:

A determinant is not altered in value if we interchange the corresponding columns and rows. Thus

$$\begin{vmatrix} a_{11} & a_{12} \\ a_{21} & a_{22} \end{vmatrix} = a_{11}a_{22} - a_{12}a_{21} = \begin{vmatrix} a_{11} & a_{21} \\ a_{12} & a_{22} \end{vmatrix} \tag{9}$$

$$\begin{vmatrix} a_{11} & a_{12} & a_{13} \\ a_{21} & a_{22} & a_{23} \\ a_{31} & a_{32} & a_{33} \end{vmatrix} = \begin{vmatrix} a_{11} & a_{21} & a_{31} \\ a_{12} & a_{22} & a_{32} \\ a_{13} & a_{23} & a_{33} \end{vmatrix} \tag{10}$$

Or, in general,

$$\begin{vmatrix} a_{11} & a_{12} & \cdots & a_{1n} \\ a_{21} & a_{22} & \cdots & a_{2n} \\ \vdots & \vdots & & \vdots \\ a_{n1} & a_{n2} & \cdots & a_{nn} \end{vmatrix} = \begin{vmatrix} a_{11} & a_{21} & \cdots & a_{n1} \\ a_{12} & a_{22} & \cdots & a_{n2} \\ \vdots & \vdots & & \vdots \\ a_{1n} & a_{2n} & \cdots & a_{nn} \end{vmatrix} \tag{11}$$

The student can readily verify this theorem for determinants of the second and third orders by direct substitution.[2] A proof can readily be given for determinants of the nth order although we shall not give it here.

Exercise

Show that by actually evaluating the determinants,

$$\begin{vmatrix} 2 & 1 & 4 \\ 2 & 2 & 0 \\ 5 & 3 & 1 \end{vmatrix} = \begin{vmatrix} 2 & 2 & 5 \\ 1 & 2 & 3 \\ 4 & 0 & 1 \end{vmatrix}$$

Theorem II: *A determinant is merely changed in sign by an interchange of any two of its columns.* Thus

$$\begin{vmatrix} a_{11} & a_{12} \\ a_{21} & a_{22} \end{vmatrix} = a_{11}a_{22} - a_{12}a_{21} = -\begin{vmatrix} a_{12} & a_{11} \\ a_{22} & a_{21} \end{vmatrix} \tag{12}$$

and

$$\begin{vmatrix} a_{11} & a_{12} & a_{13} \\ a_{21} & a_{22} & a_{23} \\ a_{31} & a_{32} & a_{33} \end{vmatrix} = -\begin{vmatrix} a_{12} & a_{11} & a_{13} \\ a_{22} & a_{21} & a_{23} \\ a_{32} & a_{31} & a_{33} \end{vmatrix} \tag{13}$$

Proof: Suppose the p'th and q'th columns are interchanged. Then each term of the first determinant can be obtained from a term of the second determinant by means of one interchange in the order of subscripts. Thus each term in one determinant has its negative as a term in the other. Consequently, the determinants themselves are the negatives of each other.

---

[2] In expanding the determinants in equations such as Eqs. (9) and (10), the student is cautioned to recall that the "row subscripts" referred to in Rules I, II, and III stand for row numbers. Thus, for example, the "row subscript" of a_{21} in the determinant on the right side of Eq. (9) is 1 as far as Rules I, II, and III are concerned. In other words, the sign of a term is determined by the *location* of its elements in the determinant, and not by any fortuitous subscripts that these elements may happen to have.

Exercise

Show that by evaluating the determinants,

$$\begin{vmatrix} 6 & 4 & 1 \\ 2 & 1 & 1 \\ -5 & 1 & -2 \end{vmatrix} = -\begin{vmatrix} 6 & 1 & 4 \\ 2 & 1 & 1 \\ -5 & -2 & 1 \end{vmatrix}$$

Theorem III: *A determinant is merely changed in sign by the interchange of any two rows.* Thus

$$\begin{vmatrix} a_{11} & a_{12} \\ a_{21} & a_{22} \end{vmatrix} = a_{11}a_{22} - a_{12}a_{21} = -\begin{vmatrix} a_{21} & a_{22} \\ a_{11} & a_{12} \end{vmatrix} \tag{14}$$

and

$$\begin{vmatrix} a_{11} & a_{12} & a_{13} \\ a_{21} & a_{22} & a_{23} \\ a_{31} & a_{32} & a_{33} \end{vmatrix} = -\begin{vmatrix} a_{21} & a_{22} & a_{23} \\ a_{11} & a_{12} & a_{13} \\ a_{31} & a_{32} & a_{33} \end{vmatrix} \tag{15}$$

Proof: By Theorem I, we can interchange the columns and rows. The present theorem then becomes the same as Theorem II.

Exercise

Show that

$$\begin{vmatrix} 6 & 4 & 1 \\ 2 & 1 & 1 \\ -5 & 1 & -2 \end{vmatrix} = -\begin{vmatrix} 2 & 1 & 1 \\ 6 & 4 & 1 \\ -5 & 1 & -2 \end{vmatrix}$$

Theorem IV: *If any two columns or any two rows of a determinant are identical, the value of the determinant is zero.* Thus

$$\begin{vmatrix} a_{11} & a_{11} \\ a_{21} & a_{21} \end{vmatrix} = a_{11}a_{21} - a_{11}a_{21} = 0 \tag{16}$$

and

$$\begin{vmatrix} a_{11} & a_{12} & a_{11} \\ a_{21} & a_{22} & a_{21} \\ a_{31} & a_{32} & a_{31} \end{vmatrix} = 0 \tag{17}$$

Proof: If we interchange the identical columns, or identical rows, the determinant remains unaltered. However, by Theorems II and III it must change sign. This is only possible if the value of the determinant is zero. Q.E.D.

One of the principal values of determinants is their use in the rapid solution of simultaneous equations. The preceding four theorems allow certain manipulations to be made which, as we shall find later, aid in the rapid evaluation of determinants. By using *minors* (to be discussed in the following paragraphs), these theorems can be brought to bear on sections of a determinant when they may not be valuable in dealing with the determinant as a whole. Thus with the aid of these theorems, in conjunction with expansion in minors, large sections of the calculations in evaluating determinants can be eliminated or greatly simplified.

The foregoing theorems are also the basis for further theorems, which culminate in §1.9, where it is proved how determinants can be used to solve simultaneous linear equations of any number.

Exercise

Show that

$$\begin{vmatrix} 4 & 4 & 2 \\ 1 & 1 & 6 \\ 7 & 7 & 3 \end{vmatrix} = 0$$

1.5. Minors

Definition: The determinant of order $n - 1$ obtained by removing the row and column crossing at a given element of a determinant of order n is called the minor of that element.

For example, in the determinant

$$\begin{vmatrix} a_{11} & a_{12} & a_{13} \\ a_{21} & a_{22} & a_{23} \\ a_{31} & a_{32} & a_{33} \end{vmatrix}$$

the minor of a_{11} is

$$\begin{vmatrix} a_{22} & a_{23} \\ a_{32} & a_{33} \end{vmatrix}$$

and is usually written A_{11}.

The minor of a_{23} is

$$\begin{vmatrix} a_{11} & a_{12} \\ a_{31} & a_{32} \end{vmatrix} = A_{23}$$

and so on.

1.6. Expansion of determinants in terms of the elements of a row or column, and their minors

Let us write

$$D = \begin{vmatrix} a_{11} & a_{12} & a_{13} \\ a_{21} & a_{22} & a_{23} \\ a_{31} & a_{32} & a_{33} \end{vmatrix} \tag{18}$$

Then $D = a_{11}a_{22}a_{33} - a_{11}a_{32}a_{23} - a_{21}a_{12}a_{33} + a_{21}a_{32}a_{13}$
$+ a_{31}a_{12}a_{23} - a_{31}a_{22}a_{13}$

$$= a_{11}(a_{22}a_{33} - a_{32}a_{23}) - a_{21}(a_{12}a_{33} - a_{32}a_{13}) + a_{31}(a_{12}a_{23} - a_{22}a_{13})$$

$$= a_{11}\begin{vmatrix} a_{22} & a_{23} \\ a_{32} & a_{33} \end{vmatrix} - a_{21}\begin{vmatrix} a_{12} & a_{13} \\ a_{32} & a_{33} \end{vmatrix} + a_{31}\begin{vmatrix} a_{12} & a_{13} \\ a_{22} & a_{23} \end{vmatrix}$$

$$= a_{11}A_{11} - a_{21}A_{21} + a_{31}A_{31} \tag{19}$$

Equation (19) is called an expansion of the determinant D in terms of the elements and minors of the first column.

It may similarly be shown that

$$D = -a_{12}A_{12} + a_{22}A_{22} - a_{32}A_{32} \tag{20}$$

$$D = a_{13}A_{13} - a_{23}A_{23} + a_{33}A_{33} \tag{21}$$

Also

$$D = a_{11}A_{11} - a_{12}A_{12} + a_{13}A_{13} \tag{22}$$

$$D = -a_{21}A_{21} + a_{22}A_{22} - a_{23}A_{23} \tag{23}$$

$$D = a_{31}A_{31} - a_{32}A_{32} + a_{33}A_{33} \tag{24}$$

These are all special cases of an important general theorem, to be given below.

Suppose we have the determinant

$$\begin{vmatrix} a_{11} & a_{12} & \cdots & a_{1n} \\ a_{21} & a_{22} & \cdots & a_{2n} \\ \vdots & \vdots & & \vdots \\ a_{n1} & a_{n2} & \cdots & a_{nn} \end{vmatrix}$$

where the first subscript of each element stands for the number of its row, and the second for the number of its column. Let A_{pq} stand for the minor of the element a_{pq}. Then we have the following theorem for the expansion of a determinant according to the minors of its k'th column.

$$D = \sum_{j=1}^{j=n} (-1)^{j+k} a_{jk} A_{jk} \tag{25}$$

Equations (19), (20), and (21) are special cases of Eq. (25). In Eq. (19) $k = 1$, in Eq. (20) $k = 2$, and in Eq. (21) $k = 3$.

For the expansion of a determinant according to the minors of its r'th row, we have the theorem

$$D = \sum_{s=1}^{s=n} (-1)^{s+r} a_{rs} A_{rs} \tag{26}$$

Equations (22), (23), and (24) are special cases of Eq. (26). In Eq. (22) $r = 1$, in Eq. (23) $r = 2$, and in Eq. (24) $r = 3$.

We will not give the derivations of Eqs. (25) and (26) here, since they are too long and involved.

A convenient way to remember the sign of a minor in accordance with $(-1)^{j+k}$ in Eq. (25) or $(-1)^{s+r}$ in Eq. (26) is to use the following diagram

$$\begin{matrix} + & - & + & - & + & - & + & - & \cdots \\ - & + & - & + & - & + & - & + & \cdots \\ + & - & + & - & + & - & + & - & \cdots \\ - & + & - & + & - & + & - & \cdots & \cdots \\ + & - & + & \cdots & \cdots & \cdots & \cdots & \cdots & \cdots \\ \cdots & \cdots & \cdots & \cdots & \cdots & \cdots & \cdots & \cdots & \cdots \end{matrix}$$

In this diagram the sign of the minor is given in terms of its designating element. Starting with a plus sign in the upper left-hand corner and moving along either columns or rows, the signs can be marked off as alternatingly plus and minus. This cannot be done in moving along diagonals.[3]

Exercise

Evaluate the determinant

$$\begin{vmatrix} 3 & 5 & 1 & 7 \\ 1 & 2 & 0 & 1 \\ 4 & 2 & 2 & 6 \\ 2 & 1 & 0 & 3 \end{vmatrix}$$

by first expanding it in minors of the third column.

1.7. Removal of factors

Before coming to the application of determinants, we must still prove a few additional theorems. The first of these is

Theorem V: *A common factor of all of the elements of the same row or column of a determinant may be divided out of the elements and*

[3] If the quantities A_{jk} are the minors in the expansion of D in Eq. (25), then the quantities $(-1)^{j+k}A_{jk}$ are called the cofactors in the expansion.

placed as a factor before the new determinant. In other words, if all the elements of a row or column are divided by n, the value of the determinant is divided by n. Thus for example

$$\begin{vmatrix} a_{11} & a_{12} & a_{13} \\ a_{21} & a_{22} & a_{23} \\ a_{31} & a_{32} & a_{33} \end{vmatrix} = n \begin{vmatrix} a_{11} & a_{12}/n & a_{13} \\ a_{21} & a_{22}/n & a_{23} \\ a_{31} & a_{32}/n & a_{33} \end{vmatrix} \tag{27}$$

To demonstrate the truth of this theorem, we need only note that each term in the expansion of the determinant contains just one element of each column and one element of each row as a factor.

1.8. Addition and subtraction

Theorem VI: *A determinant having $a_{11} + q_1$, $a_{21} + q_2$, --- as the elements of a column is equal to the sum of the determinant having a_{11}, a_{21}, --- as the elements of the corresponding column, and the determinant having q_1, q_2, --- as the elements of that column, while the elements of the remaining columns of each determinant are the same as in the given determinant.* Thus

$$\begin{vmatrix} a_{11} + q_1 & a_{12} & a_{13} \\ a_{21} + q_2 & a_{22} & a_{23} \\ a_{31} + q_3 & a_{32} & a_{33} \end{vmatrix} = \begin{vmatrix} a_{11} & a_{12} & a_{13} \\ a_{21} & a_{22} & a_{23} \\ a_{31} & a_{32} & a_{33} \end{vmatrix} + \begin{vmatrix} q_1 & a_{12} & a_{13} \\ q_2 & a_{22} & a_{23} \\ q_3 & a_{32} & a_{33} \end{vmatrix} \tag{28}$$

To prove this theorem, we expand in terms of the elements and minors of the first column.

Let $(A + Q)_1$ be the minor of $a_{11} + q_1$, etc.

Now $(A + Q)_1 = A_{11} = Q_1$, $(A + Q)_2 = A_{21} = Q_2$, and so on. Then

$$\begin{aligned}(a_{11} + q_1)(A + Q)_1 - (a_{21} + q_2)(A + Q)_2 + (a_{31} + q_3)(A + Q)_3 \\ = a_{11}(A + Q)_1 - a_{21}(A + Q)_2 + a_{31}(A + Q)_3 \\ + q_1(A + Q)_1 - q_2(A + Q)_2 + q_3(A + Q)_3 \\ = (a_{11}A_{11} - a_{21}A_{21} + a_{31}A_{31}) + (q_1Q_1 - q_2Q_2 + q_3Q_3)\end{aligned}$$

This verifies Eq. (28). It is clear that an analogous proof is possible for determinants of any order.

A similar theorem holds if columns in the above theorem are replaced by rows. Thus

$$\begin{vmatrix} a_{11}+q_1 & a_{12}+q_2 & a_{13}+q_3 \\ a_{21} & a_{22} & a_{23} \\ a_{31} & a_{32} & a_{33} \end{vmatrix} = \begin{vmatrix} a_{11} & a_{12} & a_{13} \\ a_{21} & a_{22} & a_{23} \\ a_{31} & a_{32} & a_{33} \end{vmatrix} + \begin{vmatrix} q_1 & q_2 & q_3 \\ a_{21} & a_{22} & a_{23} \\ a_{31} & a_{32} & a_{33} \end{vmatrix} \tag{29}$$

Theorem VII: *A determinant is not changed in value if we add to the elements of any column the products of the corresponding elements of another column by the same arbitrary number.* Thus for example

$$\begin{vmatrix} a_{11}+na_{12} & a_{12} & a_{13} \\ a_{21}+na_{22} & a_{22} & a_{23} \\ a_{31}+na_{32} & a_{32} & a_{33} \end{vmatrix} = \begin{vmatrix} a_{11} & a_{12} & a_{13} \\ a_{21} & a_{22} & a_{23} \\ a_{31} & a_{32} & a_{33} \end{vmatrix} \tag{30}$$

where n is any number whatsoever.

To prove this, we note that by application of Eqs. (27) and (28)

$$\begin{vmatrix} a_{11}+na_{12} & a_{12} & a_{13} \\ a_{21}+na_{22} & a_{22} & a_{23} \\ a_{31}+na_{32} & a_{32} & a_{33} \end{vmatrix} = \begin{vmatrix} a_{11} & a_{12} & a_{13} \\ a_{21} & a_{22} & a_{23} \\ a_{31} & a_{32} & a_{33} \end{vmatrix} + n\begin{vmatrix} a_{12} & a_{12} & a_{13} \\ a_{22} & a_{22} & a_{23} \\ a_{32} & a_{32} & a_{33} \end{vmatrix}$$

The last determinant has the value zero, since it has two equal columns. This establishes the proof of the theorem for a determinant of order 3. The proof can be extended to a determinant of any order.

A theorem similar to Theorem VII holds for rows as well as for columns. Thus

$$\begin{vmatrix} a_{11}+na_{21} & a_{12}+na_{22} & a_{13}+na_{23} \\ a_{21} & a_{22} & a_{23} \\ a_{31} & a_{32} & a_{33} \end{vmatrix} = \begin{vmatrix} a_{11} & a_{12} & a_{13} \\ a_{21} & a_{22} & a_{23} \\ a_{31} & a_{32} & a_{33} \end{vmatrix} \tag{31}$$

Example: To show the utility of the foregoing theorems in reducing the labor in evaluating determinants, let us find the value of

$$\begin{vmatrix} 8 & 2 & 4 & 2 \\ 3 & 1 & 1 & 1 \\ 1 & 8 & 3 & 6 \\ 6 & 3 & 3 & 4 \end{vmatrix}$$

As a first step, we multiply the third column by 2 and subtract it from the first column in accordance with Theorem VII. The determinant then becomes

$$\begin{vmatrix} 0 & 2 & 4 & 2 \\ 1 & 1 & 1 & 1 \\ -5 & 8 & 3 & 6 \\ 0 & 3 & 3 & 4 \end{vmatrix}$$

The purpose of this step is to set up as many zeros as possible in one column or row (the first column, in this case) in order to eliminate the minors of these zero elements from the evaluation calculations.

Next we expand the determinant in minors of the first column, obtaining

$$-1\begin{vmatrix} 2 & 4 & 2 \\ 8 & 3 & 6 \\ 3 & 3 & 4 \end{vmatrix} - 5\begin{vmatrix} 2 & 4 & 2 \\ 1 & 1 & 1 \\ 3 & 3 & 4 \end{vmatrix}$$

As the next step, we expand both determinants in minors of the second row. This expansion gives us two identical sets of minors to be evaluated, thus reducing the work involved.

$$\begin{aligned} &-\left[-8\begin{vmatrix} 4 & 2 \\ 3 & 4 \end{vmatrix} + 3\begin{vmatrix} 2 & 2 \\ 3 & 4 \end{vmatrix} - 6\begin{vmatrix} 2 & 4 \\ 3 & 3 \end{vmatrix}\right] \\ &-5\left[-\begin{vmatrix} 4 & 2 \\ 3 & 4 \end{vmatrix} + \begin{vmatrix} 2 & 2 \\ 3 & 4 \end{vmatrix} - \begin{vmatrix} 2 & 4 \\ 3 & 3 \end{vmatrix}\right] \\ &= -[-8(10) + 3(2) - 6(-6)] \\ &\quad -5\,[-(10) + (2) - (-6)] \\ &= 80 - 6 - 36 + 50 - 10 - 30 = 48 \end{aligned}$$

1.9. *n* simultaneous linear equations in *n* unknowns

We are now ready to extend the discussion in §1.1 to a system of n simultaneous linear equations in n unknowns.

Suppose we have n simultaneous linear equations

$$\begin{aligned} a_{11}x_1 + a_{12}x_2 + \cdots + a_{1n}x_n &= k_1 \\ a_{21}x_1 + a_{22}x_2 + \cdots + a_{2n}x_n &= k_2 \\ \vdots \qquad\quad \vdots \qquad\qquad\quad \vdots \qquad &\quad \vdots \\ a_{n1}x_1 + a_{n2}x_2 + \cdots + a_{nn}x_n &= k_n \end{aligned} \tag{32}$$

Let D denote the determinant of the coefficients of the n unknowns, i.e.

$$D = \begin{vmatrix} a_{11} & a_{12} & \cdots & a_{1n} \\ a_{21} & a_{22} & \cdots & a_{2n} \\ \vdots & \vdots & & \vdots \\ a_{n1} & a_{n2} & \cdots & a_{nn} \end{vmatrix} \tag{33}$$

Let us now multiply the first column by x_1, thereby effectively multiplying the determinant by x_1 in accordance with Theorem V. Therefore

$$Dx_1 = \begin{vmatrix} a_{11}x_1 & a_{12} & \cdots & a_{1n} \\ a_{21}x_1 & a_{22} & \cdots & a_{2n} \\ \vdots & \vdots & & \vdots \\ a_{n1}x_1 & a_{n2} & \cdots & a_{nn} \end{vmatrix} \tag{34}$$

Let us next multiply the second column by x_2 and add it to the first column. In accordance with Theorem VII, this leaves the value of the determinant unchanged. Therefore

$$Dx_1 = \begin{vmatrix} (a_{11}x_1 + a_{12}x_2) & a_{12} & \cdots & a_{1n} \\ (a_{21}x_1 + a_{22}x_2) & a_{22} & \cdots & a_{2n} \\ \vdots & \vdots & & \vdots \\ (a_{n1}x_1 + a_{n2}x_2) & a_{n2} & \cdots & a_{nn} \end{vmatrix} \tag{35}$$

Let us next multiply in turn the third column by x_3 and add it to the first column, the fourth column by x_4 and add it to the first column, and so on. These steps, in accordance with Theorem VII, leave the value of the determinant unchanged. We thus finally obtain

$$Dx_1 = \begin{vmatrix} (a_{11}x_1 + a_{12}x_2 + \cdots + a_{1n}x_n) & a_{12} & \cdots & a_{1n} \\ (a_{21}x_1 + a_{22}x_2 + \cdots + a_{2n}x_n) & a_{22} & \cdots & a_{2n} \\ \vdots & \vdots & & \vdots \\ (a_{n1}x_1 + a_{n2}x_2 + \cdots + a_{nn}x_n) & a_{n2} & \cdots & a_{nn} \end{vmatrix} \tag{36}$$

Let us next substitute for the first column in the above determinant, the corresponding values from Eqs. (32). Thus

$$Dx_1 = \begin{vmatrix} k_1 & a_{12} & --- & a_{1n} \\ k_2 & a_{22} & --- & a_{2n} \\ \vdots & \vdots & & \vdots \\ k_n & a_{n2} & --- & a_{nn} \end{vmatrix} = K_1 \tag{37}$$

where K_1 is defined as the above determinant with the k's in the first column. In a like manner we define

$$K_2 = \begin{vmatrix} a_{11} & k_1 & a_{13} & --- & a_{1n} \\ a_{21} & k_2 & a_{23} & --- & a_{2n} \\ \vdots & \vdots & \vdots & & \vdots \\ a_{n1} & k_n & a_{n3} & --- & a_{nn} \end{vmatrix} \tag{38}$$

wherein the k's replace the second column. K_3, K_4, --- K_n are defined in a corresponding manner.

Now it is clear that, if we took steps similar to those taken in deriving Eq. (37), we could show that

$$Dx_2 = K_2, \qquad Dx_3 = K_3, \qquad --- \qquad Dx_n = K_n \tag{39}$$

Therefore, provided that $D \neq 0$, Eqs. (36) and (39) supply us with the solutions for the simultaneous Eqs. (32) in the form

$$x_1 = \frac{K_1}{D}, \qquad x_2 = \frac{K_2}{D}, \qquad --- \qquad x_n = \frac{K_n}{D} \tag{40}$$

The expression of the solutions of a system of simultaneous linear equations as the quotients of determinants given by Eqs. (40) is called Cramer's Rule.

Equations (40) are the solution of our fundamental problem in this chapter.

Example: The solution of

$$\begin{aligned} 2x + 3y + 5z &= 7 \\ 3x + 5y - 9z &= -6 \\ 8x + \ y - 4z &= 2 \end{aligned} \tag{41}$$

is

$$x = \frac{\begin{vmatrix} 7 & 3 & 5 \\ -6 & 5 & -9 \\ 2 & 1 & -4 \end{vmatrix}}{\begin{vmatrix} 2 & 3 & 5 \\ 3 & 5 & -9 \\ 8 & 1 & -4 \end{vmatrix}} = \frac{-283}{-387} = \frac{283}{387} \tag{42}$$

$$y = \frac{\begin{vmatrix} 2 & 7 & 5 \\ 3 & -6 & -9 \\ 8 & 2 & -4 \end{vmatrix}}{\begin{vmatrix} 2 & 3 & 5 \\ 3 & 5 & -9 \\ 8 & 1 & -4 \end{vmatrix}} = \frac{-66}{-387} = \frac{66}{387} \tag{43}$$

$$z = \frac{\begin{vmatrix} 2 & 3 & 7 \\ 3 & 5 & -6 \\ 8 & 1 & 2 \end{vmatrix}}{\begin{vmatrix} 2 & 3 & 5 \\ 3 & 5 & -9 \\ 8 & 1 & -4 \end{vmatrix}} = \frac{-389}{-387} = \frac{389}{387} \tag{44}$$

If $D = 0$, then Eqs. (40) fail to solve the problem. In that case, either (a) the set of Eqs. (32) is inconsistent; or (b) one of the Eqs. (32) is a linear combination of some of the others.

As a simple example of case (a) we can take the set of simultaneous equations

$$\begin{aligned} 2x + 4y &= 5 \\ 2x + 4y &= 7 \end{aligned}$$

Here $D = 0$.

This set of equations is, of course, inconsistent, since it leads to the conclusion $5 = 7$.

As an example of case (b) we can take

$$\begin{aligned} x + 2y + z &= 4 \\ 2x + 3y + z &= 2 \\ 3x + 5y + 2z &= 6 \end{aligned} \tag{45}$$

Here, the third equation is the sum of the first and second. In this case also, $D = 0$. But here we cannot obtain a unique solution because not enough equations are given in Eqs. (45), since only two of the equations are independent.

As a practical matter, D will ordinarily not be zero, and Eq. (40) will give the desired solution. If $D = 0$, either not enough information is given [case (b)] or there is some error [case (a)].

1.10. Homogeneous linear equations

Definition: *An equation is called linear if it contains only constants and terms of the first degree in the variables involved.* Thus

$$ax + by + cz = d$$

is a linear equation.[4]

Definition: *An equation is called homogeneous if its terms are all of the same degree in the variables involved.*

Thus $$Ax^2 + Bxy + Cy^2 = 0$$

is a homogeneous equation. The zero term is not considered a term so far as the above definition is concerned.

A homogeneous linear equation is an equation which is both linear and homogeneous.

For example: $$ax + by + cz = 0$$

is a homogeneous linear equation. On the other hand, the equation

$$ax + by + cz = d$$

is linear, but not homogeneous.

A set of simultaneous *homogeneous linear equations,* such as

$$a_{11}x + a_{12}y + a_{13}z = 0 \tag{46}$$
$$a_{21}x + a_{22}y + a_{23}z = 0 \tag{47}$$
$$a_{31}x + a_{32}y + a_{33}z = 0 \tag{48}$$

sometimes arises in electrical problems. We now wish to point out certain facts about such a set of equations. In the first place, they have the obvious solution $x = 0$, $y = 0$, and $z = 0$. Besides being obvious, this solution also follows from the Eqs. (40), provided $D \neq 0$.

---

[4] The graph of a linear equation in two variables, $Ax + By = C$, is a straight line, which explains how the term linear came to be used.

Next, suppose that

$$D = \begin{vmatrix} a_{11} & a_{12} & a_{13} \\ a_{21} & a_{22} & a_{23} \\ a_{31} & a_{32} & a_{33} \end{vmatrix} = 0$$

In this case, a solution other than the obvious zero solution could exist. We now state the following theorem (but omit its proof because it is too long).

Theorem VIII: *A system of n simultaneous homogeneous linear equations in n unknowns has solutions other than the obvious solution* 0, 0, 0 --- 0, *if and only if the determinant of the coefficient vanishes.*

For the particular[5] case of Eqs. (46), (47), and (48) where $n = 3$, we can find the solutions by expanding the determinant D according to elements and minors of the third row. Thus

$$D = a_{31}\begin{vmatrix} a_{12} & a_{13} \\ a_{22} & a_{23} \end{vmatrix} - a_{32}\begin{vmatrix} a_{11} & a_{13} \\ a_{21} & a_{23} \end{vmatrix} + a_{33}\begin{vmatrix} a_{11} & a_{12} \\ a_{21} & a_{22} \end{vmatrix} = 0 \tag{49}$$

Comparing (49) with (48) we see that there is a set of solutions

$$x = k\begin{vmatrix} a_{12} & a_{13} \\ a_{22} & a_{23} \end{vmatrix}, \qquad y = -k\begin{vmatrix} a_{11} & a_{13} \\ a_{21} & a_{23} \end{vmatrix}, \qquad z = k\begin{vmatrix} a_{11} & a_{12} \\ a_{21} & a_{22} \end{vmatrix} \tag{50}$$

where k is any constant. The constant k shows that if each individual solution of a set is multiplied by the same constant, a new set of solutions results.

We could, of course, have expanded D, according to elements and minors of the first or second row to get a set of solutions. The result, however, would be the same as Eq. (50), any apparent difference being only a difference in the value of k used.

Example: Solve the set of simultaneous equations

$$\begin{aligned} 2x + 5y - 3z &= 0 \\ x - 5y + z &= 0 \\ 3x + 3y - 3z &= 0 \end{aligned} \tag{51}$$

By actual expansion, the determinant

$$\begin{vmatrix} 2 & 5 & -3 \\ 1 & -5 & 1 \\ 3 & 3 & -3 \end{vmatrix}$$

[5] For the general case, see Bocher, *Introduction to Higher Algebra*, Chapter IV.

vanishes. Therefore, the Eqs. (51) have the solution, given by Eq. (50)

$$\begin{aligned} x &= k(5 - 15) &&= -10k \\ y &= -k(2 + 3) &&= -5k \\ z &= k(-10 - 5) &&= -15k \end{aligned} \tag{52}$$

If we let $k = -\frac{1}{5}$, we arrive at the very simple solution

$$x = 2 \qquad y = 1 \qquad z = 3$$

Exercises

Solve the systems of simultaneous equations:

(1)
$$\begin{aligned} 2x + 3y + 4z &= 5 \\ 2y - 3z &= 7 \\ y + 5z &= -8 \end{aligned}$$

(2)
$$\begin{aligned} x - 2y + z &= 12 \\ x + 2y + 3z &= 48 \\ 6x + 4y + 3z &= 84 \end{aligned}$$

(3)
$$\begin{aligned} 2x + 3y + 4z + 2t &= 9 \\ 5x - 4y + 6z + t &= 3 \\ 3x + 2y - z - 2t &= 1 \\ x - 5y + z + 2t &= 0 \end{aligned}$$

(4)
$$\begin{aligned} 2x - y + 3z - 2t &= 4 \\ x + 7y + z - t &= 2 \\ 3x + 5y - 5z + 3t &= 0 \\ 4x - 3y + 2z - t &= 5 \end{aligned}$$

(5)
$$\begin{aligned} x + y + 4z &= 0 \\ 2x - 7y - z &= 0 \\ x - y + 2z &= 0 \end{aligned}$$

(6) Show that

$$\begin{vmatrix} a_1 & b_1 & c_1 \\ a_2 & b_2 & c_2 \\ a_3 & b_3 & c_3 \end{vmatrix} = \begin{vmatrix} a_2 & c_2 & b_2 \\ a_1 & c_1 & b_1 \\ a_3 & c_3 & b_3 \end{vmatrix}$$

1.11. Solution of a network problem

One of the most useful applications of determinants in radio engineering is in solving network problems. As soon as the networks become at all complicated, the use of determinants is a great labor-saving device. We will introduce the subject by finding the conditions for balance in a Wheatstone Bridge.

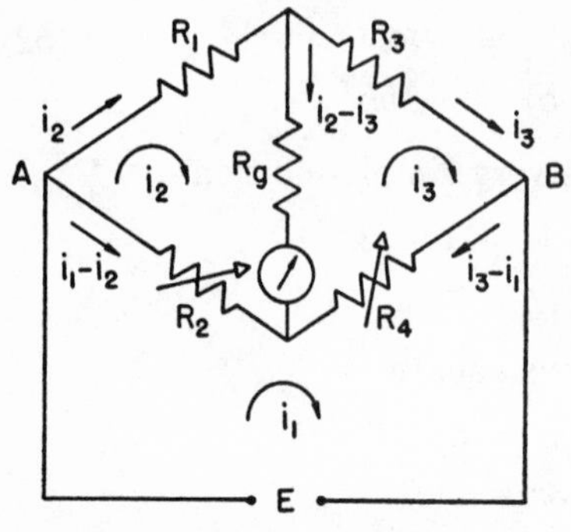

FIG. 1-1. A Wheatstone Bridge.

Figure 1-1 shows the familiar circuit of a Wheatstone bridge. A voltage E is applied between the junction points A and B, and the resistors R_2 and R_4 are varied until the current through R_g vanishes. This is called the condition of balance. We wish to find the relation between the resistors R_1, R_2, R_3, and R_4 when the bridge is balanced.

Let us first write down the circuit equations for this network. These equations are[6]

$$R_2(i_1 - i_2) + R_4(i_1 - i_3) = E \tag{53}$$
$$R_1 i_2 + R_g(i_2 - i_3) + R_2(i_2 - i_1) = 0 \tag{54}$$
$$R_3 i_3 + R_4(i_3 - i_1) + R_g(i_3 - i_2) = 0 \tag{55}$$

The condition for balance may be stated as

$$i_2 - i_3 = 0 \tag{56}$$

To solve for i_2 and i_3, let us first arrange Eqs. (53), (54), and (55) in the standard form, Eq. (32). Accordingly, we write

$$(R_2 + R_4)i_1 - R_2 i_2 - R_4 i_3 = E \tag{57}$$
$$-R_2 i_1 + (R_1 + R_2 + R_g)i_2 - R_g i_3 = 0 \tag{58}$$
$$-R_4 i_1 - R_g i_2 + (R_3 + R_4 + R_g)i_3 = 0 \tag{59}$$

Let us use the notation

$$\Delta = \begin{vmatrix} (R_2 + R_4) & -R_2 & -R_4 \\ -R_2 & R_1 + R_2 + R_g & -R_g \\ -R_4 & -R_g & (R_3 + R_4 + R_g) \end{vmatrix} \tag{60}$$

[6] It is assumed that the student has an elementary knowledge of electrical circuit theory. The fundamentals of circuit theory are discussed in Chap. 2.

for the determinant of the coefficients of the simultaneous equations. We may then write

$$i_2 - i_3 = \frac{1}{\Delta}\left\{\begin{vmatrix} R_2 + R_4 & E & -R_4 \\ -R_2 & 0 & -R_g \\ -R_4 & 0 & (R_3 + R_4 + R_g) \end{vmatrix} - \begin{vmatrix} R_2 + R_4 & -R_2 & E \\ -R_2 & (R_1 + R_2 + R_g) & 0 \\ -R_4 & -R_g & 0 \end{vmatrix}\right\}$$

$$= -\frac{E}{\Delta}\left\{\begin{vmatrix} -R_2 & -R_g \\ -R_4 & (R_3 + R_4 + R_g) \end{vmatrix} + \begin{vmatrix} -R_2 & (R_1 + R_2 + R_g) \\ -R_4 & -R_g \end{vmatrix}\right\}$$

(by expanding in minors of the second and third columns respectively)

$$= -\frac{E}{\Delta}\begin{vmatrix} -R_2 & R_1 + R_2 \\ -R_4 & R_3 + R_4 \end{vmatrix}$$

(by Theorem VI)

$$= \frac{E}{\Delta}(R_2R_3 - R_1R_4) \tag{61}$$

It follows from Eq. (61) and Eq. (56) that

$$R_2R_3 - R_1R_4 = 0 \tag{62}$$

is the required condition for balance.

Whether the use of determinants in the preceding example was really a labor-saving device may be questionable. However, the example served as a convenient introduction to the use of determinants in network problems. The simplification introduced by using determinants in the next example will be obvious.

1.12. A point-attenuation network

The following example is the design of a filter to eliminate one particular frequency. In practice, this problem arose in the design of an audio-frequency filter to eliminate the 10-kc beat note between the carrier frequencies of adjacent channels in a broadcast receiver.

Figure 1-2 shows the schematic diagram of the filter. We want to find what conditions are necessary so that, at a frequency $\omega/2\pi$, there shall be no output voltage e, even though there is an input voltage e_1. These conditions will be achieved when the current through z, and therefore the voltage across z, is zero. One fundamental condition may therefore be written

$$i_1 + i_4 = 0 \tag{63}$$

since this is the current through z.

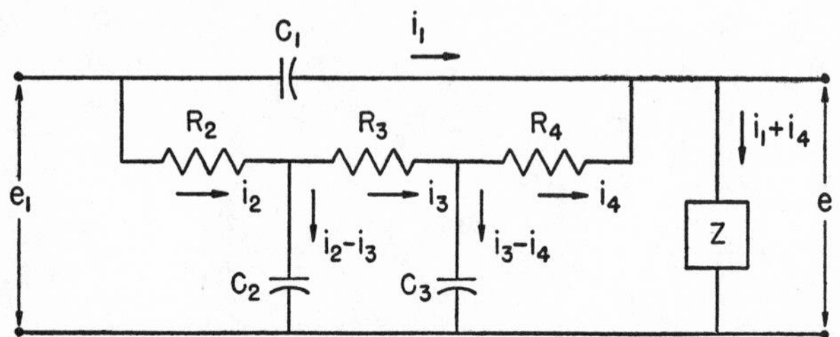

Fig. 1-2. An R-C transmission network having infinite attenuation at one frequency.

Let us next write down the steady-state-voltage equations of this network

$$\left(R_2 - \frac{j}{\omega C_2}\right) i_2 + \frac{j}{\omega C_2} i_3 = e_1 \tag{64}$$

$$\frac{j}{\omega C_2} i_2 + \left(R_3 - \frac{j}{\omega C_2} - \frac{j}{\omega C_3}\right) i_3 + \frac{j}{\omega C_3} i_4 = 0 \tag{65}$$

$$z i_1 + \frac{j}{\omega C_3} i_3 + \left(R_4 - \frac{j}{\omega C_3} + z\right) i_4 = 0 \tag{66}$$

$$-\frac{j}{\omega C_1} i_1 - R_2 i_2 - R_3 i_3 - R_4 i_4 = 0 \tag{67}$$

Solving this system of equations according to the method of Eqs. (40), we get

$$i_1 D = \begin{vmatrix} e_1 & \left(R_2 - \dfrac{j}{\omega C_2}\right) & \dfrac{j}{\omega C_2} & 0 \\ 0 & \dfrac{j}{\omega C_2} & \left(R_3 - \dfrac{j}{\omega C_2} - \dfrac{j}{\omega C_3}\right) & \dfrac{j}{\omega C_3} \\ 0 & 0 & \dfrac{j}{\omega C_3} & \left(R_4 - \dfrac{j}{\omega C_3} + z\right) \\ 0 & -R_2 & -R_3 & -R_4 \end{vmatrix} \tag{68}$$

$$\text{and } i_4 D = \begin{vmatrix} 0 & \left(R_2 - \frac{j}{\omega C_2}\right) & \frac{j}{\omega C_2} & e_1 \\ 0 & \frac{j}{\omega C_2} & \left(R_3 - \frac{j}{\omega C_2} - \frac{j}{\omega C_3}\right) & 0 \\ z & 0 & \frac{j}{\omega C_3} & 0 \\ -\frac{j}{\omega C_1} & -R_2 & -R_3 & 0 \end{vmatrix} \tag{69}$$

where

$$D = \begin{vmatrix} 0 & \left(R_2 - \frac{j}{\omega C_2}\right) & \frac{j}{\omega C_2} & 0 \\ 0 & \frac{j}{\omega C_2} & \left(R_3 - \frac{j}{\omega C_2} - \frac{j}{\omega C_3}\right) & \frac{j}{\omega C_3} \\ z & 0 & \frac{j}{\omega C_3} & \left(R_4 - \frac{j}{\omega C_3} + z\right) \\ \frac{-j}{\omega C_1} & -R_2 & -R_3 & -R_4 \end{vmatrix} \tag{70}$$

Next, interchange the first and fourth columns of the determinant in Eq. (69) in accordance with Theorem II. This makes its first column identical with that of Eq. (68). Then expand the determinants in Eqs. (68) and (69) according to elements and minors of the first column. After dividing through by e_1 and multiplying by D, Eq. (63) reduces to

$$\begin{vmatrix} \frac{j}{\omega C_2} & \left(R_3 - \frac{j}{\omega C_2} - \frac{j}{\omega C_3}\right) & \frac{j}{\omega C_3} \\ 0 & \frac{j}{\omega C_3} & \left(R_4 - \frac{j}{\omega C_3} + z\right) \\ -R_2 & -R_3 & -R_4 \end{vmatrix} - \begin{vmatrix} \frac{j}{\omega C_2} & \left(R_3 - \frac{j}{\omega C_2} - \frac{j}{\omega C_3}\right) & 0 \\ 0 & \frac{j}{\omega C_3} & +z \\ -R_2 & -R_3 & -\frac{j}{\omega C_1} \end{vmatrix} = 0 \tag{71}$$

Since the first and second columns of the determinants in Eq. (71) are identical, we expand both determinants in elements and minors of the third column. Then Eq. (71) becomes

$$\frac{j}{\omega C_3}\begin{vmatrix} 0 & \dfrac{j}{\omega C_3} \\ -R_2 & -R_3 \end{vmatrix} - \left(R_4 - \frac{j}{\omega C_3}\right)\begin{vmatrix} \dfrac{j}{\omega C_2} & \left(R_3 - \dfrac{j}{\omega C_2} - \dfrac{j}{\omega C_3}\right) \\ -R_2 & -R_3 \end{vmatrix}$$

$$+ \left(-R_4 + \frac{j}{\omega C_1}\right)\begin{vmatrix} \dfrac{j}{\omega C_2} & \left(R_3 - \dfrac{j}{\omega C_2} - \dfrac{j}{\omega C_3}\right) \\ 0 & \dfrac{j}{\omega C_3} \end{vmatrix} = 0 \quad (72)$$

Expanding Eq. (72) we get,

$$\frac{j}{\omega C_3}\cdot\frac{j}{\omega C_3}\cdot R_2 - \left(R_4 - \frac{j}{\omega C_3}\right)\left[\frac{-jR_3}{\omega C_2} + R_2\left(R_3 - \frac{j}{\omega C_2} - \frac{j}{\omega C_3}\right)\right]$$

$$+ \left(-R_4 + \frac{j}{\omega C_1}\right)\frac{j}{\omega C_2}\cdot\frac{j}{\omega C_3} = 0 \quad (73)$$

Simplifying Eq. (73) we get

$$-\frac{R_2}{\omega^2 C_3^2} + j\frac{R_4 R_3}{\omega C_2} + \frac{R_3}{\omega^2 C_2 C_3} - R_2 R_3 R_4 + j\frac{R_2 R_3}{\omega C_3}$$

$$+ j\frac{R_4 R_2}{\omega C_2} + \frac{R_2}{\omega^2 C_2 C_3} + j\frac{R_2 R_4}{\omega C_3} + \frac{R_2}{\omega^2 C_3^2} + \frac{R_4}{\omega^2 C_2 C_3}$$

$$- \frac{j}{\omega^3 C_1 C_2 C_3} = 0 \quad (74)$$

Since both real and imaginary parts of Eq. (74) must vanish separately, we have

$$\frac{R_3}{\omega^2 C_2 C_3} - R_2 R_3 R_4 + \frac{R_2}{\omega^2 C_3 C_2} + \frac{R_4}{\omega^2 C_2 C_3} = 0 \quad (75)$$

and

$$\frac{R_4 R_3}{\omega C_2} + \frac{R_2 R_3}{\omega C_3} + \frac{R_4 R_2}{\omega C_2} + \frac{R_2 R_4}{\omega C_3} - \frac{1}{\omega^3 C_1 C_2 C_3} = 0 \quad (76)$$

From Eq. (75)

$$\omega^2 = \frac{R_2 + R_3 + R_4}{R_2 R_3 R_4 C_2 C_3} \quad (77)$$

and from Eq. (76)

$$\frac{1}{C_1} = \omega^2[R_4 R_3 C_3 + R_4 R_2 C_3 + R_2 R_3 C_2 + R_2 R_4 C_2] \quad (78)$$

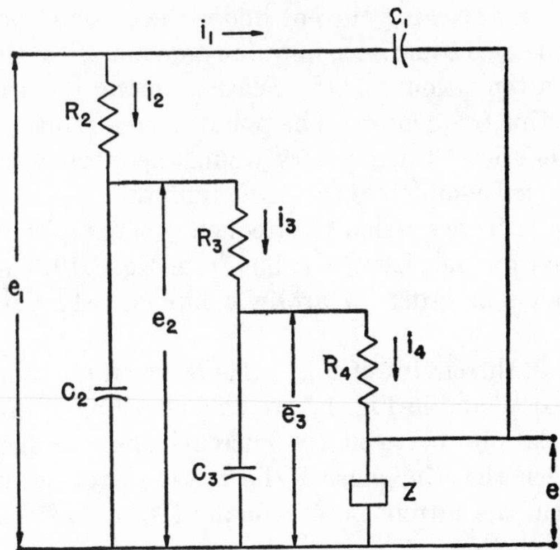

Fig. 1-3. Step diagram of the network in Fig. 1-2.

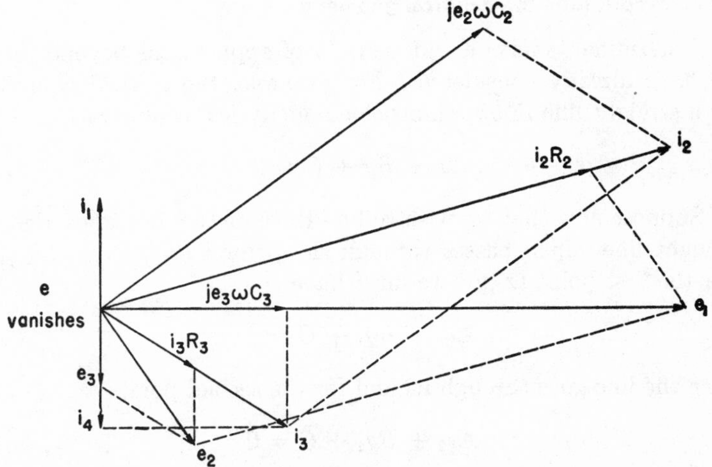

Fig. 1-4. Vector diagram of the current and voltage relations in the circuit of Fig. 1-3 (or Fig. 1-2) at the frequency of infinite attenuation.

Since z does not carry current under these conditions, and does not enter into these equations, its value does not affect the frequency of complete attenuation, nor the relation among the other network constants at this frequency. The point (single-frequency) attenuation characteristic of this network would therefore still be retained if z were removed completely (or made infinite).

From Eq. (77) we see that the frequency of complete attenuation is not affected by the size of C_1; but from Eq. (78), C_1 must be of the right value in order to attain complete attenuation at this frequency.

In Fig. 1-3, the circuit of Fig. 1-2 is redrawn to show its properties more clearly; and in Fig. 1-4 we have a vector diagram showing the phase relations between the currents and voltages involved. It may be seen that the phase of the voltage is rotated by each R-C section, so that the current in R_4 is finally 180° out of phase with the current through C_1.

All the foregoing could have been worked out without using determinants. If the student will try to do this, however, he will quickly convince himself of the utility of determinants.

1.13. Application to analytical geometry

Determinants have a wide variety of applications beyond those we have already considered. For example, the general equation for a straight line in two-dimensional analytical geometry is

$$Ax + By + C = 0 \tag{79}$$

Suppose now that we wish to find the equation of the particular straight line which passes through the points[7] (x_1,y_1) and (x_2,y_2). For the first point (x_1,y_1) we must have

$$Ax_1 + By_1 + C = 0 \tag{80}$$

since the line goes through it; and for the second point

$$Ax_2 + By_2 + C = 0 \tag{81}$$

since the line goes through it, also.

[7] This is a simplified notation for the points $(x = x_1)$, $(y = y_1)$ and $(x = x_2)$, $(y = y_2)$.

The three equations, (79), (80), and (81), for the purposes of this investigation, are therefore a system of three simultaneous homogeneous linear equations in the three unknowns—A, B, and C. According to §1.10, they will have a solution, if and only if the determinant of the coefficients vanishes; i.e.,

$$\begin{vmatrix} x & y & 1 \\ x_1 & y_1 & 1 \\ x_2 & y_2 & 1 \end{vmatrix} = 0 \tag{82}$$

Equation (82) is therefore the equation of the straight line through the points (x_1,y_1) and (x_2,y_2) in the form of a determinant.

Example: Find the equation of the straight line which passes through the points (2,1) and (5,2).

According to Eq. (82), the straight line is

$$\begin{vmatrix} x & y & 1 \\ 2 & 1 & 1 \\ 5 & 2 & 1 \end{vmatrix} = 0 \tag{83}$$

If we expand the determinant, we find the more usual expression

$$\begin{vmatrix} x & y & 1 \\ 2 & 1 & 1 \\ 5 & 2 & 1 \end{vmatrix} = -x + 3y - 1 = 0$$

or

$$x - 3y + 1 = 0 \tag{84}$$

The student can readily see that the line in Eq. (84) actually does pass through the points (2,1) and (5,2).

Exercises

1. The general equation for a circle is

$$A(x^2 + y^2) + Bx + Cy + D = 0$$

Find the equation of the circle which passes through the three points (2,1), (4,8), and (6,7).

2. In solid analytical geometry, the general equation for a plane is

$$Ax + By + Cz + D = 0$$

From this equation, tell how many points determine a plane.

1.14. Further discussion of determinants

In vector analysis, the magnitude of the vector product $\bar{A} \times \bar{B}$ of two-dimensional vectors is

$$\begin{vmatrix} A_x & B_x \\ A_y & B_y \end{vmatrix}$$

and the scalar triple product $\bar{A} \times \bar{B} \cdot \bar{C}$ of three-dimensional vectors is

$$\begin{vmatrix} A_x & B_x & C_x \\ A_y & B_y & C_y \\ A_z & B_z & C_z \end{vmatrix}$$

These determinants are particular combinations of the vector components, but it is very interesting that those particular combinations which are expressed by symmetrical determinants are of special importance.

In vector analysis, the magnitude of the *vector product* $\bar{A} \times \bar{B}$ is equal to the area of the parallelogram bounded by the vectors $\bar{A}$ and $\bar{B}$, and the scalar triple product $\bar{A} \times \bar{B} \cdot \bar{C}$ is equal to the volume of the parallelopiped determined by the vectors $\bar{A}$, $\bar{B}$, and $\bar{C}$. It is thus possible to express a determinant geometrically. Accordingly, a second-order determinant may be considered as the area of the parallelogram determined by the two vectors whose components are the elements of the determinant. Likewise, a third-order determinant may be considered as the volume of the parallelopiped determined by the three vectors whose components are the elements of the determinant. Fourth-order and still higher order determinants may likewise be considered as hypervolumes determined by sets of vectors in hyperspace.

It is quite remarkable that the particular combination of the elements of a square array given, for example, by Eq. (7) has such great importance. Nevertheless, square arrays of elements as well as rectangular arrays (where the number of columns is not equal to the number of rows) have other important properties besides their properties as determinants. These general arrays are called *matrices*, and they are a powerful tool in modern algebra. The student may also be interested in knowing that infinite-order determinants have proved useful in celestial mechanics.

Exercise

In the circuit of Fig. 1-A, show that the conditions for infinite

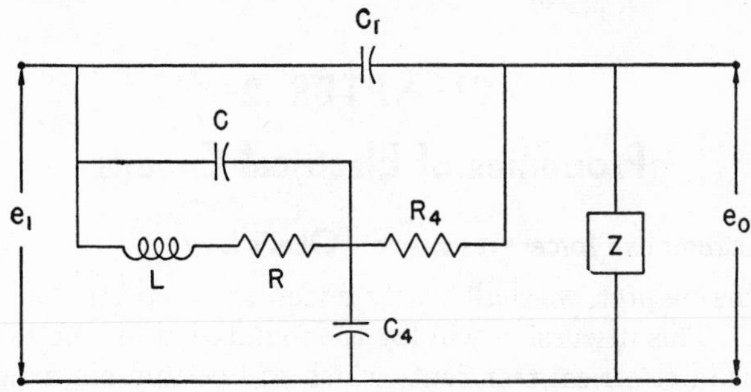

FIG. 1-A.

attenuation are

$$\frac{1}{\omega^2} = L(C + C_1) + RR_4C_1(C + C_4)$$

and

$$\frac{1}{\omega^2} = \frac{LC_1R_4(C_4 + C)}{RC_1 + R_4C_1 + RC}$$

CHAPTER 2

Properties of Electrical Circuits

2.1. Electromotive force—resistance—Ohm's Law

In this chapter, we shall briefly review the properties of electrical circuits. This discussion will lay the foundation for the solution of problems in electrical transients which will occupy our attention in most of the remainder of the book.

If a battery or a generator is connected across the terminals of a resistor, an electric current will flow (Fig. 2-1). We describe the situation by saying that the battery or generator has an electromotive force (e.m.f.) which it applies to the resistor. The ratio of the applied e.m.f. E to the current I is called the resistance R of the resistor. Thus

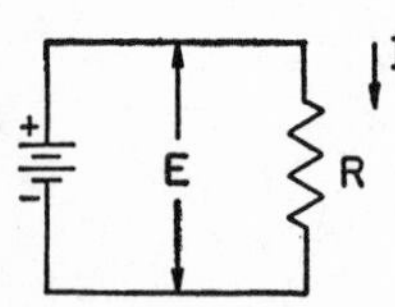

FIG. 2-1. Current flowing through a resistor due to the voltage from a battery.

$$\frac{E}{I} = R \qquad \text{or} \qquad E = IR \tag{1}$$

Equation (1) is used to define the magnitude of the resistance R. The magnitudes of E and I are defined by other means with which the student is probably familiar from his study of physics, and which we shall therefore not consider here. If R is a constant, then Eq. (1) says that E is proportional to I. This is called Ohm's Law. Consequently, a resistor whose magnitude R is independent of the amount of current which is flowing through it is called an ohmic resistor.

If the adjustment of I to changes in E, in accordance with Eq. (1), is instantaneous, then R is said to be a pure resistance. When an electric current flows through a *pure* resistor, no magnetic or electric field is produced. *The only way in which there is evidence that current is flowing through the resistor is that it generates heat energy (at the rate of I^2R).* Pure resistors, which produce no electrostatic or magnetic field as current flows, do not occur in nature.

However, the laboratory resistors which we use are good approximations to pure resistors for most practical purposes.

2.2. Counter e.m.f.

A concept which is often of value in considering electrical circuits is that of *counter e.m.f.* A counter e.m.f. is a fictitious voltage defined for analytical purposes to describe the loss of voltage in a circuit element. We say that when current flows through a resistor, there is a counter e.m.f. in the resistor of amount IR. Since $IR = E$, we can look at an electrical circuit as a balanced system in which the applied e.m.f. is equal to the counter e.m.f. From this point of view the magnitude of the current which flows is determined by the counter e.m.f. Thus the amount of current which will flow in the circuit is such that the counter e.m.f. equals the applied e.m.f.

In later paragraphs of this chapter we shall also consider the counter e.m.f. produced by capacitive and inductive elements.

2.3. Capacitance

If a voltage V is applied between the plates of a capacitor, a charge $+Q$ will collect on the positive plate and a charge $-Q$ will collect on the negative plate. We describe this by saying that the capacitor gets a charge Q. We define the capacitance C of the capacitor as the ratio of Q to V. Thus

$$C = \frac{Q}{V} \quad \text{or} \quad Q = CV \quad \text{or} \quad V = \frac{Q}{C} \tag{2}$$

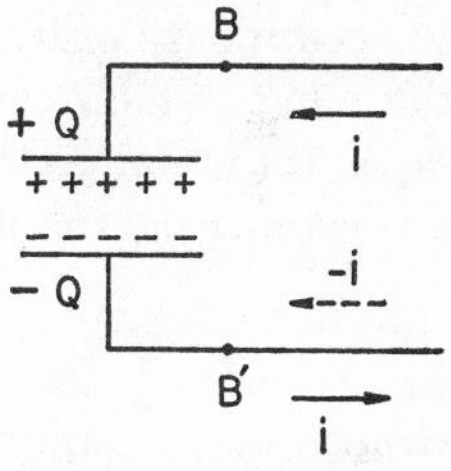

2.4. Current through a capacitor

We will now consider a very important matter; namely, what we mean by current flowing through a capacitor. Let us consider the point B in Fig. 2-2. The current at B is, by definition, the rate at which electric charge flows past it. If electric charge flows past B in the direction of the arrow, it must enter the capacitor. If i is the current at B in the direction of the arrow, then

Fig. 2-2. Current flowing through a capacitor.

$$i = \frac{dQ}{dt} \tag{3}$$

Now as soon as the charge on one plate of a capacitor changes, the electrostatic field will cause an equal and opposite change in charge on the other plate. This means that a current $-i = -dQ/dt$ will flow in the direction of the dotted arrow at B' when a current i flows in the direction of the arrow at B. This current $(-i)$ at B' is equivalent to a current $+i$ in the direction of the full arrow. Thus we may speak of the current $+i$ as flowing through the capacitor in the direction of the full arrows, even though no actual charge passes between its plates.

2.5. Potential drop and counter e.m.f. of a capacitor

The relation between the static and current properties of electricity is such that the potential difference which causes charge

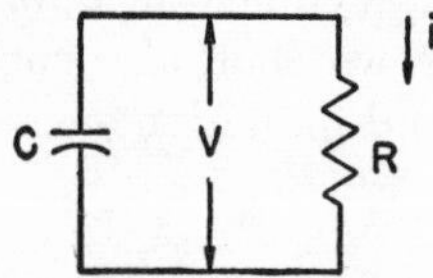

FIG. 2-3. Current flowing through a resistor due to the voltage from a charged capacitor.

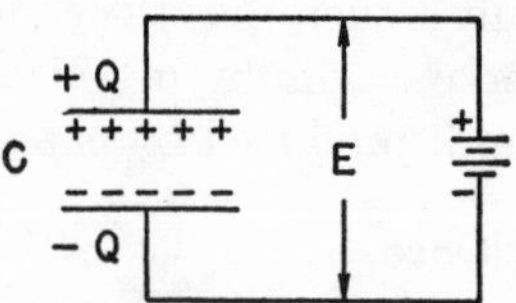

FIG. 2-4. A capacitor charged by a battery.

to accumulate on the plates of a capacitor is of the same nature as the e.m.f. which causes current to flow in a resistor. Thus, if a capacitor is charged to a potential V_0 and is then discharged through a resistance R, the initial current through R will be

$$I_0 = \frac{V_0}{R} \tag{4}$$

As the capacitor is gradually discharged by the flow of current, the magnitude of i will be decreased, but we will always have

$$i = \frac{V}{R} \tag{5}$$

where V is the instantaneous potential difference between the capacitor plates and i is the instantaneous current through R (shown in Fig. 2-3).

On the other hand, if a battery is connected across the terminals of a capacitor, as shown in Fig. 2-4, the latter will become charged.

If the e.m.f. of the battery is E, then the charge on the capacitor will be

$$Q = CE \tag{6}$$

where Q, C, and E are all measured in the same system of units (for instance coulombs, farads, and volts).

The ratio Q/C, which is the voltage across the capacitor, may be considered the counter e.m.f. produced by the capacitor. This just balances the voltage from the battery E. In other words, when a voltage E is applied to the terminals of a capacitor, it accumulates a charge Q of such amount that $Q/C = E$.

Since the current into a capacitor is

$$i = \frac{dQ}{dt}$$

it follows that

$$Q = \int i\,dt$$

Therefore, the expression for the voltage across the capacitor at any instant may be written

$$\text{voltage across capacitor} = \text{counter e.m.f. of capacitor}$$
$$= \frac{Q}{C} = \frac{\int i\,dt}{C} \tag{7}$$

2.6. Pure capacitive element

The essential electrical property of a pure capacitive element is that it has an electrostatic field around it, mostly between its plates in the case of a capacitor. Since an electrostatic field represents a certain amount of energy, we may say that a capacitor stores energy in an electrostatic field. A pure capacitor does not have a magnetic field around it as current flows through it, nor does it generate heat. The flow of current through a capacitor only changes the amount of electrostatic energy which it stores. In electrostatic theory, it is shown that the energy of a charged capacitor is

$$\text{energy} = \frac{1}{2}\frac{Q^2}{C} = \frac{1}{2}CE^2 \tag{8}$$

It follows from Eq. (7) that the maximum voltage across a capacitive element is not in step[1] with the current as in the case of a

[1] We say "in step" rather than "in phase," since we are not limited to steady-state alternating-current considerations in this chapter.

resistance. Rather, the voltage lags behind the current waiting for the accumulation of charge as described by the integral, $\int i\,dt$, before reaching its maximum value. The Eq. (7), however, is true at every instant.

Pure capacitive elements, like pure resistive elements, do not exist in practice. However, a capacitor with an air dielectric is a pretty good approximation to a pure capacitance.

2.7. Inductance of a coil and counter e.m.f.

If current is flowing through an inductor, usually a coil, the inductor is surrounded by a magnetic field, and is threaded by the magnetic flux lines of its own field (see Fig. 2-5). Let the number of flux lines threading the inductor be F. According to a law of physics, the number of flux lines is proportional to the magnitude of the current flowing through the inductor. Therefore we may write

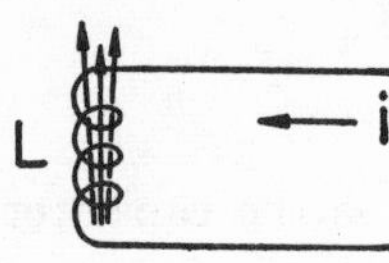

FIG. 2-5. Magnetic flux lines due to current flowing through an inductance.

$$F = Li \tag{9}$$

where L is a factor of proportionality. L is called the self inductance (or just the inductance) of the inductor.

There is a well-known law of physics (Faraday's Law) which says that if the number of magnetic flux lines threading an electrical circuit is changed, an e.m.f. is induced in the circuit. The magnitude of the e.m.f. is equal to the rate of change of the number of flux lines, and its direction is such as to oppose the change in the number of flux lines. According to this law, if the current through an inductor is changing, an e.m.f. is induced of amount

$$\text{induced e.m.f.} = \frac{-dF}{dt} = -L\frac{di}{dt} \tag{10}$$

This induced e.m.f.[2] may be considered the counter e.m.f. produced in an inductor as the current through it changes. Accordingly, we may say that if an e.m.f. E is applied to the inductor, tending to change the current through it, the rate of change of current di/dt is of such an amount that the counter e.m.f. just balances the applied

[2] If L is not a constant, but varies with time due, for example, to mechanical motion, then the form $-dF/dt$ must be used for the e.m.f.

e.m.f. Thus

$$E - L\frac{di}{dt} = 0 \qquad \text{or} \qquad E = L\frac{di}{dt} \tag{11}$$

In other words, the voltage drop across the inductor is $L\ di/dt$.

2.8. Mutual inductance

Suppose we have a coil of self-inductance L_1 through which a current i_1 flows; and a coil of self-inductance L_2 through which a current i_2 flows (see Fig. 2-6). It is common practice to call the respective coils L_1 and L_2, in this case. The magnetic field of the coil L_1 will thread the coil L_2 with a number of lines of force which we may call P. Likewise, the magnetic field of the coil L_2 will thread the coil L_1 with a number of lines of force which we may call Q. Now P is proportional to i_1 and Q is proportional to i_2. Therefore, we may write

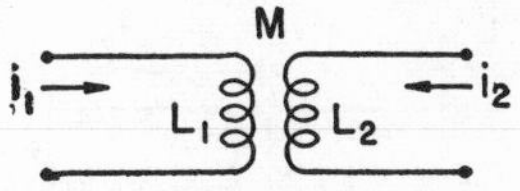

FIG. 2-6. Mutual inductance.

$$P = -M_{12}i_1 \tag{12}$$

$$Q = -M_{21}i_2 \tag{13}$$

where M_{12} and M_{21} are constants of proportionality and the minus sign is merely a sign convention. In the theory of magnetic fields, it is shown that M_{12} and M_{21} must be equal. We therefore call them by the single symbol M. Thus

$$M = M_{12} = M_{21} \tag{14}$$

Referring back to Faraday's law in §2.7 we see that a change in i_1 will induce an e.m.f. e_2 in L_2, and a change in i_2 will induce an e.m.f. e_1 in L_1, where

$$e_2 = -\frac{dP}{dt} = M\frac{di_1}{dt} \tag{15}$$

$$e_1 = -\frac{dQ}{dt} = M\frac{di_2}{dt} \tag{16}$$

It is worthwhile to point out that while L (self-inductance) is always positive, M (mutual inductance) may be either positive or negative. In practice, the sign of the mutual inductance may be changed very simply by reversing the connections of either the primary or secondary coil.

The student may wonder whether a counter e.m.f. is produced by a mutual inductance. A counter e.m.f. is produced in a circuit by the current flowing in that circuit. Thus a mutual inductance does not produce a counter e.m.f. but only produces an induced e.m.f. in other circuits. For instance, consider the case shown in Fig. 2-7. If the current i_1 changes, it will induce a voltage $M(di_1/dt)$ in circuit 2. This will cause a change in i_2 which will, in turn, induce a voltage $M(di_2/dt)$ in circuit 1. This might be considered a counter e.m.f. due to di_1/dt since a change in i_1 was its original cause. However, the magnitude of $M(di_2/dt)$ depends on conditions in circuit 2, such as the size of R_2. It is, therefore, more convenient to consider $M(di_2/dt)$ as an e.m.f. induced by circuit 2 in circuit 1, than to consider it as a counter e.m.f. due to di_1/dt.

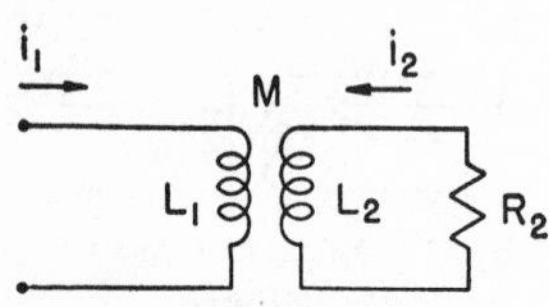

FIG. 2-7. A network with a resistive load in the secondary circuit.

All statements regarding coils in this section refer just as well to inductances in general.

2.9. Pure inductance elements

A pure inductance element has a magnetic field around it as electric current flows through it, but it generates no heat and has no electrostatic field around it. Since a magnetic field represents a certain amount of energy, we may say that an inductance stores energy in a magnetic field. This is true of both self- and mutual inductance. It may be shown that the magnetic field energy of an isolated inductance is $\frac{1}{2}Li^2$, while the magnetic energy due to mutual inductance is Mi_1i_2.

The e.m.f. due to an inductance does not follow in step with the current, but rather with the rate of change of the magnetic field, which generally means the rate of change of a current. This is described mathematically by Eqs. (10), (15), and (16).

2.10. Consideration of potentials in a circuit

In view of the close connection between difference of potential and electromotive force, it is interesting to follow the variation of potential around a circuit in which there are various types of circuit elements.

Suppose a current i is flowing in the circuit of Fig. 2-8. Let the points designated by 1, 2, 3, 4, and 5 have potentials V_1, V_2, V_3,

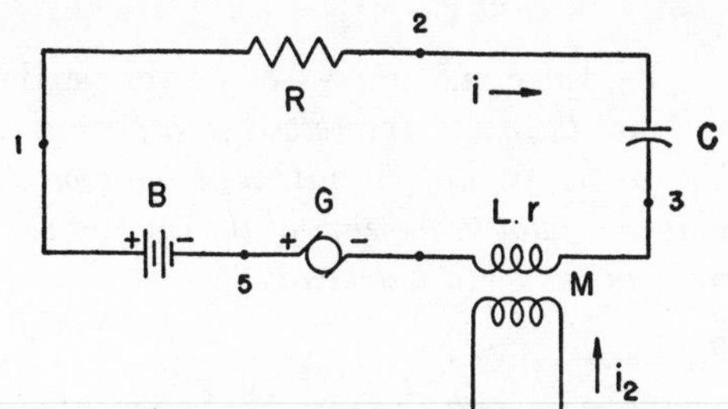

FIG. 2-8. Various potential sources and utilizations in a circuit.

V_4, and V_5, respectively. Then

$$V_1 - V_2 = iR \tag{17}$$

$$V_2 - V_3 = \frac{1}{C}\int i\,dt \tag{18}$$

$$V_3 - V_4 = L\frac{di}{dt} + ri - M\frac{di_2}{dt} \tag{19}$$

$$V_4 - V_5 = -E_g \tag{20}$$

$$V_5 - V_1 = -E_B \tag{21}$$

where E_G and E_B are the voltages generated by the generator and the battery, respectively, in the direction in which the current is flowing. Adding Eqs. (17) through (21) we get

$$0 = iR + \frac{1}{C}\int i\,dt + L\frac{di}{dt} + ri - M\frac{di_2}{dt} - E_G - E_B \tag{22}$$

or

$$E_G + E_B + M\frac{di_2}{dt} = iR + \frac{1}{C}\int i\,dt + L\frac{di}{dt} + ri \tag{23}$$

If we call E_G and E_B the internal e.m.f.'s of the generator and battery, respectively, then Eq. (23) signifies that *the sum of the internal e.m.f.'s plus the induced e.m.f.'s is equal to the sum of the counter e.m.f.'s created by the flow of current in the circuit elements.*

If we consider only a partial circuit, say the circuit from 1 to 5, in a clockwise direction, but excluding the battery, then by adding Eqs. (17) through (20) we get

$$V_1 - V_5 = iR + \frac{1}{C}\int i\,dt + L\frac{di}{dt} + ri - M\frac{di_2}{dt} - E_G \quad (24)$$

By Eq. (21),
$$V_1 - V_5 = E_B \quad (25)$$

If we call $(V_1 - V_5)$ the e.m.f. impressed on the partial circuit, then Eq. (24) tells us that *the e.m.f. impressed on a partial circuit, plus the internal e.m.f.'s of the partial circuit, plus the e.m.f.'s induced into the partial circuit are equal to the sum of the counter e.m.f.'s created by the flow of current in the circuit elements.*

2.11. Kirchhoff's Laws

We are now ready to state the two fundamental laws of electrical network analysis. These are known as Kirchhoff's Laws.

First Law: *The algebraic sum of the currents at any branch point in a network is equal to zero.*

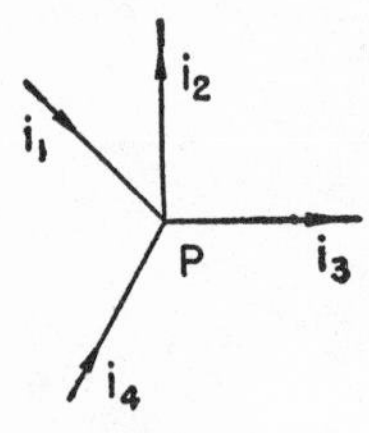

FIG. 2-9. Currents at a node.

Second Law: *The sum of the counter e.m.f.'s produced by the current in the circuit elements of any closed circuit is equal to the algebraic sum of the internal, applied, and induced e.m.f.'s in the same circuit.*

As an illustration of the First Law, consider the branch point (usually called a *node*) P, in Fig. 2-9. For this point, according to the First Law, we must have at every instant

$$i_1 + i_4 - i_2 - i_3 = 0 \quad (26)$$

Stated in other words, *the sum of the currents flowing into P must be equal to the sum of the currents flowing out of P.* This means that there can be no accumulation of charge at P.

As an illustration of the Second Law, consider the network in Fig. 2-10. Regardless of how complicated this network may be, if we follow any closed circuit, such as the one starting at A and going through R_1, C_2, R_3, L_3, R_4, R_5, C_5, and ending at A, we must have

$$R_1i_1 + \frac{\int i_2\,dt}{C_2} + R_3i_3 + L\frac{di_3}{dt} + R_4i_4 + R_5i_5 + \frac{\int i_5\,dt}{C_5}$$
$$= e_1 + e_2 + e_3 + e_4 + e_5 \quad (27)$$

In this case, each e must be taken with the proper sign. Furthermore, any or all of the terms may be zero in particular cases.

The significance of the Second Law is that the electrical potential at A, V_A, has a definite value. In proceeding around the circuit we encounter potential differences of the types shown in Eqs. (17) through (21). But when we get back to A we must again have the potential V_A. Figure 2-8 shows a special case of Kirchhoff's Second Law in which the current i is a constant around the closed circuit.

Kirchhoff's Laws in the form described in this chapter hold at every instant in any electrical network. The reader can show, as an

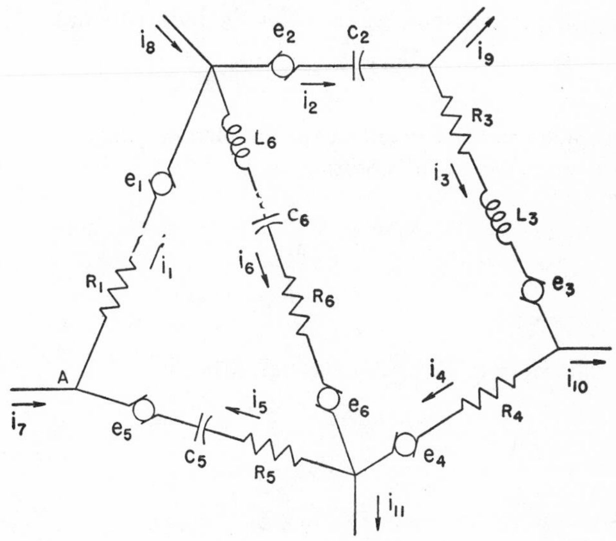

FIG. 2-10. A network.

exercise, that it must follow that these laws will then also hold in the more familiar complex impedance form for steady-state a-c systems. The above form is more fundamental, however, and can be used to obtain complete solutions to circuit problems—transient and aperiodic solutions in addition to the steady-state terms. In order to obtain these solutions, it is necessary only to solve the differential equations which arise from the application of Kirchhoff's Law to electrical networks.

2.12. Impedance functions

For assistance in setting up network equations it has been found convenient to express the counter e.m.f. in any circuit element as the product of an operational quantity called the impedance function of the circuit element, times the current through the element. Accordingly, we have for a resistance,

$$Z_R i = Ri \tag{28}$$

for a capacitance,

$$Z_C i = \frac{\int i\,dt}{C} \tag{29}$$

and for an inductance,

$$Z_L i = L\frac{di}{dt} \tag{30}$$

For a mutual inductance, we have for the induced e.m.f.

$$Z_M i' = M\frac{di'}{dt} \tag{31}$$

where i' refers to the current in the coupled circuit.

If we make use of the notation

$$p = \frac{d}{dt} \tag{32}$$

and

$$\frac{1}{p} = \int dt \tag{33}$$

then it follows from Eqs. (28) through (31) that

$$Z_R = R \tag{34}$$

$$Z_C = \frac{1}{pC} \tag{35}$$

$$Z_L = pL \tag{36}$$

$$Z_M = pM \tag{37}$$

where Z is called the impedance function of the respective circuit element. Accordingly, the counter e.m.f. in any circuit or partial circuit may be written

$$Z(p)i$$

where i is the current flowing in the circuit (or partial circuit), and $Z(p)$ is a function involving only p and the circuit constants. For this reason, if we wish to consider a circuit element or combination of circuit elements without specifying exactly of what it consists, we describe it simply as the impedance Z.

In accordance with this new notation we may now rewrite Eq. (23), for example,

$$E_G + E_B + Mpi_2 = \left[R + \frac{1}{pC} + pL + r\right] i = Zi \qquad (23')$$

where

$$Z = R + \frac{1}{pC} + pL + r \qquad (38)$$

The student has no doubt noted the close connection between the impedance functions described in this section, and the impedances of steady-state a-c theory. When a steady-state condition is reached in a network to which sinusoidal voltages of frequency $\omega/2\pi$ are applied, the currents and voltages can be found algebraically by substituting $(j\omega)$ for p in the impedance functions. But, in order to obtain complete solutions, including transient as well as steady-state terms, and in order to solve problems where the applied voltages are not sinusoidal, it is necessary to use the more fundamental impedance functions rather than steady-state impedances.

2.13. Loop or mesh analysis

Suppose we have a complicated network such as that shown in Fig. 2-11. As we have already stated, the complete solution for the currents and voltages in this network can be obtained by finding the solutions to the equations which we get by applying Kirchhoff's Laws to the network. We shall now describe a standard symmetrical method of applying Kirchhoff's Laws to complicated networks.

Kirchhoff's First Law is automatically applied by employing the concept of *circulating currents* or *loop currents.* According to this concept, the network is made up of a number of closed loops, for example the closed loops I, II, III, IV, V, and VI in Fig. 2-11. In these closed loops, the currents i_1, i_2, i_3, i_4, i_5, and i_6, respectively, are all considered to be positive when flowing in the same direction, either clockwise or counterclockwise. Accordingly, in any impedance which is common to more than one loop, the current which is flowing is the algebraic sum of the circulating currents of all the loops of which it is a common member. Thus the current through Z_C in Fig. 2-11 is $\pm(i_1 - i_2)$, the sign depending upon which direction we wish to consider positive for current through Z_C. By considering all the currents in terms of circulating currents, Kirchhoff's First Law is automatically obeyed. For example, in Fig. 2-11, the sum of the currents into the node, (d), is

$$(i_4 - i_2) + (i_2 - i_3) + (i_3 - i_4) = 0 \tag{39}$$

In order to apply Kirchhoff's Second Law to the network, we apply it successively to each independent loop[3] in the network.

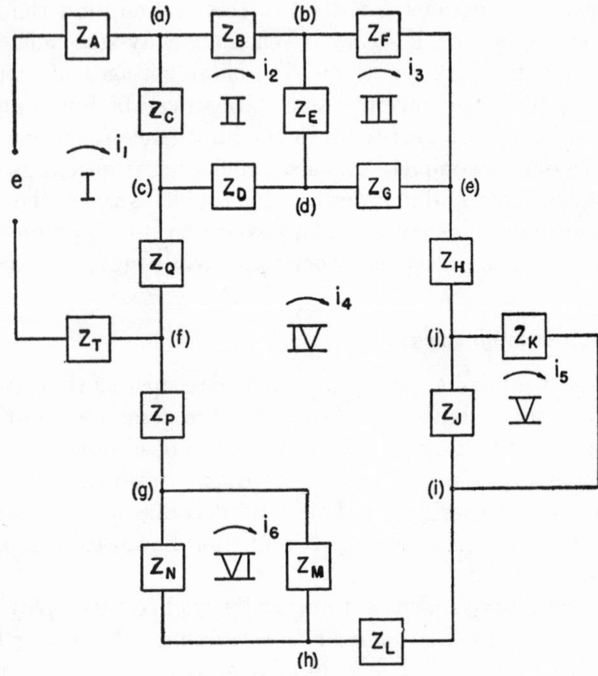

Fig. 2-11. A network of six loops displayed for loop analysis.

This gives us a number of equations equal to the number of independent loops in the network. For example, in the case of the network of Fig. 2-11, we have the six equations

[3] Loops are called independent provided that the determinant of their coefficients, such as the determinant multiplying i_1 in Eq. (49), does not vanish identically. Generally speaking, an independent loop is one which contains one or more impedances that are not included in the other independent loops of the network. It is customary to use the word *mesh* for a loop which cannot be subdivided into other loops.

$$(Z_A + Z_C + Z_Q + Z_T)i_1 - Z_C i_2 - Z_Q i_4 = e \tag{40}$$
$$-Z_C i_1 + (Z_B + Z_E + Z_D + Z_C)i_2 - Z_E i_3 - Z_D i_4 = 0 \tag{41}$$
$$-Z_E i_2 + (Z_F + Z_G + Z_E)i_3 - Z_G i_4 = 0 \tag{42}$$
$$\begin{aligned}-Z_Q i_1 - Z_D i_2 - Z_G i_3 \\ + (Z_Q + Z_D + Z_G + Z_H + Z_J + Z_L + Z_M + Z_P)i_4 \\ - Z_J i_5 - Z_M i_6 = 0\end{aligned} \tag{43}$$
$$-Z_J i_4 + (Z_J + Z_K)i_5 = 0 \tag{44}$$
$$- Z_M i_4 + (Z_M + Z_N)i_6 = 0 \tag{45}$$

These equations can also be written in the symmetrical form

$$\left.\begin{array}{ccccccc} Z_{11}i_1 + Z_{12}i_2 + Z_{13}i_3 + Z_{14}i_4 + Z_{15}i_5 + Z_{16}i_6 = E_1 \\ Z_{21}i_1 + Z_{22}i_2 + Z_{23}i_3 + Z_{24}i_4 + Z_{25}i_5 + Z_{26}i_6 = E_2 \\ \vdots \\ Z_{61}i_1 + Z_{62}i_2 + Z_{63}i_3 + Z_{64}i_4 + Z_{65}i_5 + Z_{66}i_6 = E_6 \end{array}\right\} \tag{46}$$

where $Z_{11} = (Z_A + Z_C + Z_Q + Z_T)$ is the coefficient of i_1 in Eq. (40), $Z_{12} = -Z_C$ is the coefficient of i_2 in the same equation, and so on. In the particular case considered, $E_1 = e$, and $E_2 = E_3 = E_4 = E_5 = E_6 = 0$. We note in passing that

$$Z_{pq} = Z_{qp} \tag{47}$$

for example
$$Z_{12} = -Z_C = Z_{21} \tag{48}$$

Equation (47) will always hold if the impedances consist only of ordinary M, L, R, and C circuit elements.

The symmetrical form, Eq. (46), for the circuit equations is very useful for theoretical considerations and for solution in terms of determinants. Thus we may write

$$\begin{vmatrix} Z_{11} & Z_{12} & \cdots & Z_{16} \\ Z_{21} & Z_{22} & \cdots & Z_{26} \\ \vdots & \vdots & & \vdots \\ Z_{61} & Z_{62} & \cdots & Z_{66} \end{vmatrix} i_1 = \begin{vmatrix} E_1 & Z_{12} & \cdots & Z_{16} \\ E_2 & Z_{22} & \cdots & Z_{26} \\ \vdots & \vdots & & \vdots \\ E_6 & Z_{62} & \cdots & Z_{66} \end{vmatrix} \tag{49}$$

as the integro-differential[4] equation for i_1.

---

[4] The presence of operators involving $1/p$ makes these equations integro-differential equations, rather than ordinary differential equations. We will show, however, that this does not affect the general method of solution.

After the currents have been determined, we can find the voltage drop across any impedance element by using the general formula

$$e = Zi \tag{50}$$

where i is the current through the element and Z is its impedance operator. The potentials of the nodes can then be found by a process of simple addition after one node has been chosen as a reference level. Thus in Fig. 2-11, if we consider the node (f) to be the reference level,[5] then to find the potential at (b), we write

$$\begin{aligned} V_b &= (V_b - V_a) + (V_a - V_c) + (V_c - V_f) + V_f \\ &= -Z_B i_2 + Z_c(i_1 - i_2) + Z_Q(i_1 - i_4) + V_f \end{aligned} \tag{51}$$

2.14. An example of the use of network equations in loop analysis

Let us now use the method of network equations to find the integro-differential equation for the current i_2 in Fig. 2-12. Using the standard symmetrical form, we have

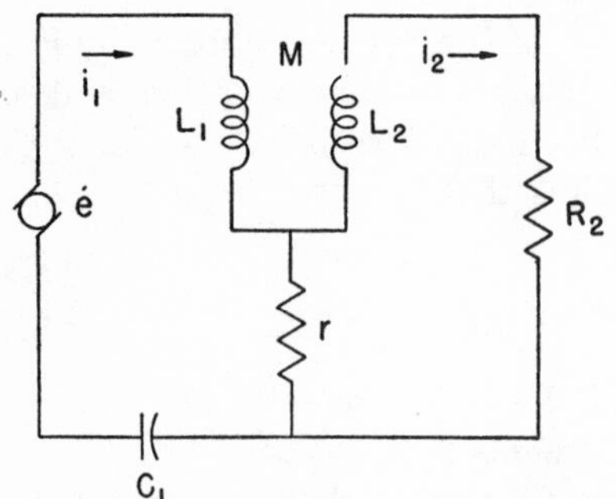

Fig. 2-12. A network with combined inductive and resistive coupling.

$$Z_{11}i_1 + Z_{12}i_2 = e \tag{52}$$

$$Z_{21}i_1 + Z_{22}i_2 = 0 \tag{53}$$

where, by mere inspection of the figure, we can write

$$Z_{11} = pL_1 + r + \frac{1}{pC_1} \tag{54}$$

$$Z_{12} = -(pM + r) = Z_{21} \tag{55}$$

$$Z_{22} = pL_2 + (r + R_2) \tag{56}$$

Solving Eqs. (52) and (53) for i_2, we obtain

$$\begin{aligned} i_2 &= \frac{\begin{vmatrix} Z_{11} & e \\ Z_{12} & 0 \end{vmatrix}}{\begin{vmatrix} Z_{11} & Z_{12} \\ Z_{12} & Z_{22} \end{vmatrix}} = \frac{-Z_{12}e}{Z_{11}Z_{22} - Z_{12}^2} \\ &= \frac{(pM + r)e}{\left(pL_1 + r + \dfrac{1}{pC_1}\right)(pL_2 + r + R_2) - (pM + r)^2} \end{aligned} \tag{57}$$

---

[5] The reference level is usually an electrical ground, and it is considered to be at zero potential.

Equation (57) is the solution for i_2 in operational form. Since p is an operator, the form of Eq. (57) is inconvenient for use. Consequently, we cross-multiply the equation to obtain

$$\left[\left(pL_1 + r + \frac{1}{pC_1}\right)(pL_2 + r + R_2) - (pM + r)^2\right] i_2 = (pM + r)e \quad (58)$$

or

$$\left[p^2(L_1L_2 - M^2) + p(L_1R_2 + L_1r + L_2r - 2Mr) + \left(rR_2 + \frac{L_2}{C_1}\right) + \frac{r + R_2}{pC_1}\right] i_2 = (pM + r)e \quad (59)$$

If we substitute for p and $1/p$ their values given by (32) and (33), we obtain from Eq. (59)

$$(L_1L_2 - M^2)\frac{d^2i_2}{dt^2} + (L_1R_2 + L_1r + L_2r - 2Mr)\frac{di_2}{dt} + \left(rR_2 + \frac{L_2}{C_1}\right) i_2 + \frac{(r + R_2)}{C_1}\int i_2\,dt = M\frac{de}{dt} + re \quad (60)$$

Equation (60) holds, regardless of the form of e. If we can solve the integro-differential equation, we will have the complete solution for i_2.

2.15. Current generators

So far, we have considered only voltage sources as the driving elements in our networks. Some driving elements, however, are more naturally considered as current sources than as voltage sources. A pentode tube may be cited as an example. Actually, in a linear network, every constant-current generator has an equivalent constant-voltage generator, and vice versa, so that, as far as conditions external to the generator are concerned, it can be considered either as a current or a voltage generator.

The equivalent generator forms are shown in Fig. 2-13. In the steady state at any one frequency, it is clear that the voltage generator with its internal impedance Z_{in} in series, will deliver the same voltage and current to the external impedance Z_{ex} as will the current generator with Z_{in} in shunt, provided that

$$e = Z_{in} \cdot i \quad (61)$$

Here e is the strength of the voltage generator in Fig. 2-13(a) and i is the strength of the current generator in Fig. 2-13(b). The voltage across Z_{ex} in either case is

$$\frac{Z_{ex}e}{Z_{ex} + Z_{in}}$$

and the current through Z_{ex} in either case is

$$\frac{Z_{in}i}{Z_{ex} + Z_{in}}$$

With the aid of the Principle of Superposition, to be derived in Chap. 4, it can be shown that the equivalence of the two generator

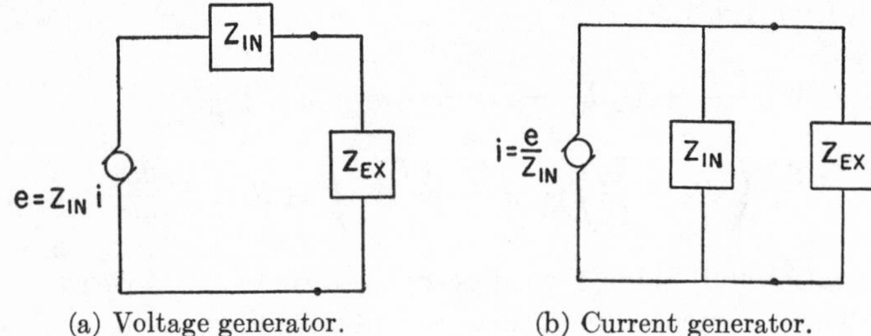

(a) Voltage generator. (b) Current generator.

FIG. 2-13. Equivalent forms of voltage and current generators.

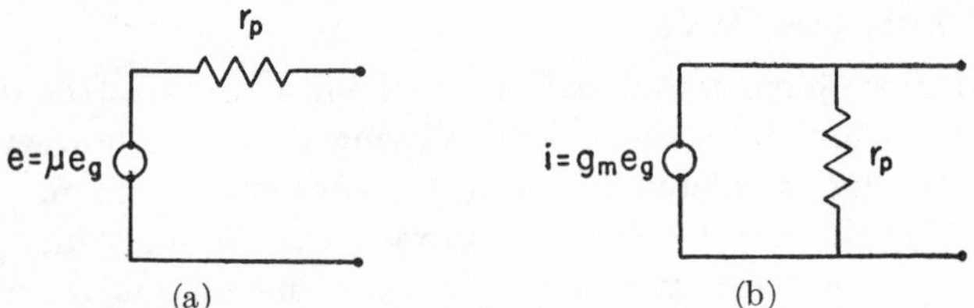

(a) (b)

FIG. 2-14. (a) Representation of an amplifier tube as a voltage generator. (b) Representation of an amplifier tube as a current generator.

representations holds in the transient as well as the steady state, provided that the impedances are linear and do not vary with time. As an example of equivalent current and voltage generator representations, we may cite an amplifier tube. This may be represented as a voltage generator of strength μe_g in series with the plate resistance r_p, or it can equally well be represented as a current generator of strength

$$\frac{\mu e_g}{r_p} = g_m e_g \tag{62}$$

in shunt with r_p, since

$$g_m = \frac{\mu}{r_p} \tag{63}$$

These equivalent forms of representation are shown in Fig. 2-14.

2.16. Node analysis

The method of *loop analysis* used in §2.13 is not always the best method for solving network problems. It is sometimes preferable to use the complementary method known as *node analysis.* In node analysis, the potentials of the various nodes with respect to some reference node take the place of the loop currents used in loop analysis. Current generators are used instead of voltage generators. Instead of impedances, their reciprocals, admittances, are used. Finally, the network equations are the expressions of Kirchhoff's First Law, namely the equality of currents going into and out of each node.

To illustrate the method of node analysis, let us analyze the network in Fig. 2-11 by means of node analysis. First, let us choose node (f) as the reference node and let us assign to it a potential zero. Then the potentials of all other nodes are their potentials with respect to node (f). Next let us replace the voltage generator e in series with Z_A and Z_T, with a current generator of strength

$$i = \frac{e}{Z_A + Z_T} \tag{64}$$

and let the current generator be in shunt with $Z_A + Z_T$ as shown in Fig. 2-15. We now write down the network equations:[6]

$$Y_B(V_a - V_b) + Y_C(V_a - V_c) + Y_{AT}V_a = i \tag{65}$$

$$Y_B(V_b - V_a) + Y_E(V_b - V_d) + Y_F(V_b - V_e) = 0 \tag{66}$$

$$Y_C(V_c - V_a) + Y_D(V_c - V_d) + Y_QV_c = 0 \tag{67}$$

$$Y_D(V_d - V_c) + Y_E(V_d - V_b) + Y_G(V_d - V_e) = 0 \tag{68}$$

$$Y_F(V_e - V_b) + Y_G(V_e - V_d) + Y_H(V_e - V_j) = 0 \tag{69}$$

---

[6] $Y_B = 1/Z_B$ is called the admittance of the branch from node (a) to node (b) with a corresponding meaning for Y_C, Y_D, etc.

$$- Y_Q V_c - Y_{AT} V_a - Y_P V_g = -i \qquad (70)$$

$$Y_P V_g + (Y_N + Y_M)(V_g - V_h) = 0 \qquad (71)$$

$$(Y_N + Y_M)(V_h - V_g) + Y_L(V_h - V_i) = 0 \qquad (72)$$

$$Y_L(V_i - V_h) + (Y_J + Y_K)(V_i - V_j) = 0 \qquad (73)$$

$$(Y_J + Y_K)(V_j - V_i) + Y_H(V_j - V_e) = 0 \qquad (74)$$

The number of independent node equations is one less than the number of nodes, since any one of the node equations is always

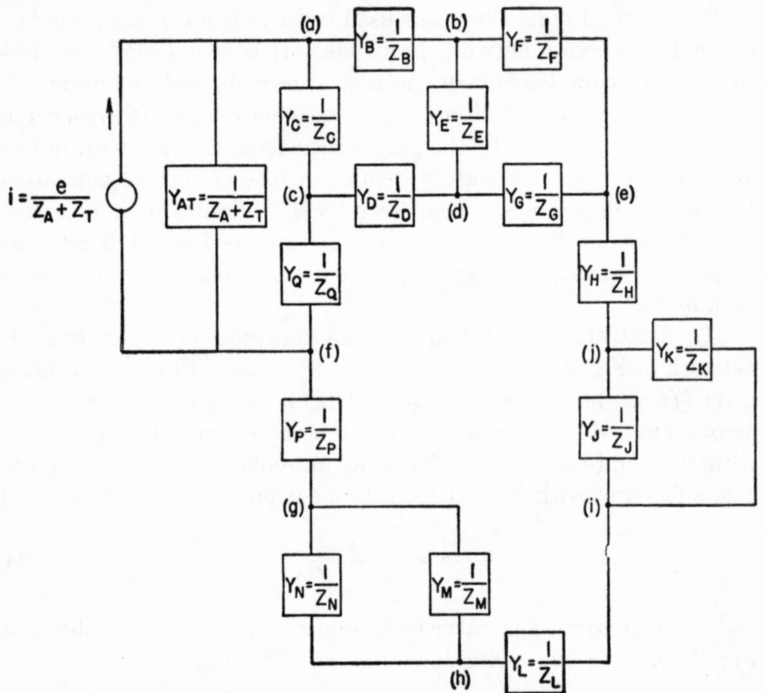

Fig. 2-15. Equivalent representation of the network of Fig. 2-11 as a network of ten nodes displayed for node analysis.

derivable from a combination of the others. (See Example 1 below.) It is therefore customary to eliminate the node equation corresponding to the reference node [node (f) in our discussion]. Equation (70) is thus superfluous, and the equation corresponding to it in any analysis is usually omitted. We may note in passing that since setting the reference-node voltage V_f equal to zero removes the f column from Eq. (81), it is to be expected that the f row will also be superfluous. Otherwise we would have more equations than unknowns, so that the equations could not all be independent.

Equations (65) through (74) may also be written in symmetrical form, corresponding to Eq. (46) for loop analysis. Thus Eq. (65) may be written

$$(Y_B + Y_C + Y_{AT})V_a - Y_BV_b - Y_CV_c = i \tag{75}$$

or

$$Y_{aa}V_a + Y_{ab}V_b + Y_{ac}V_c = i_a \tag{76}$$

where $Y_{aa} = Y_B + Y_C + Y_{AT}$ = sum of admittances from node (a) to all other neighboring nodes (77)[7]

$Y_{ab} = -Y_B$ = minus the admittance from node (a) to node (b) without going through other nodes (78)

$Y_{ac} = -Y_C$ = minus the admittance from node (a) to node (c) without going through other nodes (79)

$i_a = i$ = sum of current entering node (a) from current generators attached to it. (80)

The entire set of equations, Eqs. (65) through (74), may therefore be written in the symmetrical form

$$\begin{array}{c} Y_{aa}V_a + Y_{ab}V_b + Y_{ac}V_c + \cdots + Y_{aj}V_j = i_a \\ Y_{ba}V_a + Y_{bb}V_b + Y_{bc}V_c + \cdots + Y_{bj}V_j = i_b \\ \vdots \qquad \vdots \qquad \vdots \qquad \qquad \vdots \qquad \vdots \\ Y_{ja}V_a + Y_{jb}V_b + Y_{jc}V_c + \cdots + Y_{jj}V_j = i_j \end{array} \tag{81}$$

As mentioned above, the equation corresponding to the reference node (f) is superfluous, and may be omitted. It may also be noted that

$$Y_{pq} = Y_{qp} \tag{82}$$

The set of equations (81) can readily be solved formally for any voltage with the aid of determinants. For example, if V_a is the voltage of interest, we write

[7] A neighboring node to node (a) is one that can be reached from node (a) without going through any other node.

$$\begin{vmatrix} Y_{aa} & Y_{ab} & \cdots & Y_{aj} \\ Y_{ba} & Y_{bb} & \cdots & Y_{bj} \\ \vdots & \vdots & & \vdots \\ Y_{ja} & Y_{jb} & \cdots & Y_{jj} \end{vmatrix} V_a = \begin{vmatrix} i_a & Y_{ab} & \cdots & Y_{aj} \\ i_b & Y_{bb} & \cdots & Y_{bj} \\ \vdots & \vdots & & \vdots \\ i_j & Y_{jb} & \cdots & Y_{jj} \end{vmatrix} \tag{83}$$

Whether to use loop analysis or node analysis in solving a problem should be determined by deciding which method leads more easily to the final desired answer. In a case such as that of Fig. 2-11, where there are more independent node than loop equations (9 and 6 respectively) the decision would normally be in favor of loop analysis. In other cases, especially those involving vacuum-tube amplifiers, node analysis may be simpler and should therefore be used.[8]

Exercises

1. Write down the node equations for Fig. 2-A, and show that the equation for node (a) can be obtained by a linear combination of the equations for nodes (b), (c), and (d).

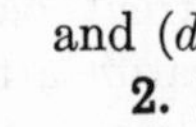

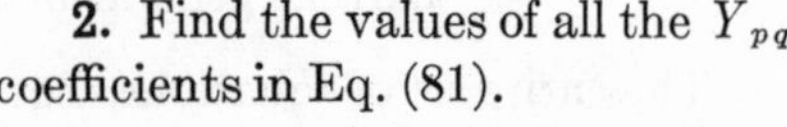

2. Find the values of all the Y_{pq} coefficients in Eq. (81).

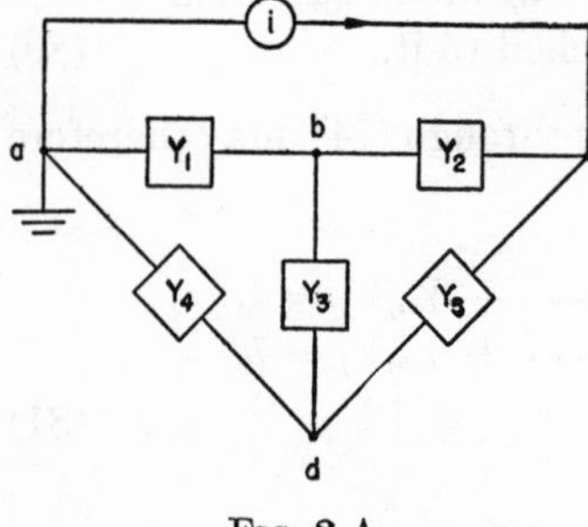

FIG. 2-A.

2.17. An example of node analysis

As a practical example of the use of node analysis, consider the video-amplifier stage in Fig. 2-16(a). Let us write down the equations to find the output voltage e_2 in terms of the input voltage e_g.

Let us first draw the circuit in the equivalent form shown in Fig. 2-16(b) which is suitable for node analysis. Using ground as the reference node, we write down the equations for the other nodes, (1) and (2).

$$\left(\frac{g_m}{\mu} + \frac{1}{R_1 + pL} + pC\right) e_1 - pCe_2 = g_m e_g \tag{84}$$

$$-pCe_1 + \left(\frac{1}{R_2} + pC + pC_2\right) e_2 = 0 \tag{85}$$

[8] For an excellent and more extensive discussion of node analysis, see Gardner and Barnes, *Transients in Linear Systems*, Chap. II.

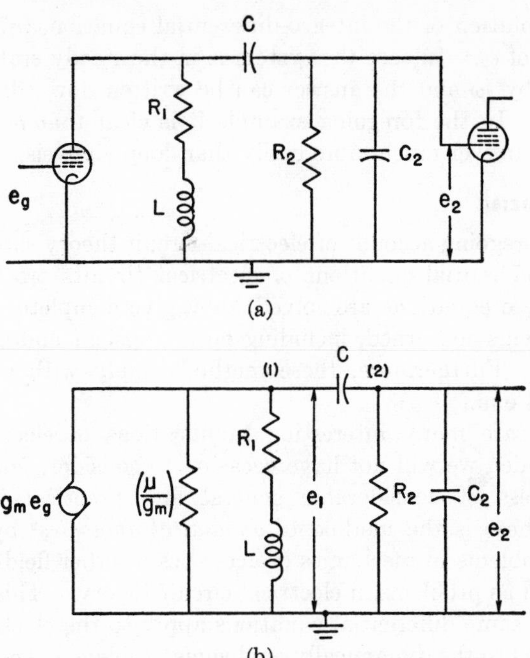

FIG. 2-16. An amplifier schematic and its equivalent display for node analysis. (a) Video amplifier stage. (b) Equivalent schematic display for node analysis.

To find e_2, we solve by determinants. Thus,

$$\begin{vmatrix} \left(\dfrac{g_m}{\mu} + \dfrac{1}{R_1 + pL} + pC\right) & -pC \\ -pC & \left(\dfrac{1}{R_2} + pC + pC_2\right) \end{vmatrix} e_2 = \begin{vmatrix} \left(\dfrac{g_m}{\mu} + \dfrac{1}{R_1 + pL} + pC\right) & g_m e_g \\ -pC & 0 \end{vmatrix} \tag{86}$$

This reduces to

$$\left[\left(\frac{g_m}{\mu} + \frac{1}{R_1 + pL} + pC\right)\left(\frac{1}{R_2} + pC + pC_2\right) - p^2C^2\right] e_2 = pCg_me_g \tag{87}$$

The solution of the integro-differential equation, (87), will give the form of e_2. In case the system is in the steady state, p can be replaced by $j\omega$ and the answer can be written down directly from Eq. (87). In the foregoing example it is clear that node analysis gives the answer much more easily than loop analysis.

2.18. General

The foregoing account of electrical-circuit theory shows how the integro-differential equations of electrical circuits are formulated. When these equations are solved, they give complete solutions to the problems concerned, including both transient and steady-state solutions. Furthermore, these methods apply with any type of impressed e.m.f.

There are many interesting ramifications of electrical-circuit theory which we will not have occasion to consider, but which are nevertheless of considerable general and practical importance. Among these is the method of *dynamical analogies*[9] by means of which problems in mechanics or acoustics or other fields of physics are solved as problems in electrical-circuit theory. This is possible when the same differential equations apply to the electrical-circuit problem as to the dynamically analogous problem. The advantage of solving such problems as electrical-circuit problems lies in the fact that electrical-circuit theory has been so thoroughly developed and is so widely known that other problems seem simpler when dealt with in the language of and with the methods of electrical-circuit theory. The method of dynamical analogies, however, works both ways, so that it is also possible, and sometimes instructive, to solve a circuit problem as a problem in some dynamically analogous field.

Further developments of circuit theory will be found in later chapters of this book, especially in Chap. 4. The solution of problems based upon circuit theory will occupy much of our attention throughout the book.

2.19. Units

All the equations of this chapter will hold directly in the mks system of units. In this system, the units used for the various quantities mentioned are as follows:

---

[9] H. F. Olson, *Dynamical Analogies*, and Chap. II of Gardner and Barnes, *op. cit.*

Quantity	*Unit*
length	meter
mass	kilogram
time	second
current	ampere
potential	volt
charge	coulomb
power	watt
energy	joule
resistance	ohm
capacitance	farad
inductance (self or mutual)	henry

Exercises

1. Write the network equations for Fig. 2-B in (1) loop form and (2) node form.

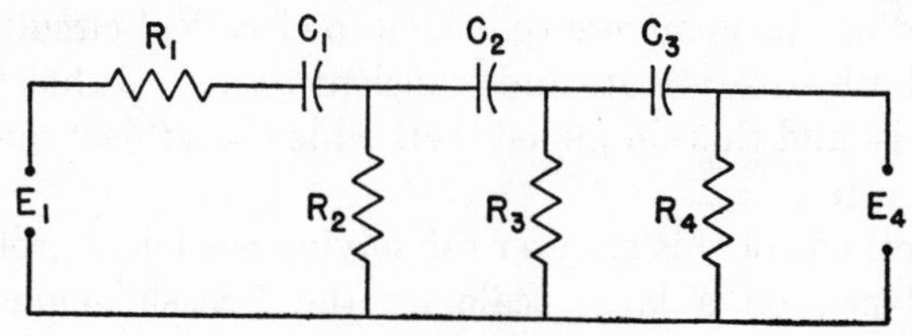

FIG. 2-B.

2. Write the loop equations for Fig. 2-C in symmetrical form. Show that

$$Z_{23} = Z_{32}$$

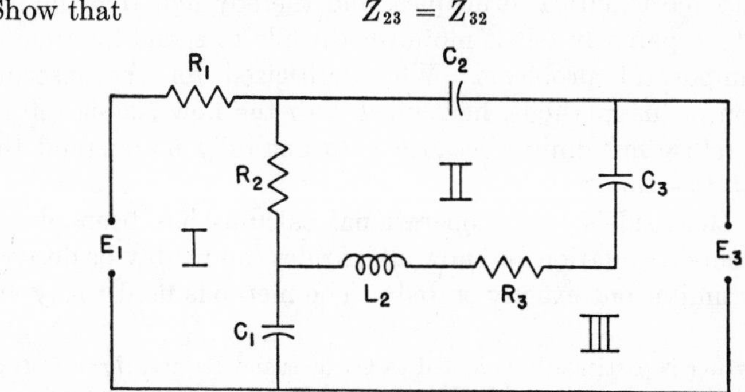

FIG. 2-C.

(In exercises (1) and (2) E_1 represents a voltage generator, but E_4 and E_3 merely represent voltages to be found.)

CHAPTER 3

Transient Solutions of Circuit Problems by Means of the Laplace Transformation[1]

3.1. The fundamental problem — a simple solution for transients — introduction

The reader is no doubt acquainted with the simple method of solving steady-state problems in terms of complex quantities. The question therefore naturally arises as to whether there is any simple way of finding the complete solutions to electrical-circuit problems, including both steady-state and transient terms. It has been found that there is, and this simplified method is the subject matter of the present chapter.

The methods of this chapter for solving electrical problems were first developed on a large scale by the British engineer, Oliver Heaviside. As developed by him, the subject was called *operational calculus* and was essentially a collection of rules which he had found would usually work. He made no great effort to derive these rules from basic mathematical principles, and thereby find their limitations. He apparently felt it more worthwhile to spend his time in solving important problems. When criticized for the insecure foundation of his methods, he replied with the now classic retort, "Shall I refuse my dinner because I do not fully understand the process of digestion?"

Since Heaviside's time,[2] operational calculus has been placed upon a secure foundation and now all its rules can readily be derived and their limitations exactly stated. The methods used today are

---

[1] The writer is particularly indebted to Gardner and Barnes, *Transients in Linear Systems*, as a background for the material presented in this chapter.

[2] It is known that many of the rules used by Heaviside were independently and sometimes previously discovered by others, and were frequently based on a more secure mathematical foundation by their discoverers. But it was Heaviside who first used these rules in a systematic study of transients.

such that the subject is more accurately named *transformation calculus*, and this is the name we employ here. Present methods can be used to treat arbitrary initial conditions in the problem, which could not easily be done by Heaviside, and more varied types of applied voltages can now be handled.

3.2. Laplace transforms

In Chap. IV of the author's *Frequency Analysis, Modulation and Noise*, the Fourier integral is applied to the solution of practical problems.[3] In many of these problems, we are given a function of time $G(t)$ which passes through a transmission system having a known frequency characteristic, and we want to find the output signal. To solve this problem we express the time function $G(t)$ in terms of its frequency composition $F(f)$ with the aid of a Fourier transformation. We then apply the frequency characteristic of the transmission system to $F(f)$ in order to obtain the frequency composition of the output signal $\bar{F}(f)$. The Fourier-integral transformation formulas are then once more used to transform $\bar{F}(f)$ into $\bar{G}(t)$, the resultant output signal.

Reviewing the procedure used in Fourier-integral analysis, we see that even though both the input and output signals are functions of time, the problem is actually solved in terms of frequency, except for initial and final transformations between time and frequency. Since it is possible to express $G(t)$ in terms of frequency, and since the characteristics of the transmission system are given in terms of frequency, solving in terms of frequency is the most practical method.

Now, it so happens that in solving the differential equations of electrical circuits, it is also possible to express the quantities involved in terms of a secondary variable. In terms of this secondary variable, we can solve the problem algebraically. Then by transforming back to the original independent variable, we obtain the solution to the original differential equation. The transformation which makes these operations possible is called the Laplace transformation.[4]

The Laplace transformation transforms $f(t)$, a function of t, into $F(s)$, a function of some new variable s, according to the equation

---

[3] A short discussion of Fourier integrals is also given in Appendix E of this book.

[4] First introduced by P. S. Laplace in 1779.

$$\int_0^\infty f(t)\epsilon^{-st}\,dt = F(s) \tag{1}$$

For example, if

$$f(t) = \epsilon^{-at} \tag{2}$$

then

$$\int_0^\infty \epsilon^{-at}\cdot\epsilon^{-st}\,dt = \int_0^\infty \epsilon^{-(a+s)t}\,dt = \frac{\epsilon^{-(a+s)t}}{-(a+s)}\bigg|_0^\infty = \frac{1}{a+s} \tag{3}$$

Therefore

$$F(s) = \frac{1}{a+s} \tag{4}$$

Thus the Laplace transformation allows ϵ^{-at} to be expressed as

$$\frac{1}{a+s}$$

The quantities ϵ^{-at} and $1/(a+s)$ are therefore called *Laplace transforms.* Specifically, $1/(a+s)$ is called the *Laplace transform* of ϵ^{-at}, while ϵ^{-at} is called the inverse transform of $1/(a+s)$.

Equation (1) is called the *direct* Laplace transformation. An *inverse* transformation which expresses $f(t)$ in terms of $F(s)$ will be derived in Chap. 7. The physical significance of t in Eq. (1) is determined by the problem at hand. Most frequently in our work it will be time, but it may also be some other variable, such as length. On the other hand, the physical significance of s is just the significance which we find for it because of its relation to t in Eq. (1). This significance will be discussed in Chap. 7, but for our present purposes we do not need to know anything more about s than that it is related to t through Eq. (1).

As we shall use it, t in Eq. (1) will be restricted to real values, but s will be allowed to take on complex values. However, the real part of s will be required to be large enough to make the integral in Eq. (1) absolutely convergent. In accordance with the foregoing, it will frequently be convenient to refer to t as the *real variable* and s as the *complex variable* in the Laplace transformation.

The form of $F(s)$ determined by an integration in which s is allowed to have any real positive value [greater than some minimum required to make the integral in Eq. (1) converge] can also be used when s is complex. This follows because the analytical extension theorem (§5.16) tells us that if

$$\int_0^\infty f(t)\epsilon^{-st}\,dt = F(s) \tag{5}$$

for a continuous range of values of s along the real axis, then the two expressions must be equal for all values of s for which both expressions are analytic. Accordingly

$$\int_0^\infty \epsilon^{-at}\epsilon^{-st}\,dt = \frac{1}{a+s} \tag{6}$$

holds for complex as well as real values of s.

Equation (1) may also be written in the form

$$\mathcal{L}[f(t)] = F(s) \tag{7}$$

in which operating with $\mathcal{L}$ on a function of t means multiplying it by ϵ^{-st} and integrating with respect to t from 0 to ∞. Thus, for example

$$\mathcal{L}[\epsilon^{-at}] = \frac{1}{a+s} \tag{8}$$

Equation (7) is called the functional form of the Laplace transformation, and is just a short-hand method of writing Eq. (1).

Exercises

Find the Laplace transforms of: **1.** $\cos \omega t$. **2.** 1. **3.** $t\epsilon^{-bt}$.

Answers:

1. $\dfrac{s}{s^2+\omega^2}$. **2.** $\dfrac{1}{s}$. **3.** $\dfrac{1}{(s+b)^2}$.

3.3. Some fundamental transformation formulas

The Laplace transformation is of outstanding importance because it can be used to transform problems in differential and integro-differential equations in t into algebraic problems in s. This property is due to the following two theorems:

Theorem I: *If*

$$\int_0^\infty f(t)\epsilon^{-st}\,dt = F(s) \tag{9}$$

then

$$\int_0^\infty \frac{d}{dt}[f(t)]\cdot\epsilon^{-st}\,dt = sF(s) - f(0+) \tag{10}$$

In the foregoing theorem, $f(0+)$ is the value of $f(t)$ as t approaches zero from the positive side. (See Fig. 3-1.)

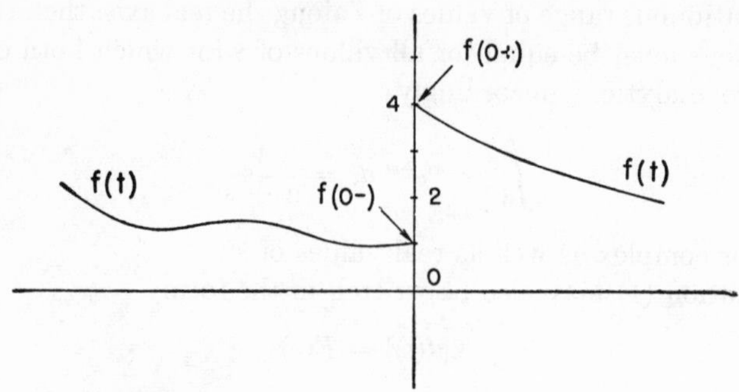

$f(0+) = 4$
$f(0-) = 1$
$f(t+) = f(t-)$ where $f(t)$ is continuous.

FIG. 3-1. + and − notation at a discontinuity.

Theorem II: *If*

$$\int_0^\infty f(t)\epsilon^{-st}\,dt = F(s) \tag{11}$$

then

$$\int_0^\infty \left\{\int_0^t f(t)\,dt\right\} \epsilon^{-st}\,dt = \frac{F(s)}{s} \tag{12}$$

In order for Theorems I and II to hold, it is, of course, necessary that all the integrals involved be convergent.

To prove Theorem I, we integrate Eq. (9) by parts. This gives[5]

$$\int_0^\infty f(t)\epsilon^{-st}\,dt = \frac{-1}{s} f(t)\epsilon^{-st}\Big|_0^\infty + \frac{1}{s}\int_0^\infty \frac{df(t)}{dt}\epsilon^{-st}\,dt$$

$$= \frac{1}{s} f(0+) + \frac{1}{s}\int_0^\infty \frac{df(t)}{dt}\epsilon^{-st}\,dt \qquad (13)^6$$

Making use of Eq. (9), we can then transform Eq. (13) directly into Eq. (10), thus proving the theorem.

To prove Theorem II, we integrate Eq. (11) by parts, but this time we let

$$u = \epsilon^{-st} \qquad \text{and} \qquad dv = f(t)\,dt$$

[5] In Eq. (13) we let $u = f(t)$ and $dv = \epsilon^{-st}\,dt$ in the equation

$$\int u\,dv = uv - \int v\,du$$

[6] In writing $f(0+)$, we anticipate the possibility that $f(t)$ may have a discontinuity at $t = 0$.

Thus

$$\int_0^\infty f(t)\epsilon^{-st}\,dt = \left\{\epsilon^{-st}\int^t f(t)\,dt\right\}\Big|_0^\infty + s\int_0^\infty\left[\int^t f(t)\,dt\right]\epsilon^{-st}\,dt$$
$$= -\int^{0+} f(t)\,dt + s\int_0^\infty\left[\int^t f(t)\,dt\right]\epsilon^{-st}\,dt \quad (14)^7$$

However,

$$\int_0^\infty \left\{\int_0^t f(t)\,dt\right\}\epsilon^{-st}\,dt$$
$$= \int_0^\infty\left\{\int^t f(t)\,dt\right\}\epsilon^{-st}\,dt - \left\{\int^{0+} f(t)\,dt\right\}\int_0^\infty \epsilon^{-st}\,dt$$
$$= \int_0^\infty\left\{\int^t f(t)\,dt\right\}\epsilon^{-st}\,dt - \frac{1}{s}\int^{0+} f(t)\,dt \quad (15)$$

Substitution of Eqs. (11) and (15) into Eq. (14) yields Eq. (12), thus proving the theorem.

If we use the notation

$$f^{-1}(t) = \int^t f(t)\,dt \quad (16)$$

and

$$f^1(t) = \frac{d}{dt}[f(t)] \quad (17)$$

then according to Eqs. (12) and (15), Theorem II may be written[8]

$$\mathcal{L}[f^{-1}(t)] = \frac{F(s)}{s} + \frac{f^{-1}(0+)}{s} \quad (18)$$

Correspondingly, Theorem I may be written

$$\mathcal{L}[f^1(t)] = sF(s) - f(0+) \quad (19)$$

In addition to the foregoing theorems, as expressed in Eqs. (10) and (12) or (18) and (19), the reader can easily prove the theorems expressed by the following formulas[9] (20–26):

---

[7] The form $\int^t$ stands for the indefinite integral, while $\int^0$ stands for the indefinite integral with 0 substituted for t.

[8] $f^{-1}(0+)$ is a shorthand method of writing $\int^{0+} f(t)\,dt$, which is the value of the indefinite integral $\int f(t)\,dt$ as t approaches zero from the positive side.

[9] The significance of $\mathcal{L}[f(t/a)]$ in Eq. (23) is

$$\int_0^\infty f\left(\frac{t}{a}\right)\epsilon^{-st}\,dt$$

not

$$\int_0^\infty f\left(\frac{t}{a}\right)\epsilon^{-s(t/a)}\,d\left(\frac{t}{a}\right)$$

In case we should have occasion to express the latter in functional form, we

$$\mathcal{L}[af(t)] = aF(s) \tag{20}$$

$$\mathcal{L}[f_1(t) + f_2(t)] = F_1(s) + F_2(s) \tag{21}$$

$$\mathcal{L}[f_1(t) - f_2(t)] = F_1(s) - F_2(s) \tag{22}$$

In Eqs. (21) and (22), $F_1(s)$ is the Laplace transform of $f_1(t)$ and $F_2(s)$ is the Laplace transform of $f_2(t)$.

$$\mathcal{L}\left[f\left(\frac{t}{a}\right)\right] = aF(as) \tag{23}$$

$$\mathcal{L}[\epsilon^{-at}f(t)] = F(s + a) \tag{24}$$

$$\mathcal{L}[\epsilon^{at}f(t)] = F(s - a) \tag{25}$$

$$\mathcal{L}\left[\frac{d^2f(t)}{dt^2}\right] = s^2F(s) - sf(0+) - f^1(0+) \tag{26}$$

All the formulas, Eqs. (20) through (26), are limited to cases in which the Laplace integrals converge.

With the aid of the foregoing general formulas, we are now in a position to derive a great number of special formulas, and thus develop a useful table of Laplace transforms as a preliminary to the solution of practical problems. All of the foregoing general formulas, along with many other general and special formulas are listed in the table in Appendix D.

Exercises

1. Assuming $f(t)$ and $F(s)$ to be related by the equation

$$\int_0^\infty f(t)\epsilon^{-st}\,dt = F(s)$$

show that $\quad \mathcal{L}\left[f\left(\frac{t}{a}\right)\right] = \int_0^\infty f\left(\frac{t}{a}\right)\epsilon^{-st}\,dt = aF(as)$

thus deriving Eq. (23).

2. If

$$\int_0^\infty t\cos\beta t\cdot\epsilon^{-st}\,dt = \frac{s^2 - \beta^2}{(s^2 + \beta^2)^2}$$

---

shall write it $\mathcal{L}_{t/a}[f(t/a)]$. When $\mathcal{L}$ has no subscript, it will be assumed that the real variable (i.e., the variable of integration and the multiplier of $-s$ in the exponent) is t.

use Eq. (23) to find the value of

$$\int_0^\infty \frac{t}{\beta} \cos t \cdot \epsilon^{-st}\, dt$$

Answer:

$$\beta \left\{ \frac{\beta^2 s^2 - \beta^2}{(\beta^2 s^2 + \beta^2)^2} \right\} = \frac{1}{\beta} \left\{ \frac{s^2 - 1}{(s^2 + 1)^2} \right\}$$

3. Derive Eqs. (24) and (25).

4. Show that Eqs. (20), (21), and (22) are immediate consequences of formulas (1), (2), and (3) of Appendix A.

5. Derive Eq. (26).

6. Let $f(t) = t^3 - t$ and verify Eq. (26) by direct differentiation and integration.

3.4. A time-displacement theorem

Another fundamental formula in dealing with Laplace transforms is expressed by the following theorem:

Theorem: *If*

$$F(s) = \mathcal{L}[f(t)]$$

and $\quad f(t) = 0 \quad$ *when* $\quad t < 0,$

then $\quad \mathcal{L}[f(t - b)] = \epsilon^{-bs} F(s)$

provided that b is a positive constant.

To prove the theorem, let

$$\tau = t - b \tag{27}$$

Then
$$\mathcal{L}[f(t - b)] = \int_{t=0}^{\infty} f(t - b)\epsilon^{-st}\, dt = \int_{\tau=-b}^{\infty} f(\tau)\epsilon^{-s(\tau+b)}\, d\tau$$
$$= \int_0^\infty f(\tau)\epsilon^{-s(\tau+b)}\, d\tau \tag{28}$$

since $f(\tau) = 0$ when $\tau < 0$. Thus

$$\mathcal{L}[f(t - b)] = \int_0^\infty f(\tau)\epsilon^{-s(\tau+b)}\, d\tau = \epsilon^{-sb} \int_0^\infty f(\tau)\epsilon^{-s\tau}\, d\tau$$
$$= \epsilon^{-sb} F(s) \tag{29}$$

which proves the theorem. This formula is very useful in dealing with wave-propagation problems and also in dealing with pulsing or switching problems where there is a discontinuity in the time function.

3.5. Development of a table of Laplace transforms

In Appendix D, as already mentioned, there is an extended table of Laplace transforms. We now wish to show how this table is developed, by deriving a number of these formulas.

In §3.2, we have already shown that

$$\int_0^\infty \epsilon^{-at}\epsilon^{-st}\,dt = \frac{1}{s+a} \tag{30}$$

so that

$$\mathfrak{L}[\epsilon^{-at}] = \frac{1}{s+a} \tag{31}$$

Let us next find the transform of sin bt, where b is a real number. Here, using standard methods of integration

$$\int_0^\infty \sin bt\epsilon^{-st}\,dt = \frac{\epsilon^{-st}(-s\sin bt - b\cos bt)}{b^2+s^2}\Bigg|_0^\infty$$

$$= \frac{b}{b^2+s^2} \tag{32}$$

Therefore

$$\mathfrak{L}[\sin bt] = \frac{b}{b^2+s^2} \tag{33}$$

We can use the same integration formula to find the transform of ϵ^{-at} sin bt, where the real part of a is positive.

Thus

$$\int_0^\infty \epsilon^{-at}\sin bt\,\epsilon^{-st}\,dt = \frac{\epsilon^{-(a+s)t}[-(a+s)\sin bt - b\cos bt]}{b^2+(a+s)^2}\Bigg|_0^\infty$$

$$= \frac{b}{b^2+(a+s)^2} \tag{34}$$

Therefore

$$\mathfrak{L}[\epsilon^{-at}\sin bt] = \frac{b}{b^2+(a+s)^2} \tag{35}$$

By entirely similar methods, we could derive the formulas

$$\mathfrak{L}[\cos bt] = \frac{s}{b^2+s^2} \tag{36}$$

$$\mathfrak{L}[\epsilon^{-at}\cos bt] = \frac{a+s}{b^2+(a+s)^2} \tag{37}$$

Actually, we could have obtained Eq. (34) from Eq. (33) and Eq. (37) from Eq. (36) directly, by using Eq. (24).

Next let us find the transform of t. Here, integrating by parts, we get

$$\int_0^\infty t\epsilon^{-st}\,dt = \frac{t\epsilon^{-st}}{-s}\Big|_0^\infty - \int_0^\infty \frac{\epsilon^{-st}}{-s}\,dt$$

$$= \frac{-1}{s}\left\{\left(t + \frac{1}{s}\right)\epsilon^{-st}\right\}\Big|_0^\infty = \frac{1}{s^2} \tag{38}$$

provided that the real part of s is positive.

Thus

$$\mathfrak{L}[t] = \frac{1}{s^2} \tag{39}$$

In a similar manner, we could find the transform of t^2 by integration. However, for the sake of practice, we prefer to do it with the aid of Eqs. (18), (20), and (39). Thus

$$\mathfrak{L}[t^2] = \mathfrak{L}\left[\int^t 2t\,dt\right] = \frac{2}{s}\left(\frac{1}{s^2}\right) + 0 = \frac{2}{s^3} \tag{40}$$

In continuing this process for higher powers of t, we could find the general formula

$$\mathfrak{L}[t^n] = \frac{n!}{s^{n+1}} \tag{41}$$

By using Eq. (24) in combination with Eq. (41), we then get

$$\mathfrak{L}[t^n\epsilon^{-at}] = \frac{n!}{(s+a)^{n+1}} \tag{42}$$

The foregoing examples will illustrate how a table of Laplace transforms can gradually be developed. Obviously it is more convenient to find transforms with the aid of a table than to find them by direct integration, except in the simplest cases. On the other hand, it is impractical to make a table of Laplace transforms so complete as to include all practical cases without making it so large as to be unwieldy. Consequently, only key forms are listed in the table, and variations from them should be handled with the aid of general formulas such as derived in the previous section. A list of such general formulas is given at the beginning of the table in Appendix D.

Exercises

1. Without the aid of the table, find the transforms of

(*a*) $\sin(at + \phi)$

(*b*) $t \sin(at + \phi)$

(c) $\cos(at + \phi)$
(d) $t\epsilon^{-at} \sin at$
(e) $t^2 + 2t + 1$

2. With the aid of the table in Appendix D, find the transforms of the functions in Exercise 1, and note the difference in time required.

3.6. The inverse transformation

Up to this point, we have concentrated upon the problem of finding the functions of the complex variable s which are the transforms of given functions of the real variable t. However, before the Laplace transforms can be of much use, the final functions of s must be transformed back into functions of t. These inverse transformations can be obtained from the regular table of Laplace transforms, and they are designated by the symbol $\mathcal{L}^{-1}$. Thus, for example, since

$$\mathcal{L}[\epsilon^{-at}] = \frac{1}{s+a} \tag{43}$$

we write

$$\mathcal{L}^{-1}\left[\frac{1}{s+a}\right] = \epsilon^{-at} \tag{44}$$

The foregoing use of the inverse transformation implicitly assumes that there is only one function, $f(t)$, whose Laplace transform is a given function,[10] $F(s)$. It can be proved that, except for cases which are of no technical interest, this one to one correspondence, sometimes called the *uniqueness property*, is actually a fact for positive values of t. Accordingly, every Laplace transformation will work backward as well as forward. For example, from Eqs. (20) and (21) it follows that

$$\mathcal{L}^{-1}[aF(s)] = af(t) \tag{45}$$

$$\mathcal{L}^{-1}[F_1(s) + F_2(s)] = f_1(t) + f_2(t) \tag{46}$$

---

[10] Regarding the direct transformation, we note that since

$$F(s) = \int_0^\infty f(t)\epsilon^{-st}\,dt$$

has a definite value for every function $f(t)$, it is clear that there is only one function, $F(s)$, which is the Laplace transform of $f(t)$.

In finding the inverse transformations which arise in practice, the table of transforms is, of course, of primary importance. However, there are certain supplementary and additional methods of sufficient importance to warrant special study. One of these is the Heaviside Expansion Theorem, which will be studied in §3.8. Another method of particular theoretical significance is the Bromwich Integral which will be studied in Chap. 7.

The Laplace transformation

$$\int_0^\infty f(t)\epsilon^{-st}\,dt = F(s)$$

deals only with the value of $f(t)$ from 0 to ∞, and is entirely independent of the values of t when t is negative. Therefore, *the formulas of the inverse transformation apply only to positive* (and zero) *values of t.* This fact should be kept in mind.

3.7. Step functions

The specification of Laplace transforms is made more precise with the aid of the unit step function. The unit step is a function of the real variable t, which has the value zero for all negative values of

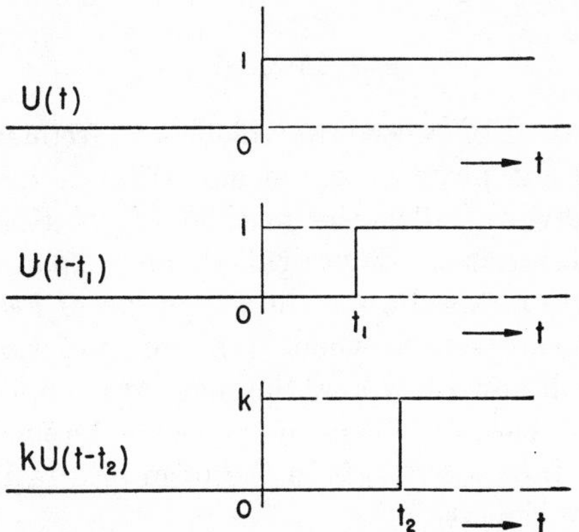

FIG. 3-2. Examples of step functions.

t, and the value unity for all positive values of t. The function has a discontinuity at $t = 0$. We shall designate the unit step as $U(t)$. A similar function, but with its discontinuity at $t = t_1$ is therefore $U(t - t_1)$. Fig. 3-2 shows a group of step functions.

The Laplace transform of the unit step can readily be determined. Thus

$$\mathfrak{L}\{U(t)\} = \int_0^\infty \epsilon^{-st}\, dt = \frac{\epsilon^{-st}}{-s}\bigg|_0^\infty = \frac{1}{s} \tag{47}$$

If we apply the time-displacement theorem of §3.4 in finding inverse transforms, it is convenient to have some automatic way of being sure that the function $f(t)$ to be found is zero when $t < 0$. This can be done by writing

$$\mathfrak{L}^{-1}\{\epsilon^{-bs}F(s)\} = f(t-b)U(t-b) \tag{48}$$

We shall find step functions very useful in problems involving discontinuities, such as pulses, the closing of switches, and so on.

Exercise

Show that $$\mathfrak{L}\{U(t-t_1)\} = \frac{\epsilon^{-st_1}}{s}$$

3.8. Heaviside's expansion theorem—the solution for *f(t)* in terms of characteristic vibrations

(a) Real Nonmultiple Roots of *B*(*s*). In applying the inverse transformation

$$\mathfrak{L}^{-1}[F(s)] = f(t) \tag{49}$$

there is one method of procedure which is so frequently used and has such important physical significance that it deserves special study. This may be called the method of solution in terms of characteristic vibrations. It was called the "expansion theorem" by Heaviside. It is based upon the expansion of $F(s)$ into partial fractions, and it can be used when $F(s)$ is of the form of a rational fraction. We will now show how the method is applied.

In a great number of problems in which the Laplace transformation is used, the function $F(s)$ is in the form of a rational fraction. In such cases, we can write

$$F(s) = \frac{A(s)}{B(s)} \tag{50}$$

where $A(s)$ and $B(s)$ are polynomials in s. Now the reader will recall from his study of algebra, or of integration, that any such rational fraction can be expanded into a sum of simple partial fractions.[11] In order to do this, let us express the denominator, $B(s)$, in factored form. Thus,

$$B(s) = C(s - s_1)(s - s_2) \cdots (s - s_n) \tag{51}$$

where $s_1, s_2 \cdots s_n$ are the n roots of

$$B(s) = 0 \tag{52}$$

Then, if there are no multiple roots, $F(s)$ can be expanded in the form

$$F(s) = \frac{A(s)}{B(s)} = \frac{K_1}{s - s_1} + \frac{K_2}{s - s_2} + \cdots + \frac{K_n}{s - s_n} \tag{53}$$

The value of any K coefficient, such as K_q, is the constant[12]

$$K_q = \left\{ \frac{A(s)}{\frac{d}{ds}[B(s)]} \right\}_{s=s_q} \tag{54}$$

$$= \left\{ (s - s_q) \frac{A(s)}{B(s)} \right\}_{s=s_q} \tag{54A}$$

The reader can construct a proof of this statement as an exercise.

In case $s = 0$ is a root, but not a multiple root, then Eq. (53) takes on the special form

$$F(s) = \frac{A(0)}{sB_1(0)} + \frac{M_1}{s - s_1} + \frac{M_2}{s - s_2} + \cdots + \frac{M_{n-1}}{s - s_{n-1}} \tag{55}$$

where

$$B_1(s) = \frac{B(s)}{s} \tag{56}$$

---

[11] If the numerator $A(s)$ is of the same or a higher degree in s than the denominator $B(s)$, algebraic division is first carried out until the denominator is of higher degree, before proceeding with the partial fraction expansion. Thus in

$$F(s) = \frac{s^2 + 3}{s^2 - 1}$$

we first carry out algebraic division to get

$$F(s) = 1 + \frac{4}{s^2 - 1}$$

and then proceed to expand $4/(s^2 - 1)$ in partial fractions. In practice, it will be found that the denominator is usually of higher degree from the very outset. In this section, it will be assumed that any common factors of $A(s)$ and $B(s)$ have already been canceled out.

[12] See the exercise on p. 73. The particular form of K_q which will be found most convenient depends upon whether or not $B(s)$ is given in factored form, so that $(s - s_q)$ can be factored out.

and
$$M_q = \left\{\frac{A(s)}{s\dfrac{d}{ds}[B_1(s)]}\right\}_{s=s_q} \tag{57}$$

$$= \left\{\frac{A(s)}{\dfrac{d}{ds}[B(s)]}\right\}_{s=s_q} \tag{57A}$$

$$= \left\{(s - s_q)\frac{A(s)}{B(s)}\right\}_{s=s_q} \tag{57B}$$

Let us now find the inverse transform of $F(s)$ as given by Eq. (53). From Eqs. (44) and (45) we know that

$$\mathfrak{L}^{-1}\left\{\frac{K_q}{s - s_q}\right\} = K_q\epsilon^{s_q t} \tag{58}$$

Therefore, according to Eqs. (53) and (46),

$$f(t) = \mathfrak{L}^{-1}[F(s)] = K_1\epsilon^{s_1 t} + K_2\epsilon^{s_2 t} + \cdots + K_n\epsilon^{s_n t} \tag{59}$$

In case $F(s)$ is given by Eq. (55), we get

$$\begin{aligned} f(t) &= \mathfrak{L}^{-1}[F(s)] \\ &= \frac{A(0)}{B_1(0)} + M_1\epsilon^{s_1 t} + M_2\epsilon^{s_2 t} + \cdots + M_{n-1}\epsilon^{s_{n-1} t} \end{aligned} \tag{60}$$

since the inverse of $1/s$ is unity for positive values of t, and our analysis applies only to positive values of t.

Equation 59 applies just as well to the case in which s is a factor of $B(s)$, but the form of Eq. (60) may be found more convenient. (See Example 2 of §3.9.)

(b) Complex Roots of $B(s)$. In case one of the roots of $B(s)$ is complex, its conjugate is also a root. To be specific, let s_1 and s_2 be the conjugate complex roots. Then we can write[13]

$$s_1 = a + j\omega \tag{61}$$

$$s_2 = a - j\omega = s_1^* \tag{62}$$

Furthermore, in this case, K_1 and K_2 as defined by Eq. (54) must

[13] The notation $s_1{}^*$ stands for the complex conjugate of s_1. The properties of complex conjugates which are used here are discussed in §6.1 and the exercises following that section.

also be conjugate. (See §6.1.) Therefore, we can write

$$K_1 = \alpha + j\beta \tag{63}$$

$$K_2 = \alpha - j\beta = K_1^* \tag{64}$$

Then

$$\begin{aligned}\frac{K_1}{s - s_1} + \frac{K_2}{s - s_2} &= \frac{K_1}{s - s_1} + \frac{K_1^*}{s - s_1^*} \\ &= \frac{K_1 s - K_1 s_1^* + K_1^* s - K_1^* s_1}{(s - a)^2 + \omega^2} \\ &= \frac{(K_1 + K_1^*)s - (K_1 s_1^* + K_1^* s_1)}{(s - a)^2 + \omega^2} \\ &= \frac{2\alpha s - 2(\alpha a + \beta\omega)}{(s - a)^2 + \omega^2}\end{aligned} \tag{65}$$

The quantity on the right of Eq. (65) can be transformed back into a function of t, with the aid of Eqs. (20), (35), and (37). We thus obtain

$$\mathcal{L}^{-1}\left\{\frac{2\alpha s - 2(\alpha a + \beta\omega)}{(s - a)^2 + \omega^2}\right\} = 2\alpha\epsilon^{at}\cos\omega t - 2\beta\epsilon^{at}\sin\omega t \tag{66}$$

Consequently, in the case of a pair of complex roots, the two terms in Eq. (59) or (60) corresponding to these two conjugate roots can be combined into a real function of t as shown in Eq. (66). In the case of complex roots of $B(s)$, it is a simple matter to replace the pair of partial fractions involving a pair of conjugate roots with a single term of the form shown on the right of Eq. (65) having a quadratic denominator, and having the known inverse transform given in Eq. (66). The quantities α and β can be determined by calculating K_1 alone, without the necessity of calculating K_2.

Thus, when there is a pair of complex roots, Eqs. (53) and (59) can be rewritten

$$F(s) = \frac{A(s)}{B(s)} = \frac{2\alpha s - 2(\alpha a + \beta\omega)}{(s - a)^2 + \omega^2} + \frac{K_3}{s - s_3} + \cdots + \frac{K_n}{s - s_n} \tag{67}$$

and

$$f(t) = 2\alpha\epsilon^{at}\cos\omega t - 2\beta\epsilon^{at}\sin\omega t + K_3\epsilon^{s_3 t} + \cdots + K_n\epsilon^{s_n t} \tag{68}$$

where a, ω, α, and β are defined by Eqs. (61) through (64).

(c) Multiple Roots of $B(s)$. If $B(s)$ has a multiple root, then we can write

$$B(s) = C(s - s_1)^p(s - s_{p+1})(s - s_{p+2}) \cdots (s - s_n) \tag{69}$$

where $B(s)$ is a polynomial of the nth order. In this case, Eq. (53) must be modified, and the terms

$$\frac{K_1}{s - s_1} + \frac{K_2}{s - s_2} + \cdots + \frac{K_p}{(s - s_p)} \tag{70}$$

corresponding to the multiple root are replaced by

$$\frac{N_1}{s - s_1} + \frac{N_2}{(s - s_1)^2} + \cdots + \frac{N_p}{(s - s_1)^p} \tag{71}$$

where any N_r is given by

$$N_r = \frac{1}{(p - r)!} \left\{ \frac{d^{p-r}}{ds^{p-r}} \left[\frac{A(s)}{B(s)} (s - s_1)^p \right] \right\}_{s=s_1} \tag{72}$$

and for the special case of N_p

$$N_p = \left\{ \frac{A(s)}{B(s)} (s - s_1)^p \right\}_{s=s_1} \tag{73}$$

The terms in Eq. (53) of the form

$$\frac{K_m}{s - s_m}$$

remain unchanged if $m > p$. Consequently, in this case,

$$f(t) = \left\{ N_1 + N_2 t + \cdots + \frac{N_p t^{p-1}}{(p-1)!} \right\} \epsilon^{s_1 t} + K_{p+1}\epsilon^{s_{p+1}t} + \cdots + K_n \epsilon^{s_n t} \tag{74}$$

where the K's are given by Eq. (54).

If there are multiple complex roots, they will of course exist in conjugate pairs. The values of the N's in Eq. (74) will then also occur in conjugate pairs which, when combined, will give damped sine and cosine waves multiplied by powers of t. The case is not of sufficient practical importance to be worked out in detail here, but the above Eqs. (69) through (74) will apply to this case just as well as to the case of multiple real roots.

(d) **General.** The foregoing discussion has indicated the method of expressing the solution for $f(t)$ in terms of a sum of a number of exponential and periodic terms, in case $F(s)$ is a rational fraction. The method is perfectly general, provided that the roots of $B(s)$ can be found. Unfortunately, if $B(s)$ is of higher order than the second in s, the determination of the factors of $B(s)$ involves the solution of algebraic equations of higher degree than the quadratic, unless the factors of $B(s)$ are known for physical reasons. This makes the solution difficult and frequently impossible. In case $B(s)$ is not of a higher degree than the fourth, or in case the coefficients of $B(s)$ are assigned numerical values, the roots can be found, as shown in text books on the theory of algebraic equations. However, the most useful and instructive practical cases occur when $B(s)$ as originally presented is already reduced to linear and quadratic factors.

Exercise

Derive Eqs. (54), (57), (72), and (73).

3.9. Examples of the expansion-theorem method of finding the inverse transforms

We will now illustrate the foregoing method by solving a few examples:

Example 1: Find the inverse transform of

$$F(s) = \frac{3s + 7}{s^2 + 5s + 6} \tag{75}$$

We first find the factors of the denominator, by solving the equation

$$s^2 + 5s + 6 = 0 \tag{76}$$

Thus
$$s = \frac{-5 \pm \sqrt{25 - 24}}{2} = \frac{-5 \pm 1}{2} = -3 \text{ or } -2 \tag{77}$$

Consequently
$$s^2 + 5s + 6 = (s + 3)(s + 2) \tag{78}$$

We may therefore resolve $F(s)$ into partial fractions according to Eq. (53) in the form

$$F(s) = \frac{3s + 7}{s^2 + 5s + 6} = \frac{K_1}{s + 3} + \frac{K_2}{s + 2} \tag{79}$$

where

$$K_1 = \left\{\frac{3s+7}{\dfrac{d}{ds}(s^2+5s+6)}\right\}_{s=-3} = \left\{\frac{3s+7}{2s+5}\right\}_{s=-3} = \frac{-2}{-1} = 2 \quad (80)$$

and

$$K_2 = \left\{\frac{3s+7}{\dfrac{d}{ds}(s^2+5s+6)}\right\}_{s=-2} = \left\{\frac{3s+7}{2s+5}\right\}_{s=-2} = \frac{1}{1} = 1 \quad (81)$$

according to Eq. (54). Consequently

$$F(s) = \frac{3s+7}{s^2+5s+6} = \frac{2}{s+3} + \frac{1}{s+2} \quad (82)$$

Then

$$f(t) = \mathfrak{L}^{-1}\left\{\frac{3s+7}{s^2+5s+6}\right\} = 2\epsilon^{-3t} + \epsilon^{-2t} \quad (83)$$

which is the desired answer.

Example 2: Find the inverse transform of

$$F(s) = \frac{6s+4}{s^2+2s} \quad (84)$$

In this case, the factors of the denominator are obvious by inspection. We may therefore write

$$F(s) = \frac{6s+4}{s(s+2)} = \frac{1}{s}\left\{\frac{6s+4}{s+2}\right\}_{s=0} + \frac{M_1}{s+2} \quad (85)$$

Now, by Eq. (57),

$$M_1 = \left\{\frac{6s+4}{s\dfrac{d}{ds}(s+2)}\right\}_{s=-2} = \left\{\frac{6s+4}{s}\right\}_{s=-2} = \frac{-12+4}{-2} = 4 \quad (86)$$

Consequently

$$F(s) = \frac{6s+4}{s(s+2)} = \frac{2}{s} + \frac{4}{s+2} \quad (87)$$

Then by Eq. (60)

$$f(t) = \mathfrak{L}^{-1}\left\{\frac{6s+4}{s(s+2)}\right\} = 2 + 4\epsilon^{-2t} \quad (88)$$

which is the desired answer.

Example 3: Find the inverse transform of

$$F(s) = \frac{3s^2+9s+5}{(s+3)(s^2+2s+2)} \quad (89)$$

As a first step, we find the factors of $s^2 + 2s + 2$. Accordingly, we set

$$s^2 + 2s + 2 = 0 \tag{90}$$

and get
$$s = \frac{-2 \pm \sqrt{4 - 8}}{2} = -1 \pm \sqrt{-1} \tag{91}$$

Therefore, following the notation of Eqs. (61) and (62), we write

$$s_1 = -1 + j \tag{92}$$

$$s_2 = -1 - j = s_1^* \tag{93}$$

Then using Eq. (53), we write

$$F(s) = \frac{3s^2 + 9s + 5}{(s + 3)(s^2 + 2s + 2)} = \frac{3s^2 + 9s + 5}{(s + 3)(s + 1 - j)(s + 1 + j)}$$

$$= \frac{K_1}{s + 1 - j} + \frac{K_2}{s + 1 + j} + \frac{K_3}{s + 3} \tag{94}$$

Now, in this case,

$$\frac{d}{ds}[B(s)] = \frac{d}{ds}[(s + 3)(s^2 + 2s + 2)]$$
$$= s^2 + 2s + 2 + (s + 3)(2s + 2)$$
$$= 3s^2 + 10s + 8 \tag{95}$$

Then, according to Eq. (54),

$$K_1 = \left\{\frac{3s^2 + 9s + 5}{3s^2 + 10s + 8}\right\}_{s=-1+j}$$
$$= \frac{3(-1 + j)^2 + 9(-1 + j) + 5}{3(-1 + j)^2 + 10s(-1 + j) + 8} = \frac{3j - 4}{4j - 2}$$
$$= 1 + \frac{j}{2} \tag{96}$$

and according to Eq. (64),

$$K_2 = K_1^* = 1 - \frac{j}{2} \tag{97}$$

Also
$$K_3 = \left\{\frac{3s^2 + 9s + 5}{3s^2 + 10s + 8}\right\}_{s=-3} = \frac{27 - 27 + 5}{27 - 30 + 8} = 1 \tag{98}$$

Thus, corresponding to Eqs. (61)–(66), we have in this case

$$a = -1, \qquad \omega = 1, \qquad \alpha = 1, \qquad \beta = \tfrac{1}{2} \tag{99}$$

Therefore, by Eqs. (59) and (66),

$$\begin{aligned} f(t) &= \mathcal{L}^{-1}\left\{\frac{3s^2 + 9s + 5}{(s+3)(s^2+2s+2)}\right\} \\ &= 2\epsilon^{-t}\cos t - \epsilon^{-t}\sin t + \epsilon^{-3t} \end{aligned} \tag{100}$$

which is the desired answer.

The foregoing three examples illustrate the method of using the expansion theorem. In many cases, however, it is possible to bypass the actual work of the expansion theorem by using the table of Laplace transforms. Accordingly, in the next section we shall solve the same three examples with the aid of the table.

Exercises

Using the expansion theorem, find the Laplace transforms of

1. $$\frac{5s + 7}{s^2 + 3s + 2}$$

2. $$\frac{2s + 1}{s(s^2 + 2s + 5)}$$

3. $$\frac{1}{(s^2 + 2s + 2)(s^2 + 4s + 13)}$$

3.10. Solution of the examples in §3.9 by reference to the table of Laplace transforms

We will next use the table of transforms to solve the same examples already solved in §3.9 by means of the expansion theorem. This will give a good comparison of the relative merits of the two methods.

Example 1: *To find the inverse transform of*

$$F(s) = \frac{3s + 7}{s^2 + 5s + 6} \tag{101}$$

This problem is of the form

$$K\frac{s + a_0}{(s + \alpha)(s + \gamma)} \tag{102}$$

which is form #12 in the table.

Here $$K = 3 \qquad \text{and} \qquad a_0 = \tfrac{7}{3} \tag{103}$$

To find α and γ, we set

$$s^2 + 5s + 6 = 0 \tag{104}$$

and solve for the roots. These are

$$s = \frac{-5 \pm \sqrt{25 - 24}}{2} = -2 \text{ or } -3 \tag{105}$$

Therefore $$s^2 + 5s + 6 = (s + 2)(s + 3) \tag{106}$$

Consequently $$\alpha = 2 \qquad \text{and} \qquad \gamma = 3 \tag{107}$$

Therefore, according to form #12 of the table,

$$\begin{aligned} f(t) &= K \frac{(a_0 - \alpha)\epsilon^{-\alpha t} - (a_0 - \gamma)\epsilon^{-\gamma t}}{\gamma - \alpha} \\ &= 3 \left\{ \frac{(\frac{7}{3} - 2)\epsilon^{-2t} - (\frac{7}{3} - 3)\epsilon^{-3t}}{1} \right\} \\ &= \epsilon^{-2t} + 2\epsilon^{-3t} \end{aligned} \tag{108}$$

This solution agrees with the result obtained in Eq. (83). And, by using the table of transforms, it is more quickly obtained than by means of the expansion theorem used in the preceding section.

Example 2: *To find the inverse transform of*

$$F(s) = \frac{6s + 4}{s^2 + 2s} \tag{109}$$

This problem is also of the form

$$\frac{K(s + a_0)}{(s + \alpha)(s + \gamma)} \tag{110}$$

which is form #12 in the table.

Here $$K = 6, \qquad a_0 = \tfrac{2}{3}, \qquad \gamma = 2, \qquad \text{and} \qquad \alpha = 0 \tag{111}$$

Therefore according to form #12 of the table,

$$\begin{aligned} f(t) &= K \left\{ \frac{a_0 - (a_0 - \gamma)\epsilon^{-\gamma t}}{\gamma} \right\} \\ &= 6 \left\{ \frac{\frac{2}{3} - (\frac{2}{3} - 2)\epsilon^{-2t}}{2} \right\} = 2 + 4\epsilon^{-2t} \end{aligned} \tag{112}$$

This solution agrees with the result in Eq. (88), and it is obtained most rapidly with the aid of the table.

Example 3: *To find the inverse transform of*

$$F(s) = \frac{3s^2 + 9s + 5}{(s + 3)(s^2 + 2s + 2)} \tag{113}$$

This problem is of the form

$$K \frac{s^2 + a_1 s + a_0}{(s + \gamma)[(s + \alpha)^2 + \beta^2]} \tag{114}$$

which is form #24 in the table.

To find α and β, we solve

$$s^2 + 2s + 2 = 0 \tag{115}$$

and get

$$s = \frac{-2 \pm \sqrt{4 - 8}}{2} = -1 \pm j \tag{116}$$

Therefore,

$$s^2 + 2s + 2 = (s + 1)^2 + 1 \tag{117}$$

or

$$\alpha = 1 \qquad \text{and} \qquad \beta = 1 \tag{118}$$

From Eqs. (113) and (114) it is evident that

$$K = 3, \qquad a_1 = 3, \qquad a_0 = \tfrac{5}{3}, \qquad \gamma = 3 \tag{119}$$

Consequently, from form #24 of the table,

$$\begin{aligned}
\frac{1}{3} f(t) &= \frac{\gamma^2 - a_1\gamma + a_0}{(\alpha - \gamma)^2 + \beta^2} \epsilon^{-\gamma t} \\
&\quad + \frac{1}{\beta} \left\{ \frac{(\alpha^2 - \beta^2 - a_1\alpha + a_0)^2 + \beta^2(a_1 - 2\alpha)^2}{(\gamma - \alpha)^2 + \beta^2} \right\}^{\frac{1}{2}} \epsilon^{-\alpha t} \sin (\beta t + \psi) \\
&= \frac{9 - 9 + \frac{5}{3}}{(1 - 3)^2 + 1} \epsilon^{-3t} \\
&\qquad + \left\{ \frac{(1 - 1 - 3 + \frac{5}{3})^2 + (3 - 2)^2}{(3 - 1)^2 + 1} \right\}^{\frac{1}{2}} \epsilon^{-t} \sin (t + \psi) \\
&= \frac{1}{3} \epsilon^{-3t} + \frac{\sqrt{5}}{3} \epsilon^{-t} \sin (t + \psi)
\end{aligned} \tag{120}$$

where[14]

---

[14] This is making use of the trigonometric formula

$$\tan^{-1} A - \tan^{-1} B = \tan^{-1} \left(\frac{A - B}{1 + AB} \right)$$

$$\begin{aligned}\psi &= \tan^{-1}\frac{\beta(a_1 - 2\alpha)}{\alpha^2 - \beta^2 - a_1\alpha + a_0} - \tan^{-1}\frac{\beta}{\gamma - \alpha}\\ &= \tan^{-1}\left(-\frac{3}{4}\right) - \tan^{-1}\left(\frac{1}{2}\right) = \tan^{-1}\left\{\frac{-\frac{3}{4} - \frac{1}{2}}{1 + (-\frac{3}{4})(\frac{1}{2})}\right\}\\ &= \tan^{-1}(-2) \end{aligned} \tag{121}$$

From Eq. (121), it follows that

$$\tan\psi = -2 = \frac{\sin\psi}{\cos\psi} \tag{122}$$

From Eq. (122) we have $\qquad \cos^2\psi = \frac{1}{4}\sin^2\psi \qquad (123)$

and from trigonometry $\qquad \cos^2\psi = 1 - \sin^2\psi \qquad (124)$

Therefore, $\qquad \frac{1}{4}\sin^2\psi = 1 - \sin^2\psi \qquad (125)$

or $\qquad \sin\psi = \frac{\pm 2}{\sqrt{5}} \qquad (126)$

Then from Eq. (122), $\qquad \cos\psi = \frac{\mp 1}{\sqrt{5}} \qquad (127)$

Consequently,

$$\begin{aligned}\sin(t + \psi) &= \sin t\cos\psi + \cos t\sin\psi\\ &= \frac{\pm 1}{\sqrt{5}}(-\sin t + 2\cos t)\end{aligned} \tag{128}$$

Using the (+) sign in Eq. (128) and substituting it in Eq. (120), we obtain

$$f(t) = \epsilon^{-3t} + \epsilon^{-t}[2\cos t - \sin t] \tag{129}$$

This solution agrees with Eq. (100). Actually, the solution was completed with Eq. (121). The purpose of the further work was only to show the equality between Eqs. (120) and (100). We note that there is an ambiguity in sign in Eq. (128). This is a disadvantage of the "phase-angle" form in the solution by formula in this particular case. The form in which the terms in $\sin\beta t$ and $\cos\beta t$ are separated would therefore have been preferable for deriving the equivalent of Eq. (100).

In comparing the solutions by formula in the present section with the solutions by the expansion-theorem method in the previous section, we conclude that solutions by formula are usually more rapid, when an appropriate formula is available. When no appropriate formula is available, the expansion theorem must be used.

Exercises

Solve by formula exercises 1 and 2 at the end of §3.9.

3.11. Example of the solution of a transient problem

As an example of the use of the Laplace transformation and of the formulas and methods of the preceding sections, we will find the complete solution for the current which flows in a series L-R-C circuit, as shown in Fig. 3-3, when a sinusoidal e.m.f. is impressed upon the circuit. The differential equation governing current flow in this circuit, according to electrical circuit theory as developed in Chap. 2, is:

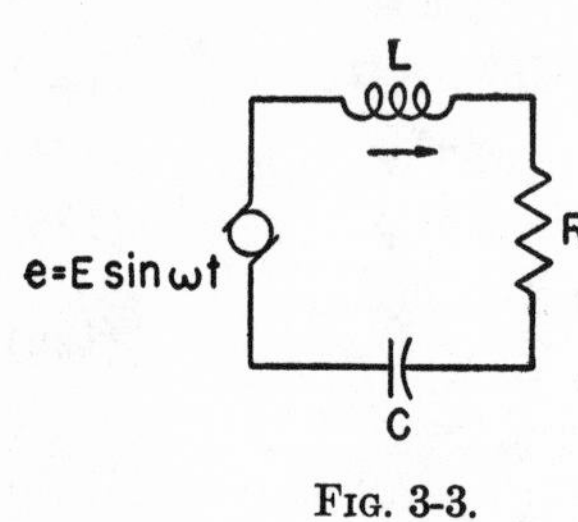

FIG. 3-3.

$$L\frac{di}{dt} + Ri + \frac{Q}{C} = L\frac{di}{dt} + Ri + \frac{\int i\,dt}{C}$$
$$= E \sin \omega t \tag{130}$$

Our problem is to find the explicit expression for i as a function of t. To obtain the solution we will transform all the quantities in Eq. (130) into functions of s, and solve the problem in terms of s. We will then transform back to t, and thereby have the solution. Accordingly, we write

$$i \equiv i(t) \tag{131}$$

thus expressing the fact that i is a function of t. We then define the Laplace transform of $i(t)$ by the equation

$$\int_0^\infty i(t)\epsilon^{-st}\,dt = I(s) \tag{132}$$

or, in short form,
$$\mathfrak{L}[i(t)] = I(s) \tag{133}$$

Then by Eqs. (18), (19), and (20),

$$\mathfrak{L}\left[L\frac{di}{dt}\right] = L[sI(s) - i(0+)] \tag{134}$$

$$\mathfrak{L}[Ri] = RI(s) \tag{135}$$

$$\mathfrak{L}\left[\frac{Q}{C}\right] = \mathfrak{L}\left[\frac{\int i\,dt}{C}\right] = \frac{1}{C}\left[\frac{I(s)}{s} + \frac{Q_0}{s}\right] \tag{136}$$

Furthermore,

$$\mathfrak{L}[E \sin \omega t] = \int_0^\infty E \sin \omega t \epsilon^{-st}\, dt = \frac{E\omega}{s^2 + \omega^2} \tag{137}$$

by direct integration.[15]

Since the left and right sides of Eq. (130) are equal, their Laplace transforms are also equal.[16] Consequently,

$$L[sI(s) - i_0] + RI(s) + \frac{1}{C}\left[\frac{I(s)}{s} + \frac{Q_0}{s}\right] = \frac{E\omega}{s^2 + \omega^2} \tag{138}$$

where i_0 is the current at time $t = 0$.

Solving Eq. (138) for $I(s)$, we obtain

$$\begin{aligned} I(s) &= \frac{1}{Ls + R + \dfrac{1}{Cs}}\left\{\frac{E\omega}{s^2 + \omega^2} + Li_0 - \frac{Q_0}{Cs}\right\} \\ &= \frac{Li_0 s^3 - (Q_0/C)s^2 + (Li_0\omega^2 + E\omega)s - (Q_0/C)\omega^2}{\left(Ls^2 + Rs + \dfrac{1}{C}\right)(s^2 + \omega^2)} \end{aligned} \tag{139}$$

$I(s)$ in Eq. (139) is of a form which can be transformed back into a function of t by the method of the expansion theorem. Let us now use the quiescent initial conditions, namely

$$i_0 = 0 \tag{140}$$

$$Q_0 = 0 \tag{141}$$

Then Eq. (139) becomes

$$I(s) = \frac{E\omega s}{\left(Ls^2 + Rs + \dfrac{1}{C}\right)(s^2 + \omega^2)} \tag{142}$$

This is of form #26 of the table, where

$$\alpha_0 = 0 \tag{143}$$

$$\lambda = \omega \tag{144}$$

$$\alpha = \frac{R}{2L} \tag{145}$$

$$\beta = \sqrt{\frac{1}{LC} - \frac{R^2}{4L^2}} \tag{146}$$

---

[15] Form #16 of the table of Laplace transforms will give the same result.

[16] This so-called uniqueness property of the Laplace transform was discussed in §3.6.

Therefore,

$$i(t) = \frac{E\omega}{L} \cdot \frac{1}{\omega} \left\{ \frac{\omega^2}{\left(\frac{1}{LC} - \omega^2\right)^2 + \frac{\omega^2 R^2}{L^2}} \right\}^{\frac{1}{2}} \sin(\omega t + \psi_1)$$

$$+ \frac{E\omega}{L} \cdot \frac{1}{\sqrt{\frac{1}{LC} - \frac{R^2}{4L^2}}} \left\{ \frac{1/LC}{\left(\frac{1}{LC} - \omega^2\right)^2 + \frac{\omega^2 R^2}{L^2}} \right\}^{\frac{1}{2}} \epsilon^{-Rt/2L}$$

$$\sin\left\{\sqrt{\frac{1}{LC} - \frac{R^2}{4L^2}}\, t + \psi_2\right\} \qquad (147)$$

where

$$\psi_1 = \tan^{-1}\frac{\lambda}{a_0} - \tan^{-1}\frac{2\alpha\lambda}{\alpha^2 + \beta^2 - \lambda^2}$$

$$= \tan^{-1}\infty - \tan^{-1}\left\{\frac{\frac{\omega R}{L}}{\frac{1}{LC} - \omega^2}\right\} = \tan^{-1}\left\{\frac{\frac{1}{LC} - \omega^2}{\frac{\omega R}{L}}\right\}$$

$$= \tan^{-1}\left\{\frac{\frac{1}{\omega C} - \omega L}{R}\right\} \qquad (148)$$

and

$$\psi_2 = \tan^{-1}\frac{\beta}{a_0 - \alpha} - \tan^{-1}\frac{-2\alpha\beta}{\alpha^2 - \beta^2 + \lambda^2} \qquad (149)$$

Since $a_0 = 0$,

$$\psi_2 = \tan^{-1} - \frac{\beta}{\alpha}\left\{\frac{\lambda^2 - \alpha^2 - \beta^2}{\lambda^2 + \alpha^2 + \beta^2}\right\}$$

$$= \tan^{-1}\left\{\frac{-\sqrt{\frac{1}{LC} - \frac{R^2}{4L^2}}}{\frac{R}{2L}} \cdot \frac{\omega^2 - \frac{1}{LC}}{\omega^2 + \frac{1}{LC}}\right\} \qquad (150)$$

By simple algebraic manipulation, Eq. (147) becomes

$$i(t) = \frac{E}{\left\{\left(\omega L - \frac{1}{\omega C}\right)^2 + R^2\right\}^{\frac{1}{2}}} \sin(\omega t + \psi_1)$$

$$+ \frac{E\sqrt{\frac{1}{LC}}\,\epsilon^{-Rt/2L}}{\sqrt{\frac{1}{LC} - \frac{R^2}{4L^2}}\sqrt{\left(\omega L - \frac{1}{\omega C}\right)^2 + R^2}}$$

$$\sin\left(\sqrt{\frac{1}{LC} - \frac{R^2}{4L^2}}\, t + \psi_2\right) \qquad (151)$$

The first term on the right of Eq. (151) is the steady-state component of the current, and the second term is the transient component. We thus see that the use of the Laplace transformation gives the complete solution, as is to be expected.

It may appear to the reader that the above method of solution with the aid of the Laplace transformation does not have much advantage, either in rapidity or simplicity, over the standard method of solving the differential equations of circuits. This, however, is not true. Many of the steps taken in this section may be bypassed, after the reader becomes better acquainted with the method. (See §3.13.) This is particularly true when the initial conditions are quiescent; i.e., when

$$i_0 = i(0+) = 0 \tag{152}$$

and

$$Q_0 = \int^{0+} i\,dt = 0 \tag{153}$$

Exercises

1. Find the current which flows in the resistor of Fig. 3-A after the switch is opened.

2. Find $i(t)$ from Eq. (142) by using the expansion-theorem method.

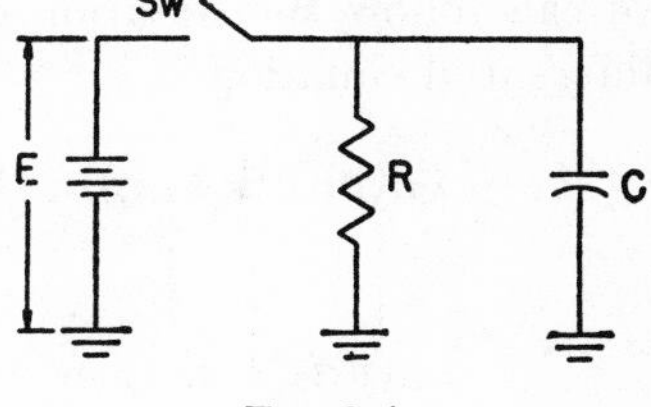

FIG. 3-A.

3.12. General theory of the solution of circuit problems and the treatment of initial conditions

The example in the preceding section illustrates the solution of the differential equation of a single circuit with a particular applied e.m.f. and particular initial conditions. In the general case, the differential equation of a single-series circuit may be written

$$L\frac{di}{dt} + Ri + \frac{\int i\,dt}{C} = e(t) \tag{154}$$

where $e(t)$ is the e.m.f. in the circuit. With the aid of Eqs. (134) through (136), Eq. (154) transforms into

$$\left[sL + R + \frac{1}{sC}\right] I(s) - Li(0) + \frac{Q_0}{Cs} = E(s) \tag{155}$$

where $E(s)$ is the Laplace transform of $e(t)$. It then follows from

Eq. (155) that

$$I(s) = \frac{E(s) + Li(0) - \frac{Q_0}{Cs}}{z(s)} \tag{156}$$

where

$$z(s) = sL + R + \frac{1}{sC} \tag{157}$$

The function $z(s)$ is the same function of s as the steady-state impedance is of $(j\omega)$. Therefore $z(s)$ is also called the impedance function.

It follows from Eq. (156) that

$$\begin{aligned} i(t) &= \mathfrak{L}^{-1}\left\{\frac{E(s) + Li(0) - Q_0/Cs}{z(s)}\right\} \\ &= \mathfrak{L}^{-1}\left\{\frac{E(s) + O(s)}{z(s)}\right\} \end{aligned} \tag{158}$$

where

$$O(s) = Li(0) - \frac{Q_0}{Cs} \tag{159}$$

When we are dealing with a network instead of a single circuit, we can follow the notation of §§2.12 and 2.13 and write for the differential equations:

$$\left.\begin{array}{l} z_{11}(p)i_1 + z_{12}(p)i_2 + \cdots + z_{1n}(p)i_n = e_1(t) \\ \vdots \\ z_{n1}(p)i_1 + z_{n2}(p)i_2 + \cdots + z_{nn}(p)i_n = e_n(t) \end{array}\right\} \tag{160}$$

The transformed equations of Eq. (160) are

$$\left.\begin{array}{l} z_{11}(s)I_1(s) + z_{12}(s)I_2(s) + \cdots + z_{1n}(s)I_n(s) = \bar{E}_1(s) \\ \vdots \\ z_{n1}(s)I_1(s) + z_{n2}(s)I_2(s) + \cdots + z_{nn}(s)I_n(s) = \bar{E}_n(s) \end{array}\right\} \tag{161}$$

where

$$E_1(s) = E_1(s) + O_{11}(s) + O_{12}(s) + \cdots + O_{1n}(s) \tag{162}$$

and so forth, and

$$O_{pq}(s) = L_{pq}i_q(0) - \frac{Q_q(0)}{C_{pq}s} \tag{163}$$

Equations (161) can then be solved for any of the I's in terms of the $\bar{E}$'s and z's in the standard manner of Chap. 1. The transforms of the $\bar{I}$'s will then be the solutions for current. The method will be illustrated by Example 5 in the next section.

In case the initial conditions are quiescent, that is, in case the currents in all inductances and the charges on all capacitors are zero at time $t = 0$, then all the functions $O(s)$ will also vanish. In this case, the $\bar{E}$'s will be simpler, and the problem may be expected to be easier to solve. For example, Eq. (156) then becomes

$$I(s) = \frac{E(s)}{z(s)} \tag{164}$$

The foregoing discussion is extended in §§4.5 and 7.8.

3.13. The solution of some practical examples

We will now apply the theory developed in this chapter to solve a number of examples.

Example 1: *Charging Curve of a Capacitor.* As a first example, let us find the charging curve of a capacitor C in series with a resistance R. Suppose that the capacitor C in Fig. 3-4 is uncharged at time $t = 0$, when the switch is closed. Let us find the subsequent charge on the capacitor.

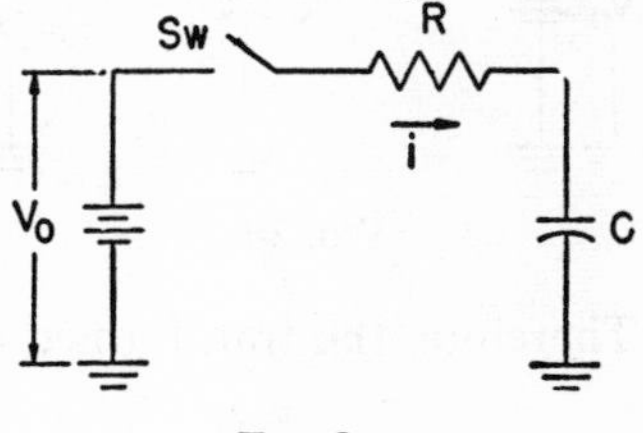

FIG. 3-4.

Applying Kirchhoff's Second Law to the circuit in Fig. 3-4, we have

$$Ri + \frac{q}{C} = R\frac{dq}{dt} + \frac{q}{C} = V_0U(t) \tag{165}$$

Now by Eq. (19)

$$\mathcal{L}\left[\frac{dq}{dt}\right] = sQ(s) - q(0+) \tag{166}$$

Consequently, Eq. (165) transforms to

$$RsQ(s) + \frac{Q(s)}{C} = \frac{V_0}{s} \tag{167}$$

since

$$q(0+) = 0$$

Thus

$$Q(s) = \frac{V_0}{s}\left[\frac{1}{\frac{1}{C} + Rs}\right] = \frac{V_0}{Rs\left(\frac{1}{RC} + s\right)} \tag{168}$$

This equation is of form #11 in the table. Therefore

$$q(t) = \frac{V_0}{R}\left[\frac{1 - \epsilon^{-t/RC}}{1/RC}\right] = V_0C(1 - \epsilon^{-t/RC}) \tag{169}$$

This is the well-known formula for the charging curve of a capacitor in series with a resistor.

Example 2: *Discharging Curve of a Capacitor.* In Fig. 3-5 is a capacitor connected to a battery of potential V_0. At time $t = 0$, the switch is opened and the capacitor starts to discharge through the resistance R. Let us find the subsequent charge on the capacitor.

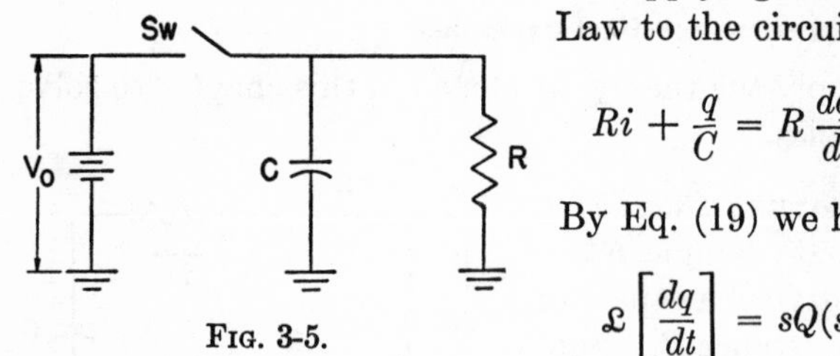

FIG. 3-5.

Applying Kirchhoff's Second Law to the circuit, we have

$$Ri + \frac{q}{C} = R\frac{dq}{dt} + \frac{q}{C} = 0 \tag{170}$$

By Eq. (19) we have

$$\mathfrak{L}\left[\frac{dq}{dt}\right] = sQ(s) - q(0+) \tag{171}$$

Therefore, the transformed equation of Eq. (170) is

$$R[sQ(s) - q(0+)] + \frac{Q(s)}{C} = 0 \tag{172}$$

or

$$Q(s) = \frac{CV_0}{s + \dfrac{1}{RC}} \tag{173}$$

since

$$q(0+) = CV_0 \tag{174}$$

The right side of Eq. (173) is of form #10 in the table. Therefore

$$q(t) = CV_0\epsilon^{-t/RC} \tag{175}$$

Equation (175) shows the charge on the capacitor as a function of time.

To get the voltage of the capacitor in either this or the preceding case, we divide the charge by the capacitance. Thus, in this case

$$\text{voltage of capacitor} = V = \frac{q(t)}{C} = V_0\epsilon^{-t/RC} \tag{176}$$

Example 3: *Current Rise in an Inductance.* Let us next find the current in the circuit of Fig. 3-6 assuming that it is zero at the instant that the switch is closed. Applying Kirchhoff's Second Law, we have for the differential equation of the circuit

$$L\frac{di}{dt} + Ri = EU(t) \tag{177}$$

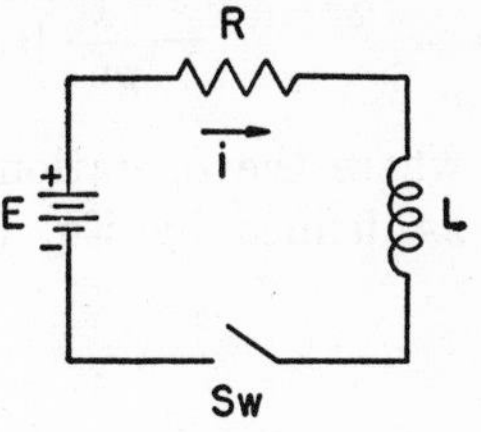

FIG. 3-6.

The terms in Eq. (177) are of types which have been used so often that by this time the reader should be able to write down the transformed equation of Eq. (177) without reference to any table.

It is[17]

$$LsI(s) + RI(s) = \frac{E}{s} \tag{178}$$

Therefore,

$$I(s) = \frac{E}{s(Ls + R)} \tag{179}$$

Then, by form #11 of the table

$$i(t) = \frac{E}{L}\left\{\frac{1 - \epsilon^{-Rt/L}}{(R/L)}\right\} = \frac{E}{R}(1 - \epsilon^{-Rt/L}) \tag{180}$$

This is the well-known formula for the current rise in an inductance.

Example 4: *A Compound R-C Network.* Consider the circuit of Fig. 3-7. Let us find the variation of e_2 with time after the instant (which we will call $t = 0$) when the input voltage is changed from a constant value of e_0 to a constant value of e_1. The solution will answer the practical question of how quickly the A.V.C. voltage at the input tube will respond to a change in the A.V.C. voltage at the detector in certain radio receivers.

Applying Kirchhoff's Second Law to Fig. 3-7, according to the method of §2.13, we have, in operational form,

---

[17] This follows because, when the initial conditions are quiescent,

$$\mathfrak{L}\left\{\frac{df(t)}{dt}\right\} = sF(s) - f(0+) = sF(s)$$

and, if A is a constant, $\mathfrak{L}\{A\} = \dfrac{A}{s}$

$$\left[R_1 + \frac{1}{pC_1}\right][i_1] - \frac{1}{pC_1}[i_2] = e_1 U(t) \tag{181}$$

$$-\frac{1}{pC_1}[i_1] + \left[R_2 + \frac{1}{pC_1} + \frac{1}{pC_2}\right] i_2 = 0 \tag{182}$$

where the operation $1/p$ stands for integration with respect to t as defined by Eq. (33) of Chap. 2, and the initial voltage e_0 is

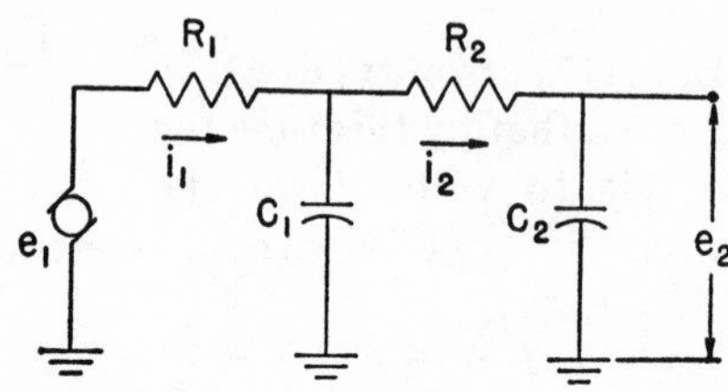

FIG. 3-7.

handled below in terms of initial charges on the capacitors. Applying the Laplace transformation to Eqs. (181) and (182), we obtain, as in Eq. (161),

$$\left(R_1 + \frac{1}{sC_1}\right) I_1(s) - \frac{1}{sC_1} I_2(s) = \frac{e_1}{s} - \frac{Q_1(0)}{sC_1} + \frac{Q_2(0)}{sC_1} \tag{183}$$

$$\left(-\frac{1}{sC_1}\right) I_1(s) + \left(R_2 + \frac{1}{sC_1} + \frac{1}{sC_2}\right) I_2(s)$$
$$= \frac{Q_1(0)}{sC_1} - \frac{Q_2(0)}{sC_1} - \frac{Q_2(0)}{sC_2} \tag{184}$$

where
$$Q_1(0) = \int^0 i_1\,dt \tag{185}$$

$$Q_2(0) = \int^0 i_2\,dt = \text{initial charge on } C_2 \tag{186}$$

and
$$Q_1(0) - Q_2(0) = \text{initial charge on } C_1 \tag{187}$$

Now
$$\frac{Q_1(0)}{C_1} - \frac{Q_2(0)}{C_1} = e_0 = \frac{Q_2(0)}{C_2} \tag{188}$$

Therefore Eqs. (183) and (184) can be rewritten

$$\left(R_1 + \frac{1}{sC_1}\right) I_1(s) - \frac{1}{sC_1} I_2(s) = \frac{e_1 - e_0}{s} \tag{189}$$

$$-\frac{1}{sC_1} I_1(s) + \left(R_2 + \frac{1}{sC_1} + \frac{1}{sC_2}\right) I_2(s) = 0 \tag{190}$$

Solving the simultaneous Eqs. (189) and (190) for $I_2(s)$, we get

$$I_2(s) = \frac{\dfrac{e_1 - e_0}{s^2C_1}}{\left(R_1 + \dfrac{1}{sC_1}\right)\left(R_2 + \dfrac{1}{sC_1} + \dfrac{1}{sC_2}\right) - \dfrac{1}{s^2C_1^2}}$$

$$= \frac{(e_1 - e_0)}{C_1\left[\dfrac{1}{C_1C_2} + \left(\dfrac{R_1}{C_1} + \dfrac{R_1}{C_2} + \dfrac{R_2}{C_1}\right)s + R_1R_2s^2\right]} \tag{191}$$

To separate the denominator into linear factors, we first find the roots of

$$R_1R_2s^2 + \left(\frac{R_1}{C_1} + \frac{R_1}{C_2} + \frac{R_2}{C_1}\right)s + \frac{1}{C_1C_2} = 0 \tag{192}$$

Calling these roots (α_1) and (α_2), we have

$$\alpha_1 = \frac{-\left(\dfrac{R_1}{C_1} + \dfrac{R_1}{C_2} + \dfrac{R_2}{C_1}\right) + \sqrt{\left(\dfrac{R_1}{C_1} + \dfrac{R_1}{C_2} + \dfrac{R_2}{C_1}\right)^2 - \dfrac{4R_1R_2}{C_1C_2}}}{2R_1R_2} \tag{193}$$

$$\text{and } \alpha_2 = \frac{-\left(\dfrac{R_1}{C_1} + \dfrac{R_1}{C_2} + \dfrac{R_2}{C_1}\right) - \sqrt{\left(\dfrac{R_1}{C_1} + \dfrac{R_1}{C_2} + \dfrac{R_2}{C_1}\right)^2 - \dfrac{4R_1R_2}{C_1C_2}}}{2R_1R_2} \tag{194}$$

Transforming Eq. (191) according to form #11 of the table, we then have

$$i_2(t) = \frac{e_1 - e_0}{R_1R_2C_1}\left[\frac{\epsilon^{\alpha_2 t} - \epsilon^{\alpha_1 t}}{\alpha_2 - \alpha_1}\right] \tag{195}$$

Therefore,

$$(e_2 - e_0) = \frac{1}{C_2}\int_0^t i_2\,dt$$

$$= \frac{e_1 - e_0}{R_1R_2C_1C_2(\alpha_2 - \alpha_1)}\left[\frac{\epsilon^{\alpha_2 t}}{\alpha_2} - \frac{\epsilon^{\alpha_1 t}}{\alpha_1} - \frac{1}{\alpha_2} + \frac{1}{\alpha_1}\right] \tag{196}$$

which is the solution to the problem.

The foregoing solution by means of transformation calculus was obtained more easily than could have been done by the standard differential equations method.[18]

Example 5: *Transient in a Secondary Circuit—Effect of Unity Coupling.* Suppose that the switch is closed in the circuit of Fig. 3-8 and we wish to find the current which flows in the secondary circuit. As a first step, we apply Kirchhoff's Second Law to Fig. 3-8. This gives

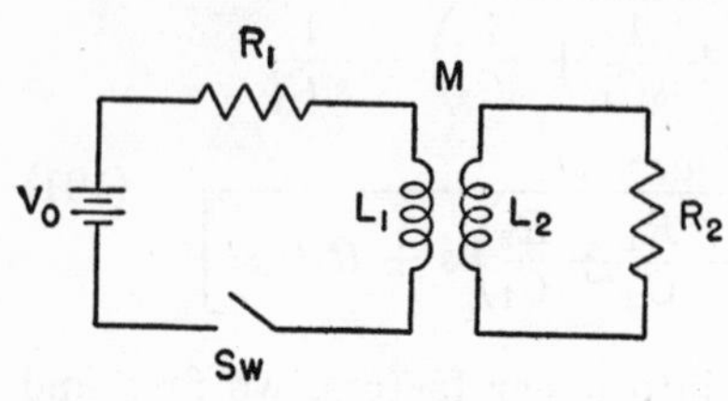

FIG. 3-8.

$$L_1 \frac{di_1}{dt} + R_1 i_1 = M \frac{di_2}{dt} + V_0 U(t) \tag{197}$$

$$L_2 \frac{di_2}{dt} + R_2 i_2 = M \frac{di_1}{dt} \tag{198}$$

Applying the Laplace transformation to Eqs. (197) and (198), and rearranging for simple solution, we get for quiescent initial conditions,

$$(sL_1 + R_1)I_1(s) - sMI_2(s) = \frac{V_0}{s} \tag{199}$$

$$-sMI_1(s) + (sL_2 + R_2)I_2(s) = 0 \tag{200}$$

Solving Eqs. (199) and (200), we have

$$I_2(s) = \frac{MV_0}{(sL_1 + R_1)(sL_2 + R_2) - s^2M^2} \tag{201}$$

Therefore
$$i_2(t) = \frac{MV_0(\epsilon^{-\alpha_2 t} - \epsilon^{-\alpha_1 t})}{(\alpha_1 - \alpha_2)(L_1L_2 - M^2)} \tag{202}$$

where

$$\alpha_1 = \frac{(L_1R_2 + L_2R_1) + \sqrt{(L_1R_2 + L_2R_1)^2 - 4R_1R_2(L_1L_2 - M^2)}}{2(L_1L_2 - M^2)} \tag{203}$$

---

[18] The time constant of the network for $e_2 - e_0$ is the time at which

$$\frac{e_2 - e_0}{e_\cdot - e_0} = \frac{1}{R_1R_2C_1C_2(\alpha_2 - \alpha_1)} \left[\frac{\epsilon^{\alpha_2 t}}{\alpha_2} - \frac{\epsilon^{\alpha_1 t}}{\alpha_1} - \frac{1}{\alpha_2} + \frac{1}{\alpha_2} \right] = 1 - \frac{1}{\epsilon}$$

$$\alpha_2 = \frac{(L_1R_2 + L_2R_1) - \sqrt{(L_1R_2 + L_2R_1)^2 - 4R_1R_2(L_1L_2 - M^2)}}{2(L_1L_2 - M^2)} \quad (204)$$

The secondary current, according to Eq. (202), thus consists of two exponentially decaying components.

In the case of unity coupling

$$L_1L_2 = M^2 \quad (205)$$

and Eq. (202) becomes indeterminate. Furthermore, in this case it is no longer true that i_1 and i_2 must be zero at the instant after the switch is closed. However, the stored magnetic energy $(\frac{1}{2}L_1i_1^2 + \frac{1}{2}L_2i_2^2 - Mi_1i_2)$ must still vanish at this instant. Using this condition, it will be found that Eq. (201) still holds and reduces to

$$I_2(s) = \frac{MV_0}{s(L_1R_2 + L_2R_1) + R_1R_2} \quad (206)$$

so that

$$i_2(t) = \frac{MV_0}{L_1R_2 + L_2R_1} \epsilon^{-\frac{R_1R_2t}{L_1R_2+L_2R_1}} \quad (207)$$

For unity coupling, the secondary transient thus consists only of a single exponential term. Physically, this means that for unity coupling, the two circuits are so tightly coupled that the transient has the form of a single-circuit transient.

Example 6: *Response of an R-C Circuit to a Square Wave.* Suppose that a square wave with voltage of height V_0 is applied to the

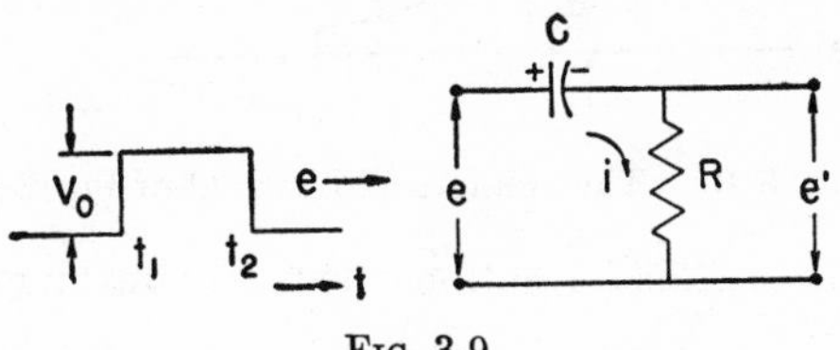

FIG. 3-9.

circuit of Fig. 3-9. Let us find the magnitude of the current which flows. This circuit is assumed quiescent before the square wave is applied. The differential equation of the circuit is

$$Ri + \frac{q}{C} = Ri + \frac{\int_0^t i\,dt}{C} = V_0[U(t - t_1) - U(t - t_2)] \quad (208)$$

Applying the Laplace transformation to Eq. (208), we get

$$RI(s) + \frac{I(s)}{sC} = V_0 \left[\frac{\epsilon^{-st_1}}{s} - \frac{\epsilon^{-st_2}}{s} \right] \tag{209}$$

Therefore

$$I(s) = \frac{V_0}{R\left(s + \frac{1}{RC}\right)} [\epsilon^{-st_1} - \epsilon^{-st_2}] \tag{210}$$

It therefore follows from formulas (a), (j), and (10) of Appendix D, that

$$i(t) = \frac{V_0}{R} \{\epsilon^{-\left(\frac{t-t_1}{RC}\right)} U(t - t_1) - \epsilon^{-\left(\frac{t-t_2}{RC}\right)} U(t - t_2)\} \tag{211}$$

Equation (211) as well as the voltages e and e' are plotted in Fig. 3-10. The simplicity of the solution of this problem illus-

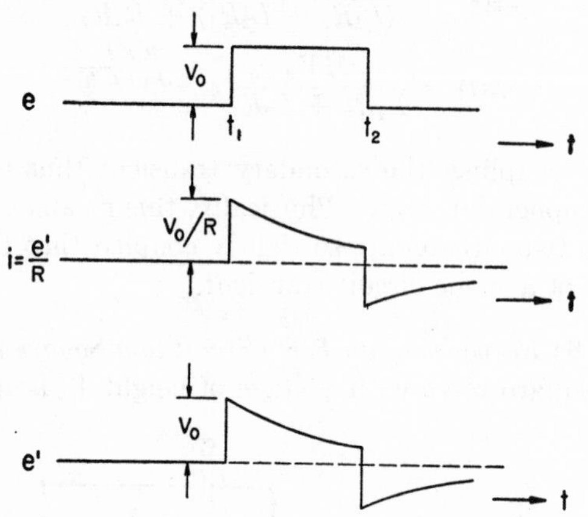

FIG. 3-10. The voltages and current of Fig. 3-9.

trates the power of transformation calculus in dealing with problems in transients.

3.14. Conclusion

In the present chapter we have developed the method for solving problems in electrical circuit transients by means of the Laplace transformation. This method has advantages of simplicity and rapidity over the method of solving the differential equations of circuits by orthodox means. The method we have used is a modernized, improved version of Heaviside's operational calculus. Our method[19] handles varieties of initial conditions and various forms of applied voltage in a more natural and straightforward manner than was achieved by Heaviside. Furthermore, the method here used has been put on a more trustworthy mathematical foundation.

In several succeeding chapters, we shall develop further the theory and methods of transformation calculus, and we shall apply them in studying various topics in circuit theory and solving certain important practical problems. The methods of transformation calculus thus developed can also be used in solving problems in other fields of physics and engineering which are governed by linear differential equations. These applications are discussed in a variety of publications.[20]

Exercises

1. A voltage, V_0, is applied to resistor R and capacitor C in series. Find the equation for the voltage across the capacitor as a function of time. Assume that the capacitor is uncharged when the voltage is first applied. (See Fig. 3-B.)

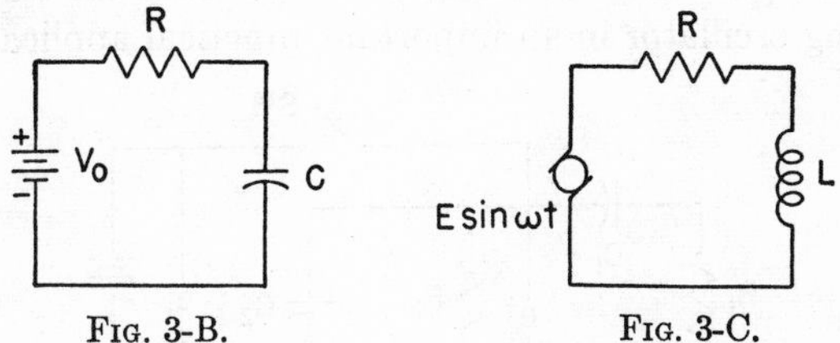

FIG. 3-B. FIG. 3-C.

2. An e.m.f. $E \sin \omega t$ is applied to a resistance and inductance in series. Find the complete expression for the current as a function of time, assuming that the current is zero when the e.m.f. is first applied. (See Fig. 3-C.)

3. Suppose that an e.m.f. $E \cos \omega t$ is applied to the network shown in Fig. 3-D. Find the value of the current i_2 in the resistor R_2, including both transient and steady-state terms. Assume that $i_1 = 0$ and $i_2 = 0$ at $t = 0$, when the voltage is first applied.

[19] The term "our method" is used as a means of distinction from Heaviside's method. The method is, of course, not original with the present author.

[20] Good general discussions will be found in Carslaw and Jaeger, *Operational Methods in Applied Mathematics*, and in Gardner and Barnes, *Transients in Linear Systems*.

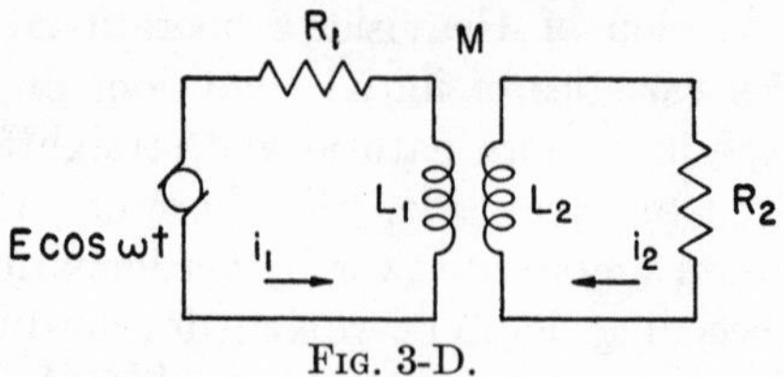

Fig. 3-D.

4. Find the transient and steady-state components of i_2 in Fig. 3-E, assuming that $Q_1 = 0$ and $Q_2 = 0$ at $t = 0$.

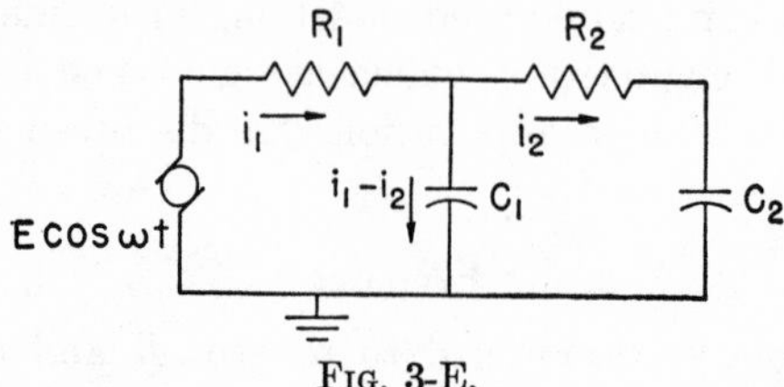

Fig. 3-E.

5. In Fig. 3-F, assume that the switch is originally closed. Then open the switch and find the equation for the decay of the voltage e. This equation is important in determining the time constant of a blocking oscillator in an important practical application.

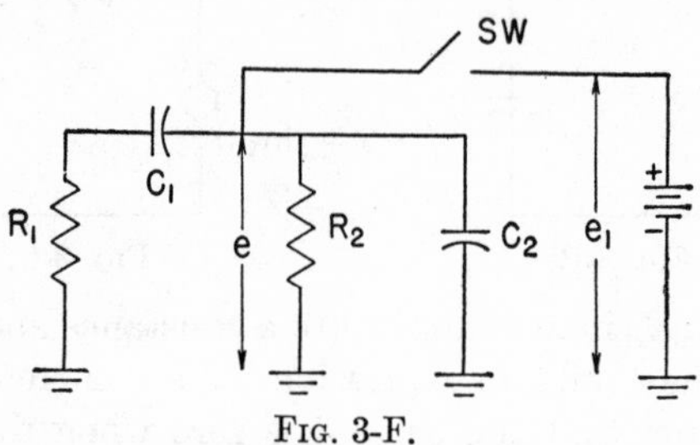

Fig. 3-F.

6. In the circuit of Fig. 3-G assume that the input is a voltage pulse of unit height and of length $T_2 - T_1$. Find the output.

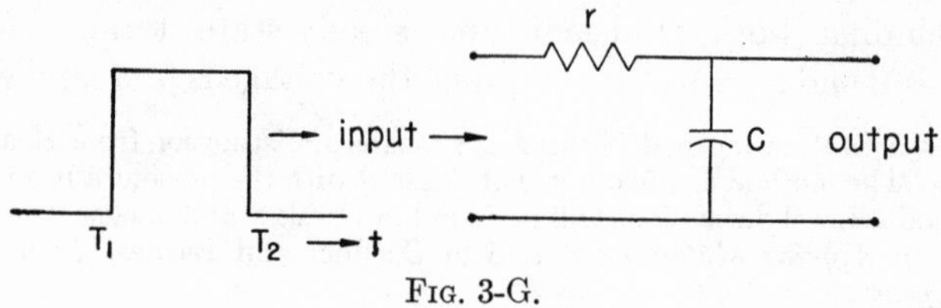

Fig. 3-G.

7. In the circuit of Fig. 3-H, find the voltage e_g as a function of time, after closing the switch.

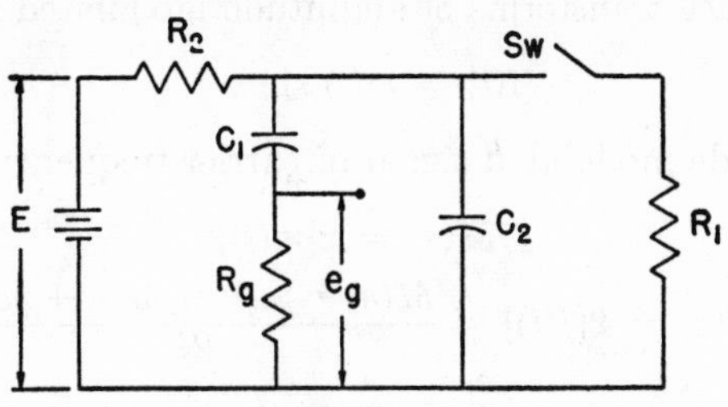

FIG. 3-H.

8. If

$$\mathcal{L}[f(t,\alpha)] = F(s,\alpha)$$

where α is a parameter, then

$$\int_0^\infty \frac{\partial}{\partial\alpha}[f(t,\alpha)\epsilon^{-st}]\,dt = \frac{\partial}{\partial\alpha}\int_0^\infty f(t,\alpha)\epsilon^{-st}\,dt = \frac{\partial}{\partial\alpha}[F(s,\alpha)]$$

Consequently $$\mathcal{L}\left[\frac{\partial}{\partial\alpha}f(t,\alpha)\right] = \frac{\partial}{\partial\alpha}F(s,\alpha)$$

This relation can be used to find new transformation pairs for the table. Thus starting from the pair

$$\mathcal{L}[\epsilon^{at}] = \frac{1}{s-a}$$

find the Laplace transforms of $t\epsilon^{at}$ and of $t^2\epsilon^{at}$.

9. (a) If

$$\mathcal{L}[f(t)] = F(s)$$

show that in general

$$\lim_{t\to\infty} f(t) = \lim_{s\to 0} s\,F(s)$$

(b) Choose three examples from the table of Laplace transforms to illustrate the foregoing theorem.

10. (a) If

$$\mathcal{L}[f(t)] = F(s)$$

show that in general

$$\lim_{t\to 0} f(t) = \lim_{s\to\infty} s\,F(s)$$

(b) Choose three examples from the table of Laplace transforms to illustrate the foregoing theorem.

11. (Laplace transforms of amplitude modulated signals): If

$$f(t) = m(t) \sin \omega_0 t$$

is an amplitude modulated signal of carrier frequency $\omega_0/2\pi$, and if

$$M(s) = \mathfrak{L}[m(t)]$$

show that $F(s) = \mathfrak{L}[f(t)] = \dfrac{M(s - j\omega_0) - M(s + j\omega_0)}{2j}$

12. If a square wave is applied to the grid of tube #1 in Fig. 3-I, find the expression for the voltage on the grid of the second

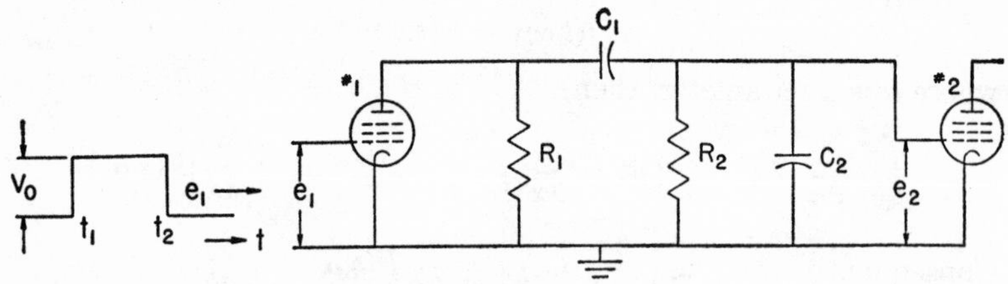

FIG. 3-I.

tube. Using this expression, draw the wave shape of e_2 in a typical case. Use node analysis.

CHAPTER 4

Some Fundamental Concepts and Relations in Circuit Theory[1]

4.1. Introduction

Circuit problems can be solved by solving the differential equations of the circuits. We followed this procedure in the foregoing chapter and it is useful for many purposes. The theory of electrical circuits is, however, not limited to the solution of specific problems, but also includes the broader considerations of what may be called the underlying physics of the situation. The frequency analysis of circuits with the aid of the Fourier integral is one variety of these more physical methods[2] of investigation. In the present chapter we shall deal with the other two methods commonly used, one based upon analysis in terms of step functions and the other based upon analysis in terms of impulse functions. We shall find the analogues of the Fourier integral in certain "superposition integrals." Finally, we shall find certain interrelations between the properties of circuits based upon the different methods of analysis. In the course of this chapter we shall also derive some of the fundamental theorems of circuit analysis.

4.2. The indicial admittance

If an impedance is initially in a quiescent state, the time function of current which enters the impedance in response to the application of a unit-step function of voltage is called the *indicial admittance* of the impedance, and is designated $A(t)$. Thus we showed in

---

[1] The writer is particularly indebted to J. R. Carson's *Electrical Circuit Theory and Operational Calculus* and Schelkunoff's *Electromagnetic Waves* as a background for the material presented in this chapter.

[2] This method is treated in detail in the author's *Frequency Analysis, Modulation and Noise*, McGraw-Hill, New York (1948). A brief discussion of Fourier integrals is given in Appendix E of the present book.

§3.13 (Example 3) that the indicial admittance of the circuit in Fig. 4-1 is

$$A(t) = \frac{1}{R}(1 - \epsilon^{-Rt/L}) \tag{1}$$

We will find the indicial admittance to be particularly important because of its use in superposition integrals which will be considered

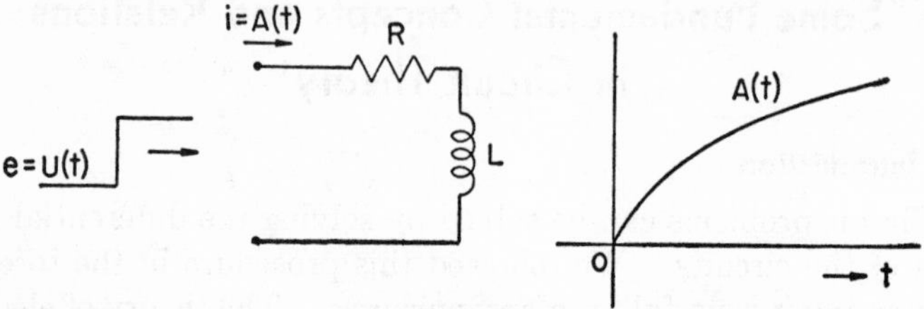

FIG. 4-1. A series R-L circuit and its indicial admittance.

later on in this chapter. However, many writers on the subject of operational calculus make the indicial admittance the central theme of the whole subject.[3] It is therefore desirable for the reader to become well acquainted with its properties.

The indicial admittance is related to its corresponding impedance by a formula known as Carson's integral equation,[4] which we will now derive for the case of a single *L-R-C* circuit. The generalization for a network can be derived by proceeding according to the methods for treating networks in §3.12. Returning to a single circuit, if the initial conditions are quiescent and a unit-step function of voltage is applied to the circuit, the Laplace transformed equation of the circuit may be written

$$I(s) = \frac{1}{sz(s)} \tag{2}$$

according to Eq. (156) of Chap. 3. It then follows that

$$A(t) = \mathfrak{L}^{-1}[I(s)] = \mathfrak{L}^{-1}\left[\frac{1}{sz(s)}\right] \tag{3}$$

or

$$\frac{1}{sz(s)} = \int_0^\infty \epsilon^{-st} A(t)\, dt \tag{4}$$

---

[3] A concise and accurate discussion of the use of the indicial admittance as the basis for operational calculus is given in Chap. X of Karman and Biot, *Mathematical Methods in Engineering*.

[4] Originated by the American engineer, John R. Carson.

which is Carson's integral equation.[5] This equation is used to express the impedance function in terms of the indicial admittance, and vice versa. The Laplace transform of the indicial admittance is thus $1/sz(s)$.

As an example, let us test the correctness of Eq. (4) by substituting the value of $A(t)$ from Eq. (1). Accordingly

$$\int_0^\infty \epsilon^{-st} \frac{1}{R} (1 - \epsilon^{-Rt/L})\, dt = \left.\frac{\epsilon^{-st}}{-sR}\right|_0^\infty - \left.\frac{\epsilon^{-(s+R/L)t}}{-\left(s + \frac{R}{L}\right) R}\right|_0^\infty$$

$$= \frac{1}{s(sL + R)} \tag{5}$$

Since

$$z(s) = sL + R \tag{6}$$

for the circuit in Fig. 4-1, it follows that Eq. (5) verifies Carson's integral equation, Eq. (4), for this particular case. Carson's equation is widely used in radio literature.

Since the instant which we choose for the origin of time does not affect the course of physical phenomena, it follows that the response of a circuit to the displaced unit step $U(t - t_1)$ must be $A(t - t_1)$.

Exercises

1. Find $A(t)$ for the circuit of Fig. 4-A.
Answer:

$$A(t) = \frac{1}{R} \epsilon^{-t/RC}$$

2. Find $A(t)$ for the circuit of Fig. 4-B.

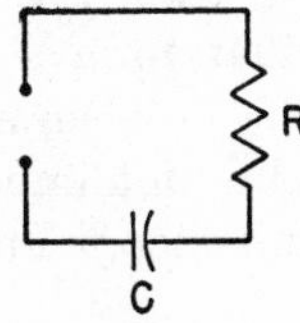

FIG. 4-A.

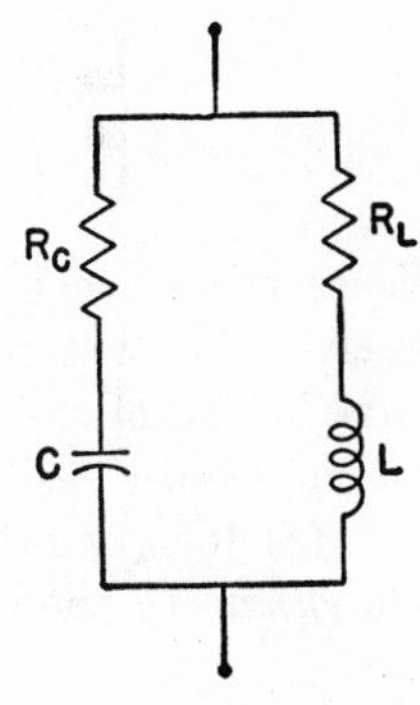

FIG. 4-B.

[5] As pointed out in §3.12, $z(s)$ is the impedance function taken as a function of s. This can perhaps most easily be found by substituting s for $j\omega$ in the steady-state impedance of the circuit.

Answer:

$$A(t) = \frac{1}{R_c}\,\epsilon^{-t/R_cC} + \frac{1}{R_L}\,(1 - \epsilon^{-R_Lt/L})$$

4.3. The unit impulse

We next wish to consider impulse functions and begin with the definition of a unit impulse, which we shall call $\delta(t)$. A *unit impulse* is a function whose value is zero except in an arbitrarily small interval around $t = 0$, where it becomes infinite in such a way that

$$\int_{-a}^{+b} \delta(t)\,dt = 1 \tag{7}$$

In Eq. (7), a and b are any finite positive quantities.

Special types of unit-impulse functions may be defined by limiting processes in various ways. For example, we can use

$$\delta(t) = \lim_{\Delta t\to 0} \frac{U\left(t + \frac{\Delta t}{2}\right) - U\left(t - \frac{\Delta t}{2}\right)}{\Delta t} \tag{8}$$

or

$$\delta(t) = \lim_{\Delta t\to 0} \frac{U(t + \Delta t) - U(t)}{\Delta t} \tag{9}$$

or

$$\delta(t) = \lim_{\Delta t\to 0} \frac{U(t) - U(t - \Delta t)}{\Delta t} \tag{10}$$

or

$$\begin{cases} \delta(t) = \lim\limits_{\Delta t\to 0} \dfrac{\epsilon^{-t/\Delta t}}{\Delta t} & \text{when} \quad t > 0 \\ \delta(t) = 0 & \text{when} \quad t \le 0 \end{cases} \tag{11}$$

These cases are illustrated in Fig. 4-2(a), (b), (c), and (d) respectively. The net result of using any of these forms is always the same in practice, so that the particular form should be chosen which is most easily manipulated in the problem at hand. Equation (8) [or (9) or (10)] shows that the unit impulse is formally equivalent to the derivative of the unit step. Furthermore,

$$\delta(t - C)$$

expresses a unit impulse at $t = C$, and it may be shown[6] that

[6] A derivation of Eq. (12) would proceed as follows:

$$\int_{-\infty}^{+\infty} g(t)\delta(t - C)\, dt = g(C) \tag{12}$$

provided that $g(t)$ is a finite and continuous function of t.

If $P(t)$ is an impulsive function in general, (i.e., not necessarily a unit impulse) then

$$\int_{t_1}^{t_2} P(t)\, dt$$

is called the *strength* or *magnitude* of the impulse, where the impulse lies entirely in the small interval $t_2 - t_1$. Accordingly, we can say that a unit impulse is an impulse of unit strength.

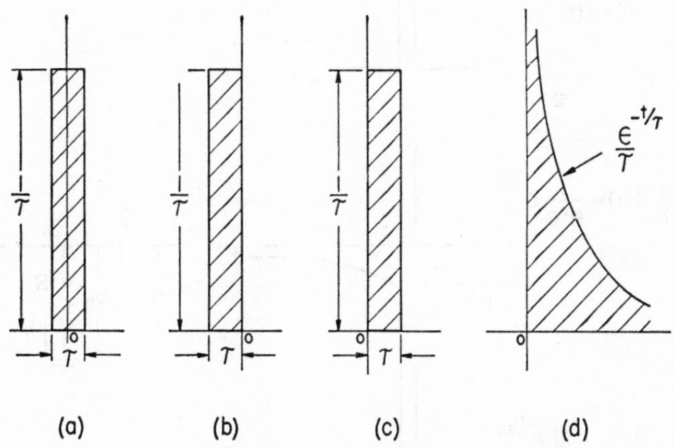

Fig. 4-2. Various pre-limit forms of unit impulses.

With the use of Eq. (12), we can easily find the Laplace transform of $\delta(t)$. Thus, using a form of $\delta(t)$ in which all the impulse is on the positive[7] side of $t = 0$, such as shown in Eq. (10) or (11) and

---

$$\int_{-\infty}^{+\infty} g(t)\delta(t - C)\, dt = \int_{C-a}^{C+a} g(t)\delta(t - C)\, dt = g(C) \int_{C-a}^{C+a} \delta(t - C)\, dt = g(C)$$

where a is a very small quantity. If one of the specific forms of $\delta(t)$ in Eqs. (8–11) is chosen, the derivation can easily be made rigorous.

[7] If a form of the unit impulse is used in which part of the active part of the function is negative, such as shown in Fig. 4-2 (a) or (b), it would be necessary to take the effect of this negative region into account in writing down the initial conditions. This would cause needless complication. We will therefore always assume a form of the unit impulse in which all the active part is in the positive region of t.

depicted in Fig. 4-2(c) or (d), we get

$$\mathcal{L}[\delta(t)] = \int_0^\infty \epsilon^{-st}\delta(t)\,dt = \int_{-\infty}^{+\infty} \epsilon^{-st}\delta(t)\,dt = \epsilon^0 = 1 \tag{13}$$

The Laplace transform of the unit impulse is therefore unity itself, and conversely

$$\mathcal{L}^{-1}(1) = \delta(t) \tag{14}$$

Step functions and impulse functions never appear in practice except as approximations. Thus the condition in which a quantity

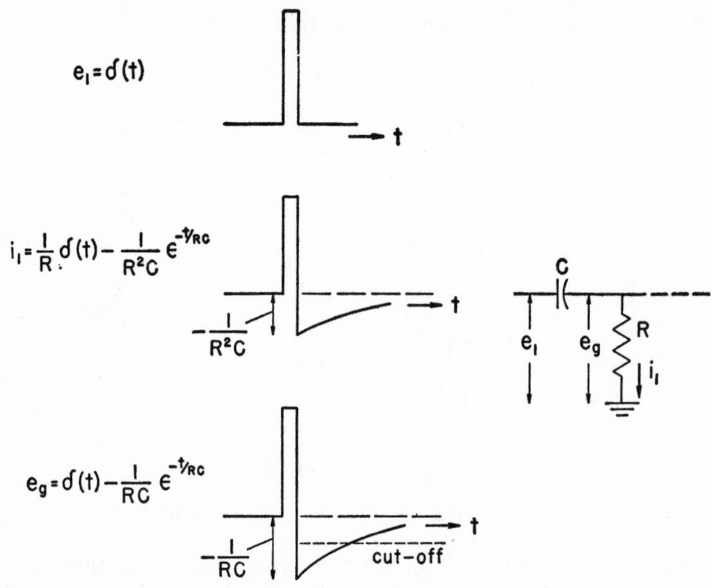

FIG. 4-3. Blocking of grid by an impulse. (The formulas in this figure assume that there is no grid current. See Exercise 4 at the end of §4.4 for the case when there is grid current.)

changes by a finite amount in an interval so short that a fraction of the interval would be of no practical interest, and in which the new value is then retained for the duration of the period of interest of the problem, is treated by specifying the quantity as a step function. As a practical example, the closing of a switch connecting a battery to a circuit is analyzed by assuming that a step function of voltage is applied to the circuit.

In a similar manner, the condition in which a quantity has so great a value in an interval of negligible duration that a finite change is effected in the state of the system is treated by specifying the quantity as an impulse function. For example, consider a voltage pulse entering the grid circuit of a vacuum tube as shown in Fig. 4-3. This pulse may be considered an impulse if its duration is negligibly short in comparison with the *R-C* time constant of the circuit and its magnitude is so great that it has an appreciable effect on the circuit despite its short duration. In the case of the impulse in Fig. 4-3, the ultimate effect is to drive the grid voltage so far negative that the tube is cut off for an appreciable length of time. The actual magnitude and duration of the voltage pulse e_1 are not separately important in this case, but the time integral of e_1 (i.e., the strength of the voltage impulse) determines how far negative the grid voltage goes and how long the tube is cut off. Thus e_1, in this case, is an impulse function.[8]

Exercise

Show that $$\mathcal{L}[\delta(t - a)] = \epsilon^{-as}$$

4.4. Green's function

If an impedance is initially in a quiescent state, the time function of current which enters the impedance in response to the application of a unit-impulse function of voltage is called *Green's function* for the impedance, and is designated $B(t)$. Accordingly, if the voltage impulse e_1 in Fig. 4-3 is of unit strength, then the current i_1 is Green's function for the series *R-C* impedance in the same figure.

Let us now find the analytical expression for

$$i_1(t) = B(t) \tag{15}$$

in Fig. 4-3. The circuit equation is

$$Ri_1 + \frac{\int i_1\,dt}{C} = e_1 = \delta(t) \tag{16}$$

Applying the Laplace transformation to Eq. (16), we get

$$RI_1 + \frac{I_1}{sC} = 1 \tag{17}$$

[8] Additional considerations of step and impulse functions, particularly concerning their energy and frequency characteristics, will be found in the author's *Frequency Analysis, Modulation and Noise.*

since the initial conditions are quiescent in accordance with the above definition, so that[9]

$$\int^{0+} i_1\,dt = 0 \tag{18}$$

Solving Eq. (17) for I_1, we get

$$I_1 = \frac{1}{R + \frac{1}{sC}} = \frac{s}{R\left(s + \frac{1}{RC}\right)} = \frac{1}{R} - \frac{1}{R^2C\left(s + \frac{1}{RC}\right)} \tag{19}$$

Consequently, $$B(t) = i_1(t) = \frac{1}{R}\,\delta(t) - \frac{1}{R^2C}\,\epsilon^{-t/RC} \tag{20}$$

by forms #1 and #10 in the table of Laplace transforms. This function is the analytical form of i_1 in Fig. 4-3, if e_1 is a unit impulse.

In practical cases, the height and duration of an impulse are always actually finite. Consequently the $\delta(t)$ in Eq. (20) is only an approximation in practice—the true value corresponding to it having about the same form as the actual voltage impulse. However, the second term on the right of Eq. (20), namely

$$\left(-\frac{1}{R^2C}\,\epsilon^{-t/RC}\right)$$

corresponds accurately, for practical purposes, to the current after

[9] When we set $\int^{0+} i_1\,dt = 0$, we are using the value of this quantity at the beginning of impulse, rather than at the end of the impulse. To justify this usage let us consider the form of $\delta(t)$ in Fig. 4-2(c), which is of the type used in deriving Eq. (13). If we consider a case in which Δt is very small but still finite in $\delta(t)$, and apply the Laplace transformation to Eq. (16), it is obvious that in that case the value

$$\int^{0+} i_1\,dt = 0$$

must be used. If now Δt is allowed to take on a succession of still smaller values, the value of

$$\int^{0+} i_1\,dt$$

is unaffected. Therefore, in the limit as Δt approaches zero, the equation

$$\int^{0+} i_1\,dt = 0$$

is still correct.

the impulse has passed. The foregoing discussion has ignored the fact that grid current may flow in the tube. For the case when grid current does flow, see Exercise 4 at the end of this section.

Let us next find the equation for $B(t)$ which corresponds to Carson's equation for $A(t)$. In this case, let a unit-impulse function of voltage be applied to a circuit having quiescent initial conditions. Then according to Eq. (156) of Chap. 3, the Laplace transformed equation of the circuit may be written

$$I(s) = \frac{1}{z(s)} \tag{21}$$

Therefore

$$B(t) = \mathcal{L}^{-1}[I(s)] = \mathcal{L}^{-1}\left[\frac{1}{z(s)}\right] \tag{22}$$

or

$$\frac{1}{z(s)} = \int_0^\infty \epsilon^{-st} B(t)\, dt \tag{23}$$

Equation (23) is the equation for $B(t)$ which corresponds to Carson's equation for $A(t)$. The above derivation was carried out for a single mesh circuit, but the same equation holds for any impedance in linear networks. Equation (22) or (23) shows that $1/z(s)$ (i.e., the circuit admittance as a function of s) is the Laplace transform of Green's function. We will discuss the significance of this fact in §4.8.

Finally, we wish to derive the relation between $B(t)$ and $A(t)$. Equation (3) gives us the relation

$$\mathcal{L}[A(t)] = \frac{1}{sz(s)} \tag{24}$$

Therefore, by Eq. (19) of Chap. 3,

$$\mathcal{L}\left[\frac{dA}{dt}\right] = \frac{1}{z(s)} - A(0+) \tag{25}$$

Consequently,

$$\frac{dA}{dt} = \mathcal{L}^{-1}\left[\frac{1}{z(s)}\right] - \mathcal{L}^{-1}[A(0+)] = B(t) - A(0+)\delta(t) \tag{26}$$

Rearranging Eq. (26), we obtain

$$B(t) = A(0+)\delta(t) + \frac{dA}{dt} \tag{27}$$

As a simple example of the use of Eq. (27), let us derive $B(t)$ for Fig. 4-3 from the value of $A(t)$ in Exercise 1 at the end of §4.2. There

$$A(t) = \frac{1}{R} \epsilon^{-t/RC} \tag{28}$$

Therefore, by Eq. (27)

$$B(t) = \frac{1}{R} \delta(t) - \frac{1}{R^2C} \epsilon^{-t/RC} \tag{29}$$

This solution agrees with that of Eq. (20), which was obtained by a different method.

Exercises

1. Find the response of the circuit in Fig. 4-C to the voltage function in Fig. 4-D.

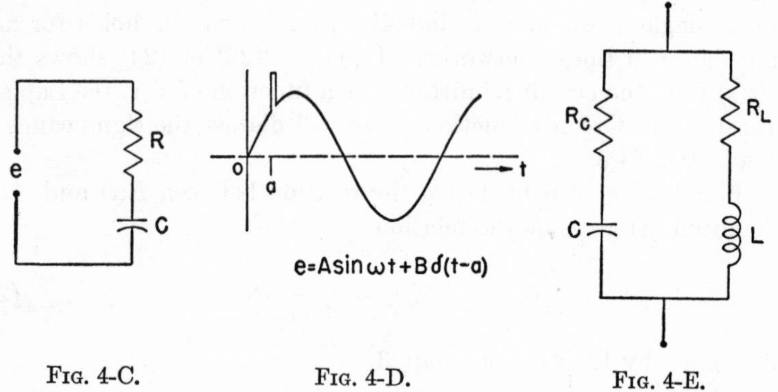

Fig. 4-C. Fig. 4-D. Fig. 4-E.

2. Carry through the formal integration in Eq. (23) for $B(t)$ as expressed in Eq. (20) and verify the correctness of Eq. (23) in this case.

3. Find $B(t)$ for the circuit in Fig. 4-E.

4. Solve for i_1 and e_g in Fig. 4-3, assuming that grid current does flow during the impulse duration. Assume that the voltage impulse has a very short but finite duration Δt, and a height $1/\Delta t$. Assume, also, that grid current is limited to the value I_s as the complete cathode emission.

Answer:

$$i_1 = \left(I_s\,\Delta t + \frac{1}{R}\right)\left[\delta(t) - \frac{1}{RC}\,\epsilon^{-t/RC}\right]$$

$$e_g = \delta(t) - \left(\frac{I_s}{C}\,\Delta t + \frac{1}{RC}\right)\epsilon^{-t/RC}$$

4.5. The principle of superposition

The analysis of electrical circuits is often greatly simplified by using a general proposition known as the *principle of superposition.* This principle is actually of very wide use, applying to all linear systems, whether electrical, mechanical, or otherwise; and applying to both transient and steady-state phenomena. We will now state the principle in a form which is particularly suitable for circuit analysis,[10] and for which we shall be able to supply a simple proof.

In a network whose circuit parameters (L, R, C, and M) are constants, if several electromotive forces are applied either in the same or in different locations and at the same or different times, the total current produced is the sum of the currents produced by the individual e.m.f.'s considered separately.

As a corollary to this principle, we have the following. *If a current or voltage function $f(t)$ can be separated into a number of parts, $f_1(t), f_2(t), \cdots f_n(t)$,* such that

$$f(t) = f_1(t) + f_2(t) + \cdots + f_n(t)$$

then any current or voltage due to $f(t)$ will be the sum of the components due to $f_1(t), f_2(t), \cdots$ and $f_n(t)$ taken separately.

A mathematical proof of the principle of superposition can be based upon the solution of the differential equations of the network by the method of Laplace transforms and the use of Eqs. (21) and (46) of Chap. 3. For simplicity, let us consider the case of a single circuit, and let a number of e.m.f.'s $e(t)$, $f(t)$, $g(t)$, $\cdots$ be applied. Accordingly, the circuit equation is

$$L\frac{di}{dt} + Ri + \int \frac{i\,dt}{C} = e(t) + f(t) + g(t) + \cdots \qquad (30)$$

[10] The following discussion will be based upon the assumption of constant values of the circuit parameters (L, R, C, and M). As one consequence of the principle, it will follow that the amplitude and phase characteristics (as a function of frequency) of any transmission system to which the principle applies will be independent of the size or form of the signal.

The Laplace transformed equation corresponding to Eq. (30) is then

$$LsI(s) + RI(s) + \frac{I(s)}{sC} = E(s) + F(s) + G(s) + \cdots + O(s) \quad (31)$$

where
$$O(s) = Li_0 - \frac{Q_0}{sC} \quad (32)$$

Therefore,
$$I(s) = \frac{E(s)}{z(s)} + \frac{F(s)}{z(s)} + \frac{G(s)}{z(s)} + \cdots + \frac{O(s)}{z(s)} \quad (33)$$

Transforming Eq. (33) back into a function of t, we obtain

$$i(t) = \mathfrak{L}^{-1}\left[\frac{E(s)}{z(s)}\right] + \mathfrak{L}^{-1}\left[\frac{F(s)}{z(s)}\right] + \mathfrak{L}^{-1}\left[\frac{G(s)}{z(s)}\right] + \cdots + \mathfrak{L}^{-1}\left[\frac{O(s)}{z(s)}\right] \quad (34)$$

In Eq. (34), $\mathfrak{L}^{-1}[E(s)/z(s)]$ is the current due to $e(t)$, $\mathfrak{L}^{-1}[F(s)/z(s)]$ is the current due to $f(t)$, $\mathfrak{L}^{-1}[G(s)/z(s)]$ is the current due to $g(t)$, etc., while $\mathfrak{L}^{-1}[O(s)/z(s)]$ is the current due to the initial state of the circuit at $t = 0$. Equation (34) thus tells us that the effects of the individual e.m.f.'s $e(t)$, $f(t)$, $g(t)$, etc., are additive, which is the principle of superposition.

Following the method used in §3.12, the foregoing demonstration can be generalized to the case of a network. Thus, in a network having the circuit differential equations[11]

$$\begin{array}{c} z_{11}(p)i_1 + z_{12}(p)i_2 + \cdots + z_{1n}(p)i_n = e_1(t) + f_1(t) + \cdots \\ \vdots \\ z_{n1}(p)i_1 + z_{n2}(p)i_2 + \cdots + z_{nn}(p)i_n = e_n(t) + f_n(t) + \cdots \end{array} \quad (35)$$

the transformed equations are

$$\begin{array}{l} z_{11}(s)I_1(s) + z_{12}(s)I_2(s) + \cdots + z_{1n}(s)I_n(s) = E_1(s) + F_1(s) + \cdots + O_1(s) \\ \vdots \\ z_{n1}(s)I_1(s) + z_{n2}(s)I_2(s) + \cdots + z_{nn}(s)I_n(s) = E_n(s) + F_n(s) + \cdots + O_n(s) \end{array} \quad (36)$$

[11] See §§2.12 and 2.13 for the meaning of $z_{jk}(p)$.

Solving Eq. (36) for one of the currents, say I_1, we have

$$\begin{aligned} I_1(s) = {} & [E_1(s) + F_1(s) + \cdots + O_1(s)] \frac{M_{11}(s)}{\Delta(s)} \\ & + [E_2(s) + F_2(s) + \cdots + O_2(s)] \frac{M_{21}(s)}{\Delta(s)} + \cdots \\ & + [E_n(s) + F_n(s) + \cdots + O_n(s)] \frac{M_{n1}(s)}{\Delta(s)} \end{aligned} \tag{37}$$

where

$$\Delta(s) = \begin{vmatrix} z_{11}(s) & \cdots & z_{1n}(s) \\ \vdots & & \vdots \\ z_{n1}(s) & \cdots & z_{nn}(s) \end{vmatrix} \tag{38}$$

and $M_{11}(s)$ is the cofactor of $z_{11}(s)$ in Eq. (38), and so on. It is clear from Eq. (37) that the current $i_1(t)$ will consist of the sum of the currents due to $e_1(t), f_1(t), \cdots e_2(t), f_2(t)$, etc., considered separately,

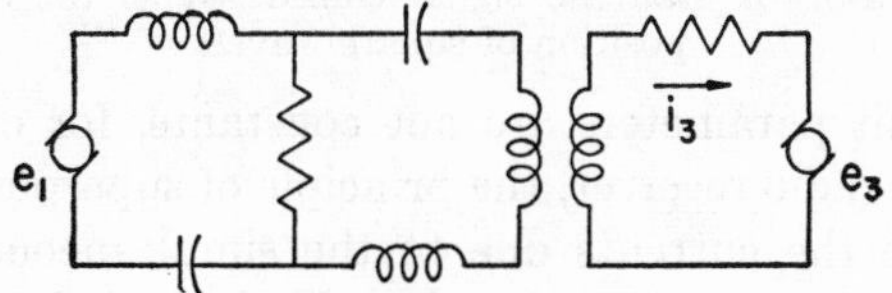

FIG. 4-4. A schematic illustrating superimposed voltages.

plus the currents due to the non-quiescent initial conditions.[12] The mathematical basis for the principle of superposition has thus been demonstrated.

As an example of the use of the principle of superposition, consider the network in Fig. 4-4. In order to find the current i_3, we can find the current i_3 which would flow due to e_1 if e_3 were zero, and the current due to e_3 if e_1 were zero. If we add these together, we then get the total current i_3 which actually flows, assuming quiescent initial conditions.

As another example, consider the e.m.f. shown in Fig. 4-5. The current in a linear network due to this e.m.f. may be calculated

[12] The non-quiescent initial conditions thus constitute an equivalent voltage. It should also be noted that each voltage function, such as $e_1(t)$, may contribute both to the transient and steady-state portions (i.e., in the language of the theory of differential equations, both to the complementary function and to the particular integral portions) of the current.

by calculating first the current due to the long pulse

$$a[U(t - t_1) - U(t - t_4)]$$

and then the current due to the short pulse

$$b[U(t - t_2) - U(t - t_3)]$$

and adding the results.

Our statement of the principle of superposition referred only to networks in which the circuit parameters were constants. In case the circuit parameters are not constants, for example in the converter of a radio receiver, the principle of superposition does not apply. There the currents due to the simultaneous operation of two different voltages cannot just be added, since there is additional current due to the interaction of the voltages. A similar condition prevails in other nonlinear circuits.

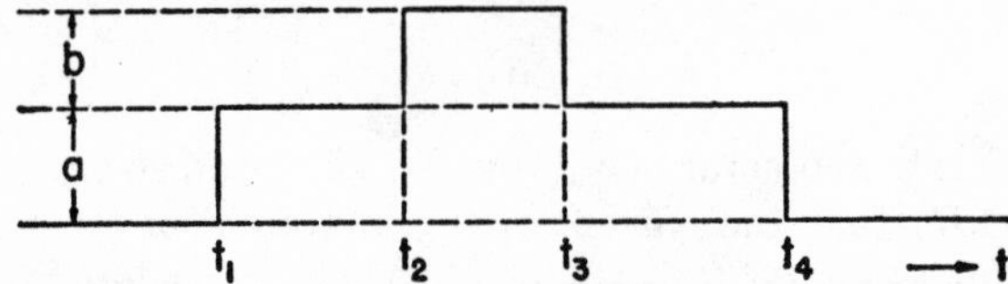

FIG. 4-5. A staircase signal considered as the superposition of square waves.

Exercises

1. Find the current in R (Fig. 4-F), (a) in the steady state; and (b) the total current starting from quiescent initial conditions.

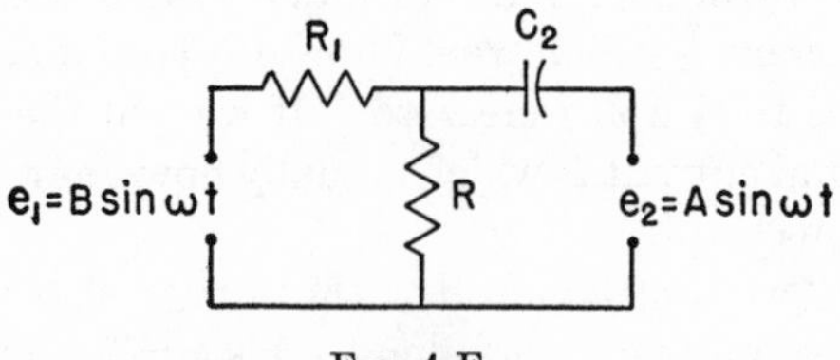

FIG. 4-F.

2. In a network whose circuit parameters L, R, C, and M do not vary with time or with the magnitude of the current passing through them, prove that

$$z_{jk} = z_{kj}$$

3. (Reciprocity Theorem): Prove that if an e.m.f. $e(t)$ of any waveshape whatsoever, located at one point in a network having constant parameters produces a current $i(t)$ at an other point in the network, then the same e.m.f. $e(t)$ located at the second point would produce the same current $i(t)$ at the first point.

4. If C and D are short-circuited together in Fig. 4-G and a unit step of voltage is applied between A and B, call the current which flows through the shorting bar $i_1(t)$. If A and B are short-circuited together and a unit step of voltage is applied between C and D, call the current which flows through the shorting bar $i_2(t)$. Show by solving the network equations that

$$i_1(t) = i_2(t)$$

This result also follows directly from the reciprocity theorem without the necessity of solving the network equations.

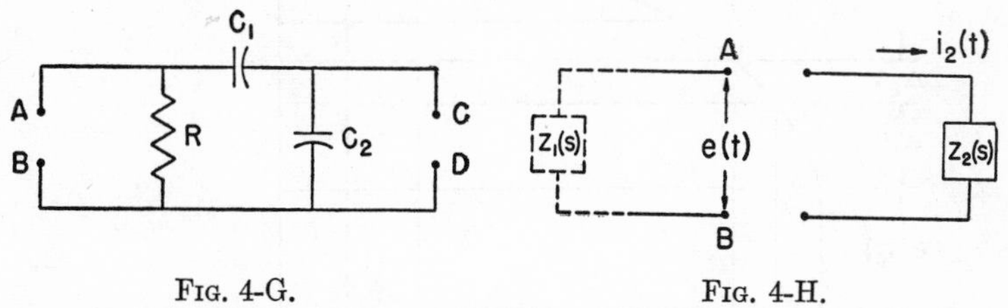

FIG. 4-G. FIG. 4-H.

5. (Thevenin's Theorem): Let the impedance looking into a network between terminals A and B in Fig. 4-H be $Z_1(s)$ and let the voltage between these be $e(t)$. Then if an impedance $Z_2(s)$ is connected between A and B, prove that the current $i_2(t)$ which will flow through $Z_2(s)$ will be

$$i_2(t) = \pounds^{-1}\left\{\frac{E(s)}{Z_1(s) + Z_2(s)}\right\}$$

where

$$E(s) = \pounds\,\{e(t)\}$$

6. If a pulse of unit height and of duration $(t_2 - t_1)$ is applied at the point indicated in Fig. 4-I, find the voltage $e'(t)$, and the values of r and C' such that the same current will flow through Z in Fig. 4-J as through Z in Fig. 4-I.

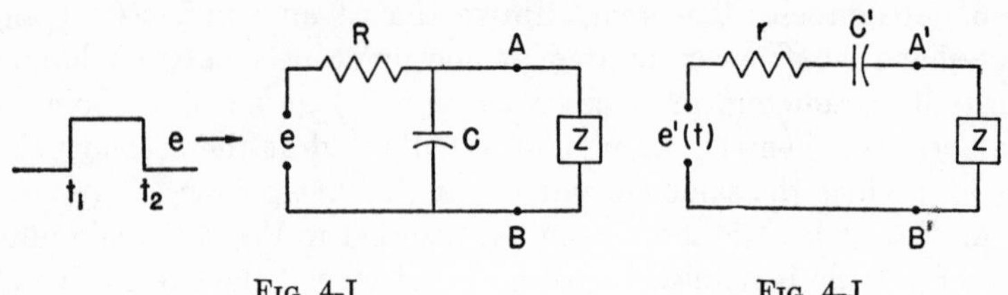

FIG. 4-I. FIG. 4-J.

4.6. The superposition integrals

We will now use the results obtained in the preceding sections to derive explicit expressions for the current due to an arbitrary e.m.f. in terms of definite integrals. These are called superposition integrals.

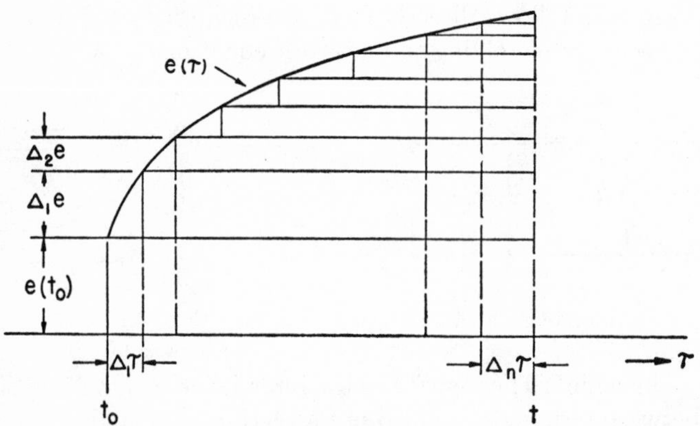

FIG. 4-6. Analysis of a general function as the superposition of step functions.

Consider an e.m.f. $e(\tau)$, as shown in Fig. 4-6, where τ is the general time variable. Suppose that this e.m.f. is zero until some time t_0 and that we wish to find the current at time t. Now in the range between t_0 and t, we may write as an approximation

$$\begin{aligned} e(\tau) = e(t_0)U(\tau - t_0) &+ \Delta_1 eU(\tau - t_0 - \Delta_1\tau) \\ &+ \Delta_2 eU(\tau - t_0 - \Delta_1\tau - \Delta_2\tau) + \cdots \\ &+ \Delta_{n-1}eU(\tau - t + \Delta_n\tau) + \Delta_n eU(\tau - t) \end{aligned} \quad (39)$$

if all the Δ quantities are very small. This is obvious from Fig. 4-6.

It then follows from the principle of superposition, and the definition of indicial admittance,[13] that

$$i(\tau) = e(t_0)A(\tau - t_0) + (\Delta_1 e)A(\tau - t_0 - \Delta_1\tau) + \cdots + (\Delta_{n-1}e)A(\tau - t + \Delta_n\tau) + \Delta_n eA(\tau - t) \quad (40)$$

In particular, if $\tau = t$, we have

$$i(t) = e(t_0)A(t - t_0) + (\Delta_1 e)A(t - t_0 - \Delta_1\tau) + (\Delta_2 e)A(t - t_0 - \Delta_1\tau - \Delta_2\tau) + \cdots + \Delta_{n-1}eA(t - t + \Delta_n\tau) + \Delta_n eA(t - t) \quad (41)$$

If we let n increase indefinitely and make all the $\Delta\tau$'s approach zero, then for any Δe we have

$$\Delta e = \left\{\frac{\partial e(\tau)}{\partial\tau}\right\} \Delta\tau \quad (42)$$

if $e(\tau)$ is a continuous function of τ.

From Eq. (39) it then follows that

$$e(t) = e(t_0)U(t - t_0) + \int_{t_0}^{t} \left\{\frac{\partial e(\tau)}{\partial\tau}\right\} U(t - \tau)\, d\tau \quad (43)$$

and Eq. (41) becomes

$$i(t) = e(t_0)A(t - t_0) + \int_{t_0}^{t} \left\{\frac{\partial e(\tau)}{\partial\tau}\right\} A(t - \tau)\, d\tau \quad (44)$$

Equation (43) is an expression for $e(t)$ as a superposition of step functions. Equation (44) gives the circuit response to this superposition of step functions. The latter is an explicit expression for $i(t)$ in terms of the voltage and of the indicial admittance of the impedance under consideration. This equation is sometimes called the *superposition theorem.*

In case $e(\tau)$ is not a continuous function between t_0 and t, but has a finite number of discontinuities as shown in Fig. 4-7, then by making the appropriate changes in Eq. (40), it follows that Eq. (44) becomes

$$i(t) = e(t_0)A(t - t_0) + \int_{t_0}^{t_a} \frac{\partial e}{\partial\tau} A(t - \tau)\, d\tau + (E_{2a} - E_{1a})A(t - t_a) + \int_{t_a}^{t_b} \left(\frac{\partial e}{\partial\tau}\right) A(t - \tau)\, d\tau + (E_{2b} - E_{1b})A(t - t_b) + \int_{t_b}^{t} \left(\frac{\partial e}{\partial\tau}\right) A(t - \tau)\, d\tau \quad (45)$$

[13] To get the total current, we would have to add to $i(\tau)$, any current in the impedance due to the initial conditions at $\tau = t_0$.

For most purposes, however, we shall use the simpler Eq. (44) as the fundamental equation, since Eq. (45) is of essentially the same form.

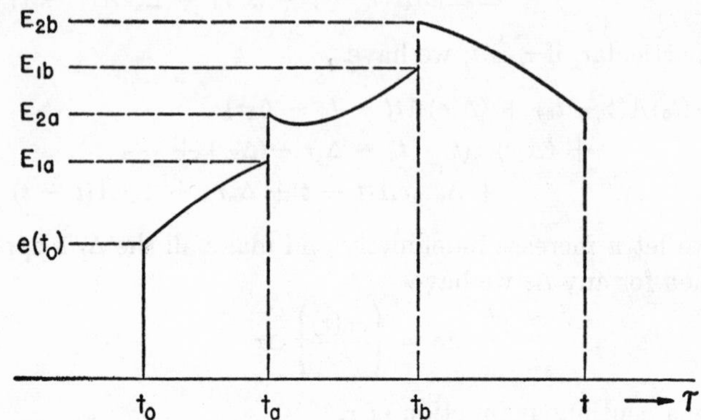

FIG. 4-7. A function having discontinuities.

Equation (44) can be changed into a number of alternative forms,[14] each of which is useful at times. These are listed below

[14] These alternative forms are derived from Eq. (44) in the following manner. In the integrand of Eq. (44) let

$$x = t - \tau + t_0 \tag{A}$$

Then

$$dx = -d\tau \tag{B}$$

because t is a constant for the integral in Eq. (44). Furthermore, then,

$$\frac{\partial}{\partial \tau} e(\tau) = \frac{\partial}{\partial t} e(t - x + t_0) \tag{C}$$

Consequently

$$\int_{\tau=t_0}^{\tau=t} \left\{ \frac{\partial}{\partial \tau} e(\tau) \right\} A(t - \tau)\, d\tau = - \int_{x=t}^{x=t_0} \left\{ \frac{\partial}{\partial t} e(t - x + t_0) \right\} A(x - t_0)\, dx$$

$$= + \int_{x=t_0}^{x=t} \left\{ \frac{\partial}{\partial t} e(t - x + t_0) \right\} A(x - t_0)\, dx \tag{D}$$

Now the value of a definite integral is a function only of the limits of integration, and not of the variable of integration. Therefore, we can substitute τ for x in the last integral of (D). Consequently

$$\int_{x=t_0}^{x=t} \frac{\partial}{\partial t} [e(t - x + t_0)]A(x - t_0)\, dx = \int_{\tau=t_0}^{\tau=t} \frac{\partial}{\partial t} [e(t - \tau + t_0)]A(\tau - t_0)\, d\tau \tag{E}$$

From (D) and (E) we then have

along with the original equation. We call them *superposition integrals.*

$$i(t) = \frac{d}{dt}\int_{t_0}^{t} e(t - \tau + t_0)A(\tau - t_0)\,d\tau \tag{46}$$

$$= \frac{d}{dt}\int_{t_0}^{t} e(\tau)A(t - \tau)\,d\tau \tag{47}$$

$$= e(t)A(0) + \int_{t_0}^{t} e(\tau)\left\{\frac{\partial}{\partial t}[A(t - \tau)]\right\} d\tau \tag{48}$$

$$= e(t)A(0) + \int_{t_0}^{t} e(t - \tau + t_0)\frac{\partial}{\partial \tau}[A(\tau - t_0)]\,d\tau \tag{49}$$

$$= e(t_0)A(t - t_0) + \int_{t_0}^{t}\left\{\frac{\partial}{\partial t}[e(t - \tau + t_0)]\right\} A(\tau - t_0)\,d\tau \tag{50}$$

$$= e(t_0)A(t - t_0) + \int_{t_0}^{t}\left\{\frac{\partial}{\partial \tau}[e(\tau)]\right\} A(t - \tau)\,d\tau \tag{51}$$

$$\int_{t_0}^{t}\left\{\frac{\partial}{\partial \tau}e(\tau)\right\} A(t - \tau)\,d\tau = \int_{t_0}^{t}\frac{\partial}{\partial t}[e(t - \tau + t_0)]A(\tau - t_0)\,d\tau \tag{F}$$

Substituting this value into Eq. (44), we get

$$i(t) = e(t_0)A(t - t_0) + \int_{t_0}^{t}\frac{\partial}{\partial t}[e(t - \tau + t_0)]A(\tau - t_0)\,d\tau \tag{G}$$

which is Eq. (50).

Next, according to the standard equation for differentiating an integral with a variable limit (See Wilson, *Advanced Calculus*, p. 283), Eq. (G) can be transformed into

$$i(t) = \frac{d}{dt}\int_{t_0}^{t} e(t - \tau + t_0)A(\tau - t_0)\,d\tau \tag{H}$$

which is Eq. (46). If we then repeat the processes of Eqs. (A), (B), (D), and (E), equation (H) is transformed into

$$i(t) = \frac{d}{dt}\int_{t_0}^{t} e(\tau)A(t - \tau)\,d\tau \tag{J}$$

which is Eq. (47).

To derive Eq. (48), we integrate Eq. (44) by parts. Thus

The preceding formulas,[15] Eqs. (46–51), are called by Carson the fundamental formulas of circuit theory. They are an expression for the current which flows in any impedance, whose indicial admittance is known, in response to any voltage. Among other things, these equations show that the applied e.m.f. and the indicial admittance have similar and equivalent effects in producing the resultant current (see also §7.8).

A set of superposition integrals corresponding to Eqs. (46) through (51) can also be found which give the current in terms of the voltage and Green's function. These integrals can either be derived directly or can be obtained by transformation from Eqs. (46–51). Because of the physical insight which is thereby gained, we shall derive one of them directly.

Consider the e.m.f. shown in Fig. 4-8 which is zero until time $\tau = t_0$, and suppose that we wish to find the current due to it at

---

$$
\begin{aligned}
i(t) &= e(t_0)A(t - t_0) + \int_{t_0}^{t} \left\{\frac{\partial}{\partial\tau} e(\tau)\right\} A(t - \tau)\, d\tau \\
&= e(t_0)A(t - t_0) + e(\tau)A(t - \tau)\Big|_{\tau=t_0}^{\tau=t} + \int_{t_0}^{t} e(\tau)\frac{\partial}{\partial\tau}[A(t - \tau)]\, d\tau \\
&= e(t_0)A(t - t_0) + e(t)A(0) - e(t_0)A(t - t_0) + \int_{t_0}^{t} e(\tau)\frac{\partial}{\partial t}[A(t - \tau)]\, d\tau \qquad \text{(K)}
\end{aligned}
$$

which is Eq. (48) after cancellation of the equal terms of opposite sign.

To derive Eq. (49) we integrate Eq. (G) by parts. Thus

$$
\begin{aligned}
i(t) &= e(t_0)A(t - t_0) + \int_{t_0}^{t} \frac{\partial}{\partial t}[e(t - \tau + t_0)]A(\tau - t_0)\, d\tau \\
&= e(t_0)A(t - t_0) - \int_{t_0}^{t} \frac{\partial}{\partial\tau}[e(t - \tau + t_0)]A(\tau - t_0)\, d\tau \\
&= e(t_0)A(t - t_0) - e(t - \tau + t_0)A(\tau - t_0)\Big|_{\tau=t_0}^{\tau=t} \\
&\qquad + \int_{t_0}^{t} e(t - \tau + t_0)\frac{\partial}{\partial\tau}[A(\tau - t_0)]\, d\tau \\
&= e(t_0)A(t - t_0) - e(t_0)A(t - t_0) + e(t)A(0) \\
&\qquad + \int_{t_0}^{t} e(t - \tau + t_0)\frac{\partial}{\partial\tau}[A(\tau - t_0)]\, d\tau \qquad \text{(L)}
\end{aligned}
$$

which is Eq. (49) after cancellation of the equal terms of opposite sign.

Equation (44) itself is Eq. (51).

[15] If it would serve any purpose, we could also replace the limits t_0 and t in the integrals in Eqs. (46-51) with $-\infty$ and $+\infty$, since the integrand of each will vanish when $\tau < t_0$ or $\tau > t$.

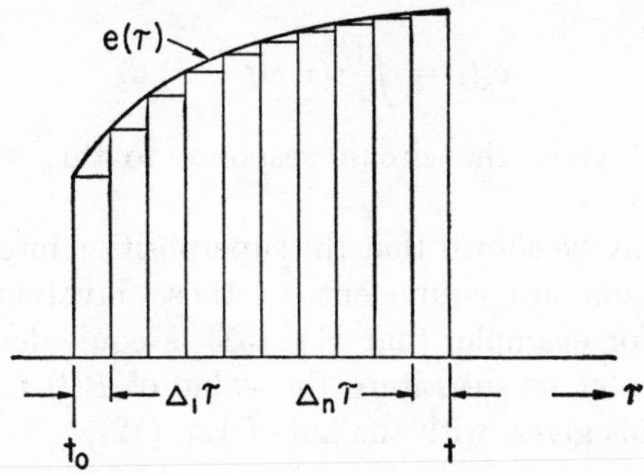

FIG. 4-8. Analysis of a general function as the superposition of impulse functions.

time $\tau = t$. Let us separate the e.m.f. into impulsive components as shown in the figure. Then, using the principle of superposition and the definition of Green's function, it follows as an approximation that[16]

$$i(t) = e(t_0)\Delta_1\tau B(t - t_0) + e(t_0 + \Delta_1\tau)\Delta_2\tau B(t - t_0 - \Delta_1\tau) + \cdots + e(t - \Delta_n\tau)\Delta_n\tau B(t - t + \Delta_n\tau) \quad (52)$$

If we let n increase indefinitely, and let all the $\Delta\tau$'s approach zero, Eq. (52) becomes

$$i(t) = \int_{t_0}^{t} e(\tau)B(t - \tau)\,d\tau \quad (53)$$

which is an exact equation and not an approximation like Eq. (52).

Equation (53) is the desired form of the superposition integral for $i(t)$ in terms of Green's function and the impressed voltage. An alternative form

$$i(t) = \int_{t_0}^{t} e(t - \tau + t_0)B(\tau - t_0)\,d\tau \quad (54)$$

can easily be obtained by the type of transformation which was used in deriving Eqs. (46–51). We will leave this to the reader.

It is worthy of note that if the applied voltage $e(t)$ is expressed as a superposition of impulse functions as shown in Fig. 4-8 in the

[16] As in the previous case, to get the total current, we would have to add to $i(t)$, any current in the impedance due to the initial conditions at $\tau = t_0$.

form

$$e(t) = \int_{t_0}^{t} e(\tau)\delta(t - \tau)\, d\tau \tag{55}$$

then Eq. (53) gives the circuit response to this superposition of impulse functions.

It can easily be shown that the superposition integrals involving Green's function are equivalent to those involving the indicial admittance; for example, that Eq. (53) is equivalent to Eq. (48). To show this, let us substitute the value of $B(t)$ in Eq. (27) into Eq. (53). This gives, with the aid of Eq. (12),

$$\begin{aligned} i(t) &= \int_{t_0}^{t} e(\tau)B(t - \tau)\, d\tau = \int_{t_0}^{t} e(\tau)\left[A(0)\delta(t - \tau) + \frac{\partial A(t - \tau)}{\partial(t - \tau)}\right] d\tau \\ &= A(0)\int_{t_0}^{t} e(\tau)\delta(t - \tau)\, d\tau + \int_{t_0}^{t} e(\tau)\frac{\partial}{\partial t}[A(t - \tau)]\, d\tau \\ &= A(0)e(t) + \int_{t_0}^{t} e(\tau)\frac{\partial}{\partial t}[A(t - \tau)]\, d\tau \end{aligned} \tag{56}$$

in agreement with Eq. (48).

4.7. An example of the use of superposition integrals

In the circuit of Fig. 4-9, let us find the current (transient and steady-state) which flows when the applied voltage is

$$e = E \sin \omega t \tag{57}$$

The capacitor C is initially uncharged.

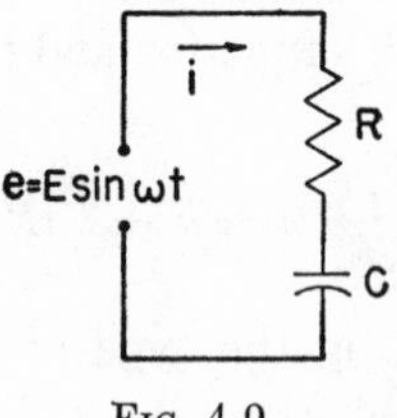

FIG. 4-9.

We will solve the example in two ways. First we shall obtain a solution by the standard method, using the table of transforms. Then we shall solve it using a superposition integral. We shall, of course, find the same answer in both cases if we solve the problem correctly. The solution with the aid of the table is actually much simpler in this case. This is usually the case when an exact solution can be obtained in closed form.

The circuit equation of Fig. 4-9 is

$$Ri + \int_0^t \frac{i\,dt}{C} = E \sin \omega t \tag{58}$$

Taking Laplace transforms of both sides, we obtain

$$\left[R + \frac{1}{sC}\right] I(s) = \frac{E\omega}{s^2 + \omega^2} \tag{59}$$

Therefore,

$$I(s) = \frac{E\omega s}{R\left(s + \dfrac{1}{RC}\right)(s^2 + \omega^2)} \tag{60}$$

By formula (23) of Appendix D, we then have

$$\begin{aligned} i(t) &= \frac{E\omega}{R}\left[\frac{1}{\left(\dfrac{1}{RC}\right)^2 + \omega^2}\right]\left\{\frac{-1}{RC}\,\epsilon^{-t/RC} + \frac{1}{RC}\cos \omega t + \omega \sin \omega t\right\} \\ &= -\frac{E\omega C}{1 + \omega^2C^2R^2}\,\epsilon^{-t/RC} + \frac{E\omega C \cos \omega t}{1 + \omega^2C^2R^2} + \frac{E}{R}\,\frac{\omega^2C^2R^2 \sin \omega t}{1 + \omega^2C^2R^2} \end{aligned} \tag{61}$$

Let us next solve the same problem using the indicial admittance and a superposition integral. To find the indicial admittance, we write

$$Ri_1 + \int_0^t \frac{i_1\,dt}{C} = U(t) \tag{62}$$

or

$$\left(R + \frac{1}{sC}\right) I_1(s) = \frac{1}{s} \tag{63}$$

Thus

$$I_1(s) = \frac{1}{R\left(s + \dfrac{1}{RC}\right)} \tag{64}$$

and

$$i_1(t) = \frac{1}{R}\,\epsilon^{-t/RC} = A(t) \tag{65}$$

Substituting this value of $A(t)$ and the applied voltage into Eq. (48), we obtain

$$
\begin{aligned}
i(t) &= \frac{E}{R}\sin\omega t + \int_0^t E\sin\omega\tau\left\{\frac{-1}{R^2C}\,\epsilon^{-(t-\tau)/RC}\right\}d\tau \\
&= \frac{E}{R}\sin\omega t - \frac{E\epsilon^{-t/RC}}{R^2C}\int_0^t \sin\omega\tau\,\epsilon^{\tau/RC}\,d\tau \\
&= \frac{E}{R}\sin\omega t - \frac{E\epsilon^{-t/RC}}{R^2C}\left\{\frac{\epsilon^{\tau/RC}\left(\dfrac{1}{RC}\sin\omega\tau - \omega\cos\omega\tau\right)}{\left[\dfrac{1}{R^2C^2}+\omega^2\right]}\right\}_{\tau=0}^{\tau=t} \\
&= \frac{E}{R}\,\frac{\omega^2C^2R^2\sin\omega t}{1+\omega^2C^2R^2} + \frac{E\omega C\cos\omega t}{1+\omega^2C^2R^2} - \frac{E\omega C}{1+\omega^2C^2R^2}\,\epsilon^{-t/RC} \qquad (66)
\end{aligned}
$$

in agreement with Eq. (61). As expected, we obtain the same answer, regardless of the method of solution.[17]

As previously pointed out, the use of a superposition integral is usually a more laborious process than a solution with the aid of a table of transforms, when an exact solution is possible. Superposition integrals are, however, very useful in theoretical investigations because of their insight into the basic physics of many situations. We shall use them for such investigations in the remainder of the chapter. They are also useful when it is possible to get a desired answer by numerical integration of a superposition integral in case the corresponding Laplace transform cannot be found by the usual methods.

Exercise

In the circuit of Fig. 4-K find the voltage at e_2 when the voltage pulse shown is applied at e_0. Solve this problem by using the table

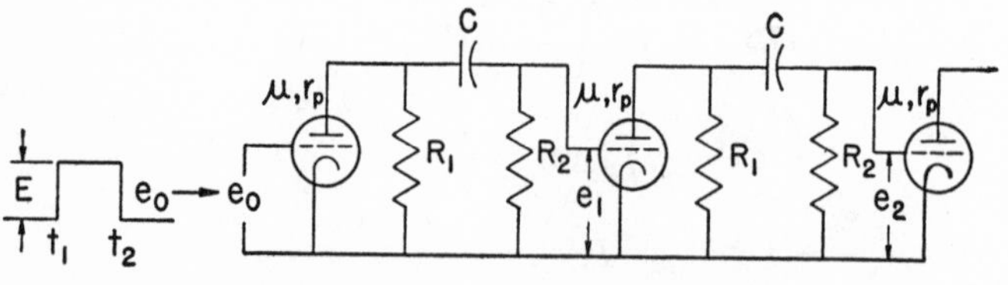

FIG. 4-K.

of transforms and then by using a superposition integral. Compare the ease of solution in the two cases.

[17] Additional examples of use of superposition integrals may be found in L. B. Arguimbau, *Vacuum Tube Circuits*, Chap. IV. New York: John Wiley & Sons, Inc., 1948.

4.8. Borel's Theorem—the inverse transform of the product of two functions

Next, we wish to use Eqs. (46) and (47) or (53) and (54) to derive an important formula in Laplace transformations. Let us write

$$\mathfrak{L}[i(t)] = I(s) \tag{67}$$

and

$$\mathfrak{L}[e(t)] = E(s) \tag{68}$$

Then, if we have not included in $i(t)$ any current due to the initial conditions of the system at $\tau = t_0$, we have

$$I(s) = E(s)\left[\frac{1}{z(s)}\right] \tag{69}$$

Furthermore, by Eq. (22),

$$\mathfrak{L}[B(t)] = \frac{1}{z(s)} \tag{70}$$

If we choose an origin of time such that $t_0 = 0$, it follows from Eqs. (53) and (69) that

$$I(s) = \mathfrak{L}[i(t)] = \mathfrak{L}\left\{\int_0^t e(\tau)B(t-\tau)\,d\tau\right\} = \frac{E(s)}{z(s)} \tag{71}$$

Since we have not specified any particular form for the voltage function $e(\tau)$ or the impedance function[18] $z(s)$, the relation in Eq. (71) is a general one and may be written

$$\mathfrak{L}\left\{\int_0^t f_1(t-\tau)f_2(\tau)\,d\tau\right\} = F_1(s)F_2(s) \tag{72}$$

where

$$\mathfrak{L}[f_1(t)] = F_1(s) \tag{73}$$

and

$$\mathfrak{L}[f_2(t)] = F_2(s) \tag{74}$$

It also follows, either from Eq. (54) or by interchanging F_1 and F_2 in Eq. (72), that

$$\mathfrak{L}\left\{\int_0^t f_1(\tau)f_2(t-\tau)\,d\tau\right\} = F_1(s)F_2(s) \tag{75}$$

Equations (72) and (75) are important general formulas in Laplace transformation theory. They can be used as an expression

---

[18] Strictly speaking, our proof of the principle of superposition was limited to cases in which $z(s)$ was a rational fraction. However, neither the truth of the principle of superposition nor of Eq. (72) is actually so limited in fact.

for the inverse transform of any function of s which is the product of two functions whose inverse transforms are known. Taken together, they are sometimes called Borel's Theorem.[19]

Exercise

Assuming that

$$\mathcal{L}^{-1}\left[\frac{1}{s+a}\right] = \epsilon^{-at}$$

and

$$\mathcal{L}^{-1}\left[\frac{1}{(s+b)^2}\right] = t\epsilon^{-bt}$$

find by means of Borel's Theorem

$$\mathcal{L}^{-1}\left[\frac{1}{(s+a)(s+b)^2}\right]$$

Answer:

$$\frac{\epsilon^{-at} + [(a-b)t - 1]\epsilon^{-bt}}{(a-b)^2}$$

4.9. Some relations between the fundamental response functions

In the preceding pages we have derived integral formulas for the response of an impedance to an e.m.f., by resolving the e.m.f. into (1) step-function components; and (2) impulse-function components. In the author's *Frequency Analysis, Modulation and Noise*, a different type of superposition integral, a Fourier integral, is used for the corresponding problem when the e.m.f. was resolved into cosine wave components. There it is shown that

$$i(t) = \frac{1}{\pi}\int_0^\infty \frac{S(\omega)}{|z(j\omega)|}\cos\left[\omega t - \phi(\omega) - N(\omega)\right] d\omega \tag{76}$$

where $e(t)$ has the frequency composition

$$e(t) = \frac{1}{\pi}\int_0^\infty S(\omega)\cos\left[\omega t - \phi(\omega)\right] d\omega \tag{77}$$

and

$$z(j\omega) = |z(j\omega)|\epsilon^{jN(\omega)} \tag{78}$$

[19] The notation

$$f_1(t)*f_2(t) \equiv \int_0^t f_1(t-\tau)f_2(\tau)\,d\tau$$

is sometimes used, where the (*) indicates on integration of the type indicated, and the process indicated by the (*) is called *convolution* of $f_1(t)$ and $f_2(t)$.

is the steady-state impedance. Other types of superposition integrals are also possible, but these three are by far the most widely used.

These integrals tell us that a knowledge of any one of the three—(a) indicial admittance, (b) Green's function, or (c) steady-state impedance as a function of frequency—in conjunction with the applied voltage, is sufficient to determine the current that flows. Any one of the above three quantities thus inherently gives a complete description of the impedance. As a matter of fact, each can be expressed completely in terms of either of the others. Equation (27) shows this relation between $A(t)$ and $B(t)$. Other relations between the fundamental response functions will be found in the next few pages.

Suppose that we have a system with the steady-state impedance $z(j\omega)$. Then let us write

$$\frac{1}{z(j\omega)} = \alpha(\omega) + j\beta(\omega) \tag{79}$$

Suppose that an e.m.f. $e_0 \sin(\omega t + \phi)$ is applied to this impedance at time $t = 0$. Then by Eq. (49),

$$\begin{aligned} i(t) &= A(0)e_0 \sin(\omega t + \phi) + \int_0^t e_0 \sin[\omega(t - \tau) + \phi] \frac{\partial A(\tau)}{\partial \tau}\, d\tau \\ &= A(0)e_0 \sin(\omega t + \phi) + e_0 \sin(\omega t + \phi) \int_0^t \cos \omega\tau \frac{\partial A(\tau)}{\partial \tau}\, d\tau \\ &\qquad - e_0 \cos(\omega t + \phi) \int_0^t \sin \omega\tau \frac{\partial A(\tau)}{\partial \tau}\, d\tau \end{aligned} \tag{80}$$

Now $i(t)$ in Eq. (80) can be resolved into a steady-state component[20]

$$\begin{aligned} i_1(t) &= A(0)e_0 \sin(\omega t + \phi) + e_0 \sin(\omega t + \phi) \int_0^\infty \cos \omega\tau \frac{\partial A(\tau)}{\partial \tau}\, d\tau \\ &\qquad - e_0 \cos(\omega t + \phi) \int_0^\infty \sin \omega\tau \frac{\partial A(\tau)}{\partial \tau}\, d\tau \end{aligned} \tag{81}$$

[20] This procedure will fail if the infinite integrals do not converge.

and a transient component

$$i_2(t) = -e_0 \sin(\omega t + \phi) \int_t^\infty \cos \omega\tau \frac{\partial A(\tau)}{\partial \tau} d\tau + e_0 \cos(\omega t + \phi) \int_t^\infty \sin \omega\tau \frac{\partial A(\tau)}{\partial \tau} d\tau \quad (82)$$

which dies away as $t \to \infty$. According to elementary steady-state theory, the steady-state current may also be written

$$i_1(t) = e_0[\alpha(\omega) \sin(\omega t + \phi) + \beta(\omega) \cos(\omega t + \phi)] \quad (83)$$

Comparing Eqs. (81) and (83), we obtain

$$\alpha(\omega) = A(0) + \int_0^\infty \cos \omega\tau \frac{\partial A(\tau)}{\partial \tau} d\tau \quad (84)$$

and

$$\beta(\omega) = -\int_0^\infty \sin \omega\tau \frac{\partial A(\tau)}{\partial \tau} d\tau \quad (85)$$

Equations (84) and (85) are means of expressing the steady-state impedance in terms of the indicial admittance. The reader can easily show that the corresponding formulas in terms of Green's function are

$$\alpha(\omega) = \int_0^\infty \cos \omega t B(t)\, dt \quad (86)$$

and

$$\beta(\omega) = -\int_0^\infty \sin \omega t B(t)\, dt \quad (87)$$

In fact, Eqs. (86) and (87) follow directly from Eq. (23).

Exercises

1. Substitute the value of $B(t)$ from Eq. (27) into Eqs. (86) and (87) and derive Eqs. (84) and (85).

2. If a voltage $e_0 \sin(\omega t + \phi)$ is applied to an impedance at time $t = 0$, show that the steady-state component of current is

$$i_1(t) = e_0 \sin(\omega t + \phi) \int_0^\infty \cos \omega\tau B(\tau)\, d\tau - e_0 \cos(\omega t + \phi) \int_0^\infty \sin \omega\tau\, B(\tau)\, d\tau$$

while the transient component is

$$i_2(t) = e_0 \cos(\omega t + \phi) \int_t^\infty \sin \omega\tau B(\tau)\, d\tau - e_0 \sin(\omega t + \phi) \int_t^\infty \cos \omega\tau B(\tau)\, d\tau$$

4.10. The indicial admittance and Green's function as Fourier integrals

We next wish to express $A(t)$ and $B(t)$ as Fourier integrals in terms of the steady-state impedance. Now we know that these functions are the responses to the unit step $U(t)$ and the unit impulse $\delta(t)$, respectively.

It is well known that the frequency compositions of these latter functions are [21]

$$U(t) = \frac{1}{2} + \frac{1}{\pi}\int_0^\infty \frac{\sin \omega t}{\omega}\,d\omega \tag{88}$$

and

$$\delta(t) = \frac{1}{\pi}\int_0^\infty \cos \omega t\,d\omega \tag{89}$$

At any frequency ω the response to a pure[22] sine wave $e_0 \sin \omega t$ is

$$i(t) = \frac{e_0 \sin \omega t}{z(j\omega)} = e_0\alpha(\omega)\sin \omega t + e_0\beta(\omega)\cos \omega t \tag{90}$$

while the response to a pure cosine wave $e_0 \cos \omega t$ is

$$i(t) = \frac{e_0 \cos \omega t}{z(j\omega)} = e_0\alpha(\omega)\cos \omega t - e_0\beta(\omega)\sin \omega t \tag{91}$$

It then follows from Eqs. (88) and (90), that the indicial admittance is

$$A(t) = \frac{\alpha(0)}{2} + \frac{1}{\pi}\int_0^\infty \frac{\alpha(\omega)}{\omega}\sin \omega t\,d\omega + \frac{1}{\pi}\int_0^\infty \frac{\beta(\omega)}{\omega}\cos \omega t\,d\omega \tag{92}$$

where $\alpha(0)$ is the d-c conductance; and, from Eqs. (89) and (91), that

$$B(t) = \frac{1}{\pi}\int_0^\infty \alpha(\omega)\cos \omega t\,d\omega - \frac{1}{\pi}\int_0^\infty \beta(\omega)\sin \omega t\,d\omega \tag{93}$$

Equations (92) and (93) are the desired expressions for the indicial admittance and for Green's function in terms of their frequency components. We can also find alternative expressions by making use of the fact that $A(t)$ and $B(t)$ as defined by Eqs. (92)

---

[21] See Appendix E.

[22] A pure sine wave has no components of other frequencies, and must therefore be an infinitely long sine-wave train. See Fig. 4, Chap. III, of the author's book cited above.

and (93) must vanish[23] when t is negative. Therefore we can write

$$A(-t) = \frac{1}{2}\alpha(0) - \frac{1}{\pi}\int_0^\infty \frac{\alpha(\omega)}{\omega} \sin \omega t \, d\omega + \frac{1}{\pi}\int_0^\infty \frac{\beta(\omega)}{\omega} \cos \omega t \, d\omega = 0 \quad (94)$$

$$B(-t) = \frac{1}{\pi}\int_0^\infty \alpha(\omega) \cos \omega t \, d\omega + \frac{1}{\pi}\int_0^\infty \beta(\omega) \sin \omega t \, d\omega = 0 \quad (95)$$

Consequently,

$$A(t) = A(t) + A(-t) = \alpha(0) + \frac{2}{\pi}\int_0^\infty \frac{\beta(\omega)}{\omega} \cos \omega t \, d\omega \quad (96)$$

and also

$$A(t) = A(t) - A(-t) = \frac{2}{\pi}\int_0^\infty \frac{\alpha(\omega)}{\omega} \sin \omega t \, d\omega \quad (97)$$

Furthermore,

$$B(t) = B(t) + B(-t) = \frac{2}{\pi}\int_0^\infty \alpha(\omega) \cos \omega t \, d\omega \quad (98)$$

$$B(t) = B(t) - B(-t) = -\frac{2}{\pi}\int_0^\infty \beta(\omega) \sin \omega t \, d\omega \quad (99)$$

Equations (96–99) are alternative equations to (92) and (93) for expressing $A(t)$ and $B(t)$ in terms of their frequency components. However, while Eqs. (92) and (93) are the expressions for the response to $U(t)$ and $\delta(t)$, respectively, for all values of t, Eqs. (96) through (99), in view of their derivation, are limited in validity to positive values of t. Nevertheless, since $A(t)$ and $B(t)$ are, generally speaking, only defined for positive values of t, this limitation is not important.

Earlier in this chapter (§4.6) we have shown that a knowledge of $A(t)$ or of $B(t)$ in conjunction with the applied voltage is sufficient to determine the current which flows in a network. We may therefore draw an interesting conclusion from Eqs. (96) and (97) or from Eqs. (98) and (99)—namely, *the behavior of a network under all circumstances is completely determined if either the real or the*

[23] These expressions must vanish when t is negative, because they are the respective responses to $U(t)$ and $\delta(t)$ as defined by Eqs. (88) and (89) for all values of t, both positive and negative. They are not limited in application to positive values of t as are oridnary expressions derived from Laplace transforms.

imaginary component of the steady-state admittance is specified over the entire frequency range.

As a further conclusion, we can then also say that *the amplitude and phase characteristics of a system cannot be chosen independently.* They must be so chosen that

$$\alpha(0) + \frac{2}{\pi}\int_0^\infty \frac{\beta(\omega)}{\omega}\cos\omega t\,d\omega = \frac{2}{\pi}\int_0^\infty \frac{\alpha(\omega)}{\omega}\sin\omega t\,d\omega \qquad (100)$$

or (its equivalent)

$$\int_0^\infty \alpha(\omega)\cos\omega t\,d\omega = -\int_0^\infty \beta(\omega)\sin\omega t\,d\omega \qquad (101)$$

for all positive values of t.

In the following section we will give further consideration to the relation between amplitude and phase characteristics. Before

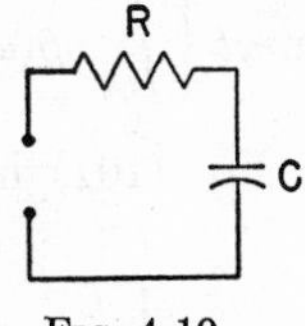

FIG. 4-10.

doing so, however, we wish now to illustrate the use of one of the above Fourier-integral formulas in a simple example. Thus let us find the indicial admittance of the series R-C circuit shown in Fig. 4-10, by the use of Eq. (96). Here

$$z(j\omega) = R + \frac{1}{j\omega C} \qquad (102)$$

Therefore,

$$\frac{1}{z(j\omega)} = \frac{1}{R + \dfrac{1}{j\omega C}} = \frac{\omega^2C^2R + j\omega C}{1 + \omega^2C^2R^2} \qquad (103)$$

Thus

$$\alpha(0) = 0 \qquad (104)$$

and

$$\beta(\omega) = \frac{\omega C}{1 + \omega^2C^2R^2} \qquad (105)$$

Substituting these values into Eq. (96), we obtain[24]

---

[24] It will be shown in Chap. 5 that

$$\int_0^\infty \frac{\cos x}{b^2 + x^2}\,dx = \frac{\pi\epsilon^{-b}}{2b}$$

$$A(t) = \frac{2}{\pi} \int_0^\infty \frac{C \cos \omega t}{1 + \omega^2 C^2 R^2} \, d\omega = \frac{1}{R} \epsilon^{-t/RC} \tag{106}$$

This solution is in agreement with the result previously calculated by the method of Chap. 3.

4.11. A relation between amplitude and phase characteristics

Equations (100) and (101) show that there are definite relations between the amplitude and phase characteristics of a system. We now wish to discuss further ramifications of this fact.

In the author's *Frequency Analysis, Modulation and Noise*, it is pointed out that[25]

$$\alpha(\omega) = \frac{2}{\pi} \int_0^\infty \cos \omega t \left\{ \int_0^\infty \alpha(\omega) \cos \omega t \, d\omega \right\} dt \tag{107}$$

and
$$\beta(\omega) = \frac{2}{\pi} \int_0^\infty \sin \omega t \left\{ \int_0^\infty \beta(\omega) \sin \omega t \, d\omega \right\} dt \tag{108}$$

Therefore, if we substitute Eq. (101) into Eqs. (107) and (108), we obtain

$$\alpha(\omega) = -\frac{2}{\pi} \int_0^\infty \cos \omega t \left\{ \int_0^\infty \beta(\omega) \sin \omega t \, d\omega \right\} dt \tag{109}$$

and
$$\beta(\omega) = -\frac{2}{\pi} \int_0^\infty \sin \omega t \left\{ \int_0^\infty \alpha(\omega) \cos \omega t \, d\omega \right\} dt \tag{110}$$

Equations (109) and (110) show one way in which the real part of the admittance function can be calculated from the imaginary part, and vice versa. Actually, however, these equations are not in the form which is most useful in practice. More practical forms will be derived in §7.9.

---

[25] Exercise (2), p. 64. The above conclusion makes use of the fact that $\alpha(\omega) + j\beta(\omega)$ is the Fourier transform of $B(t)$.

CHAPTER 5

Theory of Functions of a Complex Variable

5.1. Introduction

It is assumed that the reader has already studied the elementary properties of complex quantities. In the present chapter we wish to extend this study. This will lead us to some of the most remarkable and useful of all mathematical phenomena. With the aid of complex quantities we shall obtain new insight into the whole subject of transformation calculus in general and circuit phenomena in particular. We shall develop powerful means to investigate stability in regenerative circuits, and we shall find ways of evaluating otherwise unevaluable integrals.

In the usual study of real quantities, if Y is a function of X, such as

$$Y = X + \epsilon^X \tag{1}$$

then for every real value of X, Y has a definite value. In a similar manner if w is the same function of a complex variable z, namely

$$w = z + \epsilon^z \tag{2}$$

then for every complex value of z, w has a definite value. Thus if

$$z = 2 + j\frac{\pi}{4} \tag{3}$$

then

$$\begin{aligned} w &= \left(2 + j\frac{\pi}{4}\right) + \epsilon^{2+j\pi/4} \\ &= 2 + j\frac{\pi}{4} + \epsilon^2\left[\cos\frac{\pi}{4} + j\sin\frac{\pi}{4}\right] \\ &= \left[2 + \epsilon^2\left(\cos\frac{\pi}{4}\right)\right] + j\left[\frac{\pi}{4} + \epsilon^2\left(\sin\frac{\pi}{4}\right)\right] \end{aligned} \tag{4}$$

It is customary to designate the real component of z as x and the imaginary component as y. Thus

$$z = x + jy \tag{5}$$

Likewise, if w is a function of z, it is customary to designate the real and imaginary components of w as u and v, respectively. Thus, we write

$$w = f(z) = u + jv \tag{6}$$

For the particular case of Eqs. (3) and (4), we may then write

$$x = 2 \tag{7}$$

$$y = \frac{\pi}{4} \tag{8}$$

$$u = 2 + \epsilon^2 \cos \frac{\pi}{4} \tag{9}$$

$$v = \frac{\pi}{4} + \epsilon^2 \sin \frac{\pi}{4} \tag{10}$$

In the present chapter we shall study some of the properties of functions of a complex variable, so that we can apply them later on in the book.

5.2. Graphical representation of a function of a complex variable

The possible values of X in Eq. (1) may be designated as points on a line—i.e., the X axis; and corresponding to Eq. (1) we may draw a curve showing the values of Y corresponding to each point on the X axis. This is shown in Fig. 5-1.

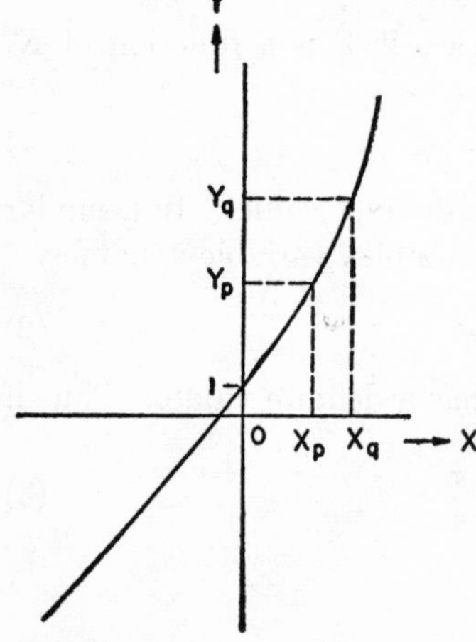

FIG. 5-1. The curve $Y = X + \epsilon^X$ in the real X, Y plane.

It would probably be very convenient if it were possible to draw corresponding graphs for the functions of a complex variable. However, since a complex variable has a real and an imaginary component, it requires a plane—i.e., the complex plane—instead of a single line like the X axis, to show the possible values of z. Two additional coordinates would then be required to give a complete graphical representation of the w surface, and since this would require four-dimensional space, it is not practical for ordinary human beings. Consequently, we must use a different type of graphical representation for functions of a complex variable. This representation will now be explained.

Since
$$z = x + jy \tag{11}$$
and
$$w = u + jv = f(z) \tag{12}$$
it follows that u and v are each functions of x and y. For example, suppose
$$w = z^2 \tag{13}$$
Then
$$w = (x + jy)^2 = (x^2 - y^2) + j2xy \tag{14}$$
Therefore,
$$u = x^2 - y^2 \tag{15}$$
and
$$v = 2xy \tag{16}$$

Next on an (x,y) plane let us draw the sets of curves in accordance with Eqs. (15) and (16) which we get by letting u and v equal the various integers. These curves are shown in Fig. 5-2. Thus, for example, $u = 2$ gives the pair of curves
$$x^2 - y^2 = 2 \tag{17}$$

With the aid of Fig. 5-2 we can now read off the values of u and v for any set of values of x and y, corresponding to the equation
$$w = u + jv = z^2 = (x + jy)^2 \tag{18}$$

We may therefore consider Fig. 5-2 as a graphical representation of Eq. (18). Since its coordinates are x and y, which are the real and imaginary components of z respectively, the plane of Fig. 5-2 may be considered a complex plane, and it is customary to call it the z plane.

An equivalent representation of the equation
$$w = z^2$$
can be made in the w plane; i.e., a plane in which the coordinates are u and v. If Eqs. (15) and (16) are solved to eliminate first x and then y, we obtain
$$u = \frac{v^2}{4y^2} - y^2 \tag{19}$$
$$u = x^2 - \frac{v^2}{4x^2} \tag{20}$$

Then, if in Eqs. (19) and (20) we let y and x equal various integers, we obtain the curves of integral values of y and x in the w plane. These are shown in Fig. 5-3. They are two families of parabolas.

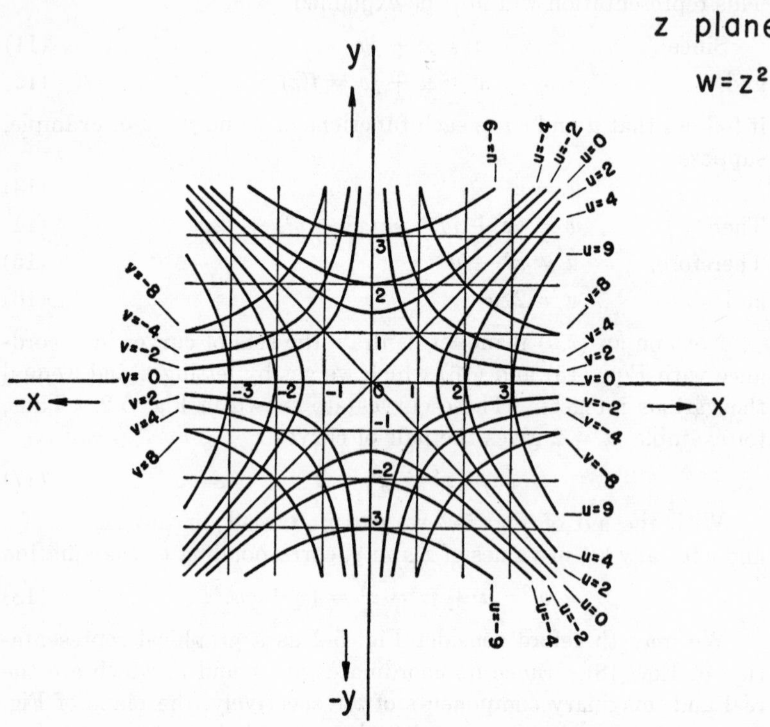

FIG. 5-2. The coordinate lines of the w plane transformed to the z plane by the transformation $w = z^2$, where $w = u + jv$ and $z = x + jy$.

We can use either Fig. 5-2 or Fig. 5-3 to find the values of w corresponding to various values of z, as well as the values of z corresponding to various values of w, in accordance with the equation

$$w = z^2 \tag{21}$$

Thus either figure shows, for example, that if

$$z = 1 + 2j \tag{22}$$

then

$$w = -3 + 4j \tag{23}$$

as required by Eq. (21). Likewise, if

$$z = 3 + j \tag{24}$$

then

$$w = 8 + 6j \tag{25}$$

Figures 5-2 and 5-3 show how the coordinate lines of the z plane are transformed into curves in the w plane, and how the coordinate

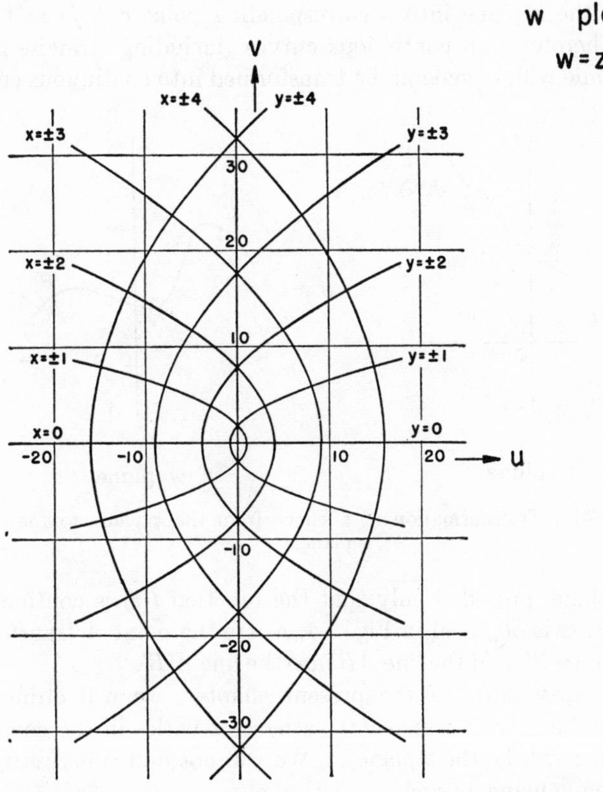

FIG. 5-3. The coordinate lines of the z plane transformed to the w plane by the transformation $w = z^2$, where $z = x + jy$ and $w = u + jv$.

lines of the w plane are transformed into curves in the z plane, by the equation

$$w = z^2$$

These, however, are but special cases of the general phenomenon, that any continuous function

$$w = f(z) \tag{26}$$

will transform any continuous curve in the z plane into another continuous curve in the w plane, and vice versa. To demonstrate this fact, we first point out that Eq. (26) transforms every point $a + jb$ in the z plane into a corresponding point $c + jd$ in the w plane. Therefore, all continuous curves (including straight lines) in the z plane will, in general, be transformed into continuous curves

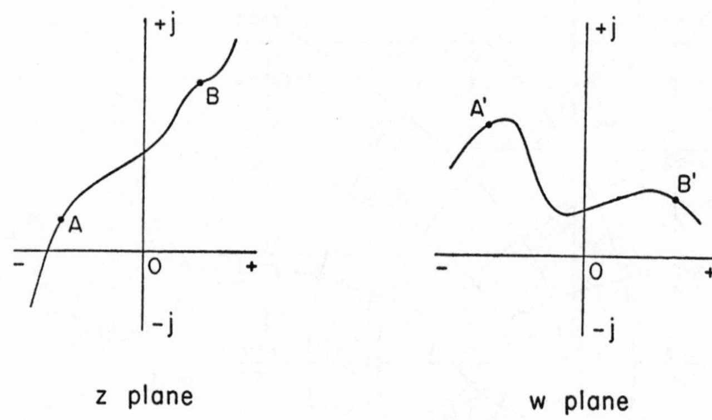

FIG. 5-4. Transformation of a curve from the z plane to the w plane.

in the w plane, provided only that the function $f(z)$ is continuous. This situation is depicted in Fig. 5-4, where the point A transforms into A', B into B', and the line AB into the line $A'B'$.

In the early parts of the present chapter, we will ordinarily study only the way in which $f(z)$ varies as z varies in the complex plane (which will be the z plane). We will not find it necessary to consider the w plane as such.

Exercises

1. If $x = 2$, $y = 3$ in Eq. 18, find the values of u and v from Fig. 5-2.

2. If $u = 4$, $v = 2$ in Eq. 18, find the values of x and y from Fig. 5-2.

5.3. Analytic functions

If $f(X)$ is a function of a real variable X then the ratio

$$\lim_{\Delta X \to 0} \frac{f(X + \Delta X) - f(X)}{\Delta X} = \frac{df}{dX} \tag{27}$$

approaches the same limit whether ΔX is taken in the positive or the negative direction, in most cases of interest. There are exceptions. For example, there are cases in which a function has different left-hand and right-hand derivatives at a point. But in functions of practical interest these cases occur only at isolated points, if at all. Consequently, we can speak of the value of the derivative of $f(X)$ at a point, without specifying the particular manner in which ΔX approaches zero.

Let us now consider a function $f(z)$, where z can vary over the entire complex plane and is not limited to the real axis. The question then arises as to what conditions are necessary in order for the derivative of $f(z)$ with respect to z to have a value at every point which is independent of the manner in which Δz approaches zero. This question is important practically, because if the conditions are not satisfied, it is then not possible to differentiate $f(z)$ with respect to z by means of simple formulas. The question is even more important fundamentally, because it is found that functions having derivatives which are independent of direction have remarkably useful properties.

As a first step in finding the conditions for a single valued derivative, let us write

$$w = f(z) = u + jv \tag{28}$$

where

$$z = x + jy \tag{29}$$

Let us now find the value of the ratio

$$\lim_{\Delta z \to 0} \left(\frac{\Delta w}{\Delta z} \right)$$

if Δz approaches zero parallel to the real axis (as shown by $\Delta_1 z$ in Fig. 5-5). In this case we can write

$$\Delta z = \Delta x \tag{30}$$

and

$$\lim_{\Delta z \to 0} \frac{\Delta w}{\Delta z} = \lim_{\Delta x \to 0} \frac{u(x + \Delta x,y) - u(x,y)}{\Delta x} + j \frac{v(x + \Delta x,y) - v(x,y)}{\Delta x}$$

$$= \frac{\partial u}{\partial x} + j \frac{\partial v}{\partial x} \tag{31}$$

Let us next find the value of the ratio

$$\lim_{\Delta z \to 0} \left(\frac{\Delta w}{\Delta z} \right)$$

if Δz approaches zero parallel to the imaginary axis (as shown by

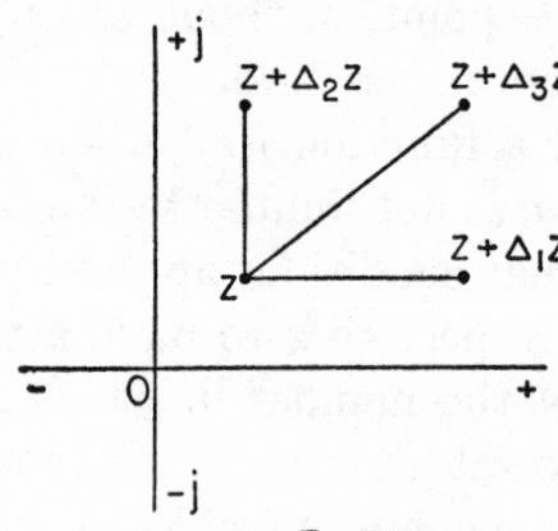

FIG. 5-5. Illustration of different possibilities for the direction of Δz.

$\Delta_2 z$ in Fig. 5-5). In this case we can write

$$\Delta z = j\, \Delta y \tag{32}$$

and

$$\lim_{\Delta z \to 0} \frac{\Delta w}{\Delta z} = \lim_{j\,\Delta y \to 0} \frac{u(x,y + \Delta y) - u(x,y)}{j\, \Delta y} + j \frac{v(x,y + \Delta y) - v(x,y)}{j\, \Delta y}$$

$$= \frac{1}{j} \left\{ \frac{\partial u}{\partial y} + j \frac{\partial v}{\partial y} \right\} = \frac{\partial v}{\partial y} - j \frac{\partial u}{\partial y} \tag{33}$$

If now the value of the derivative

$$\frac{df}{dz} = \lim_{\Delta z \to 0} \left(\frac{\Delta w}{\Delta z} \right) \tag{34}$$

is to be independent of the direction in which Δz approaches zero, it is necessary that the quantities on the right of Eqs. (31) and (33) shall be equal. Thus

$$\frac{\partial u}{\partial x} + j\frac{\partial v}{\partial x} = \frac{\partial v}{\partial y} - j\frac{\partial u}{\partial y} \tag{35}$$

Equating real and imaginary parts, we have

$$\frac{\partial u}{\partial x} = \frac{\partial v}{\partial y} \tag{36}$$

$$\frac{\partial v}{\partial x} = -\frac{\partial u}{\partial y} \tag{37}$$

The pair of equations (36) and (37) are called the *Cauchy-Riemann differential equations.* In view of the foregoing, they are a necessary requirement in order that the derivative df/dz shall be independent of the manner in which $\Delta z \to 0$.

We will next show that they are also a sufficient requirement, by showing that if Eqs. (36) and (37) hold, then the value of

$$\lim_{\Delta z \to 0} \left(\frac{\Delta w}{\Delta z}\right)$$

is the same as that given by Eq. (31) or Eq. (33), even though $\Delta z \to 0$ from an arbitrary direction (such as $\Delta_3 z$ in Fig. 5-5). In this case we write

$$\Delta z = \Delta x + j\,\Delta y \tag{38}$$

In accordance with the theory of total differentials[1] we can also write

$$\begin{aligned}\Delta w &= \Delta u + j\,\Delta v \\ &= \frac{\partial u}{\partial x}\Delta x + \frac{\partial u}{\partial y}\Delta y + j\left\{\frac{\partial v}{\partial x}\Delta x + \frac{\partial v}{\partial y}\Delta y\right\} \\ &\qquad + \text{terms of higher order in } \Delta x \text{ and } \Delta y\end{aligned} \tag{39}$$

Since we are assuming that Eqs. (36) and (37) hold, we may rewrite Eq. (39) (neglecting higher-order terms), as

$$\begin{aligned}\Delta w &= \frac{\partial u}{\partial x}\Delta x - \frac{\partial v}{\partial x}\Delta y + j\left\{\frac{\partial v}{\partial x}\Delta x + \frac{\partial u}{\partial x}\Delta y\right\} \\ &= \left(\frac{\partial u}{\partial x} + j\frac{\partial v}{\partial x}\right)(\Delta x + j\,\Delta y)\end{aligned} \tag{40}$$

Then $$\frac{dw}{dz} = \lim_{\Delta z \to 0}\left(\frac{\Delta w}{\Delta z}\right) = \frac{\partial u}{\partial x} + j\frac{\partial v}{\partial x} = \frac{\partial v}{\partial y} - j\frac{\partial u}{\partial y} \tag{41}$$

[1] See Wilson, *Advanced Calculus*, p. 95.

The value of the derivative is thus independent of the direction of Δz, and it agrees with both Eqs. (31) and (33). The Cauchy-Riemann equations are thus sufficient, as well as necessary, conditions for the derivative dw/dz to have a value which is independent of the way in which Δz approaches zero. A function

$$w = f(z) \tag{42}$$

whose derivative has this property is called an *analytic function.*

Example 1: We will now show that the function

$$w = z^2 \tag{43}$$

is analytic. From Eq. (43) it follows that

$$w = u + jv = (x + jy)^2 = x^2 - y^2 + j2xy \tag{44}$$

Therefore,

$$u = x^2 - y^2 \tag{45}$$

$$v = 2xy \tag{46}$$

Then

$$\frac{\partial u}{\partial x} = 2x = \frac{\partial v}{\partial y} \tag{47}$$

$$\frac{\partial v}{\partial x} = 2y = -\frac{\partial u}{\partial y} \tag{48}$$

The Cauchy-Riemann equations are thus satisfied, so that the function $w = z^2$ is analytic.

Example 2: Consider the function

$$w = u + jv = x + j2y \tag{49}$$

Here

$$u = x \tag{50}$$

$$v = 2y \tag{51}$$

Then

$$\frac{\partial u}{\partial x} = 1, \qquad \frac{\partial v}{\partial y} = 2 \tag{52}$$

Equation (36) is therefore not satisfied, so that the function w of Eq. (49) is not an analytic function of z.

5.4. Further discussion of analytic functions

Most functions

$$w = u(x,y) + j\,v(x,y) \tag{53}$$

which might be set up at random, would not turn out to be analytic functions. We have already seen a case in point in Example (2) of the last section. However, if w can be expressed in the form

$$w = f(z) = f(x + jy) \tag{54}$$

where the function f is any of the ordinary types of functions used for real quantities, such as a polynomial, sine, or logarithm, then the function $w = f(z)$ can be shown to be analytic. This is another of those remarkable phenomena of mathematics, which we have so often had occasion to mention. Furthermore, in this case the derivative df/dz can be obtained by the ordinary formulas of differential calculus. Thus

$$\frac{d}{dz}(z^n) = nz^{n-1} \tag{55}$$

$$\frac{d}{dz}(\sin z) = \cos z \tag{56}$$

$$\frac{d}{dz}(\log z) = \frac{1}{z} \tag{57}$$

$$\frac{d}{dz}(\epsilon^z) = \epsilon^z \tag{58}$$

and so forth.

We shall not take the space to prove all the foregoing statements at this time, although we shall use them. However, the reader will readily be able to prove those not derived in the text after reading the remainder of the chapter, especially §5.16. At this point we will illustrate the general phenomenon by deriving formula (55) for the special case in which $n = 2$. Thus let

$$w = z^2 = x^2 - y^2 + j2xy = u + jv \tag{59}$$

Then by Eq. (33),

$$\frac{dw}{dz} = \frac{\partial v}{\partial y} - j\frac{\partial u}{\partial y} = 2x + j2y = 2z \tag{60}$$

everywhere in the z plane for derivatives in the direction of the y axis. Since we have already shown in Eqs. (47) and (48) that the function is analytic, it follows that

$$\frac{d}{dz}(z^2) = 2z \tag{61}$$

in all directions throughout the complex plane.

In the foregoing discussion, we have talked about $\sin z$, ϵ^z, $\log z$, and so forth, when z is a complex variable, without defining what we mean by these functions when z is complex. If z is limited to real values, then we know that $\sin z$ is related to the properties of a real angle z, and ϵ^z is defined fundamentally by the notion of multiplying ϵ by itself z times. If z is allowed to take on complex values, then the above ideas become meaningless, unless we choose to assign a meaning to them. There is, however, one method of definition of the above functions which continues to have meaning, even when z is complex. This is the definition of the function in terms of a power series. Accordingly, many functions are defined for complex values of z in terms of their power series. Thus we define

$$\epsilon^z = 1 + z + \frac{z^2}{2!} + \cdots \tag{62}$$

$$\sin z = z - \frac{z^3}{3!} + \frac{z^5}{5!} \cdots \tag{63}$$

$$\cos z = 1 - \frac{z^2}{2!} + \frac{z^4}{4!} - \cdots \tag{64}$$

and so forth.

In terms of these power-series definitions, all the common functions are analytic, and their derivatives can be found by the ordinary formulas of differentiation, as mentioned above.[2]

It is also noteworthy that practically all the general relations between functions which hold for real values of z also continue to hold for complex values in terms of the above definitions. Thus, for example,

$$a^{z_1} \cdot a^{z_2} = a^{z_1+z_2} \tag{65}$$

$$a^0 = 1 \tag{66}$$

$$\cos(z_1 + z_2) = \cos z_1 \cos z_2 - \sin z_1 \sin z_2 \tag{67}$$

$$\sin(z_1 + z_2) = \sin z_1 \cos z_2 + \cos z_1 \sin z_2 \tag{68}$$

$$\tan z = \frac{\sin z}{\cos z} \tag{69}$$

$$\sin^2 z + \cos^2 z = 1 \tag{70}$$

and so on.

---

[2] For a proof of these statements, see, for example, Goursat-Hedrick, *Mathematical Analysis*, Vol. 2, Part 1. The method of proof is outlined in the exercises for this section.

Exercises

1. Using the binomial expansion, prove that

$$\frac{d}{dz}(z^m) = mz^{m-1}$$

2. Prove that

(*a*) $$\frac{d}{dz}(\sin z) = \cos z$$

(*b*) $$\frac{d}{dz}(\cos z) = -\sin z$$

(*c*) $$\frac{d}{dz}(\epsilon^z) = \epsilon^z$$

using the result of Exercise 1 and the power-series definition of the functions.

3. Prove that

$$\epsilon^{jz} = \cos z + j \sin z$$

4. Using the result in Exercise 3, prove that

$$\cos z = \frac{\epsilon^{jz} + \epsilon^{-jz}}{2} \quad \text{and} \quad \sin z = \frac{\epsilon^{jz} - \epsilon^{-jz}}{2j}$$

5. Using the result in Exercise 4, prove that

$$\sin (z_1 + z_2) = \sin z_1 \cos z_2 + \cos z_1 \sin z_2$$

6. What is the real part of $\epsilon^{(2+j\pi/4)}$?

Answer:

$$\epsilon^2 \cos\left(\frac{\pi}{4}\right)$$

7. What is the imaginary part of $\sin (2 + 3j)$?

Answer:

$$j \cos 2 \left(\frac{\epsilon^3 - \epsilon^{-3}}{2}\right) = j \cos 2 \sinh 3$$

8. (a) Prove that

$$\cos z = \cos (x + jy)$$

is analytic by showing that its real and imaginary parts satisfy the Cauchy-Riemann equations.

(b) Do the same for

$$\cosh z = \frac{\epsilon^z + \epsilon^{-z}}{2}$$

5.5. The logarithm

The function $\log z$ deserves special treatment, both because of its peculiarities and because of its importance. To begin with, $\log z$ cannot be expressed as a power series in z, for we recall that the function $\log x$ has a singularity at the origin. We could express $\log z$ as a power series in $(z - 1)$, but instead of doing that, let us consider the equation

$$\epsilon^w = z$$

Accordingly,

$$\epsilon^w = \epsilon^{u+jv} = \epsilon^u \cdot \epsilon^{jv} = z = x + jy = r\epsilon^{j\phi} \tag{71}$$

where $\quad r = \sqrt{x^2 + y^2} \quad$ and $\quad \phi = \tan^{-1}\left(\frac{y}{x}\right)$

u, v, x, y, r, and ϕ are all real quantities.

From Eq. (71) it follows that[3]

$$u = \log r \tag{72}$$

and

$$v = \phi = \phi_0 + 2\pi n \tag{73}$$

where ϕ_0 is the value of ϕ between zero and 2π, and n is any positive or negative integer, including zero.

Let us now define the general logarithm in accordance with the original elementary definition

$$\epsilon^{\text{Log } z} = z \tag{74}$$

Then if $w = \text{Log } z$, we have,[4] from Eqs. (71–74),

$$\text{Log } z = w = u + jv = \log r + j(\phi_0 + 2\pi n) \tag{75}$$

The logarithm is thus a multiple-valued function, its value depending upon the value chosen for n. Therefore, every quantity, whether real or complex (excepting zero), has an infinite number of

---

[3] $\log r$ means, of course $\log_\epsilon r$, unless there is some statement to the contrary.

[4] The multiple-valued logarithm will be written with a capital L to distinguish it from its particular value when $n = 0$, which is written with a small l. Thus

$$\text{Log } z = \log z + j2\pi n$$

logarithms. In case z is real and positive, then $\phi_0 = 0$ and

$$\text{Log } z = \log r + j2\pi n \tag{76}$$

In this case $\log z = \log r$ is real.

If z is real and negative, then $\phi_0 = \pi$ and

$$\text{Log } z = \log r + j2\pi(n + \tfrac{1}{2}) \tag{77}$$

while

$$\log z = \log r + j\pi \tag{78}$$

Therefore, the logarithm of a negative number is never real.

If z_1 and z_2 are two complex quantities, then

$$z_1 = r_1\epsilon^{j\phi_1} \tag{79}$$

$$z_2 = r_2\epsilon^{j\phi_2} \tag{80}$$

$$z_1z_2 = r_1r_2\epsilon^{j(\phi_1+\phi_2)} \tag{81}$$

Thus

$$\text{Log } z_1 = \log r_1 + j(\phi_1 + 2\pi n) \tag{82}$$

$$\text{Log } z_2 = \log r_2 + j(\phi_2 + 2\pi m) \tag{83}$$

and

$$\begin{aligned} \text{Log } (z_1z_2) &= \log (r_1r_2) + j[(\phi_1 + \phi_2) + 2\pi p] \\ &= \text{Log } z_1 + \text{Log } z_2 \end{aligned} \tag{84}$$

since p can take on any integral value, which therefore includes $m + n$. The logarithm of a product is thus the sum of the logarithms of its factors, for complex quantities as well as reals.

Let us next consider briefly the way in which the logarithm varies. Suppose that z varies continuously along any curve in the complex plane not passing through the origin. Then $\log r$ and ϕ will likewise vary continuously, so that Log z will vary continuously. Now if z describes a closed curve and returns to its initial position, several distinct cases exist depending upon whether or not the closed curve has the origin within it. These cases are shown in Fig. 5-6. If the curve does not enclose the origin, the value of ϕ will return to its initial value. However, if the curve does enclose the origin, the value of ϕ will be increased by 2π for each loop that the curve has made about the origin in a counterclockwise direction and will be decreased by 2π for each loop about the origin in a clockwise direction. This property of the logarithm will be of interest in connection with the theory of residues.

The function

$$w = z^m \tag{85}$$

has already been defined for the case in which m is real and integral. If m has any complex value whatever, we can define z^m by the equation

$$z^m = \epsilon^{m \log z} \tag{86}$$

More generally we can define z^m as

$$z^m = \epsilon^{m \operatorname{Log} z} \tag{87}$$

which makes z^m a multiple-valued function just like the logarithm, unless m is an integer (see Example 3). Furthermore, if m is not an integer, then

$$\epsilon^{z^m} = 1 + z^m + \frac{z^{2m}}{2!} + \frac{z^{3m}}{3!} + \cdots \tag{88}$$

is also multiple-valued.

If a point P, such as the origin in Fig. 5-6, has the property that a function $f(z)$ takes on multiple values if z varies along a path

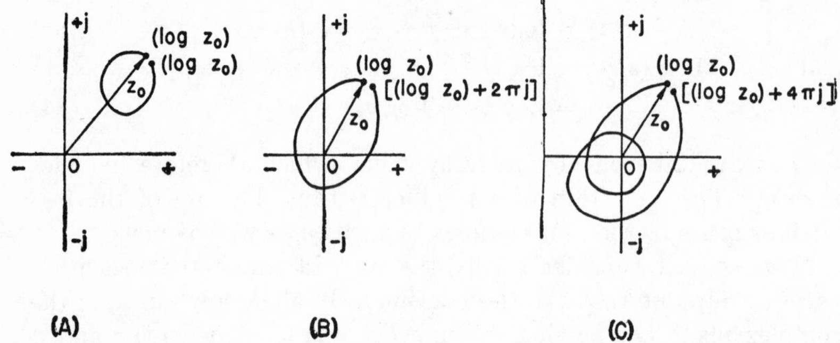

FIG. 5-6. The effect on the value of Log z caused by moving z around the origin.

enclosing P, then P is called a *branch point* or *critical point* of the function $f(z)$. It is clear that a function cannot be analytic at a branch point. From the preceding discussion, we see that Log z has a branch point at the origin. Likewise, provided m is not an integer, z^m and ϵ^{z^m} also have branch points at the origin. The discussion of branch points is extended in §5.17.

Exercises

1. From Eqs. (75) and (41), show that

$$\frac{d}{dz}(\operatorname{Log} z) = \frac{1}{z}$$

2. From Eq. (88) and the equation

$$\frac{d}{dz}(\epsilon^Z) = \epsilon^Z \frac{dZ}{dz}$$

show that

$$\frac{d}{dz}(z^m) = mz^{m-1}$$

for all values of m.

3. If m is an integer, show that

$$z^m = \epsilon^{m \operatorname{Log} z}$$

is single-valued.

5.6. Integration

In the integration of a real function $f(x)$, we define the definite integral between the values $x = a$ and $x = b$, as [see Fig. 5-7(a)]

$$\int_a^b f(x)\,dx = \lim_{\substack{\Delta x \to 0 \\ n \to \infty}} \sum_{p=1}^{n} \overline{f(x)_p}\,\Delta x_p \tag{89}$$

This definition is given in books on calculus, which also show that the integral can be represented as an area. In the case of a function $f(z)$ of a complex variable z, we similarly define a definite integral as a summation in the form

$$\int_{(C)} f(z)\,dz = \lim_{\substack{\Delta z \to 0 \\ n \to \infty}} \sum_{p=1}^{n} \overline{f(z)_p}\,\Delta z_p \tag{90}$$

where $\overline{f(z)_p}$ is the average value of $f(z)$ in the interval Δz_p.

In the case of a complex variable, it is necessary to specify the entire path of integration C, since there is more than one continuous path (see Fig. 5-7) between the end points z_1 and z_2. Furthermore, it is not possible to represent the integral in Eq. (90) as an area or its equivalent in the same simple way as is done with the integral in Eq. (89), since four-dimensional space would be required for an analogous representation.

In order to separate Eq. (90) into its real and imaginary components, we write

$$f(z) = u + jv \tag{91}$$

$$z = x + jy \tag{92}$$

as the notation for the real and imaginary components of $f(z)$ and z. Then

$$\begin{aligned}
\int_{(C)} f(z)\,dz &= \lim_{\substack{\Delta z \to 0 \\ n \to \infty}} \sum_{p=1}^{n} \overline{f(z)}_p\,\Delta z_p \\
&= \lim_{\substack{\Delta x \to 0 \\ \Delta y \to 0 \\ n \to \infty}} \sum_{p=1}^{n} (u_p + jv_p)(\Delta x_p + j\,\Delta y_p) \\
&= \lim_{\substack{\Delta x \to 0 \\ \Delta y \to 0 \\ n \to \infty}} \sum_{p=1}^{n} [(u_p\,\Delta x_p - v_p\,\Delta y_p) + j(v_p\,\Delta x_p + u_p\,\Delta y_p)] \\
&= \int_{(C)} (u\,dx - v\,dy) + j\int_{(C)} (v\,dx + u\,dy) \qquad (93)
\end{aligned}$$

We note also that if the direction of integration is reversed—i.e., if the integral is taken from z_2 to z_1 but along the same path C,

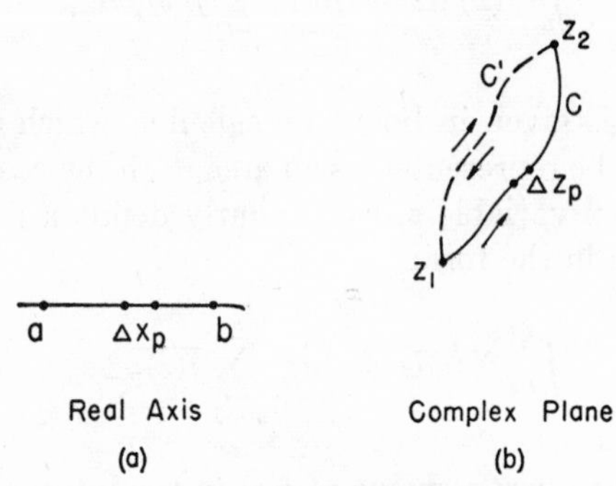

FIG. 5-7. Paths of integration in the real and complex domains.

then the value of the integral just changes sign. This follows because the values of u and v are unchanged at every point but the values of Δx and Δy change sign. Therefore

$$\int_{\substack{z_1 \\ C}}^{z_2} f(z)\,dz = -\int_{\substack{z_2 \\ -C}}^{z_1} f(z)\,dz \qquad (94)$$

Now in the integration of a real function $f(x)$ with respect to the real variable x, we know that there generally exists a function $F(x)$, such that

$$\int_a^b f(x)\,dx = F(b) - F(a) \tag{95}$$

and
$$\frac{d}{dx}[F(x)] = f(x) \tag{96}$$

$F(x)$ is called the indefinite integral of $f(x)$.

The question therefore naturally arises as to whether we can find a corresponding function $F(z)$ for the function $f(z)$ in the complex plane so that equations corresponding to Eqs. (95) and (96) will hold true. In other words, can we find a function $F(z)$ such that the integral in Eq. (93) can be expressed as

$$\int_{z_1 \atop C}^{z_2} f(z)\,dz = F(z_2) - F(z_1) \tag{97}$$

and such that
$$\frac{d}{dz}[F(z)] = f(z) \tag{98}$$

This question will now be examined.

Equation (97) expresses the value of the definite integral in terms of the end points alone. In order for this to be possible, the value of the integral along the path C must be equal to its value along every other path C' having the same end points, z_1 and z_2. It therefore follows from Eq. (94) that the value of the integral taken around a closed path (usually called a closed contour) and returning to the same point must vanish. Thus, for Eq. (97) to hold, it is necessary that

$$\oint f(z)\,dz = \int_{z_1 \atop C}^{z_2} f(z)\,dz + \int_{z_2 \atop C'}^{z_1} f(z)\,dz = 0 \tag{99}$$

In order to understand the significance of Eq. (99), we recall the following theorem which is proved in books on advanced calculus[5] when they take up the subject of line integrals:

A necessary and sufficient condition that the integral

$$\oint [M(x,y)\,dx + N(x,y)\,dy]$$

around every closed contour shall vanish in a given region R (see Fig. 5-8) *of the x, y plane is that*

$$\frac{\partial M}{\partial y} = \frac{\partial N}{\partial x}$$

[5] Wilson, *Advanced Calculus*, p. 298.

The theorem also requires that M, N, $\partial M/\partial y$, and $\partial N/\partial x$ shall be continuous and single-valued, and that the region R shall be *simply connected.*[6]

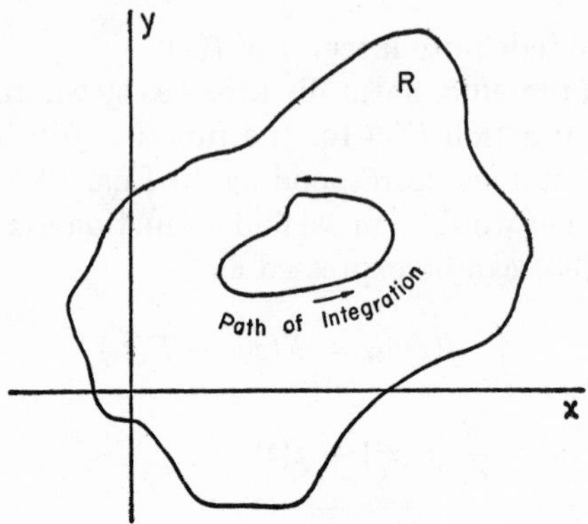

FIG. 5-8. A path of integration lying wholly inside a region R.

If we separate the closed-contour integral in Eq. (99) into its real and imaginary parts, we have

$$\oint f(z)\,dz = \oint (u\,dx - v\,dy) + j\oint (v\,dx + u\,dy) = 0 \qquad (100)$$

Since the real and imaginary parts must vanish separately, Eq. (99) is thus equivalent to the two equations

$$\oint (u\,dx - v\,dy) = 0 \qquad (101)$$

$$\oint (v\,dx + u\,dy) = 0 \qquad (102)$$

[6] A *simply connected* region is defined as a region such that any closed curve drawn in it can be shrunk to a point by a continuous deformation without

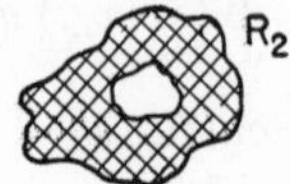

FIG. 5-A. Simply connected and multiply connected regions.

crossing the boundary of the region. Thus R_1 in Fig. 5-A is simply connected, while R_2 is not.

Applying the foregoing theorem to Eqs. (101) and (102), we obtain the equations

$$\frac{\partial u}{\partial y} = -\frac{\partial v}{\partial x} \tag{103A}$$

$$\frac{\partial v}{\partial y} = \frac{\partial u}{\partial x} \tag{103B}$$

as the necessary and sufficient conditions that the real and imaginary parts of the closed-contour integral in Eq. (100) shall vanish. We recognize Eqs. (103A) and (103B) as the familiar Cauchy-Riemann equations. Therefore *the closed-contour integral*

$$\oint f(z)\,dz$$

will vanish for all contours in a region if, and only if,[7] *$f(z)$ is analytic in that region.*

We have already pointed out that the vanishing of all closed-contour integrals in a region is equivalent to integrals being independent of the path of integration. We may therefore restate the result of the last paragraph in the following form:

A necessary and sufficient condition that the value of the integral

$$\int_{z_1}^{z_2} f(z)\,dz$$

shall be a function only of the end points, z_1 and z_2, is that the function $f(z)$ shall be analytic.

If we keep one end point fixed, the integral then becomes a function of the other end point alone. We may therefore write

$$\int_{z_0}^{z} f(z)\,dz = F(z) \tag{104}$$

where z_0 is the fixed end point and z is used both as the symbol for the variable end point and the variable of integration. While this terminology is somewhat ambiguous, it is legitimate, since the value of the end point z is not substituted into $F(z)$ until after the integration is performed. It follows from Eq. (104) that (see Fig. 5-9)

---

[7] The theorem may fail to be true if u and v and their derivatives are not single-valued and continuous, as required by the previous theorem.

$$\int_{z_1}^{z_2} f(z)\,dz = \int_{z_0}^{z_2} f(z)\,dz - \int_{z_0}^{z_1} f(z)\,dz = F(z_2) - F(z_1) \quad (105)$$

which is the analogue of Eq. (95) in complex form. A complex analogue of Eq. (95) therefore exists if, and only if, $f(z)$ is analytic.

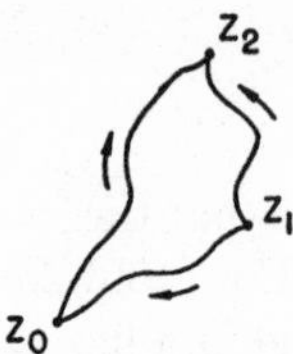

FIG. 5-9. Two different paths of integration between z_1 and z_2.

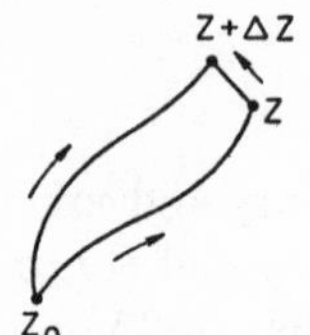

FIG. 5-10. Two different paths of integration between z_0 and $z + \Delta z$.

Let us next vary the end point z in Eq. (104) (see Fig. 5-10) and find the value of the derivative

$$\frac{d}{dz}[F(z)]$$

Accordingly, we write

$$\begin{aligned}\frac{d}{dz}[F(z)] &= \lim_{\Delta z\to 0}\left\{\frac{F(z+\Delta z) - F(z)}{\Delta z}\right\}\\ &= \lim_{\Delta z\to 0}\frac{1}{\Delta z}\left\{\int_{z_0}^{z+\Delta z} f(z)\,dz - \int_{z_0}^{z} f(z)\,dz\right\}\\ &= \lim_{\Delta z\to 0}\frac{1}{\Delta z}\int_{z}^{z+\Delta z} f(z)\,dz = f(z) \qquad (106)\end{aligned}$$

The contraction of the two integrals into one integral in Eq. (106) was possible only because the value of the integral was independent of the path of integration. Equation (106) therefore holds true if $f(z)$ is analytic. It is the analogue of Eq. (96) for real variables.

Equations (105) and (106) show that analytic functions of a complex variable can be integrated in the same way as functions of a real variable. Furthermore, since we have previously pointed out that the same differentiation formulas hold in general for complex variables as for real variables, it follows from Eqs. (105) and (106) that the same integration formulas also hold. Thus

$$\int z^n\,dz = \frac{z^{n+1}}{n+1} + \text{constant}$$

$$\int \frac{dz}{z} = \text{Log}\,z + \text{constant}$$

$$\int \epsilon^z\,dz = \epsilon^z + \text{constant}$$

$$\int \sin z\,dz = -\cos z + \text{constant}$$

and so forth.

5.7. Examples of integration in the complex plane

Example 1: *A Nonanalytic Function Integrated Around a Closed Contour.* We will now give a few examples of integration in the complex plane. We will start with a function that is not analytic and show that the integral of this function around a closed contour does not vanish. Accordingly, let us take the function

$$f(z) = u + jv = x - j2y \quad (107)^8$$

and integrate it around the closed contour shown in Fig. 5-11, starting at the point 1, j.

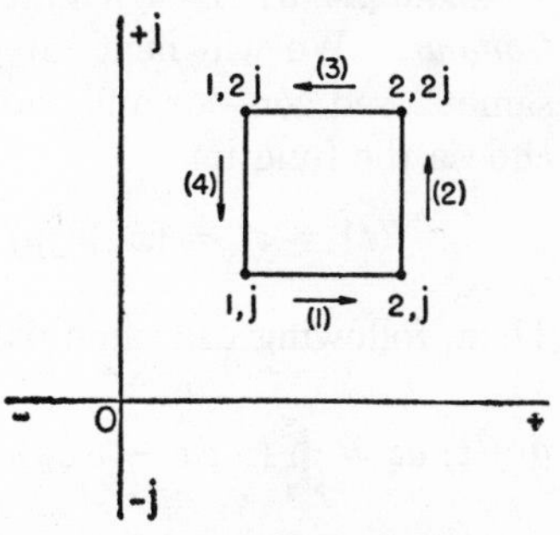

FIG. 5-11. A closed contour in the z plane.

Let us call the sides of the square contour (1), (2), (3), and (4), respectively. Then along side (1), $dy = 0$ and $y = 1$. Along side (2), $dx = 0$ and $x = 2$. Along side (3), $dy = 0$ and $y = 2$. Along side (4), $dx = 0$ and $x = 1$. We may therefore write

$$\begin{aligned}\oint f(z)\,dz &= \oint (u + jv)(dx + j\,dy)\\ &= \oint (u\,dx - v\,dy) + j\oint (v\,dx + u\,dy)\\ &= \underset{(1)}{\int_1^2 x\,dx} + j\underset{(1)}{\int_1^2 (-2)\,dx} + \underset{(2)}{\int_1^2 + 2y\,dy} + j\underset{(2)}{\int_1^2 2\,dy}\end{aligned}$$

---

[8] It is ordinarily not possible to express a nonanalytic function explicitly as a function of z, since, as we have already pointed out, all the ordinary func-

$$+ \underset{(3)}{\int_2^1 x\,dx} + j \underset{(3)}{\int_2^1 (-4)\,dx} + \underset{(4)}{\int_2^1 2y\,dy} + j \underset{(4)}{\int_2^1 dy}$$

$$= \frac{x^2}{2}\Big|_1^2 - j2x\Big|_1^2 + y^2\Big|_1^2 + j2y\Big|_1^2 + \frac{x^2}{2}\Big|_2^1 - j4x\Big|_2^1 + y^2\Big|_2^1 + jy\Big|_2^1$$

$$= (2 - \tfrac{1}{2}) - j(4 - 2) + (4 - 1) + j(4 - 2) + (\tfrac{1}{2} - 2)$$

$$- j(4 - 8) + (1 - 4) + j(1 - 2) = 3j \quad (108)$$

Thus
$$\oint (x - j2y)\,dz = 3j \quad (109)$$

and accordingly it does not vanish. This fact is not surprising, since $(x - j2y)$ is not an analytic function. We will next show, however, that when we integrate an analytic function around a closed contour, the integral does vanish.

Example 2: *An Analytic Function Integrated Around a Closed Contour.* We will next integrate an analytic function around the same closed contour and show that it actually does vanish. Let us choose the function

$$f(z) = z^2 = (x + jy)^2 = (x^2 - y^2) + j2xy = u + jv \quad (110)$$

Then, following the same path as before, we obtain

$$\oint f(z)\,dz = \oint (u\,dx - v\,dy) + j \oint (v\,dx + u\,dy)$$

$$= \underset{(1)}{\int_1^2 (x^2 - 1)\,dx} + j \underset{(1)}{\int_1^2 2x\,dx}$$

$$+ \underset{(2)}{\int_1^2 - 4y\,dy} + j \underset{(2)}{\int_1^2 (4 - y^2)\,dy} + \underset{(3)}{\int_2^1 (x^2 - 4)\,dx}$$

$$+ j \underset{(3)}{\int_2^1 4x\,dx} + \underset{(4)}{\int_2^1 - 2y\,dy} + j \underset{(4)}{\int_2^1 (1 - y^2)\,dy}$$

---

tions of z can be proved to be analytic. We must therefore express a non-analytic function of z in terms of the real and imaginary components of z; i.e., in terms of x and y. The function is still, however, a function of z, since it has a definite value for every value of z.

$$
\begin{aligned}
&= \left(\frac{x^3}{3} - x\right)\Bigg|_1^2 + jx^2\Bigg|_1^2 - 2y^2\Bigg|_1^2 + j\left(4y - \frac{y^3}{3}\right)\Bigg|_1^2 \\
&\qquad + \left(\frac{x^3}{3} - 4x\right)\Bigg|_2^1 + j2x^2\Bigg|_2^1 - y^2\Bigg|_2^1 + j\left(y - \frac{y^3}{3}\right)\Bigg|_2^1 \\
&= \left(\tfrac{8}{3} - 2 - \tfrac{1}{3} + 1\right) + j(4 - 1) - (8 - 2) \\
&\qquad + j\left(8 - \tfrac{8}{3} - 4 + \tfrac{1}{3}\right) + \left(\tfrac{1}{3} - 4 - \tfrac{8}{3} + 8\right) + j(2 - 8) \\
&\qquad - (1 - 4) + j\left(1 - \tfrac{1}{3} - 2 + \tfrac{8}{3}\right) \\
&= 0
\end{aligned} \tag{111}
$$

Thus

$$\oint z^2\,dz = 0 \tag{112}$$

as was to be expected, since

$$f(z) = z^2 = (x^2 - y^2) + j2xy$$

is an analytic function.

Example 3: *An Analytic Function Integrated along Two Different Paths with the Same End Points.* We will now give an example of the fact, proved in §5.6, that the integral of an analytic function between two points is independent of the path of integration. As our example, we will integrate the function

$$f(z) = z^2 = (x^2 - y^2) + j2xy \tag{113}$$

between the points $(1, j)$ and $(2, 2j)$ along (a) the diagonal (5) in Fig. 5-12, and (b) the broken path (1), (2) in the same figure. We will then compare the results.

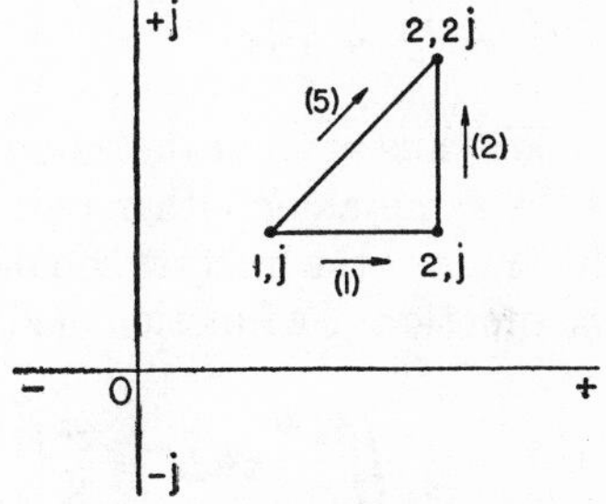

Fig. 5-12. Two different paths of integration between the points $(1, j)$ and $(2, 2j)$.

(a) We note first that along the diagonal

$$y = x \tag{114}$$

Therefore, along the diagonal

$$\int_{1,j}^{2,2j} f(z)\,dz = \int_{1,j}^{2,2j} z^2\,dz = \underset{(5)}{\int_{1,1}^{2,2}} (u\,dx - v\,dy) + j \underset{(5)}{\int_{1,1}^{2,2}} (v\,dx + u\,dy)$$

$$= \underset{(5)}{\int_{1,1}^{2,2}} \{(x^2 - y^2)\,dx - 2xy\,dy\} + j \underset{(5)}{\int_{1,1}^{2,2}} \{2xy\,dx + (x^2 - y^2)\,dy\}$$

$$= \underset{(5)}{\int_{1,1}^{2,2}} \{(x^2 - x^2)\,dx - 2y^2\,dy\} + j \underset{(5)}{\int_{1,1}^{2,2}} \{2x^2\,dx + (y^2 - y^2)\,dy\}$$

$$= -\frac{2y^3}{3}\Big|_1^2 + j\frac{2x^3}{3}\Big|_1^2 = -\frac{14}{3} + j\frac{14}{3} \tag{115}$$

(b) Along the broken path (1), (2), we have, just as in Example 2,

$$\int_{1,j}^{2,2j} z^2\,dz = \underset{(1)}{\int_1^2} (x^2 - 1)\,dx + j \underset{(1)}{\int_1^2} 2x\,dx + \underset{(2)}{\int_1^2} -4y\,dy + j \underset{(2)}{\int_1^2} (4 - y^2)\,dy$$

$$= \left(\frac{x^3}{3} - x\right)\Big|_1^2 - jx^2\Big|_1^2 - 2y^2\Big|_1^2 + j\left(4y - \frac{y^3}{3}\right)\Big|_1^2$$

$$= (\tfrac{8}{3} - 2 - \tfrac{1}{3} + 1) + j(4 - 1) - (8 - 2) + j(8 - \tfrac{8}{3} - 4 + \tfrac{1}{3})$$

$$= -\tfrac{14}{3} + j\tfrac{14}{3} \tag{116}$$

We thus see that the value of the integral between the two points is the same along either path. Now in §5.6, we also proved that the value of the integral should be obtainable directly by integrating the function as a function of z. To test this, we write

$$\int_{1+j}^{2+2j} z^2\,dz = \frac{z^3}{3}\Big|_{1+j}^{2+2j} = \frac{(2 + 2j)^3}{3} - \frac{(1 + j)^3}{3}$$

$$= -\tfrac{14}{3} + j\tfrac{14}{3} \tag{117}$$

This result agrees with Eqs. (116) and (115) and thus verifies the fact that the integration can be carried out directly in terms of z.

Exercises

1. Integrate the function ϵ^z along path (5) in Fig. 5-12 and then show that the same result is obtained by integration in terms of z directly and substituting the values of the end points.

2. Do the same for the function z^3.

5.8. Integration of analytic functions, in multiply connected regions

Suppose we have a region, such as R in Fig. 5-13, which is not simply connected.[9] Let us designate the outer boundary of the region as C, and let the various inner boundaries be called C_1, C_2, --- C_n, respectively, as shown in Fig. 5-13.

Next, suppose that a function $f(z)$ is analytic everywhere within and at the boundaries of the shaded region R, but that it may fail to be analytic outside of C, or inside of C_1, C_2, etc. We will now prove that

$$\oint_C f(z)\,dz = \oint_{C_1} f(z)\,dz + \oint_{C_2} f(z)\,dz + \cdots + \oint_{C_n} f(z)\,dz \tag{118}$$

where C_1, --- C_n are all of the interior boundaries, and the integration in all cases is taken in the same direction (i.e., clockwise or counterclockwise). The theorem does not apply in cases where $f(z)$ has a branch point within C, and is thus multiple-valued.

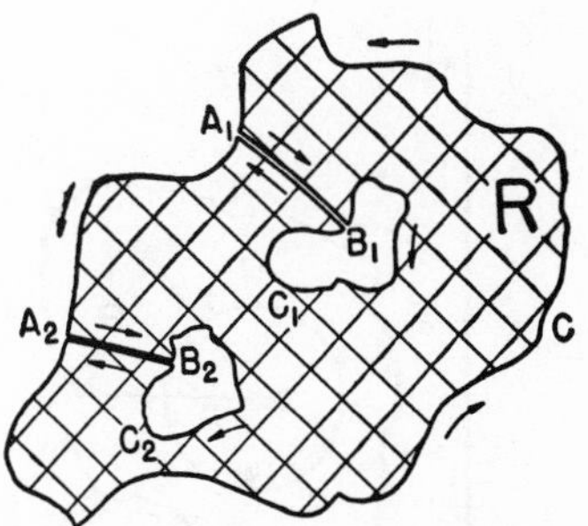

FIG. 5-13. A closed contour which avoids encircling the regions inside C_1 and C_2.

In order to prove the theorem, we draw a series of connecting lines A_1B_1, A_2B_2, --- A_nB_n between the interior boundaries C_1, --- C_n and the exterior boundary C, in such a way that none of the connecting lines cross each other. We then integrate the function along the contour designated by the arrows in Fig. 5-13. Within this contour the function is everywhere analytic. The contour integral therefore vanishes. Furthermore, the integral along each connecting line AB in one direction is canceled by the integral along the same connecting line in the opposite direction.[10] Therefore the vanishing of the complete contour integral is equivalent to the equation

[9] Regions which are not *simply connected* are called *multiply connected*. A good discussion of multiply connected regions will be found in Wilson, *Advanced Calculus*, p. 89.

[10] The value of an integral $\int f(z)\,dz$ in one direction along a given curve between two points is equal to the negative of the same integral taken in the

$$\oint_C f(z)\,dz + \oint_{C_1} f(z)\,dz + \cdots + \oint_{C_n} f(z)\,dz = 0 \qquad (119)$$

We note that the integrals along the inner boundaries $C_1, C_2 \cdots C_n$ are taken in the opposite direction from that of the integral along the outer boundary. If we reverse the directions of the integrals along the inner boundaries, we reverse the signs[11] of these integrals, and Eq. (119) becomes

$$\oint_C f(z)\,dz = \oint_{C_1} f(z)\,dz + \cdots + \oint_{C_n} f(z)\,dz \qquad (120)$$

This result is the same as Eq. (118), and thus the theorem is proved.

5.9. Cauchy's integral formulas

We will next derive a remarkable set of formulas which are of great importance in the further development of our subject.

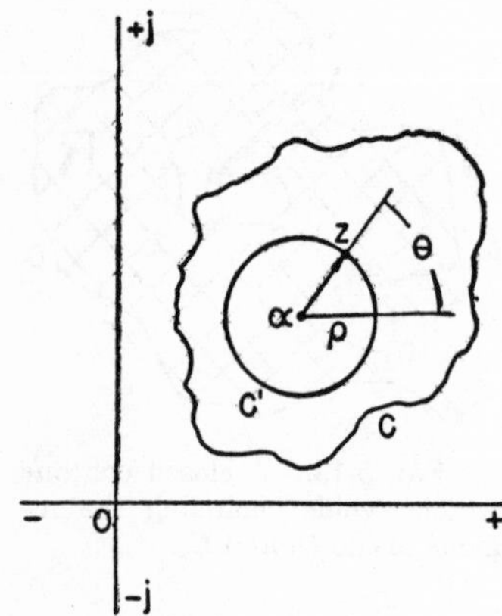

FIG. 5-14. A circle C', lying wholly within the contour C.

Consider a function $f(z)$ which is analytic everywhere within a closed contour C as well as at its boundary. (See Fig. 5-14.) Let α be some fixed point inside C. Then the function

$$\frac{f(z)}{z - \alpha}$$

is analytic everywhere within and at the boundary of C except at α. It is even analytic at α, in case $f(z)$ has $(z - \alpha)$ as a factor, but this is not important for our present purposes. Let us next draw a circle of small radius ρ around α, and let us call the circular contour C'. Then, by the theorem of §5.8,

opposite direction. The reason for this is that dz changes sign when the direction of integration is reversed, while $f(z)$ remains the same at each point. The whole argument of this section will, of course, break down if $f(z)$ has a branch point within C; for then the values of $f(z)$ may be different for the opposite directions of integration along the lines A_qB_q.

[11] Note the reversals in the direction of the arrows in some of the integrals of Eqs. (119) and (120).

$$\oint_C \frac{f(z)}{z - \alpha} dz = \oint_{C'} \frac{f(z)}{z - \alpha} dz \tag{121}$$

We will now evaluate the integral on the left, by finding the value of the integral on the right as the radius ρ becomes very small. On the circular contour, we can write

$$z - \alpha = \rho(\cos\theta + j\sin\theta) = \rho\epsilon^{j\theta} \tag{122}$$

$$dz = j\rho\epsilon^{j\theta}\, d\theta \tag{123}$$

Furthermore, along the infinitesimal circular contour, we may write

$$f(z) = f(\alpha) \tag{124}$$

Therefore

$$\oint_{C'} \frac{f(z)}{z - \alpha} dz = \oint_{C'} \frac{f(\alpha)}{\rho\epsilon^{j\theta}} \cdot j\rho\epsilon^{j\theta}\, d\theta = jf(\alpha) \oint_{C'} d\theta = 2\pi j f(\alpha) \tag{125}$$

Substituting (125) into (121), we obtain

$$\oint_C \frac{f(z)}{z - \alpha} dz = 2\pi j \cdot f(\alpha) \tag{126}$$

Equation (126) tells us that *the value of an analytic function* $f(z)$ *at any point* α *is completely determined by its value along any closed contour enclosing* α, *provided that the function is analytic everywhere along and within the contour. In particular,*

$$f(\alpha) = \frac{1}{2\pi j} \oint_C \frac{f(z)}{z - \alpha} dz \tag{127}$$

Equation (127) is called Cauchy's integral formula. It is of fundamental importance.

We will next find a formula corresponding to Eq. (127) for the derivative of $f(\alpha)$ with respect to α. Accordingly, we write[12]

[12] We herein make use of the identity

$$\frac{1}{z - (\alpha + \Delta\alpha)} - \frac{1}{z - \alpha} = \frac{\Delta\alpha}{(z - \alpha)[z - (\alpha + \Delta\alpha)]}$$

$$\begin{aligned} f'(\alpha) &= \frac{d}{d\alpha}[f(\alpha)] = \lim_{\Delta\alpha\to 0} \frac{f(\alpha+\Delta\alpha) - f(\alpha)}{\Delta\alpha} \\ &= \lim_{\Delta\alpha\to 0} \frac{1}{2\pi j\,\Delta\alpha}\left\{\oint_C \frac{f(z)}{z-(\alpha+\Delta\alpha)}\,dz - \oint_C \frac{f(z)}{z-\alpha}\,dz\right\} \\ &= \lim_{\Delta\alpha\to 0} \frac{1}{2\pi j\,\Delta\alpha}\left\{\Delta\alpha \oint_C \frac{f(z)}{(z-\alpha)(z-\alpha-\Delta\alpha)}\,dz\right\} \\ &= \frac{1}{2\pi j}\oint_C \frac{f(z)\,dz}{(z-\alpha)^2} \end{aligned} \tag{128}$$

In a similar manner we would find

$$f''(\alpha) = \frac{2!}{2\pi j}\oint_C \frac{f(z)\,dz}{(z-\alpha)^3} \tag{129}$$

$$f^n(\alpha) = \frac{n!}{2\pi j}\oint_C \frac{f(z)\,dz}{(z-\alpha)^{n+1}} \tag{130}$$

It is worth while noting that the foregoing method of derivation indicates that an analytic function must have derivatives of all orders.

Since α may be any point in the complex plane, it will be found convenient for future use to rewrite Eqs. (127) through (130) as

$$f(z) = \frac{1}{2\pi j}\oint_C \frac{f(t)}{t-z}\,dt \tag{131}$$

$$f'(z) = \frac{1}{2\pi j}\oint_C \frac{f(t)}{(t-z)^2}\,dt \tag{132}$$

$$f''(z) = \frac{2!}{2\pi j}\oint_C \frac{f(t)}{(t-z)^3}\,dt \tag{133}$$

$$f^n(z) = \frac{n!}{2\pi j}\oint_C \frac{f(t)}{(t-z)^{n+1}}\,dt \tag{134}$$

where t is the variable of integration in the above equations, and z is any point in the complex plane where $f(z)$ is analytic.

5.10. Taylor's series

Cauchy's integral formulas can be used to derive Taylor series for a function of a complex variable. To show this, let $f(t)$ be an analytic function of the complex variable t everywhere on the boundary and in the interior of a circle whose center is at a. (See Fig. 5-15.) Then if z is any point within the circle, we have, from Eq. (131),

$$f(z) = \frac{1}{2\pi j} \oint_C \frac{f(t)}{t - z}\, dt = \frac{1}{2\pi j} \oint_C \frac{f(t)}{t - a} \left(\frac{1}{1 - \dfrac{z - a}{t - a}} \right) dt \tag{135}$$

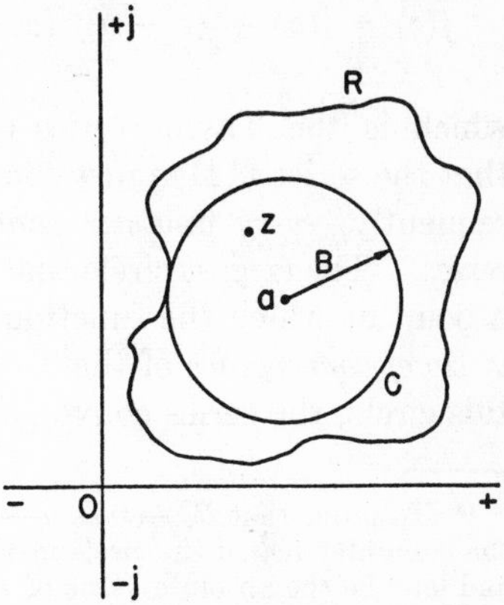

Fig. 5-15. The largest circle with center at $z = a$ which lies wholly within the contour C.

where the contour C is the circle. Now if p is any quantity whatever,

$$\frac{1}{1 - p} = 1 + p + p^2 + \cdots + p^{n-1} + \frac{p^n}{1 - p} \tag{136}$$

Substituting (136) into (135) and letting

$$p = \frac{z - a}{t - a} \tag{137}$$

we obtain

$$f(z) = \frac{1}{2\pi j} \left\{ \oint_C \frac{f(t)}{t - a}\, dt + (z - a) \oint_C \frac{f(t)}{(t - a)^2}\, dt + \cdots + (z - a)^{n-1} \oint_C \frac{f(t)}{(t - a)^n}\, dt \right\} + R_n \tag{138}$$

where

$$R_n = \frac{(z - a)^n}{2\pi j} \oint_C \frac{f(t)}{(t - a)^n (t - z)}\, dt \tag{139}$$

Making use of Eqs. (131–134), (138) becomes

$$f(z) = f(a) + (z - a)f'(a) + \cdots + \frac{(z - a)^{n-1}}{(n - 1)!} f^{n-1}(a) + R_n \tag{140}$$

As n becomes infinite, it can readily be shown that R_n approaches zero.[13] Therefore (140) can be changed to

$$f(z) = f(a) + (z - a)f'(a) + \cdots + \frac{(z-a)^n}{n!}f^n(a) + \cdots \qquad (141)$$

which is the Taylor series expansion of $f(z)$. It can be proved that the series (141) must converge if z lies within the circle. Consequently, *every analytic function can be expanded into a Taylor series.* The largest circle that can be drawn about a before reaching a point at which the function $f(z)$ fails to be analytic, is called the *circle of convergence* of the Taylor series (141). Everywhere within this circle, the series converges.[14]

---

[13] To prove that $R_n \to 0$ as $n \to \infty$, let M be the greatest value of $f(t)$ along the circumference of the circle in Fig. 5-15. Let B be the radius of the circle, and let r be the absolute value of $z - a$. Then if t lies on the circle

$$|t - z| \geqq B - r$$

In other words,

$$\left|\frac{1}{t - z}\right| \leqq \frac{1}{B - r}$$

Therefore,

$$|R_n| = \left|\frac{(z-a)^n}{2\pi j}\oint_C \frac{f(t)}{(t-a)^n(t-z)}\,dt\right| < \frac{1}{2\pi}\left(\frac{r}{B}\right)^n \frac{M}{B-r}2\pi B = \frac{MB}{B-r}\left(\frac{r}{B}\right)^n$$

Since $\frac{r}{B} < 1$, the factor $\left(\frac{r}{B}\right)^n \to 0$ as $n \to \infty$. Therefore $R_n \to 0$ also.

[14] For any analytic function $f(z)$ whose Taylor series has only real coefficients

$$[f(j\omega)]^* = f(-j\omega)$$

where the asterisk stands for the complex conjugate. To prove this, let

$$f(z) = a_0 + a_1 z + a_2 z^2 + a_3 z^3 + a_4 z^4 + \cdots$$

be the Taylor expansion of $f(z)$. Then

$$f(j\omega) = a_0 + ja_1\omega - a_2\omega^2 - ja_3\omega^3 + a_4\omega^4 + \cdots$$

and

$$[f(j\omega)]^* = a_0 - ja_1\omega - a_2\omega^2 + ja_3\omega^3 + a_4\omega^4 + \cdots$$
$$= f(-j\omega)$$

Similarly, we could also show that

$$f(j\omega) = [f(-j\omega)]^*$$

5.11. Laurent's expansion

In the preceding section, we showed how a function $f(z)$ can be expanded in a power series about any point at which the function is analytic. This is the familiar Taylor series. We will now derive an important generalization of Taylor series and show how a function can be expanded in a type of power series even about points at which it is not analytic.

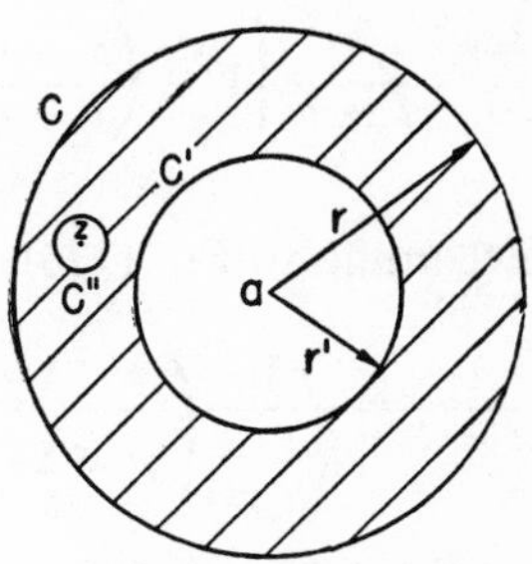

FIG. 5-16. Significant contours in deriving Laurent's expansion.

Consider a function $f(t)$ and a point a in the complex plane. About a as center, let us draw two concentric circles, C and C'. (See Fig. 5-16.) Let us assume that $f(t)$ is analytic in the area between C and C' as well as on the circles themselves. Elsewhere the function may or may not be analytic. Next consider a point z in the area between C and C' where $f(t)$ is analytic. About z, let us draw a small circle C'' lying entirely between C and C'. Then the function

$$\frac{f(t)}{t - z}$$

is analytic everywhere inside C, if the areas inside C' and C'' are excluded. Therefore, by Eq. (120),

$$\oint_C \frac{f(t)}{t - z}\, dt = \oint_{C'} \frac{f(t)}{t - z}\, dt + \oint_{C''} \frac{f(t)}{t - z}\, dt \tag{142}$$

Now $f(t)$ itself is analytic everywhere within C'', so that by Eq. (131)

$$\oint_{C''} \frac{f(t)}{t - z}\, dt = 2\pi j\, f(z) \tag{143}$$

Furthermore,

$$\oint_{C'} \frac{f(t)}{t - z}\, dt = -\oint_{C'} \frac{f(t)}{z - t}\, dt \tag{144}$$

Substituting (143) and (144) into (142), we get

$$f(z) = \frac{1}{2\pi j} \oint_C \frac{f(t)}{t - z}\, dt + \frac{1}{2\pi j} \oint_{C'} \frac{f(t)}{z - t}\, dt \tag{145}$$

Now

$$\frac{1}{t-z} = \frac{1}{t-a}\left(\frac{1}{1-\dfrac{z-a}{t-a}}\right)$$

$$= \frac{1}{t-a}\left\{1 + \left(\frac{z-a}{t-a}\right) + \left(\frac{z-a}{t-a}\right)^2 + \cdots + \left(\frac{z-a}{t-a}\right)^n + \cdots\right\} \tag{146}$$

according to Eq. (136). In a similar manner

$$\frac{1}{z-t} = \frac{1}{z-a}\left(\frac{1}{1-\dfrac{t-a}{z-a}}\right)$$

$$= \frac{1}{z-a}\left\{1 + \frac{t-a}{z-a} + \left(\frac{t-a}{z-a}\right)^2 + \cdots + \left(\frac{t-a}{z-a}\right)^n + \cdots\right\} \tag{147}$$

The series Eq. (146) converges if t lies only on C, since then

$$\left|\frac{z-a}{t-a}\right| < 1$$

Likewise, the series Eq. (147) converges if t lies only on C', since then

$$\left|\frac{t-a}{z-a}\right| < 1$$

Substituting Eqs. (146) and (147) into Eq. (145), we obtain

$$f(z) = \left\{\frac{1}{2\pi j}\oint_C \frac{f(t)}{t-a}\,dt + \frac{(z-a)}{2\pi j}\oint_C \frac{f(t)}{(t-a)^2}\,dt + \cdots \right.$$

$$\left. + \frac{(z-a)^n}{2\pi j}\oint_C \frac{f(t)}{(t-a)^{n+1}}\,dt + \cdots\right\} + \left\{\frac{1}{z-a}\cdot\frac{1}{2\pi j}\oint_{C'} f(t)\,dt \right.$$

$$+ \frac{1}{(z-a)^2}\cdot\frac{1}{2\pi j}\oint_{C'} (t-a)f(t)\,dt$$

$$\left. + \frac{1}{(z-a)^n}\cdot\frac{1}{2\pi j}\oint_{C'} (t-a)^{n-1}f(t)\,dt + \cdots\right\}$$

$$= A_0 + A_1(z-a) + A_2(z-a)^2 + \cdots + A_n(z-a)^n + \cdots$$

$$+ \frac{A_{-1}}{(z-a)} + \frac{A_{-2}}{(z-a)^2} + \cdots + \frac{A_{-m}}{(z-a)^m} + \cdots \tag{148}$$

where
$$A_p = \frac{1}{2\pi j} \oint \frac{f(t)\,dt}{(t-a)^{p+1}} \tag{149}$$

Equation (149) holds for all positive and negative integral values of p, including zero. If p is a positive integer or zero, then the integral is taken over the contour C. If p is a negative integer, then the integral is taken over the contour C'. However, since all the functions

$$\frac{f(t)}{(t-a)^{p+1}}$$

are analytic between C and C', we can actually use either contour C or C' or any concentric contour between them in evaluating the integrals in Eq. (149). It can easily be shown that the series Eq. (148) converges and is equal to $f(z)$ provided only that z lies in the region where $f(z)$ is analytic. It is *not* necessary that $f(z)$ should be analytic at the point a.

Equation (148) is called *Laurent's expansion.*[15] In case the function $f(t)$ is analytic everywhere inside C, including the point a, then the coefficients A_{-q} of the negative power terms in Eq. (148) all vanish,[16] and Laurent's expansion reduces to a Taylor series. If $f(t)$ is not analytic at a, then the general Laurent expansion must be used. It is generally more difficult to carry through the numerical evaluation of the coefficients of a Laurent expansion than a Taylor series; since the former requires integration as shown in Eq. (149), while the latter is determined by differentiation, which is usually simpler.

---

[15] The part of the function consisting of the constant plus the series in positive powers of $(z-a)$ is called the *regular part* of $f(z)$. The series of inverse power terms is called the *principal part.* Accordingly, a function is the sum of its regular part plus its principal part.

[16] If $f(t)$ is analytic everywhere within the contour C, including the point a, then $(t-a)^q f(t)$ is also analytic and

$$A_{-q} = \frac{1}{2\pi j} \oint (t-a)^q f(t)\,dt = 0$$

5.12. Singular points[17]

If the coefficients of the negative power terms (A_{-1}, A_{-2}, etc.) in the Laurent expansion do not all vanish, then the function is said to have a *singular point*[18] at $z = a$. As z approaches a, each negative-power term whose coefficient does not vanish approaches infinity. If there is only a finite number of nonvanishing coefficients, then the singular point a is called a *pole*.[19] If there is an infinite number of nonvanishing coefficients, the singular point a is called an *essential singularity.*

If a is a *pole*, then the function $f(z)$ may be expanded about a in the form

$$f(z) = \frac{A_{-m}}{(z-a)^m} + \frac{A_{-(m-1)}}{(z-a)^{m-1}} + \cdots + \frac{A_{-1}}{z-a} + A_0 + A_1(z-a) + \cdots + A_n(z-a)^n + \cdots \quad (150)$$

If A_{-m} is the highest order nonvanishing coefficient of the inverse power terms, then a is called a *pole of the m'th order.*[20] As z approaches a pole at a, the absolute value of $f(z)$ approaches infinity, regardless of the manner in which z approaches a. An example of a function having poles is

$$f(z) = \frac{1}{(z+c)(z-c)^2} \quad (151)$$

This function has a pole of the first order at $z = -c$ and a pole of the second order at $z = +c$.

If a is an *essential singularity*, then the function $f(z)$ may be expanded about a in the form

---

[17] Laurent's expansion, since it ultimately depends upon Eq. (118), does not apply to cases in which $f(z)$ has a branch point at $z = a$. Cases of branch points are also excluded from the discussion in §5.12.

[18] If all the coefficients of the negative power terms do vanish at $z = a$, the function is said to have an *ordinary point* at a, sometimes called a *regular point* at a.

[19] It may be shown that if $f(z)$ has a *pole* at $z = a$, then $[1/f(z)]$ has a *regular point* at $z = a$.

[20] If $f(z)$ has a regular point at $z = a$, but is equal to zero there, then $f(z)$ is said to have a zero of the nth order, if all the A coefficients in Eq. (150) vanish up to, but not including, A_n.

$$f(z) = A_0 + A_1(z - a) + \cdots + A_n(z - a)^n + \cdots$$
$$+ \frac{A_{-1}}{z - a} + \frac{A_{-2}}{(z - a)^2} + \cdots + \frac{A_{-m}}{(z - a)^m} + \cdots \quad (152)$$

where the series of the inverse power terms, at least, is an infinite series. The remarkable theorem[21] may be proved that as z approaches an essential singularity a, $f(z)$ may be made to approach any finite or infinite value whatever, chosen at will, by choosing the proper manner for z to approach a. As an example of a function having an essential singularity, we cite

$$\sin\frac{1}{z} = \frac{1}{z} - \frac{1}{3!}\cdot\frac{1}{z^3} + \frac{1}{5!}\cdot\frac{1}{z^5} + \cdots \quad (153)$$

which has an essential singularity at $z = 0$.

5.13. Residues

If a is a regular point of $f(z)$, then as we have shown, the integral of $f(z)$ along a closed contour surrounding a, but not enclosing any singular points, will vanish. On the other hand, if a is a singular point of $f(z)$, then the integral

$$\oint f(z)\,dz$$

along a closed contour surrounding a will not necessarily[22] vanish. Since, however, the integral along every closed contour surrounding a, but no other singular point, will have the same value, according to Eq. (118), its value must be a property only of the function with respect to the singular point, but not of the particular path of integration. We therefore assign a special name to the value of this integral, or rather to the integral divided by $2\pi j$. We call

$$R = \frac{1}{2\pi j}\oint f(z)\,dz \quad (154)$$

---

[21] For a proof, see Goursat-Hedrick, *Functions of a Complex Variable*, Section 42.

[22] Because the real and imaginary components u and v of $f(z)$ do not remain continuous at the singular point a, we cannot say that the closed-contour integral will definitely not vanish, because continuity is required for the theorems in §5.6 to apply.

the *residue* of the function $f(z)$ with respect to the singular point a. We shall find residues to be of great importance in engineering applications.

We will now show that the residue R is equal to the coefficient A_{-1} of the Laurent expansion. To show this, let us express $f(z)$ in terms of its Laurent expansion. Accordingly

$$f(z) = A_0 + A_1(z - a) + \cdots + A_n(z - a)^n + \cdots + \frac{A_{-1}}{z - a} + \frac{A_{-2}}{(z - a)^2} + \cdots + \frac{A_{-m}}{(z - a)^m} + \cdots \qquad (155)$$

Now at every point on the actual path of integration, the series (155) is uniformly convergent and equal to $f(z)$. It can therefore be integrated term by term. When this is done, the integral of each term for which n is zero or positive vanishes because the integrand is analytic everywhere within the contour. If n is negative, and not (-1), then the terms vanish by application of Eq. (134). Therefore,

$$\oint A_n(z - a)^n\,dz = 0 \qquad (n \neq -1) \qquad (156)$$

and[23]

$$\oint \frac{A_{-1}}{z - a}\,dz = 2\pi j A_{-1} \qquad (157)$$

according to Eq. (131).

Consequently,

$$\oint f(z)\,dz = 2\pi j A_{-1} \qquad (158)$$

and therefore,

$$A_{-1} = R = \text{the residue of } f(z) \text{ with respect to the singular point } a. \qquad (159)$$

The residue of a function with respect to a singular point is thus the A_{-1} coefficient of its Laurent expansion.

If a is a pole of the mth order for $f(z)$, then the product

$$(z - a)^m f(z) \qquad (160)$$

has a regular point at a, and can therefore be expanded about a in a Taylor series. The coefficient of $(z - a)^{m-1}$ in the Taylor expansion of the expression (160) will then clearly be the residue of $f(z)$ with

[23] See Fig. 5-6(B).

respect to the point a. This is often a convenient method of finding residues.

Suppose $f(z)$ is of the form

$$f(z) = \frac{P(z)}{Q(z)} \tag{161}$$

where both $Q(z)$ and $P(z)$ are regular at the point a. Suppose also that $f(z)$ has a *pole* at a, and that $Q(a) = 0$ and $P(a) \neq 0$. Then it is easy to show that the residue of $f(z)$ with respect to a is[24]

$$\frac{P(a)}{Q'(a)} \tag{162}$$

where $Q'(z)$ is $\frac{d}{dz}[Q(z)]$.

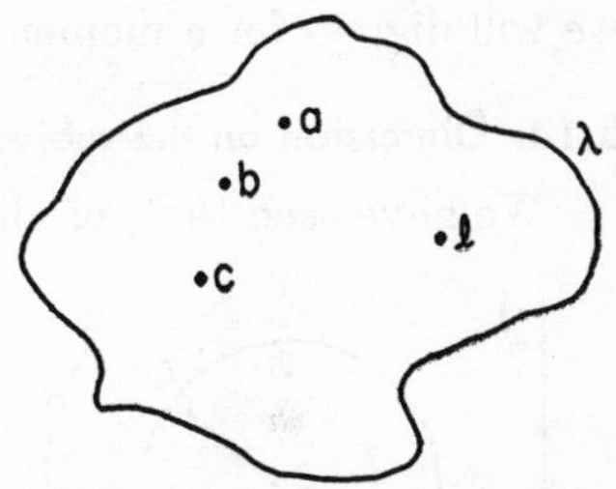

FIG. 5-17. The contour λ within which lie the singular points, $a, b, c \text{---} l$.

Consider next a function $f(z)$ which is analytic along a closed contour λ and has in the interior of the contour λ a finite number of singular points, $a, b \text{---} l$, respectively (see Fig. 5-17). Let $A, B, \text{---} L$, be the corresponding residues at these singular points. Then, by Eqs. (120) and (154),

$$\oint_\lambda f(z)\,dz = 2\pi j(A + B + \text{---} + L) \tag{163}$$

Stating Eq. (163) in words, we have the theorem:

---

[24] To find the residue of $P(z)/Q(z)$ at $z = a$, where $Q(a) = 0$ and $P(a) \neq 0$, take the integral

$$\frac{1}{2\pi j}\oint \frac{P(z)}{Q(z)}\,dz$$

around an arbitrarily small circle about $z = a$. Then, since $P(z)$ and $Q(z)$ are both regular at a,

$$P(z) = P(a) + (z - a)P'(a) + \text{---} = P(a)$$

except for infinitesimals, if z remains close enough to a.

$$Q(z) = Q(a) + (z - a)Q'(a) + \text{---} = (z - a)Q'(a)$$

except for infinitesimals of higher order. Consequently,

$$\text{residue of } \frac{P(z)}{Q(z)} \text{ at } a = \frac{1}{2\pi j}\oint \frac{P(z)}{Q(z)}\,dz = \frac{1}{2\pi j}\frac{P(a)}{Q'(a)}\oint \frac{dz}{z - a} = \frac{P(a)}{Q'(a)}$$

The integral $\oint_\lambda f(z)\,dz$ *of* $f(z)$ *taken in a counterclockwise direction along the closed contour* λ *is equal to the product of* $2\pi j$ *times the sum of the residues of* $f(z)$ *with respect to the singular points inside* λ.

We are now ready to apply the theory of residues to the evaluation of real definite integrals. In later chapters, we shall apply it in the study of transformation calculus. However, the subject of residues is of such great importance in engineering problems, that we will digress for a moment to consider it more closely.

5.14. Digression on the subject of residues

We have seen that, of all the terms in the Laurent expansion of $f(z)$, only the term

$$\frac{A_{-1}}{z-a}$$

contributes to the closed-contour integral

$$\oint f(z)\,dz$$

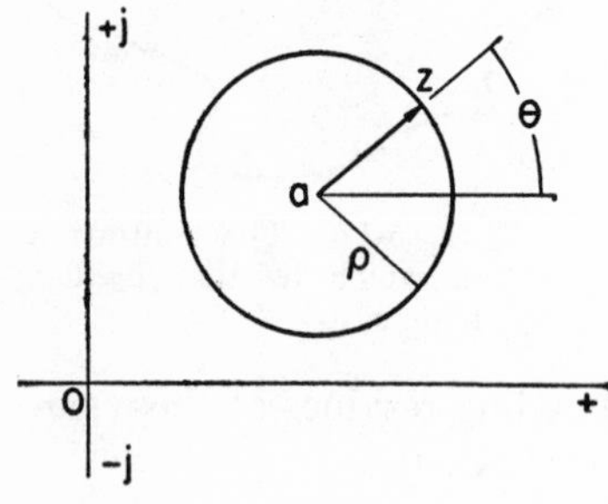

FIG. 5-18. A circular contour of integration.

To get a clearer insight into what is happening, let us choose a circular contour of radius ρ, with its center at a, as the path of integration (see Fig. 5-18). Let θ be the angle that the vector $z - a$ makes with the axis of reals. Then

$$z - a = \rho(\cos\theta + j\sin\theta) = \rho\epsilon^{j\theta} \tag{164}$$

and

$$dz = \rho(-\sin\theta + j\cos\theta)\,d\theta = j\rho\epsilon^{j\theta}\,d\theta \tag{165}$$

Therefore,

$$\oint \frac{A_{-1}}{z-a}\,dz = \oint_{\theta_0}^{\theta_0+2\pi} \frac{A_{-1}\rho(-\sin\theta + j\cos\theta)}{\rho(\cos\theta + j\sin\theta)}\,d\theta$$

$$= \int_{\theta_0}^{\theta_0+2\pi} A_{-1}j\,d\theta = j2\pi A_{-1} \tag{166}$$

and if $n \neq -1$,

$$\oint A_n(z-a)^n\,dz = \int_{\theta_0}^{\theta_0+2\pi} A_n\rho^n(\cos\theta + j\sin\theta)^n \rho(-\sin\theta + j\cos\theta)\,d\theta$$

$$= A_n\rho^{n+1} \int_{\theta_0}^{\theta_0+2\pi} [-\sin (n+1)\theta + j\cos (n+1)\theta]\, d\theta$$

$$= \frac{A_n\rho^{n+1}}{n+1} \{\cos (n+1)\theta + j \sin (n+1)\theta\} \Big|_{\theta_0}^{\theta_0+2\pi} = 0 \quad (167)$$

Looking at the integrand in Eq. (167), we see that both the real and the imaginary components have equal positive and negative portions during a cycle, giving a net result of zero upon closed-contour integration. In the case of Eq. (166), however, the integrand has the constant value jA_{-1}, so that the integral does not vanish.

The residue of a function with respect to a point is thus analogous to an average value or a d-c component of the function with respect to movement along a circular contour about the point as center.

There is a close analogy to a residue in certain physical problems. Thus if a steady current of strength I is flowing through a straight wire, the magnetic field strength at a distance r from the wire is

$$H = \frac{2I}{r}$$

in a direction concentric with the wire (see Fig. 5-19). The work done in taking a unit magnetic pole around any closed curve in a plane at right angles to the wire is then $4\pi I$, if the curve encloses the wire. If the curve does not enclose the wire, the algebraic value of the work done is zero. The strength of current in this problem is thus analogous to the residue of a function at a singular point.

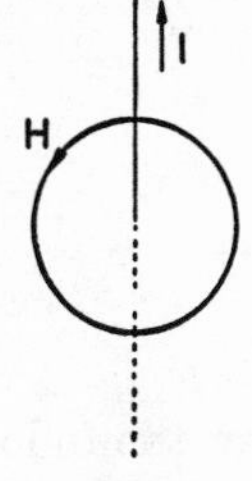

FIG. 5-19. A magnetic flux line encircling a straight wire which conducts electric current.

5.15. The evaluation of real definite integrals by the method of contour integration in the complex plane

With the aid of contour integration in the complex plane, a large number of important real definite integrals can be evaluated, whose value it would be difficult to determine by any other means. The method can best be explained by solving a few actual examples.

Example 1: *Evaluation of*

$$\int_0^\infty \frac{\cos x}{b^2 + x^2}\, dx$$

Consider the function

$$\frac{\epsilon^{jz}}{b^2 + z^2}$$

This function is analytic for finite values of z except at the points

$$z = \pm jb \tag{168}$$

If we integrate the function around the path shown in Fig. 5-20, we

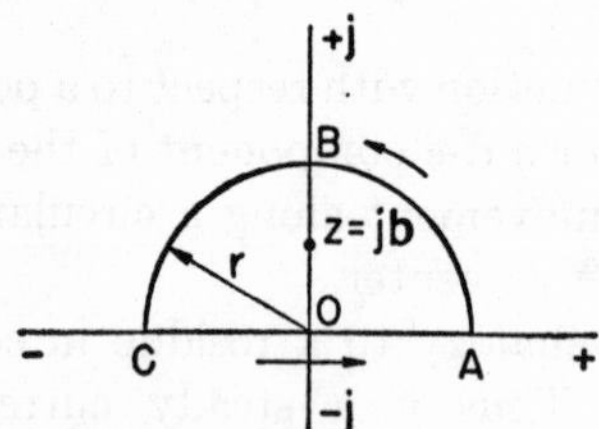

FIG. 5-20. The path of integration in Example 1.

get the following result:

$$\int_{(OA)} \frac{\epsilon^{jz}}{b^2 + z^2}\, dz + \int_{(AC)} \frac{\epsilon^{jz}}{b^2 + z^2}\, dz + \int_{(CO)} \frac{\epsilon^{jz}}{b^2 + z^2}\, dz = 2\pi j R_{jb} \tag{169}$$

where R_{jb} is the residue of the function about the point $z = jb$.

Now along the real axis $z = x$, so that

$$\int_{(OA)} \frac{\epsilon^{jz}}{b^2 + z^2}\, dz = \int_0^r \frac{\epsilon^{jx}}{b^2 + x^2}\, dx \tag{170}$$

and

$$\int_{(CO)} \frac{\epsilon^{jz}}{b^2 + z^2}\, dz = \int_{-r}^0 \frac{\epsilon^{jx}}{b^2 + x^2}\, dx = -\int_r^0 \frac{\epsilon^{-jx'}}{b^2 + x'^2}\, dx'$$

$$= \int_0^r \frac{\epsilon^{-jx'}}{b^2 + x'^2}\, dx' \tag{171}$$

where $x' = -x$.

Furthermore, since a definite integral is not a function of the variable of integration, but only of the end points, it follows that

$$\int_{(CO)} \frac{\epsilon^{jz}}{b^2 + z^2}\, dz = \int_0^r \frac{\epsilon^{-jx'}}{b^2 + x'^2}\, dx' = \int_0^r \frac{\epsilon^{-jx}}{b^2 + x^2}\, dx \tag{172}$$

Along the path (AC), we may write

$$z = r(\cos\theta + j\sin\theta) = r\epsilon^{j\theta} \tag{173}$$

so that

$$\int_{(AC)} \frac{\epsilon^{jz}}{b^2 + z^2}\, dz = \int_0^\pi \frac{(\epsilon^{-r\sin\theta})(\epsilon^{jr\cos\theta})}{b^2 + r^2\epsilon^{j2\theta}}\, jr\epsilon^{j\theta}\, d\theta \tag{174}$$

Now between 0 and π, $\sin\theta$ is always positive, so that

$$\left|\epsilon^{-r\sin\theta}\right| < 1 \tag{175}$$

Furthermore,

$$\left|\epsilon^{jr\cos\theta}\right| = 1 = \left|\epsilon^{j\theta}\right| \tag{176}$$

Now

$$\left|b^2 + r^2\epsilon^{j2\theta}\right| \geq \left|r^2 - b^2\right| \tag{177}$$

for all values of θ.
Therefore, if $r \to \infty$,

$$\left|\int_{(AC)} \frac{\epsilon^{jz}}{b^2 + z^2}\, dz\right| < \left|\int_0^\pi \frac{r}{r^2 - b^2}\, d\phi\right| \to 0 \tag{178}$$

To find R_{jb}, we form the product

$$(z - jb) \cdot \frac{\epsilon^{jz}}{(b^2 + z^2)} = \frac{\epsilon^{jz}}{z + jb} \tag{179}$$

as described by the expression (160). Since the m of Eq. (160) is unity in this case, the residue R_{jb} is the constant term in the Taylor series of

$$\frac{\epsilon^{jz}}{z + jb}$$

expanded about the point $z = jb$. Thus

$$R_{jb} = \frac{\epsilon^{j(jb)}}{jb + jb} = \frac{\epsilon^{-b}}{j2b} \tag{180}$$

Substituting Eqs. (180), (178), (172), and (170) into Eq. (169), and letting $r \to \infty$, we get

$$\int_0^\infty \frac{\epsilon^{jx} + \epsilon^{-jx}}{b^2 + x^2}\,dx = \int_0^\infty \frac{2\cos x\,dx}{b^2 + x^2} = \frac{\pi\epsilon^{-b}}{b} \tag{181}$$

Therefore,

$$\int_0^\infty \frac{\cos x}{b^2 + x^2}\,dx = \frac{\pi\epsilon^{-b}}{2b} \tag{182}$$

which is the desired result. This integral was used in §4.9.

Example 2: *Evaluation of*

$$\int_0^\infty \frac{\sin x}{x}\,dx$$

Consider the function

$$\frac{\epsilon^{jz}}{z}$$

This function is analytic for finite values of z, except at the point

$$z = 0$$

Let us integrate the function about the path $(ABMB'A'NA)$ as shown in Fig. 5-21. Let ρ be the radius of the inner circle and r be

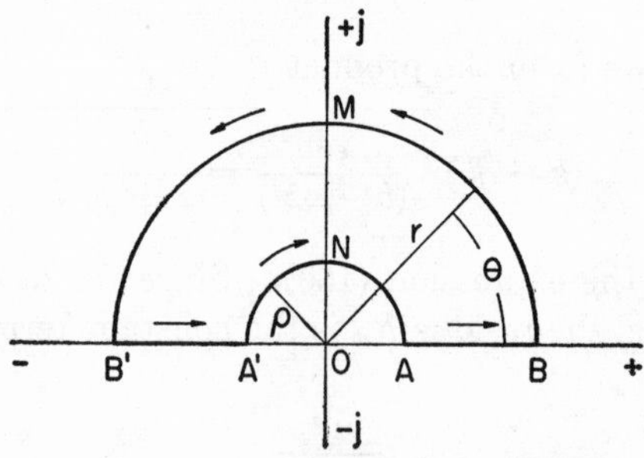

FIG. 5-21. The path of integration in Example 2.

the radius of the outer circle. Since this path encloses no singular point, the closed-contour integral vanishes. Therefore

$$\int_\rho^r \frac{\epsilon^{jx}}{x}\,dx + \int_{(BMB')} \frac{\epsilon^{jz}}{z}\,dz + \int_{-r}^{-\rho} \frac{\epsilon^{jx}}{x}\,dx + \int_{(A'NA)} \frac{\epsilon^{jz}}{z}\,dz = 0 \tag{183}$$

Now

$$\int_{-r}^{-\rho} \frac{\epsilon^{jx}}{x}\,dx = \int_{r}^{\rho} \frac{\epsilon^{-jx'}}{x'}\,dx' = -\int_{\rho}^{r} \frac{\epsilon^{-jx'}}{x'}\,dx' = -\int_{\rho}^{r} \frac{\epsilon^{-jx}}{x}\,dx \qquad (184)$$

in a manner similar to the derivation of Eq. (172).

Along the path (BMB')

$$z = r(\cos\theta + j\sin\theta) = r\epsilon^{j\theta} \qquad (185)$$

$$dz = jr\epsilon^{j\theta}\,d\theta \qquad (186)$$

Therefore,

$$\left|\int_{(BMB')} \frac{\epsilon^{jz}}{z}\,dz\right| = \left|\int_0^{\pi} \frac{\epsilon^{jr(\cos\theta + j\sin\theta)}}{r\epsilon^{j\theta}}\,jr\epsilon^{j\theta}\,d\theta\right|$$

$$= \left|\int_0^{\pi} j(\epsilon^{-r\sin\theta})\epsilon^{jr\cos\theta}\,d\theta\right|$$

$$< \int_0^{\pi} \epsilon^{-r\sin\theta}\,d\theta = 2\int_0^{\pi/2} \epsilon^{-r\sin\theta}\,d\theta \qquad (187)$$

Now

$$\sin\theta \geq \frac{2}{\pi}\theta \qquad (188)$$

for all values of θ between zero and $\pi/2$. Consequently,

$$2\int_0^{\pi/2} \epsilon^{-r\sin\theta}\,d\theta < 2\int_0^{\pi/2} \epsilon^{-r(2\theta/\pi)}\,d\theta = \left.\frac{\epsilon^{-r(2\theta/\pi)}}{(-r/\pi)}\right|_0^{\pi/2}$$

$$= \frac{\pi}{r}[1 - \epsilon^{-r}] \qquad (189)$$

and if $r \to \infty$

$$\int_{(BMB')} \frac{\epsilon^{jz}}{z}\,dz \to 0 \qquad (190)$$

Along the path $(A'NA)$ we expand the integrand in a Laurent series. Thus

$$\frac{\epsilon^{jz}}{z} = \frac{1}{z}[1 + jz + (jz)^2 + \text{---}]$$

$$= \frac{1}{z} + P(z) \qquad (191)$$

where $P(z)$ is analytic at the origin.

Therefore
$$\int_{(A'NA)} \frac{\epsilon^{jz}}{z} \, dz = \int_{(A'NA)} \frac{dz}{z} + \int_{(A'NA)} P(z) \, dz$$
$$= \int_{\pi}^{0} \frac{j\rho\epsilon^{j\theta} \, d\theta}{\rho\epsilon^{j\theta}} + \int_{(A'NA)} P(z) \, dz$$
$$= -j\pi + \int_{(A'NA)} P(z) \, dz \tag{192}$$

since
$$z = \rho\epsilon^{j\theta} \tag{193}$$
and
$$dz = j\rho\epsilon^{j\theta} \, d\theta \tag{194}$$

along the path $(A'NA)$.

Let K be the maximum value of $P(z)$ on the semicircle of radius ρ. Then

$$\left| \int_{(A'NA)} P(z) \, dz \right| \leq \pi\rho K \tag{195}$$

Consequently, if $\rho \to 0$,

$$\int_{(A'NA)} P(z) \, dz \to 0$$

and
$$\int_{(A'NA)} \frac{\epsilon^{jz}}{z} \, dz = -j\pi \tag{196}$$

Therefore, if we let $r \to \infty$ and $\rho \to 0$, Eq. (183) becomes

$$\int_0^\infty \frac{\epsilon^{jx} - \epsilon^{-jx}}{x} \, dx - j\pi = 0 \tag{197}$$

or
$$\int_0^\infty \frac{\sin x}{x} \, dx = \frac{\pi}{2} \tag{198}$$

This is an important result. It is used in studying the unit-step function.

The two examples just worked out are typical of the contour-integration method of evaluating definite integrals. The general principle involved is to use contour integration to transform a definite integral whose value cannot readily be determined into quantities whose value can be determined. There is no prescribed method of procedure. Experience, and especially ingenuity, are the most important guides.[25]

Exercises

Evaluate the following definite integrals—(Goursat)

1.
$$\int_0^\infty \frac{\sin mx\, dx}{x(x^2 + a^2)^2}$$

where m and a are real.

2.
$$\int_{-\infty}^{+\infty} \frac{\cos ax}{1 + x^4}\, dx$$

where a is real.

3.
$$\int_0^\infty \frac{\cos ax - \cos bx}{x^2}\, dx$$

where a and b are real and positive.

5.16 The analytical extension theorem

We next wish to prove an important theorem: *If two analytic functions are equal for a finite length along any arc in a region in which both are analytic, then they are equal everywhere in the region.*

For convenience in reference, we shall call this theorem the *analytical extension theorem.* The name is appropriate because the proof is carried out by a process known as analytical extension (or analytical continuation).

To prove the theorem, let us call the functions $f_1(z)$ and $f_2(z)$, and let us suppose that they are equal along the finite arc (ab) in Fig. 5-22. Let us further suppose that both functions are analytical in the region R except in a few areas which are removed from R by shading. We can then expand both $f_1(z)$ and $f_2(z)$ about the point a in Taylor series. Thus

$$f_1(z) = f_1(a) + (z - a)f_1'(a) + \frac{(z - a)^2}{2!}f_1''(a) + \cdots \quad (199)$$

and
$$f_2(z) = f_2(a) + (z - a)f_2'(a) + \frac{(z - a)^2}{2!}f_2''(a) + \cdots \quad (200)$$

---

[25] Another example of the evaluation of integrals by contour integration will be found in §8.6, where the Fourier transform of the Gaussian error function is evaluated.

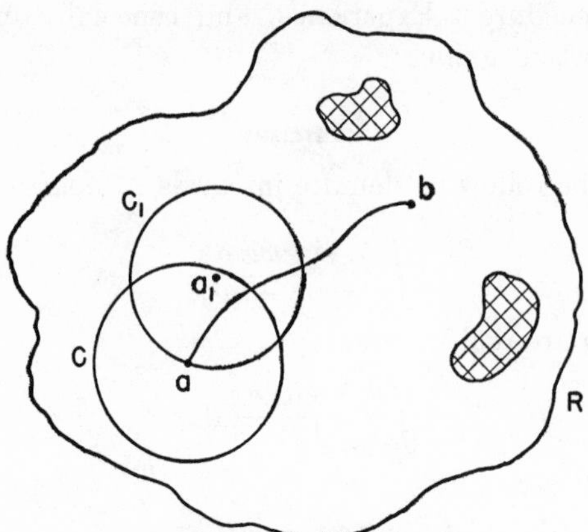

FIG. 5-22. Contours used in deriving the analytical extension theorem.

Now by hypothesis the functions are equal along a finite length of the arc (ab). Their derivatives of all orders must consequently be equal along this arc. Since the derivative of an analytic function is independent of direction, and since the derivative is another analytic function, it follows that

$$\left.\begin{aligned} f_1(a) &= f_2(a) \\ f_1'(a) &= f_2'(a) \\ f_1''(a) &= f_2''(a) \\ f_1^n(a) &= f_2^n(a) \end{aligned}\right\} \tag{201}$$

for all directions about a, since these expressions are equal along the arc (ab). The coefficients of (199) and (200) are thus equal. It follows that

$$f_1(z) = f_2(z) \tag{202}$$

everywhere within any circle C, which is smaller than the circle of convergence of the above power series.

Let us next choose a point a_1, near the edge of C, and let us expand $f_1(z)$ and $f_2(z)$ in Taylor series about a_1. Thus

$$f_1(z) = f_1(a_1) + (z - a_1)f_1'(a_1) + \frac{(z - a_1)^2}{2!} f_1''(a_1) + \cdots \tag{203}$$

$$f_2(z) = f_2(a_1) + (z - a_1)f_2'(a_1) + \frac{(z - a_1)^2}{2!} f_2''(a_1) + \cdots \tag{204}$$

Since $f_1(z)$ and $f_2(z)$ are equal along an arc between a_1 and a, it follows as before that

$$\left.\begin{array}{l} f_1(a_1) = f_2(a_1) \\ \vdots \qquad\quad \vdots \\ f_1^n(a_1) = f_2^n(a_1) \end{array}\right\} \tag{205}$$

The coefficients of Eqs. (203) and (204) are thus identical. It follows that $f_1(z)$ and $f_2(z)$ are therefore equal everywhere within C_1, the circle of convergence of this series. If we proceed in this manner we can extend the region of proved equality of $f_1(z)$ and $f_2(z)$ to the entire area in which both functions are analytic. Thus the theorem is proved.

The analytical extension theorem is very useful in many applications. In practice, the original arc of equality is usually the real axis, or a portion of it. We shall now apply the theorem to a few examples.

Example 1: Suppose $\sin^2 z$ and $\cos^2 z$ are defined in such a way that they agree with the ordinary definition of the sine and cosine when z is real. Suppose, further, that $\sin^2 z$ and $\cos^2 z$ are analytic, except for a finite number of singular points, in any finite portion of the complex plane. Now on the real axis

$$\sin^2 x = 1 - \cos^2 x \tag{206}$$

It follows that

$$\sin^2 z = 1 - \cos^2 z \tag{207}$$

at all points in the complex plane at which $\sin^2 z$ and $\cos^2 z$ are analytic.

Example 2: Suppose $f_1(z)$ is a function which is analytic except for a finite number of singular points in any finite portion of the complex plane. Suppose, further, that

$$f_1(z) = f_2(x) \tag{208}$$

everywhere along the real axis. Then if $f_2(x)$ has the power series expansion

$$f_2(x) = a_0 + a_1 x + a_2 x^2 + \cdots \tag{209}$$

for real values of x, then $f_1(z)$ must have the power series expansion

$$f_1(z) = a_0 + a_1(z) + a_2 z^2 + \cdots \tag{210}$$

with the same coefficients as Eq. (209), at all points in the complex plane where the series Eq. (210) converges.

This example shows why the power series expansion of a function of a real variable can be used to extend the definition of a function to the complex plane.

5.17. Conformal representation—branch points—Riemann surfaces[26]

(a) Conformal Representation. We will next briefly extend our study of the graphical representation of functions of a complex

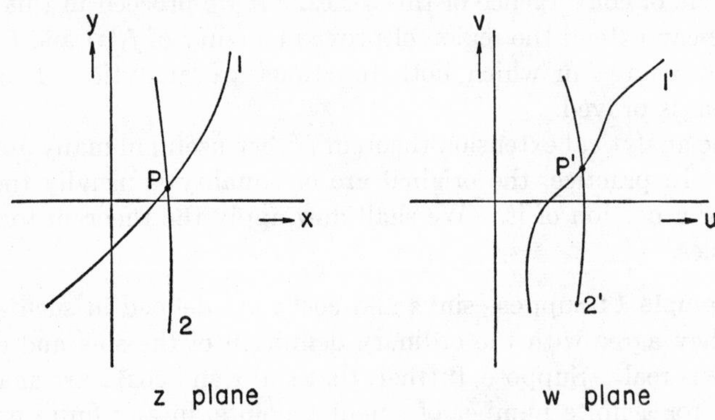

FIG. 5-23. Illustration of conformal transformation, showing a pair of curves transformed from the z plane to the w plane and having the same angle of intersection in both planes.

variable begun in §5.2. We will first consider the matter of conformal representation. Let

$$z = x + jy \tag{211}$$

and

$$w = u + jv \tag{211-A}$$

be complex variables, and let

$$w = f(z) \tag{212}$$

In §5.2, it was pointed out that any curve in the z plane is transformed into a corresponding curve in the w plane by Eq. (212). Now suppose we draw two intersecting curves in the z plane, and the corresponding curves in the w plane (see Fig. 5-23). We will

[26] For an excellent discussion of the subjects of conformal representation and Riemann surfaces, which are only touched upon here, the reader is referred to E. J. Townsend, *Functions of a Complex Variable*, Chaps. IV and VIII.

now show that the angle of intersection of the two curves in the z plane is the same as the angle of intersection between the ccr-responding curves in the w plane, unless P is a singular point of $f(z)$. Since angles of intersection are preserved in transforming curves from the z plane to the w plane or vice versa, the w plane is said to give an *isogonal* or *conformal representation* of the z plane.

The proof of equality of angles will now be given. Consider the curves 1 and 2 of the z plane intersecting at P, and the corresponding curves 1′ and 2′ of the w plane intersecting at P', obtained by the transformation Eq. (212). It is clear that the point of intersection P must be transformed into the point of intersection P' by Eq. (212) since these points are the points of equality of both curves in their corresponding planes. Now if Δz_1 and Δz_2 are small increments starting from P along the curves 1 and 2, and if we express Δz_1 and Δz_2 in polar form,

$$\Delta z_1 = |\Delta z_1| \epsilon^{j\phi_{\Delta z_1}} \tag{213}$$

and

$$\Delta z_2 = |\Delta z_2| \epsilon^{j\phi_{\Delta z_2}} \tag{214}$$

Then if Δz_2 and Δz_1 are made infinitesimally small,

$$\lim_{\substack{\Delta z_2 \to 0 \\ \Delta z_1 \to 0}} \{\phi_{\Delta z_2} - \phi_{\Delta z_1}\} = \text{angle of intersection of curves 1 and 2} \tag{215}$$

Similarly, in the w plane

$$\Delta w_1 = |\Delta w_1| \epsilon^{j\phi_{\Delta w_1}} \tag{216}$$

$$\Delta w_2 = |\Delta w_2| \epsilon^{j\phi_{\Delta w_2}} \tag{217}$$

and

$$\lim_{\substack{\Delta w_2 \to 0 \\ \Delta w_1 \to 0}} \{\phi_{\Delta w_2} - \phi_{\Delta w_1}\} = \text{angle of intersection of curves 1' and 2'} \tag{218}$$

From Eqs. (213) and (217) it follows that

$$\frac{\Delta w_1}{\Delta z_1} = \left|\frac{\Delta w_1}{\Delta z_1}\right| \epsilon^{j(\phi_{\Delta w_1} - \phi_{\Delta z_1})} \tag{220}$$

However, if we express $\Delta w_1/\Delta z_1$ in polar form directly, we have

$$\frac{\Delta w_1}{\Delta z_1} = \left|\frac{\Delta w_1}{\Delta z_1}\right| \epsilon^{j\phi\left(\frac{\Delta w_1}{\Delta z_1}\right)} \tag{221}$$

From Eqs. (220) and (221) it follows that

$$\phi_{\Delta w_1} - \phi_{\Delta z_1} = \phi_{\left(\frac{\Delta w_1}{\Delta z_1}\right)} \tag{222}$$

In a similar manner, we could also show that

$$\phi_{\Delta w_2} - \phi_{\Delta z_2} = \phi_{\left(\frac{\Delta w_2}{\Delta z_2}\right)} \tag{223}$$

Since w is an analytic function of z, we know from §5.3 that dw/dz is the same in all directions. Consequently, as the increments become vanishingly small,

$$\phi_{\left(\frac{\Delta w_2}{\Delta z_2}\right)} = \phi_{\left(\frac{\Delta w_1}{\Delta z_1}\right)} \tag{224}$$

Therefore,
$$\phi_{\Delta w_1} - \phi_{\Delta z_1} = \phi_{\Delta w_2} - \phi_{\Delta z_2}$$
or
$$\phi_{\Delta w_2} - \phi_{\Delta w_1} = \phi_{\Delta z_2} - \phi_{\Delta z_1} \tag{225}$$

provided only that P is a *regular* point of $f(z)$. Thus, the angle of intersection between curves 1 and 2 is equal to the angle of intersection between curves 1′ and 2′. It should be noted that these angles are not only equal in magnitude, but are also of the same sign, so that the direction of rotation from 1 to 2 is the same as the direction of rotation from 1′ to 2′.

As an example of conformal representation, we refer to Fig. 5-3 and note that the x and y coordinate lines which intersect at right angles in the z plane transform into other curves which intersect at right angles in the w plane. Furthermore the direction of rotation between the x and y coordinate lines is retained.

(b) Multiple-Valued Functions—Branch Points and Riemann Surfaces. If z is a multiple-valued function of w, such as

$$z = \sqrt{w} \qquad \text{or} \qquad z = \log w \qquad \text{or} \qquad z = \sin^{-1} w \tag{226}$$

then the previous discussion still applies in general, but a certain amount of clarification is required. Consider the function

$$z = \sqrt[3]{w} \tag{227}$$

and let us express z and w in polar form

$$w = r(\cos\phi + j\sin\phi) \tag{228}$$

$$z = R(\cos\theta + j\sin\theta) \tag{229}$$

Substituting Eqs. (228) and (229) into Eq. (227), we obtain

$$R(\cos\theta + j\sin\theta) = r^{\frac{1}{3}}\left[\cos\left(\frac{\phi}{3}\right) + j\sin\left(\frac{\phi}{3}\right)\right] \tag{230}$$

or
$$R = r^{\frac{1}{3}} \quad \text{and} \quad \theta = \frac{\phi}{3} \tag{231}$$

According to Eq. (231), the entire w plane can be transformed into any one of the three regions marked I, II, or III in the z plane of Fig. 5-24. In this case, the region I corresponds to the w plane for ϕ between 0 and 2π, while the region II corresponds to ϕ between 2π and 4π, and the region III corresponds to ϕ between 4π and 6π.

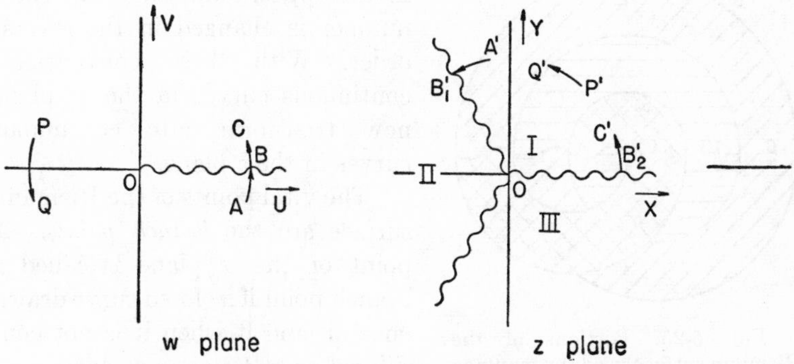

FIG. 5-24. Transformation of the curves PQ and ABC from the w plane to the z plane by the transformation $z = \sqrt[3]{w}$.

If ϕ is between 6π and 8π, we come back to the region I in the z plane, after which the process continues in an obvious manner. This triple presentation, however, has a flaw from the viewpoint of transforming curves from the w plane to the z plane. If we try to transform a curve, such as AB which crosses the demarcation line OU, the corresponding curve in the region I of the z plane will not be a single curve, but rather will be two segments $A'B_1'$, and $B_2'C'$.

To avoid this difficulty, the idea of a *Riemann surface* is introduced. A Riemann surface is an idealized representation of a plane into a number of superimposed sheets for the purpose of allowing a multiple-valued function to have most of the geometrical transformation properties of a single-valued function. In the case of Fig. 5-24, the w plane may be considered a Riemann surface.

This surface consists of 3 sheets which we can mark I, II, and III to correspond with the regions of the z plane. Whenever the positive real axis of w is crossed by a continuous curve, the curve goes from one sheet to another. If the w plane is a Riemann surface, the curve ABC in Fig. 5-24 is not a continuous curve in the w plane (if its transform lies entirely in region I of the z plane) but is two segments, AB and BC. It is therefore not surprising that it transforms into the two segments $A'B_1'$ and $B_2'C'$. If the positive real axis of w is crossed by a continuous curve in a counterclockwise direction, the sheet number is changed in the cyclical order, I, II, III, I, II, III, I, etc. If the crossing takes place in the opposite direction, the sheet number is changed in the reverse order. With these conventions, continuous curves in the w plane now transform into continuous curves in the z plane.

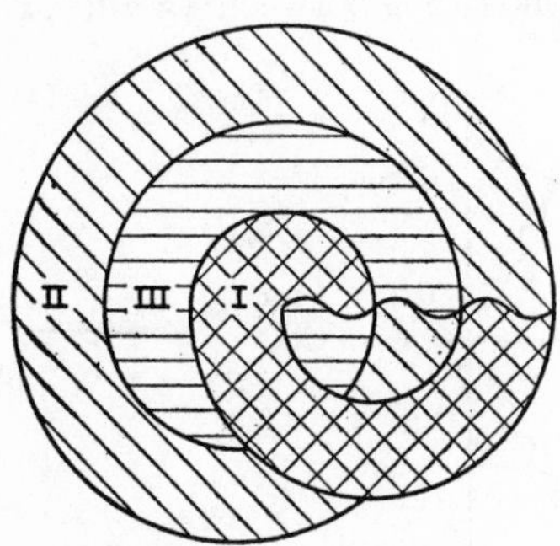

FIG. 5-25. Portions of the Riemann surface used for mapping the values of w corresponding to the transformation $w = z^3$.

The vital points of the Riemann surface are the *branch points*. A point of the w plane is called a branch point if a closed curve drawn once around it when it is not considered as a Riemann surface, does not transform into a closed curve in the z plane. Thus the point O of the w plane in Fig. 5-24 is a branch point. In order to prevent encircling of a branch point, we draw through it a demarcation line called a *branch cut*, and in the Riemann surface representation we consider that a line goes from one sheet to another of the Riemann surface if it crosses the branch cut. The positive part of the real axis of the w plane in Fig. 5-24 is a branch cut. The choice of the branch cuts is arbitrary, so long as they go through the branch points. Thus, in the w plane of Fig. 5-24 we might, for example, have chosen the negative half of the real axis as the branch cut. If we had done so, the regions in the z plane would have been rotated 60° from their present position, but the transformation of curves from the w plane to the z plane would be just as satisfactory, provided that the w plane is considered a Riemann surface. Furthermore, the branch cuts can be curved lines just as well as straight ones. A diagram of a portion of the Riemann surface of the w plane is shown in Fig. 5-25.

We conclude our very brief discussion of multiple-valued functions and Riemann surfaces by pointing out that if Riemann surfaces are used to obtain one-to-one correspondence between the values of the dependent and independent variables w and z, then there is conformal transformation of intersecting curves, provided only that the curves do not go through a branch point or a singular point.

If the relation between z and w is any multiple-valued relation, not necessarily that of Eq. (227), and if an open curve in the z plane

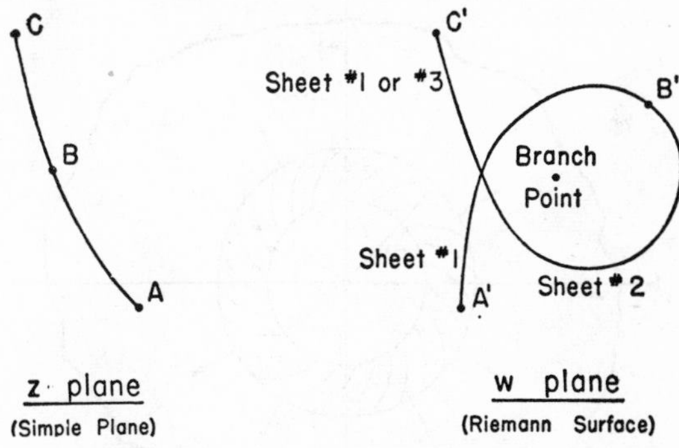

FIG. 5-26. Passage between sheets of a Riemann surface.

transforms into a curve in the w plane which includes a closed loop, then there must always be a branch point within the loop. Consequently, as the curve crosses the point where the loop is closed, we may consider that it enters a different sheet of the Riemann surface. This is illustrated in Fig. 5-26.

5.18. The point at infinity

The behavior of an analytic function $f(z)$ of a complex variable z as z approaches infinity is such that one may, in many ways, consider the entire infinite region as a single point in the complex plane. Thus, we will now show that as $z \to \infty$ in any direction whatever, the function $f(z)$ will have either a regular point at infinity, or a pole, or an essential singularity. In order to simplify our demonstration, we will assume that the function is regular for all *finite* values of z whose absolute value is greater than some value R. Then if we choose $R' > R$ (see Fig. 5-27), the function $f(z)$ can be expanded in the Laurent expansion

$$f(z) = \sum_{n=-\infty}^{+\infty} A_n z^n \tag{232}$$

in the region between the circles centered at the origin and of radius R and R', respectively. Since $f(z)$ has no singularity for any finite

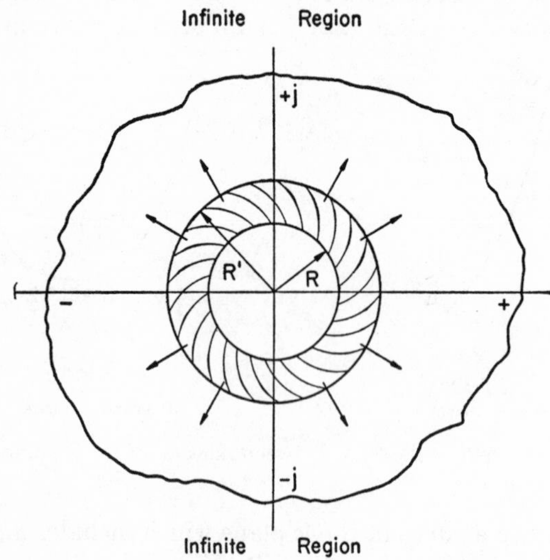

FIG. 5-27. An expanding circle R' approaching the infinite region.

value of z of absolute value greater than R, we can increase R' indefinitely, so that the expansion (232) is valid all the way out to, but not including, infinity. As $z \to \infty$, we will then say that

(1) $f(z)$ has a regular point at infinity if all the coefficients in Eq. (232) vanish for $n > 0$.

(2) $f(z)$ has a pole at infinity if only a finite number of coefficients in Eq. (232) do not vanish, for positive values of n. The order of the pole is then the largest value of n among the coefficients which do not vanish.

(3) $f(z)$ has an essential singularity at infinity if an infinite number of coefficients in Eq. (232) do not vanish for positive values of n.

The practical utility of talking about the point at infinity arises from the fact that a number of important functions have regular points and a number have poles at infinity. This is especially true of functions used in circuit theory.

In case a function $f(z)$ has a regular point at infinity, the function can be expanded in the inverse power series

$$f(z) = A_0 + \frac{A_{-1}}{z} + \frac{A_{-2}}{z^2} + \cdots + \frac{A_{-n}}{z^n} + \cdots \tag{233}$$

This expansion will be useful in finding relations between attenuation and phase characteristics of network functions.

5.19. Further discussion of functions of a complex variable

In the foregoing chapter we have given an introduction to the theory of functions of a complex variable, covering those topics which will be useful in our later work. We shall use these especially in further developments in transformation calculus and transient analysis. Both complex quantities and the theory of functions of a complex variable have numerous other applications in mathematics and physics.

The importance and wide field of application of complex quantities is indeed surprising, since, as the terminology implies, they do seem like an imaginary creation of man. Nevertheless, the properties of these quantities and especially of their analytic functions constitute some of the most remarkable and useful phenomena of mathematics. Because of this, we wish briefly to look further into the nature and foundations of these phenomena.

Probably the most remarkable single fact about functions of a complex variable is that, although we might naturally anticipate that the laws governing them would be more complicated than those governing real variables, they are often actually simpler. For example, every algebraic equation of the nth degree, with n complex coefficients, has n complex roots. No correspondingly simple rule holds for real quantities. Furthermore, all powers and roots of complex quantities exist as complex quantities. The same cannot be said for real quantities; i.e., not all powers and roots of real quantities exist as real quantities.

As another example, every function having a single-valued derivative in the complex plane can be expanded in a Taylor series, but the corresponding rule has exceptions in the case of real variables.[27] Numerous other examples could also be cited. Thus it appears in a way as though variables and functions behave more simply and naturally if they are allowed to range over complex values than if they are restricted to values that are real.

In looking for a reason for the more "natural" behavior of complex variables, we are struck with their rotational properties; i.e., their properties related to variation along closed contours. No corresponding properties exist for real variables, for they are restricted to variation along the real axis. Thus, there is nothing for real variables corresponding to the Cauchy-integral formula

$$f(z) = \frac{1}{2\pi j} \oint \frac{f(t)\,dt}{t - z}$$

for complex variables. There is consequently no such simple systematic theory of singular points and residues for real variables as there is for the complex variable case.

In the case of a function of a complex variable, if it has a derivative which is the same in all directions, then its components satisfy the Cauchy-Riemann equations, its line integral about any closed contour vanishes, and it can be expanded in a Taylor series. In fact, any function having any one of these properties, must also have all the others. This is a systematic relationship between the properties of functions which is largely tied in with their rotational and directional properties. Functions of real variables have no adequate counterpart.

It has sometimes been remarked that the study of an analytic function

$$w = f(z) = u + jv$$

of a complex variable

$$z = x + jy$$

---

[27] For example, ϵ^{-1/x^2} cannot be expanded in a Taylor series in x, even though *all* of its derivatives are single-valued and continuous at $x = 0$. The corresponding function ϵ^{-1/z^2} has an essential singularity at $z = 0$, and therefore has not even a single-valued first derivative.

amounts essentially to the study of a pair of real functions $u(x,y)$ and $v(x,y)$ which satisfy the Cauchy-Riemann equations. While in a sense this is true, the student should not get the impression that the quantity $\sqrt{-1}$ is introduced purely as a convenient and shorthand method of notation. That would be analogous to believing that one can describe a beautiful girl in terms of her weight and dimensions, and other measurable attributes, while ignoring the characteristics of the girl which are due to the over-all combination.[28]

---

[28] The equation

$$\epsilon^{j\pi} = -1$$

has been called the eutectic point of mathematics. This is a very appropriate metaphor, for no matter how you boil down and explain this equation, which relates four of the most remarkable numbers of mathematics, it still has a certain mystery about it that cannot be explained away.

CHAPTER 6

Loci of Complex Functions

6.1. The circle and straight line

In this chapter we shall consider the subject of curves in the complex plane and their application to electrical problems. As a preliminary, we will review some properties of conjugate complex quantities, and will introduce the concept of inversion and the unit circle.[1]

Suppose we have a complex quantity

$$z = x + jy = r(\cos \phi + j \sin \phi) = r\epsilon^{j\phi} \tag{1}$$

Then, its conjugate is defined as

$$z^* = x - jy = r(\cos \phi - j \sin \phi) = r\epsilon^{-j\phi} \tag{2}$$

Furthermore, $$\frac{1}{z} = \frac{1}{r}\,\epsilon^{-j\phi} = \frac{1}{r}\,(\cos \phi - j \sin \phi) \tag{3}$$

and $$\frac{1}{z^*} = \frac{1}{r}\,\epsilon^{j\phi} = \frac{1}{r}\,(\cos \phi + j \sin \phi) \tag{4}$$

These relations are depicted graphically in Fig. 6-1. The amplitudes of z and z^* are equal, and their amplitudes are the reciprocals of those of $1/z^*$ and $1/z$.

Two complex quantities, such as z and $1/z^*$, whose angles are the same but whose amplitudes are reciprocal to each other, are said to be inverse with respect to the unit circle. We note in passing that the amplitude of z is

$$|z| = r = \sqrt{zz^*} \tag{5}$$

and that all complex quantities on the unit circle have an amplitude

[1] Some general relations between complex quantities and their conjugates will be found in the exercises at the end of §6.1. It will be assumed that the reader is acquainted with these relations.

equal to unity. We can therefore define the unit circle by means of the following equation:

$$z \cdot z^* = 1 \tag{6}$$

where z is any point on the unit circle.

Equation (6) suggests that other curves in the complex plane may be expressible in terms of simple equations. This is actually

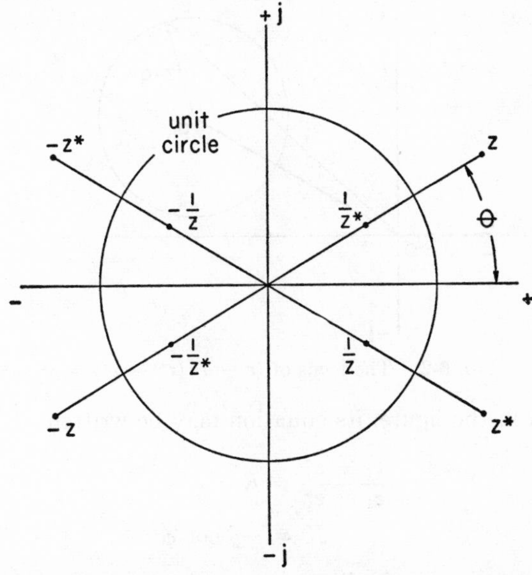

FIG. 6-1. Location of conjugates, reciprocals, and inverse points in the complex plane.

the case. Thus clearly (see Fig. 6-2), any circle of radius ρ about a point a in the complex plane may be expressed as

$$(z - a)(z^* - a^*) = \rho^2 \tag{7}$$

where z is any point on the circle.

Expanding Eq. (7), we obtain

$$zz^* - a^*z - az^* + aa^* - \rho^2 = 0 \tag{8}$$

which may also be written

$$zz^* + Az + A^*z^* + BB^* = 0 \tag{9}$$

where
$$a = -A^* \tag{10}$$
and[2]
$$\rho = \sqrt{AA^* - BB^*} \tag{11}$$

Any of the forms Eqs. (7), (8), or (9) may be considered as the general equation for a circle.

In order to find the equation for a straight line, let us first consider a straight line passing through the origin (see Fig. 6-3). As

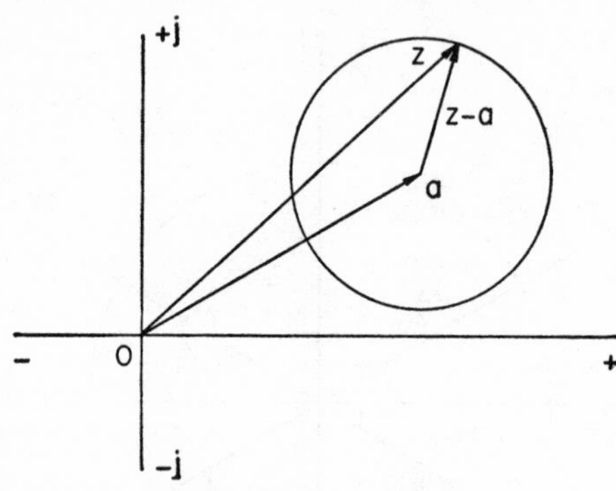

FIG. 6-2. The locus of $(z - a)(z^* - a^*) = \rho^2$.

can be seen in the figure, its equation may be written

$$\frac{z_1 + z_1^*}{z_1 - z_1^*} = K \tag{12}$$

where
$$K = -j \cot \phi \tag{13}$$

and z_1 is any point on the line.

Rewriting Eq. (12) we have

$$z_1(1 - K) + z_1^*(1 + K) = 0 = z_1(1 - K) + z_1^*(1 - K)^* \tag{14}$$

since
$$1 + K = (1 - K)^* \tag{15}$$

The z_1 line will be transformed into the z line, by adding to every z_1 the constant[3]

$$c = C(\sin \phi - j \cos \phi) \tag{16}$$

---

[2] The magnitude of B is fixed by the equation

$$B \cdot B^* = aa^* - \rho^2$$

The phase of B is arbitrary.

[3] More generally, $c = C(\sin \phi - j \cos \phi) + M(\cos \phi + j \sin \phi)$ where M is any real constant.

where C is the perpendicular distance between the lines z_1 and z. If we substitute

$$z = z_1 + c \tag{17}$$

into Eq. (14), we get

$$(z - c)(1 - K) + (z^* - c^*)(1 - K)^* = 0 \tag{18}$$

as the equation for any straight line. Rewriting Eq. (18), we have

$$Az + A^*z^* + BB^* = 0 \tag{19}$$

where
$$A = 1 - K \tag{20}$$

and
$$BB^* = -c(1 - K) - c^*(1 - K)^* \tag{21}$$

Equation (19) may also be considered as a limiting form of Eq. (8) when ρ and a become infinite. For this reason, a straight

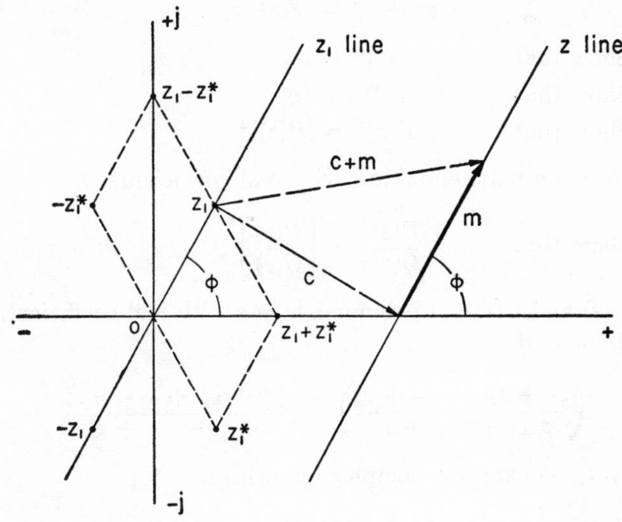

FIG. 6-3. The straight line loci of Eqs. (14), (18), and (19).

line may be considered as a circle of infinite radius. In the remainder of this chapter, when we refer to circles in general we shall wish to include straight lines as a special case.

Exercises

1. If

$$z = x + jy = r\epsilon^{j\phi}$$

is a complex quantity, and

$$z^* = x - jy = r\epsilon^{-j\phi}$$

is its complex conjugate, show that

(a) $zz^* = x^2 + y^2 = r^2$ is a pure real quantity;
(b) $z + z^* = 2x = 2r \cos \phi$ is a pure real quantity;
(c) $z - z^* = j2y = j2r \sin \phi$ is a pure imaginary quantity.

Note that $z \cdot z^*$ is the square of the absolute value of z.

2. If z_1 and z_2 are complex quantities, show that

(a) $$z_1^* \cdot z_2^* = (z_1 \cdot z_2)^*$$

(b) $$\frac{z_1^*}{z_2^*} = \left(\frac{z_1}{z_2}\right)^*$$

(c) $$z_1^* + z_2^* = (z_1 + z_2)^*$$

3. Show that $$(z^*)^* = z$$

4. Show that $$(z^*)^n = (z^n)^*$$

5. Show that $$P(z^*) = [P(z)]^*$$

where $P(z)$ is a polynomial in z with real coefficients.

6. Show that $$\frac{P(z^*)}{Q(z^*)} = \left[\frac{P(z)}{Q(z)}\right]^*$$

where $Q(z)$ and $P(z)$ are polynomials in z with real coefficients.

7. Show that

$$\left(\frac{z_1 + z_2 + \cdots + z_n}{z_{n+1} + \cdots + z_m}\right)^* = \frac{z_1^* + z_2^* + \cdots + z_n^*}{z_{n+1}^* + \cdots + z_m^*}$$

where $z_1, z_2, \cdots$ are any complex quantities.

6.2. Transformations

In certain cases of interest, it may happen that a complex variable w is a function of another complex variable z. Thus in Fig. 6-4, R_1 and R_2 are fixed resistances while z is subject to variation as the capacitance C is varied. The impedance, say w, looking into the network is

$$w = R_1 + \frac{zR_2}{z + R_2} = \frac{(R_1 + R_2)z + R_1R_2}{z + R_2} \tag{22}$$

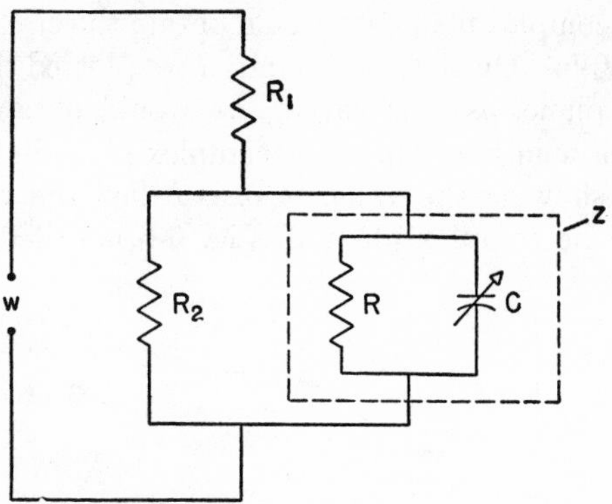

Fig. 6-4. Schematic diagram showing the impedance w as a function of the impedance z.

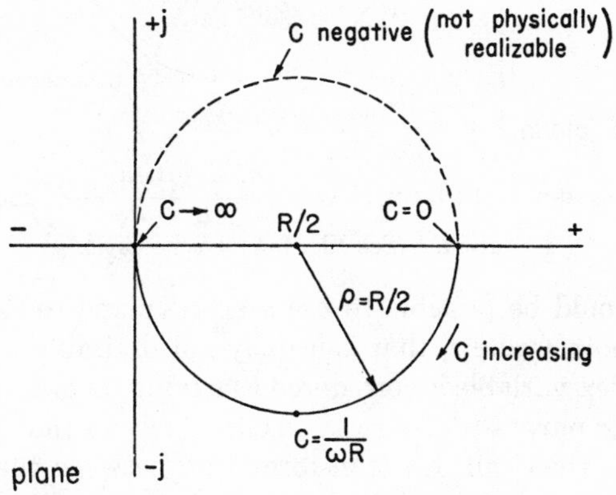

Fig. 6-5. The locus of $z = \dfrac{-jR}{R\omega C - j}$ as C is varied. (See Fig. 6-4 for schematic.)

The complex variable w is therefore a function of the complex variable z in this case.

If now the capacitance C is varied from zero to infinity, and the impedance

$$z = \frac{\dfrac{R}{j\omega C}}{R + \dfrac{1}{j\omega C}} = \frac{-jR}{R\omega C - j} = \frac{R - jR^2\omega C}{R^2\omega^2C^2 + 1} \tag{23}$$

is plotted in a complex plane, we would obtain the circular locus for z shown in Fig. 6-5. On the other hand, if we plotted the values of w in a complex plane, as C is varied, we would obtain the circular locus shown for w in Fig. 6-6. The complex plane in Fig. 6-5, since it is used for showing the value of z, is called the z plane. Correspondingly, the complex plane in Fig. 6-6 is called the w plane.

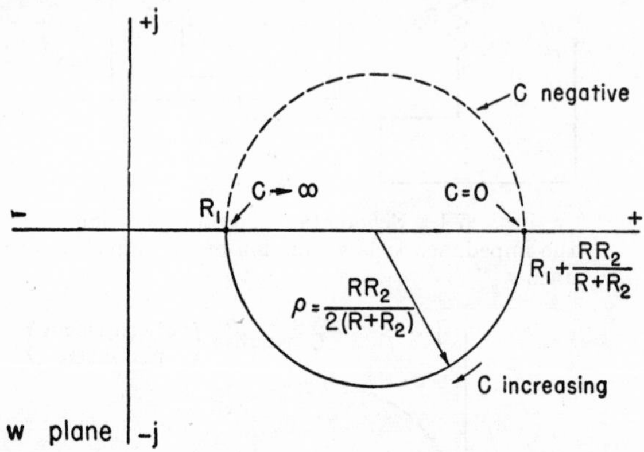

FIG. 6-6. The locus of $w = \dfrac{(R_1 - R_2)z + R_1R_2}{z + R_2}$ as C is varied. (See Fig. 6-4 for schematic.)

While it would be possible to use a single plane to show the locus curves of both w and z, that is usually not desirable. Accordingly, each complex variable is considered as having its own complex plane for plotting purposes. A relationship, such as that expressed by Eq. (22), is then called a transformation between the z plane and the w plane.

The important theorem can easily be proved[4] that the transformation[5]

$$w = \frac{az + b}{cz + d} \tag{24}$$

---

[4] See Exercise 4.

[5] A function such as

$$\frac{az + b}{cz + d}$$

which is linear in z in both the numerator and denominator is called a *bilinear* function of z.

transforms circles in the z plane (including straight lines) into circles in the w plane, where a, b, c, and d are any complex constants whatsoever. Since Eq. (24) can be solved to give

$$z = \frac{-dw + b}{cw - a} \tag{25}$$

the same relation also transforms circles in the w plane into circles in the z plane. As an example, the bilinear transformation, Eq. (22), transforms a circular locus in the z plane into a circular locus in the w plane, as illustrated in Figs. 6-5 and 6-6.

Exercises

1. Find the equation of the circle whose center is at $2 + j3$ and whose radius is 5.

2. Find the equation of the straight line passing through the points $1 + j4$ and $3 + j6$.

3. Prove that

$$\left(\frac{az + b}{cz + d}\right)^* = \frac{a^*z^* + b^*}{c^*z^* + d^*}$$

4. By substituting Eq. (25) into Eq. (9), show with the aid of Exercise 3 that the transformation Eq. (24) transforms circles in the z plane into circles in the w plane.

5. Show that if

$$dd^* - A\,dc^* - A^*d^*c + BB^*cc^* = 0$$

the circle Eq. (9) is transformed into a straight line by Eq. (24).

6.3. Complex functions of real variables—radio circuit examples

If s is a real variable, then the locus of the function

$$z = F(s) = \frac{as + b}{cs + d} \tag{26}$$

represents a circle in the complex plane, where a, b, c, and d are any complex constants. This must be true since the possible values of s lie on the real axis, which must be transformed into a circle by Eq. (26), according to Eq. (24). With the aid of Eq. (26), we can show that many complex functions of importance in radio have circular locus curves. Furthermore, if a function $F(s)$ has a circular locus curve, its reciprocal $1/F(s)$ also has a circular locus curve. This is shown by letting b and c equal one, and d and a equal zero, in Eq. (25).

We can easily locate the center of the locus circle of $z = F(s)$ and also find its radius. To do so, we apply the transformation Eq. (26) to the real axis in the s plane; namely,

$$s = s^* \tag{27}$$

which will give us the locus curve of $F(s)$ in the z plane. From Eq. (26) and Exercise 3 above, it follows that

$$z^* = \frac{a^*s^* + b^*}{c^*s^* + d^*} \tag{28}$$

Solving Eq. (26) for s and Eq. (28) for s^* and substituting into Eq. (27), we obtain

$$s = \frac{b - dz}{-a + cz} = s^* = \frac{b^* - d^*z^*}{-a^* + c^*z^*} \tag{29}$$

Cross-multiplying Eq. (29), we have

$$-a^*b + a^*\,dz + bc^*z^* - dc^*zz^* = -ab^* + ad^*z^* + b^*cz - d^*czz^* \tag{30}$$

or

$$zz^* + \frac{a^*d - b^*c}{d^*c - dc^*}z + \frac{bc^* - ad^*}{d^*c - dc^*}z^* + \frac{ab^* - a^*b}{d^*c - dc^*} = 0 \tag{31}$$

Comparing Eq. (31) with Eq. (8), we see that the center of the locus circle is at

$$z = \frac{ad^* - bc^*}{d^*c - dc^*} \tag{32}$$

and the radius is

$$\rho = \sqrt{\frac{(a^*d - b^*c)(bc^* - ad^*)}{(d^*c - dc^*)^2} - \frac{ab^* - a^*b}{d^*c - dc^*}} \tag{33}$$

We shall find formulas (32) and (33) to be very useful in many locus problems. (See Example 2 below.)

Example 1. It follows from Eq. (26) that

$$R + j\omega L$$

as well as its reciprocal

$$\frac{1}{R + j\omega L}$$

have circular locus curves as functions of ω. These are illustrated in Fig. 6-7.

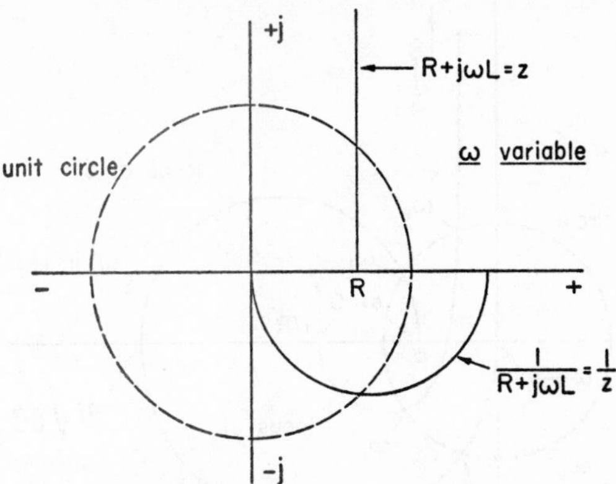

FIG. 6-7. Impedance and admittance loci of a series R-L combination for variable ω.

Example 2. The impedance and admittance loci of the parallel *L-R-C* combination in Fig. 6-8 are given by the equation

$$z = \frac{R + j\omega L}{1 + jR\omega C - \omega^2 LC} \tag{34}$$

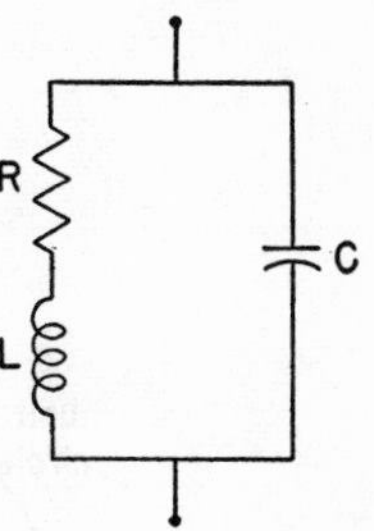

FIG. 6-8. Parallel *L-R-C* combination.

and its reciprocal. The loci of z and $(1/z)$ as functions of ω in this case are not circles.[6] On the other hand, they are circles as functions of C. The situation is depicted in Fig. 6-9. It is in agreement with Eq. (26).

Since we know that z as defined by Eq. (34) describes a circle as the capacitance C is varied, it is of interest in this case to locate the center and find the radius of the circle. To do this we first note that if z in Eq. (34) is considered as a bilinear function of C of the form of Eq. (26), then

$$a = 0 \tag{35}$$

$$b = R + j\omega L \tag{36}$$

$$c = (-\omega^2 L + j\omega R) \tag{37}$$

$$d = 1 \tag{38}$$

[6] In case this is a high Q circuit ($\sqrt{L/C} \gg R$) the locus is approximately circular near resonance, as shown in Example 1 of §6.4.

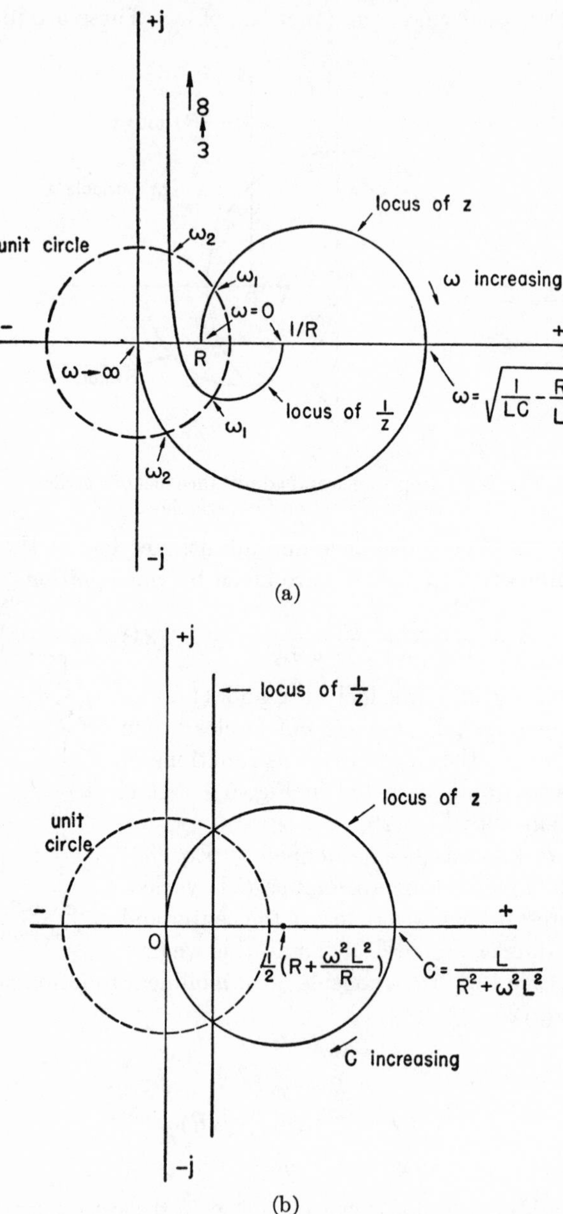

FIG. 6-9. Loci of z and $1/z$ for the impedance of Fig. 6-8. (a) ω variable. (b) C variable.

Substituting these values into Eq. (32), we find that the center of the circle is at

$$z = \frac{ad^* - bc^*}{d^*c - dc^*} = \frac{-(R + j\omega L)(-\omega^2 L - j\omega R)}{(-\omega^2 L + j\omega R) - (-\omega^2 L - j\omega R)}$$

$$= \frac{(R\omega^2 L - R\omega^2 L) + j(\omega^3 L^2 + \omega R^2)}{2j\omega R} = \frac{1}{2}\left(R + \frac{\omega^2 L^2}{R}\right) \tag{39}$$

Next, substituting into Eq. (33), we find for the radius of the circle

$$\rho = \sqrt{\frac{(a^*d - b^*c)(bc^* - ad^*)}{(d^*c - dc^*)^2} - \frac{ab^* - a^*b}{d^*c - dc^*}}$$

$$= \sqrt{\frac{(R - j\omega L)(-\omega^2 L + j\omega R)(R + j\omega L)(-\omega^2 L - j\omega R)}{[(-\omega^2 L + j\omega R) - (-\omega^2 L - j\omega R)]^2}}$$

$$= \frac{1}{2}\left(R + \frac{\omega^2 L^2}{R}\right) \tag{40}$$

In the light of Eqs. (39) and (40), it follows that the circle must pass through the origin, as shown in Fig. 6-9(b). Since the locus of z passes through the origin, the locus of $1/z$ in the z plane must pass through infinity; and since the locus of $1/z$ is of circular type, it must be a straight line. Two points on this line are the intersections of the locus of z and the unit circle, since these two points are their own inverse points with respect to the unit circle. These two points determine the locus of $1/z$.

6.4. A universal-locus curve of resonant circuits

The method of impedance loci can be used to advantage in investigating the parallel resonant circuit in Fig. 6-10(a) and the series resonant circuit in Fig. 6-10(b). Let us first consider the parallel resonant circuit. Its impedance is given by the equation

$$\frac{1}{z} = \frac{1}{r} + \frac{1}{j\omega L} + j\omega C \tag{41}$$

To study its properties in the neighborhood of resonance, we introduce the fractional frequency deviation from resonance, defined as

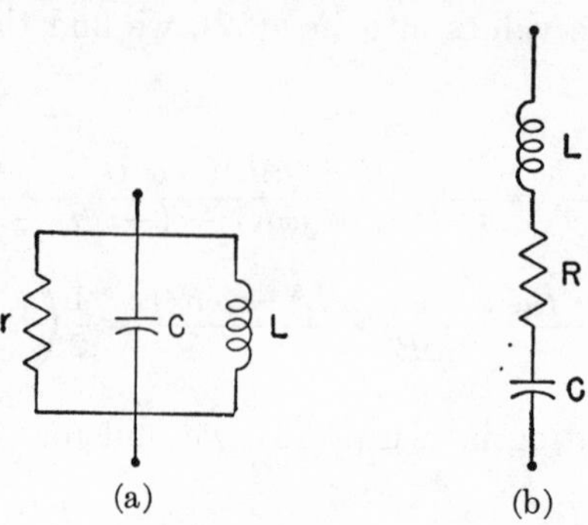

FIG. 6-10. Simple parallel- and series-tuned circuits.

$$\delta = \frac{\omega - \omega_0}{\omega_0} \tag{42}$$

where

$$\omega_0 = \frac{1}{\sqrt{LC}} \tag{43}$$

is the resonant frequency. We also define the quality factor Q of the circuit as

$$Q = r\sqrt{\frac{C}{L}} \tag{44}$$

It also follows from Eqs. (43) and (44) that

$$Q = \frac{r}{\omega_0 L} = \omega_0 Cr \tag{45}$$

We next introduce the resonant reactance

$$X_0 = \omega_0 L = \frac{1}{\omega_0 C} = \sqrt{\frac{L}{C}} \tag{46}$$

With the aid of these quantities, Eq. (41) becomes

$$\begin{aligned} z &= \frac{1}{\frac{1}{r} + j\left(\omega C - \frac{1}{\omega L}\right)} = \frac{1}{\frac{1}{r} + j\left[\omega_0(1+\delta)C - \frac{1}{\omega_0(1+\delta)L}\right]} \\ &= QX_0\left\{\frac{1}{1 + jQ\delta\left(\frac{2+\delta}{1+\delta}\right)}\right\} \end{aligned} \tag{47}$$

Near resonance, when $|\delta| \ll 1$, Eq. (47) reduces to

$$z = QX_0 \left\{ \frac{1}{1 + j2Q\delta} \right\} = QX_0 \left\{ \frac{1}{1 + 4Q^2\delta^2} - j \frac{2Q\delta}{1 + 4Q^2\delta^2} \right\} \quad (48)$$

If the impedance z is plotted as a function of frequency in terms of δ in the neighborhood of resonance, the middle form of Eq. (48) shows that the locus curve is a circle. Substitution of the constants of the middle form of Eq. (48) into Eqs. (32) and (33) shows that

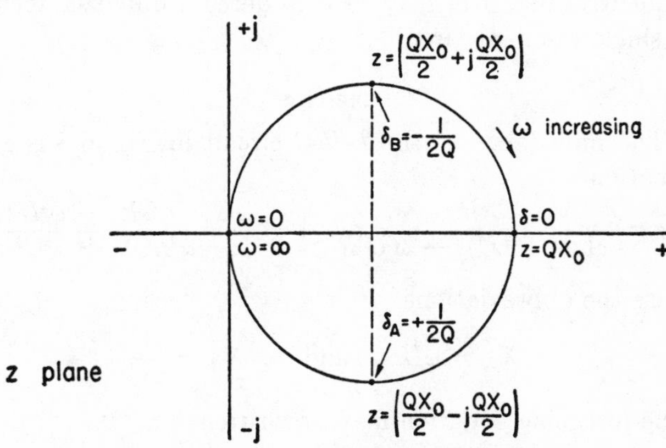

FIG. 6-11. Universal locus curve for the impedance of a parallel resonant circuit. (The same curve will serve as the locus of the admittance of a series resonant circuit if z is interpreted as admittance and X_0 as resonant susceptance).

the center of the circle is at $z = QX_0/2$ and its radius is $QX_0/2$. Equation (48) is plotted in Fig. 6-11.

The points $\delta = \pm 1/2Q$ correspond to the half-power points, since the magnitude of z is equal to $1/\sqrt{2}$ times its resonant value at these points. By definition, the bandwidth of the circuit is equal to the frequency spacing between the half-power points. Therefore,

$$\text{bandwidth} = f_A - f_B = f_0(\delta_A - \delta_B) = f_0 \left(\frac{1}{2Q} + \frac{1}{2Q} \right) = \frac{f_0}{Q} \quad (49)$$

Consequently,

$$Q = \frac{f_0}{\text{bandwidth}} \quad (50)$$

Since the ratio on the right of Eq. (50) is also defined as the circuit selectivity, we have thus shown that Q, as defined in Eqs. (44) or (45), is also equal to the selectivity.

The admittance y of the series L-R-C circuit in Fig. 6-10(b) has a circular locus curve in the complex y plane with completely analogous properties to those of Fig. 6-11. The reader can show this fact as an exercise. Furthermore, as shown in Example 1 below, a parallel-tuned circuit of the type shown in Fig. 6-8 has the same properties near resonance as the circuit of Fig. 6-10(a). Consequently, Fig. 6-11 may be considered a universal locus curve for all single resonant circuits.

Exercises

1. The impedance of the L-R-C circuit in Fig. 6-8 is given by the equation

$$z = \frac{R}{(1 - \omega^2LC)^2 + \omega^2C^2R^2} + j\frac{\omega L - \omega CR^2 - \omega^3L^2C}{(1 - \omega^2LC)^2 + \omega^2C^2R^2}$$

If we use the abbreviations

$$X_L = \omega L \qquad \text{and} \qquad X_C = \frac{1}{\omega C}$$

then the foregoing equation may be written

$$z = \frac{RX_C^2}{(X_C - X_L)^2 + R^2} + j\frac{X_L(X_C - X_L) - R^2}{(X_C - X_L)^2 + R^2}X_C$$

For a high Q circuit, only the factors $(X_C - X_L)$ in the foregoing equation vary appreciably in the neighborhood of resonance. Accordingly, show with the aid of Taylor series that in the neighborhood of resonance the impedance is approximately

$$z = \frac{RQ^2}{1 + S^2} - j\frac{RQ^2S}{1 + S^2} = \frac{RQ^2}{1 + jS}$$

where $$\omega_0 = \frac{1}{\sqrt{LC}} \qquad Q = \frac{1}{R}\sqrt{\frac{L}{C}}$$

and $$S = 2Q\left(\frac{\omega - \omega_0}{\omega_0}\right)$$

Draw the locus curve of z and note its values at $\omega = 0$, $\omega = \infty$, and its shape and values in the neighborhood of resonance.

2. Show that the impedance of the parallel R-C combination in Fig. 6-A has a circular locus as either ω, R, or C is varied. Locate the center of the circle in each case and find its radius.

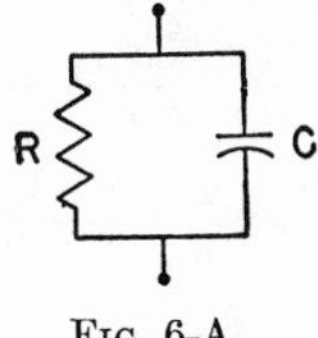

Fig. 6-A.

3. Derive and plot the locus curve of the admittance of the series L-R-C circuit in Fig. 6-10(b).

6.5. Some properties of the derivative of a complex function of a real variable

Let z be a complex function of a real variable ω. Then z will have a locus curve in the complex plane such as shown in Fig. 6-12.

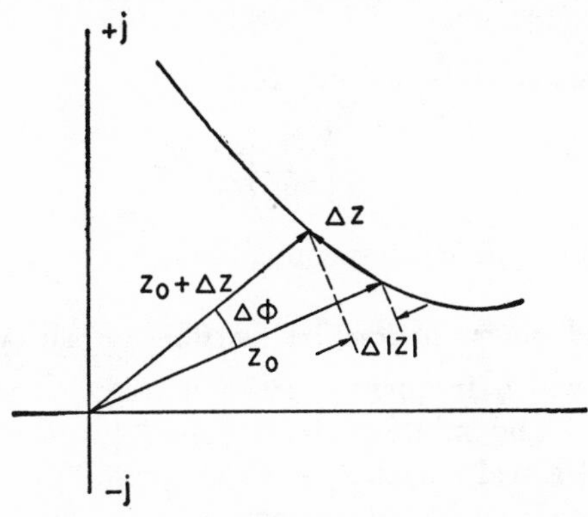

Fig. 6-12. Differential quantities along a general locus curve.

We now wish to consider some properties of the derivative $dz/d\omega$. By definition

$$\frac{dz}{d\omega} = \lim_{\Delta\omega \to 0} \frac{(z + \Delta z) - z}{\Delta\omega} = \lim_{\Delta\omega \to 0} \frac{\Delta z}{\Delta\omega} \tag{51}$$

In Fig. 6-12, we can see that as $\Delta\omega \to 0$ and consequently $\Delta z \to 0$, Δz becomes tangent to the locus curve. Therefore, since ω is a real quantity, $dz/d\omega$ is also tangent to the locus curve.

We shall find it convenient to resolve $dz/d\omega$ into components parallel and perpendicular to z. To do this, we write

$$z = |z|\epsilon^{j\phi} \tag{52}$$

Then[7]

$$\begin{aligned} \frac{dz}{d\omega} &= \frac{\partial z}{\partial |z|}\frac{d|z|}{d\omega} + \frac{\partial z}{\partial \phi}\frac{d\phi}{d\omega} \\ &= \epsilon^{j\phi}\frac{d|z|}{d\omega} + j|z|\epsilon^{j\phi}\frac{d\phi}{d\omega} \\ &= z\left\{\frac{1}{|z|}\frac{d|z|}{d\omega} + j\frac{d\phi}{d\omega}\right\} \end{aligned} \tag{53}$$

Since

$$\frac{1}{|z|}\frac{d|z|}{d\omega}$$

and

$$\frac{d\phi}{d\omega}$$

are both real, it follows that

$$z\left\{\frac{1}{|z|}\frac{d|z|}{d\omega}\right\}$$

is the component of $dz/d\omega$ parallel to z, while

$$z\left\{j\frac{j\phi}{d\omega}\right\}$$

is the component of $dz/d\omega$ perpendicular to z.

6.6. Maxima and minima of complex functions of real variables[8]

A problem which frequently arises in radio engineering is to find the maxima and minima of a complex function (impedance, current, etc.) of a real variable (ω, R, C, etc.). In Fig. 6-13 is the locus curve of such an impedance shown as a function of ω. The maxima and minima of the real or of the imaginary component of z are best found by setting the derivative of this component with respect to ω equal to zero, in the ordinary way. Finding the maxima and minima of $|z|$ and ϕ is, however, usually a more complicated matter, since it is cumbersome to find $d|z|/d\omega$ and $d\phi/d\omega$.

---

[7] In general, $|dz/d\omega| \neq d|z|/d\omega$ because $\Delta|z|$ is the change in length of z and is not the length of Δz.

[8] This method was first used in radio engineering by W. Van B. Roberts, *Proc. I.R.E.*, Vol. 14 (1926), p. 689.

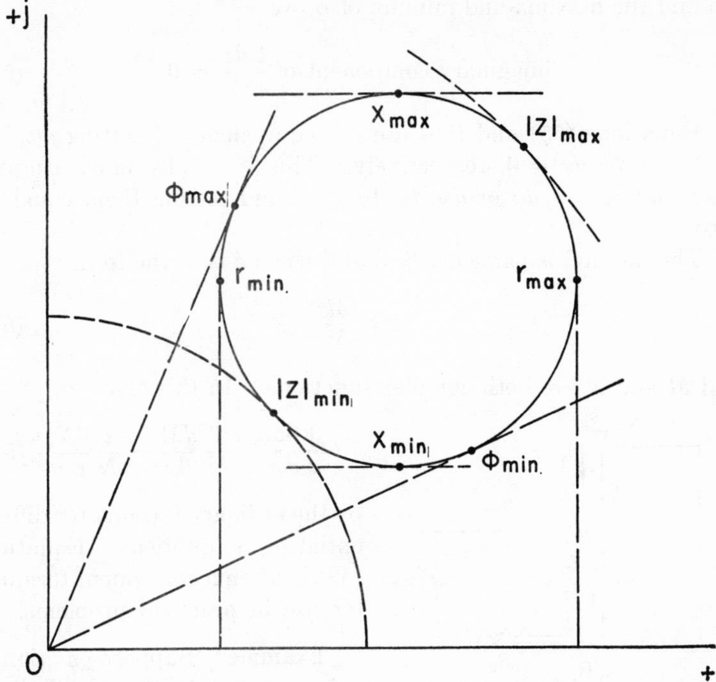

FIG. 6-13. Illustration of the various maxima and minima in the locus curve of a complex impedance $z = r + jx$.

However, let us transform Eq. (53) into

$$\frac{1}{z}\frac{dz}{d\omega} = \frac{1}{|z|}\frac{d|z|}{d\omega} + j\frac{d\phi}{d\omega} \tag{54}$$

In this form we see that

$$\frac{1}{|z|}\frac{d|z|}{d\omega}$$

is the real component of

$$\frac{1}{z}\frac{dz}{d\omega}$$

and $d\phi/d\omega$ is its imaginary component. Therefore, to find the maxima and minima of $|z|$, we need only set

$$\text{real component of } \frac{1}{z}\frac{dz}{d\omega} = 0 \tag{55}$$

To find the maxima and minima of ϕ, we set

$$\text{imaginary component of } \frac{1}{z}\frac{dz}{d\omega} = 0 \tag{56}$$

Equations (55) and (56) are the equivalents of setting $d|z|/d\omega = 0$ and $d\phi/d\omega = 0$, respectively. This is usually much simpler than finding $d|z|/d\omega$ or $d\phi/d\omega$ directly, and setting them equal to zero.

The method is particularly useful when z is of the form

$$z = \frac{M}{N} \tag{57}$$

and M and N are both complex functions. In this case

$$\frac{1}{z}\frac{dz}{d\omega} = \frac{1}{M}\frac{dM}{d\omega} - \frac{1}{N}\frac{dN}{d\omega} \tag{58}$$

by the ordinary formula for differentiating a quotient. Equation (58) is often a convenient formula for use in practical problems.

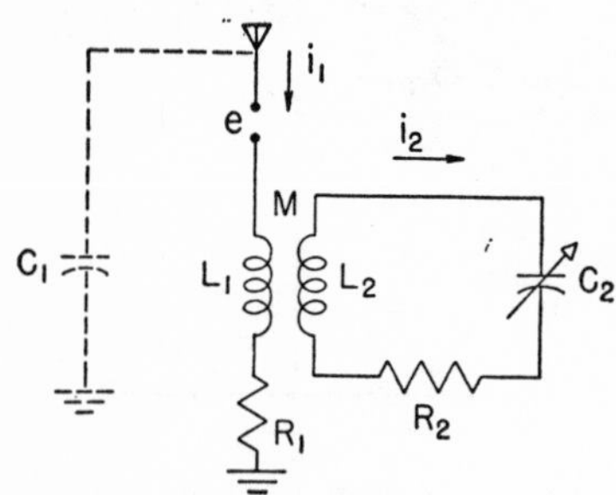

Fig. 6-14. An antenna and input circuit.

Example: Suppose a signal voltage e is generated in the antenna of Fig. 6-14. Let us find the value of C_2 which makes the secondary current a maximum. The circuit equations in this case are

$$i_1z_1 + i_2z_m = e \tag{59}$$

$$i_1z_m + i_2z_2 = 0 \tag{60}$$

where

$$z_1 = R_1 + j\left(\omega L_1 - \frac{1}{\omega C_1}\right) \tag{61}$$

$$z_2 = R_2 + j\left(\omega L_2 - \frac{1}{\omega C_2}\right) \tag{62}$$

$$z_m = j\omega M \tag{63}$$

Solving Eqs. (59) and (60), we get

$$i_2 = \frac{-ez_m}{z_1z_2 - z_m^2} \tag{64}$$

According to Eq. (55), i_2 will be a maximum when

$$\text{real component of } \frac{1}{i_2}\frac{di_2}{dC_2} = 0 \tag{65}$$

Now

$$\frac{di_2}{dC_2} = \frac{di_2}{dz_2}\cdot\frac{dz_2}{dC_2} = \frac{ez_m z_1}{(z_1 z_2 - z_m^2)^2}\cdot\frac{j}{\omega C_2^2} \tag{66}$$

Consequently,

$$\frac{1}{i_2}\frac{di_2}{dC_2} = \frac{-z_1}{z_1 z_2 - z_m^2}\cdot\frac{j}{\omega C_2^2} \tag{67}$$

The same result could also have been obtained by using Eq. (58).

For maximum i_2, the real part of Eq. (67) must equal zero. Therefore, the imaginary part of

$$\frac{z_1}{z_1 z_2 - z_m^2} = 0 \tag{68}$$

This means that $\dfrac{z_1}{z_1 z_2 - z_m^2}$ must be real. Therefore, its reciprocal

$$\frac{z_1 z_2 - z_m^2}{z_1} = z_2 - \frac{z_m^2}{z_1}$$

must also be real. Now

$$z_2 - \frac{z_m^2}{z_1} = R_2 + j\left(\omega L_2 - \frac{1}{\omega C_2}\right) + \frac{\omega^2 M^2}{R_1 + j\left(\omega L_1 - \dfrac{1}{\omega C_1}\right)}$$

$$= R_2 + j\left(\omega L_2 - \frac{1}{\omega C_2}\right) + \frac{\omega^2 M^2\left\{R_1 - j\left(\omega L_1 - \dfrac{1}{\omega C_1}\right)\right\}}{R_1^2 + \left(\omega L_1 - \dfrac{1}{\omega C_1}\right)^2} \tag{69}$$

The imaginary part of this equals zero. Therefore

$$\omega L_2 - \frac{1}{\omega C_2} - \frac{\omega^2 M^2\left(\omega L_1 - \dfrac{1}{\omega C_1}\right)}{R_1^2 + \left(\omega L_1 - \dfrac{1}{\omega C_1}\right)^2} = 0 \tag{70}$$

for maximum secondary current. In other words,

$$\omega L_2 - \frac{1}{\omega C_2} = \frac{\omega^2 M^2 \left(\omega L_1 - \frac{1}{\omega C_1}\right)}{R_1^2 + \left(\omega L_1 - \frac{1}{\omega C_1}\right)^2} \tag{71}$$

is the condition which gives the value of C_2 for maximum secondary current.

Exercises

1. Find the value of M in Fig. 6-14 which makes i_2 a maximum, assuming that all the other circuit constants remain fixed. Equation (64) may be used as a basis.

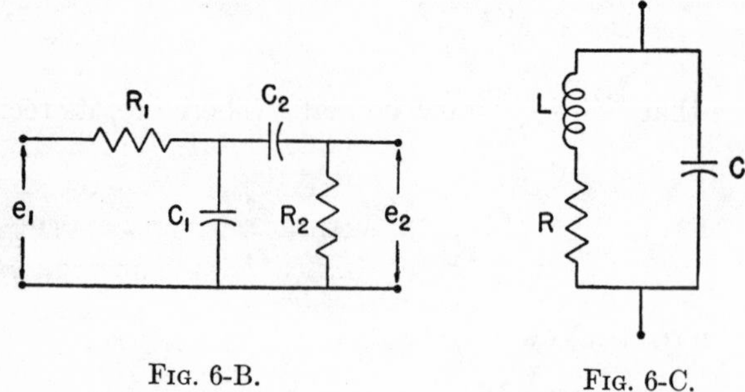

FIG. 6-B. FIG. 6-C.

2. In the circuit of Fig. 6-B, find the frequency for which $|e_2|$ is a maximum.

3. Find the exact frequency at which the impedance of the parallel tuned circuit in Fig. 6-C is a maximum.

CHAPTER 7

The Inversion Theorem and Related Topics

7.1. Introduction

In Chap. 3, we said that the Laplace transformation

$$\int_0^\infty f(t)\epsilon^{-st}\,dt = F(s) \tag{1}$$

transforms $f(t)$, a function of t, into $F(s)$, a function of s. This is analogous to the Fourier transformation formula[1]

$$\int_{-\infty}^{+\infty} \epsilon^{-j\omega t}G(t)\,dt = \Omega(\omega) \tag{2}$$

which transforms a function of time $G(t)$ into $\Omega(\omega)$, a function of ω. In the case of Fourier integrals, we also have an explicit form for the inverse transformation; namely,

$$\frac{1}{2\pi}\int_{-\infty}^{+\infty} \epsilon^{j\omega t}\Omega(\omega)\,d\omega = G(t) \tag{3}$$

There is likewise a corresponding expression for the inverse transformation in the case of Laplace transforms. This direct expression for the inverse transformation, and its uses and significance, will be the principal subject matter of the present chapter.

The explicit form of the inverse transformation will be derived in §7.3, but before proceeding with this derivation, certain preliminary matters will be investigated. In the first place, let us examine the significance of the Fourier transformations, Eqs. (2) and (3). To be specific, let us consider a rectangular pulse. It is well known that a rectangular pulse as shown in Fig. 7-1(a) has a distribution of frequency components as shown[2] in Fig. 7-1(b). More specifically, it is known that a superposition of frequency

[1] See Appendix E.

[2] See Goldman, *Frequency Analysis, Modulation and Noise*, §3.4.

components of the form

$$\epsilon^{j\omega t} = \cos \omega t + j \sin \omega t$$

and of amounts

$$\Omega(\omega) = \left|\frac{2}{\omega} \sin\left(\frac{\omega T}{2}\right)\right| \epsilon^{j \tan^{-1}\left(\frac{\cos \omega T - 1}{\sin \omega T}\right)} = S(\omega)\epsilon^{j\phi(\omega)}$$

will give a resultant function of t with a real component as shown in Fig. 7-1(a) and a zero imaginary component. Assuming that $G(t)$ is a real function of t, it is also possible to combine corresponding

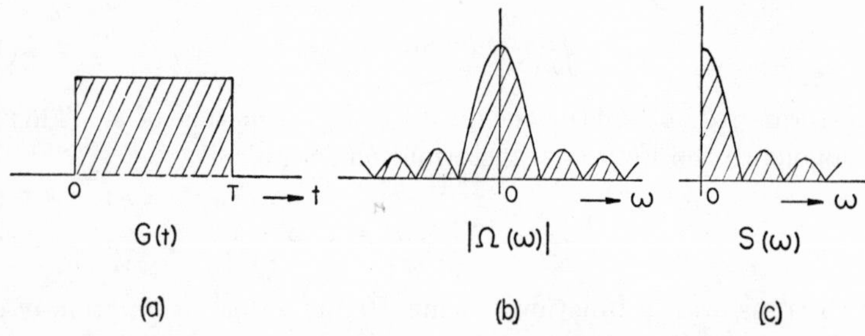

FIG. 7-1. A rectangular pulse and its frequency distributions.

positive and negative frequency components in accordance with the equation

$$\Omega(\omega)\epsilon^{j\omega t} + \Omega(-\omega)\epsilon^{j(-\omega)t} = 2S(\omega) \cos (\omega t + \phi)$$

Equation (3) then becomes

$$G(t) = \frac{1}{\pi}\int_0^{\infty} S(\omega) \cos (\omega t + \phi)\, d\omega \tag{4}$$

In this form, the Fourier integral has the significance of a superposition of real frequency components for all positive real values of ω, which, thinking in the general terms of complex variables, amounts to an integration along the positive portion of the real axis of ω. In the form

$$G(t) = \frac{1}{2\pi}\int_{-\infty}^{+\infty} \epsilon^{j\omega t}\Omega(\omega)\, d\omega \tag{5}$$

the Fourier integral has the significance of an integration of the complex function $\epsilon^{j\omega t}\Omega(\omega)$ along the entire real axis of ω.

So far we have not discussed the significance of the variable s, other than to say that it may be complex and that its real part must be of such magnitude that

$$\int_0^\infty f(t)\epsilon^{-st}\,dt = F(s) \tag{6}$$

will converge. We now wish to develop means for expressing $f(t)$ as an integral with respect to s in analogy with Eq. (3), and we may then understand better the significance of s.

7.2. The unit step and the unit impulse as contour integrals

Consider the complex s plane shown in Fig. 7-2. Suppose the contour (C) extends along the imaginary axis from $-j\infty$ to $+j\infty$, except for an essentially infinitesimal semicircle by-passing the origin on the right. We will now show that a unit step may be expressed as a contour integral by the equation

$$\frac{1}{2\pi j}\int_C \frac{\epsilon^{s(t-t_1)}}{s}\,ds = U(t-t_1) \tag{7}$$

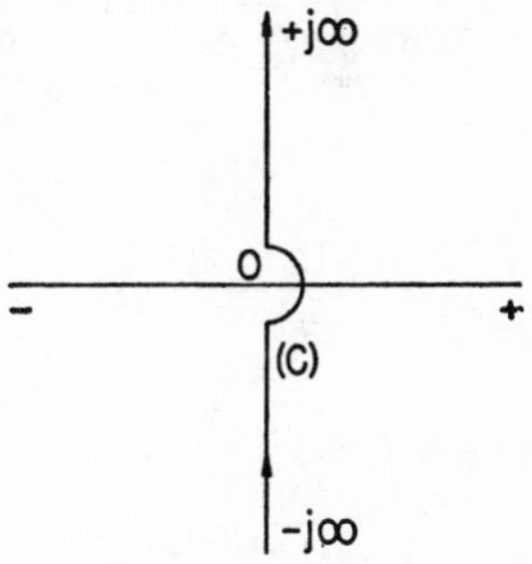

FIG. 7-2. The contour C.

To do this, we break up the contour (C) into its straight and semicircular parts and carry out the integration directly. Along the straight portions of the contour, $s = jy$, while along the semicircular portion, $s = \rho(\cos\theta + j\sin\theta) = \rho\epsilon^{j\theta}$. Therefore

$$\begin{aligned}
\frac{1}{2\pi j}\int_C \frac{\epsilon^{s(t-t_1)}}{s}\,ds &= \frac{1}{2\pi j}\int_{-\infty}^{-\rho} \frac{\epsilon^{jy(t-t_1)}}{jy}\,j\,dy \\
&\quad + \frac{1}{2\pi j}\int_{-\pi/2}^{+\pi/2} \frac{\epsilon^{\rho(\cos\theta + j\sin\theta)(t-t_1)}}{\rho\epsilon^{j\theta}}\,\rho\epsilon^{j\theta}\,j\,d\theta + \frac{1}{2\pi j}\int_\rho^\infty \frac{\epsilon^{jy(t-t_1)}}{jy}\,j\,dy \\
&= \frac{1}{2\pi j}\int_{-\infty}^{-\rho} \frac{\cos[y(t-t_1)] + j\sin[y(t-t_1)]}{y}\,dy \\
&\quad + \frac{1}{2\pi}\int_{-\pi/2}^{+\pi/2} \epsilon^{\rho(\cos\theta + j\sin\theta)(t-t_1)}\,d\theta \\
&\quad + \frac{1}{2\pi j}\int_\rho^\infty \frac{\cos[y(t-t_1)] + j\sin[y(t-t_1)]}{y}\,dy
\end{aligned} \tag{8}$$

Now

$$\int_{-\infty}^{-\rho} \frac{\cos [y(t - t_1)]}{y} dy = -\int_{\rho}^{\infty} \frac{\cos [y(t - t_1)]}{y} dy \tag{9}$$

and

$$\int_{-\infty}^{-\rho} \frac{\sin [y(t - t_1)]}{y} dy = \int_{\rho}^{\infty} \frac{\sin [y(t - t_1)]}{y} dy \tag{10}$$

Also,

$$\lim_{\rho \to 0} \int_{-\pi/2}^{+\pi/2} \epsilon^{\rho(\cos\theta + j\sin\theta)(t-t_1)}\, d\theta = \int_{-\pi/2}^{+\pi/2} d\theta = \pi \tag{11}$$

Substituting Eqs. (9), (10), and (11) into Eq. (8) and letting $\rho \to 0$, we obtain

$$\frac{1}{2\pi j} \int_C \frac{\epsilon^{s(t-t_1)}}{s} ds = \frac{1}{2} + \frac{1}{\pi} \int_0^{\infty} \frac{\sin y(t - t_1)}{y} dy \tag{12}$$

Now

$$\int_0^{\infty} \frac{\sin y(t - t_1)}{y} dy \begin{array}{l} = +\frac{\pi}{2} \text{ if } (t - t_1) \text{ is positive} \\ = -\frac{\pi}{2} \text{ if } (t - t_1) \text{ is negative} \end{array} \tag{13}$$

Therefore,

$$\frac{1}{2\pi j} \int_C \frac{\epsilon^{s(t-t_1)}}{s} ds = \begin{array}{c} +1 \text{ if } t - t_1 \text{ is positive} \\ 0 \text{ if } t - t_1 \text{ is negative} \end{array} = U(t - t_1) \tag{14}$$

which is what we started out to prove. The similarity between (12) and the expression for the unit step as a Fourier integral suggests that the significance of the imaginary component of s is closely related to $j\omega$, where ω is 2π times the frequency of sinusoidal functions of t.

Next we wish to show that

$$U(t - t_1) = \frac{1}{2\pi j} \int_{\gamma - j\infty}^{\gamma + j\infty} \frac{\epsilon^{s(t-t_1)}}{s} ds \tag{15}$$

where γ is any positive constant and the path of integration is the vertical straight line which passes at a distance γ to the right of the origin. This expression for $U(t - t_1)$ differs from Eq. (14) only in the path of integration, but it will be found useful in certain cases in which Eq. (14) cannot be used.

To carry out the proof, we note first that we have already shown that

$$U(t - t_1) = \frac{1}{2\pi j} \int_C \frac{\epsilon^{s(t-t_1)}}{s}\, ds \tag{16}$$

where the path of integration is along the contour C from $-j\infty$ to $+j\infty$. Furthermore, it was shown in §5.6 that the same integral taken along any other path between the same end points will yield the same value, provided no singular point of the integrand lies between the two paths of integration. Consequently, it follows from Eq. (16) that

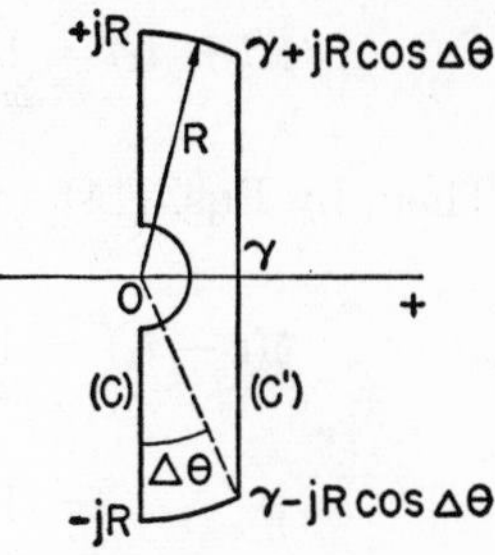

FIG. 7-3. The contours C and C' between $-jR$ and $+jR$ in the complex s plane.

$$U(t - t_1) = \frac{1}{2\pi j} \int_{-j\infty}^{\gamma - j\infty} \frac{\epsilon^{s(t-t_1)}}{s}\, ds + \frac{1}{2\pi j} \int_{\gamma - j\infty}^{\gamma + j\infty} \frac{\epsilon^{s(t-t_1)}}{s}\, ds + \frac{1}{2\pi j} \int_{\gamma + j\infty}^{j\infty} \frac{\epsilon^{s(t-t_1)}}{s}\, ds \tag{17}$$

Now (see Fig. 7-3) let $\qquad \Delta\theta = \sin^{-1}\left(\frac{\gamma}{R}\right) \qquad (18)$

Then

$$\left|\frac{1}{2\pi j} \int_{-j\infty}^{\gamma - j\infty} \frac{\epsilon^{s(t-t_1)}}{s}\, ds\right| = \lim_{R\to\infty} \left|\frac{1}{2\pi j} \int_{-\pi/2}^{-\pi/2+\Delta\theta} \frac{\epsilon^{R(\cos\theta + j\sin\theta)(t-t_1)} jR\epsilon^{j\theta}\, d\theta}{R\epsilon^{j\theta}}\right|$$

$$< \lim_{R\to\infty} \left|\frac{1}{2\pi} \epsilon^{\gamma(t-t_1)} \int_{-\pi/2}^{-\pi/2+\Delta\theta} \epsilon^{jR\sin\theta(t-t_1)}\, d\theta\right| < \lim_{\Delta\theta\to 0} \frac{\Delta\theta}{2\pi} \epsilon^{\gamma(t-t_1)} \to 0 \tag{19}$$

Similarly,

$$\left|\frac{1}{2\pi j} \int_{\gamma + j\infty}^{j\infty} \frac{\epsilon^{s(t-t_1)}}{s}\, ds\right| \to 0 \tag{20}$$

Therefore,

$$U(t - t_1) = \frac{1}{2\pi j} \int_{\gamma - j\infty}^{\gamma + j\infty} \frac{\epsilon^{s(t-t_1)}}{s}\, ds \tag{21}$$

thus proving Eq. (15)

In order to find the expression for a unit impulse as a contour integral, we use the definition

$$\delta(t - t_1) = \lim_{\Delta t_1 \to 0} \frac{U(t - t_1) - U(t - t_1 - \Delta t_1)}{\Delta t_1} \tag{22}$$

Then, by Eqs. (14) and (21),

$$\begin{aligned} \delta(t - t_1) &= \lim_{\Delta t_1 \to 0} \frac{1}{2\pi j} \int_C \frac{\epsilon^{s(t-t_1)} - \epsilon^{s(t-t_1-\Delta t_1)}}{s\,\Delta t_1}\,ds \\ &= \lim_{\Delta t_1 \to 0} \frac{1}{2\pi j} \int_C \left\{\frac{1 - \epsilon^{-s\,\Delta t_1}}{s\,\Delta t_1}\right\} \epsilon^{s(t-t_1)}\,ds \\ &= \lim_{\Delta t_1 \to 0} \frac{1}{2\pi j} \int_{\gamma - j\infty}^{\gamma + j\infty} \left\{\frac{1 - \epsilon^{-s\,\Delta t_1}}{s\,\Delta t_1}\right\} \epsilon^{s(t-t_1)}\,ds \end{aligned} \tag{23}$$

Although
$$\lim_{\Delta t_1 \to 0} \left\{\frac{1 - \epsilon^{-s\,\Delta t_1}}{s\,\Delta t_1}\right\} = 1 \tag{24}$$

we will leave the expression for $\delta(t - t_1)$ in the form of Eq. (23). In this way, we will have available an exact expression for the type of quasi-impulses that occur in practice, in which Δt_1 is very small but still finite. In theoretical cases such as will be met in the following section, in which we deal with true impulses, we can also let $\Delta t_1 \to 0$.

7.3. The inversion theorem

In Eqs. (14) and (21), we found means for expressing the unit step $U(t - t_1)$ as an integral of s components, and in Eq. (23) we found a means for expressing the unit impulse as an integral of s components. We will now extend this work and find means for expressing an arbitrary function of t, $f(t)$, as an integral of its s components, $F(s)$. This will give us a new method for finding $f(t)$ in solving problems such as those dealt with in Chap. 3. It will also give us a new insight into many other important questions.

A direct method of approach for finding an expression for $f(t)$ as an integral of s components is to break up the whole function[3] $f(t)$, as shown in Fig. 7-4, into impulses of strength $f(\tau)\,\Delta\tau$ at the loca-

---

[3] In conformity with the work in Chap. 3, we shall deal only with functions $f(t)$ which are zero when $t < 0$.

tions $t = \tau$. We see first of all from Fig. 7-4 that

$$f(t) = \int_0^\infty \delta(t - \tau)f(\tau)\, d\tau \tag{25}$$

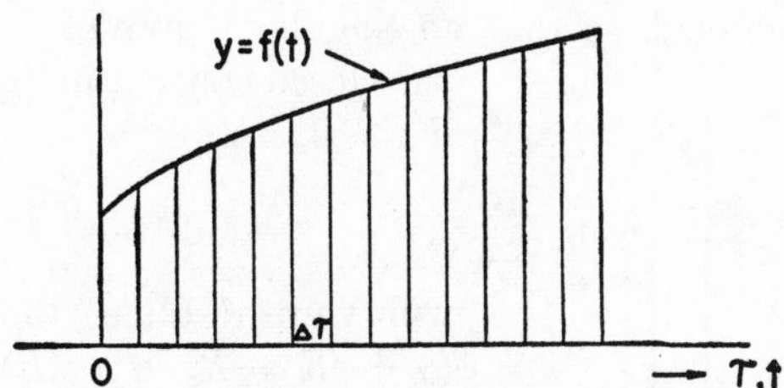

Fig. 7-4. Representation of a function as the superposition of successive impulses in accordance with Eq. (25).

Equation (25) is also just a restatement of Eq. (55) of Chap. 4. Next, substituting Eq. (23) into Eq. (25), we have

$$\begin{aligned} f(t) &= \int_0^\infty \left\{ \lim_{\Delta\tau \to 0} \frac{1}{2\pi j} \int_{\gamma - j\infty}^{\gamma + j\infty} \left[\frac{1 - \epsilon^{-s\,\Delta\tau}}{s\,\Delta\tau} \right] \epsilon^{s(t-\tau)}\, ds \right\} f(\tau)\, d\tau \\ &= \frac{1}{2\pi j} \int_{\gamma - j\infty}^{\gamma + j\infty} \left\{ \int_0^\infty \epsilon^{-s\tau} f(\tau)\, d\tau \right\} \epsilon^{st}\, ds = \frac{1}{2\pi j} \int_{\gamma - j\infty}^{\gamma + j\infty} F(s)\epsilon^{st}\, ds \end{aligned} \tag{26}$$

where[4]

$$F(s) = \int_0^\infty \epsilon^{-st} f(t)\, dt \tag{27}$$

We recognize $F(s)$ as the Laplace transform of $f(t)$.

In the above derivation of Eq. (26), we have inverted the order of integration. This is justified only if the integrals involved are absolutely convergent. It can be shown that this will be the case provided that γ is greater than the real coordinate of every singular point of $F(s)$.[5]

---

[4] In this derivation, since we were dealing with theoretically true impulses, we passed to the limit $\Delta\tau \to 0$, so that

$$\lim_{\Delta\tau \to 0} \left[\frac{1 - \epsilon^{-s\,\Delta\tau}}{s\,\Delta\tau} \right] = 1$$

[5] See §5.12 for a discussion of singular points.

Next suppose that $F(s)$ is of such form that[6]

$$|F(s)| < CR^{-k} \tag{28}$$

where k is a positive constant and R is the radius of a circular arc at least large enough so that no singular points of $F(s)$ lie outside the closed contour in Fig. 7-5. Then if $t > 0$,

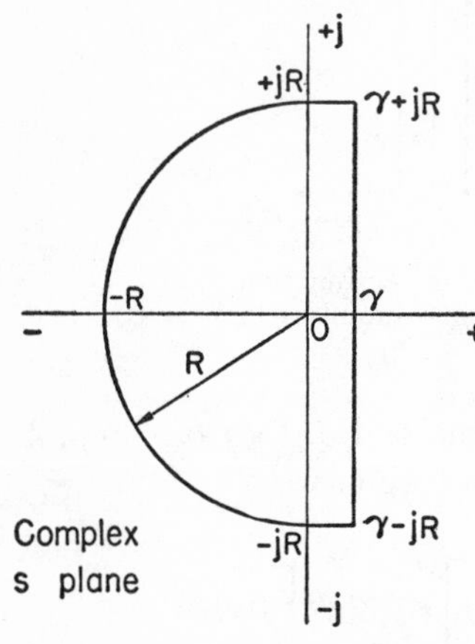

Fig. 7-5. The basic contour of the inversion theorem (as $R \to \infty$).

$$\int F(s)\epsilon^{st}\, ds$$

will vanish[7] along the circular arc $(\gamma + jR,\ -R,\ \gamma - jR)$ if $R \to \infty$. It then follows from Eq. (26) that

$$f(t) = \frac{1}{2\pi j}\oint F(s)\epsilon^{st}\, ds \tag{29}$$

where the integral is taken along the closed contour in Fig. 7-5, with R infinite. According to §5.8, *the contour in Eq. (29) can also be replaced by any closed contour which encloses all the singular points of* $F(s)$.

Equations (29) and (27), or their equivalent, Eqs. (26) and (27), are called the *inversion theorem.* Comparing Eq. (29) with Eq. (163) of Chap. 5, we see that the inversion theorem can be stated in the following form:

---

[6] In many future applications of Eq. (29), $F(s)$ will be of the form $E(s)/Z(s)$, where $E(s)$ is the Laplace transform of an applied voltage function $e(t)$. Now the Fourier integral energy theorem in conjunction with §7.7 shows that the value of $E(s)$ as $s \to \pm j\infty$ is determined by the energy content of $e(t)$ at infinite frequencies. In all actual voltages, this energy content will vanish at least exponentially as $\omega \to \infty$, and generally speaking $E(s)$ will also vanish to the same order along the circular arc in Fig. 7-5. Consequently, Eq. (29) can be used, even though the form used for $F(s)$ may not at first seem to satisfy Eq. (28), if $Z(s)$ alone is considered. This footnote is inserted at this point for reference purposes, even though its meaning may not be clear to the reader until he has read the remainder of the chapter.

[7] The reader can supply the proof that the integral along the infinite circular arc will vanish by following the method used in the derivation of Eq. (190) of Chap. 5, and Eq. (19) of this chapter.

If $F(s)$ is defined by the Laplace transformation

$$F(s) = \int_0^\infty f(t)\epsilon^{-st}\,dt$$

then

$$f(t) = \frac{1}{2\pi j}\oint F(s)\epsilon^{st}\,ds$$

and therefore, *$f(t)$ is the sum of the residues of the function*

$$F(s)\epsilon^{st}$$

with respect to all its singular points.

Equation (29) itself is an explicit formula for calculating the inverse of the Laplace transformation, and it is therefore called the inverse transformation. It can be used for finding $f(t)$ from $F(s)$ when the given form of $F(s)$ cannot be treated with the aid of available tables of transforms. In fact, pairs of Laplace transforms, $f(t)$ and $F(s)$, to be used for compiling a table, can be obtained from the inverse transformation (29) just as readily as from the direct Laplace transformation. The inverse transformation is also useful as the general expression for $f(t)$ in theoretical investigations, as we shall see.

The contour integral on the right of Eq. (26) or Eq. (29) is sometimes called the Bromwich integral or the Bromwich-Wagner[8] integral.

In case the function $F(s)$ has a branch point to the left of the vertical straight line $(\gamma - jR,\ \gamma + jR)$ in Fig. 7-5, then it is not possible to change from the vertical path of integration in Eq. (26) to the closed contour in Eq. (29). In such cases we must start from Eq (26), in order to calculate $f(t)$, and where necessary we must work out new contours which are not closed (see §11.7).

7.4. Solutions for $f(t)$ by contour integration—poles and residues

We shall next apply the inverse transformation to the direct calculation of the solutions to some problems already solved in Chap. 3 by means of the expansion theorem or with the aid of a table of Laplace transforms. This will give us a good comparison

---

[8] T. J. Bromwich, "Normal Coordinates in Dynamical Systems," *Proc. Lond. Math. Soc.*, Vol. 2, No. 15, 1916.

K. W. Wagner, "Über Eine Formel von Heaviside zur Berechnung von Einschaltvorgaenge," *Arch. Electro-tech.*, Vol. 4, 1916.

between the different methods. The procedure is the same in all the different methods up to the point of finding the function $F(s)$ which is the transform of the desired function $f(t)$. The methods differ only in the method of finding $f(t)$ from $F(s)$. We have already had practice in the application of the expansion theorem and in use of a table of transforms. We will now see how $f(t)$ is found by means of contour integration.

Example 1: *Charging Curve of a Capacitor.* As a first example we will find the charging curve of a capacitor C connected to a

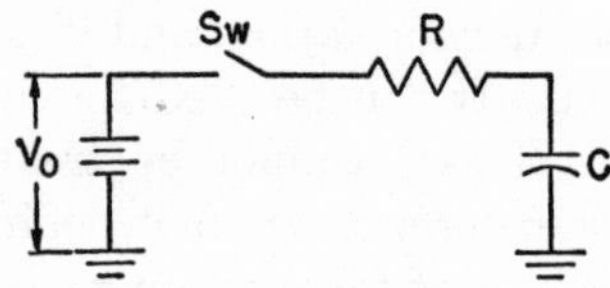

FIG. 7-6.

battery of voltage V_0 through a resistor R, as shown in Fig. 7-6. The same problem was solved in §3.13 with the aid of the table of Laplace transforms.

Applying Kirchhoff's Second Law to the circuit of Fig. 7-6, we have

$$Ri + \frac{q}{C} = R\frac{dq}{dt} + \frac{q}{C} = V_0 \tag{30}$$

The transformed equation of (30) is

$$R[sQ(s) - q(0+)] + \frac{Q(s)}{C} = \frac{V_0}{s} \tag{31}$$

Since the initial conditions are quiescent,

$$q(0+) = 0 \tag{32}$$

Therefore, Eq. (31) may be written

$$Q(s) = \frac{V_0}{Rs\left(\frac{1}{RC} + s\right)} \tag{33}$$

According to the inversion theorem, we may then write

$$q(t) = \frac{1}{2\pi j} \oint \frac{V_0 \epsilon^{st}\, ds}{Rs\left(\frac{1}{RC} + s\right)} \tag{34}$$

Comparing Eq. (34) with Eq. (163) of Chap. 5, we see that $q(t)$ is the sum of the residues of the function

$$\frac{V_0 \epsilon^{st}}{Rs\left(\frac{1}{RC} + s\right)} \tag{35}$$

This function clearly has poles at

(I) $$s = 0$$

and (II) $$s = -\frac{1}{RC}$$

Now, according to Eq. (162) of Chap. 5, the residue of Eq. (35) at any pole $s = a$ is

$$\left\{\frac{V_0 \epsilon^{st}}{\frac{d}{ds}\left[Rs\left(\frac{1}{RC} + s\right)\right]}\right\}_{s=a} = \left\{\frac{V_0 \epsilon^{st}}{R\left(\frac{1}{RC} + s\right) + Rs}\right\}_{s=a}$$

$$= \frac{V_0 \epsilon^{at}}{R\left(\frac{1}{RC} + a\right) + Ra} \tag{36}$$

Therefore, the residue at the pole $s = 0$ is

$$\frac{V_0}{R\left(\frac{1}{RC}\right)} = V_0 C$$

and the residue at the pole $s = -1/RC$ is

$$\frac{V_0 \epsilon^{-t/RC}}{R\left(-\frac{1}{RC}\right)} = -V_0 C \epsilon^{-t/RC}$$

Consequently,

$$q(t) = V_0 C(1 - \epsilon^{-t/RC}) \tag{37}$$

since $q(t)$ is the sum of the residues at the poles. This solution, of course, agrees with the answer found in §3.13 even though the result was obtained by an entirely different method.

Example 2: *Series L-R-C Circuit, with Sinusoidal Applied E.M.F.* We will next solve the problem of §3.11. As shown in Fig. 7-7, a

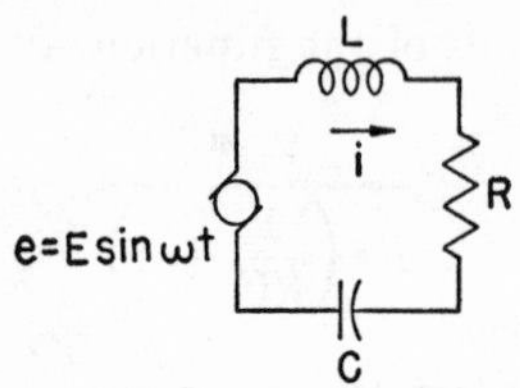

FIG. 7-7. Series L-R-C circuit with sinusoidal applied e.m.f.

sinusoidal e.m.f. is applied to a series L-R-C circuit, starting with quiescent initial conditions. The circuit equation in this case is

$$L\frac{di}{dt} + Ri + \frac{\int i\,dt}{C} = E \sin \omega t \tag{38}$$

Since the initial conditions are quiescent, and since the Laplace transform of sin ωt is

$$\frac{\omega}{s^2 + \omega^2}$$

Eq. (38) may be written in the equivalent form

$$I(s) = \frac{1}{Ls + R + \dfrac{1}{sC}}\left[\frac{E\omega}{s^2 + \omega^2}\right] \tag{39}$$

According to the inversion theorem, we may then write

$$i(t) = \frac{1}{2\pi j}\oint \frac{E\omega s\epsilon^{st}\,ds}{\left(Ls^2 + Rs + \dfrac{1}{C}\right)(s^2 + \omega^2)} \tag{40}$$

Comparing Eq. (40) with Eq. (163) of Chap. 5 just as in the previous example, we see that $i(t)$ is the sum of the residues of the function

$$\frac{E\omega s\epsilon^{st}}{\left(Ls^2 + Rs + \frac{1}{C}\right)(s^2 + \omega^2)} \tag{41}$$

This function has poles at

(I) $$s = +j\omega \tag{42}$$

(II) $$s = -j\omega \tag{43}$$

(III) $$s = -\frac{R}{2L} + j\sqrt{\frac{1}{LC} - \frac{R^2}{4L^2}} \tag{44}$$

(IV) $$s = -\frac{R}{2L} - j\sqrt{\frac{1}{LC} - \frac{R^2}{4L^2}} \tag{45}$$

According to Eq. (162) of Chap. 5, the residue of Eq. (41) at any pole $s = a$ is

$$\left[\frac{E\omega s\epsilon^{st}}{\frac{d}{ds}\left\{\left(Ls^2 + Rs + \frac{1}{C}\right)(s^2 + \omega^2)\right\}}\right]_{s=a} = \left\{\frac{E\omega s\epsilon^{st}}{(2Ls + R)(s^2 + \omega^2) + \left(Ls^2 + Rs + \frac{1}{C}\right)2s}\right\}_{s=a}$$

$$= \frac{E\omega a\epsilon^{at}}{(2La + R)(a^2 + \omega^2) + \left(La^2 + Ra + \frac{1}{C}\right)2a} \tag{46}$$

Consequently, the respective residues are

(I) $$\frac{jE\omega^2\epsilon^{j\omega t}}{\left(-\omega^2 L + j\omega R + \frac{1}{C}\right)2j\omega} \tag{47}$$

(II) $$\frac{-jE\omega^2\epsilon^{-j\omega t}}{\left(-\omega^2 L - j\omega R + \frac{1}{C}\right)(-2j\omega)} \tag{48}$$

$$\text{(III)}\quad \frac{E\omega\left(-\frac{R}{2L}+j\sqrt{\frac{1}{LC}-\frac{R^2}{4L^2}}\right)\epsilon^{-\left(\frac{R}{2L}+j\sqrt{\frac{1}{LC}-\frac{R^2}{4L^2}}\right)t}}{\left[2L\left(-\frac{R}{2L}+j\sqrt{\frac{1}{LC}-\frac{R^2}{4L^2}}\right)+R\right]\left[\frac{R^2}{2L^2}-\frac{1}{LC}-j\frac{R}{L}\sqrt{\frac{1}{LC}-\frac{R^2}{4L^2}}+\omega^2\right]} \tag{49}$$

$$\text{(IV)}\quad \frac{E\omega\left(-\frac{R}{2L}-j\sqrt{\frac{1}{LC}-\frac{R^2}{4L^2}}\right)\epsilon^{-\left(\frac{R}{2L}-j\sqrt{\frac{1}{LC}-\frac{R^2}{4L^2}}\right)t}}{\left[2L\left(-\frac{R}{2L}-j\sqrt{\frac{1}{LC}-\frac{R^2}{4L^2}}\right)+R\right]\left[\frac{R^2}{2L^2}-\frac{1}{LC}+j\frac{R}{L}\sqrt{\frac{1}{LC}-\frac{R^2}{4L^2}}+\omega^2\right]} \tag{50}$$

The sum of the residues (I), (II), (III), and (IV) is then equal to $i(t)$. A little algebraic manipulation will reduce $i(t)$ as thus found to the same form as Eq. (151) of Chap. 3. The reader may carry this through as an exercise, but we will not consume space with it here.

On the whole, it may be concluded from the two preceding examples that the method of contour integration is a more lengthy process than the use of a table of Laplace transforms. The use of a table is therefore preferable in solving most practical problems. However, the method of contour integration is much more versatile for theoretical and research work, since the use of a table is limited essentially to problems of particular forms. In many of the succeeding sections of this and other chapters, we shall use the method of contour integration in important theoretical investigations.

7.5. Derivation of the expansion theorem by contour integration

The foregoing examples suggest a general method of finding inverse transforms which we will now derive. Suppose that a function $F(s)$ is given and we wish to find the corresponding function of t, $f(t)$. The inversion theorem tells us that

$$f(t) = \frac{1}{2\pi j}\oint F(s)\epsilon^{st}\,ds \tag{51}$$

According to Eq. (163) of Chap. 5, as we have already had occasion to note, the value of this integral is the sum of the residues of the function

$$F(s)\epsilon^{st}$$

at all its singular points.[9] Since ϵ^{st} has no singularities in the finite plane, the singular points in question are those of $F(s)$.

In case $F(s)$ can be put in the form

$$F(s) = \frac{P(s)}{Q(s)} \tag{52}$$

and $P(s)$ has no singularities in the finite plane, so that all singularities of $F(s)$ are due to zeros of $Q(s)$, and if these singularities are all poles, then Eq. (51) can be evaluated in a relatively simple form. According to §5.13, the residue of

$$F(s)\epsilon^{st} \tag{53}$$

at any pole $s = a$ is

$$\frac{P(a)\epsilon^{at}}{Q'(a)} \tag{54}$$

where

$$Q'(a) = \left\{\frac{d}{ds}\,Q(s)\right\}_{s=a} \tag{55}$$

Therefore, if $F(s)$ has only n singular points, and these are poles due to zeros of $Q(s)$ at $s = a_1, a_2, \cdots a_n$, respectively, then

$$f(t) = \frac{1}{2\pi j}\oint F(s)\epsilon^{st}\,ds = \frac{P(a_1)\epsilon^{a_1t}}{Q'(a_1)} + \frac{P(a_2)\epsilon^{a_2t}}{Q'(a_2)} + \cdots + \frac{P(a_n)\epsilon^{a_nt}}{Q'(a_n)} \tag{56}$$

We recognize[10] Eq. (56) as Heaviside's expansion theorem already

---

[9] We need consider only singular points in the finite plane, ordinarily, since the finite energy content of signals will usually ensure the fact that there is no residue at infinity. See footnote (6).

[10] As derived in Chap. 3, the expansion theorem dealt only with forms of $F(s)$ which were rational fractions. However, it may be shown (see Goursat, Page 133) that a single-valued function, all of whose singularities are poles, is a rational fraction. Consequently, Eq. (56) is essentially the same as the expansion theorem derived in Chap. 3. In Chap. 10, we shall meet a function having an infinite number of poles (plus an essential singularity at infinity). This is handled by the inversion theorem in combination with expression (54) which thereby constitutes a generalization of the expansion theorem for non-algebraic cases.

derived in Chap. 3. The foregoing derivation, however, gives a deeper insight into the significance of the expansion theorem.

In case the function $F(s)$ has singularities other than poles due to zeros of $Q(s)$, the corresponding residues have to be added to the right side of Eq. (56) to get the complete solution for $f(t)$. When the residues can be found, the inversion theorem yields a generalization to the expansion theorem as originally derived, which can be used even when $F(s)$ is not in the form of a rational fraction.

In a large number of the problems in which transformation calculus is used, the function of the complex variable s is present in a form such as

$$I(s) = \frac{E(s)}{Z(s)} \tag{57}$$

where $E(s)$ is the transform of the voltage or force function, and $Z(s)$ is the impedance function. In that case, some of the terms in the response function $i(t)$ are due to the singularities of $1/Z(s)$ [i.e., zeros of $Z(s)$], and are characteristic of the form of the impedance. The other terms in the response function are due to the singularities of $E(s)$, and are characteristic of the form of the voltage or force function. In case the voltage is of periodic form, the latter are called the steady-state response, while the former are called the transient response.

7.6. Relations between Laplace and Fourier transforms—interchangeability of tables

The Laplace-transformation formulas

$$F(s) = \int_0^\infty f(t)\epsilon^{-st}\,dt \tag{58}$$

and

$$f(t) = \frac{1}{2\pi j}\oint F(s)\epsilon^{st}\,ds \tag{59}$$

bear a striking resemblance to the Fourier-transformation formulas[11]

$$F_1(f) = \int_{-\infty}^{+\infty} G(t)\epsilon^{-j2\pi ft}\,dt \tag{60}$$

and

$$G(t) = \int_{-\infty}^{+\infty} F_1(f)\epsilon^{j2\pi ft}\,df \tag{61}$$

[11] The notation $F_1(f)$ is used rather than $F(f)$ so as not to cause confusion with the function $F(s)$.

In fact, if we substitute $j\omega = j2\pi f$ for s in Eqs. (58) and (59), the formal identity is complete, except for the paths of integration. In case $F(s)$ has no poles on the imaginary axis or to the right of it and if the contour integral

$$\int F(s)\epsilon^{st}\,ds$$

vanishes on the infinite semicircle to the left of the imaginary axis, and if $G(t)$ is real and vanishes for negative values of t, the two sets of equations have identical significance. Actually these conditions are satisfied in the majority of cases of practical interest, so that to a large extent a table of Fourier pairs can be used as a table of Laplace transforms, and vice versa. Thus the Campbell and Foster table,[12] which is perhaps the most extensive table of Fourier pairs in existence, is also an extensive table of Laplace transforms.

For the reader's convenience, the following sets of rules have been tabulated for interchangeability of such tables.

I. To Get Laplace Transforms from a Table of Fourier Pairs:

1. Make sure that $G(t)$ is real. (Otherwise the form is not suited for use as a Laplace transform.)

2. Substitute $f(t)$ for $G(t)$.

3. (a) If $G(t) = 0$ for $t < 0$, substitute $(s/2\pi j)$ for f in $F_1(f)$ to get $F(s)$.

(b) If $G(t)$ is an even function, i.e., $G(t) = G(-t)$, substitute $(s/2\pi j)$ for f in $F_1(f)$ and divide[13] by 2 to get $F(s)$.

(c) If $G(t) \neq 0$ for $t < 0$, and if $G(t)$ is not an even function of t, and if $G(t)$ cannot be put into either of the foregoing forms by a change of variable, then the form is not suited for use as a Laplace transform.

II. To Get Fourier Pairs from a Table of Laplace Transforms:

1. Make sure that $F(s)$ has no poles on the imaginary axis or to the right of it. (Otherwise the form is not suited for use as a Fourier pair.)

---

[12] Bell System Monograph B584.

[13] In this case

$$F_1(f) = \int_{-\infty}^{+\infty} G(t)\epsilon^{-j2\pi ft}\,dt = \int_0^{\infty} G(t)[\epsilon^{-j2\pi ft} + \epsilon^{j2\pi ft}]\,dt = F(s) + [F(s)]^* = 2F(s)$$

since $F_1(f)$ is real when $G(t)$ is an even function.

2. Substitute $G(t)$ for $f(t)$. [$G(t)$ will consequently vanish for negative values of t.]
3. Substitute $(j2\pi f)$ for s in $F(s)$ to get $F_1(f)$.

As an example of the foregoing rules, we give the following pairs of equivalent transforms:

$$\begin{cases} G(t) = \epsilon^{-\beta t} \text{ for } t > 0 \\ F_1(f) = \dfrac{1}{j2\pi f + \beta} \end{cases} \qquad \begin{cases} f(t) = \epsilon^{-\beta t} \text{ for } t > 0 \\ F(s) = \dfrac{1}{s + \beta} \end{cases}$$

7.7. Relations between Laplace and Fourier transforms—impedance characteristics versus frequency characteristics

The fact that Laplace and Fourier transforms are formally equivalent in the majority of cases, if s is substituted for $j\omega$, leads us to inquire further into the relation between impedance characteristics and frequency characteristics. According to the Fourier-integral method of solution, the driving function $e(t)$ is expressed as a Fourier integral of frequency components in the form

$$e(t) = \frac{1}{2\pi} \int_{-\infty}^{+\infty} E(j\omega)\epsilon^{j\omega t}\, d\omega \tag{62}$$

where[14]

$$E(j\omega) = \int_0^\infty e(t)\epsilon^{-j\omega t}\, dt \tag{63}$$

assuming that $e(t) = 0$ when $t < 0$. Then the response $i(t)$ can be written in the form

$$i(t) = \frac{1}{2\pi} \int_{-\infty}^{+\infty} \frac{E(j\omega)}{Z(j\omega)} \epsilon^{j\omega t}\, d\omega \tag{64}$$

If the integration in Eq. (64) can be carried out, the result is the desired solution for $i(t)$. On the other hand, according to the method of transformation calculus,

$$i(t) = \frac{1}{2\pi j} \oint \frac{E(s)}{Z(s)} \epsilon^{st}\, ds \tag{65}$$

where

$$E(s) = \int_0^\infty e(t)\epsilon^{-st}\, dt \tag{66}$$

---

[14] The function $E(j\omega)$ is used instead of $F_1(f)$ so that a function of the same form as $E(s)$ in Eq. (66) will be obtained.

Since (64) can be rewritten

$$i(t) = \frac{1}{2\pi j} \int_{j\omega=-j\infty}^{j\omega=+j\infty} \frac{E(j\omega)}{Z(j\omega)} \epsilon^{j\omega t} d(j\omega) \tag{67}$$

a comparison of Eqs. (65) and (67) shows that use of the Fourier integral is formally identical with integration along the imaginary axis of the s plane in using the Laplace transformation.

From a practical point of view we can say that the methods of transformation calculus are ordinarily used to solve problems given in terms of impedances or differential equations, while the methods of Fourier integrals are generally used for problems given in terms of frequency characteristics. Actually, transformation calculus can solve the problems of Fourier integrals, but when this is done the two methods are identical. Practically, we can distinguish between the two methods by saying that *when a problem is solved by an explicit integration along the imaginary axis of the s plane, we say that the Fourier-integral method is used; but when the problem is solved by adding the residues at the singularities, the method used is that of transformation calculus.* The two methods are just alternative procedures for evaluating the same contour integrals.

In case the integrand of Eq. (65)

$$I(s)\epsilon^{st} = \frac{E(s)}{Z(s)} \epsilon^{st} \tag{68}$$

has a singularity on the imaginary axis or to the right of it, the integral Eq. (63) will fail to converge; so that the Fourier-integral method of solution cannot be used. However, it is still possible to use the method of transformation calculus and use a contour in Eq. (65) which passes to the right of all poles of $I(s)$. The method of transformation calculus is thus more general than the method of Fourier integrals.

As an example, suppose that starting at $t = 0$, an e.m.f. ϵ^{at} in which a is a positive constant, is applied across a resistance R. Then according to Eq. (63)

$$E(j\omega) = \int_0^\infty \epsilon^{at}\epsilon^{-j\omega t}\, dt = \left.\frac{\epsilon^{(a-j\omega)t}}{a - j\omega}\right|_0^\infty \tag{69}$$

which does not converge. Therefore, the Fourier-integral method cannot be used.[15] On the other hand, by transformation calculus

$$E(s) = \int_0^\infty \epsilon^{at}\epsilon^{-st}\,dt = \left.\frac{\epsilon^{(a-s)t}}{a-s}\right|_0^\infty = \frac{1}{s-a} \tag{70}$$

where the real part of s is greater than a. Then

$$i(t) = \frac{1}{2\pi j}\oint \frac{\epsilon^{st}}{R(s-a)}\,ds \tag{71}$$

The integrand of Eq. (71) has only one pole, at $s = a$. Therefore, by Eq. (56),

$$i(t) = \frac{\epsilon^{at}}{R} \tag{72}$$

which we know is the correct answer.

Cases in which poles of $I(s)$ lie to the right of the imaginary axis are rare in practice. They are due either to negative resistances or to continually rising applied voltages. They are thus associated with unstable conditions. Cases in which poles of $I(s)$ lie *on* the imaginary axis are due to pure reactances or to steady-state applied voltages which continue indefinitely. These cases may be approximated in practice, and are therefore frequently important. However, in the vast majority of actual cases, the poles of $I(s)$ lie to the left of the imaginary axis, and the problem can be solved, at least in the abstract, by either the methods of transformation calculus or those of Fourier integrals.

The method of Fourier integrals has one aspect of greater generality than that of transformation calculus in that it can treat functions of the real variable t in which $G(t) \neq 0$ when t is negative. Transformation calculus cannot handle such functions. In practice, however, this advantage is not of any consequence in the types of problems which we have so far treated, since the origin of t can always be moved so far to the left that $f(t)$ vanishes everywhere to the left of it. However, in certain traveling wave problems this

[15] In any physically realizable case, the e.m.f. cannot continue its exponential rise indefinitely. The Fourier integral of any actual e.m.f. (from which the direct current has been subtracted) will always converge, so that in theory the Fourier-integral method will always work. However, it may become very complicated. Therefore, if an actual e.m.f. is approximately exponential over a particularly wide range of interest, it is convenient to have a simple method to calculate its transient response from its simple exponential behavior.

advantage is important. It should also be mentioned that in generalized Fourier integral theory, in which the frequency is allowed to become complex, there is no longer any difference between the two points of view.

Finally, a word is in order concerning the relation of s and $j\omega$ to p, where

$$p \equiv \frac{d}{dt} \tag{73}$$

This matter has already been settled in §4.5, where it was shown that p is equivalent to s if the initial conditions at $t = 0$ are replaced by a corresponding voltage. When the initial conditions at $t = 0$ are quiescent, p and s are exactly equivalent.[16]

7.8. Characteristics and correspondence of impedances and voltages

Earlier in this chapter we have shown that the current which flows in any branch of a network is equal to the sum of the residues of the poles of the function

$$I(s)\epsilon^{st} = \frac{E(s)}{Z(s)}\,\epsilon^{st} \tag{74}$$

It is clear that these poles and residues can arise either from $E(s)$ or $Z(s)$ and that the roles of $E(s)$ and of $1/Z(s)$ are entirely equivalent in their effect on the current response. Furthermore, the current will involve the various characteristic exponentials which are due to the location of the poles of both $E(s)$ and $1/Z(s)$.

In Table I we have illustrated this phenomenon by recording the responses of ten different impedances to seven different applied voltages. This table gives the complete solution to seventy different circuit problems, some of great and some of trivial importance. In the table we see, for example, that the pole at

$$s = -\frac{1}{RC} \tag{75}$$

of the function

$$\frac{1}{Z(s)} = \frac{s}{R\left(s + \dfrac{1}{RC}\right)} \tag{76}$$

[16] Because of the close relationship of p and s, many writers use the symbol p both for d/dt and for the Laplace complex variable s. Since the two are not exactly equivalent, we have preferred to follow those writers who use separate symbols for them.

TABLE I

i(t) / I(s)	e(t)	E(s)	I Z(s) = sL	II R	III $1/sC$	IV $R+\frac{1}{sC}$	V $sL+\frac{1}{sC}=\frac{L}{s}(s^2+\frac{1}{LC})$	VI $R+sL$
A — i(t)	$\delta(t)$	1	$U(t)/L$	$\frac{1}{R}\delta(t)$	DOUBLET IMPULSE	$\frac{1}{R}\delta(t)-\frac{1}{R^2C}\epsilon^{-t/RC}$	$\frac{1}{L}\cos(\frac{t}{\sqrt{LC}})$	$\frac{1}{L}\epsilon^{-Rt/L}$
A — I(s)			$\frac{1}{sL}$	$\frac{1}{R}$	sC	$\frac{1}{R}\left[1-\frac{1}{1+sCR}\right]$	$\frac{s}{L(s^2+\frac{1}{LC})}$	$\frac{1}{R+sL}$
B — i(t)	$U(t)$	$1/s$	t/L	$\frac{1}{R}U(t)$	$C\delta(t)$	$\frac{1}{R}\epsilon^{-t/RC}$	$\sqrt{\frac{C}{L}}\sin(\frac{t}{\sqrt{LC}})$	$\frac{1}{R}(1-\epsilon^{-Rt}$
B — I(s)			$\frac{1}{s^2L}$	$1/sR$	c	$\frac{C}{1+sCR}$	$\frac{1}{L(s^2+\frac{1}{LC})}$	$\frac{1}{s(R+sL)}$
C — i(t)	t	$1/s^2$	$t^2/2L$	t/R	$CU(t)$	$C(1-\epsilon^{-t/RC})$	$C\left[1-\cos(\frac{t}{\sqrt{LC}})\right]$	$\frac{t}{R}-\frac{L}{R^2}(1-\epsilon^{-Rt}$
C — I(s)			$\frac{1}{s^3L}$	$1/s^2R$	$\frac{C}{s}$	$\frac{C}{s(1+sCR)}$	$\frac{1}{Ls(s^2+1/LC)}$	$\frac{1}{s^2(R+sL)}$
D — i(t)	t^2	$2/s^3$	$t^3/6L$	$t^2/2R$	Ct	$Ct+RC^2\left[\epsilon^{-t/RC}-1\right]$	$C\sqrt{LC}\left[\frac{t}{\sqrt{LC}}-\sin\frac{t}{\sqrt{LC}}\right]$	$\frac{t^2}{2R}-\frac{Lt}{R^2}+\frac{L^2}{R^3}(1-\epsilon^{-Rt/L}$
D — I(s)			$\frac{1}{s^4L}$	$1/s^3R$	$\frac{C}{s^2}$	$\frac{C}{s^2(1+sCR)}$	$\frac{1}{Ls^2(s^2+1/LC)}$	$\frac{1}{s^3(R+sL)}$
E — i(t)	ϵ^{-at}	$\frac{1}{s+a}$	$\frac{1-\epsilon^{-at}}{La}$	$\frac{\epsilon^{-at}}{R}$	$C\delta(t)-Ca\epsilon^{-at}$	$\frac{1}{aR-1/C}\left[a\epsilon^{-at}-\frac{1}{CR}\epsilon^{-t/CR}\right]$	$\frac{-a\epsilon^{-at}+a\cos(t/\sqrt{LC})+\frac{1}{\sqrt{LC}}\sin(t/\sqrt{LC})}{L(a^2+\frac{1}{CL})}$	$\frac{1}{R-aL}(\epsilon^{-at}-\epsilon^{-Rt/L}$
E — I(s)			$\frac{1}{sL(s+a)}$	$\frac{1}{R(s+a)}$	$\frac{sC}{s+a}$	$\frac{s}{R(s+\frac{1}{CR})(s+a)}$	$\frac{s}{L(s+a)(s^2+1/LC)}$	$\frac{1}{(s+a)(R+sL)}$
F — i(t)	$\sin\omega t$	$\frac{\omega}{s^2+\omega^2}$	$\frac{1}{\omega L}(1-\cos\omega t)$	$\frac{\sin\omega t}{R}$	$\omega C\cos\omega t$	$\frac{\omega C\left[\cos\omega t+R\omega C\sin\omega t-\epsilon^{-t/RC}\right]}{1+\omega^2C^2R^2}$	$-\frac{\frac{\omega}{L}\left\{\cos\omega t-\cos(\frac{t}{\sqrt{LC}})\right\}}{\frac{1}{LC}-\omega^2}$	$\frac{\omega L\epsilon^{-Rt/L}-\omega L\cos\omega t+R\sin\omega t}{R^2+\omega^2L^2}$
F — I(s)			$\frac{\omega}{sL(s^2+\omega^2)}$	$\frac{\omega}{R(s^2+\omega^2)}$	$\frac{s\omega C}{s^2+\omega^2}$	$\frac{\omega s}{R(s+\frac{1}{CR})(s^2+\omega^2)}$	$\frac{\omega s}{L(s^2+\omega^2)(s^2+\frac{1}{LC})}$	$\frac{\omega}{(R+sL)(s^2+\omega^2)}$
G — i(t)	$\cos\omega t$	$\frac{s}{s^2+\omega^2}$	$\frac{1}{\omega L}\sin\omega t$	$\frac{\cos\omega t}{R}$	$C\delta(t)-\omega C\sin\omega t$	$\frac{\omega C\left[R\omega C\cos\omega t-\sin\omega t+\frac{1}{R\omega C}\epsilon^{-t/RC}\right]}{1+\omega^2C^2R^2}$	$\frac{(\omega/L)\left[\sin\omega t-\frac{1}{\omega\sqrt{LC}}\sin(\frac{t}{\sqrt{LC}})\right]}{\omega^2-1/LC}$	$\frac{-R\epsilon^{-Rt/L}+R\cos\omega t+\omega L\sin\omega t}{R^2+\omega^2L^2}$
G — I(s)			$\frac{1}{L(s^2+\omega^2)}$	$\frac{s}{R(s^2+\omega^2)}$	$\frac{s^2C}{s^2+\omega^2}$	$\frac{s^2}{R(s+1/CR)(s^2+\omega^2)}$	$\frac{s^2}{L(s^2+\omega^2)(s^2+\frac{1}{LC})}$	$\frac{s}{(R+sL)(s^2+\omega^2)}$

LIST OF SYMBOLS $Z=\sqrt{(\omega L-\frac{1}{\omega C})^2+R^2}$ $\quad\psi_1=\tan^{-1}\left\{\frac{\frac{1}{\omega C}-\omega L}{R}\right\}$

$\beta=\sqrt{\frac{1}{LC}-\frac{R^2}{4L^2}}$ $\quad\psi_2=\tan^{-1}\left\{-\frac{2\beta L}{R}\left(\frac{\omega^2LC-1}{\omega^2LC+1}\right)\right\}$

for the series R-C circuit (IV), gives rise to a characteristic factor $\epsilon^{-t/RC}$, which appears in the response of this impedance to each of the seven different applied voltages. In a similar manner, the pair of poles at

$$s=-\frac{R}{2L}\pm j\sqrt{\frac{1}{LC}-\frac{R^2}{4L^2}} \tag{77}$$

of the function

$$\frac{1}{Z(s)}=\frac{s}{L\left\{s^2+\frac{sR}{L}+\frac{1}{LC}\right\}} \tag{78}$$

TABLE I (*Cont.*)

VII	VIII	IX	X
$R+sL+\frac{1}{sC}$	$\frac{R(R_CsC+1)}{sC(R+R_C)+1}$	$\frac{(R_L+sL)(R_CsC+1)}{s^2LC+sC(R_L+R_C)+1}$	$\frac{R+sL}{s^2LC+sRC+1}$
$\epsilon^{-Rt/2L}\left\{\frac{1}{L}\cos\beta t-\left(\frac{R}{2\beta L^2}\right)\sin\beta t\right\}$	$\left[\frac{1}{R}+\frac{1}{R_C}\right]\delta(t)-\frac{1}{R_C^2C}\epsilon^{-t/R_CC}$	$\frac{1}{R}\delta(t)+\frac{1}{L}\epsilon^{-R_Lt/L}-\frac{1}{R_C^2C}\epsilon^{-t/R_CC}$	DOUBLET IMPULSE $+\frac{1}{L}\epsilon^{-Rt/L}$
$\frac{s}{L(s^2+sR/L+1/LC)}$	$\frac{sC(R+R_C)+1}{R(sR_CC+1)}$	$\frac{s^2LC+sC(R_L+R_C)+1}{(R_L+sL)(R_CsC+1)}$	$\frac{s^2LC+sRC+1}{R+sL}$
$\frac{(\epsilon^{-Rt/2L}\sin\beta t)}{\beta L}$	$\frac{1}{R}+\frac{1}{R_C}\epsilon^{-t/R_CC}$	$\frac{1}{R_L}(1-\epsilon^{-R_Lt/L})+\frac{1}{R_C}\epsilon^{-t/R_CC}$	$C\delta(t)+\frac{1}{R}(1-\epsilon^{-Rt/L})$
$\frac{1}{L(s^2+sR/L+1/LC)}$	$\frac{sC(R+R_C)+1}{sR(sR_CC+1)}$	$\frac{s^2LC+sC(R_L+R_C)+1}{s(R_L+sL)(R_CsC+1)}$	$\frac{s^2LC+sRC+1}{s(R+sL)}$
$C\left\{\epsilon^{-Rt/2L}\left[-\frac{R}{2\beta L}\sin\beta t-\cos\beta t\right]+1\right\}$	$\frac{t}{R}+C(1-\epsilon^{-t/R_CC})$	$\frac{t}{R_L}-\left[\frac{L}{R_L^2}-C\right]+\frac{L}{R_L^2}\epsilon^{-Rt/L}-C\epsilon^{-t/R_CC}$	$\frac{t}{R}-\left(\frac{L}{R^2}-C\right)+\frac{L}{R^2}\epsilon^{-Rt/L}$
$\frac{1}{Ls(s^2+sR/L+1/LC)}$	$\frac{sC(R+R_C)+1}{s^2R(sR_CC+1)}$	$\frac{s^2LC+sC(R_L+R_C)+1}{s^2(R_L+sL)(R_CsC+1)}$	$\frac{s^2LC+sRC+1}{s^2(R+sL)}$
$\left[\frac{C^2R^2}{4\beta L}-LC^2\beta\right]\epsilon^{-Rt/2L}\sin\beta t+Ct+RC^2\epsilon^{-Rt/2L}(\cos\beta t-1)$	$\frac{t^2}{2R}+Ct+R_CC^2\left[\epsilon^{-t/R_CC}-1\right]$	$\frac{t^2}{2R_L}-\left[\frac{L}{R_L^2}-C\right]t+\left[\frac{L^2}{R_L^3}-R_CC^2\right]-\frac{L^2}{R_L^3}\epsilon^{-Rt/L}+R_CC^2\epsilon^{-t/R_CC}$	$\frac{t^2}{2R}-\left[\frac{L}{R^2}-C\right]t+\frac{L^2}{R^3}(1-\epsilon^{-Rt/L})$
$\frac{1}{Ls^2(s^2+sR/L+1/LC)}$	$\frac{sC(R+R_C)+1}{s^3R(sR_CC+1)}$	$\frac{s^2LC+sC(R_L+R_C)+1}{s^3(R_L+sL)(R_CsC+1)}$	$\frac{s^2LC+sRC+1}{s^3(R+sL)}$
$\frac{1}{L\left\{\beta^2+\left(a-\frac{R}{2L}\right)^2\right\}}\left\{-a\epsilon^{-at}+a\epsilon^{-Rt/2L}\cos\beta t+\frac{1}{\beta}\left[\frac{1}{LC}-\frac{aR}{2L}\right]\epsilon^{-Rt/2L}\sin\beta t\right\}$	$\frac{\epsilon^{-at}}{R}+\frac{1}{aR_C-\frac{1}{C}}\left[a\epsilon^{-at}-\frac{1}{R_CC}\epsilon^{-t/R_CC}\right]$	$\left[\frac{1}{R_L-aL}+\frac{1}{R_C-\frac{1}{aC}}\right]\epsilon^{-at}-\frac{1}{R_L-aL}\epsilon^{-R_Lt/L}-\frac{1}{R_C-\frac{1}{aC}}\left(\frac{1}{aCR_C}\right)\epsilon^{-t/R_CC}$	$C\delta(t)+\left(\frac{1}{R-aL}-aC\right)\epsilon^{-at}-\frac{1}{R-aL}\epsilon^{-Rt/L}$
$\frac{s}{L(s+a)(s^2+sR/L+1/LC)}$	$\frac{sC(R+R_C)+1}{R(s+a)(sR_CC+1)}$	$\frac{s^2LC+sC(R_L+R_C)+1}{(s+a)(R_L+sL)(R_CsC+1)}$	$\frac{s^2LC+sRC+1}{(s+a)(R+sL)}$
$\frac{\sin(\omega t+\psi_1)}{Z}+\frac{\frac{1}{\sqrt{LC}}\epsilon^{-Rt/2L}\sin(\beta t+\psi_2)}{\beta Z}$	$\frac{\sin\omega t}{R}+\frac{\omega C\left[\cos\omega t+R_C\omega C\sin\omega t-\epsilon^{-t/R_CC}\right]}{1+\omega^2C^2R_C^2}$	$\frac{X_L}{Z_L^2}\epsilon^{-R_Lt/L}-\frac{X_C}{Z_C^2}\epsilon^{-t/R_CC}-\left(\frac{X_L}{Z_L^2}+\frac{X_C}{Z_C^2}\right)\cos\omega t+\left(\frac{R_L}{Z_L^2}+\frac{R_C}{Z_C^2}\right)\sin\omega t$	$\frac{X_L}{Z_L^2}\epsilon^{-Rt/L}-\left(\frac{X_L}{Z_L^2}-\frac{1}{X_C}\right)\cos\omega t+\frac{R}{Z_L^2}\sin\omega t$
$\frac{s\omega}{L(s^2+\omega^2)(s^2+sR/L+1/LC)}$	$\frac{\omega[sC(R+R_C)+1]}{R(sR_CC+1)(s^2+\omega^2)}$	$\frac{\omega[s^2LC+sC(R_L+R_C)+1]}{(s^2+\omega^2)(R_L+sL)(R_CsC+1)}$	$\frac{\omega[s^2LC+sRC+1]}{(s^2+\omega^2)(R+sL)}$
$\frac{\cos(\omega t+\psi_1)}{Z}+\frac{1}{\omega\beta Z\sqrt{LC}}\epsilon^{-Rt/2L}\left\{\beta\cos(\beta t+\psi_2)-\frac{R}{2L}\sin(\beta t+\psi_2)\right\}$	$\frac{\cos\omega t}{R}+\frac{\omega C\left[R_C\omega C\cos\omega t-\sin\omega t+\frac{\epsilon^{-t/R_CC}}{R_C\omega C}\right]}{1+\omega^2C^2R_C^2}$	$-\frac{R_L}{Z_L^2}\epsilon^{-R_Lt/L}+\frac{X_C^2}{R_CZ_C^2}\epsilon^{-t/R_CC}+\left(\frac{R_L}{Z_L^2}+\frac{R_C}{Z_C^2}\right)\cos\omega t+\left(\frac{X_L}{Z_L^2}+\frac{X_C}{Z_C^2}\right)\sin\omega t$	$C\delta(t)-\frac{R}{Z_L^2}\epsilon^{-Rt/L}+\frac{R}{Z_L^2}\cos\omega t+\left(\frac{X_L}{Z_L^2}-\frac{1}{X_C}\right)\sin\omega t$
$\frac{s^2}{L(s^2+\omega^2)(s^2+sR/L+1/LC)}$	$\frac{s[sC(R+R_C)+1]}{R(sR_CC+1)(s^2+\omega^2)}$	$\frac{s[s^2LC+sC(R_L+R_C)+1]}{(s^2+\omega^2)(R_L+sL)(R_CsC+1)}$	$\frac{s[s^2LC+sRC+1]}{(s^2+\omega^2)(R+sL)}$

$X_L=\omega L$ $\quad$ $X_C=\frac{1}{\omega C}$

$Z_L^2=\omega^2L^2+R_L^2$

$Z_C^2=\frac{1}{\omega^2C^2}+R_C^2=\frac{1+\omega^2C^2R_C^2}{\omega^2C^2}$

for the series L-R-C circuit (VII) gives rise to characteristic factors of the form

$$\epsilon^{-\frac{Rt}{2L}}\cos\left\{\left(\sqrt{\frac{1}{LC}-\frac{R^2}{4L^2}}\right)t+\phi\right\}$$

which appear in all the response functions of this impedance. The poles of the voltage function $E(s)$ similarly affect all the response functions in which the corresponding voltage is involved.

In the case of parallel impedances, such as (VIII), (IX), and (X), the currents through the different branches are additive, making it a simple matter to calculate the total response by the simple addition of known responses of simpler circuits. In systems in which addition of this type prevails, it is sometimes possible to cancel undesired terms in the response function by the coupling to the network of the proper impedance acted upon by the proper voltage.[17]

Table I will serve as a handy reference for the type of response that can be obtained from various impedances and voltages. The speed with which such a table can be calculated from the $I(s)$ function is an excellent example of the labor-saving qualities of transformation calculus.

In the case of a network, it is ordinarily true that the same natural frequencies and exponential damping factors appear in the current of every branch of the network, regardless of the nature of the applied e.m.f. and of the part of the network in which it is applied. Physically, the reason for this is that each exponential term in the expansion-theorem solution for the current in one branch of the network will, through coupling, induce a term of the same type in every other branch of the network.[18] Mathematically, the reason for this can be seen by examining Eq. (37) of Chap. 4. There we see that all the poles of any $I_k(s)$ which are due to poles of the transformed voltage functions or to zeros of $\Delta(s)$, will also be present in every other $I_k(s)$.

An exceptional case will occur when there are additional[19] poles due to the minors or to a linear combination in the numerator of Eq. (37) of Chap. 4. Another exceptional case will occur when poles present in some $I_j(s)$ will fail to be present in some other $I_k(s)$, because of the vanishing of the coupling minor $M_{jk}(s)$. When these exceptional cases involve a pole of a transformed voltage function, they give rise to types of filters or bridge circuits.

Another type of exceptional case exists in which a mesh, having

---

[17] If $R = R_L = R_C = \sqrt{L/C}$ in impedance (IX), then $Z(s)$ reduces to R. The responses should then reduce to the applied voltage divided by R. This fact can be used to check errors in Column IX of the table. Another check is dimensional homogeneity.

[18] Exponential factors of the form ϵ^{mt}, where m may be complex, are of a specially permanent form, because they retain their form through differentiation and integration. They therefore retain their form through any type of coupling in a linear network.

[19] The case of coincident poles is another special case, but will not be treated here.

a certain characteristic exponential term,[20] has zero coupling with the rest of the network for this particular exponential term. This exponential term can then be aroused only when an e.m.f. is applied in the particular mesh in question, and even then it will appear only in this circuit. This condition is described as an *isolated mode*, and it is due to the vanishing of all the coupling minors $M_{jk}(s)$, $k \neq j$, for particular values of k and s. *Isolated modes* have been investigated by Guillemin.[21]

7.9. The relations between attenuation and phase characteristics[22]

(a) Some Properties of Impedance and Admittance Functions—Symmetry. In §4.11 we showed that the real and imaginary components of an admittance function cannot be specified independently throughout the frequency range. We now wish to deal with this subject more thoroughly, since it is a matter of great importance, especially in the design of feedback amplifiers.

In the present chapter we have seen that the impedances and admittances[23] of all linear networks with simple elements are analytic functions of s. In Chap. 10 we will find that linear networks are still analytic functions of s, even if they involve transmission-line elements. The fact that the immittances of linear networks are analytic functions of s is the reason for the relations between their amplitude and phase characteristics; and in finding these relations, we shall make use of the properties of analytic functions, especially contour integration. We note in passing that the analytic character of the network functions is still retained if

---

[20] It is unusual for a circuit in a network to have characteristic exponential terms of its own. The exponents themselves are usually affected by the coupling. This may be seen in Examples (4) and (5) of §3.13.

[21] E. A. Guillemin, *Proc. I.R.E.*, 15, p. 935 (1927).

[22] This section is largely based upon material in H. W. Bode's *Network Analysis and Feedback Amplifier Design*, New York: D. Van Nostrand, 1945. The most important parts of it originate in Bode's patent No. 2,123,178 and his paper "Relations between Amplitude and Phase in Feedback Amplifier Design," *Bell Sys. Tech. Jour.*, 19, p. 421 (July, 1940). An alternative approach based upon orthogonal functions and Hilbert transforms is due to N. Wiener and Y. W. Lee. See U. S. patents No. 2,024,900; 2,124,599; and 2,128,257. Also see Lee's paper in the June, 1932, issue of *Jour. Math. and Phys.*

[23] Hereafter, following the terminology of Bode, we shall use the term *immittance*, to stand for either an impedance or an admittance when the discussion refers equally well to both.

the network includes linear amplifiers. The reader can show this as an exercise.

We will next find some general properties of network immittances. Let $T(s)$ represent the immittance of a linear network with lumped-circuit components,[24] so that $T(j\omega)$ is the steady-state immittance in question. Since $T(s)$ is the ratio of two polynomials in s with real coefficients, it is analytic, and furthermore we can expand it in a Taylor series with real coefficients. Therefore,

$$\begin{aligned} T(j\omega) &= a_0 + a_1(j\omega) + a_2(j\omega)^2 + a_3(j\omega)^3 + \cdots \\ &= a_0 - a_2\omega^2 + a_4\omega^4 \cdots + j[a_1\omega - a_3\omega^3 + a_5\omega^5 \cdots] \\ &= \alpha(\omega) + j\beta(\omega) \end{aligned} \tag{79}$$

We see that the real part $\alpha(\omega)$ of the steady-state immittance is an even function of frequency, while the imaginary part $\beta(\omega)$ is odd.[25]

Let us next express $T(j\omega)$ in exponential form. Thus

$$T(j\omega) = \alpha(\omega) + j\beta(\omega) = |T(j\omega)|\epsilon^{j\phi} = \epsilon^{a(\omega)+j\phi(\omega)} \tag{80}$$

where

$$a(\omega) = \log_\epsilon |T(j\omega)| \tag{81}$$

Accordingly, $a(\omega)$ and $\phi(\omega)$ may be called the attenuation and phase shift, respectively, in case we are dealing with a transfer immittance. Since $\alpha(\omega)$ is an even function, and $\beta(\omega)$ is odd, it follows that

$$T[j(-\omega)] = \alpha(-\omega) + j\beta(-\omega) = \alpha(\omega) - j\beta(\omega) = [T(j\omega)]^* \tag{82}$$

Consequently

$$\epsilon^{a(-\omega)+j\phi(-\omega)} = T[j(-\omega)] = [T(j\omega)]^* = \epsilon^{a(\omega)-j\phi(\omega)} \tag{83}$$

Thus $a(\omega)$ is an even function of ω, and $\phi(\omega)$ is an odd function. The attenuation and phase thus have the same symmetry as the real and imaginary parts of the immittance.

(b) The Location of the Poles and Zeros of Physically Realizable Immittances—Minimum-Phase-Shift Networks. If a self- or transfer immittance of a network is energized by the application of a small impulse of voltage of strength K, the response of the

---

[24] Either a self- or transfer impedance or admittance.

[25] In §4.4 of the author's *Frequency Analysis, Modulation and Noise,* these symmetry properties are proved for any physical network without being limited to lumped-circuit networks.

network will be given by the integral

$$i(t) = \frac{1}{2\pi j} \oint \frac{K\epsilon^{st}\,ds}{Z(s)} = \frac{1}{2\pi j} \oint K\epsilon^{st}Y(s)\,ds \tag{84}$$

In case $Z(s)$ has a zero [or $Y(s)$ has a pole] for a value of

$$s = c + jd \tag{85}$$

having a positive real part, the term in $i(t)$ corresponding to this zero (or pole) will have a multiplier ϵ^{ct} which ultimately increases without limit. Clearly, no stable network could have such a characteristic. We therefore conclude that no stable network has any self- or transfer admittance with a pole to the right of the imaginary axis. All networks referred to as *physically realizable* must be stable and have the symmetry properties discussed in subsection (a).[26]

The foregoing criterion on the poles $Y(s)$ or the zeros of $Z(s)$ is an important criterion on the stability of an immittance. In the remainder of this section we will make important use of this criterion. In addition, however, we will usually want to specify that the immittances with which we shall be dealing will not only be physically realizable, but also that they will be of the *minimum-phase-shift type.*[27] Mathematically, this will mean that the admittances will have no zeros and the impedances no poles on the imaginary axis or to the right of it. Thus physically realizable immittances of the minimum-phase-shift type have neither poles nor zeros in the right half of the s plane.

The physical significance of a transfer immittance of the minimum-phase-shift type is that such an immittance has the least phase shift of all immittances which have its particular attenuation characteristic as a function of frequency.[28] Most network impedances ordinarily used are of the minimum-phase-shift type if

---

[26] Physically realizable immittances also have certain other properties. Thus their real parts must be positive on the frequency axis. The term *physically realizable immittance* as used here is limited to immittances which are physically realizable with passive circuit elements. An extended discussion of physical realizability is given in Bode's book, to which reference has already been made.

[27] If we are dealing with a self-immittance, this will then mean an impedance of the minimum-reactance type or an admittance of the minimum-susceptance type.

[28] See Bode, §11.5.

transmission-line sections are not used. However, there are important exceptions. The transfer immittance between the input and output of a network bridge is often not of the minimum-phase type. An obvious example of an immittance which is not of minimum-phase type is shown in Fig. 7-8. The transfer immittance between the voltage E_1 and the current I_2 through R is of minimum-phase-shift type when the length of the loss-less transmission line is

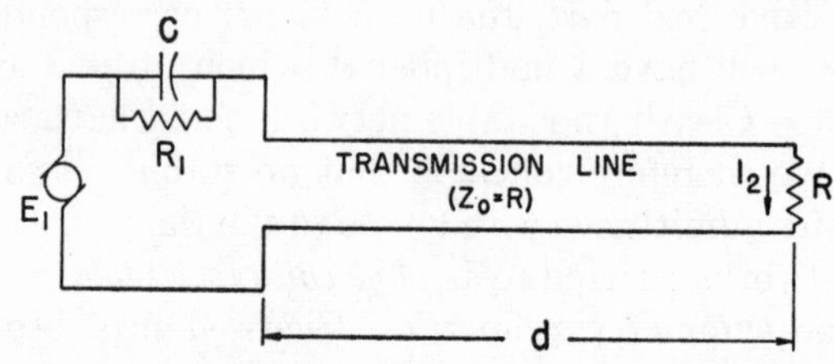

FIG. 7-8. The admittance $Y_{12} = \dfrac{I_2(s)}{E_1(s)}$, an illustration of a transfer immittance which is not of minimum-phase-shift type. (If the transmission line length is made zero, Y_{12} becomes of minimum-phase-shift type.)

zero. When the line length is not zero, the attenuation is unaffected, but the phase shift is increased.[29]

We next note that $a(\omega)$ in Eq. (80) has a pole at every zero of $T(j\omega)$. Consequently, the restriction to minimum-phase-shift immittances makes the functions

$$T(j\omega) = \alpha(\omega) + j\beta(\omega) \tag{86}$$

and

$$W(j\omega) = \log_\epsilon [T(j\omega)] = a(\omega) + j\phi(\omega) \tag{87}$$

remarkably similar in their properties. Thus the real part of each is an even function of ω, while the imaginary part is odd. If $T(s)$ is analytic at infinity in the s plane so is $W(s)$, and vice versa. Fur-

[29] In the case of Fig. 7-8, the transfer admittance

$$Y_{12} = \frac{\epsilon^{-s\sqrt{lc}\,d}}{\left(R + \dfrac{R_1}{1+sCR_1}\right)}$$

has a zero at $s = \infty$ in the right half of the s plane unless $d = 0$. For a more thorough discussion of minimum-phase-shift immittances the reader is referred to Chap. XI of Bode's book.

thermore, neither has a pole in the right half of the s plane. We shall now derive certain relations between the real and imaginary parts of functions having these properties, and they will be relations between $a(\omega)$ and $\phi(\omega)$ as well as relations between $\alpha(\omega)$ and $\beta(\omega)$.

(c) **The Attenuation-Integral Theorem.** Suppose we have an analytic function $S(s)$ having no poles or zeros in the right half of the s plane, and let us assume that it is analytic at $s = 0$ and as $s \to \infty$. We can then expand the function in the Taylor series

$$S(s) = A_0 + B_0 s + A_1 s^2 + B_1 s^3 + \cdots \tag{88}$$

about $s = 0$, and in the Taylor series

$$S(s) = A_\infty - \frac{B'_\infty}{s} + \frac{A'_1}{s^2} - \frac{B'_1}{s^3} + \cdots \tag{89}$$

about the point at infinity. Along the imaginary axis, we can write[30]

$$S(j\omega) = A(\omega) + jB(\omega) \tag{90}$$

We will now use contour integration to derive important relations between the real and imaginary parts of $S(j\omega)$. First, let us integrate

$$S(s) - A_\infty$$

along the closed contour in Fig. 7-9. Since there are no singularities within the contour,

$$\oint [S(s) - A_\infty]\, ds = 0 \tag{91}$$

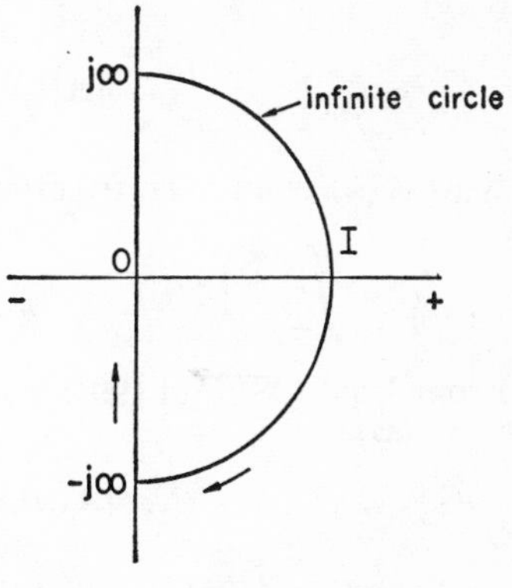

FIG. 7-9. A path of integration in the complex s plane.

Let us now separate this into the integral along the imaginary axis and the integral along the infinite semicircle (I). Thus

$$\int_{-j\infty}^{+j\infty} [A(\omega) + jB(\omega) - A_\infty]d(j\omega) + \int_{\mathrm{I}} \left[-\frac{B'_\infty}{s} + \frac{A'_1}{s^2} - \frac{B'_1}{s^3} + \cdots \right] ds = 0 \tag{92}$$

[30] The relations which we shall derive between A and B will be relations between $a(\omega)$ and $\phi(\omega)$ as well as relations between $\alpha(\omega)$ and $\beta(\omega)$.

Now
$$\int_{-j\infty}^{+j\infty} jB(\omega)d(j\omega) = 0 \tag{93}$$

because $B(\omega)$ is an odd function of ω. Furthermore, along the infinite semicircle we can write

$$s = R\epsilon^{j\theta} \tag{94}$$

and
$$ds = jR\epsilon^{j\theta}\, d\theta \tag{95}$$

where R is the radius of the infinite semicircle. Thus

$$\int_{\text{I}} \frac{-B'_\infty}{s}\, ds = \int_{\pi/2}^{-\pi/2} \frac{-B'_\infty jR\epsilon^{j\theta}\, d\theta}{R\epsilon^{j\theta}} = j\pi B'_\infty \tag{96}$$

and
$$\int_{\text{I}} \frac{ds}{s^n} = 0 \qquad \text{if} \qquad n > 1 \tag{97}$$

Substituting these values into Eq. (92), we have, after dividing by j,

$$\int_{-\infty}^{+\infty} [A(\omega) - A_\infty]d\omega + \pi B'_\infty = 0 \tag{98}$$

Now $A(\omega)$ is an even function of ω, so that

$$\int_{-\infty}^{+\infty} [A(\omega) - A_\infty]\, d\omega = 2\int_0^\infty [A(\omega) - A_\infty]\, d\omega \tag{99}$$

From Eqs. (98) and (99), we have finally

$$\int_0^\infty [A(\omega) - A_\infty]\, d\omega = -\frac{\pi}{2} B'_\infty \tag{100}$$

Equation (100) is called the attenuation-integral theorem. It is clear from the earlier discussion in this section, that this equation holds if A and B are, respectively, the real and imaginary parts of an immittance, and also if they are the attenuation and phase of an immittance of minimum-phase-shift type.

To illustrate the theorem, consider the real and imaginary parts of the impedance of the network in Fig. 7-10. Here

$$z = \frac{R\left(\dfrac{1}{j\omega C}\right)}{R + \dfrac{1}{j\omega C}} = \frac{R}{1 + \omega^2C^2R^2} - \frac{jR^2\omega C}{1 + \omega^2C^2R^2} \tag{101}$$

so that
$$A(\omega) = \frac{R}{1 + \omega^2 C^2 R^2} \tag{102}$$
and
$$B(\omega) = -\frac{R^2 \omega C}{1 + \omega^2 C^2 R^2} \tag{103}$$
Thus
$$A_\infty = 0 \tag{104}$$
and[31]
$$B'_\infty = \frac{-1}{C} \tag{105}$$

The attenuation-integral theorem, Eq. (100), then tells us that

$$\int_0^\infty \frac{R}{1 + \omega^2 C^2 R^2}\, d\omega = \frac{\pi}{2C} \tag{106}$$

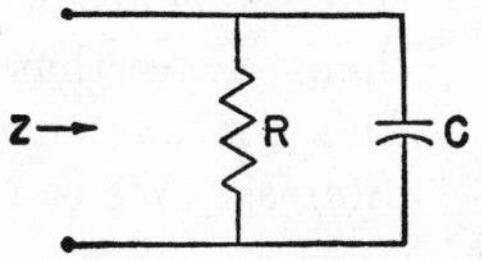

FIG. 7-10. The impedance z, consisting of R and C in parallel.

The reader can confirm this fact by direct integration.

Exercises

1. Confirm the attenuation-integral theorem for the attenuation and phase of the impedance in Fig. 7-10.

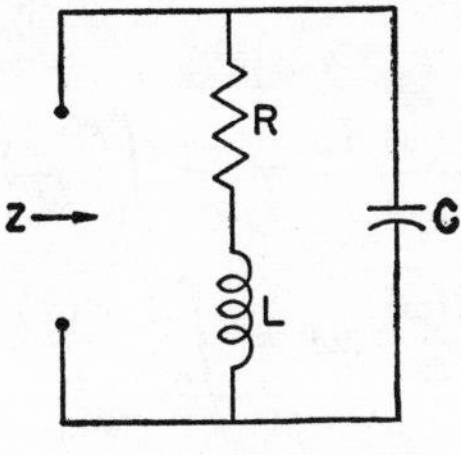

FIG. 7-A.

2. Confirm the attenuation integral theorem for the real and imaginary parts of the impedance in Fig. 7-A.

---

[31] The reader will note that the value of B'_∞ is not the value of $B(\omega)$ as $\omega \to \infty$. The quantity B'_∞ is defined in Eq. (89). A comparison of Eqs. (89) and (90) shows that $B'_\infty = \lim_{\omega \to \infty} [\omega B(\omega)]$.

(d) **The Phase-Area Theorem.** In order to evaluate the attenuation integral, we set up the function $[S(s) - A_\infty]$ whose integral reduced to that of the attenuation integral along the frequency axis and whose integral along the infinite semicircle was finite. A corresponding function for a phase integral, which would have the desired symmetry properties on the frequency axis and the desired magnitude at infinity is $[S(s)/s]$. This function, however, has a pole at $s = 0$, so that the contour of integration must be changed to that shown in Fig. 7-11. This contour encloses no singularity of $[S(s)/s]$. We can therefore write

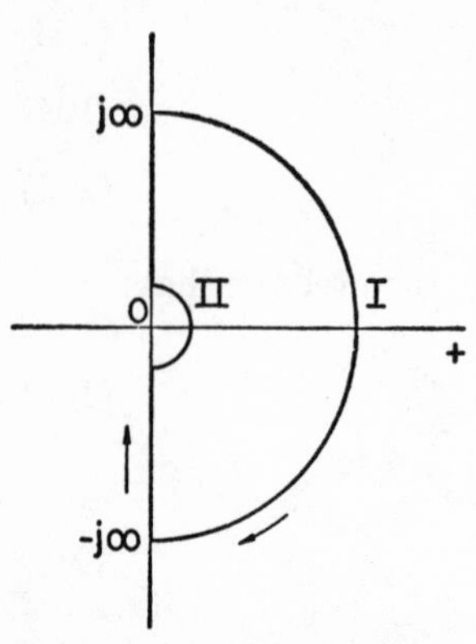

FIG. 7-11. A path of integration in the complex s plane.

$$\oint \frac{S(s)}{s}\, ds = 0 \tag{107}$$

Separating Eq. (107) into the different parts of the contour, we have

$$\int_{-\infty}^{0} \frac{A(\omega) + jB(\omega)}{j\omega}\, d(j\omega) + \int_{\text{II}} \frac{S(s)}{s}\, ds + \int_{0}^{\infty} \frac{A(\omega) + jB(\omega)}{j\omega}\, d(j\omega) + \int_{\text{I}} \frac{S(s)}{s}\, ds = 0 \tag{108}$$

Now
$$\int_{-\infty}^{0} \frac{A(\omega)\, d\omega}{\omega} = -\int_{0}^{\infty} \frac{A(\omega)}{\omega}\, d\omega \tag{109}$$

and
$$\int_{-\infty}^{0} \frac{B(\omega)}{\omega}\, d\omega = \int_{0}^{\infty} \frac{B(\omega)}{\omega}\, d\omega \tag{110}$$

by symmetry. Furthermore

$$\int_{\text{II}} \frac{S(s)}{s}\, ds = \int_{\text{II}} \frac{[A_0 + B_0 s + A_1 s^2 + \text{---}]}{s}\, ds = jA_0\pi \tag{111}$$

$$\int_{\text{I}} \frac{S(s)}{s}\, ds = \int_{\text{I}} \frac{\left[A_\infty - \dfrac{B}{s} + \dfrac{A_1'}{s^2}\right]}{s}\, ds = -jA_\infty\pi \tag{112}$$

Therefore, Eq. (108) reduces to

$$2j \int_0^\infty \frac{B(\omega)}{\omega}\, d\omega + jA_0\pi - jA_\infty\pi = 0 \tag{113}$$

or

$$\int_0^\infty \frac{B(\omega)}{\omega}\, d\omega = \frac{\pi}{2}\,(A_\infty - A_0) \tag{114}$$

Equation (114) may be called the phase-integral theorem. If we make the frequency scale logarithmic by introducing the new variable

$$u = \log \omega \tag{115}$$

then Eq. (114) becomes

$$\int_{-\infty}^{+\infty} B(\omega)\, du = \frac{\pi}{2}\,(A_\infty - A_0) \tag{116}$$

Equation (116) is called the phase-area theorem.

The phase-area theorem is illustrated in Fig. 7-12, where the attenuation curves of three different immittances are shown, each having the same values for $A_0 = a(0)$, and $A_\infty = a(\infty)$. We see that in accordance with the phase-area theorem, each has the same area under the phase-shift curve in the phase diagram. This fact has important practical consequences. For example, in the design of feedback amplifiers, it is desirable to keep the phase shift low over a wide range of frequencies. The phase-area theorem shows that, for fixed values of $a(0)$ and $a(\infty)$, it is then necessary to spread the phase shift over a wide range of octaves.

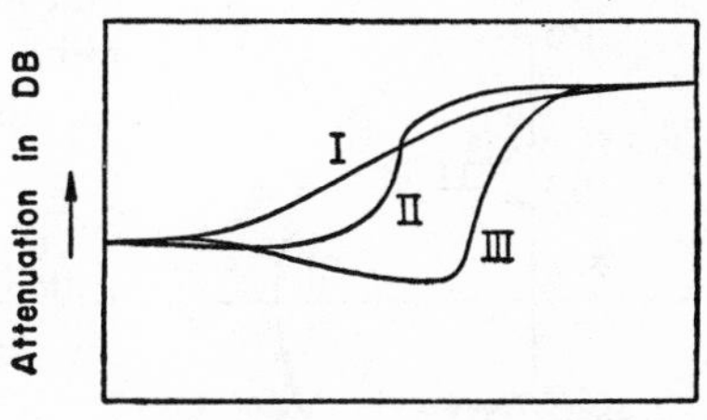

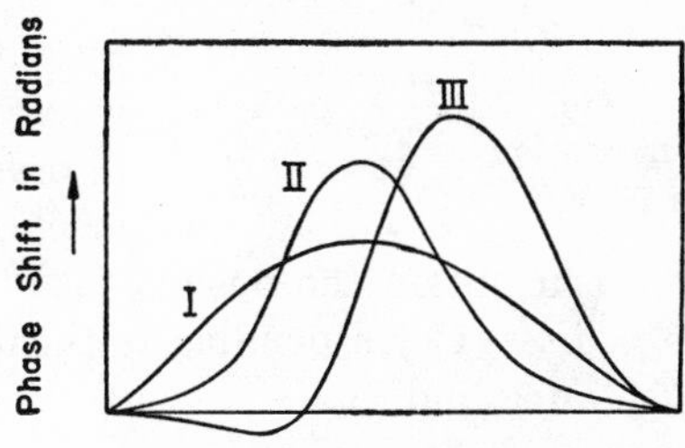

FIG. 7-12. Illustration of the phase-area theorem.

Just as in the case of the attenuation-integral theorem, the phase-area theorem applies to the relation between attenuation and phase as well as to the relation between the real and imaginary part of an immittance. However, in order for it to apply to attenuation and phase, the immittance must again be of the minimum-phase-shift type.

Exercise

Show that the phase-area theorem applies to the real and imaginary parts of the impedance of the R-C circuit in Fig. 7-10 by actually carrying out the integration.

(e) Determination of the Phase Shift from the Attenuation Characteristic. The foregoing theorems, although quite interesting and instructive, are insufficient to determine the phase shift at any arbitrary specific frequency. This is most often the information which is wanted, especially in feedback-amplifier design. We will now derive an equation which will give us this information.

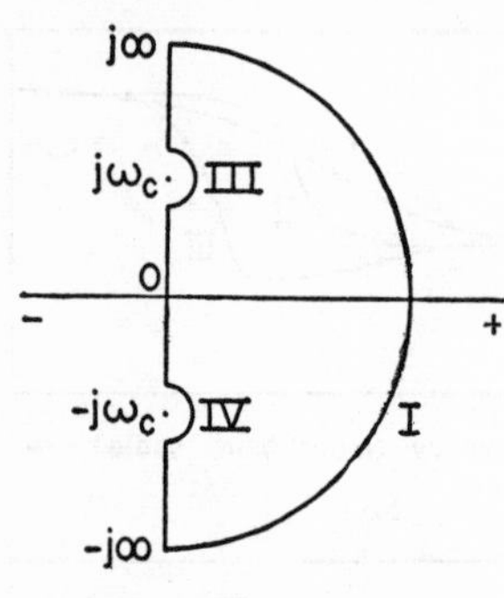

FIG. 7-13. A path of integration in the complex s plane.

If we consider the derivation of the phase-integral theorem, we note that we obtained the attenuation at $\omega = 0$ by integrating around a pole at $s = 0$ whose residue was A_0. Consequently, in order to find the phase shift B_C at an arbitrary frequency $\omega_C/2\pi$, let us see if we can obtain the desired result by integrating around a pole at $s = j\omega_C$. Corresponding to the methods previously used, we choose the integrand[32] as

$$\frac{S(s) - A_C}{s^2 + \omega_C^2}$$

and integrate it along the contour shown in Fig. 7-13. This integrand has the desired symmetry along the frequency axis, it has a pole at ω_C, its leading term has B_C as a factor at this pole so that the result will give B_C, and the integrand does not have a pole at infinity, so that the phase shift at infinity will not be involved. Accordingly,

[32] A_C and B_C are defined by the equation,

$$S(j\omega_C) = A_C + jB_C$$

Then, also,

$$S(-j\omega_C) = A_C - jB_C$$

$$\oint \frac{S(s) - A_C}{s^2 + \omega_C^2}\,ds = \int_{-j\infty}^{-j(\omega_C+r)} \frac{A(\omega) + jB(\omega) - A_C}{-\omega^2 + \omega_C^2}\,d(j\omega)$$
$$+ \int_{\text{IV}} \frac{-jB_C}{s^2 + \omega_C^2}\,ds + \int_{-j(\omega_C-r)}^{+j(\omega_C-r)} \frac{A(\omega) + jB(\omega) - A_C}{-\omega^2 + \omega_C^2}\,d(j\omega)$$
$$+ \int_{\text{III}} \frac{jB_C}{s^2 + \omega_C^2}\,ds + \int_{j(\omega_C+r)}^{j\infty} \frac{A(\omega) + jB(\omega) - A_C}{-\omega^2 + \omega_C^2}\,d(j\omega)$$
$$+ \int_{\text{I}} \frac{S(s) - A_C}{s^2 + \omega^2}\,ds = 0 \quad (117)$$

where r is the radius of the small semicircles around the poles. Now

$$\int_{\text{IV}} \frac{-jB_C}{s^2 + \omega_C^2}\,ds = \int_{\text{IV}} \frac{-jB_C}{(s + j\omega_C)(s - j\omega_C)}\,ds$$
$$= \int_{-\pi/2}^{+\pi/2} \frac{-jB_C \cdot jr\epsilon^{j\phi}\,d\phi}{r\epsilon^{j\phi}(-2j\omega_C)} = \frac{j\pi B_C}{2\omega_C} \quad (118)$$

where $$s = -j\omega_C + r\epsilon^{j\phi} \text{ along IV} \quad (119)$$

and $$ds = jr\epsilon^{j\phi}\,d\phi \quad (120)$$

and $$s - j\omega_C = r\epsilon^{j\phi} - 2j\omega_C \rightarrow -2j\omega_C \quad \text{as} \quad r \rightarrow 0 \quad (121)$$

Similarly, $$\int_{\text{III}} \frac{jB_C}{s^2 + \omega_C^2}\,ds = \frac{j\pi B_C}{2\omega_C} \quad (122)$$

Furthermore, $$\int_{\text{I}} \frac{S(s) - A_C}{s^2 + \omega_C^2}\,ds = 0 \quad (123)$$

and $$\int_{-j\infty}^{+j\infty} \frac{B(\omega)}{-\omega^2 + \omega_C^2}\,d(j\omega) = 0 \quad (124)$$

while $$\int_{-j\infty}^{+j\infty} \frac{A(\omega) - A_C}{-\omega^2 + \omega_C^2}\,d(j\omega) = -2j \int_0^{\infty} \frac{A(\omega) - A_C}{\omega^2 - \omega_C^2}\,d\omega \quad (125)$$

Finally,[33] $$\int_{\omega_C - r}^{\omega_C + r} \frac{A(\omega) - A_C}{\omega^2 - \omega_C^2}\,d\omega \rightarrow 0 \quad \text{as} \quad r \rightarrow 0 \quad (126)$$

---

[33] The residue of the pole of

$$\left[\frac{S(s) - A_C}{s^2 + \omega_C{}^2}\right]$$

at $s = \pm j\omega_C$ is due entirely to the imaginary component $\dfrac{jB_C}{s^2 + \omega_C{}^2}$.

Equation (117) thus reduces to

$$B_C = \frac{2\omega_C}{\pi} \int_0^\infty \frac{A(\omega) - A_C}{\omega^2 - \omega_C^2} d\omega \tag{127}$$

Equation (127) is an equation of the desired type for the determination of the phase shift at an arbitrary frequency from the attenuation curve. An alternative form which is obtained by transforming to a logarithmic frequency scale is actually more useful. Thus, starting from Eq. (127), we write

$$B_C = \frac{2}{\pi} \int_0^\infty \frac{A(\omega) - A_C}{\omega/\omega_C - \omega_C/\omega} \frac{d\omega}{\omega} = \frac{2}{\pi} \int_{-\infty}^{+\infty} \frac{A(\omega) - A_C}{\epsilon^u - \epsilon^{-u}} du$$

$$= \frac{1}{\pi} \int_{-\infty}^{+\infty} \frac{A - A_C}{\sinh u} du \tag{128}$$

where
$$u = \log \frac{\omega}{\omega_C} \tag{129}$$

and, by definition,
$$A = A(\omega) \tag{130}$$

In order to obtain a more usable form of Eq. (128), we integrate by parts. Thus

$$\begin{aligned} B_C &= \frac{1}{\pi} \int_{-\infty}^0 \frac{A - A_C}{\sinh u} du + \frac{1}{\pi} \int_0^\infty \frac{A - A_C}{\sinh u} du \\ &= \frac{1}{\pi} \left[(A - A_C) \log \coth \left(\frac{-u}{2} \right) \right]_{-\infty}^0 \\ &+ \frac{1}{\pi} \int_{-\infty}^0 \frac{dA}{du} \log \coth \left(\frac{-u}{2} \right) du + \frac{1}{\pi} \left[(A - A_C) \log \coth \left(\frac{+u}{2} \right) \right]_0^\infty \\ &+ \frac{1}{\pi} \int_0^\infty \frac{dA}{du} \log \coth \left(\frac{+u}{2} \right) du \end{aligned} \tag{131}$$

Now as $u \to \infty$, $\log \coth u \to 0$. On the other hand, as $u \to 0$, $A \to A_C$ and $\log \coth \frac{u}{2} \to \infty$, but

$$(A - A_C) \log \coth \left(\frac{u}{2} \right) \to u \frac{dA}{du} \left[- \log \left(\frac{u}{2} \right) \right] \to 0$$

Therefore the integrated portions of the right side of Eq. (131) vanish, and the equation reduces to

$$B_C = \frac{1}{\pi}\int_{-\infty}^{0} \frac{dA}{du} \log\coth\left(\frac{-u}{2}\right) du + \frac{1}{\pi}\int_{0}^{\infty} \frac{dA}{du} \log\coth\left(\frac{+u}{2}\right) du$$

$$= \frac{1}{\pi}\int_{-\infty}^{+\infty} \frac{dA}{du} \log\coth\left|\frac{u}{2}\right| du \tag{132}$$

As an alternative form of Eq. (132), we can also write[34,35]

$$B_C = \frac{1}{\pi}\int_{-\infty}^{+\infty} \left[\frac{dA}{du} - \left(\frac{dA}{du}\right)_C\right] \log\coth\left|\frac{u}{2}\right| du$$

$$+ \frac{1}{\pi}\int_{-\infty}^{+\infty} \left(\frac{dA}{du}\right)_C \log\coth\left|\frac{u}{2}\right| du$$

$$= \frac{\pi}{2}\left(\frac{dA}{du}\right)_C + \frac{1}{\pi}\int_{-\infty}^{+\infty} \left[\frac{dA}{du} - \left(\frac{dA}{du}\right)_C\right] \log\coth\left|\frac{u}{2}\right| du \tag{133}$$

Equations (132) and (133) are very valuable in showing the relations between attenuation and phase characteristics. The factor

$$\log\coth\left|\frac{u}{2}\right| = \log\left|\frac{\omega + \omega_C}{\omega - \omega_C}\right| \tag{134}$$

in the integrand is plotted in Fig. 7-14, which shows that this factor is symmetrical about ω_C on a logarithmic frequency scale. We can draw the following conclusions from the foregoing equations and Fig. 7-14.

(a) There is a phase shift at any frequency due to the rate of change of the attenuation. (It amounts to 180 degrees when the attenuation is varying at the rate of 12 db per octave.)

(b) If dA/du plotted on a logarithmic frequency scale is antisymmetrical about ω_C, the slope of the attenuation curve at ω_C alone

---

[34] If A is attenuation in Eqs. (132) and (133), dA/du is measured in nepers per unit change in u. This is the same as decibels per octave divided by $20 \log_{10} 2 = 6.02$. Accordingly, Eq. (133) is sometimes written

$$\phi_C = \frac{\pi}{12}\left(\frac{da}{du}\right)_C + \frac{1}{6\pi}\int_{-\infty}^{+\infty}\left[\frac{da}{du} - \left(\frac{da}{du}\right)_C\right] \log\coth\left|\frac{u}{2}\right| du$$

where da/du is measured in decibels per octave, ϕ_C is in radians, and $u = \log_\epsilon (\omega/\omega_C)$.

[35]
$$\int_{-\infty}^{+\infty} \log\coth\left|\frac{u}{2}\right| du = \frac{\pi^2}{2}$$

determines the phase shift at ω_C. If

$$\left[\frac{dA}{du} - \left(\frac{dA}{du}\right)_C\right]$$

has a component which is symmetrical about ω_C, this component also contributes to the phase shift, the most heavily weighted portions of the contribution coming from the frequency ranges nearest ω_C.

Conclusion (a) is clearly illustrated in Fig. 7-12. Conclusion (b), since it deals with a smaller term, is not so obviously depicted.

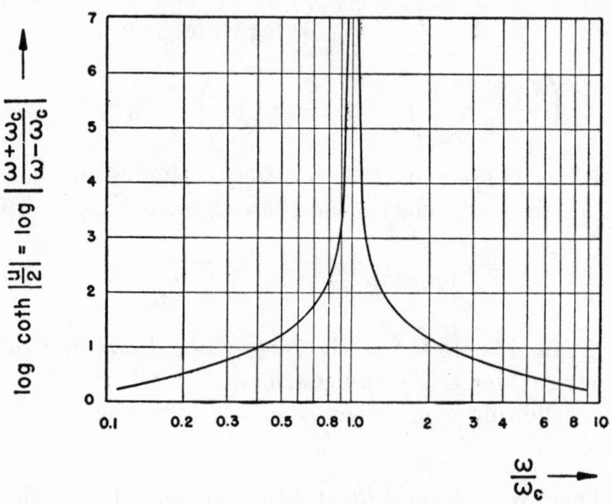

FIG. 7-14. Plot of log coth $(u/2)$ on a logarithmic frequency scale.

Equations (127), (132), and (133) will, of course, apply to the real and imaginary part of the immittance, just as well as to the attenuation and phase.

Exercises

1. Derive the formula

$$A_C - A_0 = -\frac{\omega_C}{\pi}\int_{-\infty}^{+\infty} \frac{d}{du}\left(\frac{B}{\omega}\right) \log \coth \frac{|u|}{2}\, du$$

2. Derive the formulas

$$A_C - A_\infty = -\frac{1}{\pi\omega_C}\int_0^\infty \frac{d(\omega B)}{d\omega} \log \left|\frac{\omega + \omega_C}{\omega - \omega_C}\right| d\omega$$

and $$A_C - A_0 = -\frac{\omega_C}{\pi}\int_0^\infty \frac{d}{d\omega}\left(\frac{B}{\omega}\right)\log\left|\frac{\omega + \omega_C}{\omega - \omega_C}\right| d\omega$$

(f) General. In addition to the relations between $A(\omega)$ and $B(\omega)$ which we have derived, a large number of other relations are given by Bode.[36] These formulas give means to determine

1. $A(\omega)$ when $B(\omega)$ is prescribed over the complete frequency range;
2. $B(\omega)$ when $A(\omega)$ is prescribed over the complete frequency range;
3. $A(\omega)$ and $B(\omega)$ over the entire range when $A(\omega)$ is prescribed over part of the range and $B(\omega)$ over the rest of it.

Special charts and curves are also given so that these calculations can be done expeditiously. Practical applications of these various relations in the design of feedback amplifiers are discussed briefly in our Chap. 12. Applications of these relations in the design of servomechanisms are described elsewhere.[37]

Since the foregoing relations, when they refer to attenuation and phase, are limited to minimum-phase-shift networks, it is sometimes possible to get around the restrictions imposed by these relations by the use of networks which are not of the minimum-phase-shift type.

Equation (133) shows that rapid change in attenuation causes large phase shifts. This is the underlying cause of the overshoot and striations associated with sharp cutoff.[38,39] It is probably also the cause of many diffraction phenomena in optics, when properly interpreted in terms of space variables.

---

[36] These are listed in tables at the end of his Chaps. XIII and XIV.

[37] For example, see James, Nichols, and Phillips, *Theory of Servomechanisms*. McGraw-Hill Book Co., Inc., 1947.

[38] See Goldman, *Frequency Analysis, Modulation and Noise*, §4.19.

[39] The large phase shifts associated with sharp cutoff show that transmission systems having sharp cutoff have great time delays. Because of these great time delays the so-called anticipatory transients which precede the output signal actually take place after the input signal has started. Anticipatory transients in the output therefore do not precede the input signal so that there is no violation of the Law of Cause and Effect. (See p. 81 of the author's book cited above.)

Exercise

(*The Wiener-Lee condition for physical realizability.*) If the variable ω in an immittance $T(j\omega)$ is changed to ϕ where

$$\omega = \tan \frac{\phi}{2}$$

the range $(-\infty < \omega < +\infty)$ is changed to the range $(-\pi < \phi < +\pi)$. Under these circumstances, Wiener and Lee have shown that a physically realizable immittance can be expressed

$$T(j\omega) = \sum_{n=0}^{\infty} a_n \epsilon^{-jn\phi}$$

where

$$a_n = \frac{1}{2\pi} \int_{-\pi}^{+\pi} T\left(j \tan \frac{\phi}{2}\right) \epsilon^{jn\phi}\, d\phi$$

Show that the coefficients a_n must be real. Show also that if we write

$$T(j\omega) = A(\omega) + jB(\omega) = A'(\phi) + jB'(\phi)$$

then $A'(\phi)$ and $B'(\phi)$ can be expanded in the Fourier series

$$A'(\phi) = a_0 + a_1 \cos \phi + a_2 \cos 2\phi + \cdots$$

and

$$B'(\phi) = a_1 \sin \phi + a_2 \sin 2\phi + \cdots$$

where the a_n coefficients are the same in both series.

CHAPTER 8

Gamma and Error Functions

8.1. Introduction

In this chapter we shall discuss the properties of two interesting functions, the *gamma function* and the *error function*. These functions are remarkable for the variety of ways in which they appear to be at the heart of many important problems and operations. We shall consider first the gamma function.

8.2. The gamma function and the factorial

If n is a positive quantity, then

$$\Gamma(n) = \int_0^\infty x^{n-1}\epsilon^{-x}\,dx \tag{1}$$

is defined as the *gamma function* of n. This seems like a very artificial function, but we will now show that for integral values of n,

$$\Gamma(n) = (n-1)! \tag{2}$$

To show this, let us assume that $n > 0$, and integrate by parts the equation for $\Gamma(n+1)$. Thus

$$\Gamma(n+1) = -[x^n\epsilon^{-x}]\Big|_0^\infty + n\int_0^\infty x^{n-1}\epsilon^{-x}\,dx \tag{3}$$

Now

$$[x^n\epsilon^{-x}]\Big|_0^\infty$$

vanishes for both limits, so that Eq. (3) may be written

$$\Gamma(n+1) = n\int_0^\infty x^{n-1}\epsilon^{-x}\,dx = n\Gamma(n) \tag{4}$$

Furthermore,

$$\Gamma(1) = \int_0^\infty \epsilon^{-x}\,dx = -[\epsilon^{-x}]\Big|_0^\infty = 1 \tag{5}$$

From (4) and (5), it follows that

$$\Gamma(2) = 1\Gamma(1) = 1 \tag{6}$$

$$\Gamma(3) = 2\Gamma(2) = 2 \cdot 1 \tag{7}$$

$$\Gamma(4) = 3\Gamma(3) = 3 \cdot 2 \cdot 1 \tag{8}$$

and finally

$$\Gamma(n) = (n - 1)! \tag{9}$$

provided that n is a positive integer. We have thus proved Eq. (2), and have established the first important property of the gamma function.

In many mathematical operations, the factorial of a parameter or of a subsidiary variable appears in the solution of a problem, for integral values of the parameter. For example, the Taylor expansion for $f(x)$,

$$f(x) = f(b) + \frac{x - b}{1!} f'(b) + \frac{(x - b)^2}{2!} f''(b) + \cdots + \frac{(x - b)^n}{n!} f^n(b) + \cdots \tag{10}$$

involves *factorial* n as the denominator of all the terms on the right after the first. To make Eq. (10) completely symmetrical, the first term should be

$$\frac{f(b)}{0!}$$

In terms of the ordinary definition of a factorial, however, $0!$ has no meaning. On the other hand, if we used Eq. (9) as the definition of a generalized factorial in the form

$$n! = \Gamma(n + 1) \tag{11}$$

then we have, according to Eq. (5),

$$0! = \Gamma(1) = 1 \tag{12}$$

With this definition of $0!$, Eq. (10) becomes completely symmetrical. It thus appears that the gamma function is more fundamental than the ordinary factorial in Taylor series expansions. A similar situation is found in many types of series expansions. Furthermore it is found that many expressions involving $n!$, which would become meaningless if n were not integral, when the elementary definition is used for the factorial, can actually be used for nonintegral values of n, if $n!$ is interpreted in accordance with Eq. (11). For example, the Laplace transform

$$\mathcal{L}\{t^n\} = \frac{n!}{s^{n+1}} \tag{13}$$

which holds for integral values of n, can be generalized, as shown in §8.5, to

$$\mathcal{L}(t^n) = \frac{\Gamma(n+1)}{s^{n+1}} \tag{14}$$

for either integral or nonintegral values of n, provided that

$$(n+1) > 0 \tag{15}$$

and the result will still be correct.

8.3. The evaluation of an important definite integral

We will now show how to evaluate some important definite integrals used in this chapter. These depend on the evaluation of

$$\int_0^\infty \epsilon^{-x^2}\,dx$$

which can be accomplished by a special device.

First we note that

$$\int_0^\infty \epsilon^{-x^2}\,dx = \int_0^\infty \epsilon^{-y^2}\,dy \tag{16}$$

where x and y are any variables whatever, since the value of any definite integral is a function of the limits of integration and not of the variable of integration. We may therefore write

$$\begin{aligned}\int_0^\infty \epsilon^{-x^2}\,dx &= \left\{\int_0^\infty \epsilon^{-x^2}\,dx \cdot \int_0^\infty \epsilon^{-y^2}\,dy\right\}^{\frac{1}{2}} \\ &= \left\{\int_0^\infty \int_0^\infty \epsilon^{-x^2-y^2}\,dx\,dy\right\}^{\frac{1}{2}} \end{aligned} \tag{17}$$

This last step is justified because neither of the limits of integration involves either variable of integration.

Let us now interpret x and y as rectangular coordinates, and transform from rectangular to polar coordinates. Accordingly

$$x^2 + y^2 = r^2 \tag{18}$$

and[1]

$$dx\,dy = r\,dr\,d\theta \tag{19}$$

so that

$$\int_0^\infty \int_0^\infty \epsilon^{-x^2-y^2}\,dx\,dy = \int_0^{\pi/2} \int_0^\infty \epsilon^{-r^2} r\,dr\,d\theta$$

$$= \int_0^{\pi/2} \left\{ \frac{-\epsilon^{-r^2}}{2} \Big|_0^\infty \right\} d\theta$$

$$= \int_0^{\pi/2} \frac{1}{2}\,d\theta = \frac{\pi}{4} \tag{20}$$

This transformation is justified because $\int \epsilon^{-r^2}\,dr$ vanishes exponentially in the area between the infinite circle and the infinite square. From Eqs. (17) and (20), it then follows that

$$\int_0^\infty \epsilon^{-x^2}\,dx = \tfrac{1}{2}\sqrt{\pi} \tag{21}$$

If we write

$$x = at \tag{22}$$

then Eq. (21) may be written

$$\int_0^\infty \epsilon^{-a^2t^2}\,dt = \frac{\sqrt{\pi}}{2a} \tag{23}$$

We shall make frequent use of this important equation in the remainder of the present chapter. We shall use it first to evaluate $\Gamma(\frac{1}{2})$.

8.4. The gamma function for half-integral arguments

Let us write

$$\Gamma(\tfrac{1}{2}) = \int_0^\infty x^{-\frac{1}{2}} \epsilon^{-x}\,dx \tag{24}$$

according to Eq. (1).

Now let

$$x = y^2 \tag{25}$$

so that

$$dx = 2y\,dy \tag{26}$$

Then

$$\Gamma(\tfrac{1}{2}) = \int_0^\infty x^{-\frac{1}{2}} \epsilon^{-x}\,dx = 2\int_0^\infty \epsilon^{-y^2}\,dy = \sqrt{\pi} \tag{27}$$

according to Eq. (23).

---

[1] The reader to whom these operations are new will find them discussed in any text on advanced calculus.

From Eqs. (4) and (27), it follows that

$$\Gamma\left(\frac{3}{2}\right) = \frac{1}{2}\Gamma\left(\frac{1}{2}\right) = \frac{\sqrt{\pi}}{2} \tag{28}$$

$$\Gamma\left(\frac{5}{2}\right) = \frac{3}{2}\Gamma\left(\frac{3}{2}\right) = \frac{3\sqrt{\pi}}{2^2} \tag{29}$$

and in general,

$$\Gamma\left(\frac{n+1}{2}\right) = \frac{1 \cdot 3 \cdot 5 \cdots (n-1)}{2^{(n/2)}}\sqrt{\pi} \tag{30}$$

Equations (27) through (30) are important relations in the theory of transmission-line transients.

8.5. The Laplace transform of t^m, when $m > -1$, but is not necessarily an integer

Let us next find the Laplace transform of t^m for nonintegral values of m. By definition we have

$$\mathcal{L}[t^m] = \int_{t=0}^{t=\infty} t^m \epsilon^{-st}\, dt \tag{31}$$

In order to evaluate the integral in Eq. (31), let us make the substitution

$$x = st \tag{32}$$

Then Eq. (31) becomes

$$\mathcal{L}[t^m] = \int_{x/s=0}^{x/s=\infty} \frac{x^m \epsilon^{-x}}{s^{m+1}}\, dx = \frac{1}{s^{m+1}} \int_0^\infty x^m \epsilon^{-x}\, dx = \frac{\Gamma(m+1)}{s^{m+1}} \tag{33}$$

Equation (33) is limited to cases in which $m > -1$ because Eq. (1) is limited to cases in which $n > 0$. Furthermore, Eq. (33) is limited to values of s with positive real parts, since for zero and negative values of the real part of s, the upper limit of the integral would not be $+\infty$. The limitation[2] on s is, however, not important, since the same restriction is placed upon s in the original definition of the Laplace transformation.

---

[2] Although the integration in Eq. (33) is carried out for positive real values of s, the analytical extension theorem tells us that the results thus obtained,

8.6. Further discussion of the gamma function[3]

The definition of the gamma function $\Gamma(n)$, which was defined in Eq. (1) for positive values of n, can be generalized[4] to cover also negative and complex values of the argument. This general gamma function, $\Gamma(z)$, is defined by the equation

$$\frac{1}{\Gamma(z)} = z\epsilon^{Cz} \prod_{m=1}^{+\infty} \left(1 + \frac{z}{m}\right) \epsilon^{-z/m} \tag{34}$$

In Eq. (34), C is Euler's constant[5] and is defined as

$$\begin{aligned} C &= \lim_{p\to\infty} \left\{\left[1 + \frac{1}{2} + \frac{1}{3} + \cdots + \frac{1}{p}\right] - \log p\right\} \\ &= 0.577215665 \cdots \end{aligned} \tag{35}$$

The symbol $\prod_{m=1}^{+\infty}$

in Eq. (34) denotes an infinite product; i.e.,

$$\prod_{m=1}^{\infty} \left(1 + \frac{z}{m}\right) \epsilon^{-z/m} = [(1 + z)\epsilon^{-z}] \left[\left(1 + \frac{z}{2}\right) \epsilon^{-z/2}\right] \left[\left(1 + \frac{z}{3}\right) \epsilon^{-z/3}\right] \cdots \tag{36}$$

---

namely,

$$\int_0^\infty t^m \epsilon^{-st}\, dt = \frac{\Gamma(m+1)}{s^{m+1}} \tag{A}$$

will also be true for complex values of s, since it is true for a continuous range of real values of s, provided that no singular points or branch cuts are crossed in transforming the path of integration.

[3] For the derivation of the formulas set down and discussed in this section, the reader is referred to: N. W. McLachlan, *Complex Variable and Operational Calculus*, Chap. V. Goursat-Hedrick, *Mathematical Analysis*, Vol. I, pp. 183, 279, 290; Vol. II, Part I, pp. 100, 229. E. B. Wilson, *Advanced Calculus*, Chap. XIV. Whittaker and Watson, *Modern Analysis*, Chap. XII. (The last book is especially complete.)

[4] N. W. McLachlan, *Complex Variable and Operational Calculus*, Chap. V. Whittaker and Watson, *Modern Analysis*, Chap. XII.

[5] Euler's constant is also used in discussing the properties of $Ci(x)$. See Goldman, *Frequency Analysis, Modulation and Noise*, p. 92.

It may be shown[6] that if z is real and positive, the definition of $\Gamma(z)$ in Eq. (34) agrees with Eq. (1). Furthermore, the equation

$$\Gamma(z + 1) = z\Gamma(z) \quad (37)$$

holds for all positive, negative, and even complex values of z.

In Fig. 8-1 is a graph of the values of $\Gamma(n)$ for real values of n, both positive and negative. We see that for all integral values[7] of n less than $(+1)$, $\Gamma(n) \to \infty$. In the most important section of the graph—i.e., when $n > 0$, $\Gamma(n)$ has a minimum at

$$n = 1.4616321 \cdots \quad (38)$$

where the value of $\Gamma(n)$ is

$$\Gamma(n) = 0.8856032 \cdots \quad (38A)$$

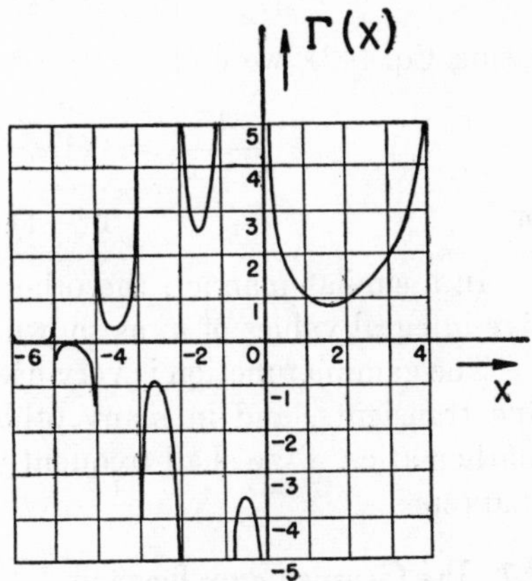

FIG. 8-1. The gamma function $\Gamma(x)$.

As $n \to \infty$, it is also true that $\Gamma(n) \to \infty$. However, it may be shown that for large values of n

$$\Gamma(n + 1) = \sqrt{2n}\; n^n \epsilon^{-n} \left(\sqrt{\pi} + \frac{b}{\sqrt{2n}}\right) \quad (39)$$

where b lies between -1 and $+1$. Therefore, by taking the logarithm of both sides of Eq. (39), we get the famous and useful approximation of Stirling, for very large values of n,

$$\log (n!) = (n + \tfrac{1}{2}) \log n - n + \tfrac{1}{2} \log 2\pi \quad (40)$$

by neglecting

$$\frac{b}{\sqrt{2n}}$$

Eq. (40) is very useful in probability and noise theory.

Another general formula of interest in connection with gamma functions is

---

[6] Goursat-Hedrick, *Mathematical Analysis*, Vol. II, Part I, p. 230.

[7] In fact, these are the only singular points of $\Gamma(z)$ in the entire complex plane.

$$\frac{1}{\Gamma(z)\Gamma(1-z)} = \frac{\sin \pi z}{\pi} \tag{41}$$

or

$$\frac{1}{\Gamma(z)} = \Gamma(1-z)\,\frac{\sin \pi z}{\pi} \tag{42}$$

Using Eq. (42), we find

$$\frac{1}{\Gamma(-1)} = \Gamma(1+1)\,\frac{\sin(-\pi)}{\pi} = 0 \tag{43}$$

or

$$\Gamma(-1) = \infty \tag{44}$$

In a similar manner, the other infinite values of $\Gamma(n)$ for negative integral values of n, as shown in Fig. 8-1, can be verified.

The gamma function is very useful in the theory of transmission-line transients, and in many other branches of pure and applied mathematics. We shall frequently have occasion to use it in later chapters.

8.7. The Gaussian error function

Among the functions of outstanding importance in transformation calculus, as well as in other branches of mathematics, are the Gaussian error function,[8]

$$g(k,x) = \frac{k}{\sqrt{\pi}}\,\epsilon^{-k^2x^2} \tag{45}$$

and various integrals in which it is involved. A curve of $g(k,x)$ is shown in Fig. 8-2. In Eq. (45), x is the variable and k may be considered a parameter.

The name "error function" arises from the fact that, in any operation in which it is desired to obtain a particular value, but in which the actual value obtained deviates from the desired value due to *random* causes, the relative frequencies of occurrence of deviations from the desired value by amounts x will be given by $g(k,x)$. The original errors to which the function in Eq. (45) was applied were the errors in astronomers' observations of the locations of the stars. The same function will, however, apply to random errors of all kinds. For example, in a radio-tube factory in which it is desired to manufacture a tube with a transconductance

[8] The Gaussian error function is often called the "normal distribution function" in probability theory.

of G_0 micromhos, the variations from G_0 will generally be distributed in frequency of occurrence by a curve of the form of Eq. (45). The same function also governs the behavior of many natural phenomena having random distributions, such as the velocities of molecules in a gas, and various quantities in the theory of random noise.

If $g(k,x)$ is integrated from $(-\infty)$ to $(+\infty)$, we obtain from Eq. (23), and using the fact that $g(k,x)$ is an even function,

$$\int_{-\infty}^{+\infty} g(k,x)\,dx = \int_{-\infty}^{+\infty} \frac{k}{\sqrt{\pi}} \epsilon^{-k^2x^2}\,dx = 2\int_0^{\infty} \frac{k}{\sqrt{\pi}} \epsilon^{-k^2x^2}\,dx = 1 \tag{46}$$

We may therefore conclude that, for probability purposes, the constants in Eq. (45) are so arranged that $g(k,x)$ represents the

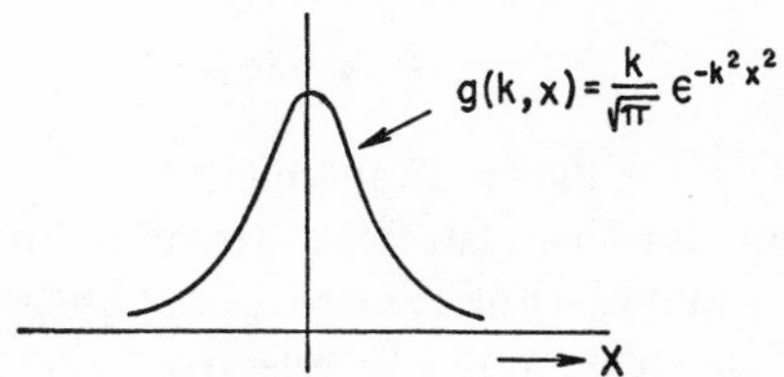

FIG. 8-2. The Gaussian error function $g(k,x)$.

fractional probability that the actual deviation shall lie within a block of unit width centered about the deviation x. The constant k is very important because it gives a convenient measure of the accuracy of the process. If k is large, the curve in Fig. 8-2 is high and thin, and the process is very accurate. If k is small, the curve in Fig. 8-2 is low and broad, and the process is very inaccurate.

8.8. A radio manufacturing example

As a matter of general interest, we will now give a practical example of how the Gaussian error curve can be used in radio engineering. Let us suppose that a radio-tube factory is making a type of tube with a desired transconductance (g_m) of 2,200 micromhos. Suppose that a 50-micromho measuring interval is chosen and that it is found in actual production that 20 percent of the tubes have transconductances between 2,175 and 2,225 and 5 percent of the tubes have transconductances between 2,375 and 2,425. Let us assume that the transconductances are distributed about 2,200 according to a Gaussian error curve. (This is to be expected if the deviations are due to random[9] causes.) From the foregoing data, we know that deviations (in the 50-micromho measuring interval) of +200 micromhos above the desired value of 2,200 occur one-fourth as frequently as values in the measuring interval around 2,200 itself. For the case in question, we then have[10]

$$\frac{\frac{k}{\sqrt{\pi}}\epsilon^{-k^2x_0^2}}{\frac{k}{\sqrt{\pi}}\epsilon^{-k^2x_1^2}} = 4 \tag{47}$$

where
$$x_0 = 0 \tag{48}$$
and
$$x_1 = 200 \tag{49}$$
Consequently,
$$\epsilon^{(200k)^2} = 4 \tag{50}$$
or
$$k = 0.0059 \tag{51}$$

Equation (51) gives us the fundamental information about the manufacturing deviations. Starting from it we can calculate what we want to know. For example, suppose we wish to know what fraction of the tubes would be rejected if the permitted deviation were ±300 micromhos. This fraction would be[11]

$$\begin{aligned}\text{fraction rejected} &= 2\int_{300}^{\infty}\frac{k}{\sqrt{\pi}}\epsilon^{-k^2x^2}\,dx = \frac{2}{\sqrt{\pi}}\int_{300k}^{\infty}\epsilon^{-y^2}\,dy \\ &= \text{erfc}\,(300k) = \text{erfc}\,(1.77) = 0.0124\end{aligned} \tag{52}$$

[9] If some particular manufacturing fault, such as a bent shaft in one production machine, is the main reason for the deviations, the deviations can no longer be expected to be distributed according to a Gaussian error curve.

[10] To be more accurate, we should write

$$\frac{\int_{-25}^{+25}\frac{k}{\sqrt{\pi}}\epsilon^{-k^2x^2}\,dx}{\int_{175}^{225}\frac{k}{\sqrt{\pi}}\epsilon^{-k^2x^2}\,dx} = 4$$

Equation (47), however, gives a good approximation if the measuring interval is small.

[11] The function erfc (x) is defined in Eq. (55), and its numerical values can be obtained from Fig. 8-3. For values of x greater than 1.5, the asymptotic expansion [Eq. (35) of Chap. 11] can be used.

Thus if the tolerance were set at ± 300 micromhos, 1.24 percent of the tubes would be rejected. On the other hand, if the tolerance were set at ± 200 micromhos, the fraction rejected would be

$$\begin{aligned} \text{fraction rejected} &= \text{erfc } (200k) = \text{erfc } (1.18) \\ &= 0.0959 = 9.6 \text{ percent} \end{aligned} \tag{53}$$

The foregoing method gives us a rapid means of determining the effect of tolerances upon the percentage of rejects, which is a very important question in manufacturing.

8.9. The functions erf (*x*) and erfc (*x*), and some Laplace transformation formulas

The importance of the Gaussian error function in transformation calculus arises from the fact that its integrals

$$\text{erf } (x) = 2 \int_0^x g(1,x)\, dx = \frac{2}{\sqrt{\pi}} \int_0^x \epsilon^{-x^2}\, dx \tag{54}$$

and

$$\text{erfc } (x) = 2 \int_x^\infty g(1,x) = \frac{2}{\sqrt{\pi}} \int_x^\infty \epsilon^{-x^2}\, dx - 1 - \text{erf } (x) \tag{55}$$

appear in many important Laplace transforms. The notation *erf* is a contraction of "error function" and the notation *erfc* is a contraction of "complementary error function." The error function of Eq. (54) is an integral of the Gaussian error function. It might thus more properly be called an error integral. However, although this confusion of terminology exists in the literature, the function erf (x) is always defined as in Eq. (54) and erfc (x) as in Eq. (55). Graphs of erf (x) and erfc (x) are shown in Fig. 8-3.

We will now derive some important Laplace transformations in which these functions appear. Let us first find

$$\mathfrak{L}^{-1} \left\{ \frac{1}{\sqrt{s}(s-1)} \right\}$$

Now,

$$\mathfrak{L}^{-1} \left\{ \frac{1}{\sqrt{s}} \right\} = \frac{t^{-\frac{1}{2}}}{\Gamma(\frac{1}{2})} = \frac{1}{\sqrt{\pi t}} \tag{56}$$

by Eqs. (33) and (27), and by Eq. (10) of Appendix D

$$\mathfrak{L}^{-1} \left\{ \frac{1}{s-1} \right\} = \epsilon^t \tag{57}$$

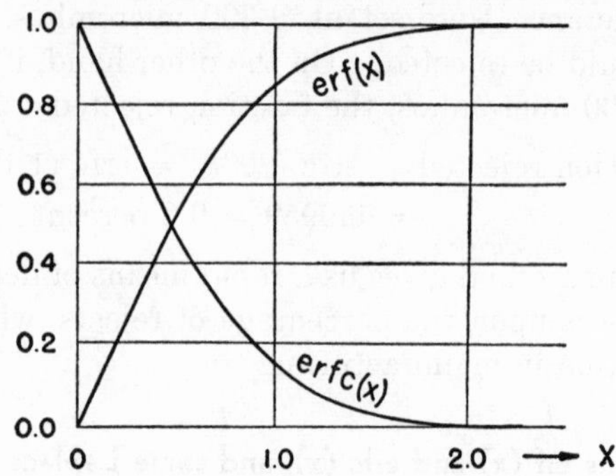

FIG. 8-3. Graphs of erf(x) and erfc(x).

Therefore, by Eqs. (72), (73), and (74) of Chap. 4,

$$\mathfrak{L}^{-1}\left\{\frac{1}{\sqrt{s}\,(s-1)}\right\} = \int_0^t \frac{1}{\sqrt{\pi\tau}}\,\epsilon^{(t-\tau)}\,d\tau = \frac{\epsilon^t}{\sqrt{\pi}}\int_0^t \frac{\epsilon^{-\tau}\,d\tau}{\sqrt{\tau}} \quad (58)$$

In Eq. (58) let us make the substitution

$$\tau = x^2 \quad (59)$$

Then

$$d\tau = 2x\,dx \quad (60)$$

Thus $$\mathfrak{L}^{-1}\left\{\frac{1}{\sqrt{s}\,(s-1)}\right\} = \frac{\epsilon^t}{\sqrt{\pi}}\int_{x=0}^{x=\sqrt{t}} 2\epsilon^{-x^2}\,dx = \epsilon^t \operatorname{erf}(\sqrt{t}) \quad (61)$$

Equation (61) is an important transform in its own right. Other transforms can also be derived from it. For example, applying Eq. (24) of Chap. 3, and letting $a = 1$, Eq. (61) becomes

$$\mathfrak{L}^{-1}\left\{\frac{1}{s\sqrt{s+1}}\right\} = \operatorname{erf}(\sqrt{t}) \quad (62)$$

By a somewhat similar procedure of transformations and substitutions, the formula

$$\mathfrak{L}^{-1}\left\{\frac{1}{s}\,\epsilon^{-k\sqrt{s}}\right\} = \operatorname{erfc}\left(\frac{k}{2\sqrt{t}}\right) \quad \text{where} \quad k \geq 0 \quad (63)$$

can be derived.[12]

[12] See Churchill, *Modern Operational Mathematics in Engineering.*

Equations (61–63) and similar formulas listed in the table of Laplace transforms are important in the theory of transmission-line transients.

8.10. Fourier transforms of the Gaussian error function calculated by contour integration

In the author's *Frequency Analysis, Modulation and Noise* (p. 133), it is mentioned that when $k = \sqrt{\pi}$, the Gaussian error function

$$g(k,t) = \frac{k}{\sqrt{\pi}} \epsilon^{-k^2t^2} \tag{64}$$

is its own Fourier transform. We are now in a position to prove this fact by an actual integration.

The Fourier transform of $g(k,t)$ is

$$F(f) = \int_{-\infty}^{+\infty} \epsilon^{-j2\pi ft} \frac{k}{\sqrt{\pi}} \epsilon^{-k^2t^2}\, dt \tag{65}$$

Now
$$\epsilon^{-j2\pi ft}\epsilon^{-k^2t^2} = \epsilon^{-\left(kt+\frac{j\pi f}{k}\right)^2} \cdot \epsilon^{-\frac{\pi^2f^2}{k^2}} \tag{66}$$

Therefore,
$$F(f) = \frac{k}{\sqrt{\pi}} \epsilon^{-\frac{\pi^2f^2}{k^2}} \int_{-\infty}^{+\infty} \epsilon^{-\left(kt+j\frac{\pi f}{k}\right)^2} dt \tag{67}$$

Now suppose we let
$$z = kt + j\frac{\pi f}{k} \tag{68}$$

Then Eq. (67) becomes

$$F(f) = \frac{k}{\sqrt{\pi}} \epsilon^{-\frac{\pi^2f^2}{k^2}} \int_{-\infty+j\frac{\pi f}{k}}^{+\infty+j\frac{\pi f}{k}} \frac{\epsilon^{-z^2}}{k}\, dz \tag{69}$$

where the path of integration is now the line parallel to the real axis and $\pi f/k$ units above it (see Fig. 8-4). However, the integrand of (69) has no singularity between the path of integration and the real axis; and furthermore the integrand vanishes to a much higher order than $1/z$ between $-\infty$ and

$$-\infty + j\frac{\pi f}{k}$$

and between $+\infty$ and

$$+\infty + j\frac{\pi f}{k}$$

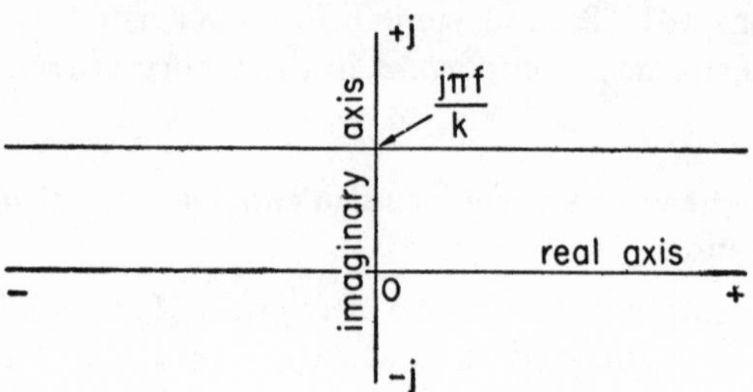

Fig. 8-4.

Therefore the path of integration in Eq. (69) can be replaced by the real axis. Consequently,

$$F(f) = \frac{k}{\sqrt{\pi}} \epsilon^{-\frac{\pi^2 f^2}{k^2}} \int_{-\infty}^{+\infty} \frac{\epsilon^{-z^2}}{k} \, dz \tag{70}$$

By Eq. (23),

$$\int_{-\infty}^{+\infty} \frac{\epsilon^{-z^2}}{k} \, dz = 2 \int_0^{\infty} \frac{\epsilon^{-z^2}}{k} \, dz = \frac{2}{k} \frac{\sqrt{\pi}}{2} = \frac{\sqrt{\pi}}{k} \tag{71}$$

Therefore,

$$F(f) = \epsilon^{-\frac{\pi^2 f^2}{k^2}} \tag{72}$$

is the Fourier transform of

$$g(k,t) = \frac{k}{\sqrt{\pi}} \epsilon^{-k^2 t^2} \tag{73}$$

For the special case in which

$$k = \sqrt{\pi} \tag{74}$$

$$g(\sqrt{\pi},t) = \epsilon^{-\pi t^2} \tag{75}$$

and

$$F(f) = \epsilon^{-\pi f^2} \tag{76}$$

so that the Fourier transforms are identical as functions of time and frequency.[13] The more general relations, Eqs. (72) and (73), are also important.

---

[13] Campbell and Foster, *Fourier Integrals for Practical Applications*, give other examples of identical transforms.

CHAPTER 9

Bessel Functions

9.1. Introduction[1]

In the past, many engineers have been accustomed to consider Bessel functions as very complicated, and there has been a tendency to avoid them. Actually, Bessel functions are somewhat similar to sines and cosines, but their significance has appeared obscure because the engineers in question have not been familiar with their most commonly used properties. This is a situation which should be corrected; and in the current chapter we shall attempt to present and discuss the most important and useful properties of Bessel functions, with the hope that the reader will become almost as familiar with them as he now is with sines and cosines. Bessel functions appear in the solution of so many important radio problems that the time required to become thoroughly acquainted with them is well spent.

9.2. Definitions of Bessel functions—Bessel's differential equation

The differential equation

$$\frac{d^2y}{dt^2} + \omega^2 y = 0 \tag{1}$$

may be called the equation of *simple harmonic motion*, or just the "*circular*" *equation*, and it has the general solution

$$y = A \cos \omega t + B \sin \omega t \tag{2}$$

where A and B are arbitrary constants. If we describe this situation in the terminology of Bessel functions, we would say that $\cos \omega t$ is a *circular function* of the *first* kind, of order ω, and argument t, and is a solution of the "circular equation" Eq. (1). Similarly, we

[1] G. N. Watson, *Treatise on Bessel Functions*, is a comprehensive and authoritative source on Bessel functions and related topics.

would call sin ωt a *circular function* of the second kind of order ω and say that it is also a solution of the "circular equation" Eq. (1).

Corresponding to the circular equation Eq. (1), let us consider Bessel's differential equation

$$\frac{d^2y}{dt^2} + \frac{1}{t}\frac{dy}{dt} + \left(1 - \frac{\nu^2}{t^2}\right)y = 0 \tag{3}$$

where ν^2 is a constant. This equation has the general solution

$$y = AJ_\nu(t) + BY_\nu(t) \tag{4}$$

The functions $J_\nu(t)$ and $Y_\nu(t)$ which arise in the solution of Eq. (3) are called Bessel functions. $J_\nu(t)$ is called the Bessel function of the *first kind* of *order* ν and *argument* t, while $Y_\nu(t)$ is called the Bessel function of the *second kind* of *order* ν and *argument* t. Equation (2) seems quite simple to us since we are all well acquainted with the numerical properties of cos ωt and of sin ωt. In the next section we will present the quantitative properties of $J_\nu(t)$ and of $Y_\nu(t)$ in the hope that the reader will become almost as familiar with them.

Three remarkable properties[2] of simplicity are enjoyed by the circular functions cos ωt and sin ωt which, however, are not enjoyed by the Bessel functions. These are:

1. The circular functions are completely periodic; i.e., their values are repeated exactly when t is increased by $2\pi/\omega$.

2. The curves of circular functions of all orders are exactly similar[3] in shape, differing only in a "stretching" factor which is proportional to $1/\omega$.

3. Curves of circular functions of the second kind are exactly similar to those of circular functions of the first kind, the only differ-

[2] The physical significance of this simplicity is discussed in §1.14 of the author's *Frequency Analysis, Modulation and Noise.*

[3] "Similar" in this case does not mean exactly the same thing as it does in geometry. When we say that the curves of all circular functions are similar, we mean that any one can be obtained by uniformly stretching any other in the x direction and in the y direction. In order to be considered "similar" in geometry, the "stretching" factors in the x and y directions must be equal. Thus, only a few curves such as circles or parabolas are considered similar in geometry. The reason that we have used the word *similar* for all circular functions, despite the geometrical definition, is that all circular functions can be made *geometrically similar* by a proper separate choice of the unit length along the abscissa and ordinate.

ence between them being a displacement of amount $\pi/2$ along the direction of the abscissa.

The Bessel functions do not enjoy this simplicity; but, on the other hand, their properties correspond to those of certain physical phenomena of importance in radio engineering. This is the reason for their importance to us.

9.3. The numerical values of the Bessel functions—series expansions and graphs

Bessel's equation Eq. (3) is a linear differential equation, but it does not have constant coefficients. It therefore cannot be solved by the simple methods available for solving linear differential equations with constant coefficients. We can, however, solve it by the method known as *solution in series.* The general theory of differential equations tells us that Bessel's equation

$$\frac{d^2y}{dt^2} + \frac{1}{t}\frac{dy}{dt} + \left(1 - \frac{\nu^2}{t^2}\right)y = 0 \tag{5}$$

has the general solution

$$y = C_1 f_1(t) + C_2 f_2(t) \tag{6}$$

where $f_1(t)$ and $f_2(t)$ are (linearly independent[4]) particular solutions of Eq. (5) and C_1 and C_2 are arbitrary constants.[5] Our problem is,

---

[4] That is, $f_1(t) \neq af_2(t) + b$.

[5] We can easily verify that Eq. (6) is a solution of Eq. (5) as follows:

Let $$y = C_1 f_1(t) + C_2 f_2(t)$$

Then $$\frac{dy}{dt} = C_1 \frac{d}{dt}[f_1(t)] + C_2 \frac{d}{dt}[f_2(t)]$$

and $$\frac{d^2y}{dt^2} = C_1 \frac{d^2}{dt^2}[f_1(t)] + C_2 \frac{d^2}{dt^2}[f_2(t)]$$

Therefore,

$$\begin{aligned}\frac{d^2y}{dt^2} + \frac{1}{t}\frac{dy}{dt} + \left(1 - \frac{\nu^2}{t^2}\right)y &= C_1\left\{\frac{d^2}{dt^2}[f_1(t)] + \frac{1}{t}\frac{d}{dt}[f_1(t)] + \left(1 - \frac{\nu^2}{t^2}\right)f_1(t)\right\} \\ &\quad + C_2\left\{\frac{d^2}{dt^2}[f_2(t)] + \frac{1}{t}\frac{d}{dt}[f_2(t)] + \left(1 - \frac{\nu^2}{t^2}\right)f_2(t)\right\} \\ &= 0\end{aligned}$$

since by hypothesis, $f_1(t)$ and $f_2(t)$ are each particular solutions of Eq. (5).

therefore, to find $f_1(t)$ and $f_2(t)$. These will then be identified with the Bessel functions $J_\nu(t)$ and $Y_\nu(t)$.

Let us then start by finding a particular solution to Eq. (5) and let us begin with the special case in which $\nu = 0$. In other words, let us find a particular solution of the equation

$$\frac{d^2y}{dt^2} + \frac{1}{t}\frac{dy}{dt} + y = 0 \tag{7}$$

According to the method of *solution in series*, we will assume a solution in the form

$$y = a_0 + a_1 t + a_2 t^2 + a_3 t^3 + \cdots \tag{8}$$

and proceed to determine the values of the coefficients. From Eq. (8) it follows that

$$\frac{dy}{dt} = a_1 + 2a_2 t + 3a_3 t^2 + \cdots \tag{9}$$

and

$$\frac{d^2y}{dt^2} = 2a_2 + 2 \cdot 3a_3 t + 3 \cdot 4a_4 t^2 + \cdots \tag{10}$$

Substituting Eqs. (8), (9), and (10) into Eq. (7), we have

$$\frac{a_1}{t} + (2a_2 + 2a_2 + a_0) + (6a_3 + 3a_3 + a_1)t + (12a_4 + 4a_4 + a_2)t^2 + \cdots = 0 \tag{11}$$

In order for Eq. (11) to hold for a continuous range of values of t, and not just for isolated values, it is necessary that the coefficient of each power of t in Eq. (11) shall vanish separately. Therefore, we must have

$$a_1 = 0 \tag{12}$$

$$4a_2 + a_0 = 0 \tag{13}$$

$$9a_3 + a_1 = 0 \tag{14}$$

$$12a_4 + 4a_4 + a_2 = 0 \tag{15}$$

and so on.

From Eq. (12), we know that a_1 vanishes, and from Eq. (14) it then follows that a_3 also vanishes. From Eq. (13), we have

$$a_2 = -\frac{a_0}{4} \tag{16}$$

and from Eq. (15),

$$a_4 = -\frac{a_2}{16} = \frac{a_0}{4 \cdot 16} \tag{17}$$

Proceeding in this manner and substituting the values of the coefficients thus found into Eq. (8), we obtain a particular solution in the form

$$y = a_0\left[1 - \frac{t^2}{2^2} + \frac{t^4}{2^2 \cdot 4^2} - \frac{t^6}{2^2 \cdot 4^2 \cdot 6^2} + \cdots\right] \tag{18}$$

Since we have not specified the value of a_0, we may let it equal anything we please. Consequently, to get the simplest particular solution, we let

$$a_0 = 1 \tag{19}$$

We call this particular solution $J_0(t)$. Thus

$$J_0(t) = 1 - \frac{t^2}{2^2} + \frac{t^4}{2^2 4^2} - \frac{t^6}{2^2 \cdot 4^2 \cdot 6^2} + \cdots + (-1)^r \frac{t^{2r}}{2^{2r}(r!)^2} + \cdots \tag{20}$$

Application of Cauchy's ratio test (see Wilson, *Advanced Calculus*, p. 422) shows that the series must converge for all values of t.

Logically, we should next proceed to derive expressions for $Y_0(t)$ and then the general functions $J_\nu(t)$ and $Y_\nu(t)$. This, however, would be a lengthy process which would be outside the real purpose of this book. We will therefore record the expressions for these functions and refer the reader elsewhere for their derivation.[6] The expressions are

$$Y_0(t) = \frac{2}{\pi}\left\{\left[C + \log\left(\frac{t}{2}\right)\right] J_0(t) + \left(\frac{t}{2}\right)^2 - \frac{(t/2)^4}{(2!)^2}\left(1 + \frac{1}{2}\right) + \cdots + \frac{(-1)^{r+1}(t/2)^{2r}}{(r!)^2}\left[1 + \frac{1}{2} + \cdots + \frac{1}{r}\right] + \cdots\right\} \tag{21}$$

[6] Derivations of the expansions of the Bessel functions will be found in Whittaker and Watson, *Modern Analysis*, and in N. W. McLachlan, *Bessel Functions for Engineers*. The latter book also contains a valuable list of formulas involving Bessel functions and a readable discussion of the whole subject in relation to engineering problems.

where C in the above equation is Euler's constant, which we have already met in the last chapter. We recall here that

$$C = 0.577216 \cdots \tag{22}$$

$$J_\nu(t) = \frac{t^\nu}{2^\nu\Gamma(\nu+1)}\left(1 - \frac{t^2}{2^2(\nu+1)} + \frac{t^4}{2\cdot 2^4(\nu+1)(\nu+2)} + \cdots + \frac{(-1)^r t^{2r}}{r!2^{2r}(\nu+1)(\nu+2)\cdots(\nu+r)} + \cdots\right)$$

$$= \sum_{r=0}^{\infty} \frac{(-1)^r (t/2)^{\nu+2r}}{r!\Gamma(\nu+r+1)} \tag{23}$$ [7]

$$Y_\nu(t) = \frac{J_\nu(t)\cos\nu\pi - J_{-\nu}(t)}{\sin\nu\pi} \tag{24}$$ [8]

if ν is not an integer. If $\nu = n$, an integer, then $Y_n(t)$ is the limit of (24) as $\nu \to n$ and may be expressed as the power series

$$\pi Y_n(t) = 2J_n(t)\left[\log\frac{t}{2} + C\right] - \left(\frac{t}{2}\right)^{-n} \sum_{r=0}^{n-1} \frac{(n-r-1)!}{r!}\left(\frac{t}{2}\right)^{2r}$$

$$- \left(\frac{t}{2}\right)^{n} \sum_{r=0}^{\infty} \frac{(-1)^r\,(t/2)^{2r}}{r!(r+n)!}$$

$$\left\{\frac{1}{r+n} + \frac{1}{r+n-1} + \cdots + 1 + \frac{1}{r} + \frac{1}{r-1} + \cdots + 1\right\} \tag{24A}$$

---

[7] $\Gamma(\nu + 1)$ here represents the gamma function of $(\nu + 1)$ discussed in the last chapter.

[8] Not all writers use the same form for the function of the second kind. The form defined in Eq. (24) is known as Weber's form and is the most commonly used. Many texts use the symbol $N_\nu(t)$ instead of $Y_\nu(t)$ for this function. If any constant multiple of $J_\nu(t)$ is added to $Y_\nu(t)$, as defined in Eq. (24), it would still serve as $Y_\nu(t)$ in Eq. (4). Accordingly,

$$\frac{\pi}{2} Y_\nu(t) + (\log_e 2 - \nu)J_\nu(t)$$

is sometimes used as the definition of the function of the second kind.

When ν is not an integer, it follows from Eqs. (4) and (24) that

$$y = CJ_\nu(t) + DJ_{-\nu}(t)$$

is a general solution of Bessel's differential equation, Eq. (3), where C and D are arbitrary constants.

Equations (23) and (24A) appear quite formidable. Tables of these functions, however, have been calculated and curves drawn so that it is rarely necessary in practice to use the foregoing equations for the actual evaluation of Bessel functions.

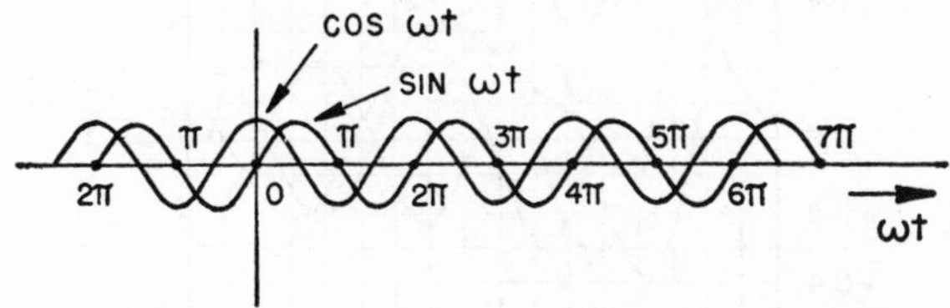

FIG. 9-1. The circular functions sin ωt and cos ωt.

Tables of the Bessel functions may be found in various places.[9] In Figs. 9-2, 9-3, and 9-4 are curves of the Bessel functions and these can be compared with the familiar curves of the sine and cosine in Fig. 9-1. For a more general picture, Fig. 9-5 shows a surface of $J_\nu(t)$ as a function of both ν and t which can be compared

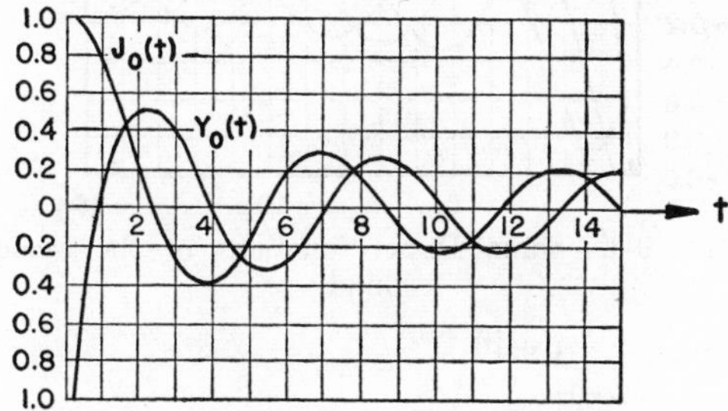

FIG. 9-2. The Bessel functions of zero order.

with the surface in Fig. 9-6, which shows sin ωt as a function of ω and t.

For large values of t, as will be shown in §11.3(b), both $J_\nu(t)$

---

[9] Extensive tables of Bessel functions may be found in Jahnke-Emde, *Tables of Functions;* N. W. McLachlan, *Bessel Functions for Engineers;* and G. N. Watson, *Treatise on Bessel Functions.* Recently, very extensive tables of Bessel functions have been calculated with the aid of the electronic computer of the Computation Laboratory of Harvard University. Volumes of these tables are currently being published. For approximate purposes, the values of various Bessel functions may be taken from the curves in the figures of the present chapter.

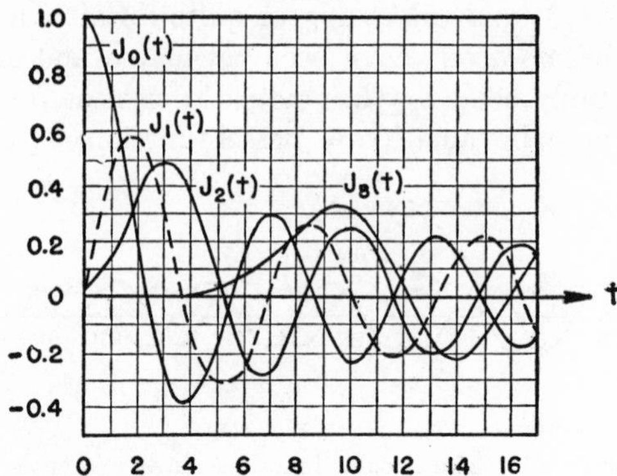

FIG. 9-3. Some Bessel functions of the first kind.

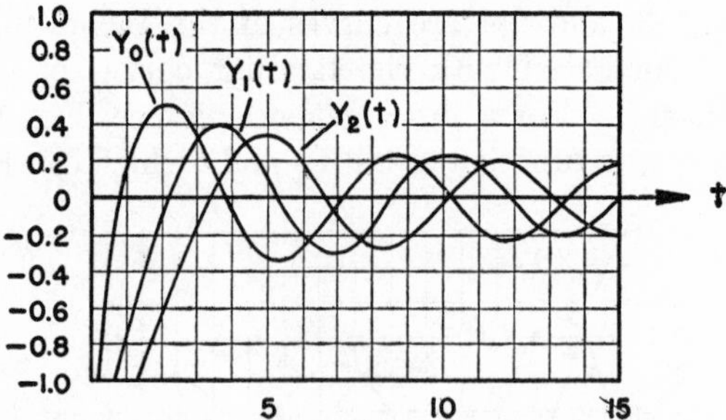

FIG. 9-4. Some Bessel functions of the second kind.

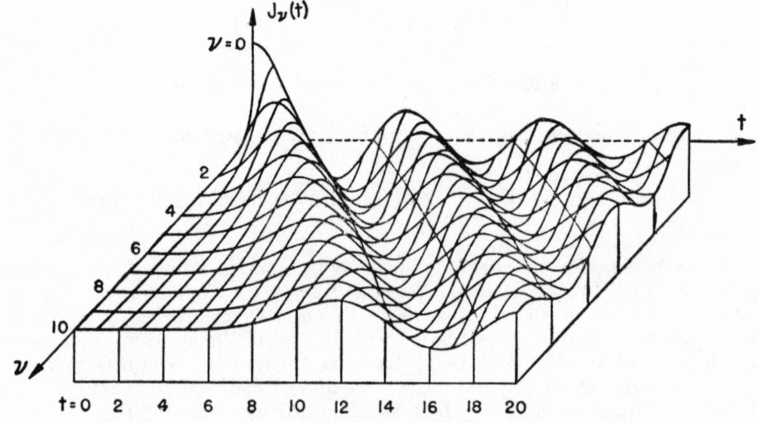

FIG. 9-5. $J_\nu(t)$ shown as a function of both ν and t.

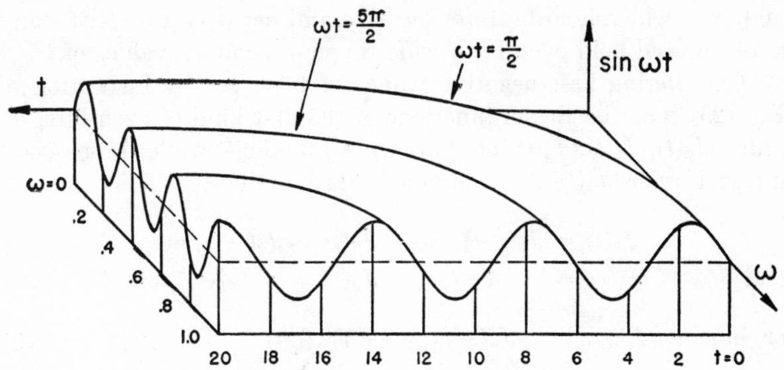

FIG. 9-6. Sin ωt shown as a function of both ω and t.

and $Y_\nu(t)$ approach the form of sine waves slowly decreasing in amplitude. In particular, when t is large

$$J_0(t) \to \sqrt{\frac{2}{\pi t}} \cos\left(t - \frac{\pi}{4}\right) \tag{25}$$

$$Y_0(t) \to \sqrt{\frac{2}{\pi t}} \sin\left(t - \frac{\pi}{4}\right) \tag{26}$$

Exercises

1. From the curves in Figs. 9-2, 9-3, and 9-4, find the values of $J_0(6)$, $J_0(10.3)$, $Y_0(5)$, $Y_0(2.1)$, $J_1(1)$, $J_1(2)$, $J_2(1)$, $J_2(6)$, $J_8(8)$, $Y_2(4)$. Check your values against those found in Jahnke-Emde's tables.

2. Derive the series expansions of sin ωt and cos ωt from Eq. (1).

3. Show that

$$\frac{\pi}{2} Y_0(t) = J_0(t)\left\{\log\left(\frac{t}{2}\right) + C\right\} + \left(\frac{t}{2}\right)^2 - \frac{(1 + \frac{1}{2})(t/2)^4}{(2!)^2} + \left(1 + \frac{1}{2} + \frac{1}{3}\right)\frac{(t/2)^6}{(3!)^2} \cdots$$

4. Derive Eq. (23) from Eq. (3).

9.4. Negative value of ν and t

Let us next for a moment consider the properties of the Bessel functions for negative values of the quantities ν and t. These properties can all be deduced from the general equations, Eqs. (23)

and (24), which hold both for positive and negative values of ν and t, and indeed hold even for a wide range of complex values of t.

Considering first negative values of t, we see by inspection of Eq. (23) that the Bessel functions of the first kind of even integral order [$J_0(t)$, $J_2(t)$, $J_4(t)$, etc.] are even functions, while those of odd integral order [$J_1(t)$, $J_3(t)$, etc.] are odd functions. Thus

$$J_0(t) = J_0(-t), \qquad J_2(t) = J_2(-t), \text{ etc.} \tag{27}$$

and

$$J_1(t) = -J_1(-t), \qquad J_3(t) = -J_3(-t), \text{ etc.} \tag{28}$$

or, in general,[10]

$$J_n(-t) = (-1)^n J_n(t) \tag{29}$$

However, when the order ν is nonintegral, then $(-t)^\nu$ is complex, so that $J_\nu(-t)$ is also complex, and the situation does not lend itself to general conclusions. The Bessel function of the second kind $Y_\nu(t)$ is complex for negative values of t, regardless of whether ν is integral or not. Consequently, Bessel functions, excepting those of the first kind of integral order, do not conveniently lend themselves to numerical evaluation for negative values of t.

Let us next consider negative values of the order ν. In this case, the values of both $J_\nu(t)$ and $Y_\nu(t)$ are still real (for all positive values of t), as we can see from[11] Eqs. (23) and (24). The functions, however, do not show any obvious types of symmetry, excepting

$$J_{-n}(t) = (-1)^n J_n(t) \tag{30}$$

$$Y_{-n}(t) = (-1)^n Y_n(t) \tag{30A}$$

if n is an integer. Equations (30) and (30A) can be derived from the final form of Eq. (23) and from Eq. (24A) by remembering that

$$\frac{1}{\Gamma(\nu + r + 1)} = 0$$

if ν is a negative integer greater than or equal to $(r + 1)$ in absolute value. The reader can verify this by writing out the actual expansions. We shall find that Eq. (30), especially, is an important and useful relation.

[10] It is customary to write $J_n(t)$ for $J_\nu(t)$, when ν is limited to integral values.
[11] The summation form of Eq. (23) must be used if ν is a negative integer.

9.5. Alternative definition of $J_n(t)$

Sines and cosines as we originally meet them are defined in terms of properties of triangles and are later expressed in terms of power series long before we think of them as solutions of Eq. (1). It is therefore of interest to know that $J_n(t)$, at least, when n is an integer, can be defined in a manner which is distinct from the differential Eq. (3). To show this definition, let us express

$$\epsilon^{\frac{1}{2}t\left(x-\frac{1}{x}\right)} = \epsilon^{\frac{tx}{2}} \cdot \epsilon^{-\frac{t}{2x}} \tag{31}$$

as the product of two power series. Thus we obtain

$$\epsilon^{\frac{1}{2}t\left(x-\frac{1}{x}\right)} = \left[1 + \frac{tx}{2} + \frac{1}{2!}\left(\frac{tx}{2}\right)^2 + \frac{1}{3!}\left(\frac{tx}{2}\right)^3 + \cdots\right] \cdot \left[1 - \frac{t}{2x} + \frac{1}{2!}\left(\frac{t}{2x}\right)^2 - \frac{1}{3!}\left(\frac{t}{2x}\right)^3 + \cdots\right] \tag{32}$$

These two series are both absolutely convergent for all values of x and t, excepting $x = 0$. Therefore, the series may be multiplied together like polynomials. Arranging the product terms in the order of powers of x, we obtain

$$\begin{aligned}
\epsilon^{\frac{1}{2}t\left(x-\frac{1}{x}\right)} &= \left(1 - \frac{t^2}{2^2} + \frac{t^4}{2^2 \cdot 4^2} - \right) \\
&\quad + x\left(\frac{t}{2} - \frac{t^3}{2^3 \cdot 2!} + \frac{t^5}{2! \cdot 2^5 \cdot 3!} - \right) + \cdots \\
&\quad + \frac{1}{x}\left(-\frac{t}{2} + \frac{t^3}{2^3 \cdot 2!} - \frac{t^5}{2! \cdot 2^5 \cdot 3!} + \right) + \cdots \\
&= J_0(t) + xJ_1(t) + x^2J_2(t) + \cdots + \frac{1}{x}J_{-1}(t) + \frac{1}{x^2}J_{-2}(t) + \cdots \\
&= \sum_{n=-\infty}^{+\infty} x^n J_n(t)
\end{aligned} \tag{33}$$

where n takes on all integral values from $-\infty$ to $+\infty$. We have thus established a new definition for $J_n(t)$; namely, as the coefficients in the expansion of

$$\epsilon^{\frac{t}{2}\left(x-\frac{1}{x}\right)}$$

Probably the majority of the radio applications of Bessel functions involve principally Bessel functions of the first kind of integral orders. It is therefore not surprising that the expansion, Eq. (33), appears as the basis of many of these applications.

9.6. Some important formulas involving $J_n(t)$

If, in Eq. (33), we let

$$x = \epsilon^{j\phi} \tag{34}$$

then we obtain the relation

$$\begin{aligned}\epsilon^{\frac{t}{2}(\epsilon^{j\phi} - \epsilon^{-j\phi})} &= \epsilon^{jt \sin \phi} \\ &= J_0(t) + \{J_1(t)\epsilon^{j\phi} + J_{-1}(t)\epsilon^{-j\phi}\} \\ &\quad + \{J_2(t)\epsilon^{j2\phi} + J_{-2}(t)\epsilon^{-j2\phi}\} + \cdots\end{aligned} \tag{35}$$

According to Eq. (30) and the equations

$$\epsilon^{jx} = \cos x + j \sin x \tag{36}$$

$$\sin x = \frac{\epsilon^{jx} - \epsilon^{-jx}}{2j} \tag{37}$$

$$\cos x = \frac{\epsilon^{jx} + \epsilon^{-jx}}{2} \tag{38}$$

we may rewrite Eq. (35) as

$$\begin{aligned}\epsilon^{jt \sin \phi} &= \cos (t \sin \phi) + j \sin (t \sin \phi) \\ &= J_0(t) + 2\{J_2(t) \cos 2\phi + J_4(t) \cos 4\phi + \cdots\} \\ &\quad + j2\{J_1(t) \sin \phi + J_3(t) \sin 3\phi + \cdots\}\end{aligned} \tag{39}$$

Equating real and imaginary parts of Eq. (39), we get the important relations

$$\cos (t \sin \phi) = J_0(t) + 2\{J_2(t) \cos 2\phi + J_4(t) \cos 4\phi + \cdots\} \tag{40}$$

$$\sin (t \sin \phi) = 2\{J_1(t) \sin \phi + J_3(t) \sin 3\phi + \cdots\} \tag{41}$$

It is interesting to note that for every particular value of t, Eqs. (40) and (41) are Fourier-series expansions. This fact immediately suggests another expression for the Bessel functions, namely,

$$J_n(t) = \frac{1}{\pi} \int_0^\pi \cos (t \sin \phi) \cos n\phi \, d\phi \tag{42}$$

if n is an even positive integer,

$$J_n(t) = \frac{1}{\pi}\int_0^\pi \sin\,(t \sin\phi)\sin n\phi\,d\phi \tag{43}$$

if n is an odd positive integer, and

$$J_0(t) = \frac{1}{\pi}\int_0^\pi \cos\,(t\sin\phi)\,d\phi \tag{44}$$

To derive Eqs. (42), (43), and (44), we need only multiply through Eq. (40) or (41), by the appropriate $\cos n\phi$, $\sin n\phi$ or unity and integrate from zero to π. All the integrals except one will then vanish, and the desired answer will be obtained.

The integral on the right of Eq. (43) will vanish if n is an even integer, while the integral in (42) will vanish if n is odd. Combining these facts with Eqs. (42) and (43), we obtain by addition

$$\begin{aligned}\frac{1}{\pi}\int_0^\pi \{\cos n\phi \cos\,(t\sin\phi) + \sin n\phi \sin\,(t\sin\phi)\}\,d\phi &= J_n(t)\\ &= \frac{1}{\pi}\int_0^\pi \cos\,(n\phi - t\sin\phi)\,d\phi \end{aligned}\tag{45}$$

where n is any positive integer. Equation (45) is sometimes used as the starting point for the whole theory of Bessel functions.

A corresponding set of formulas to Eqs. (39–45) can be derived by changing ϕ in Eq. (39) to

$$\left(\frac{\pi}{2} - \phi\right)$$

and obtaining

$$\begin{aligned}\epsilon^{jt\cos\phi} = J_0(t) &- 2\{J_2(t)\cos 2\phi - J_4(t)\cos 4\phi + \cdots\}\\ &+ j2\{J_1(t)\cos\phi - J_3(t)\cos 3\phi + \cdots\}\end{aligned}\tag{46}$$

Equating real and imaginary parts of Eq. (46), we have

$$\cos\,(t\cos\phi) = J_0(t) - 2\{J_2(t)\cos 2\phi - J_4(t)\cos 4\phi + \cdots\} \tag{47}$$

and

$$\begin{aligned}\sin\,(t\cos\phi) = 2\{J_1(t)\cos\phi &- J_3(t)\cos 3\phi\\ &+ J_5(t)\cos 5\phi - \cdots\}\end{aligned}\tag{48}$$

If in Eqs. (47) and (48) we set $\phi = 0$, we obtain

$$\cos t = J_0(t) - 2\{J_2(t) - J_4(t) + J_6(t) + \cdots\} \tag{49}$$

and

$$\sin t = 2\{J_1(t) - J_3(t) + J_5(t) - \cdots\} \tag{50}$$

Equations (49) and (50) show a striking relationship between the circular functions and the Bessel functions of the first kind.

In the foregoing section we have derived a number of the more important relationships involving Bessel functions of the first kind of integral order. In the following sections, we will take up additional relations between Bessel functions and round out what may be called, in analogy with circular functions, the trigonometry and calculus of Bessel functions. These new relations to be discussed will *not* be limited to functions of the first kind of integral order.

Exercise

1. Show that

$$\int_0^\infty J_1(t)\,dt = 1$$

It may be shown that, for all values of n,

$$\int_0^\infty J_n(t)\,dt = 1$$

9.7. Recurrence formulas—differentiation and integration

The definitions of $J_\nu(t)$ and $Y_\nu(t)$ in Eqs. (23) and (24) express these functions as uniformly convergent series. Therefore, they may usually be differentiated and integrated term by term. The actual carrying through of these operations is tedious, but the reader may at his leisure perform any of the operations which he desires. However, a number of useful formulas can thus be derived which we will record below.[12]

$$t\frac{d}{dt}[J_\nu(t)] = \nu J_\nu(t) - tJ_{\nu+1}(t) \tag{51}$$

$$t\frac{d}{dt}[Y_\nu(t)] = \nu Y_\nu(t) - tY_{\nu+1}(t) \tag{52}$$

$$t\frac{d}{dt}[J_\nu(t)] = -\nu J_\nu(t) + tJ_{\nu-1}(t) \tag{53}$$

[12] The notation $J'_\nu(t)$ is frequently used for $\frac{d}{dt}[J_\nu(t)]$ and $Y'_\nu(t)$ for $\frac{d}{dt}[Y_\nu(t)]$.

$$t\frac{d}{dt}[Y_\nu(t)] = -\nu Y_\nu(t) + tY_{\nu-1}(t) \tag{54}$$

$$\frac{d}{dt}[J_\nu(t)] = \frac{1}{2}\{J_{\nu-1}(t) - J_{\nu+1}(t)\} \tag{55}$$

$$\frac{d}{dt}[Y_\nu(t)] = \frac{1}{2}\{Y_{\nu-1}(t) - Y_{\nu+1}(t)\} \tag{56}$$

$$\frac{2\nu}{t}J_\nu(t) = J_{\nu+1}(t) + J_{\nu-1}(t) \tag{57}$$

$$\frac{2\nu}{t}Y_\nu(t) = Y_{\nu+1}(t) + Y_{\nu-1}(t) \tag{58}$$

$$\frac{d}{dt}[J_0(t)] = -J_1(t) \tag{59}$$

$$\frac{d}{dt}[Y_0(t)] = -Y_1(t) \tag{60}$$

$$\frac{d}{dt}\{t^{-\nu}J_\nu(t)\} = -t^{-\nu}J_{\nu+1}(t) \tag{61}$$

$$\frac{d}{dt}\{t^{-\nu}Y_\nu(t)\} = -t^{-\nu}Y_{\nu+1}(t) \tag{62}$$

$$\int^t t^{-\nu}J_{\nu+1}(t)\,dt = -t^{-\nu}J_\nu(t) \tag{63}$$

$$\int^t t^{-\nu}Y_{\nu+1}(t)\,dt = -t^{-\nu}Y_\nu(t) \tag{64}$$

$$\frac{d}{dt}\{t^\nu J_\nu(t)\} = t^\nu J_{\nu-1}(t) \tag{65}$$

$$\frac{d}{dt}\{t^\nu Y_\nu(t)\} = t^\nu Y_{\nu-1}(t) \tag{66}$$

$$\int^t t^\nu J_{\nu-1}(t)\,dt = t^\nu J_\nu(t) \tag{67}$$

$$\int^t t^\nu Y_{\nu-1}(t)\,dt = t^\nu Y_\nu(t) \tag{68}$$

We can readily see from the foregoing that these formulas are identical for functions of the first and second kinds. Equations (57) and (58) are known as recurrence formulas. The remainder are formulas of differentiation and integration. To while away the time on a warm summer afternoon the reader can meditate upon the similarities and dissimilarities between these formulas and corresponding formulas for sines and cosines.[13]

---

[13] A large number of other formulas will be found in Jahnke-Emde, *Tables of Functions*, and N. W. McLachlan, *Bessel Functions for Engineers*.

9.8. Half-integral orders

Bessel functions become remarkably simplified when the orders are half-integrals $\left(\text{i.e., } \frac{1}{2}, \frac{3}{2}, \frac{5}{2}, \cdots \frac{-1}{2}, \frac{-3}{2}, \cdots\right)$. Thus, if we let $\nu = \frac{1}{2}$ in Eq. (23), then with the help of Eq. (30) of Chap. 8, we get

$$J_{\frac{1}{2}}(t) = \sqrt{\frac{2}{\pi t}}\left\{t - \frac{t^3}{3!} + \frac{t^5}{5!} \cdots\right\} = \sqrt{\frac{2}{\pi t}} \sin t \tag{69}$$

In a similar manner, we obtain

$$J_{-\frac{1}{2}}(t) = \sqrt{\frac{2}{\pi t}} \cos t \tag{70}$$

Therefore, by Eq. (24)

$$Y_{\frac{1}{2}}(t) = \frac{J_{\frac{1}{2}}(t) \cos \frac{\pi}{2} - J_{-\frac{1}{2}}(t)}{\sin \frac{\pi}{2}} = -J_{-\frac{1}{2}}(t) = -\sqrt{\frac{2}{\pi t}} \cos t \tag{71}$$

$$Y_{-\frac{1}{2}}(t) = \frac{J_{-\frac{1}{2}}(t) \cos\left(-\frac{\pi}{2}\right) - J_{\frac{1}{2}}(t)}{\sin\left(-\frac{\pi}{2}\right)} = J_{\frac{1}{2}}(t) = \sqrt{\frac{2}{\pi t}} \sin t \tag{72}$$

To get $J_{\frac{3}{2}}(t)$, we let $\nu = \frac{1}{2}$ in Eq. (57), and obtain

$$J_{\frac{3}{2}}(t) = \frac{1}{t} J_{\frac{1}{2}}(t) - J_{-\frac{1}{2}}(t) = \sqrt{\frac{2}{\pi t}}\left[\frac{\sin t}{t} - \cos t\right] \tag{73}$$

To get $J_{-\frac{3}{2}}(t)$, we let $\nu = -\frac{1}{2}$ in Eq. (57), to obtain

$$J_{-\frac{3}{2}}(t) = -\frac{1}{t} J_{-\frac{1}{2}}(t) - J_{\frac{1}{2}}(t) = -\sqrt{\frac{2}{\pi t}}\left[\sin t + \frac{\cos t}{t}\right] \tag{74}$$

By similar means, we can obtain the Bessel functions of any half-integral order.

9.9. Hankel functions

In the earlier sections of this chapter, we found a certain amount of correspondence between Bessel functions and circular functions.

It is therefore not surprising that corresponding to the functions

$$\epsilon^{j\omega t} = \cos \omega t + j \sin \omega t \tag{75}$$

and

$$\epsilon^{-j\omega t} = \cos \omega t - j \sin \omega t \tag{76}$$

which are so frequently used, there is also a set of Bessel functions. These functions are known as Hankel functions, or Bessel functions of the third kind, and are defined by the equations

$$H_\nu^{(1)}(t) = J_\nu(t) + jY_\nu(t) \tag{77}$$

$$H_\nu^{(2)}(t) = J_\nu(t) - jY_\nu(t) \tag{78}$$

The Hankel functions are thus complex quantities. Their most common field of application is in problems of traveling waves. In terms of the Hankel functions, the solution of Eq. (3) may be written

$$y = CH_\nu^{(1)}(t) + DH_\nu^{(2)}(t) \tag{79}$$

where C and D are arbitrary constants.[14] For large values of t,

$$H_0^{(1)}(t) \rightarrow \sqrt{\frac{2}{\pi t}}\,\epsilon^{j(t-\pi/4)} \tag{80}$$

$$H_0^{(2)}(t) \rightarrow \sqrt{\frac{2}{\pi t}}\,\epsilon^{-j(t-\pi/4)} \tag{81}$$

which emphasizes the correspondence between the Hankel functions and the complex exponentials.

9.10. Modified Bessel functions—complex values of t

When dealing with differential equations of the Bessel type in practice, we often find the equations in the form

$$\frac{d^2y}{dt^2} + \frac{1}{t}\frac{dy}{dt} + \left(k^2 - \frac{\nu^2}{t^2}\right) y = 0 \tag{82}$$

This equation can be reduced to the form (3) by making the substitution

$$x = kt \tag{83}$$

---

[14] This solution is actually the same as Eq. (4) with $C = \dfrac{A - jB}{2}$ and $D = \dfrac{A + jB}{2}$.

Equation (82) then becomes

$$\frac{d^2y}{dx^2} + \frac{1}{x}\frac{dy}{dx} + \left(1 - \frac{\nu^2}{x^2}\right) y = 0 \tag{84}$$

Consequently the solution of Eq. (82) is

$$y = AJ_\nu(kt) + BY_\nu(kt) \tag{85}$$

Now suppose we let

$$k = \sqrt{-1} = j \tag{86}$$

in Eq. (82). Then the latter becomes

$$\frac{d^2y}{dt^2} + \frac{1}{t}\frac{dy}{dt} - \left(1 + \frac{\nu^2}{t^2}\right) y = 0 \tag{87}$$

whose formal solution is

$$y = AJ_\nu(jt) + BY_\nu(jt) \tag{88}$$

The actual solutions to Eq. (87) of interest are usually real solutions, so that $AJ_\nu(jt)$ and $BY_\nu(jt)$ are usually real quantities. To put them into real form we therefore define two new functions:

$$\begin{aligned} I_\nu(t) &= \frac{J_\nu(jt)}{(j)^\nu} \\ &= \frac{t^\nu}{2^\nu\Gamma(\nu+1)}\left\{1 + \frac{t^2}{2(2\nu+2)} + \frac{t^4}{2\cdot 4(2\nu+2)(2\nu+4)} + \cdots\right\} \end{aligned} \tag{89}$$

and[15]

$$K_\nu(t) = \frac{\pi/2}{\sin \nu\pi}\,[I_{-\nu}(t) - I_\nu(t)] \tag{90}$$

We then rewrite Eq. (88) in the form

$$y = aI_\nu(t) + bK_\nu(t) \tag{91}$$

where all the quantities in Eq. (91) are now real, for most cases of interest.

Equation (87) is known as the *modified Bessel equation*, and its solutions, $I_\nu(t)$ and $K_\nu(t)$, are known as *modified Bessel functions*

[15] When $\nu = n$, an integer, $K_n(t)$ is the limit approached by Eq. (90) as $\nu \to n$. This may also be written

$$K_n(t) = \frac{2}{\cos n\pi}\left(\frac{\partial I_{-n}}{\partial n} - \frac{\partial I_n}{\partial n}\right)$$

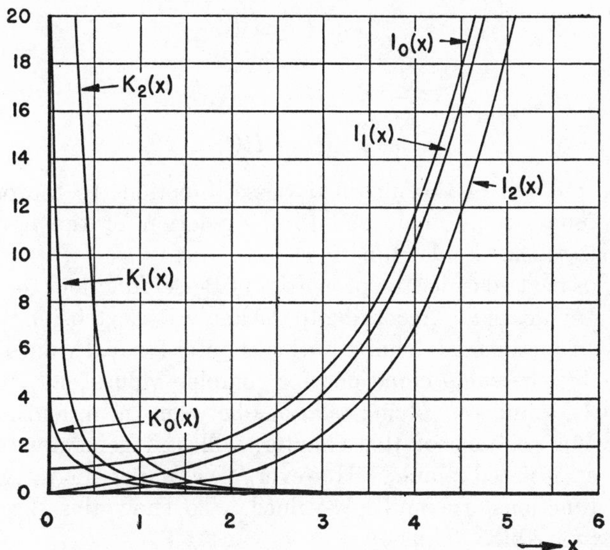

FIG. 9-7. Some of the modified Bessel functions.

of the first and second kind respectively.[16] These functions are not of an oscillating type, like the ordinary Bessel functions, but behave more like exponential functions. Some curves of $I_n(t)$ and $K_n(t)$ are shown in Fig. 9-7. For large values of t,

$$I_0(t) \to \frac{\epsilon^t}{\sqrt{2\pi t}} \tag{92}$$

$$K_0(t) \to \epsilon^{-t} \sqrt{\frac{\pi}{2t}} \tag{93}$$

The modified Bessel functions have recurrence formulas, and formulas of differentiation and integration, which can be derived from the corresponding formulas for the ordinary Bessel functions. We note in particular

[16] A table of values of $I_0(x) = J_0(\sqrt{-1}\,x)$ appears on pp. 226 and 228 of Jahnke-Emde. A table of $I_1(x) = -\sqrt{-1}\,J_1(\sqrt{-1}\,x)$ appears on pp. 227 and 229. Tables of other modified Bessel functions and of Hankel functions appear in later pages of the same book.

$$\frac{d}{dt}\{I_0(t)\} = I_1(t) \tag{94}$$

$$\frac{d}{dt}\{K_0(t)\} = -K_1(t) \tag{95}$$

$$I_{-n}(t) = I_n(t) \tag{96}$$

The relation of the modified Bessel functions to the ordinary Bessel functions is analogous to the relation of the hyperbolic functions to the circular functions.

Let us next consider the properties of Bessel functions for general complex values of t. According to the analytical extension theorem, if Bessel functions as defined in this chapter for real values of t are defined by the same equations for complex values of t, then the principal formulas involving relations between them, and recorded in previous sections of this chapter, will still generally be valid except at isolated points. However, if ν is not an integer, the Bessel functions are multiple-valued. To show this, let t be a complex variable. Thus

$$t = R\epsilon^{j\phi} \tag{97}$$

Then

$$t^\nu = R^\nu\epsilon^{j\nu(\phi+2m\pi)} \tag{98}$$

where m is any integer. Consequently, if ν is not an integer, t^ν is a multiple-valued function. It then follows from the definition of $J_\nu(t)$ in Eq. (23), and the subsequent definitions of the other Bessel functions, that they are also multiple-valued, when ν is not an integer. However, if nothing is said to the contrary, it will always be assumed that the complex phase angle of t will be given its value in the range $-\pi < \phi \leq +\pi$.

Exercises

1. From Eq. (89), find the series expansions of $I_0(x)$ and $I_1(x)$.

2. Find the values of $J_{\frac{1}{2}}(jt)$, $J_{-\frac{1}{2}}(jt)$, and $J_{\frac{3}{2}}(jt)$.

3. Show that

$$K_0(az) = \int_0^\infty \epsilon^{az\cosh\theta}\, d\theta$$

4. Show that

(a) $$J_n(z)Y_n'(z) - Y_n(z)J_n'(z) = \frac{2}{\pi z}$$

(b) $$I_n(z)K_n'(z) - K_n(z)I'(z) = -\frac{1}{z}$$

9.11. Other related functions

In addition to the functions already discussed, there are a number of other functions, closely related to the Bessel functions, which may be mentioned here. First, there are the ber and bei functions defined by the equation

$$I_0[j^{\frac{1}{2}}z] = J_0[j^{\frac{3}{2}}z] = \text{ber } z + j \text{ bei } z \tag{99}$$

These functions are important in radiation theory and in dealing with other space effects at high frequencies, such as skin effect.

Another group of useful functions are the ker and kei functions defined by the equation

$$K_0(j^{\frac{1}{2}}z) = \text{ker } z + \text{kei } z = j\frac{\pi}{2} H_0^{(1)}(j^{\frac{3}{2}}z) \tag{100}$$

These are also useful in radiation theory. Tables of these functions, as well as of other functions related to Bessel functions, will be found in some of the more extensive works on Bessel functions and related subjects.

9.12. Zeros of Bessel functions—expansion of an arbitrary function as a series of Bessel functions

The values of t for which

$$J_n(t) = 0 \tag{101}$$

are called the zeros of $J_n(t)$ or the roots of Eq. (101). These values can be located on the graphs or in the tables of $J_n(t)$ and they can also be located by analytical means.[17] It may be shown that the distances between roots of Eq. (101) approach π as t becomes large. There are consequently an infinite number of zeros. It may also be shown that the zeros of $J_n(t)$ and $J_{n+1}(t)$ alternate in location except at $t = 0$. Numerous other properties of the zeros can be demonstrated and are of practical importance.

An interesting application of the zeros of Bessel functions is in the expansion of an arbitrary function as a series of Bessel functions.[18] This corresponds to a Fourier series for circular functions.

---

[17] See Jahnke-Emde, *Tables of Functions*, p. 143.

[18] A general treatment of the expansion of an arbitrary function into a series of orthogonal functions of any kind will be found in the second chapter of Courant-Hilbert, *Methoden der Mathematischen Physik*.

Thus it may be shown that any ordinary function $f(x)$ can be expanded in the form

$$f(x) = \sum_{i=1}^{\infty} a_i J_n(\lambda_i x) \tag{102}$$

where

$$a_i = \frac{2 \int_0^1 x f(x) J_n(\lambda_i x)\, dx}{[J'_n(\lambda_i)]^2} \tag{103}$$

and the quantities λ_i are the roots of

$$J_n(x) = 0 \tag{104}$$

Other types of expansions for an arbitrary function in terms of Bessel functions are given by Whittaker and Watson.

9.13. General

The radio applications of Bessel functions are very numerous. Most of them, however, can be put into three general classes:

(1) Problems related to the series expansion of, or integrals involving, $\epsilon^{jz \sin \phi}$ or $\epsilon^{jz \cos \phi}$.

(2) Solutions of differential equations of the Bessel type, and

(3) Laplace transformations involving fractional powers of functions of s (see Chaps. 10 and 11).

These classes are not unrelated, so that a given problem may fall into more than one of the above classes. However, the list will give a general idea of the type of problem in which Bessel functions may be expected to arise. Wave-propagation problems in systems having circular symmetry almost always give rise to Bessel functions.

In addition to the account of Bessel functions presented in this chapter,[19] we will discuss the asymptotic expansions of Bessel functions, for large values of the argument, in §11.3(b).

Circular functions and Bessel functions both exemplify systems of functions which can be built up into what are known as orthogonal sets. Examples of orthogonal sets are the $J_n(t)$'s in Eqs. (40) and (41), or the $J_n(\lambda_i x)$'s in Eq. (102), or the sin $(n\omega t - \phi_n)$'s in a Fourier series. One of the important properties of an orthogonal

---

[19] For derivations of the Laplace transforms of the Bessel functions listed in Appendix D, see Watson, *Theory of Bessel Functions.*

set of functions is that it is possible to expand an arbitrary function as an infinite series of these functions multiplied by the proper constants. The proper set of functions to use for a particular expansion is the one whose terms and coefficients have the most significance and the one which gives the simplest solution to the problems at hand. Thus a Fourier series is usually best for a periodic function.

CHAPTER 10

Transients in Transmission Lines—Solution of Partial Differential Equations[1]

10.1. Laplace transformation of the partial differential equations of a transmission line

It is shown in Appendix C that the fundamental equations which govern phenomena in a transmission line are

$$L\frac{\partial i}{\partial t} + Ri = -\frac{\partial e}{\partial x} \tag{1}$$

and

$$C\frac{\partial e}{\partial t} + Ge = -\frac{\partial i}{\partial x} \tag{2}$$

These are *simultaneous partial differential equations*, and the independent variables are x and t. The final solutions will therefore be explicit solutions expressing i and e as functions of x and t of the form

$$i = i(x,t) \tag{3}$$

$$e = e(x,t) \tag{4}$$

Thus the final solution, if found, will tell us the value of current and voltage at every instant and every location.

In Appendix C will be found the *steady-state solutions* to the simultaneous Eqs. (1) and (2). In this chapter, we will attempt to find the more difficult *transient solutions*.

As a first step, let us multiply through Eq. (1) with ϵ^{-st} and integrate from zero to infinity. Then

$$\int_0^\infty L\frac{\partial i}{\partial t}\epsilon^{-st}\,dt + \int_0^\infty Ri\epsilon^{-st}\,dt = \int_0^\infty -\frac{\partial e}{\partial x}\epsilon^{-st}\,dt \tag{5}$$

[1] The writer is particularly indebted to J. R. Carson's *Electrical Circuit Theory and Operational Calculus*, and to Carslaw and Jaeger's *Operational Methods in Mathematical Physics* as a background for the material presented in this chapter.

Now, integrating by parts, we have

$$\int_0^\infty L \frac{\partial i}{\partial t} \epsilon^{-st}\, dt = [Li\epsilon^{-st}]_0^\infty + Ls \int_0^\infty i\epsilon^{-st}\, dt$$

$$= -Li(x,0) + Ls\bar{I}(x,s) \tag{6}$$

where[2]

$$\bar{I}(x,s) = \int_0^\infty i(x,t)\epsilon^{-st}\, dt \tag{7}$$

so that $\bar{I} = \bar{I}(x,s)$ is the Laplace transform of $i(x,t)$. Furthermore,

$$\int_0^\infty -\frac{\partial e}{\partial x} \epsilon^{-st}\, dt = -\frac{\partial}{\partial x} \int_0^\infty e \cdot \epsilon^{-st}\, dt = -\frac{\partial \bar{E}(x,s)}{\partial x} \tag{8}$$

where $\bar{E}(x,s)$ is the Laplace transform of $e(x,t)$. The partial differentiation with respect to x can be taken outside the integral sign in Eq. (8), since the limits of integration are not functions of x.

Substituting Eqs. (6) and (8) into Eq. (5), we obtain

$$[Ls + R]\bar{I} = -\frac{\partial \bar{E}}{\partial x} + Li(x,0) \tag{9}$$

as the transformed equation corresponding to Eq. (1). In an entirely similar manner, Eq. (2) transforms into

$$[Cs + G]\bar{E} = -\frac{\partial \bar{I}}{\partial x} + Ce(x,0) \tag{10}$$

Equations (9) and (10) are the transmission-line equations in terms of the variables x and s. Since s is not a function of x, and since there are no derivatives with respect to s in Eqs. (9) and (10), these can be solved as a pair of simultaneous ordinary differential equations. Accordingly, let us eliminate $\bar{E}$. Thus multiplying Eq. (9) by $(Cs + G)$, and differentiating Eq. (10) with respect to x, and adding the results, we obtain

$$\frac{\partial^2 \bar{I}}{\partial x^2} - [Ls + R][Cs + G]\bar{I} = C\frac{\partial e(x,0)}{\partial x} - L(Cs + G)i(x,0) \tag{11}$$

---

[2] The bar is used above I so that there will be no confusion with other uses of I in Appendix C. For simplicity, we will use the abbreviations $\bar{I}$ for $\bar{I}(x,s)$, $\bar{E}$ for $\bar{E}(x,s)$, i for $i(x,t)$, and e for $e(x,t)$ except in cases in which it appears desirable to emphasize the independent variables.

Similarly, we find,

$$\frac{\partial^2 \bar{E}}{\partial x^2} - [Ls + R][Cs + G]\bar{E} = L\frac{\partial i(x,0)}{\partial x} - C[Ls + R]e(x,0) \quad (12)$$

If we make the substitution

$$n = +\sqrt{(Ls + R)(Cs + G)} \quad (13)$$

then the complementary functions of both Eqs. (11) and (12) are of the form

$$\bar{I} = A_1\epsilon^{-nx} + B_1\epsilon^{nx} \quad (14)$$

and

$$\bar{E} = A_2\epsilon^{-nx} + B_2\epsilon^{nx} \quad (14A)$$

where A and B are independent of x, but are arbitrary functions of s to be determined by the conditions of the problem.

If we can find $\bar{I}$ and $\bar{E}$ from Eqs. (9), (10), (11), and (12), and can then find their inverse Laplace transforms, i and e, either by contour integration or with the aid of tables, then we will have found the desired solution. This is rarely a simple matter, but in the following sections we will show how various transmission-line transient problems can be solved.

10.2. Propagation of signals in an infinite transmission line—distortionless transmission

Let us now consider the propagation of a signal in a transmission line of infinite length (see Fig. 10-1). Let this signal originate as a

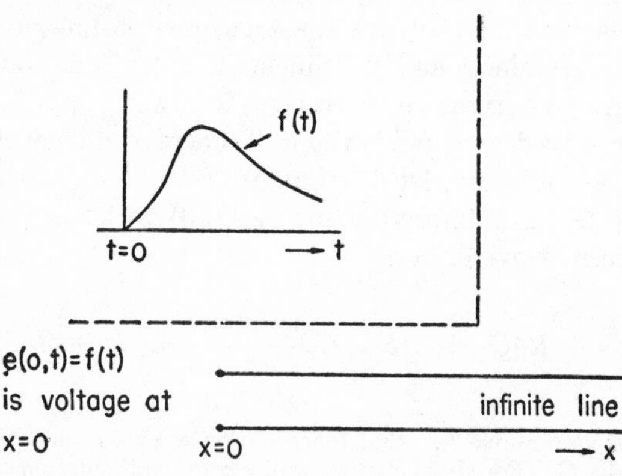

FIG. 10-1. An infinite line with voltage applied at the input.

voltage

$$e(0,t) = f(t) \tag{15}$$

at the beginning of the line, where $x = 0$.

Prior to and at time $t = 0$, we will assume that there is no current or voltage in the line. Therefore, the terms on the right of Eqs. (11) and (12) will vanish,[3] so that the transformed equations of the line reduce to

$$\frac{\partial^2 \bar{I}}{\partial x^2} - [Ls + R][Cs + G]\bar{I} = 0 \tag{16}$$

$$\frac{\partial^2 \bar{E}}{\partial x^2} - [Ls + R][Cs + G]\bar{E} = 0 \tag{17}$$

The solutions to Eqs. (16) and (17) are

$$\bar{I} = A_1\epsilon^{-nx} + B_1\epsilon^{nx} \tag{18}$$

and

$$\bar{E} = A_2\epsilon^{-nx} + B_2\epsilon^{nx} \tag{19}$$

The A's and B's are functions of s which are to be determined by the conditions of the problem. A_2 and B_2 can be determined from A_1 and B_1 and vice versa, with the aid of Eqs. (9) and (10). Let us first determine A_2 and B_2 from the conditions of the problem.

In the first place, let x be infinite. Since E must[4] remain finite even when x is infinite, for a signal of finite total energy, it follows from Eq. (19) that

$$B_2 = 0 \tag{20}$$

Next let $x = 0$. Now from Eqs. (19) and (20) it follows that

$$\bar{E}(0,s) = A_2 \tag{21}$$

and from Eq. (15), it follows that

$$\bar{E}(0,s) = \mathcal{L}\{e(0,t)\} = \mathcal{L}\{f(t)\} = F(s) \tag{22}$$

where $F(s)$ is the Laplace transform of $f(t)$. It therefore follows from Eqs. (13), (19), (20), (21), and (22) that

$$\bar{E} = \bar{E}(x,s) = F(s)\epsilon^{-nx} = F(s)\epsilon^{-x\sqrt{(Ls+R)(Cs+G)}} \tag{23}$$

---

[3] A case in which these terms do not vanish is considered in §10.5.

[4] The fact that $\bar{E}$ must remain finite is perhaps best seen with the aid of the Fourier-integral energy theorem. (See Appendix E.)

Now, if we can find $F(s)$ from the form given for $f(t)$ and if we can find the inverse transform of the right side of Eq. (23), we then have the solution to the problem of propagation in the infinite transmission line. While this may sometimes be difficult, in the special case in which

$$R = G = 0 \tag{24}$$

so that there is no dissipation, the solution is very simple. In this case, Eq. (23) reduces to

$$\bar{E}(x,s) = F(s)\epsilon^{-x\sqrt{LC}s} \tag{25}$$

Therefore it follows from formula (j) of Appendix D that

$$\begin{aligned} e(x,t) &= \mathfrak{L}^{-1}\{\bar{E}(x,s)\} = \mathfrak{L}^{-1}\{F(s)\epsilon^{-x\sqrt{LC}s}\} \\ &= f(t - x\sqrt{LC}) \end{aligned} \tag{26}$$

Thus the voltage at the point $x = x$ is exactly similar to the voltage at the point $x = 0$ except that there is a time lag of amount $x\sqrt{LC}$. In other words, signals are propagated along the line with a velocity[5] $1/\sqrt{LC}$, and without attenuation or change of wave form.

Another case of distortionless transmission occurs when

$$\frac{R}{L} = \frac{G}{C} \tag{27}$$

In this case, Eq. (23) becomes

$$\bar{E}(x,s) = F(s)\epsilon^{-x\sqrt{\frac{C}{L}}(Ls+R)} = F(s)\epsilon^{-x\sqrt{\frac{C}{L}}R}\,\epsilon^{-x\sqrt{LC}s} \tag{28}$$

It therefore follows from formula (j) of Appendix D that

$$\begin{aligned} e(x,t) &= \mathfrak{L}^{-1}\{\bar{E}(x,s)\} = \mathfrak{L}^{-1}\{F(s)\epsilon^{-x\sqrt{\frac{C}{L}}R}\,\epsilon^{-x\sqrt{LC}s}\} \\ &= \epsilon^{-x\sqrt{\frac{C}{L}}R} f(t - x\sqrt{LC}) \end{aligned} \tag{29}$$

---

[5] It is worth pointing out that $1/\sqrt{LC}$ is a true signal velocity (group velocity) in this case, since an actual signal containing information is traveling with this velocity. The velocity $\omega/\beta = 1/\sqrt{LC}$ for the steady state is a phase velocity. The two happen to be equal in this case because the phase velocity in a uniform lossless line is independent of frequency. (See §4.16 of the author's *Frequency Analysis, Modulation and Noise.*)

Consequently in this case signals are propagated without a change in wave form and with a velocity $1/\sqrt{LC}$, but there is attenuation (see Fig. 10-2) expressed by the factor

$$\epsilon^{-x\sqrt{\frac{C}{L}}R}$$

Transmission lines whose electrical constants are related by Eq. (27) are called distortionless lines of the Heaviside type, since

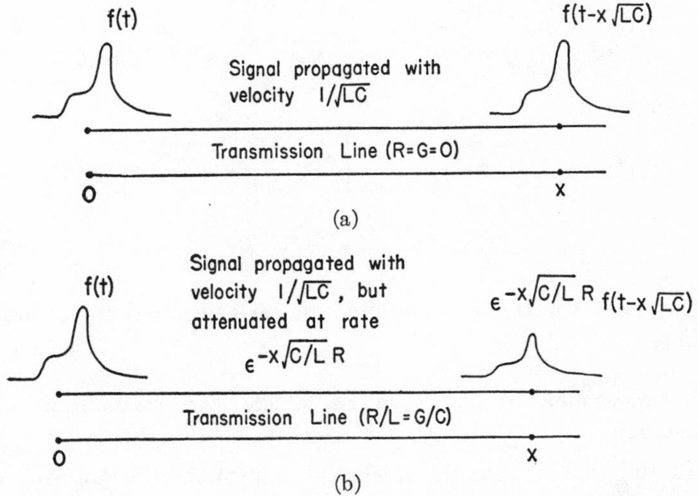

FIG. 10-2. Signal propagation in distortionless lines. (a) Lossless line. (b) Heaviside-type line.

it was Heaviside who first pointed out that such lines would have distortionless transmission.

In Eqs. (26) and (29) we found general expressions for the voltage. To find the general expression for the current, we first substitute Eq. (23) in Eq. (9). This gives

$$\bar{I} = \frac{-1}{Ls + R}\frac{\partial \bar{E}}{\partial x} = \frac{+F(s)\sqrt{(Ls + R)(Cs + G)}}{Ls + R}\epsilon^{-x\sqrt{(Ls+R)(Cs+G)}}$$

$$= F(s)\sqrt{\frac{Cs + G}{Ls + R}}\epsilon^{-x\sqrt{(Ls+R)(Cs+G)}} \tag{30}$$

since

$$i(x,0) = 0 \tag{30A}$$

Comparing Eqs. (23) and (30), we see that for an infinite line with quiescent initial conditions

$$\bar{I}(x,s) = \sqrt{\frac{Cs + G}{Ls + R}}\,\bar{E}(x,s) \tag{31}$$

Now for the case of a line in which, say,

$$\frac{R}{L} = \frac{G}{C} \tag{32}$$

Eq. (30) becomes

$$\bar{I} = F(s)\sqrt{\frac{C}{L}}\,\epsilon^{-x\sqrt{\frac{C}{L}}(Ls+R)} = F(s)\sqrt{\frac{C}{L}}\,\epsilon^{-x\sqrt{\frac{C}{L}}R}\,\epsilon^{-x\sqrt{LC}s} \tag{33}$$

Therefore,

$$i(x,t) = \mathfrak{L}^{-1}\{\bar{I}(x,s)\} = \mathfrak{L}^{-1}\left\{F(s)\sqrt{\frac{C}{L}}\,\epsilon^{-x\sqrt{\frac{C}{L}}R}\,\epsilon^{-x\sqrt{LC}s}\right\}$$

$$= \sqrt{\frac{C}{L}}\,\epsilon^{-x\sqrt{\frac{C}{L}}R}\,f(t - x\sqrt{LC}) \tag{34}$$

The current for the lossless line can be calculated in a similar manner.

10.3. Propagation of signals in an infinite line—transmission with distortion

In the general case in which the transmission is not without distortion, it is necessary to choose specific signals in order to study

Fig. 10-3. A square wave.

propagation. Accordingly, let us study the propagation of the square wave of voltage shown in Fig. 10-3. This wave may be expressed analytically as

$$f(t) = K[U(t - t_1) - U(t - t_2)] \tag{35}$$

Therefore,

$$F(s) = \frac{K}{s}\{\epsilon^{-t_1 s} - \epsilon^{-t_2 s}\} \tag{36}$$

Substituting this value into Eq. (23) we have

$$\bar{E}(x,s) = \frac{K}{s}\{\epsilon^{-t_1 s} - \epsilon^{-t_2 s}\}\epsilon^{-x\sqrt{(Ls+R)(Cs+G)}} \tag{37}$$

The function of s on the right of Eq. (37) does not appear in our table of Laplace transforms. However, the related form (No. 40)

$$\mathcal{L}^{-1}\{\epsilon^{-k\sqrt{s^2-a^2}} - \epsilon^{-ks}\} = \frac{ak}{\sqrt{t^2-k^2}} I_1(a\sqrt{t^2-k^2})U(t-k) \tag{38}$$

does appear,[6] and with its aid we shall find the transform of Eq. (37) and solve our problem.

Let us first make the substitution

$$(Ls+R)(Cs+G) = \frac{1}{v^2}[s+\rho)^2 - \sigma^2] \tag{39}$$

where

$$v = \frac{1}{\sqrt{LC}} \tag{40}$$

$$\rho = \frac{R}{2L} + \frac{G}{2C} \tag{41}$$

$$\sigma = \frac{R}{2L} - \frac{G}{2C} \tag{42}$$

Then by Eqs. (38) and (39) of this chapter in conjunction with (i), (j), and (1) of Appendix D, we have[7]

$$\mathcal{L}^{-1}\{\epsilon^{-x\sqrt{(Ls+R)(Cs+G)}}\} = \mathcal{L}^{-1}\{\epsilon^{-\frac{x}{v}\sqrt{(s+\rho)^2-\sigma^2}}\}$$

$$= \mathcal{L}^{-1}\{\epsilon^{-\frac{x}{v}(s+\rho)}\} + \mathcal{L}^{-1}\{\epsilon^{-\frac{x}{v}\sqrt{(s+\rho)^2-\sigma^2}} - \epsilon^{-\frac{x}{v}(s+\rho)}\}$$

$$= \epsilon^{-\frac{x\rho}{v}}\delta\left(t-\frac{x}{v}\right) + \frac{\epsilon^{-\rho t}\frac{\sigma x}{v}}{\sqrt{t^2-\frac{x^2}{v^2}}} I_1\left(\sigma\sqrt{t^2-\frac{x^2}{v^2}}\right)U\left(t-\frac{x}{v}\right) \tag{43}$$

Then by Eqs. (43) and (37) of this chapter in conjunction with (d) and (j) of Appendix D, we have

[6] I_1 is the modified Bessel function of the first kind and first order.

[7] $\delta(t)$ is the unit impulse discussed in Chap. 4.

$$e(x,t) =$$

$$\left\{K\epsilon^{-\frac{x\rho}{v}} + K\frac{\sigma x}{v}\int_{\tau=\frac{x}{v}}^{\tau=t-t_1} \frac{\epsilon^{-\rho\tau}}{\sqrt{\tau^2 - \frac{x^2}{v^2}}} I_1\left(\sigma\sqrt{\tau^2 - \frac{x^2}{v^2}}\right) d\tau\right\} U\left(t - t_1 - \frac{x}{v}\right)$$

$$- \left\{K\epsilon^{-\frac{x\rho}{v}} + K\frac{\sigma x}{v}\int_{\tau=\frac{x}{v}}^{\tau=t-t_2} \frac{\epsilon^{-\rho\tau}}{\sqrt{\tau^2 - \frac{x^2}{v^2}}} I_1\left(\sigma\sqrt{\tau^2 - \frac{x^2}{v^2}}\right) d\tau\right\}$$

$$U\left(t - t_2 - \frac{x}{v}\right) \quad (44)$$

Equation (44) is the solution to our problem. It is rather difficult to interpret this solution, although for any specific values of x and t, it is always possible to evaluate the integrals. Since the signal is zero when

$$t < \left(t_1 + \frac{x}{v}\right)$$

we can draw the general conclusion that the head of the signal travels with a velocity v. However, since Eq. (44) is not, in general, similar to Eq. (35), there is change in wave shape—i.e., distortion—as the signal proceeds down the line. Equation (44) can be used to study the distortion of signals in transmission lines. If v, ρ and σ are given, it is possible to plot the wave shape anywhere along the line by using this equation.

10.4. The finite line with terminal impedances—multiple reflections

Let us next consider the more important practical case of a finite line with terminal impedances as shown in Fig. 10-4. We will assume that the line is quiescent before the signal $f(t)$ is applied at $t = 0$. Accordingly, the terms on the right of Eqs. (11) and (12) will vanish and the solutions of Eqs. (11) and (12) will be

$$\bar{I} = A_1\epsilon^{-nx} + B_1\epsilon^{nx} \quad (45)$$

and

$$\bar{E} = A\epsilon^{-nx} + B\epsilon^{nx} \quad (46)$$

where A_1, B_1, A, and B are arbitrary functions[8] of s.

[8] Whenever it appears that it will add to the clarity of the argument, we will write A as $A(s)$ and B as $B(s)$ to show that they are functions of s. We

For quiescent initial conditions, Eq. (9) tells us that

$$\bar{I} = \frac{-1}{Ls + R} \frac{\partial \bar{E}}{\partial x} \tag{47}$$

Therefore, Eq. (45) may be rewritten

$$\bar{I} = \frac{n}{Ls + R} (A\epsilon^{-nx} - B\epsilon^{nx})$$

$$= \sqrt{\frac{Cs + G}{Ls + R}} (A\epsilon^{-nx} - B\epsilon^{nx}) = \frac{1}{Z_0} [A\epsilon^{-nx} - B\epsilon^{nx}] \tag{48}$$

where we have used the notation

$$Z_0(s) = \sqrt{\frac{Ls + R}{Cs + G}} \tag{49}$$

in analogy with the surge impedance in Appendix C.

Equations (46) and (48) together express $\bar{I}$ and $\bar{E}$ in terms of only two arbitrary functions of s—namely A and B.

FIG. 10-4. A finite line with terminal impedances.

Let us now find A and B from the terminal conditions. At the input end, since the voltage across Z_G is $[f(t) - e(0,t)]$, we can use the method of §3.12 and write for the transformed voltage equation,

$$Z_G(s)\bar{I}(0,s) = F(s) - \bar{E}(0,s) \tag{50}$$

where

$$F(s) = \mathcal{L}\{f(t)\} \tag{51}$$

Similarly, at the output end of the line, we have

$$Z_T(s)\bar{I}(d,s) = \bar{E}(d,s) \tag{52}$$

---

have followed a similar practice regarding $\bar{I} = \bar{I}(x,s)$, $\bar{E} = \bar{E}(x,s)$, and other functions.

Substituting the values of Eqs. (48) and (46) into Eq. (50), we obtain

$$\frac{Z_G(s)}{Z_0(s)}[A(s) - B(s)] = F(s) - [A(s) + B(s)] \tag{53}$$

In a like manner, Eq. (52) becomes

$$\frac{Z_T(s)}{Z_0(s)}[A(s)\epsilon^{-n(s)d} - B(s)\epsilon^{n(s)d}] = [A(s)\epsilon^{-n(s)d} + B(s)\epsilon^{n(s)d}] \tag{54}$$

where the notation $n(s)$ is used to emphasize that n is also a function of s. Solving Eqs. (53) and (54) as simultaneous equations for $A(s)$ and $B(s)$, we obtain

$$A = \frac{\dfrac{Z_0}{Z_0 + Z_G}}{1 - \left(\dfrac{Z_0 - Z_G}{Z_0 + Z_G}\right)\left(\dfrac{Z_0 - Z_T}{Z_0 + Z_T}\right)\epsilon^{-2nd}} F \tag{55}$$

$$B = -\frac{\left(\dfrac{Z_0}{Z_0 + Z_G}\right)\left(\dfrac{Z_0 - Z_T}{Z_0 + Z_T}\right)\epsilon^{-2nd}}{1 - \left(\dfrac{Z_0 - Z_G}{Z_0 + Z_G}\right)\left(\dfrac{Z_0 - Z_T}{Z_0 + Z_T}\right)\epsilon^{-2nd}} F \tag{56}$$

Substituting these values into Eqs. (46) and (48), we have finally

$$\bar{E} = \frac{\left(\dfrac{Z_0}{Z_0 + Z_G}\right)\left\{\epsilon^{-nx} - \left(\dfrac{Z_0 - Z_T}{Z_0 + Z_T}\right)\epsilon^{-n(2d-x)}\right\} F}{1 - \left(\dfrac{Z_0 - Z_G}{Z_0 + Z_G}\right)\left(\dfrac{Z_0 - Z_T}{Z_0 + Z_T}\right)\epsilon^{-2nd}} \tag{57}$$

$$\bar{I} = \frac{\dfrac{1}{Z_0 + Z_G}\left\{\epsilon^{-nx} + \left(\dfrac{Z_0 - Z_T}{Z_0 + Z_T}\right)\epsilon^{-n(2d-x)}\right\} F}{1 - \left(\dfrac{Z_0 - Z_G}{Z_0 + Z_G}\right)\left(\dfrac{Z_0 - Z_T}{Z_0 + Z_T}\right)\epsilon^{-2nd}} \tag{58}$$

The similarity of Eq. (58) above to Eq. (80) of Appendix C suggests that the foregoing equations can be expanded in terms of multiple reflections. Accordingly, we let

$$M(s) = \frac{Z_0 - Z_G}{Z_0 + Z_G} \tag{59}$$

and

$$N(s) = \frac{Z_0 - Z_T}{Z_0 + Z_T} \tag{60}$$

and expand the denominators of Eqs. (57) and (58) as

$$\frac{1}{1 - MN\epsilon^{-2nd}} = 1 + MN\epsilon^{-2nd} + M^2N^2\epsilon^{-4nd} + M^3N^3\epsilon^{-6nd} + \cdots \tag{61}$$

since

$$|MN\epsilon^{-2nd}| < 1 \tag{62}$$

Then Eqs. (57) and (58) become

$$\bar{E} = \frac{Z_0F}{Z_G + Z_0}\{\epsilon^{-nx} - N\epsilon^{-n(2d-x)} + MN\epsilon^{-n(2d+x)} - MN^2\epsilon^{-n(4d-x)} + \cdots\} \tag{63}$$

$$\bar{I} = \frac{F}{Z_G + Z_0}\{\epsilon^{-nx} + N\epsilon^{-n(2d-x)} + MN\epsilon^{-n(2d+x)} + MN^2\epsilon^{-n(4d-x)} + \cdots\} \tag{64}$$

Equations (63) and (64) are similar in form to Eqs. (85) and (84) of Appendix C, which suggests that the above expressions may also be interpreted in terms of multiple reflections. We will now show that this is true. We will treat the voltage equation (63), but the treatment of the current is entirely analogous.

The analogue of Eq. (63) in the case of the infinite line is Eq. (23), namely

$$\bar{E} = F(s)\epsilon^{-nx} = F(s)\epsilon^{-x\sqrt{(Ls+R)(Cs+G)}} \tag{65}$$

Now according to Eq. (46) of Chap. 3, we know that the inverse transform of Eq. (63) consists of the sum of the inverse transforms of the individual terms in Eq. (63), each taken with the proper sign. Furthermore, each term in Eq. (63) is of the same form as that of Eq. (65) as far as propagation is concerned. For example, the term

$$\frac{Z_0F}{Z_G + Z_0} MN^2\epsilon^{-n(4d-x)} \tag{66}$$

in Eq. (63) has the factor

$$\frac{-Z_0F}{Z_G + Z_0} MN^2 \tag{67}$$

which is a function of s but not of x, and is the analogue of $F(s)$

in Eq. (65), and the factor

$$\epsilon^{-n(4d-x)} \tag{68}$$

which is the analogue of ϵ^{-nx} in Eq. (65). The expression $(4d - x)$ in Eq. (68) is independent of s and is always positive and takes the place of x, which has the same properties in Eq. (65). Consequently the voltage, which is

$$e(x,t) = \mathfrak{L}^{-1}\{\bar{E}(x,s)\} \tag{69}$$

consists of the superposition of a direct signal

$$e_1(x,t) = \mathfrak{L}^{-1}\left\{\frac{Z_0F}{Z_G + Z_0}\right\} \tag{70}$$

after it has been propagated a distance x along the line, plus a reflected signal from Z_T

$$e_2(x,t) = \mathfrak{L}^{-1}\left\{\frac{-Z_0NF}{Z_G + Z_0}\right\} \tag{71}$$

after it has been propagated a distance $(2d - x)$ along the line, plus a signal reflected from Z_T and then Z_G

$$e_3(x,t) = \mathfrak{L}^{-1}\left\{\frac{Z_0MNF}{Z_G + Z_0}\right\} \tag{72}$$

after it has been propagated a distance $(2d + x)$ along the line, plus the various other multiply reflected signals indicated by Eq. (63). The functions $N(s)$ and $M(s)$, since they affect the wave shape, may properly be called wave-shape operators of Z_T and Z_G, respectively. These are analogous to the reflection coefficients[9] $N(j\omega)$ and $M(j\omega)$ of Appendix C.

Although the foregoing discussion shows some of the general properties of the transmission of signals in a finite line with terminal impedances, and shows how problems in this field can be solved, it is clear that the solution of any but the simplest problems of this

---

[9] Actually the effect of $N(s)$ and $M(s)$ is the superposition of the effects of $N(j\omega)$ and $M(j\omega)$ acting upon the Fourier integral frequency components of the signal.

type will be very lengthy and tedious. Accordingly, we shall choose a very simple case as an example—namely, a lossless line with resistive terminations. Such a line is shown in Fig. 10-5.

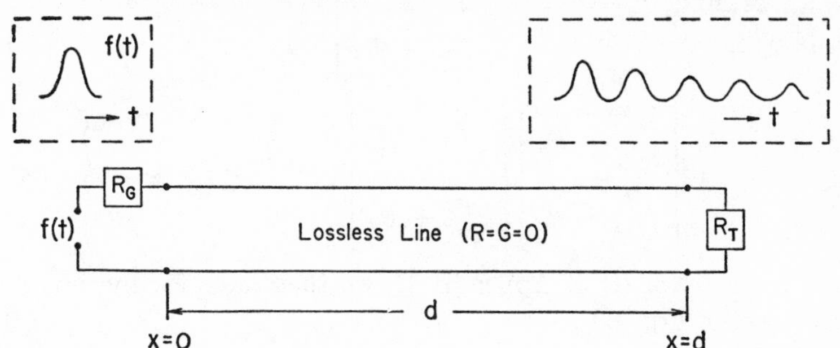

FIG. 10-5. A distortionless line with distortionless terminations, but exhibiting multiple reflections.

For this case

$$R = G = 0 \tag{73}$$

$$Z_G = R_G \tag{74}$$

and

$$Z_T = R_T \tag{75}$$

Thus,

$$Z_0 = \sqrt{\frac{Ls + R}{Cs + G}} = \sqrt{\frac{L}{C}} \tag{76}$$

Therefore, according to Eqs. (59) and (60),

$$M = \frac{\sqrt{\frac{L}{C}} - R_G}{\sqrt{\frac{L}{C}} + R_G} \tag{77}$$

$$N = \frac{\sqrt{\frac{L}{C}} - R_T}{\sqrt{\frac{L}{C}} + R_T} \tag{78}$$

so that both M and N are constants, being independent of s. Thus M and N cause no change in wave shape, but only a reduction in amplitude.

Furthermore,

$$n = \sqrt{(Ls + R)(Cs + G)} = s\sqrt{LC} \tag{79}$$

Substituting these values into (63), we have

$$\bar{E} = \frac{F\sqrt{\frac{L}{C}}}{R_G + \sqrt{\frac{L}{C}}}\left\{\epsilon^{-s\sqrt{LC}x} - \left[\frac{\sqrt{\frac{L}{C}} - R_T}{\sqrt{\frac{L}{C}} + R_T}\right]\epsilon^{-s\sqrt{LC}(2d-x)} + \left[\frac{\sqrt{\frac{L}{C}} - R_G}{\sqrt{\frac{L}{C}} + R_G}\right]\left[\frac{\sqrt{\frac{L}{C}} - R_T}{\sqrt{\frac{L}{C}} + R_T}\right]\epsilon^{-s\sqrt{LC}(2d+x)} + \cdots\right\} \tag{80}$$

By form No. (j) of Appendix D, we then have for the inverse transform of Eq. (80),

$$e(x,t) = \frac{\sqrt{\frac{L}{C}}}{R_G + \sqrt{\frac{L}{C}}}\left\{f(t - x\sqrt{LC}) - \left[\frac{\sqrt{\frac{L}{C}} - R_T}{\sqrt{\frac{L}{C}} + R_T}\right] f[t - (2d - x)\sqrt{LC}] + \left[\frac{\sqrt{\frac{L}{C}} - R_G}{\sqrt{\frac{L}{C}} + R_G}\right]\left[\frac{\sqrt{\frac{L}{C}} - R_T}{\sqrt{\frac{L}{C}} + R_T}\right] f[t - (2d + x)\sqrt{LC}] + \cdots\right\} \tag{81}$$

This is the signal at the location x and time t. We see that it consists of a direct signal plus a series of reflection echoes, of the same wave form as the original signal but of decreased intensity, all moving along the line with the velocity $1/\sqrt{LC}$.

If either R_T or R_G is less than the surge impedance $\sqrt{L/C}$ some of these echoes will be negative in sign. If the transmitted signal is a television signal, such negative echoes will appear as echoes which are photographic negatives of the original signal.

10.5. Nonquiescent initial conditions—pulse-forming line

Let us next consider a case in which the initial conditions are not quiescent. As an example we shall study the behavior and find the output of one of the so-called pulse-forming lines. Such a line is shown in Fig. 10-6. The line is of length d, and is open-circuited at one end and terminated in its surge impedance at the other end after time $t = 0$. Prior to this time, the line is charged to a potential E_0. At time $t = 0$, the two sides of the line are connected together through the resistor $R = Z_0$. The problem is to find the current through R as a function of time.

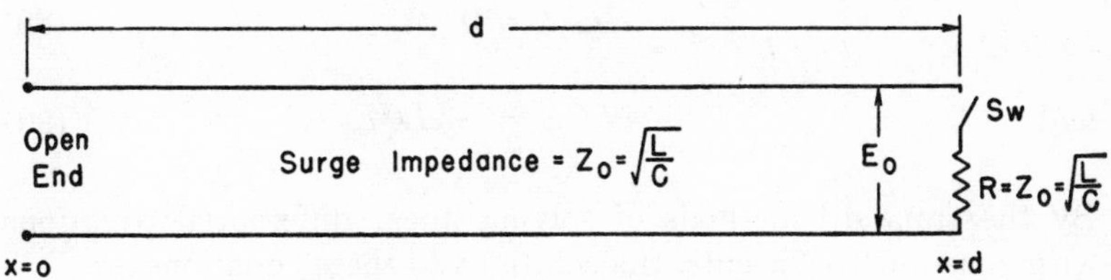

FIG. 10-6. A pulse-forming line.

In order to solve this problem, we start with Eqs. (11) and (12). In the case of practical interest, the line may be considered as having no dissipation. Therefore

$$R = G = 0 \tag{82}$$

so that Eqs. (11) and (12) reduce to

$$\frac{\partial^2 \bar{I}}{\partial x^2} - s^2LC\bar{I} = C\frac{\partial e(x,0)}{\partial x} - LCsi(x,0) \tag{83}$$

and

$$\frac{\partial^2 \bar{E}}{\partial x^2} - s^2LC\bar{E} = L\frac{\partial i(x,0)}{\partial x} - LCse(x,0) \tag{84}$$

Prior to time $t = 0$,

$$e(x,0) = E_0 \tag{85}$$

and

$$i(x,0) = 0 \tag{86}$$

Since we found in §10.3 that the velocity of propagation of the head of a signal is $1/\sqrt{LC}$, it follows that these equations also hold at the instant after $t = 0$ except at $x = d$. The point $x = d$ is a singular point. On the line side of $x = d$, in other words everywhere that Eqs. (83) and (84) apply, the foregoing initial conditions are valid. It also follows from Eqs. (85) and (86) that

$$\frac{\partial e(x,0)}{\partial x} = 0 \tag{87}$$

and

$$\frac{\partial i(x,0)}{\partial x} = 0 \tag{88}$$

Substituting these values into Eqs. (83) and (84), the latter become

$$\frac{\partial^2 \bar{I}}{\partial x^2} - s^2 LC\bar{I} = 0 \tag{89}$$

and

$$\frac{\partial^2 \bar{E}}{\partial x^2} - s^2 LC\bar{E} = -sLCE_0 \tag{90}$$

By the standard methods of solving linear differential equations with constant coefficients, the solutions to these equations are

$$\bar{I} = A_1 \epsilon^{-n_0 x} + B_1 \epsilon^{+n_0 x} \tag{91}$$

and

$$\bar{E} = A_2 \epsilon^{-n_0 x} + B_2 \epsilon^{+n_0 x} + \frac{E_0}{s} \tag{92}$$

where

$$n_0 = s\sqrt{LC} \tag{93}$$

A_1 and B_1 are arbitrary constants,[10] as are also A_2 and B_2; but one set can be obtained from the other. Thus from Eqs. (9) and (92) and the various conditions listed above, we have

$$\bar{I} = \frac{-1}{Ls}\frac{\partial \bar{E}}{\partial x} = -\frac{1}{Ls}\{-n_0 A_2 \epsilon^{-n_0 x} + n_0 B_2 \epsilon^{+n_0 x}\} \tag{94}$$

Comparing Eqs. (91) and (94), we have

$$A_1 = \frac{n_0}{Ls} A_2 = \sqrt{\frac{C}{L}}\, A_2 \tag{95}$$

$$B_1 = -\frac{n_0}{Ls} B_2 = -\sqrt{\frac{C}{L}}\, B_2 \tag{96}$$

In order to find the actual values of the arbitrary constants, we must use the given conditions of the problem. Thus we have given that, at $x = 0$, the line is open. Therefore, with the use of Eq. (91),

---

[10] When we say that the A's and B's are constant in this case, we mean that they are independent of x. They are, however, functions of s.

we have

$$\bar{I}(0,s) = 0 = A_1 + B_1 \tag{97}$$

or

$$A_1 = -B_1 \tag{98}$$

At the other end of the line, at $x = d$, for positive values of t

$$i(d,t) = \frac{e(d,t)}{R} = \sqrt{\frac{C}{L}}\, e(d,t) \tag{99}$$

so that

$$\bar{I}(d,s) = \sqrt{\frac{C}{L}}\, \bar{E}(d,s) \tag{100}$$

Now, by Eqs. (91) and (98)

$$\bar{I}(d,s) = A_1\{\epsilon^{-n_0d} - \epsilon^{+n_0d}\} \tag{101}$$

while by Eqs. (92), (95), (96), and (98),

$$\bar{E}(d,s) = \sqrt{\frac{L}{C}}\, A_1[\epsilon^{-n_0d} + \epsilon^{+n_0d}] + \frac{E_0}{s} \tag{102}$$

Substituting Eqs. (101) and (102) into Eq. (100), we obtain

$$A_1[\epsilon^{-n_0d} - \epsilon^{+n_0d}] = A_1[\epsilon^{-n_0d} + \epsilon^{+n_0d}] + \sqrt{\frac{C}{L}}\frac{E_0}{s} \tag{103}$$

which reduces to

$$A_1 = -\frac{1}{2}\sqrt{\frac{C}{L}}\frac{E_0}{s}\,\epsilon^{-n_0d} \tag{104}$$

Consequently, from Eq. (98),

$$B_1 = +\frac{1}{2}\sqrt{\frac{C}{L}}\frac{E_0}{s}\,\epsilon^{-n_0d} \tag{105}$$

Substituting these values of A_1 and B_1 and the value of n_0 from Eq. (93) into Eq. (91), we obtain

$$\begin{aligned}\bar{I}(x,s) &= -\frac{1}{2}\sqrt{\frac{C}{L}}\frac{E_0}{s}\,\epsilon^{-s\sqrt{LC}d}\{\epsilon^{-s\sqrt{LC}x} - \epsilon^{+s\sqrt{LC}x}\} \\ &= \frac{1}{2}\sqrt{\frac{C}{L}}\,E_0\left\{\frac{\epsilon^{-s\sqrt{LC}(d-x)}}{s} - \frac{\epsilon^{-s\sqrt{LC}(d+x)}}{s}\right\}\end{aligned} \tag{106}$$

The inverse transform of Eq. (106) is[11]

$$i(x,t) = \frac{1}{2}\sqrt{\frac{C}{L}}\,E_0\{U[t - \sqrt{LC}\,(d - x)] - U[t - \sqrt{LC}\,(d + x)]\} \tag{107}$$

Equation (107) is the complete solution for the current anywhere along the line. Before interpreting this solution, let us also find the voltage. From Eqs. (92), (93), (95), (96), (104), and (105), we have

$$\begin{aligned} \bar{E}(x,s) &= -\frac{1}{2}\frac{E_0}{s}\,\epsilon^{-n_0d}\epsilon^{-n_0x} - \frac{1}{2}\frac{E_0}{s}\,\epsilon^{-n_0d}\epsilon^{+n_0x} + \frac{E_0}{s} \\ &= E_0\left\{\frac{1}{s} - \frac{1}{2}\frac{\epsilon^{-s\sqrt{LC}(d-x)}}{s} - \frac{1}{2}\frac{\epsilon^{-s\sqrt{LC}(d+x)}}{s}\right\} \end{aligned} \tag{108}$$

The inverse transform of Eq. (108) is

$$\begin{aligned} e(x,t) = E_0\{U(t) - \tfrac{1}{2}U[t - \sqrt{LC}\,(d - x)] \\ - \tfrac{1}{2}U[t - \sqrt{LC}\,(d + x)]\} \end{aligned} \tag{109}$$

Equation (109) is the complete solution for the voltage.

Let us now investigate the meaning of Eqs. (107) and (109). According to Eq. (107), as depicted in Fig. 10-7, the current consists of two traveling rectangular pulses of opposite sign but constant magnitude

$$\left(\frac{1}{2}\sqrt{\frac{C}{L}}\,E_0\right)$$

traveling in opposite directions along the line with a velocity $1/\sqrt{LC}$. The pulse traveling in the negative direction is reflected at the open end of the line at $x = 0$ with a change of sign in addition to the change of direction of travel. The pulse traveling in the positive direction is completely absorbed in the terminating resistor $R = Z_0$ at $x = d$.

According to Eq. (109) as depicted in Fig. 10-8, the voltage consists of two traveling rectangular pulses of the same sign and constant magnitude $(E_0/2)$, traveling in opposite directions along

---

[11] Formulas (j) and (2) of Appendix D give

$$\mathfrak{L}^{-1}\left[\frac{\epsilon^{-ks}}{s}\right] = U(t - k)$$

the line with a velocity $1/\sqrt{LC}$. The pulse traveling in the negative direction is reflected at the open end of the line at $x = 0$, without changing its sign, thus changing only its direction of travel. The pulse traveling in the positive direction is completely absorbed in the terminating resistor $R = Z_0$ at $x = d$.

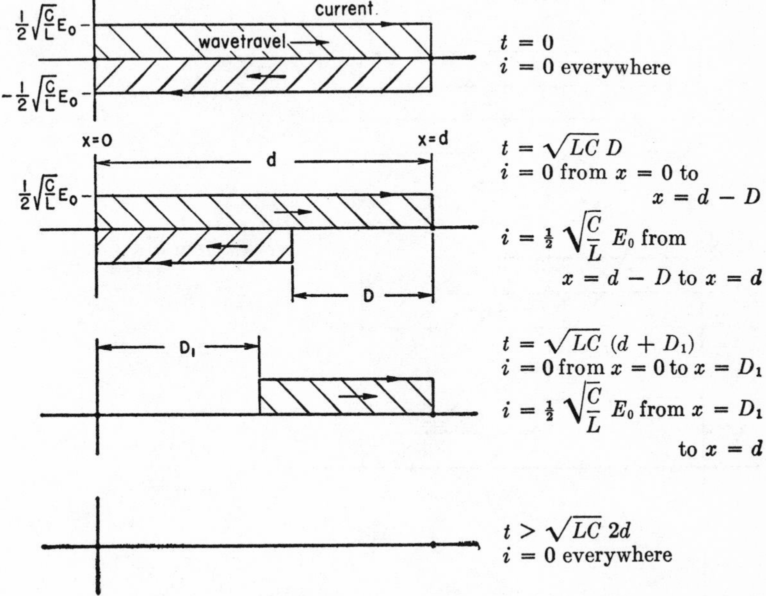

FIG. 10-7. Life history of the current wave in a pulse-forming line.

According to the foregoing description, we see that the initial charge on the line gives rise to voltage waves in both directions. Each voltage gives rise to a current of magnitude

$$i = \frac{e}{Z_0} = \sqrt{\frac{C}{L}}\, e \qquad (110)$$

in the direction of wave travel. However, since current toward $x = 0$ is negative, the negative traveling current wave is also negative in sign.

Let us next find the output of this line, namely the current through R. This is the current at $x = d$. To find this current we need only to substitute d for x in Eq. (107). Thus

$$i(d,t) = \frac{1}{2}\sqrt{\frac{C}{L}}\,E_0\{U(t) - U[t - \sqrt{LC}\,2d]\}$$
$$= \frac{E_0}{2R}\,\{U(t) - U[t - \sqrt{LC}\,2d]\} \quad (111)$$

The current through R is thus a rectangular pulse of height $E_0/2R$ and duration $2d\,\sqrt{LC}$.

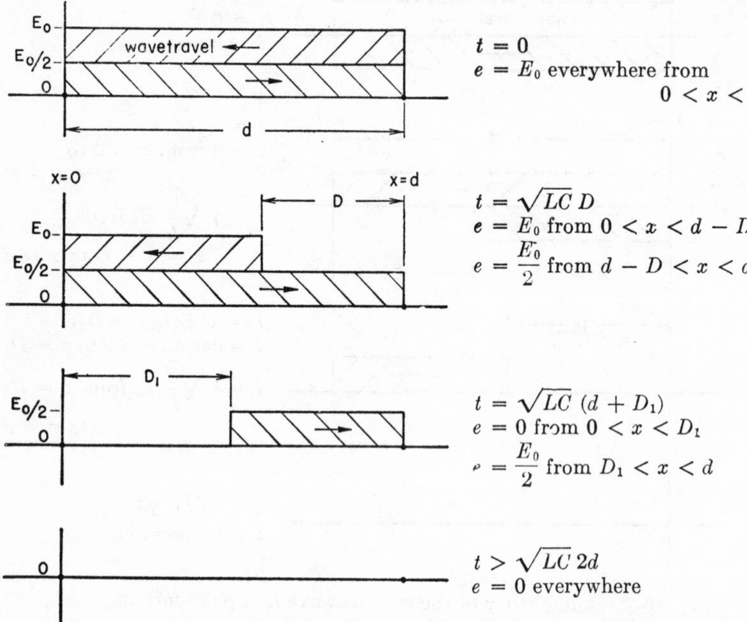

FIG. 10-8. Life history of the voltage wave in a pulse-forming line.

It is of interest to see whether the energy dissipated by the pulse in R is equal to the initial energy stored in the line. For the energy initially stored in the line, we have

$$\tfrac{1}{2}(Cd)E_0^2 \quad (112)$$

On the other hand, if $T = 2d\,\sqrt{LC}$ is the duration of the pulse, we have, for the energy dissipated in R,

$$i^2RT = \left(\frac{1}{2}\sqrt{\frac{C}{L}}\,E_0\right)^2\sqrt{\frac{L}{C}}\cdot 2d\,\sqrt{LC}$$
$$= \tfrac{1}{2}CdE_0^2 \quad (113)$$

in agreement with Eq. (112). Our solution thus is in accord with the conservation of energy.

Charged lines are very useful for the generation of short pulses of known duration. The duration is, of course, determined by the length of the line.

Exercises

1. Find the voltage at the open end of the line as a function of time.

2. Find the current at the center of the line ($x = d/2$) as a function of time.

10.6. Signaling through a leakage-free, noninductive cable

If in a transmission line

$$L = G = 0 \tag{114}$$

then we have the historically important case of a leakage-free, noninductive cable. This was solved by Lord Kelvin in order to determine the practicability of a transoceanic cable. We will arrive at the same answer as Kelvin, but we will use the methods of transformation calculus, whereas he used the orthodox methods of solving partial differential equations.

Let us consider the case of an infinitely long cable and let the applied voltage at $x = 0$ be a unit step function. Then, substituting Eq. (114) into Eq. (23), we have

$$\bar{E}(x,s) = \frac{\epsilon^{-x\sqrt{RCs}}}{s} \tag{115}$$

since

$$F(s) = \frac{1}{s} \tag{116}$$

for the unit step. By Eq. (63) of Chap. 8, the inverse transform of Eq. (115) is

$$e(x,t) = \operatorname{erfc}\left\{\frac{x\sqrt{RC}}{2\sqrt{t}}\right\} \tag{117}$$

The complementary error function (erfc) is defined in §8.9 and is plotted in Fig. 8-3. It is customary to use the abbreviation

$$\tau = \frac{4t}{x^2RC} \tag{118}$$

Accordingly, Eq. (117) may be written

$$e(x,t) = \operatorname{erfc}\left\{\frac{1}{\sqrt{\tau}}\right\} = 1 - \frac{2}{\sqrt{\pi}}\int_0^{1/\sqrt{\tau}} \epsilon^{-y^2}\,dy \tag{119}$$

We will next find the current. According to Eqs. (114), (116), and (30) we may write

$$\bar{I}(x,s) = \frac{1}{s}\sqrt{\frac{Cs}{R}}\,\epsilon^{-x\sqrt{RCs}} = \sqrt{\frac{C}{sR}}\,\epsilon^{-x\sqrt{RCs}} \tag{120}$$

Equation (120) may be solved as No. 35 in the table of transforms, and its inverse is

$$i(x,t) = \sqrt{\frac{C}{\pi Rt}}\,\epsilon^{\frac{-x^2RC}{4t}} = \sqrt{\frac{C}{\pi Rt}}\,\epsilon^{\frac{-1}{\tau}} \tag{121}$$

Let us now see how a square wave of voltage, as shown in Fig. 10-9, is transmitted along the cable. By the principle of super-

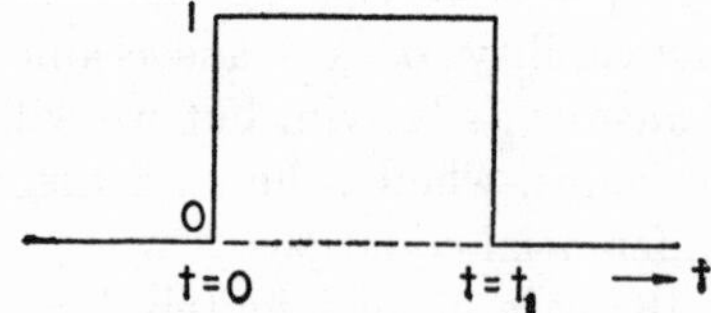

Fig. 10-9. A square wave of unit height.

position, in conjunction with Eq. (119), we may write for the propagation of the signal in Fig. 10-9,

$$e(x,t) = \operatorname{erfc}\left\{\frac{1}{\sqrt{\tau}}\right\} - \operatorname{erfc}\left\{\frac{1}{\sqrt{\tau-\tau_1}}\right\} = \frac{2}{\sqrt{\pi}}\int_{1/\sqrt{\tau}}^{1/\sqrt{\tau-\tau_1}} \epsilon^{-y^2}\,dy \qquad (\text{when } \tau > \tau_1)$$

$$= \operatorname{erfc}\left\{\frac{1}{\sqrt{\tau}}\right\} \text{---} \qquad (\text{when } 0 \le \tau \le \tau_1) \tag{122}$$

where

$$\tau_1 = \frac{4t_1}{x^2RC} \tag{123}$$

Equation (122) is plotted as a function of τ in Fig. 10-10 for seven values of τ_1. Figure 10-10, when interpreted in conjunction with Eqs. (123) and (118), gives a great deal of information about the propagation of signals. The wave shape of the signal at the location x for an input square wave at $x = 0$ is obtained by finding the value of τ_1 in Eq. (123) and seeing what wave shape corresponds to this value of τ_1 in Fig. 10-10. However, using this interpretation of wave shape, when the value of x is increased the time scale is stretched in accordance with Eq. (118). Thus if x is doubled, the time scale is stretched by a factor of four. These facts are illustrated

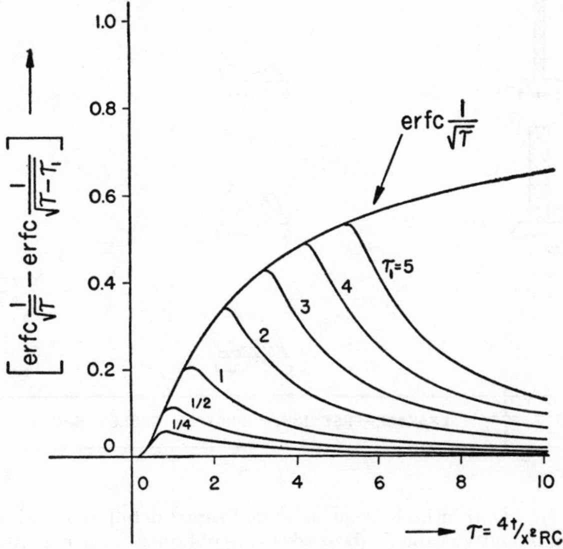

FIG. 10-10. Graphical representation of Eq. (122) for various values of τ_1.

in Fig. 10-11(A), showing the propagation of an original square wave of length

$$t_1 = \tfrac{1}{2}x_0^2RC \tag{124}$$

At the location of $x = x_0$, the signal has the shape of the $\tau_1 = 2$ curve of Fig. 10-10; while at the location of $x = 2x_0$, the signal has the shape of the $\tau_1 = \frac{1}{2}$ curve, but with the horizontal axis stretched by a factor of four. Fig. 10-11 shows clearly the loss of high-frequency components and the loss of resolving power as the distance from the source is increased.

It may be noted that the curves of $\tau_1 = 1$, $\tau_1 = \frac{1}{2}$, and $\tau_1 = \frac{1}{4}$ in Fig. 10-10 are very similar in shape except for vertical contraction. As τ_1 is still further decreased, the similarity becomes more complete, with the dimension of the ordinates being about proportional[12] to τ_1. It follows that the limit in signaling "speed"[13] is reached when $\tau_1 = 1$. Further reduction in t_1 does not change

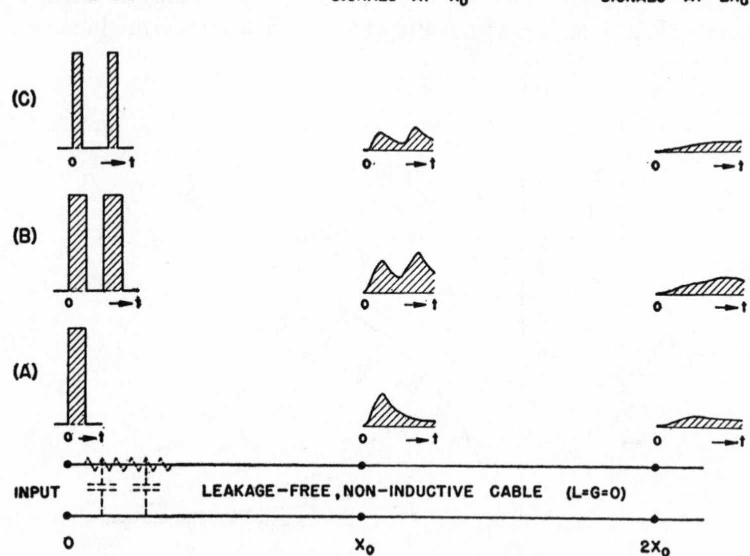

FIG. 10-11. Loss of high frequencies and signal detail along a leakage-free non-inductive cable. (Scale drawing obtained from Fig. 10-10.)

the resolution or duration of the signal, for given values of x, R, and C, but only decreases the voltage level. [See Fig. 10-11(C).] This means that even if dots are made shorter than $x^2RC/4$, the spacing between their centers cannot be decreased, if they are to be resolved.

---

[12] This must be true because

$$\lim_{\tau_1 \to 0} \left\{ \operatorname{erfc} \frac{1}{\sqrt{\tau}} - \operatorname{erfc} \frac{1}{\sqrt{\tau - \tau_1}} \right\} = \tau_1 \frac{d}{d\tau} \left\{ \operatorname{erfc} \frac{1}{\sqrt{\tau}} \right\}$$

A similar result will be true for any response of the form

$$\{f(\tau) - f(\tau - \tau_1)\}$$

[13] Number of dots per second.

The ultimate speed of signaling is therefore inversely proportional[14] to x^2RC. Comparison with Fig. 8 of Chap. IV of the author's *Frequency Analysis, Modulation and Noise* indicates that $2/x^2RC$ is more or less equivalent to the effective bandwidth of the cable for a given length.

There is no distinct velocity of propagation in the case of the noninductive cable. According to Fig. 10-10, there is some very small amount of signal even at great distances immediately after $t = 0$. This would indicate an infinite velocity of propagation for the head of the signal. This is not actually true physically, but is a consequence of our having neglected the inductance of the cable. Signals, such as those in a noninductive cable, which have no true velocity of propagation, are said to be "diffused" rather than "propagated" along the line. If the inductance L of the line is increased,[15] so that the line exhibits more clearly the properties of signal propagation, then there is no longer so much loss of resolution with distance, and consequently the "speed" of signaling can be increased.

10.7. An expansion-theorem solution involving an infinite number of poles—the finite cable short-circuited at its far end

We next wish to consider a type of solution which is of considerable historical interest, and which is also of practical interest today,

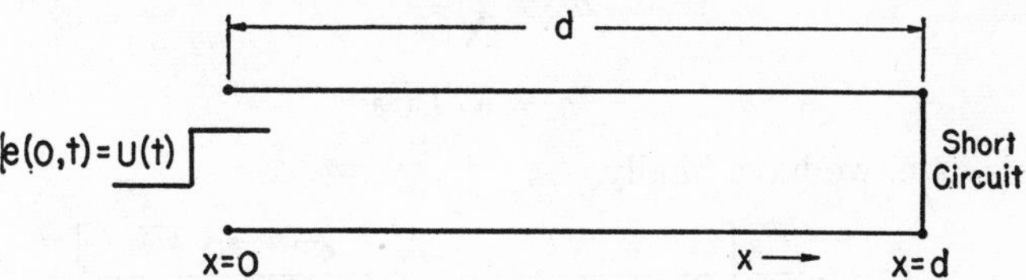

FIG. 10-12. A unit-step function of voltage applied to a cable of finite length, short-circuited at its far end.

but usually in fields other than radio engineering. This is an expansion-theorem solution involving an infinite number of poles. We will find such a solution by determining the indicial admittance of a leakage-free, inductanceless cable of finite length, short-circuited at its far end.

---

[14] This is the *KR* law of Kelvin concerning submarine-cable transmission.

[15] Modern submarine cables are continuously loaded with permalloy to produce this effect.

Let (see Fig. 10-12)

$$d = \text{length of cable}$$

Then, according to Eqs. (46) and (48), we have

$$\bar{E} = A\epsilon^{-nx} + B\epsilon^{nx} \tag{125}$$

$$\bar{I} = \frac{1}{Z_0}[A\epsilon^{-nx} - B\epsilon^{nx}] \tag{126}$$

Since we are to determine the indicial admittance, we have at $x = 0$,

$$\bar{E}(0,s) = \frac{1}{s} = A + B \tag{127}$$

Then, since the line is short-circuited at $x = d$, we have

$$\bar{E}(d,s) = 0 = A\epsilon^{-nd} + B\epsilon^{nd} \tag{128}$$

Solving Eqs. (127) and (128) as simultaneous equations, we obtain

$$A = \frac{1}{s(1 - \epsilon^{-2nd})} \tag{129}$$

and

$$B = \frac{-\epsilon^{-2nd}}{s(1 - \epsilon^{-2nd})} \tag{130}$$

Substituting Eqs. (129) and (130) into Eq. (126), and making use of the fact that

$$Z_0 = \sqrt{\frac{R}{Cs}} \tag{131}$$

and

$$n = \sqrt{RCs} \tag{132}$$

in this case, we have finally

$$\begin{aligned}\bar{I} &= \sqrt{\frac{Cs}{R}}\left[\frac{\epsilon^{-x\sqrt{RCs}}}{s(1 - \epsilon^{-2d\sqrt{RCs}})} + \frac{\epsilon^{-(2d-x)\sqrt{RCs}}}{s(1 - \epsilon^{-2d\sqrt{RCs}})}\right] \\ &= \sqrt{\frac{C}{Rs}}\frac{\epsilon^{(d-x)\sqrt{RCs}} + \epsilon^{-(d-x)\sqrt{RCs}}}{\epsilon^{d\sqrt{RCs}} - \epsilon^{-d\sqrt{RCs}}} \\ &= \sqrt{\frac{C}{Rs}}\frac{\cosh[(d-x)\sqrt{RCs}]}{\sinh[d\sqrt{RCs}]}\end{aligned} \tag{133}$$

Now,

$$\begin{aligned}\sinh[d\sqrt{RCs}] &= -j\sin[jd\sqrt{RCs}] \\ &= -j\sin[d\sqrt{-RCs}]\end{aligned} \tag{134}$$

Therefore,

$$\sinh [d\sqrt{RCs}] = 0 \tag{135}$$

if

$$\sqrt{-RCs} = \pm \frac{m\pi}{d} \tag{136}$$

for all positive integral values of m, including zero. Consequently, the expression on the right of Eq. (133) has singular points at

$$s = \frac{-m^2\pi^2}{d^2RC} \tag{137}$$

In addition, because of the factor $\sqrt{C/Rs}$, there is also a singular point at

$$s = 0 \tag{138}$$

but this coincides with the singular point indicated by Eq. (137) when $m = 0$, and is therefore already included in Eq. (137).

All the singular points of

$$\sqrt{\frac{C}{Rs}}\,\frac{\cosh (d - x)\sqrt{RCs}}{\sinh d\sqrt{RCs}} \tag{139}$$

are poles, since the reciprocal of Eq. (139)—namely,

$$\sqrt{\frac{Rs}{C}}\,\frac{\sinh [d\sqrt{RCs}]}{\cosh [(d - x)\sqrt{RCs}]} \tag{140}$$

—has a regular point wherever Eq. (139) vanishes. We can show that there are no *branch points* by expanding the numerator and denominator in series. Thus

$$\begin{aligned}
&\sqrt{\frac{C}{Rs}}\,\frac{\cosh [(d - x)\sqrt{RCs}]}{\sinh [d\sqrt{RCs}]} \\
&\qquad = \sqrt{\frac{C}{Rs}}\left\{\frac{1 + \frac{1}{2}[(d - x)\sqrt{RCs}]^2 + \cdots}{d\sqrt{RCs} + \frac{1}{6}[d\sqrt{RCs}]^3 + \cdots}\right\} \\
&\qquad = \frac{1 + \frac{1}{2}(d - x)^2RCs + \frac{1}{24}(d - x)^4(RCs)^2 + \cdots}{dRs + \frac{1}{6}d^3R^2Cs^2 + \cdots}
\end{aligned} \tag{141}$$

The right side of Eq. (141) does not involve s in any fractional exponents and is therefore *single-valued.* Consequently, there are no *branch points.*

According to the inversion theorem[16] (see §7.3) the inverse transform of Eq. (133) is the sum of the residues of

$$\sqrt{\frac{C}{Rs}}\frac{\cosh\,[(d-x)\sqrt{RCs}]\epsilon^{st}}{\sinh\,[d\sqrt{RCs}]} \tag{142}$$

with respect to the above-indicated poles. Now the residue of Eq. (142) with respect to any of the poles indicated by Eq. (137), excepting $s = 0$, is [according to Eq. (162) of Chap. 5]

$$\text{residue} = -\frac{\dfrac{jdC}{m\pi}\cosh\left[j(d-x)\dfrac{m\pi}{d}\right]\epsilon^{\frac{-m^2\pi^2}{d^2RC}t}}{\dfrac{d^2RC}{2jm\pi}\cosh jm\pi} \tag{143}$$

since

$$\frac{d}{ds}\{\sinh\,[d\sqrt{RCs}]\} = \cosh\,[d\sqrt{RCs}]\,\frac{d}{ds}\,[d\sqrt{RCs}]$$

$$= \frac{d\sqrt{RC}}{2\sqrt{s}}\cosh\,[d\sqrt{RCs}] \tag{144}$$

Reducing Eq. (143) still further, we have

$$\text{residue} = \frac{2}{dR}\left[\cos\frac{m\pi x}{d}\right]\epsilon^{\frac{-m^2\pi^2}{d^2RC}t} \tag{145}$$

When $m = 0$ in Eq. (137), so that $s = 0$, the residue of Eq. (142) is[17]

$$\text{residue}_0 = \frac{\sqrt{C/R}}{\dfrac{d}{ds}\{\sqrt{s}\sinh\,[d\sqrt{RCs}]\}_{s=0}} = \frac{1}{dR} \tag{146}$$

---

[16] The proof of the inversion theorem in Chap. 7 would require some changes in order to cover the present case. However, these changes are easily made and we will not spend time with them here.

[17] The simplest way of finding the derivative of the denominator is to express the sinh as a power series. Thus

$$\sqrt{s}\sinh\,[d\sqrt{RCs}] = \sqrt{s}\left[d\sqrt{RCs} + \frac{d^3}{3}(\sqrt{RCs})^3 + \cdots\right]$$

$$= sd\sqrt{RC} + \frac{s^2d^3}{6}(\sqrt{RC})^3 + \cdots$$

Then $\dfrac{d}{ds}\{\sqrt{s}\sinh\,[d\sqrt{RCs}]\} = d\sqrt{RC}$ for $s = 0$

Therefore, since $i(x,t)$ is the sum of the residues at all the singular points, we have, from Eqs. (145) and (146),

$$i(x,t) = \frac{1}{dR} + \frac{2}{dR} \sum_{m=1}^{\infty} \left[\cos \frac{m\pi x}{d} \right] \epsilon^{\frac{-m^2\pi^2}{d^2RC}t} \tag{147}$$

Equation (147) is the general formula for the indicial admittance anywhere along the line. In striking contrast to the solutions obtained in §10.4, the above equation expresses the answer in terms of the so-called characteristic vibrations of the system, rather than in terms of multiple reflections. Of the two, the multiple-reflection expressions have more physical significance, especially to a radio engineer. However, in noninductive cables, where there is no true propagation, the multiple-reflection interpretation loses distinctness; and it is in just these cases that the characteristic vibration expressions, such as Eq. (147), become practical. Consequently, both types of solutions are important.

It may be noted that Eq. (147) is a Fourier series in terms of the x variable. This type of solution is closely related to the classical heat-conduction and mechanical-resonance problems to which Fourier series were first applied.

10.8. General

The solution of partial differential equations is an important subject in many branches of mathematical physics, and the application of transformation calculus in finding the solution is by no means limited to the field of transmission lines.[18] Applications in heat conduction, hydrodynamics, electromagnetic field problems, and problems in mechanical vibrations are very numerous.

It is, of course, also possible to transform other variables than the t variable into a complex plane, when such a procedure will help in solving the problems at hand.

---

[18] A variety of applications are discussed in Carslaw and Jaeger's *Operational Methods in Mathematical Physics.*

CHAPTER 11

Solutions in Series[1]

11.1. Introduction

When problems in mathematical analysis are complicated, a favorite method for arriving at a solution by relatively simple means is to use a power series. It is therefore not surprising that such series were applied to transformation calculus early in the development of the subject.

It is historically interesting that, while working in this field, Heaviside discovered a phenomenon of mathematics[2] that he proceeded to use without supplying the proof of its correctness that is considered "proper" in polite mathematical society. He thereby incurred the displeasure of mathematicians to such an extent that his scientific standing became a *cause célèbre.* In later years, however, other mathematicians have investigated his procedures and have been able to show that they are generally legitimate, and they have also found out under what circumstances they may be expected to give erroneous results. This more solid foundation for Heaviside's procedure has greatly increased the confidence which can be put into its results, and has thereby enhanced its value. Nevertheless, Heaviside must still be given the credit for discovering a phenomenon which rigor and analysis alone would not have found.[3]

---

[1] The writer is particularly indebted to Carson, *Electrical Circuit Theory and Operational Calculus;* Bush, *Operational Circuit Analysis;* and McLachlan, *Complex Variable and Operational Calculus,* as a background for the material presented in this chapter.

[2] Heaviside's Asymptotic Solution.

[3] Needless to say, the story of Heaviside should not encourage the student to use carelessly procedures which he cannot justify. Heaviside's discovery was the result of intimate association with the problems involved, which guided him to the right solution. Nevertheless, his discoveries could not be used with confidence by other mathematicians until the necessary proofs were at hand. The reason that the discovery of a mathematical phenomenon is more impor-

Generally speaking, the fundamental problem in transformation calculus is to find the form of a function $f(t)$. When this is found as a series of positive powers of t in the form

$$f(t) = a_0 + a_1t + a_2t^2 + \cdots \tag{1}$$

the result has the disadvantage that it converges very slowly for large values of t and is then impractical for computation. It is therefore desirable that, in addition to the series in Eq. (1), other series which can be computed more rapidly for large values of t should also be available. One type of such series we shall find to be of the form

$$b_0 + \frac{b_1}{t} + \frac{b_2}{t^2} + \frac{b_3}{t^3} + \cdots \tag{2}$$

Series of the type (1), when they exist at all, can usually be arrived at by fairly standard and rigorous methods. It will be the series of type (2) which will require more extended study on our part. Such study will repay us, however, because it will acquaint us with many new and interesting facts, besides bringing us to the solutions to some of our problems.

11.2. Power-series solutions for small values of *t*

Let us first look into the matter of power-series solutions—i.e., solutions in a series of terms in positive integral powers of t, such as given by Eq.(1). Now, since

$$\mathcal{L}[a_nt^n] = \frac{a_nn!}{s^{n+1}} \tag{3}$$

it follows from Eq. (21) of Chap. 3 that

$$\mathcal{L}[a_0 + a_1t + a_2t^2 + \cdots] = \frac{a_0}{s} + \frac{a_1}{s^2} + \frac{2!a_2}{s^3} + \frac{3!a_3}{s^4} + \cdots \tag{4}$$

provided that the two series on either side of Eq. (4) are convergent. This solution suggests that, to find a power-series solution for $f(t)$ when $F(s)$ is given, the latter should be expanded in an inverse power series such as that shown on the right side of Eq. (4), from which the corresponding series in t can be found.

---

tant than its proof is that more men are capable of supplying the proof than are able to make the discovery.

As an example, consider the case of

$$I(s) = \frac{E}{s(sL + R)} \tag{5}$$

Here

$$I(s) = \mathfrak{L}[i(t)] \tag{6}$$

where $i(t)$ is the current in Fig. 11-1 after the switch is closed. In order to expand $I(s)$ in a form similar to the right side of Eq. (4) by the standard means of using a Taylor series, we must first express $I(s)$ as a function of $(1/s)$. Accordingly, we rewrite Eq. (5) as

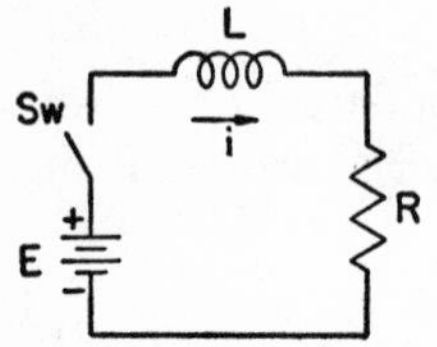

$$I(s) = \frac{1}{s^2}\left[\frac{E}{L + R\,(1/s)}\right] \tag{7}$$

FIG. 11-1.

Expanding Eq. (7) in series we have

$$I(s) = \frac{E}{R}\left\{\left(\frac{R}{L}\right)\frac{1}{s^2} - \left(\frac{R}{L}\right)^2\frac{1}{s^3} + \left(\frac{R}{L}\right)^3\frac{1}{s^4} - \left(\frac{R}{L}\right)^4\frac{1}{s^5} + \cdots\right\} \tag{8}$$

Comparing Eq. (8) with Eq. (4) or Eq. (3), we then have

$$i(t) = \frac{E}{R}\left\{\left(\frac{Rt}{L}\right) - \frac{(Rt/L)^2}{2!} + \frac{(Rt/L)^3}{3!} + \cdots\right\} \tag{9}$$

That Eq. (9) is really the correct solution is clear from the fact that it is the series expansion of

$$i(t) = \frac{E}{R}\,[1 - \epsilon^{-Rt/L}] \tag{10}$$

which we know is the correct solution by the methods of Chap. 3. Of course, when a solution in closed form, such as Eq. (10), can be found, there is no need to find a power-series solution. The foregoing example, however, serves as an excellent illustration of the method.

Finally, we note that a power series is useful only for computation purposes, and cannot be used to recognize the general properties of the solution such as are obvious by inspection of Eq. (10), except in the unusual case when the series can be recognized as the expansion of a closed-form combination of known functions. This feature is even more pronounced when the closed-form solution contains periodic terms with phase angles, facts which are completely concealed in the power-series solution. The foregoing feature greatly detracts from the usefulness of a power-series solution.

Whenever $F(s)$ can be expanded in an inverse power series such as that shown on the right side of Eq. (4), then, provided the series converges to $F(s)$ at least for values of s greater than some fixed value, and provided the corresponding t series converges, a correct power-series solution can be found by the methods described in this section. To show this fact, we note that if

$$a_0 + a_1 t + a_2 t^2 + \cdots \tag{11}$$

converges for any range of positive values of t, then the series

$$\epsilon^{-st} a_0 + \epsilon^{-st} a_1 t + \epsilon^{-st} a_2 t^2 + \cdots \tag{12}$$

will converge for all values of t, if s is sufficiently large. Consequently, Eq. (12) can be integrated term by term between the limits 0 and ∞. Thus we have

$$\int_0^\infty \epsilon^{-st}[a_0 + a_1 t + a_2 t^2 + \cdots]\, dt = \frac{a_0}{s} + \frac{a_1}{s^2} + \frac{2!a_2}{s^3} + \cdots = F(s) \tag{13}$$

Therefore,

$$\mathfrak{L}^{-1}[F(s)] = a_0 + a_1 t + a_2 t^2 + \cdots \tag{14}$$

The discussion of solutions in ascending powers of t is amplified in §11.9, and various examples are given in the exercises. Generally speaking, however, ascending power-series solutions are not of great practical importance in transformation calculus.

11.3. Asymptotic series

(a) **Introduction and Definitions.** As already mentioned, for large values of t, series in positive powers of t converge very slowly, if at all, and thus become almost useless for practical purposes. In such cases it is sometimes possible to use series in negative powers of t to good advantage. One type of such series, the *asymptotic expansion*, which we shall now describe, has turned out to be particularly practical in transformation calculus.

Consider the series

$$1 - \frac{1}{t} + \frac{1 \cdot 3}{t^2} - \frac{1 \cdot 3 \cdot 5}{t^3} + \frac{1 \cdot 3 \cdot 5 \cdot 7}{t^4} + \cdots + \frac{(2n-1)!}{2^{n-1}(n-1)!(-t)^n} + \cdots \tag{15}$$

This series happens to be divergent for all values of t. It has a special property, however, in that the values of the terms first decrease and then, after passing through a minimum, increase until finally each individual term tends toward infinity. If t is large, the values of the smallest terms are quite small. Furthermore, the larger the value of t, the further out in the series one must go before reaching the minimum. Thus in the series of Eq. (15), if $t = 10$, the series becomes

$$1 - \tfrac{1}{10} + \tfrac{3}{100} - \tfrac{15}{1000} + \cdots \tag{16}$$

and the minimum term is the sixth

$$\frac{1 \cdot 3 \cdot 5 \cdot 7 \cdot 9}{10^5} = 0.00945 \tag{17}$$

If $t = 100$, the minimum term is the fifty-first, whose value is

$$\text{fifty-first term} = 3.3 \times 10^{-35} \tag{18}$$

While the series of Eq. (15) does not converge, it can be shown that it, and other inverse power series like it which arise in transformation calculus, can be used for series expansions of functions for large values of the variable. In such cases if the series is what is called the *asymptotic expansion* of a function $f(t)$ then for sufficiently large values of t the sum of first n terms of the series differs from the value of $f(t)$ by less than the $(n + 1)$th term. Therefore, if the series is carried out only to the minimum term, it gives a good approximation to the value of the function. Furthermore, the larger the value of t, the closer the approximation.

The formal definition of an asymtotic expansion is as follows: Let $S_n(t)$ be the sum of the first $(n + 1)$ terms of the series

$$A_0 + \frac{A_1}{t} + \frac{A_2}{t^2} + \cdots + \frac{A_n}{t^n} + \cdots \tag{19}$$

and let

$$R_n(t) = t^n\{f(t) - S_n(t)\} \tag{20}$$

Then, if

$$\lim_{t \to \infty} R_n(t) = 0 \tag{21}$$

for a fixed value of n, even though

$$\lim_{n \to \infty} |R_n(t)| \to \infty \tag{22}$$

for a fixed value of t, we say that Eq. (19) is the *asymptotic expansion* of $f(t)$. In this case it is customary to write

$$f(t) \sim A_0 + \frac{A_1}{t} + \frac{A_2}{t^2} + \cdots + \frac{An}{t^n} + \cdots \tag{23}$$

(b) Examples of Asymptotic Expansions. The method for deriving asymptotic expansions is not so simple or universal as the method for deriving Taylor series. A fairly universal method for practical problems in transformation calculus will be supplied by Heaviside's solution, discussed later in this chapter. For the moment, however, we wish to derive a few asymptotic expansions by methods with which we are already familiar.

1. Let us derive an asymptotic expansion for the function

$$f(t) = \int_t^\infty \frac{\epsilon^{t-x}}{x}\,dx \tag{24}$$

We will find this expansion by successive integration by parts. Thus

$$\begin{aligned} f(t) &= \int_t^\infty \frac{\epsilon^{t-x}}{x}\,dx = \frac{-\epsilon^{t-x}}{x}\bigg|_{x=t}^{x=\infty} - \int_t^\infty \frac{\epsilon^{t-x}}{x^2}\,dx = \frac{1}{t} - \int_t^\infty \frac{\epsilon^{t-x}}{x^2}\,dx \\ &= \frac{1}{t} + \frac{\epsilon^{t-x}}{x^2}\bigg|_{x=t}^{x=\infty} + 2\int_t^\infty \frac{\epsilon^{t-x}}{x^3}\,dx = \frac{1}{t} - \frac{1}{t^2} + 2\int_t^\infty \frac{\epsilon^{t-x}}{x^3}\,dx \end{aligned} \tag{25}$$

Continuing the integration by parts, we find ultimately

$$\begin{aligned} f(t) = \frac{1}{t} - \frac{1}{t^2} + \frac{2!}{t^3} + \cdots + \frac{(-1)^n n!}{t^{n+1}} \\ + (-1)^{n+1}(n+1)!\int_t^\infty \frac{\epsilon^{t-x}\,dx}{x^{n+2}} \end{aligned} \tag{26}$$

In the case of Eq. (26)

$$S_n(t) = \frac{1}{t} - \frac{1}{t^2} + \frac{2!}{t^3} + \cdots + \frac{(-1)^n n!}{t^{n+1}} \tag{27}$$

and

$$R_n(t) = t^n\{f(t) - S_n(t)\} = (-1)^{n+1}(n+1)!t^n \int_t^\infty \frac{\epsilon^{t-x}\,dx}{x^{n+2}} \tag{28}$$

In this case,

$$\lim_{t\to\infty} R_n(t) = 0$$

for a fixed value of n, and

$$\lim_{n\to\infty} |R_n(t)| \to \infty$$

for a fixed value of t. Therefore $f(t)$ has the asymptotic expansion

$$f(t) \sim \frac{1}{t} - \frac{1}{t^2} + \frac{2}{t^3} + \cdots + \frac{(-1)^n n!}{t^{n+1}} + \cdots \tag{29}$$

2. Let us next derive an asymptotic expression for the function erfc (t) which we have already studied in Chap. 8. Starting with the definition

$$\operatorname{erfc}(t) = \frac{2}{\sqrt{\pi}} \int_{x=t}^{\infty} \epsilon^{-x^2}\, dx \tag{30}$$

we make the substitution

$$v = x^2 \tag{31}$$

Then, $\qquad dv = 2x\, dx \qquad$ or $\qquad dx = \dfrac{dv}{2x} = \dfrac{dv}{2\sqrt{v}} \qquad (32)$

and the limit $x = t$ becomes the limit $v = x^2 = t^2$. Thus Eq. (30) becomes

$$\operatorname{erfc}(t) = \frac{1}{\sqrt{\pi}} \int_{t^2}^{\infty} \frac{\epsilon^{-v}}{\sqrt{v}}\, dv \tag{33}$$

We will now subject the right side of Eq. (33) to successive integration by parts, to obtain

$$\begin{aligned}
\operatorname{erfc}(t) &= \frac{1}{\sqrt{\pi}} \int_{t^2}^{\infty} \frac{\epsilon^{-v}}{\sqrt{v}}\, dv \\
&= \frac{-1}{\sqrt{\pi}} \frac{\epsilon^{-v}}{\sqrt{v}}\Bigg|_{v=t^2}^{v=\infty} - \frac{1}{2\sqrt{\pi}} \int_{t^2}^{\infty} \frac{\epsilon^{-v}}{v^{\frac{3}{2}}}\, dv \\
&= + \frac{\epsilon^{-t^2}}{t\sqrt{\pi}} - \frac{1}{2\sqrt{\pi}} \int_{t^2}^{\infty} \frac{\epsilon^{-v}}{v^{\frac{3}{2}}}\, dv
\end{aligned} \tag{34}$$

If we continue the integration by parts, we obtain finally

$$\begin{aligned}
\operatorname{erfc}(t) \sim \frac{\epsilon^{-t^2}}{t\sqrt{\pi}} \bigg\{ 1 &- \frac{1}{2t^2} + \frac{1 \cdot 3}{(2t^2)^2} - \frac{1 \cdot 3 \cdot 5}{(2t^2)^3} + \cdots \\
&+ (-1)^n \frac{1 \cdot 3 \cdot 5 \cdots (2n-1)}{(2t^2)^n} + \cdots \bigg\}
\end{aligned} \tag{35}$$

Equation (35), because of the factor ϵ^{-t^2}, is not a true asymptotic expansion of erfc (t) as defined by Eq. (23). It, however, describes the behavior of erfc (t) for large values of t, and if the series is terminated at its minimum term, it gives a very close approximation to erfc (t) for large values of t. We may therefore call Eq. (35) an *asymptotic expression*, to distinguish it from a true asymptotic expansion. Equation (35) does give us a true asymptotic expansion for

$$\left(\frac{\text{erfc }(t)}{\epsilon^{-t^2}}\right)$$

The reason for making such a point of asymptotic expansions is that they have certain simple rules of manipulation which will be described below. Actually, the majority of the asymptotic expressions which are used in transformation calculus are not true asymptotic expansions.

3. We next wish briefly to discuss the asymptotic expressions for the Bessel functions. We shall omit[4] their derivations, since they are quite complicated. The expressions are as follows:

(for x real and positive)

$$I_n(x) \sim \frac{\epsilon^x}{\sqrt{2\pi x}}\left\{1 + \frac{1^2 - 4n^2}{8x} + \frac{(1^2 - 4n^2)(3^2 - 4n^2)}{2!(8x)^2} + \cdots\right\} \tag{36}$$

$$K_n(x) \sim \epsilon^{-x}\sqrt{\frac{\pi}{2x}}\left\{1 - \frac{1^2 - 4n^2}{8x} + \frac{(1^2 - 4n^2)(3^2 - 4n^2)}{2!(8x)^2} - \cdots\right\} \tag{37}$$

$$J_n(x) \sim \sqrt{\frac{2}{\pi x}}\left\{U \cos\left(x - \frac{n\pi}{2} - \frac{\pi}{4}\right) + V \sin\left(x - \frac{n\pi}{2} - \frac{\pi}{4}\right)\right\} \tag{38}$$

$$Y_n(x) \sim \sqrt{\frac{2}{\pi x}}\left\{U \sin\left(x - \frac{n\pi}{2} - \frac{\pi}{4}\right) - V \cos\left(x - \frac{n\pi}{2} - \frac{\pi}{4}\right)\right\} \tag{39}$$

---

[4] These derivations can be found in Bromwich, *Theory of Infinite Series;* Whittaker and Watson, *Modern Analysis;* or any of the advanced texts on Bessel functions.

where

$$U = 1 - \frac{(1^2 - 4n^2)(3^2 - 4n^2)}{2!(8x)^2} + \frac{(1^2 - 4n^2) \cdots (7^2 - 4n^2)}{4!(8x)^4} - \cdots \tag{40}$$

and

$$V = \frac{1^2 - 4n^2}{8x} - \frac{(1^2 - 4n^2)(3^2 - 4n^2)(5^2 - 4n^2)}{3!(8x)^3} + \cdots \tag{41}$$

When x is large in absolute value and x is also large in comparison with n, these expressions reduce to the simple approximations

$$I_n(x) \sim \frac{\epsilon^x}{\sqrt{2\pi x}} \tag{42}$$

$$K_n(x) \sim \epsilon^{-x}\sqrt{\frac{\pi}{2x}} \tag{43}$$

$$J_n(x) \sim \sqrt{\frac{2}{\pi x}} \cos\left(x - \frac{n\pi}{2} - \frac{\pi}{4}\right) \tag{44}$$

$$Y_n(x) \sim \sqrt{\frac{2}{\pi x}} \sin\left(x - \frac{n\pi}{2} - \frac{\pi}{4}\right) \tag{45}$$

These expressions are convenient and instructive in describing the behavior of the Bessel functions for very large values of the argument.

(c) **Further Discussion of Asymptotic Expansions.** Just as a Maclaurin series

$$f(t) = a_0 + a_1 t + a_2 t^2 + \cdots \tag{46}$$

may be considered as the expansion of a function about the point $t = 0$, so an asymptotic series

$$f(t) = A_0 + \frac{A_1}{t} + \frac{A_2}{t^2} + \cdots \tag{47}$$

may be considered as an expansion about the point $t = \infty$. As t approaches the point about which the expansion takes place in either case, only the earlier terms of the series have an appreciable value. Thus the early terms of the series describe the behavior of the function in the neighborhood of the point of expansion.

In the study of Taylor series it is noted that some uncommon functions, such as ϵ^{-1/t^2}, cannot be expanded in an infinite Taylor series even though all the derivatives exist, because the Taylor remainder does not approach zero. Thus all the derivatives of ϵ^{-1/t^2} vanish at $t = 0$, so that a formal Taylor expansion would give

$$\epsilon^{-1/t^2} = 0 + 0 + 0 + \cdots \tag{48}$$

which is obviously absurd. Furthermore, a Taylor expansion of $\sin \omega t + \epsilon^{-1/t^2}$ would give

$$\sin \omega t + \epsilon^{-1/t^2} = \omega t - \frac{(\omega t)^3}{3!} + \frac{(\omega t)^5}{5!} - \cdots \tag{49}$$

which is the Taylor expansion of $\sin \omega t$ alone. Equation (49) likewise cannot be used as an infinite Taylor series for the function on the left, since it also does not satisfy the requirement of a Taylor remainder which approaches zero. Equations (48) and (49) illustrate the general fact that functions which have terms that vanish exponentially about the point of expansion cannot generally be expanded in Taylor series.[5]

A corresponding situation exists in the case of asymptotic expansions, but here the phenomenon is much more important. Functions of the very common form ϵ^{-bt}, where b is a positive constant, have a string of zeros as their asymptotic expansion. Consequently, in general, any terms which vanish exponentially at infinity will not affect the asymptotic expansion of a function. Therefore, corresponding to the restriction that the Taylor remainder must vanish for an infinite Taylor series to be valid, it is customary to point out that an asymptotic expansion differs from the value of the function by less than the minimum term in the expansion *except for terms in the function which vanish exponentially at infinity*. For very large values of the variable, however, the exponentially vanishing terms ultimately become so small that they cause only a negligible error.

While it is true, as just pointed out, that more than one function may have a given asymptotic expansion, it is nevertheless true that only one asymptotic expansion can represent a given function for all values of the independent variable. In other words, a function cannot have two different asymptotic expansions.

[5] Though true, this is not a matter of great importance, since functions of this type occur rarely, if at all, in practice.

(d) **Manipulation of Asymptotic Expansions.** True asymptotic expansions, as defined in §11.3(a), can, in many ways, be manipulated like polynomials. Thus, any two asymptotic expansions can be added or multiplied together. Furthermore, every asymptotic expansion can be integrated term by term.[6] Furthermore, if it is known that the derivative of the original function has an asymptotic expansion, then this derivative can be obtained by term-by-term differentiation of the asymptotic expansion of the original function. It does not follow, however, from the fact that a function has an asymptotic expansion, that its derivative will also have one.

Many differential equations can also be solved in asymptotic series by a substitution method similar to our solution (see §9.3) of Bessel's equation in power series (see Exercise 1).

Exercise

1. Solve the differential equation

$$\frac{dy}{dx} = \frac{a}{x} + by$$

where b is a positive constant, by assuming a solution in asymptotic series; i.e.,

$$y \sim A_0 + \frac{A_1}{x} + \frac{A_2}{x^2} + \cdots$$

Answer:

$$y \sim -\frac{a}{bx}\left\{1 - \frac{1}{bx} + 2!\left(\frac{1}{bx}\right)^2 - 3!\left(\frac{1}{bx}\right)^3 + \cdots\right\}$$

11.4. Impulses of higher order

If, corresponding to the power series for $f(t)$ to be used for small values of t, we try to develop asymptotic solutions for large values of t by methods analogous to those used in §11.2, we run into difficulty. Thus

[6] Proofs of these properties will be found in Bromwich, *Theory of Infinite Series*, Chap. XII; or Whittaker and Watson, *Modern Analysis*, Chap. VIII.

$$\mathfrak{L}\left[A_0 + \frac{A_1}{t} + \frac{A_2}{t^2} + \cdots\right] = \frac{A_0}{s} + ? \qquad (50)$$

since

$$\int_0^\infty \epsilon^{-st}\left(\frac{A_n}{t^n}\right) dt$$

does not converge if $n > 0$.

We must therefore use a different method in order to obtain asymptotic solutions. As a preliminary, it seems worth while to investigate the significance of the inverse transforms of positive integral powers of s.

In Chap. 4 we have already found that the inverse transform of s to the zero power is a unit impulse. This discovery was not surprising since the usual significance of multiplying $F(s)$ by s is to take the derivative of $f(t)$. Therefore, since

$$\mathfrak{L}[U(t)] = s^{-1}$$

we would expect that $\mathfrak{L}^{-1}[s^0]$ would be zero everywhere except at t, where it would be infinite. However, $\mathfrak{L}^{-1}[s^0]$—i.e., $\delta(t)$—has a singular point at $t = 0$, just as $U(t)$ has, so that we would not expect $\delta(t)$ to behave like an ordinary function at a regular point. In particular, we found that $\delta(t)$ could be considered as the limiting case of any of several different types of functions (see Fig. 4-2).

Proceeding with this line of thought, let us consider the various functions shown in Fig. 11-2. Each of these is like the derivative of the preceding one, to the same extent that the unit impulse is like the derivative of the unit step.[7] Furthermore the Laplace trans-

---

[7] The shaded areas in each impulse correspond to discontinuities in the impulse of next lower order, and the heights of the shaded areas are proportional to the magnitudes of the corresponding discontinuities. In this sense each impulse is like the derivative of the impulse of next lower order. Analytically, we have

$$\delta^{n+1}(t) = \lim_{\Delta t \to 0} \frac{\delta_n(t) - \delta_n(t - \Delta t)}{\Delta t}$$

Although $\delta(t)$ has only an infinitesimal duration, we found in Chap. 4 that its effect may persist for a finite time. To get a physical idea of the effect of $\delta^{n+1}(t)$ for finite values of t, we note that if $\delta^n(t)$ is followed by the negative impulse $[-\delta^n(t - \Delta t)]$ at time Δt later, the latter tends to cancel the effect of the former, and the cancellation becomes more complete as Δt decreases. If $\delta^n(t)$ and $-\delta^n(t - \Delta t)$ are simultaneously increased by the factor $1/\Delta t$, the effect will generally remain finite. This is reminiscent of the behavior of a dipole.

forms of their limiting cases are the various integral powers of s. They may therefore be considered as *impulses of various orders*.

As an example of these Laplace transformations, consider the impulse in Fig. 11-2(d). Here we have

$$\delta''(t) = \lim_{c \to 0} \frac{U(t) - 3U(t-c) + 3U(t-2c) - U(t-3c)}{c^3} \tag{51}$$

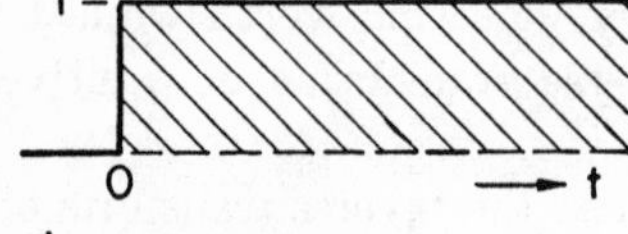

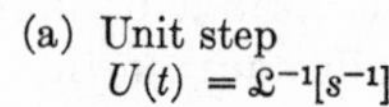
(a) Unit step
$U(t) = \mathcal{L}^{-1}[s^{-1}]$

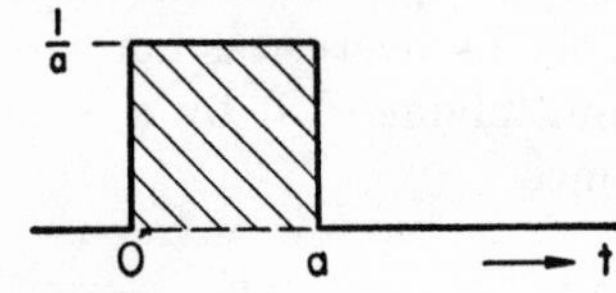

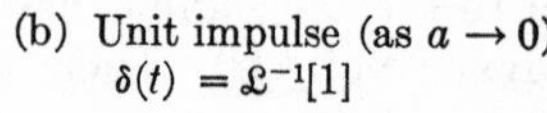
(b) Unit impulse (as $a \to 0$)
$\delta(t) = \mathcal{L}^{-1}[1]$

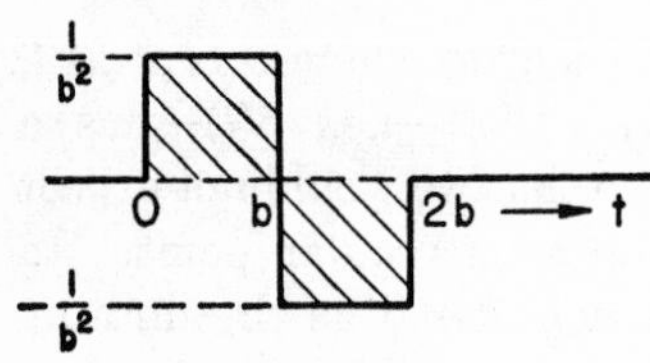

(c) Unit doublet impulse (as $b \to 0$)
$\delta'(t) = \mathcal{L}^{-1}[s]$

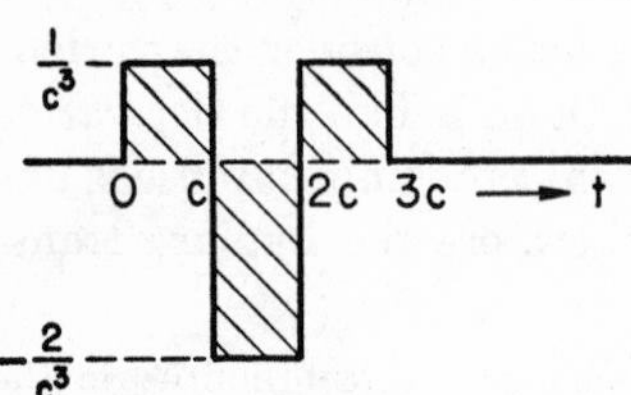

(d) Unit triplet impulse (as $c \to 0$)
$\delta''(t) = \mathcal{L}^{-1}[s^2]$

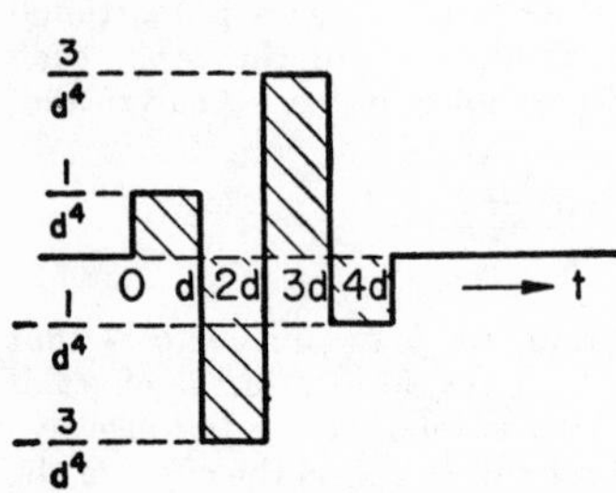

(e) Unit quadruplet impulse (as $d \to 0$)
$\delta'''(t) = \mathcal{L}^{-1}[s^3]$

FIG. 11-2. Impulses of different orders. The heights of shaded blocks are proportional to the binomial coefficients, i.e. $+1$, -1 for $\delta'(t)$: $+1$, -2, $+1$ for $\delta''(t)$; $+1$, -3, $+3$, -1 for $\delta'''(t)$; etc.

Therefore,

$$\mathcal{L}[\delta''(t)] = \lim_{c\to 0}\left\{\frac{1 - 3\epsilon^{-cs} + 3\epsilon^{-2cs} - \epsilon^{-3cs}}{c^3 s}\right\}$$

$$= \lim_{c\to 0}\left\{\frac{1 - 3\left(1 - cs + \frac{c^2s^2}{2} - \frac{c^3s^3}{3!} + \cdots\right) + 3\left(1 - 2cs + \frac{4c^2s^2}{2!} - \frac{8c^3s^3}{3!} + \cdots\right)}{c^3 s}\right.$$

$$\left.\frac{-1\left(1 - 3cs + \frac{9c^2s^2}{2!} - \frac{27c^3s^3}{3!} + \cdots\right)}{c^3 s}\right\}$$

$$= \lim_{c\to 0}\left\{\frac{0 + cs\cdot 0 + c^2s^2\cdot 0 + c^3s^3\cdot 1 + \cdots}{c^3 s}\right\} = s^2 \tag{52}$$

The other transforms can be derived in a similar manner.

Just as in the case of the unit impulse shown in Fig. 4-2, the impulses of higher order may also be considered as the limiting forms of a number of different sets of functions,[8] as long as their Laplace transforms are the proper powers of s. Because of the relation between s and $j\omega$, the frequency distribution of $\delta'(t)$ rises linearly with frequency, that of $\delta''(t)$ rises as the square of frequency, and so on.[9] It is shown in Appendix E by Fourier analysis that the frequency distribution of $\delta(t)$ is independent of frequency, and that that of $U(t)$ is inversely proportional to frequency.

The integrated value (i.e., the so-called d-c component) of all the impulses of order higher than $\delta(t)$ is zero. This can easily be demonstrated physically. Thus if a voltage wave of the form of an impulse is applied to a resistanceless capacitor, the current which flows has the wave shape of the impulse of next higher order. Now the value of the voltage wave returns to zero for finite values of t

[8] One such set which is different from Fig. 11-2 is given by Campbell and Foster in Bell System Monograph B-584, page 17.

[9] Waveshapes of the forms of the higher-order impulses (as shown in Fig. 11-2 before they have passed to the limit) will have the corresponding rising frequency characteristics in the low-frequency range. The limit to this range occurs when the pulse length is an appreciable fraction of a wavelength. Doublet impulses are used from this point of view in the discussion of shot effect at high frequencies in the author's *Frequency Analysis, Modulation and Noise.*

after $t = 0$, so that the charge on the capacitor returns to zero for all the curves in Fig. 11-2 except the unit step. Since the final charge on the condenser represents the integrated value of current, the integrated values of all the impulses of order higher than $\delta(t)$ will vanish.

11.5. "Fractional differentiation"—impulses of half-integral orders

In the preceding section, we found a group of functions which could be used as the inverse transforms of integral powers of s. In the next section we will also find it desirable to have inverse transforms for the half-integral powers of s; i.e., $s^{\frac{1}{2}}$, $s^{\frac{3}{2}}$, $s^{\frac{5}{2}}$, etc. Let us therefore proceed to find such a set of functions.

In Chap. 8 we derived the general formula [Eq. (33) of that chapter]

$$\mathcal{L}(t^m) = \frac{\Gamma(m+1)}{s^{m+1}} = \Gamma(m+1)s^{-(m+1)} \tag{53}$$

provided $m > -1$.

For the inverse transforms of the positive half-integral powers of s, m is less than (-1), so that we really have no right to use Eq. (53). Accordingly, we seem to have come to an impasse. In a case like this, it might be practical to take the attitude that we should try Eq. (53) anyway, and if the result is reasonable, we can then see if we can justify it. Heaviside would certainly have approved of this attitude, since it is essentially what he did. However, he never justified the procedure, as we shall do in §11.8.

In the case of the positive integral powers of s, we can find the inverse transform of s^{n+1} by a process akin to differentiation of the inverse transform of s^n. If we could obtain the inverse transform of $s^{n+\frac{1}{2}}$ from s^n by some process, then, by analogy, this process might be called "*fractional differentiation,*" or specifically, "*half-differentiation.*" Actually this is not done, but we do find the inverse transform of $s^{n+\frac{1}{2}}$ by differentiating $s^{n-\frac{1}{2}}$ when we use Eq. (53), for

$$\frac{d}{dt}\left[\frac{t^{-n-\frac{1}{2}}}{\Gamma(-n+\frac{1}{2})}\right] = \frac{(-n-\frac{1}{2})t^{-n-\frac{3}{2}}}{\Gamma(-n+\frac{1}{2})} = \frac{t^{-n-\frac{3}{2}}}{\Gamma(-n-\frac{1}{2})} \tag{54}$$

according to Eq. (37) of Chap. 8. Thus

$$\frac{d}{dt}\{\mathcal{L}^{-1}[s^{n-\frac{1}{2}}]\} = \mathcal{L}^{-1}[s^{n+\frac{1}{2}}] \tag{55}$$

according to Eqs. (53) and (54). Consequently, the use of Eq. (53) for obtaining the inverse transforms of the positive half-integral powers of s is sometimes called "*fractional differentiation.*"[10]

If we start with the *true* equation

$$\mathcal{L}^{-1}(s^{-\frac{1}{2}}) = \frac{t^{-\frac{1}{2}}}{\Gamma(+\frac{1}{2})} = \frac{1}{\sqrt{\pi t}} \tag{56}$$

we can find by differentiation the fictitious or, perhaps better, the *quasi-equations*

$$\mathcal{L}^{-1}(s^{+\frac{1}{2}}) \cong \frac{d}{dt}\left(\frac{1}{\sqrt{\pi t}}\right) = \frac{1}{\sqrt{\pi t}}\left[\frac{-1}{2t}\right] \tag{57}$$

$$\mathcal{L}^{-1}(s^{\frac{3}{2}}) \cong \frac{d}{dt}\{\mathcal{L}^{-1}(s^{\frac{1}{2}})\} \cong \frac{1}{\sqrt{\pi t}}\left[\frac{+3}{(2t)^2}\right] \tag{58}$$

$$\mathcal{L}^{-1}(s^{\frac{5}{2}}) \cong \frac{d}{dt}\{\mathcal{L}^{-1}(s^{\frac{3}{2}})\} \cong \frac{1}{\sqrt{\pi t}}\left[\frac{-1\cdot 3\cdot 5}{(2t)^3}\right] \tag{59}$$

and so on. We could, of course, have obtained Eqs. (57–59) directly from Eq. (53), if we had a table of the gamma functions of the negative half-integers handy.

Formulas (57–59) are not true equations. For example, in the case of Eq. (57), the Laplace transform of

$$\frac{1}{\sqrt{\pi t}}\left(\frac{-1}{2t}\right)$$

is

$$\int_0^\infty \frac{-\epsilon^{-st}}{2t\sqrt{\pi t}}\,dt = \infty \tag{60}$$

Consequently, any results which we obtain by using these formulas will have to be justified after the results are obtained.

It is worthy of note that the interpretation of the inverse transforms of positive integral powers of s as impulses of higher order is not inconsistent with Eq. (53). For these cases, $\Gamma(m+1)$ becomes the gamma function of the various negative integers, which is always infinite. Thus, according to Eq. (53)

$$\mathcal{L}^{-1}[s^n] = \frac{1}{\Gamma(-n)\cdot t^{n+1}} \tag{61}$$

The inverse transforms of positive integral powers of s should there-

[10] For a discussion of more general theories of fractional differentiation, see Doetsch, *Laplace Transformation*, p. 298.

fore vanish for all values of t, according to Eq. (53) or Eq. (61), except at $t = 0$, where they are indeterminate.

In an analogous manner the expressions on the right of Eqs. (57–59), etc. may be called impulses of half-integral orders. Each $\mathcal{L}^{-1}[(s^{n+\frac{1}{2}})]$ can be obtained from the corresponding $\mathcal{L}^{-1}[(s^{n-\frac{1}{2}})]$ by differentiation. These functions are similar to the integral order impulses in that they have a singular point at $t = 0$. They are different, however, in having values differing from zero for positive values of t. This latter fact is the reason why it is possible, as we shall see, to express a great many functions in asymptotic expansions as the sum of a series of half-integral order impulses; whereas impulses of integral order cannot be used for this purpose.

11.6. Heaviside's asymptotic solution

As mentioned earlier in the chapter, a power-series solution is unsatisfactory for large values of t because of the increasing slowness of its convergence. It is therefore very fortunate that a series type of solution has been discovered whose form and computation become increasingly simple as the value of t is increased. This series solution was discovered by Heaviside, but he never supplied the necessary proofs to justify it. Furthermore, he failed to develop the complete theory, so that his method frequently gives the wrong answer. In §11.7 we shall not only supply the complete and rigorous theory, but we shall also gain insight into the mathematical significance of the phenomenon.

The problem as proposed and solved by Heaviside amounted to finding the response of an impedance $Z(s)$ to a unit step of voltage. Thus he tried to find

$$i(t) = \mathcal{L}^{-1}\left[\frac{E(s)}{Z(s)}\right] = \mathcal{L}^{-1}\left[\frac{1}{sZ(s)}\right] \tag{62}$$

since
$$E(s) = \frac{1}{s} \tag{63}$$

for a unit step of voltage. The solution arrived at by Heaviside was to expand $1/Z(s)$ in a series of integral and half-integral powers of s of the form

$$\frac{1}{Z(s)} = a_0 + a_1 s + a_2 s^2 + \cdots + a_n s^n + \cdots$$
$$+ \sqrt{s}\,(b_0 + b_1 s + b_2 s^2 + \cdots + b_n s^n + \cdots) \tag{64}$$

After finding the values of the a and b constants, by some method of expansion of $1/Z(s)$, he wrote as the solution for *large* values of t,

$$i(t) = a_0 + \frac{1}{\sqrt{\pi t}}\left[b_0 - b_1\frac{1}{2t} + b_2\frac{1\cdot 3}{(2t)^2} - b_3\frac{1\cdot 3\cdot 5}{(2t)^3} + \cdots\right] \tag{65}$$

Let us look into the significance of this solution. In the first place, we note that, according to (62) and (64),

$$I(s) = \mathcal{L}[i(t)] = \frac{1}{sZ(s)} = \frac{a_0}{s} + a_1 + a_2 s + a_3 s^2 + \cdots + \frac{b_0}{s^{\frac{1}{2}}} + b_1 s^{\frac{1}{2}} + b_2 s^{\frac{3}{2}} + \cdots \tag{66}$$

Therefore, according to the discussion in §§11.4 and 11.5, Heaviside's solution amounts to assuming the validity of Eq. (53) for all values of s and using it to find the inverse transform of Eq. (66). We may also describe Heaviside's solution as a solution in a series of impulses of integral and half-integral orders.

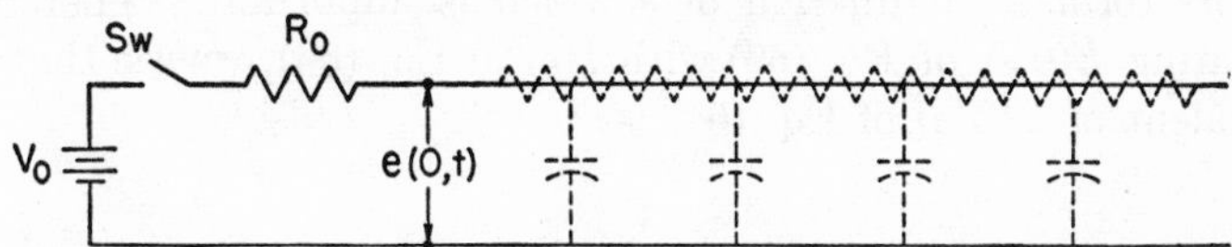

FIG. 11-3. An inductanceless, leakage-free cable in series with a resistor to which a step function of voltage can be applied by closing the switch SW.

This is an example of Heaviside's experimental method of attacking difficult mathematical problems. However, it will be found by studying Heaviside's discussion on the "Nature and Effect of Multiple Impulses"[11] that there was also physical reasoning behind his method. We shall generalize the method and put it on a more modern rigorous basis in §11.7. Hence we will not attempt further justification of the method at this point.

Let us now use Heaviside's method to solve an actual problem. For example, let us consider the case of an inductanceless, leakage-free cable connected in series with a resistance R_0 (see Fig. 11-3). Using the notation of Chap. 10, let us find the voltage at the input of the cable $e(0,t)$ for values of time relatively long after the switch is

[11] O. Heaviside, *Electromagnetic Theory*, Vol. II, p. 63 (Edition of 1899).

closed. Here the voltage equation is

$$V_0 - R_0 i(0,t) = e(0,t) \tag{67}$$

and the transformed equation is

$$\frac{V_0}{s} - R_0 I(0,s) = E(0,s) \tag{67A}$$

Now from Eq. (31) of Chap. 10, with $L = G = 0$, we have

$$I(0,s) = \sqrt{\frac{Cs}{R}}\, E(0,s) \tag{68}$$

so that

$$E(0,s) = \frac{V_0}{s\left[1 + R_0\sqrt{\frac{Cs}{R}}\right]} \tag{69}$$

As far as the mathematics is concerned, it will, of course, make no difference whether $E(0,s)$ stands for a voltage or a current. It is only its form as a function of s which is important. Therefore, comparing $E(0,s)$ of Eq. (69) with $I(s)$ in Eq. (66), we see that the equivalent of $1/Z(s)$ of Eq. (64) is

$$\frac{V_0}{\left[1 + R_0\sqrt{\frac{Cs}{R}}\right]}$$

in our case. Expanding this in a power series in the variable $\left(R_0\sqrt{\frac{Cs}{R}}\right)$, we have

$$\begin{aligned}\frac{V_0}{1 + R_0\sqrt{\frac{Cs}{R}}} &= V_0\left\{1 - \left[\frac{R_0^2C}{R}\,s\right]^{\frac{1}{2}} + \left[\frac{R_0^2C}{R}\,s\right]\right. \\ &\qquad \left. - \left[\frac{R_0^2C}{R}\,s\right]^{\frac{3}{2}} + \left[\frac{R_0^2C}{R}\,s\right]^{2} + \cdots\right\} \\ &= V_0 + \frac{V_0R_0^2C}{R}\,s + \frac{V_0R_0^4C^2}{R^2}\,s^2 + \cdots \\ &\quad + \sqrt{s}\left[-V_0R_0\left(\frac{C}{R}\right)^{\frac{1}{2}} - V_0R_0^3\left(\frac{C}{R}\right)^{\frac{3}{2}} s - \cdots\right]\end{aligned} \tag{70}$$

Therefore, by Eq. (65), we have

$$e(0,t) = V_0 - \frac{V_0}{\sqrt{\pi t}}\left[R_0\left(\frac{C}{R}\right)^{\frac{1}{2}} - R_0^3\left(\frac{C}{R}\right)^{\frac{3}{2}}\left(\frac{1}{2t}\right) + R_0^5\left(\frac{C}{R}\right)^{\frac{5}{2}}\frac{1\cdot 3}{(2t)^2} - R_0^7\left(\frac{C}{R}\right)^{\frac{7}{2}}\frac{1\cdot 3\cdot 5}{(2t)^3} + \cdots\right] \tag{71}$$

Equation (71) gives the voltage $e(0,t)$ at the input to the cable in Fig. 11-3 as an asymptotic function of time. For large values of t, the sum of the first few terms gives a very close approximation to the true value.

While the Heaviside method which we have just applied is very simple, it is only human to lack confidence in it because of its insecure foundation. In the next section we will therefore show how the solution can be derived, when it is correct, and we will also show how to find a correct solution in many cases where the original Heaviside solution is in error.

11.7. Rigorous derivation of asymptotic-series solutions by contour integration

Equation (26) of Chap. 7

$$f(t) = \frac{1}{2\pi j}\int_{\gamma - j\infty}^{\gamma + j\infty} F(s)\epsilon^{st}\,ds \tag{72}$$

gives us a general method of finding $f(t)$ from $F(s)$, and it is therefore of interest to see whether we can use it to derive Heaviside's asymptotic solution. Thus, suppose $F(s)$ can be expressed in the finite-series form

$$F(s) = \frac{A_0}{s} + \frac{B_0}{s^{\frac{1}{2}}} + A_1 + B_1 s^{\frac{1}{2}} + A_2 s + B_2 s^{\frac{3}{2}} + A_3 s^2 + \cdots + A_n s^{n-1} + B_n s^{n-\frac{1}{2}} + R_n(s) \tag{73}$$

where $R_n(s)$ is a remainder. If the B coefficients in Eq. (73) do not all vanish, then $F(s)$ will have a branch point at the origin. However, provided $F(s)$ does not have any other singular points, and provided $F(s)$ conforms to Eq. (28) of Chap. 7, then by the argument in §7.3, we can change from the original path of integration [of Eq. (72)] shown as C_1 in Fig. 11-4, to the new path shown as C_2 in Fig. 11-4. We may therefore write

$$f(t) = \frac{1}{2\pi j}\int_{C_1} F(s)\epsilon^{st}\,ds = \frac{1}{2\pi j}\int_{C_2} F(s)\epsilon^{st}\,ds$$
$$= \frac{1}{2\pi j}\int_{C_2} \epsilon^{st}\left\{\frac{A_0}{s} + \frac{B_0}{s^{\frac{1}{2}}} + A_1 + B_1 s^{\frac{1}{2}} + A_2 s + \cdots + B_n s^{n-\frac{1}{2}} + R_n(s)\right\} ds \quad (74)$$

The two arms of C_2 are infinitely close to the negative half of the real axis and are connected by a circle of infinitesimal radius r

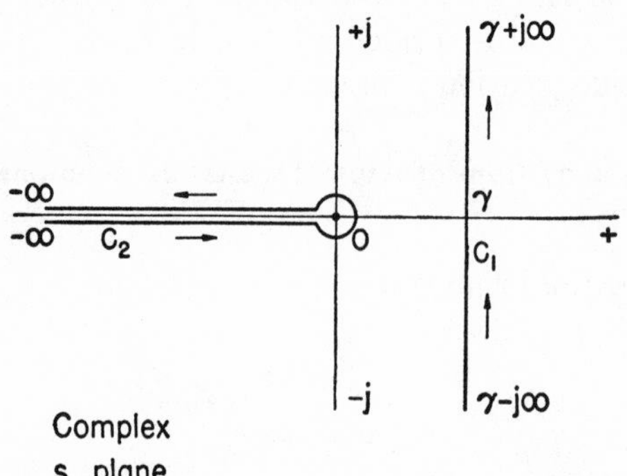

FIG. 11-4. The basic inversion theorem integration contour C_1, and the contour C_2, which is equivalent to C_1 when the only singular point is a branch point at the origin.

around the branch point at the origin. For the general terms in Eq. (74), we may therefore let $u = -s$ and write

$$\int_{C_2} \epsilon^{st} A_p s^{p-1}\,ds = -\int_{\infty}^{0} A_p \epsilon^{-ut}(-u)^{p-1}\,du + \int_{-\pi}^{+\pi} A_p \epsilon^{rt(\cos\phi + j\sin\phi)} r^{p-1}\epsilon^{j\phi(p-1)} j r \epsilon^{j\phi}\,d\phi - \int_{0}^{\infty} A_p \epsilon^{-ut}(-u)^{p-1}\,du \quad (75)$$

and[12]

$$\int_{C_2} \epsilon^{st} B_p s^{p-\frac{1}{2}}\, ds = -\int_{\infty}^{0} B_p \epsilon^{-ut}(-u)^{p-1}(-j\sqrt{u})\, du + \int_{-\pi}^{+\pi} B_p \epsilon^{rt(\cos\phi + j\sin\phi)} r^{p-\frac{1}{2}} \epsilon^{j\phi(p-\frac{1}{2})} jr\epsilon^{j\phi}\, d\phi - \int_0^{\infty} B_p \epsilon^{-ut}(-u)^{p-1}(+j\sqrt{u})\, du \qquad (76)$$

Now the terms due to integration around the infinitesimal circle in Eqs. (75) and (76) will vanish because of the infinitesimal value of r, except in the special case of[13]

$$\int_{-\pi}^{+\pi} A_0 \epsilon^{rt(\cos\phi + j\sin j\phi)} r^{-1} \epsilon^{-j\phi} jr\epsilon^{j\phi}\, d\phi = \int_{-\pi}^{+\pi} jA_0\, d\phi = j2\pi A_0 \qquad (77)$$

Furthermore, the first and third terms on the right side of Eq. (75) cancel, while the first and third terms on the right side of Eq. (76) are equal. Therefore, we have

$$\int_{C_2} \epsilon^{st} A_p s^{p-1}\, ds = 0 \qquad (p \neq 0) \qquad (78)$$

$$\int_{C_2} \epsilon^{st} A_0 s^{-1}\, ds = j2\pi A_0 \qquad (79)$$

and

$$\int_{C_2} \epsilon^{st} B_p s^{p-\frac{1}{2}}\, ds = j2 \int_0^{\infty} B_p \epsilon^{-ut} u^{p-\frac{1}{2}} (-1)^p\, du = (-1)^p j2B_p \frac{\Gamma(p+\frac{1}{2})}{t^{p+\frac{1}{2}}} \qquad (80)$$

by letting $x = ut$ and $n = p + \frac{1}{2}$ in Eq. (1) of Chap. 8. Therefore

---

[12] Along the lower arm of C_2,

$$s = |s|\epsilon^{-j\pi}$$

and along the upper arm of C_2,

$$s = |s|\epsilon^{+j\pi}$$

Therefore

$$s^{\frac{1}{2}} = |s|^{\frac{1}{2}}\epsilon^{-j\pi/2} = -j|s|^{\frac{1}{2}}$$

along the lower arm, while

$$s^{\frac{1}{2}} = |s|^{\frac{1}{2}}\epsilon^{+j\pi/2} = +j|s|^{\frac{1}{2}}$$

along the upper arm.

[13] We note that

$$\epsilon^{rt(\cos\phi + j\sin\phi)} = 1$$

because of the infinitesimal value of r.

Eq. (74) becomes

$$f(t) = A_0 + \frac{1}{\sqrt{\pi t}} \left\{ B_0 - B_1 \left(\frac{1}{2t}\right) + B_2 \frac{1 \cdot 3}{(2t)^2} - B_3 \frac{1 \cdot 3 \cdot 5}{(2t)^3} + \cdots \right.$$
$$\left. + (-1)^n B_n \frac{1 \cdot 3 \cdot 5 \cdots (2n-1)}{(2t)^n} \right\} + \frac{1}{2\pi j} \int_{C_2} \epsilon^{st} R_n(s) \, ds \quad (81)$$

In all cases where we can show that the remainder integral is negligible we have a rigorous basis for Heaviside's solution. His solution has thus been derived from the inversion theorem by the

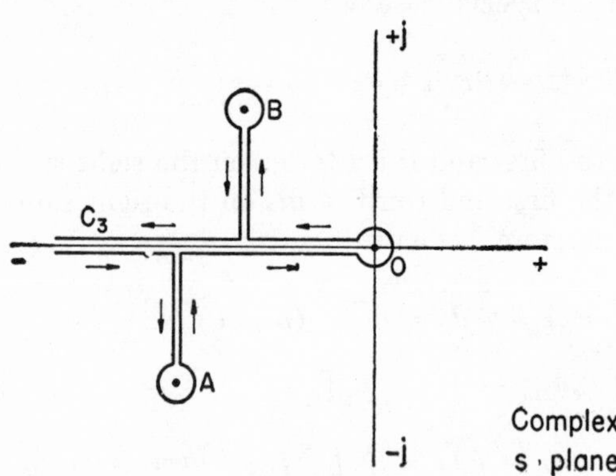

Fig. 11-5. The integration contour C_3, which can be used when $F(s)$ has poles at A and B as well as a branch point at the origin.

proper choice of the path of integration.[14] We also see that the half-power terms do not vanish because they have a branch point at the origin.[15] The series inside the braces in Eq. (81) is the beginning of an asymptotic series.

If $F(s)$ has poles, the problem can still be solved by modifying the path of integration. For example, suppose that $F(s)$ has poles at A and B in Fig. 11-5. Then the path of integration C_2 (of Fig. 11-4) must be changed to send out arms which encircle the poles,

[14] We have followed McLachlan, *Complex Variable and Operation Calculus*, in this choice of the path of integration.

[15] If terms had been used in Eq. (74) in which s were raised to a power less than (-1), these terms would not have given a finite result in Eq. (81). Consequently, Eq. (74) is the most general series in integral and half-integral terms which our method will allow.

as shown by C_3 in Fig. 11-5, in order to be a justifiable deformation of C_1. The values of the integral in the two directions along these vertical arms will cancel, since the integrand returns to its original value after encircling a pole. The value of the integral around the path encircling a pole, however, will be $2\pi j$ times the residue of the pole. Therefore each side arm adds to the value of $f(t)$ an amount equal to the residue of $[F(s)\epsilon^{st}]$, with respect to the pole. It therefore follows that if $F(s)$ has poles, the residues of $F(s)\epsilon^{st}$ at these poles must be added to Heaviside's series to get the complete solution for $f(t)$.

The Heaviside solution depends on the fact that $F(s)$ has only one branch point, and that one is at the origin. If $F(s)$ has only one branch point, but the branch point is not at the origin, it will frequently be possible to transform this branch point to the origin with the aid of Eq. (24) of Chap. 3, and then the Heaviside solution can be used. In case $F(s)$ has more than one branch point, the Heaviside solution is no longer applicable, unless the branch points all lie inside C_2. When this is not true, it is necessary to find new contours in order to make it practical to carry out the integration.[16] The Heaviside solution is of great practical importance because many transmission-line problems involve only branch points inside C_2, or those which can be transformed into that location.

It is sometimes difficult, with the contour-integration method of deriving the Heaviside solution, to show that the remainder integral is negligible. The series in Eq. (73) can usually be derived with the aid of Taylor series.

11.8. Examples of asymptotic solutions by contour integration

1. As a first example, let us solve the problem already solved in §11.6. Starting with Eq. (69) (up to which point the two methods are identical), we have

$$F(s) = E(0,s) = \frac{V_0}{s\left[1 + R_0\sqrt{\frac{Cs}{R}}\right]} \tag{82}$$

---

[16] See McLachlan (*op. cit.*), especially Chap. IV, for other practical contours of integration.

This function has only one branch point, at $s = 0$. The Heaviside method is therefore applicable. Expanding[17] the function into a finite series by algebraic division, we have

$$F(s) = \frac{V_0}{s}\left[1 - R_0\left(\frac{C}{R}\right)^{\frac{1}{2}} s^{\frac{1}{2}} + R_0^2\left(\frac{C}{R}\right) s - \cdots \right.$$

$$\left. + (-1)^{2n-1}R_0^{2n-1}\left(\frac{C}{R}\right)^{n-\frac{1}{2}} s^{n-\frac{1}{2}} + \frac{(-1)^{2n}R_0^{2n}\left(\frac{C}{R}\right)^n s^n}{1 + R_0\sqrt{\frac{Cs}{R}}}\right] \tag{83}$$

Therefore, by Eqs. (81) and (74),

$$f(t) = V_0 - \frac{V_0}{\sqrt{\pi t}}\left\{R_0\left(\frac{C}{R}\right)^{\frac{1}{2}} - R_0^3\left(\frac{C}{R}\right)^{\frac{3}{2}}\frac{1}{2t} + R_0^5\left(\frac{C}{R}\right)^{\frac{5}{2}}\frac{1\cdot 3}{(2t)^2} + \cdots \right.$$

$$\left. + (-1)^{n-1}R_0^{2n-1}\left(\frac{C}{R}\right)^{n-\frac{1}{2}}\frac{1\cdot 3\cdot 5\cdot \cdots (2n-3)}{(2t)^{n-1}}\right\}$$

$$+ \frac{V_0}{2\pi j}\int_{C_2}\frac{\epsilon^{st}(-1)^{2n}R_0^{2n}\left(\frac{C}{R}\right)^n s^n}{1 + R_0\sqrt{\frac{Cs}{R}}}\,ds \tag{84}$$

To show that the remainder integral becomes negligible for large values of n, we first note that around the infinitesimal circle at the origin,

$$\frac{V_0}{2\pi j}\int_{C_2}\frac{\epsilon^{st}(-1)^{2n}R_0^{2n}\left(\frac{C}{R}\right)^n s^n}{1 + R_0\sqrt{\frac{Cs}{R}}}\,ds$$

$$= \frac{V_0}{2\pi j}\int_{-\pi}^{+\pi}\frac{R_0^{2n}\left(\frac{C}{R}\right)^n r^n\epsilon^{jn\phi}jr\epsilon^{j\phi}\,d\phi}{1} = 0 \tag{85}$$

Furthermore, along the two arms of C_2, the absolute value of the denominator is greater than 1, since it is

---

17 $$\frac{1}{1+x} = 1 - x + x^2 - x^3 + \cdots + (-1)^q x^q + \frac{(-1)^{q+1}x^{q+1}}{1+x}$$

$$|\text{denominator}| = \left|1 \pm jR_0\sqrt{\frac{Cu}{R}}\right| \tag{86}$$

where u is the absolute value of s. It therefore follows that

$$\left|\frac{V_0}{2\pi j}\int_{C_2}\frac{\epsilon^{st}(-1)^{2n}R_0^{2n}\left(\frac{C}{R}\right)^n s^n}{1 + R_0\sqrt{\frac{Cs}{R}}}\,ds\right| < \left|\frac{V_0}{2\pi}\int_{\infty}^{0}\epsilon^{-ut}R_0^{2n}\left(\frac{C}{R}\right)^n u^n\,du\right|$$
$$+ \left|\frac{V_0}{2\pi}\int_0^{\infty}\epsilon^{-ut}R_0^{2n}\left(\frac{C}{R}\right)^n u^n\,du\right| = \frac{V_0}{\pi}R_0^{2n}\left(\frac{C}{R}\right)^n\frac{n!}{t^{n+1}} \tag{87}$$

Consequently, for values of t much larger than nR_0^2C/R, corresponding to the minimum in the asymptotic expansion, the remainder integral becomes negligible. Therefore we have finally

$$f(t) \sim V_0 - \frac{V_0}{\sqrt{\pi t}}\left\{R_0\left(\frac{C}{R}\right)^{\frac{1}{2}} - R_0^3\left(\frac{C}{R}\right)^{\frac{3}{2}}\frac{1}{(2t)}\right.$$
$$\left. + R_0^5\left(\frac{C}{R}\right)^{\frac{5}{2}}\frac{1\cdot 3}{(2t)^2} - \cdots\right\} \tag{88}$$

in which the asymptotic expansion is the complete solution for large values of t. This agrees with Eq. (71), but it has this time been derived by rigorous means.

Fig. 11-6. A sine wave generator connected to a leakage-free noninductive cable of infinite length.

2. As our next example, let us consider a case in which the residues at the poles make an important contribution to the final solution. In this case, the original Heaviside method would fail to give the complete solution. The case which we will consider is that of a sine-wave generator connected to a leakage-free, noninductive cable as shown in Fig. 11-6; and it is our object to find the current which enters the cable as a function of time.

In the present example,

$$e(0,t) = V_0 \sin \omega t \tag{89}$$

so that

$$E(0,s) = \mathcal{L}[e(0,t)] = \frac{\omega V_0}{s^2 + \omega^2} \tag{90}$$

Then, by Eq. (31) of Chap. 10,

$$I(0,s) = \sqrt{\frac{Cs}{R}}\, E(0,s) = \sqrt{\frac{Cs}{R}}\, \frac{\omega V_0}{s^2 + \omega^2} \tag{91}$$

since, in this case,

$$L = G = 0 \tag{92}$$

Our problem is to find

$$i(0,t) = \mathcal{L}^{-1}[I(0,s)] \tag{93}$$

To do so, we first express $i(0,t)$ as a contour integral. Thus, from Eqs. (91) and (93),

$$i(0,t) = \frac{1}{2\pi j} \int_{C_1} \epsilon^{st} \sqrt{\frac{Cs}{R}}\, \frac{\omega V_0}{s^2 + \omega^2}\, ds \tag{94}$$

The integrand of Eq. (94) has poles at

$$s = \pm j\omega \tag{95}$$

and a branch point at the origin, so that C_1 can be transformed to C_4 of Fig. 11-7 as a preliminary to asymptotic expansion of $i(0,t)$.

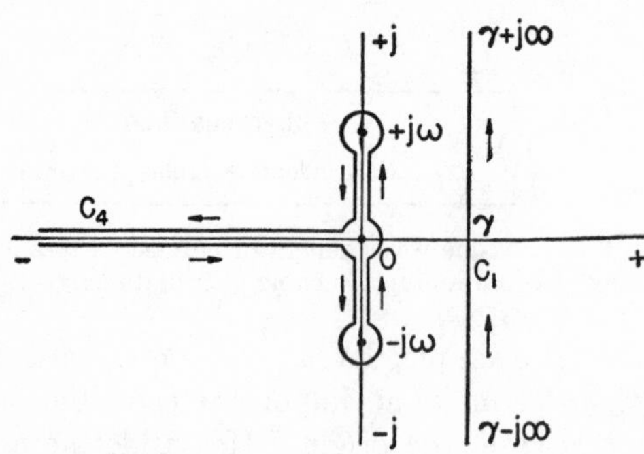

FIG. 11-7. The integration contour C_4, which can be used when $F(s)$ has a branch point at the origin and poles at $\pm j\omega$, the latter caused by an impressed steady-state sine wave.

By Eq. (54) of Chap. 7, the residue of the integrand of Eq. (94) with respect to the pole at

$$s = +j\omega \tag{96}$$

is
$$\epsilon^{j\omega t}\sqrt{\frac{C(j\omega)}{R}}\,\frac{\omega V_0}{2j\omega} = \frac{V_0}{2j}\sqrt{\frac{C}{R}}\,\sqrt{j\omega}\,\epsilon^{j\omega t} \tag{97}$$

and the residue with respect to the pole at

$$s = -j\omega \tag{98}$$

is
$$\epsilon^{-j\omega t}\sqrt{\frac{C(-j\omega)}{R}}\,\frac{\omega V_0}{2(-j\omega)} = \frac{-V_0}{2j}\sqrt{\frac{C}{R}}\,\sqrt{-j\omega}\,\epsilon^{-j\omega t} \tag{99}$$

The sum of the residues at the poles is the sum of Eqs. (97) and (99), and is, accordingly,

$$\frac{V_0}{2j}\sqrt{\frac{C}{R}}\,\sqrt{j\omega}\,\epsilon^{j\omega t} - \frac{V_0}{2j}\sqrt{\frac{C}{R}}\,\sqrt{-j\omega}\,\epsilon^{-j\omega t}$$

$$= V_0\sqrt{\frac{C}{R}}\,\sqrt{\omega}\left(\frac{\epsilon^{j\omega t+\frac{\pi}{4}} - \epsilon^{-j\omega t-\frac{\pi}{4}}}{2j}\right) = V_0\sqrt{\frac{\omega C}{R}}\sin\left(\omega t + \frac{\pi}{4}\right) \tag{100}$$

Substituting this expression into Eq. (94), we have

$$\begin{aligned} i(0,t) &= \frac{1}{2\pi j}\int_{C_1}\epsilon^{st}\sqrt{\frac{Cs}{R}}\,\frac{\omega V_0}{s^2+\omega^2}\,ds = \frac{1}{2\pi j}\int_{C_4}\epsilon^{st}\sqrt{\frac{Cs}{R}}\,\frac{\omega V_0}{s^2+\omega^2}\,ds \\ &= V_0\sqrt{\frac{\omega C}{R}}\sin\left(\omega t + \frac{\pi}{4}\right) + \frac{1}{2\pi j}\int_{C_2}\epsilon^{st}\sqrt{\frac{Cs}{R}}\,\frac{\omega V_0}{s^2+\omega^2}\,ds \end{aligned} \tag{101}$$

In order to find the asymptotic series portion of the solution, we first expand the denominator of the integral into a finite power series by algebraic division. Thus

$$\frac{1}{s^2+\omega^2} = \frac{1}{\omega^2}\left[1 - \frac{s^2}{\omega^2} + \frac{s^4}{\omega^4} - \cdots + (-1)^{n-1}\left(\frac{s}{\omega}\right)^{2n-2} + \frac{(-1)^n\left(\frac{s}{\omega}\right)^{2n}}{s^2+\omega^2}\right] \tag{102}$$

Substituting this value into the integral we have

$$\int_{C_2} \epsilon^{st} \sqrt{\frac{Cs}{R}} \frac{\omega V_0}{s^2 + \omega^2}\, ds = \int_{C_2} \epsilon^{st} \sqrt{\frac{C}{R}} \frac{V_0}{\omega} s^{\frac{1}{2}} \left[1 - \frac{s^2}{\omega^2} + \frac{s^4}{\omega^4} + \cdots \right.$$

$$\left. + (-1)^{n-1} \left(\frac{s}{\omega}\right)^{2n-2} + \frac{(-1)^n \left(\frac{s}{\omega}\right)^{2n}}{s^2 + \omega^2} \right] ds \quad (103)$$

It then follows from Eqs. (74) and (81) that

$$\frac{1}{2\pi j} \int_{C_2} \epsilon^{st} \sqrt{\frac{Cs}{R}} \frac{\omega V_0}{s^2 + \omega^2}\, ds$$

$$= \frac{V_0}{\omega} \sqrt{\frac{C}{R}} \frac{1}{\sqrt{\pi t}} \left[-\frac{1}{(2t)} + \frac{1 \cdot 3 \cdot 5}{\omega^2 (2t)^3} - \frac{1 \cdot 3 \cdot 5 \cdot 7 \cdot 9}{\omega^4 (2t)^5} - \cdots \right.$$

$$\left. + (-1)^n \frac{1 \cdot 3 \cdot 5 \cdot \cdots (4n - 3)}{\omega^{2n-2} (2t)^{2n-1}} \right]$$

$$+ (-1)^n \int_{C_2} \epsilon^{st} \sqrt{\frac{C}{R}} \frac{V_0 s^{2n+\frac{1}{2}}}{\omega^{2n+1}(s^2 + \omega^2)}\, ds \quad (104)$$

By methods entirely similar to those used in Example 1, it may be shown that the remainder integral becomes negligible in the neighborhood of the minimum term of the asymptotic expansion. Therefore, substituting Eq. (104) into Eq. (101), we have for large[18] values of t

$$i(0,t) \sim V_0 \sqrt{\frac{\omega C}{R}} \sin\left(\omega t + \frac{\pi}{4}\right)$$

$$+ \frac{V_0}{\omega} \sqrt{\frac{C}{R}} \frac{1}{\sqrt{\pi t}} \left[-\frac{1}{2t} + \frac{1 \cdot 3 \cdot 5}{\omega^2 (2t)^3} - \frac{1 \cdot 3 \cdot 5 \cdot 7 \cdot 9}{\omega^4 (2t)^5} + \cdots \right] \quad (105)$$

We note that here, just as in the case of ordinary lumped-impedance phenomena, the poles of the voltage function give rise to a steady-state term.

3. As the next example we shall obtain a series solution for the problem already solved in finite form in §10-5, where it was solved with the aid of the table of Laplace transforms. This is the problem of the propagation of voltage along a leakage-free, noninductive cable, when a unit step of voltage is applied at the input. Accord-

[18] I e., values for which the remainder integral is negligible.

ingly, we can start with Eq. (115) of Chap. 10, namely

$$\bar{E}(x,s) = \frac{\epsilon^{-x\sqrt{RCs}}}{s} \tag{106}$$

Then

$$e(x,t) = \frac{1}{2\pi j}\int_{C_1} \frac{\epsilon^{st}\epsilon^{-x\sqrt{RCs}}}{s}\,ds \tag{107}$$

The integrand of Eq. (107) has a pole and a branch point at $s = 0$, but otherwise has no singularities. We can therefore get a complete solution by integrating along C_2. The series expansion in this case is obtained by expanding

$$\epsilon^{-x\sqrt{RCs}}$$

in a Taylor series in $x\sqrt{RCs}$ in accordance with the well-known form. Thus

$$\begin{aligned} e(x,t) &= \frac{1}{2\pi j}\int_{C_1} \frac{\epsilon^{st}\epsilon^{-x\sqrt{RCs}}}{s}\,ds = \frac{1}{2\pi j}\int_{C_2} \frac{\epsilon^{st}\epsilon^{-x\sqrt{RCs}}}{s}\,ds \\ &= \frac{1}{2\pi j}\int_{C_2} \frac{\epsilon^{st}}{s}\left[1 - x\sqrt{RCs} + \frac{x^2RCs}{2!} - \cdots \right. \\ &\qquad \left. + \frac{(-x\sqrt{RCs})^{2n-1}}{(2n-1)!} + \frac{(-x\sqrt{RCs})^{2n}\epsilon^{-x\sqrt{RC\theta s}}}{(2n)!}\right] ds \end{aligned} \tag{108}$$

where the last term inside the brackets in Eq. (108) is the Taylor remainder and $0 \le \theta \le 1$.

The expansion of $\epsilon^{-x\sqrt{RCs}}$ about the branch point at $s = 0$ in the form shown in Eq. (108) can be justified by the analytical extension theorem. We note that the expansion is valid if s is real and positive. It is therefore also valid for any other contour into which the positive real axis can be deformed without crossing a singular point or branch cut, in particular for the contour C_2.

If we now apply Eqs. (74) and (81) to Eq. (108), we obtain

$$\begin{aligned} e(x,t) &= 1 + \frac{1}{\sqrt{\pi t}}\left\{-(x^2RC)^{\frac{1}{2}} + \frac{(x^2RC)^{\frac{3}{2}}}{3!2t} - \frac{1\cdot 3(x^2RC)^{\frac{5}{2}}}{5!(2t)^2}\right. \\ &\qquad \left. + \cdots + (-1)^n \frac{1\cdot 3\cdot 5\cdot \cdots (2n-3)(x^2RC)^{n-\frac{1}{2}}}{(2n-1)!(2t)^{n-1}}\right\} \\ &\qquad + \frac{1}{2\pi j}\int_{C_2} \frac{\epsilon^{st}(-x\sqrt{RCs})^{2n}\epsilon^{-x\sqrt{RC\theta s}}}{s(2n)!}\,ds \end{aligned} \tag{109}$$

Let us next examine the behavior of the remainder integral. Thus

$$\left|\frac{1}{2\pi j}\int_{C_2}\frac{\epsilon^{st}(-x\sqrt{RCs})^{2n}\epsilon^{-x\sqrt{RC\theta s}}}{s(2n)!}\,ds\right|$$
$$\leq\left|\frac{x^{2n}(RC)^n}{2\pi(2n)!}\right|\left\{\left|\int_{\infty}^{0}\epsilon^{-ut}u^{n-1}\,du\right|+\left|\int_{-\pi}^{+\pi}r^n\epsilon^{jn\phi}\,d\phi\right|\right.$$
$$\left.+\left|\int_0^\infty\epsilon^{-ut}u^{n-1}\,du\right|\right\} \quad (110)$$

The value of the integral around the infinitesimal circle vanishes because of the infinitesimal value of r. Furthermore, the absolute values of the first and third terms inside the braces are equal. Therefore

$$\text{remainder integral} \leq \frac{2\cdot x^{2n}(RC)^n}{2\pi(2n)!}\int_0^\infty \epsilon^{-ut}u^{n-1}\,du$$
$$=\frac{n!x^{2n}(RC)^n}{\pi(2n)!t^n} \quad (111)$$

We shall show in a moment that the series in Eq. (109) is absolutely convergent. It is therefore of interest to examine the value of the remainder integral when $n\to\infty$. Accordingly, we note that

$$\lim_{n\to\infty}\left\{\frac{n!x^{2n}(RC)^n}{\pi(2n)!t^n}\right\}=0 \quad (112)$$

Therefore, when $n\to\infty$, the remainder integral vanishes for all values of t after $t=0$. Thus, if we let $\alpha = x^2RC$, Eq. (109) becomes

$$e(x,t) = 1-\sqrt{\frac{\alpha}{\pi t}}\left\{1-\frac{\alpha}{3!2t}+\frac{1\cdot 3\alpha^2}{5!(2t)^2}-\cdots\right.$$
$$\left.+\frac{1\cdot 3\cdot\cdots(2n-1)\alpha^n}{(2n+1)!(2t)^n}+\cdots\right\}$$
$$=1-\sqrt{\frac{\alpha}{\pi t}}\left\{1-\frac{1}{3}\left(\frac{\alpha}{4t}\right)+\frac{1}{5\cdot 2!}\left(\frac{\alpha}{4t}\right)^2-\frac{1}{7\cdot 3!}\left(\frac{\alpha}{4t}\right)^3\right.$$
$$\left.+\cdots+\frac{1}{(2n+1)n!}\left(\frac{\alpha}{4t}\right)^n-\cdots\right\} \quad (113)$$

In this last form it is clear that an application of Cauchy's ratio test[19] will show that the series is absolutely convergent for all values of $(\alpha/4t)$. We thus see that it is possible for the inverse power series to be convergent.

The student can also show that Eq. (113) agrees with the solution obtained as Eq. (119) in Chap. 10, by integrating the latter in series.

4. As the next example, let us consider the current which enters a leakage-free cable when a unit step of voltage is applied. In this case

$$G = 0 \tag{114}$$

and

$$\bar{E}(0,s) = \frac{1}{s} \tag{115}$$

so that Eq. (31) of Chap. 10 reduces to

$$\bar{I}(0,s) = \frac{1}{s}\sqrt{\frac{Cs}{Ls + R}} = \sqrt{\frac{C}{s(Ls + R)}} \tag{116}$$

Therefore,

$$i(0,t) = \frac{1}{2\pi j}\int_{C_1} \epsilon^{st}\sqrt{\frac{C}{s(Ls + R)}}\,ds \tag{117}$$

The integrand of Eq. (117) has branch points at

$$s = 0 \qquad \text{and} \qquad s = -\frac{R}{L} \tag{118}$$

Since both of these lie within C_2 we can proceed with the asymptotic solution in the regular manner, except to bypass $s = -R/L$ with infinitesimal semicircles as shown in Fig. 11-8. Accordingly, let us expand in a Taylor series as follows:

$$\begin{aligned}\sqrt{\frac{C}{s(Ls + R)}} &= \sqrt{\frac{C}{L}}\, s^{-\frac{1}{2}} \sqrt{\frac{1}{s + R/L}} \\ &= \sqrt{\frac{C}{L}}\, s^{-\frac{1}{2}} \left[\frac{1}{(R/L)^{\frac{1}{2}}} - \frac{s}{2(R/L)^{\frac{3}{2}}} + \frac{1 \cdot 3s^2}{2!2^2(R/L)^{\frac{5}{2}}} - \cdots \right. \\ &\quad \left. + \frac{(-1)^n 1 \cdot 3 \cdot 5 \cdots (2n - 1)}{n!2^n(R/L)^{n+\frac{1}{2}}}\, s^n + R_n\right]\end{aligned} \tag{119}$$

[19] See Wilson, *Advanced Calculus*, p. 422.

in which the Taylor remainder is

$$R_n = \frac{(-1)^{n+1} 1 \cdot 3 \cdot 5 \cdots (2n+1)}{(n+1)!2^{n+1}(R/L + \theta s)^{n+\frac{3}{2}}} s^{n+1} \tag{120}$$

where θ is a quantity between zero and one.

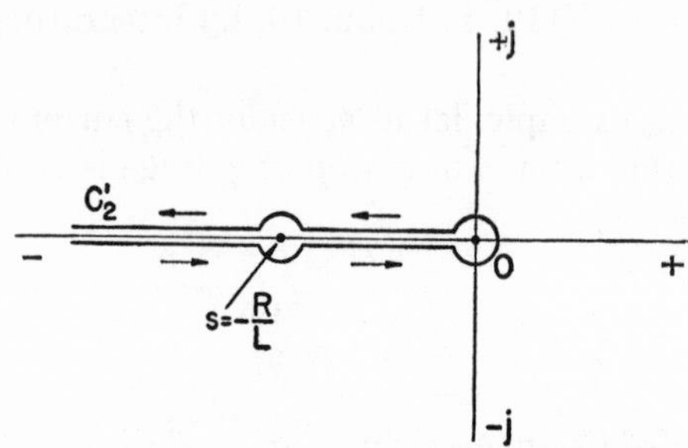

FIG. 11-8. The integration contour C_2', which can be used when $F(s)$ has a branch point at the origin and another singular point at $s = -R/L$ on the negative side of the real axis.

Substituting Eq. (119) into Eq. (117) and integrating along C_2', we obtain, according to Eqs. (74) and (81),

$$i(0,t) = \left(\sqrt{\frac{C}{L}}\right) \frac{1}{\sqrt{\pi t}} \frac{1}{\sqrt{R/L}} \left\{1 + \frac{1}{4Rt/L} + \frac{(1 \cdot 3)^2}{2!(4Rt/L)^2} + \cdots \right.$$

$$\left. + \frac{[1 \cdot 3 \cdot 5 \cdots (2n-1)]^2}{n!(4Rt/L)^n}\right\}$$

$$+ \frac{\sqrt{C/L}}{2\pi j} \int_{C'_2} \frac{\epsilon^{st}(-1)^{n+1} 1 \cdot 3 \cdot 5 \cdots (2n+1) s^{n+1}}{(n+1)!2^{n+1}\left(\frac{R}{L} + \theta s\right)^{n+\frac{3}{2}} s^{\frac{1}{2}}} ds \tag{121}$$

Our next step should properly be to show that the remainder integral is negligible in the neighborhood of the minimum of the asymptotic series. The process of doing so is similar to that used in Examples 1 and 2, and we shall therefore leave the details to the reader. We shall also leave to the reader the demonstration that the integral in Eq. (117) along the infinitesimal semicircles which bypass $s = -\dfrac{R}{L}$ in Fig. 11-8 will vanish.

It follows from the preceding discussion and Eq. (121) that for large values of t we can express $i(0,t)$ as the asymptotic expansion

$$i(0,t) \sim \sqrt{\frac{C}{R}}\sqrt{\frac{1}{\pi t}}\left\{1 + \frac{1}{4Rt/L} + \frac{(1\cdot 3)^2}{2!(4Rt/L)^2} + \cdots + \frac{[1\cdot 3\cdot 5 \cdots (2n-1)]^2}{n!(4Rt/L)^n} + \cdots\right\} \tag{122}$$

Comparing Eq. (122) with Eq. (36), we see that, at least for large values of t,

$$i(0,t) \sim \sqrt{\frac{C}{L}}\,\epsilon^{-Rt/2L} I_0\left(\frac{Rt}{2L}\right) \tag{123}$$

where I_0 is the modified Bessel function of the first kind of zero order. When, as in this case, the asymptotic expansion can be recognized as a function whose properties are known, the solution becomes much more useful for practical purposes.

11.9. Power-series solution in ascending half-integral powers of t

In the foregoing sections, we have found series in descending half-integral powers of t to be especially useful in solutions for large values of t. It is therefore of interest to see whether series in half-integral ascending powers of t are correspondingly useful for small values of t. Consider, for instance, Example 2 of §11.8. There the problem was to find the inverse transform of

$$I(0,s) = \sqrt{\frac{Cs}{R}}\frac{\omega V_0}{s^2+\omega^2} \tag{124}$$

In order to find $i(0,t)$ in a series of ascending half-integral powers of t, we therefore follow the experience of §11.2 and expand as follows:

$$\begin{aligned} I(0,s) &= \sqrt{\frac{Cs}{R}}\frac{\omega V_0}{s^2+\omega^2} = \sqrt{\frac{Cs}{R}}\frac{\omega V_0}{s^2}\left\{1 - \frac{\omega^2}{s^2} + \frac{\omega^4}{s^4} - \frac{\omega^6}{s^6} + \cdots\right\} \\ &= \omega V_0\sqrt{\frac{C}{R}}\left\{\frac{1}{s^{\frac{3}{2}}} - \frac{\omega^2}{s^{\frac{7}{2}}} + \frac{\omega^4}{s^{\frac{11}{2}}} - \frac{\omega^6}{s^{\frac{15}{2}}} + \cdots\right\} \end{aligned} \tag{125}$$

The series in the braces is absolutely convergent for values of s greater than ω. It can therefore be integrated[20] along C_1 and

[20] If C_1 is made to pass to the right of $s = \omega$.

transformed by the standard Laplace transformation formula

$$\mathfrak{L}^{-1}\left(\frac{1}{s^n}\right) = \frac{t^{n-1}}{\Gamma(n)} \tag{126}$$

Substituting Eq. (126) into Eq. (125) we then obtain

$$\begin{aligned} i(0,t) &= \omega V_0 \sqrt{\frac{C}{R}} \left\{ \frac{t^{\frac{1}{2}}}{\Gamma(\frac{3}{2})} - \frac{\omega^2 t^{\frac{5}{2}}}{\Gamma(\frac{7}{2})} + \frac{\omega^4 t^{\frac{9}{2}}}{\Gamma(\frac{11}{2})} - \cdots \right\} \\ &= 2\omega V_0 \sqrt{\frac{Ct}{\pi R}} \left\{ 1 - \frac{(2\omega t)^2}{1 \cdot 3 \cdot 5} + \frac{(2\omega t)^4}{1 \cdot 3 \cdot 5 \cdot 7 \cdot 9} - \cdots \right\} \end{aligned} \tag{127}$$

The series in Eq. (127) is absolutely convergent, which fact in conjunction with the convergence of Eq. (125) along C_1, makes Eq. (127) a true solution for $i(0,t)$ for all values of t. For small values of t, the series in Eq. (127) is useful for calculation, but for large values of t the asymptotic series is far better. As might be expected, the asymptotic solution separates the transient and steady-state terms, which the ascending power series fails to do.

It is worthy of mention that we cannot obtain a solution in positive whole-integral powers of t in this case, because of the branch point of $\bar{I}(0,s)$ at $s = 0$.

11.10. General

The foregoing account of asymptotic series solutions for $f(t)$ could be greatly extended. Solutions in series of Bessel functions have been treated by Fry,[21] and a variety of other types of solutions are treated by Doetsch.[22] It is fair to say, however, that the foregoing account of asymptotic series solutions is adequate for the present needs of a radio engineer.

---

[21] T. C. Fry, "The Solution of Circuit Problems," *Phys. Rev.*, August 1919, p. 115.

[22] G. Doetsch, *Laplace-Transformation* (1937).

CHAPTER 12

Some Additional Applications to Electrical Engineering

12.1. Introduction

In the foregoing chapters, we have developed the powerful methods of transformation calculus, and we have used them to solve a number of engineering problems. We shall now illustrate their use in some additional practical applications. It is important for the engineer to learn what types of problems can be handled, and what the limitations are to the practical use of mathematics. As far as the present chapter is concerned, we shall treat only a few of the problems which cannot be handled by ordinary steady-state theory, and which therefore appear appropriate for the application of transformation calculus.

12.2. Differentiating and integrating circuits

(a) General. Many modern systems of radio communication, particularly television, use pulses for purposes of synchronization and control.

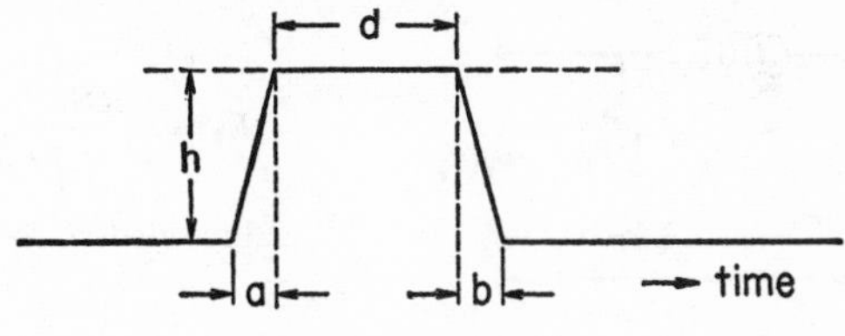

FIG. 12-1. A pulse.

An example of a pulse is shown in Fig. 12-1. Generally speaking, the important characteristics of a pulse are its length and height, and the location and rate of rise or fall of its edges. Consequently, there has been considerable activity in the development of.circuits which will make the best use of these pulse characteristics.

Quite frequently, the characteristics of a pulse can be accentuated and put into sharp relief by what are known as *differentiating*

$E_1(s) = \mathcal{L}[e_1(t)]$ $E_2(s) = \mathcal{L}[e_2(t)]$

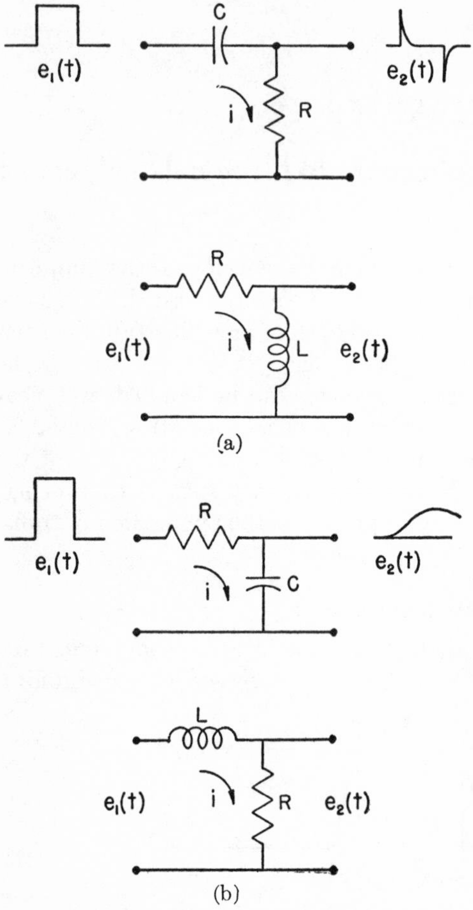

$$E_2 = \frac{RE_1}{R + \frac{1}{sC}} = sCRE_1 \quad \text{(approx.)}$$

provided $sCR \ll 1$, which means i.e. $\begin{bmatrix}\text{average voltage}\\\text{drop across } R\end{bmatrix} \ll \begin{bmatrix}\text{average voltage}\\\text{drop across } C\end{bmatrix}$

$$E_2 = \frac{sLE_1}{R + sL} = \frac{sL}{R} E_1 \quad \text{(approx.)}$$

provided $sL \ll R$

(a)

$$E_2 = \frac{\frac{E_1}{sC}}{R + \frac{1}{sC}} = \frac{E_1}{1 + sCR} = \frac{E_1}{sCR} \quad \text{(approx.)}$$

provided $sCR \gg 1$

$$E_2 = \frac{RE_1}{R + sL} = \frac{R}{sL} E_1 \quad \text{(approx.)}$$

provided $sL \gg R$

(b)

FIG. 12-2. (a) Differentiating circuits. These accentuate high-frequency components of signal. (b) Integrating circuits. These accentuate low-frequency components of signal. (Note that inequalities show that average output is much less than input for clean differentiation or integration.)

circuits and *integrating circuits*, simple forms of which are shown in Fig. 12-2. The operating characteristics of these circuits are also clearly shown by the formulas in the same figure. In Fig. 12-3 are shown the results of passing pulses through severe differentiating and integrating circuits. We see that differentiating circuits are useful in locating the edges of pulses and determining the rate of rise, while integrating circuits can be used to determine pulse lengths. When used in combination with limiters, differentiating and integrating circuits can be used for pulse shaping. This subject is discussed at length in television literature.

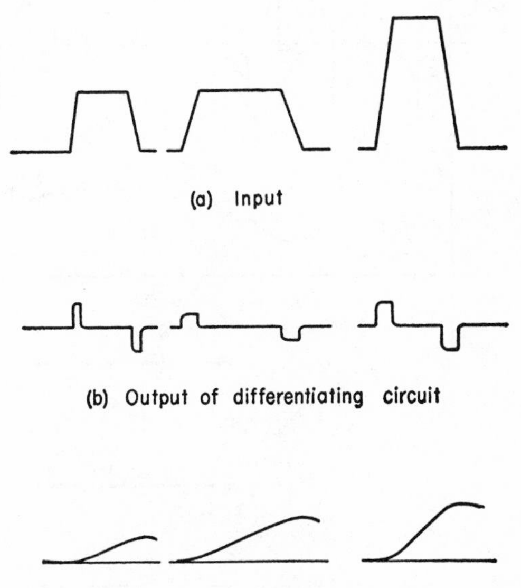

Fig. 12-3. Effect of differentiating and of integrating circuits on pulse signals.

(b) Complete Calculation for Repeated Pulses.[1] The analytical forms of the output signals of differentiating and integrating circuits can readily be determined by means of transformation calculus. Let us consider, for example, the special case of frequent interest in which the input pulses are rectangular and of identical shape and are repeated at regular intervals. Such a train of pulses is

---

[1] See also C. W. Carnahan, *Proc. I. R. E.*, Vol. 23, p. 1393 (Nov. 1935).

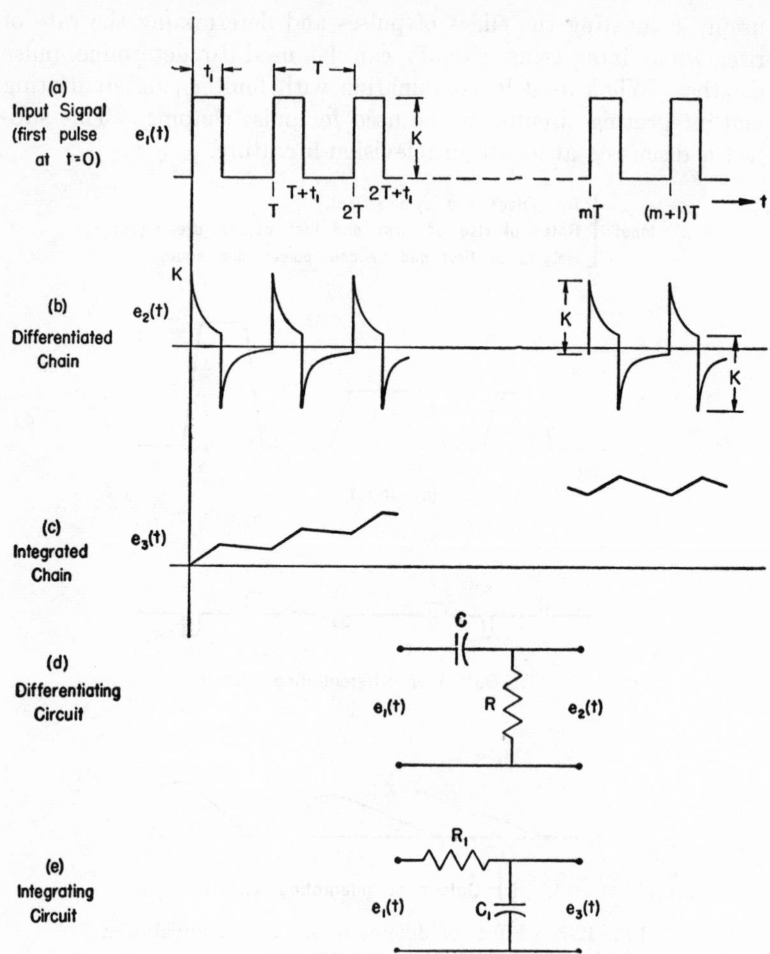

Fig. 12-4. Effect of differentiating and of integrating circuits on a chain of repeated pulses.

shown in Fig. 12-4(a). Here t is the independent variable, t_1 is the pulse length and T is the period of repetition. Then the input pulse may be written as

$$e_1(t) = K\{U(t) - U(t - t_1) + U(t - T) - U(t - T - t_1) + U(t - 2T) - U(t - 2T - t_1) + \cdots\} \quad (1)$$

Consequently, its Laplace transform is

$$E_1(s) = K\left\{\frac{1}{s} - \frac{\epsilon^{-t_1 s}}{s} + \frac{\epsilon^{-Ts}}{s} - \frac{\epsilon^{-(T+t_1)s}}{s} + \frac{\epsilon^{-2Ts}}{s} - \frac{\epsilon^{-(2T+t_1)s}}{s} + \cdots\right\} \quad (2)$$

Now the transformed output of the differentiating circuit in Fig. 12-4(d) is (without any approximation)

$$\begin{aligned} E_2(s) &= \frac{RE_1(s)}{R + \frac{1}{sC}} = \frac{sE_1(s)}{s + \frac{1}{CR}} \\ &= \frac{K}{s + \frac{1}{CR}}\{1 - \epsilon^{-t_1 s} + \epsilon^{-Ts} - \epsilon^{-(T+t_1)s} + \epsilon^{-2Ts} \\ &\qquad - \epsilon^{-(2T+t_1)s} + \cdots\} \end{aligned} \quad (3)$$

The output signal is then the inverse transform of Eq. (3), which is

$$\begin{aligned} e_2(t) &= K\{\epsilon^{-\frac{t}{CR}} - \epsilon^{-\frac{t-t_1}{CR}} + \epsilon^{-\frac{t-T}{CR}} - \epsilon^{-\frac{t-T-t_1}{CR}} \\ &\qquad + \epsilon^{-\frac{t-2T}{CR}} - \epsilon^{-\frac{t-2T-t_1}{CR}} + \cdots\} \\ &= K\epsilon^{-\frac{t}{CR}}\{[1 + \epsilon^{\frac{T}{CR}} + \epsilon^{\frac{2T}{CR}} + \cdots] \\ &\qquad - \epsilon^{\frac{t_1}{CR}}[1 + \epsilon^{\frac{T}{CR}} + \epsilon^{\frac{2T}{CR}} + \cdots]\} \end{aligned} \quad (4)$$

The two series inside brackets in Eq. (4) are not infinite but rather have only a finite number of terms. For example, in the interval

$$mT \leq t \leq mT + t_1 \quad (5)$$

during which time the pulse is on, the first series is

$$1 + \epsilon^{\frac{T}{CR}} + \epsilon^{\frac{2T}{CR}} + \cdots + \epsilon^{\frac{mT}{CR}} \quad (6)$$

and the second series is

$$1 + \epsilon^{\frac{T}{CR}} + \epsilon^{\frac{2T}{CR}} + \cdots + \epsilon^{\frac{(m-1)T}{CR}} \quad (7)$$

On the other hand, in the interval

$$mT + t_1 < t < (m+1)T \tag{8}$$

during which time the pulse is off, the first series is unchanged, but the second series adds another term, thus making it identical with the first series.

Let us now determine the response in the steady state; i.e., when m is very large. While the pulse is on, Eq. (4) becomes, as a consequence[2] of Eqs. (6) and (7),

$$
\begin{aligned}
e_2(t) &= K\epsilon^{-\frac{t}{CR}} \Big\{\Big[1 + \epsilon^{\frac{T}{CR}} + \epsilon^{\frac{2T}{CR}} + \cdots + \epsilon^{\frac{mT}{CR}}\Big] \\
&\qquad\qquad - \epsilon^{\frac{t_1}{CR}} \Big[1 + \epsilon^{\frac{T}{CR}} + \cdots + \epsilon^{\frac{(m-1)T}{CR}}\Big]\Big\} \\
&= K\epsilon^{-t/CR} \left\{\left[\frac{\epsilon^{\frac{(m+1)T}{CR}} - 1}{\epsilon^{T/CR} - 1}\right] - \epsilon^{t_1/CR} \left[\frac{\epsilon^{\frac{mT}{CR}} - 1}{\epsilon^{T/CR} - 1}\right]\right\} \\
&= \frac{K\epsilon^{-t/CR}}{\epsilon^{T/CR} - 1} \Big\{\Big[\epsilon^{\frac{(m+1)T}{CR}} - 1\Big] - \epsilon^{\frac{t_1}{CR}} \Big[\epsilon^{\frac{mT}{CR}} - 1\Big]\Big\}
\end{aligned} \tag{9}
$$

In the steady state, as we have said, m is very large, and furthermore $T \gg CR$ for a differentiating circuit, so that

$$\epsilon^{\frac{(m+1)T}{CR}} \qquad \text{and} \qquad \epsilon^{\frac{mT}{CR}}$$

are very much greater than one. Therefore, in the steady state, Eq. (9) reduces to

$$
\begin{aligned}
e_2(t) &= \frac{K\epsilon^{-\left(\frac{t-mT}{CR}\right)}}{\epsilon^{T/CR} - 1} \{\epsilon^{T/CR} - \epsilon^{t_1/CR}\} \\
&= K\epsilon^{-\left(\frac{t-mT}{CR}\right)} \left\{\frac{1 - \epsilon^{-\left(\frac{T-t_1}{CR}\right)}}{1 - \epsilon^{-T/CR}}\right\}
\end{aligned} \tag{10}
$$

In a similar manner, we find that, in the steady state during the intervals when the pulse is off,

---

[2] Here we have made use of the formula

$$1 + x + x^2 + \cdots + x^n = \frac{x^{n+1} - 1}{x - 1}$$

$$e_2(t) = -K\epsilon^{-\left(\frac{t-mT-t_1}{CR}\right)}\left\{\frac{1 - \epsilon^{-t_1/CR}}{1 - \epsilon^{-T/CR}}\right\} \tag{11}$$

Equations (10) and (11) are shown graphically in their proper places in Fig. 12-4(b).

Let us next find the result of sending the pulses through the integrating circuit in Fig. 12-4(e). Calling the output $e_3(t)$ and its transform $E_3(s)$, we have

$$E_3(s) = \frac{E_1/sC_1}{R_1 + \frac{1}{sC_1}} = \frac{E_1/R_1C_1}{s + \frac{1}{R_1C_1}}$$

$$= \frac{K}{sR_1C_1\left(s + \frac{1}{R_1C_1}\right)}\{1 - \epsilon^{-t_1s} + \epsilon^{-Ts} - \epsilon^{-(T+t_1)s} + \cdots\} \tag{12}$$

Therefore,

$$e_3(t) = \frac{K}{R_1C_1}(-R_1C_1)\{(\epsilon^{-\frac{t}{R_1C_1}} - 1) - (\epsilon^{-\frac{t-t_1}{R_1C_1}} - 1) + (\epsilon^{-\frac{t-T}{R_1C_1}} - 1) - \cdots\}$$

$$= -K\epsilon^{-t/R_1C_1}\left\{\left[\frac{\epsilon^{\frac{(m+1)T}{R_1C_1}} - 1}{\epsilon^{T/R_1C_1} - 1}\right] - \epsilon^{t_1/R_1C_1}\left[\frac{\epsilon^{\frac{mT}{R_1C_1}} - 1}{\epsilon^{T/R_1C_1} - 1}\right]\right\} + K \tag{13}$$

during pulses, and

$$= -K\epsilon^{-t/R_1C_1}\left\{\left[\frac{\epsilon^{\frac{(m+1)T}{R_1C_1}} - 1}{\epsilon^{T/R_1C_1} - 1}\right] - \epsilon^{t_1/R_1C_1}\left[\frac{\epsilon^{\frac{(m+1)T}{R_1C_1}} - 1}{\epsilon^{T/R_1C_1} - 1}\right]\right\} \tag{14}$$

between pulses, using the same methods as in the differentiating circuit case. When m is so large that $mT \gg R_1C_1$, these reduce to

$$e_3(t) = K\left\{1 - \epsilon^{-\left(\frac{t-mT}{C_1R_1}\right)}\left[\frac{1 - \epsilon^{-\left(\frac{T-t_1}{C_1R_1}\right)}}{1 - \epsilon^{-T/C_1R_1}}\right]\right\} \tag{15}$$

during pulses, and between pulses

$$e_3(t) = K\epsilon^{-\left(\frac{t-mT-t_1}{C_1R_1}\right)}\left[\frac{1 - \epsilon^{-t_1/C_1R_1}}{1 - \epsilon^{-T/C_1R_1}}\right] \tag{16}$$

Equations (15) and (16) are shown graphically in Fig. 12-4(c). In comparing Eqs. (15) and (16) with (10) and (11), it should be remembered that the time constant R_1C_1 of the integrating circuit is much longer than the time constant RC of the differentiating circuit.

Exercises

1. (*Differentiating Circuits*). Using Eqs. (10) and (11),

(a) Show that the positive peaks of $e_2(t)$ in Fig. 12-4(b) for large values of m are

$$K\left\{\frac{1-\epsilon^{-(T-t_1)/CR}}{1-\epsilon^{-T/CR}}\right\}$$

(b) Show that the negative peaks of $e_2(t)$ in Fig. 12-4(b) for large values of m are

$$K\left\{\frac{1-\epsilon^{-t_1/CR}}{1-\epsilon^{-T/CR}}\right\}$$

(c) Show that the magnitude of the discontinuous jump in $e_2(t)$ at the beginning and at the end of the pulse is exactly K.

2. (*Integrating Circuits*)

(a) Using Eqs. (13) and (14), show that during the early pulses (when $mT \ll R_1C_1$),

$$e_3(t) = \frac{K(m+1)t_1}{R_1C_1} \text{ (approximately)}$$

between pulses, and

$$e_3(t) = \frac{K}{R_1C_1}[t - m(T - t_1)] \text{ (approximately)}$$

during pulses.

(b) Using Eqs. (15) and (16), show that for large values of m (when $mT \gg R_1C_1$ while $R_1C_1 \gg T$)

$$e_3(t) = K\frac{t_1}{T}\left[1 - \left(\frac{t - mT - t_1}{R_1C_1}\right)\right] \text{ (approximately)}$$

between pulses, and

$$e_3(t) = K\frac{t_1}{T} + K\left(\frac{t - mT}{C_1R_1}\right)\left(1 - \frac{t_1}{T}\right) \text{ (approximately)}$$

during pulses.

(In making the approximations in Exercise 2, care must be taken to use the proper number of terms to fit the case in the series expansions of the exponentials.)

12.3. Compensated amplifiers for increased pass band

Another interesting application for transformation calculus is in the study of compensated amplifiers for increased bandwidth and improved television pictures. As an example, let us consider the simplified circuit of a single stage of a resistance-coupled amplifier [shown in Fig. 12-5(a)]. In this circuit, r is the plate

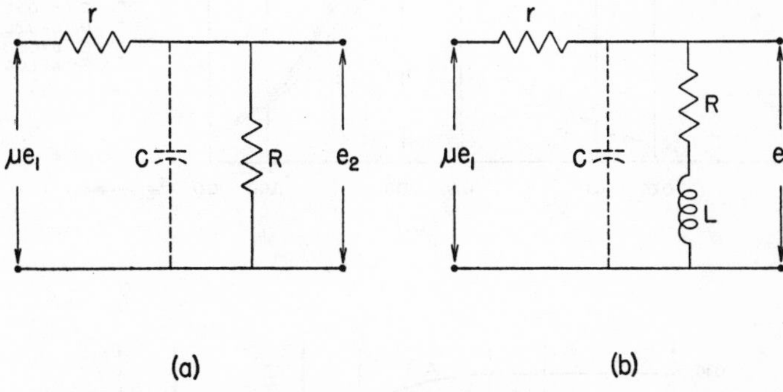

FIG. 12-5. (a) Simplified schematic diagram of a resistance-coupled video amplifier stage. (b) Same as (a) but with inductance compensation to improve the high-frequency response.

resistance of the tube; R is the load resistance; C is the equivalent effect of the tube and stray circuit capacitances; e_1 is the input voltage to the stage; μ is the amplification factor of the tube; and e_2 is the input voltage to the next stage. Now the effect of C will be to cause a loss of high-frequency components. This is shown in the A curves of Fig. 12-6, which shows the steady-state frequency characteristic of the stage. The result of such a loss of high frequencies, as is well known, will be to cause a deterioration of fine signal detail; and it should therefore be compensated.

One of the simplest and most commonly used methods of compensation is shown in Fig. 12-5(b). Here an inductance is inserted in series with the load resistance. The effect of the inductance is to increase the high-frequency response, and the effect of various values

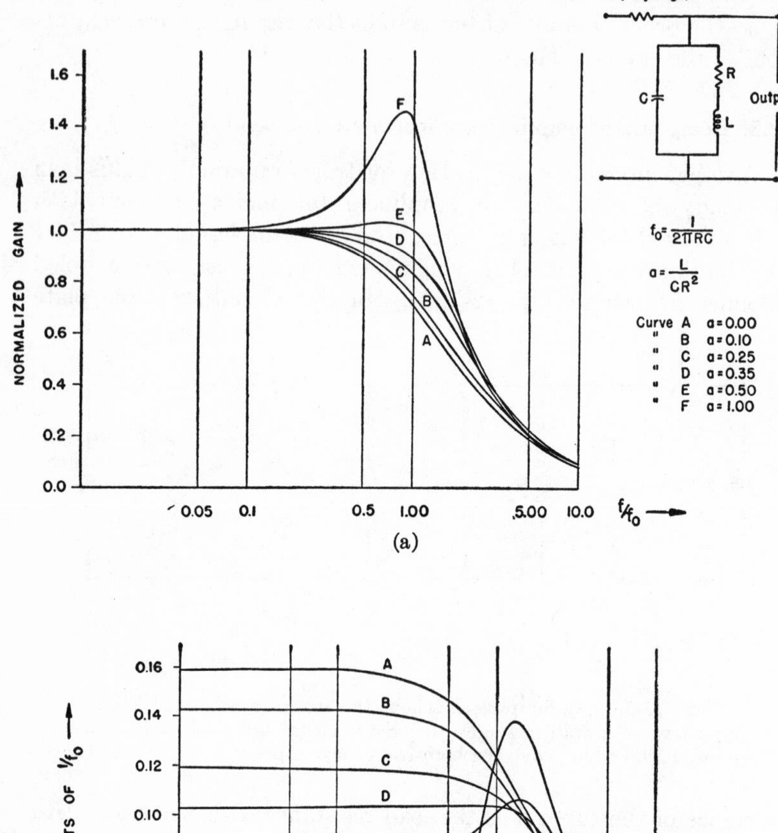

(a)

(b)

Fig. 12-6. Effect of compensating inductance on the steady-state frequency characteristics of a stage. (a) Gain versus frequency. (b) Time delay versus frequency.

of inductance on the steady-state response characteristic is shown[3] in Fig. 12-6. We now wish to determine the value of inductance which should be used for best picture quality.

In the author's *Frequency Analysis, Modulation and Noise*, it is pointed out that the two characteristics which are most important in determining the effect of a transmission system on picture quality are: (1) the reproduction of sharp edges; and (2) the reproduction of fine detail. To find the first of these characteristics we calculate the output when a unit step [shown in Fig. 12-7(a)] is sent into the

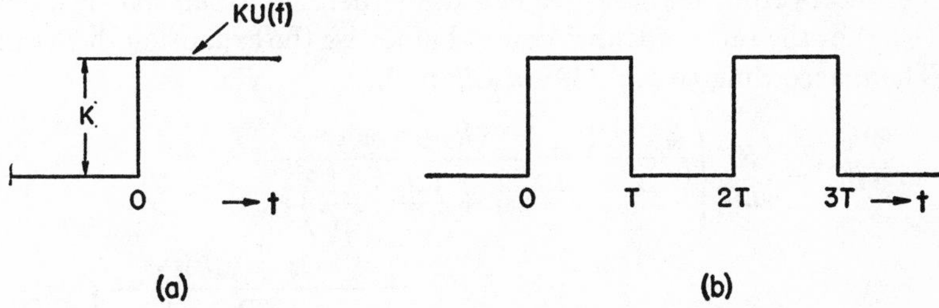

FIG. 12-7. Test input signals.

system; and to find the second, we calculate the output when a pair of rectangular pulses [as shown in Fig. 12-7(b)] is sent into the system. This we shall now proceed to do for the circuit of Fig. 12-5(b).

If in the circuit of Fig. 12-5(b)

$$\mu e_1 = KU(t) \tag{17}$$

then the Laplace transform of the input voltage is

$$\mu E_1(s) = \frac{K}{s} \tag{17A}$$

The impedance function of the parallel L-R-C circuit in Fig. 12-5(b), as we have found on previous occasions, is

$$\frac{R + sL}{s^2LC + sRC + 1} \tag{18}$$

[3] The author is indebted to Mr. R. W. Tuttle for Fig. 12-6.

Therefore the Laplace transform of the output voltage is

$$E_2 = \frac{K}{s}\left\{\frac{\dfrac{R+sL}{s^2LC+sRC+1}}{r+\dfrac{R+sL}{s^2LC+sRC+1}}\right\}$$

$$= \frac{K}{srLC}\left\{\frac{R+sL}{s^2+s\left(\dfrac{R}{L}+\dfrac{1}{rC}\right)+\left(\dfrac{r+R}{rLC}\right)}\right\} \tag{19}$$

To find e_2 from Eq. (19) we can use either the expansion theorem (§3.8) or the table of transforms. Let us use the expansion theorem. Then, according to Eq. (59) of Chap. 3,

$$e_2(t) = \frac{K}{rLC}\left\{\frac{R(rLC)}{(r+R)} + \frac{(R+s_1L)\epsilon^{s_1t}}{2s_1^2+\left(\dfrac{R}{L}+\dfrac{1}{rC}\right)s_1} + \frac{(R+s_2L)\epsilon^{s_2t}}{2s_2^2+\left(\dfrac{R}{L}+\dfrac{1}{rC}\right)s_2}\right\} \tag{20}$$

where

$$s_1 = -\frac{1}{2}\left(\frac{R}{L}+\frac{1}{rC}\right)+\sqrt{\frac{1}{4}\left(\frac{R^2}{L^2}+\frac{1}{r^2C^2}\right)-\frac{1}{LC}\left(1+\frac{R}{2r}\right)} \tag{21}$$

and

$$s_2 = -\frac{1}{2}\left(\frac{R}{L}+\frac{1}{rC}\right)-\sqrt{\frac{1}{4}\left(\frac{R^2}{L^2}+\frac{1}{r^2C^2}\right)-\frac{1}{LC}\left(1+\frac{R}{2r}\right)} \tag{22}$$

In most practical cases, r is sufficiently large, so that $1/rC$ and $R/2r$ can be neglected in the above equations. Therefore, Eq. (20) becomes

$$e_2(t) = \frac{KR}{r} + \frac{K}{rLC}\left\{\frac{\left[\dfrac{R}{2}+L\sqrt{\dfrac{R^2}{4L^2}-\dfrac{1}{LC}}\right]\epsilon^{\left(\frac{-R}{2L}+\sqrt{\frac{R^2}{4L^2}-\frac{1}{LC}}\right)t}}{\dfrac{R^2}{2L^2}-\dfrac{2}{LC}-\dfrac{R}{L}\sqrt{\dfrac{R^2}{4L^2}-\dfrac{1}{LC}}} + \frac{\left[\dfrac{R}{2}-L\sqrt{\dfrac{R^2}{4L^2}-\dfrac{1}{LC}}\right]\epsilon^{\left(-\frac{R}{2L}-\sqrt{\frac{R^2}{4L^2}-\frac{1}{LC}}\right)t}}{\dfrac{R^2}{2L^2}-\dfrac{2}{LC}+\dfrac{R}{L}\sqrt{\dfrac{R^2}{4L^2}-\dfrac{1}{LC}}}\right\} \tag{23}$$

In case
$$\frac{1}{LC} > \frac{R^2}{4L^2} \tag{24}$$

then[4]
$$e_2(t) = \frac{KR}{r}\left\{1 - \epsilon^{\alpha t}\cos\beta t - \frac{\epsilon^{\alpha t}}{2\beta}\left[\frac{R}{L} - \frac{2}{RC}\right]\sin\beta t\right\} \tag{25}$$

where
$$\beta = \sqrt{\frac{1}{LC} - \frac{R^2}{4L^2}} \tag{26}$$

and
$$\alpha = -\frac{R}{2L} \tag{27}$$

In order to reduce the foregoing equations to a universal form, let us make the substitution

$$a = \frac{L}{CR^2} \tag{28}$$

thus defining the circuit parameter a. Then Eq. (25) becomes[5]

$$e_2(t) = \frac{KR}{r}\left[1 - \epsilon^{\alpha t}\cos\beta t + \epsilon^{\alpha t}\left(\frac{2a-1}{\sqrt{4a-1}}\right)\sin\beta t\right] \tag{29}$$

where
$$\beta = \frac{1}{2aCR}\sqrt{4a-1} \tag{30}$$

and
$$\alpha = -\frac{1}{2aCR} \tag{31}$$

---

[4] When $1/LC > R^2/4L^2$, the quantity inside the braces of Eq. (23) is of the form

$$\frac{A}{B}\epsilon^{(\alpha+j\beta)t} + \frac{A^*}{B^*}\epsilon^{(\alpha-j\beta)t} = \epsilon^{\alpha t}\left(\frac{A}{B}\epsilon^{j\beta t} + \frac{A^*}{B^*}\epsilon^{-j\beta t}\right)$$

$$= \epsilon^{\alpha t}\left[\left(\frac{A}{B} + \frac{A^*}{B^*}\right)\cos\beta t + j\left(\frac{A}{B} - \frac{A^*}{B^*}\right)\sin\beta t\right]$$

$$= \frac{\epsilon^{\alpha t}}{B\cdot B^*}\left[(AB^* + A^*B)\cos\beta t + j(AB^* - A^*B)\sin\beta t)\right]$$

With the aid of this formula, Eq. (23) reduces to Eq. (25).

In the literature, the sine and cosine terms of Eq. (25) are combined into a single term in cos $(\beta t + \theta)$, and θ is expressed as a phase angle. This involves θ in an ambiguity of 180°, which can easily give rise to numerical errors in calculations, with much loss of time before the cause of the trouble is found. It is therefore desirable to avoid the use of phase angles wherever such a procedure will lead to ambiguity in calculations.

[5] An equivalent equation has been derived by McLachlan, *Phil. Mag.*, Sept. (1936), p. 481.

At the outset, we stated that the object of this investigation was to determine the optimum value of L. Let us therefore use[6] Eq. (29) and its equivalents and plot the output due to a unit-step

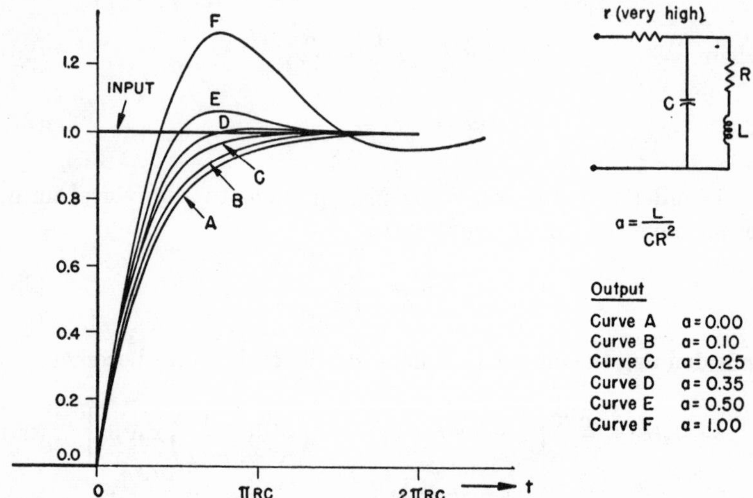

FIG. 12-8. Effect of compensating inductance on the sharpness of edges.

input for various values of a. This is shown in Fig. 12-8. By superposition of the outputs of positive unit steps at $t = 0$ and $t = 2\pi RC$, and negative unit steps at $t = \pi RC$ and $t = 3\pi RC$, we

[6] The reader can show as an exercise that

$$e_2(t) = \frac{KR}{r}\left\{1 + \frac{1 + \sqrt{1 - 4a}}{\frac{1}{a}(1 - \sqrt{1 - 4a}) - 4}\,\epsilon^{-[1-\sqrt{1-4a}]t/2aCR} + \frac{1 - \sqrt{1 - 4a}}{\frac{1}{a}(1 + \sqrt{1 - 4a}) - 4}\,\epsilon^{-[1+\sqrt{1-4a}]t/2aCR]}\right\}$$

when $$\frac{1}{LC} < \frac{R^2}{4L^2}$$

and $$e_2(t) = \frac{KR}{r}\left\{1 - \epsilon^{-t/2aCR} - \frac{t}{4aCR}\,\epsilon^{-t/2aCR}\right\}$$

when $$\frac{1}{LC} = \frac{R^2}{4L^2}$$

have also plotted Fig. 12-9. Thus Fig. 12-8 shows the effect of L on the sharpness of edges while Fig. 12-9 shows its effect on fine detail. The optimum value to be chosen for a depends upon the

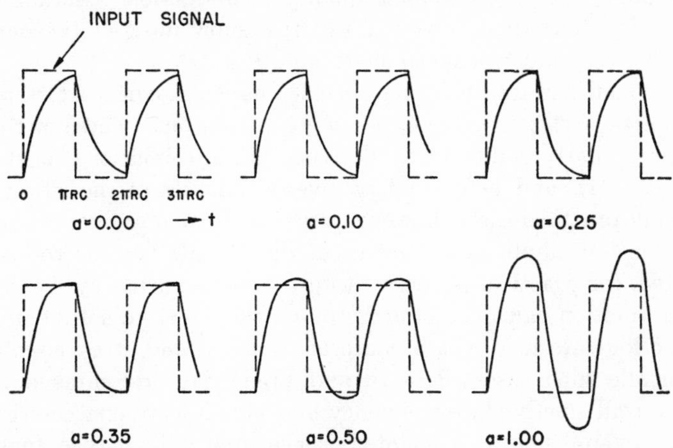

FIG 12-9. Effect of compensating inductance on the reproduction of fine detail. [See Fig. 12-5(b) for schematic and Eq. (28) for significance of a.]

requirements of the system. For clean, sharp edges with very little overshoot, the figures show that a value of

$$a = 0.35 \tag{32}$$

is about optimum, while for clean, well-shaped detail a value of

$$a = 0.50 \tag{33}$$

looks the best. It is obvious that there is nothing critical about these values.

Finally, a word should be said about the choice of R. Equation (29) shows that the output signal amplitude is proportional to R, so that it is desirable to use as large a value of R as can be done without disturbing picture quality. On the other hand, the time scale in Fig. 12-9 is proportional to RC. Now C itself is fixed by the tube which is to be used and may therefore be considered as predetermined. Consequently, if T is the length of the smallest signal detail which is expected to be resolved, Fig. 12-9 shows that

$$R = \frac{T}{\pi C} \tag{34}$$

is capable of giving excellent quality reproduction. Actually, a value of R four times as great will still show most of the detail, but with very much reduced sharpness.

The methods of transformation calculus can also be used to study the effects of various other types of compensation. These methods are particularly valuable in deriving general relations, such as Eqs. (32–34), and in getting an over-all picture of the situation. In many practical cases, however, especially when several stages of compensated amplification are used, the circuits become too complicated, for practical purposes, to use direct solution by means of transformation calculus. Furthermore, the effective actual circuit connections are in doubt because of feedback and stray coupling. To handle such cases, Bedford and Fredendall[7] recommend that the over-all steady-state frequency and phase-delay characteristics of the system be either calculated or measured. They then analyze an infinite set of equally spaced pulses, of the type shown in Fig. 12-9, in a Fourier series. The amplitudes and phases of these Fourier-series components are then operated upon as required by the steady-state characteristics of the system and the resultant components are then superimposed to get the final output signal. Bedford and Fredendall report that this is the most rapid and practical method of obtaining the over-all transient response of a multistage video amplifier, a conclusion which appears to be quite reasonable.

12.4. Feedback and stability in linear systems—conditions for oscillation

A matter of great importance in radio engineering is the question of the stability of feedback amplifiers. If the amplifier is known to be in a stable condition and in the steady state, the system can readily be analyzed by elementary methods, as we shall presently show. However, in order for such an analysis to have any value, we must also know that the system is in a stable condition. This will require the use of transformation calculus. For the sake of

[7] *Proc. I.R.E.*, April (1939), p. 277.

simplicity, we will limit our discussion to linear systems, and we will begin with a discussion of stable systems in the steady state.

(a) Stable Systems in the Steady State. In Fig. 12-10 is a diagram of a feedback amplifier. A sinusoidal voltage

$$\bar{e}_i = |\bar{e}_i| \sin \omega t \tag{35}$$

is impressed upon the input of the system from the outside and a

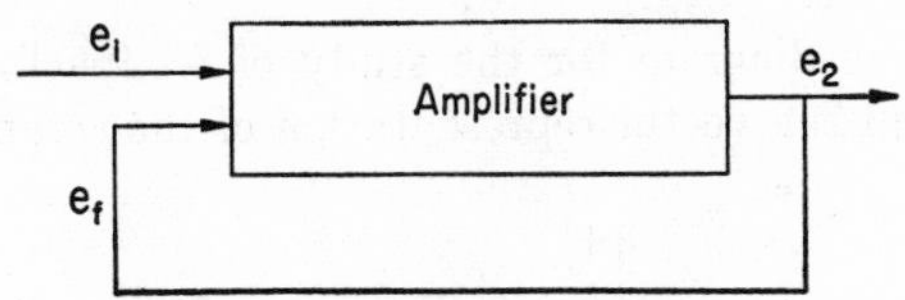

FIG. 12-10. A feedback amplifier system.

voltage $\bar{e}_f$ is fed back from the output to the input of the system. Thus we have

$$\text{total input voltage} = \bar{e}_1 = \bar{e}_i + \bar{e}_f \tag{36}$$

Let us suppose that the system is stable and in the steady state, and that the amplifier has a gain $A\epsilon^{j\alpha}$, that is

$$\text{output voltage} = \bar{e}_2 = A\epsilon^{j\alpha}\bar{e}_1 \tag{37}$$

where $\bar{e}_2$ and $\bar{e}_1$ are complex quantities representing the amplitudes and phases of the output and input voltages. Then if the connections are such that

$$\bar{e}_f = B\epsilon^{j\beta}\bar{e}_2 = AB\epsilon^{j(\alpha+\beta)}\bar{e}_1 \tag{38}$$

we can solve Eqs. (36) through (38) to obtain

$$\frac{\bar{e}_2}{\bar{e}_i} = \frac{A\epsilon^{j\alpha}}{1 - AB\epsilon^{j(\alpha+\beta)}} \tag{39}$$

The ratio $(\bar{e}_2/\bar{e}_i)$ represents the complete gain of the system, including the effect of feedback. If

$$\left|\frac{\bar{e}_2}{\bar{e}_i}\right| > \left|\frac{\bar{e}_2}{\bar{e}_1}\right| \tag{40}$$

then feedback has increased the gain, and the amplifier is said to have positive feedback. On the other hand, if

$$\left|\frac{\bar{e}_2}{\bar{e}_i}\right| < \left|\frac{\bar{e}_2}{\bar{e}_1}\right| \tag{41}$$

then feedback has decreased the gain, and the amplifier is said to have negative feedback. Systems having positive feedback are called regenerative, while systems having negative feedback are called degenerative.[8]

An instructive diagram for the study of feedback is shown in Fig. 12-11, which is a vector representation of the complex voltages

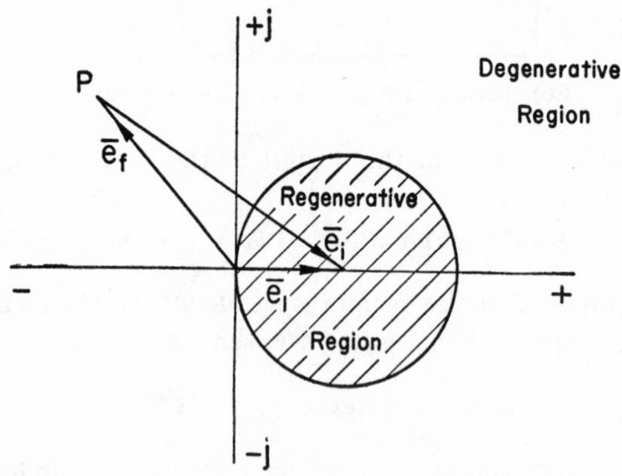

FIG. 12-11. Complex plane diagram of the voltages in a feedback amplifier, showing degenerative and regenerative conditions of feedback.

in Eq. (36). In this diagram, the total input voltage (usually the effective input grid voltage in an amplifier) is laid out as a unit vector along the positive direction of the real axis. Now it follows from Eqs. (40) and (41) that the amplifier is regenerative if $|\bar{e}_1| > |\bar{e}_i|$ and is degenerative if $|\bar{e}_1| < \bar{e}_i|$. It therefore is clear from Fig. 12-11 that if the end of the vector of the feedback voltage $\bar{e}_f$ lies within the unit circle (shaded region) centered at $e_1(1 + j0)$, the system is regenerative; but if the end of the feedback-voltage vector lies outside the circle (in the unshaded region), the system is degen-

[8] Both regenerative and degenerative amplifiers are useful in radio engineering. A discussion of these topics will be found in any modern textbook on radio engineering.

erative. In case the end of the vector $\bar{e}_f$ coincides with the center of the circle, then no input voltage is required for finite output, so that the system is an oscillator.

The foregoing discussion is applicable only if we know that the system is in the steady state and is stable. However, it leaves unanswered the question of whether or not the system really is stable. This matter will next be investigated after we prove a useful theorem.

(b) **A Contour Theorem.** Suppose that $f(z)$ is a function of a complex variable z, and let it be supposed that the function has no singularities other than poles within a particular closed contour. The function may also have zeros within this contour. We will now develop an equation relating to the number of zeros and the number of poles within the contour.

Let
$$w = f(z) \tag{42}$$
Then
$$\operatorname{Log} w = \operatorname{Log} f(z) \tag{43}$$
and
$$\frac{d}{dz}(\operatorname{Log} w) = \frac{1}{w}\frac{dw}{dz} = \frac{f'(z)}{f(z)} \tag{44}$$
where
$$f'(z) = \frac{d}{dz}[f(z)] \tag{45}$$
Accordingly,
$$\oint d(\operatorname{Log} w) = \oint \frac{1}{w}\,dw = \oint \frac{f'(z)}{f(z)}\,dz \tag{46}$$

where the integration in the z plane is along the above-mentioned contour and the integration in the w plane is along the transform of this contour into the w plane.

The integrand of Eq. (46) is analytic except at the poles and zeros of $f(z)$. Let z_0 be a point at which $f(z)$ has a zero or a pole. Then we can write

$$f(z) = (z - z_0)^n g(z) \tag{47}$$

where $g(z)$ is analytic and not zero at z_0, and n is positive for a zero and negative for a pole. The order of the pole or zero is $|n|$.

From Eq. (47) it follows that

$$f'(z) = n(z - z_0)^{n-1}g(z) + (z - z_0)^n g'(z) \tag{48}$$

Therefore
$$\frac{f'(z)}{f(z)} = \frac{n}{z - z_0} + \frac{g'(z)}{g(z)} \tag{49}$$

Since
$$\frac{g'(z)}{g(z)}$$

is analytic at z_0, it follows from §5.13 that

$$\frac{f'(z)}{f(z)}$$

has a first order pole of residue n at $z = z_0$. It likewise follows from §5.13 that the integral in a counterclockwise direction around the complete contour in Eq. (46) is equal to $2\pi j$, times the sum of the residues of $f'(z)/f(z)$ at all its poles. Now at points where $f(z)$ has a zero of the n'th order, the residue of $f'(z)/f(z)$ will be $(+n)$ and at points where $f(z)$ has a pole of the m'th order, the residue of $f'(z)/f(z)$ will be $(-m)$. Accordingly, we may write

$$\oint \frac{f'(z)}{f(z)}\, dz = 2\pi j(N - P) \tag{50}$$

where N is the number of zeros and P is the number of poles within the contour, each multiple zero or multiple pole being weighted according to its multiplicity.

Let us next separate Log w into its real and imaginary parts as

$$\operatorname{Log} w = A + jB \tag{51}$$

If, now, we use the subscripts 1 and 2 for the values of Log w at the beginning and at the end of the contour in Eq. (50), we have

$$(A_2 - A_1) + j(B_2 - B_1) = 2\pi j(N - P) \tag{52}$$

It follows that

$$A_2 = A_1 \tag{53}$$

and

$$B_2 - B_1 = 2\pi(N - P) \tag{54}$$

Interpreting Eq. (54) in the light of §5.5, it follows that the number $(N - P)$ is the number of times that the contour in the w plane in Eq. (46) encircles the origin in a counterclockwise direction as z encircles the original contour in the z plane once in a counterclockwise direction. According to the foregoing convention of signs, clockwise encirclements of the origin in the w plane will be considered negative. The same significance of $(N - P)$ will, however, hold if the original contour in the z plane is encircled in a clockwise direction and clockwise encirclements are considered positive in the w plane. We have thus arrived at the following important result:

Theorem: *If a function* $w = f(z)$ *is analytic, except for possible poles within and on a given contour taken in a clockwise direction in the* *z plane, then the number of times that the transform of this contour into the w plane encircles the origin in the w plane in a clockwise direction is equal to the number of zeros diminished by the number of poles of $f(z)$ inside the contour in the z plane, each pole or zero being counted in accordance with its multiplicity.* We will find this theorem very useful in our studies of stability.

(c) Nyquist's Criterion for Stability.[9] For the purposes of our discussion, we will say that a system is *stable* if a small impressed disturbance, which itself dies out, results in a response which dies out. We will call the system *unstable* if such a disturbance results in a response which goes on indefinitely and increases until it is limited by the nonlinearity of the system. The possibility of the disturbance giving rise to a response which goes on indefinitely at a relatively small value in a linear system will also be included in our discussion, but it is so completely unlikely that it is unimportant. However, for purposes of classification, we will also call the corresponding system unstable.

Let us consider the system in Fig. 12-10. However, this time let the impressed voltage be of the form

$$e_i = e_i(t) \tag{55}$$

where $e_i(t)$ is any function whose value differs appreciably from zero for only a finite length of time. Let

$$e_1 = e_1(t) \tag{56}$$

be the total input voltage, including feedback, due to e_i, and let

$$e_2 = e_2(t) \tag{57}$$

be the total output voltage, and

$$e_f = e_f(t) \tag{58}$$

be the feedback voltage.

In accordance with our customary notation, let us now write

$$E_1(s) = \mathfrak{L}[e_1(t)] \tag{59}$$

$$E_2(s) = \mathfrak{L}[e_2(t)] \tag{60}$$

$$E_i(s) = \mathfrak{L}[e_i(t)] \tag{61}$$

$$E_f(s) = \mathfrak{L}[e_f(t)] \tag{62}$$

[9] This treatment is based upon the classic paper of Nyquist, "Regeneration Theory," *B.S.T.J.*, Jan. (1932), p. 126.

Since we are dealing with a linear system, governed by linear differential equations, it follows in a manner similar to the discussion in §4.5 that[10]

$$\frac{E_f(s)}{E_1(s)} = H(s) \tag{63}$$

where $H(s)$ depends only on the constants and connections of the system, and is independent of the forms of the voltages.

Now, by the principle of superposition, we know that

$$e_1(t) = e_i(t) + e_f(t) \tag{64}$$

It therefore follows that

$$E_1(s) = E_i(s) + E_f(s) = E_i(s) + E_1(s)H(s) \tag{65}$$

which can be solved to give

$$E_1(s) = \frac{E_i(s)}{1 - H(s)} \tag{66}$$

Now let us write

$$G(s) = \frac{E_2(s)}{E_1(s)} \tag{67}$$

Then

$$E_2(s) = G(s)E_1(s) = \frac{G(s)E_i(s)}{1 - H(s)} \tag{68}$$

According to the inversion theorem (§7.3), it then follows from Eq. (68) that

$$e_2(t) = \frac{1}{2\pi j}\oint \frac{G(s)E_i(s)\epsilon^{st}}{1 - H(s)}\,ds \tag{69}$$

The generalized expansion theorem (§7.5) tells us that as a consequence of Eq. (69), $e_2(t)$ is equal to the sum of the residues of the integrand at its various singular points in the s plane.[11] Now

---

[10] The ratios of the other transformed voltages,

$$\frac{E_2(s)}{E_1(s)}, \qquad \frac{E_f(s)}{E_2(s)}$$

and so forth, are, of course, likewise independent of the forms of the voltages.

[11] This statement assumes that the integrand of Eq. (69) satisfies Eq. (28) of Chap. 7. If the initiating pulse $e_i(t)$ has only a finite amount of energy (this rules out impulses of infinite height) then, in the light of the Fourier integral energy theorem, $E_i(s)$ will vanish to a sufficiently high order along the infinite

the only factors in any of these residues which involve time are exponentials of the form

$$\epsilon^{s_q t}$$

where s_q is the pole at which the residue occurs. Because of this simple form of the residues, it is easy to tell whether the system is stable or not. Thus if any s_q has a positive real part, the corresponding residue rises exponentially in value, and the system is unstable. On the other hand, if the real part of every s_q is negative, then the response ultimately falls off exponentially, and the system is stable. In the physically unlikely case that the real part of an s_q should be exactly equal to zero, the corresponding response would be of a steady-state oscillatory type, and this system would also be classified as unstable.

Stated in other words, we may say that if all the poles of the integrand of Eq. (69) lie to the left of the imaginary axis in the s plane, the system is stable; but if one or more poles of the integrand lie on the imaginary axis or to the right of it, the system is unstable.

Let us next examine the integrand of Eq. (69) more closely to determine the location of its poles. In the first place, we recall that, by hypothesis, the impressed voltage $e_i(t)$ has a value which differs appreciably from zero for only a finite length of time. Consequently any poles of $E_i(s)$ lie to the left of the imaginary axis. Furthermore, since $G(s)$ is the gain function of the amplifier without a feedback connection, it represents a stable transfer function and has no poles in the right half of the s plane. Therefore, any poles of the integrand which lie to the right of the imaginary axis would have to arise from a root of the equation

$$1 - H(s) = 0 \tag{70}$$

in which the real part of s was positive.

In order to find out whether $[1 - H(s)]$ has any roots for values of s having positive real parts, we make use of the theorem of

---

circular arc in Fig. 7-5 so that the above-noted condition will be satisfied as far as $E_i(s)$ is concerned. For lumped-constant networks $G(s)$ and $H(s)$ will give no trouble. If, however, transmission-line or wave-guide sections are involved which give rise to essential singularities at infinity, then the methods of the present section have to be revised. Accordingly, we limit our discussion to lumped-constant networks.

§12.4(b). Thus we transform the contour encircling the entire right half of the s plane as indicated by the contour $AOBCA$ in Fig. 12-12(a) into $H(j\omega)$ in the H plane as shown in Fig. 12-12(b). The infinite arc BCA in the s plane will ordinarily transform into a single point[12] in the H plane, as shown in Fig. 12-12(b), in all actual cases, but it could theoretically transform into another infinite arc, as would occur in the unrealistic case shown in Fig. 12-14. In order

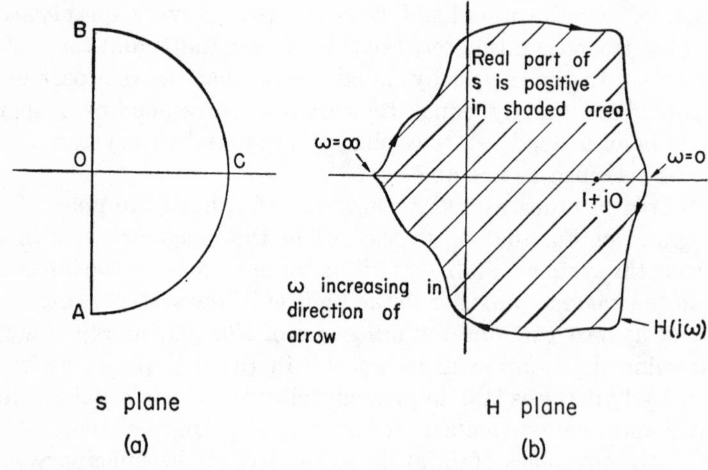

Fig. 12-12. A transformation of the right half of the complex s plane into a closed area in the complex H plane. [The perimeter $H(j\omega)$ of the shaded area in the H plane is the transform of the imaginary axis in the s plane. The infinite arc BCA transforms into a single point.]

to find out whether Eq. (70) has any roots with positive real parts, we rephrase the theorem of §12.4(b) to state for this case "The number of times that the locus of $H(j\omega)$ encircles the point $1 + j0$ in the H plane in a clockwise direction is equal to the number of

---

[12] The properties of a function of a complex variable when the variable becomes infinite are treated in §5.18. It is found that the function does one of three things. Either it approaches the same constant value for all infinite values of the variable, or else it becomes infinite for all infinite values of the variable, or else it approaches any desired value as the variable becomes infinite. In other words, the function behaves as though all of the infinite region were just a single point at which the function either had a regular point, a pole, or an essential singularity.

zeros diminished by the number of poles of $[1 - H(s)]$ for values of s having positive real parts."[13]

Now the feedback transfer function $H(s)$ will have no poles in the right half of the s plane, unless the feedback network itself is unstable even before it is connected to the input. Although this may occur in some multiloop feedback systems, we will usually confine our attention to cases in which this does not occur. Furthermore, if $H(s)$ has no poles in the right half of the s plane, $[1 - H(s)]$ will likewise have no poles in this region. We thus arrive at Nyquist's criterion:

If the locus of

$$H(j\omega) = \frac{E_f(j\omega)}{E_1(j\omega)} \tag{71}$$

encircles the point $1 + j0$ *in a clockwise direction as* ω *is varied from* $-\infty$ *to* $+\infty$, *then the system is unstable. If the locus does not encircle* $1 + j0$, *then [provided that* $H(s)$ *itself has no poles for values of* s *having positive real parts] the system is stable.*

In case $H(s)$ has poles for values of s with positive real parts, each of these poles will cancel the effect of one root of

$$1 - H(s) = 0 \tag{72}$$

as far as encirclements are concerned. In such cases stability is not assured by the fact that the point $1 + j0$ is not encircled by $H(j\omega)$. Except in certain multiloop servo systems, however, the feedback loop itself is stable, so that the Nyquist criterion can be used to give an unambiguous answer.

Some illustrative diagrams showing contours of $H(j\omega)$ are shown in Fig. 12-13. It is worthy of note that since $H(j\omega)$ is conjugate to $H(-j\omega)$, the locus of $H(j\omega)$ for negative values of ω will be a mirror image of the locus for positive values of ω. We also note that at extremely high frequencies the feedback voltage in all actual cases will be short-circuited by stray capacities, while at extremely low frequencies the feedback voltage is usually reduced to zero by blocking capacitors. $H(j\omega)$ will therefore usually comprise a locus for positive values of ω which begins and ends at the origin. The locus of $H(j\omega)$ for negative values of ω will be the mirror image of the

---

[13] We note that the function $[-H(s)]$ will encircle the origin in the H plane in the same direction as will $H(s)$.

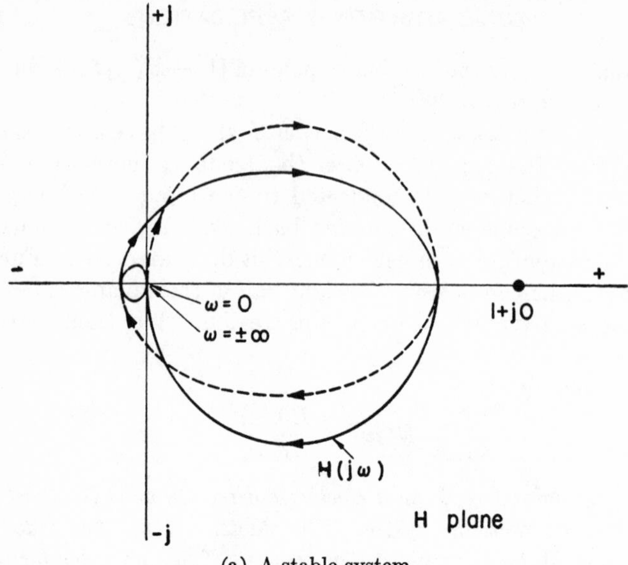

(a) A stable system.

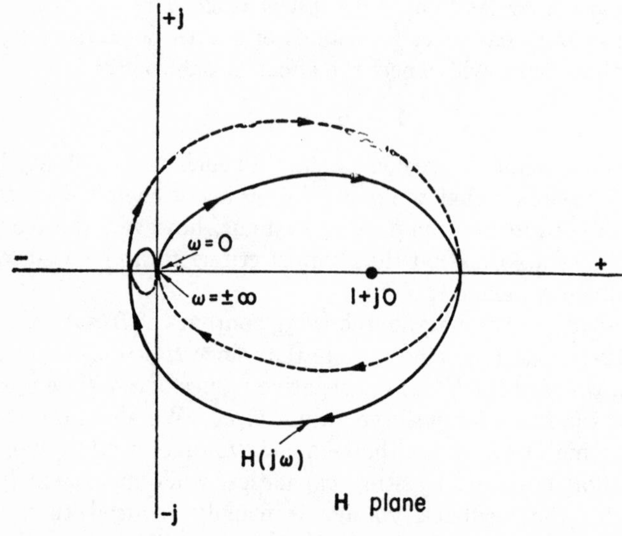

(b) An unstable system.

FIG. 12-13. Illustrative loci of the feedback transfer function $H(j\omega)$. (Direction of arrows indicates direction of increasing frequency. The solid curves indicate the positive frequency ranges while the dashed curves indicate the negative frequency ranges.)

positive locus reflected in the real axis. We note, however, that both locus curves will encircle the point $1 + j0$ in the same direction of rotation, if they encircle it at all. It is therefore sufficient to draw the positive locus curve in applications of Nyquist's criterion.

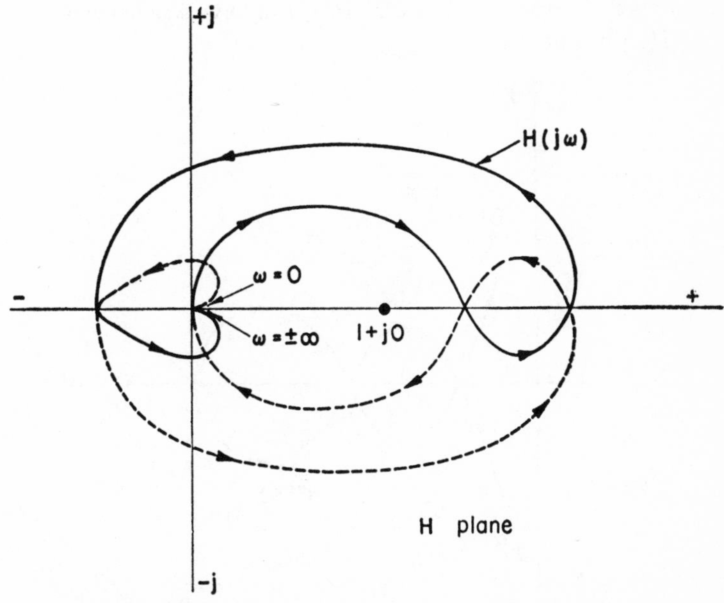

FIG. 12-13. (*Cont.*). (c) An unstable system. [The point $1 + j0$ is not encircled by the locus, according to the test in footnote (15). The locus, however, does have a closed contour with counterclockwise rotation and will therefore be unstable according to footnote (14)].

Figure 12-14 shows a theoretically possible but unrealistic case in which $H(j\omega)$ does not vanish at $\omega = \infty$ and $\omega = 0$. Such cases are sometimes useful in theoretical discussions. Figure 12-15(a) shows a case in which the feedback voltage is unstable,[14,15] so that the

---

[14] $H(s)$ will have a pole in the right half of the s plane, and the feedback voltage will then be unstable, in case the locus of $H(j\omega)$ has a closed contour with counterclockwise rotation anywhere in the H plane. To show this, let H_0 be any point within the closed contour in question. Then the locus of $[H(j\omega) - H_0]$ will encircle the origin in a counterclockwise direction. Therefore $[H(s) - H_0]$ and consequently $H(s)$ itself will have a pole for a value of s with a positive real part.

[15] The test of whether a point, say H_0, is encircled or not is to draw a vector

system is unstable even though the point $1 + j0$ is not encircled. On the other hand, Fig. 12-15(b) shows a case in which the feedback voltage is unstable, but the complete system may be stable nevertheless. In the latter case the point $1 + j0$ is encircled in a counterclockwise direction so that the number of poles of $[1 - H(s)]$ exceeds the number of zeros. In this case $H(s)$ can have a pole even though $[1 - H(s)]$ has no zero.

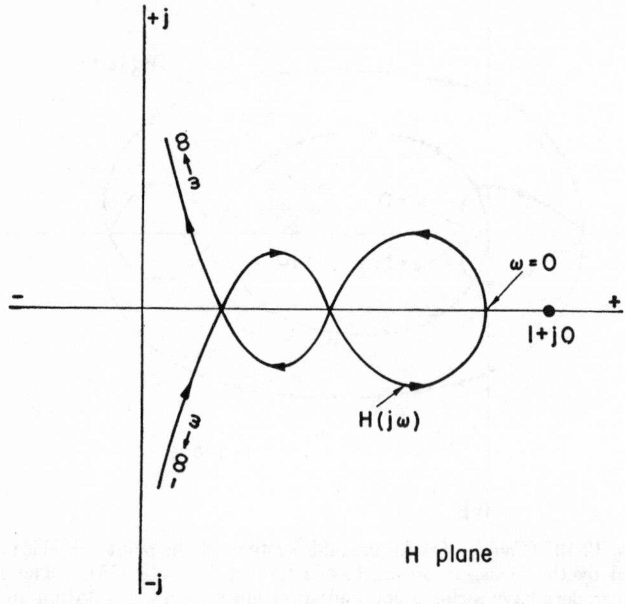

FIG. 12-14. A theoretically possible, but unrealistic locus curve.

Let us now compare Nyquist's criterion with the discussion in §12.4(a) and the picture in Fig. 12-11. According to Eq. (71), the end-point of $\bar{e}_f/\bar{e}_1$ in Fig. 12-11 corresponds to the value of $H(j\omega)$ for the steady-state frequency in question. Consequently, the locus of the end-point of $\bar{e}_f/\bar{e}_1$ for variable frequency will coincide with the locus of $H(j\omega)$ in Fig. 12-12. If this locus passes to the right of the point $1 + j0$, then the system has the correct phase

from H_0 to the locus of $H(j\omega)$. If the total rotation of this vector is zero as ω varies from $-\infty$ to $+\infty$, then the point is not encircled. The total rotation divided by 2π is equal to the number of times that the point is encircled.

shift and more than enough gain to produce oscillation. It would therefore not be surprising if such a system were unstable, since the cumulative amplification of a transient could easily drive the system

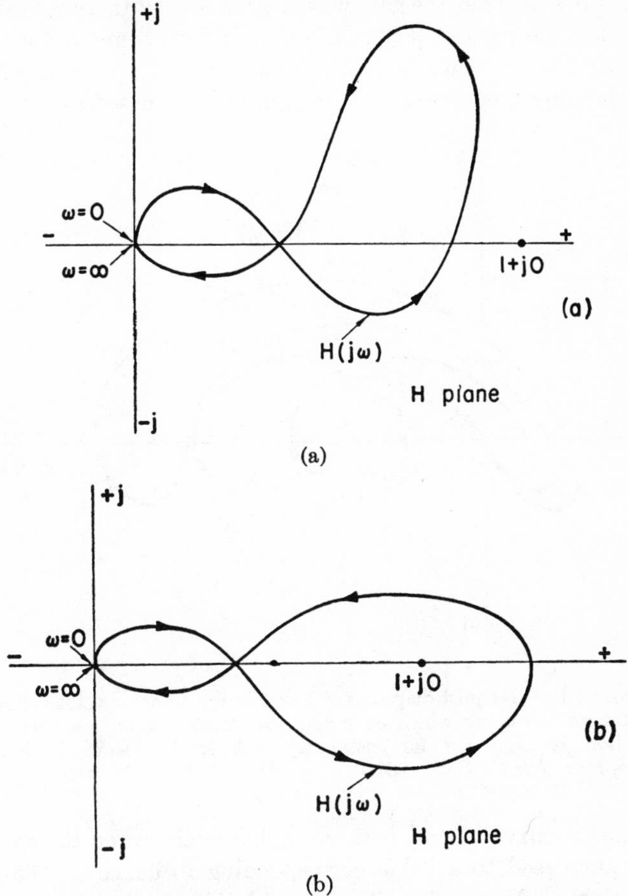

FIG. 12-15. Loci of systems in which the feedback voltage itself is unstable. (Only the positive frequency ranges are shown.) (a) Over-all system is unstable. (b) Over-all system may be stable.

into nonlinear operation and thereby reduce the over-all gain until $\bar{e}_f$ coincided with $\bar{e}_1$. Hence it might appear that the Nyquist criterion derived above does not actually add very much to what could be predicted from steady-state studies. Some experiments of

Peterson, Kreer, and Ware[16] are therefore of special interest. These men set up a system whose gain they could vary so that the locus of $H(j\omega)$ was changed from curve a (in Fig. 12-16)[17] to curve b and then to curve c as the gain was increased. Of these curves, only b encircled the point $1 + j0$. They found, as a matter of experiment, that the system was stable for a gain corresponding to curve a, but became unstable when the gain was increased to that corresponding to curve b, and became stable again when the gain was further increased to a value corresponding to curve c. This is a verification of Nyquist's criterion, and is a result which steady-state considerations could not have predicted.

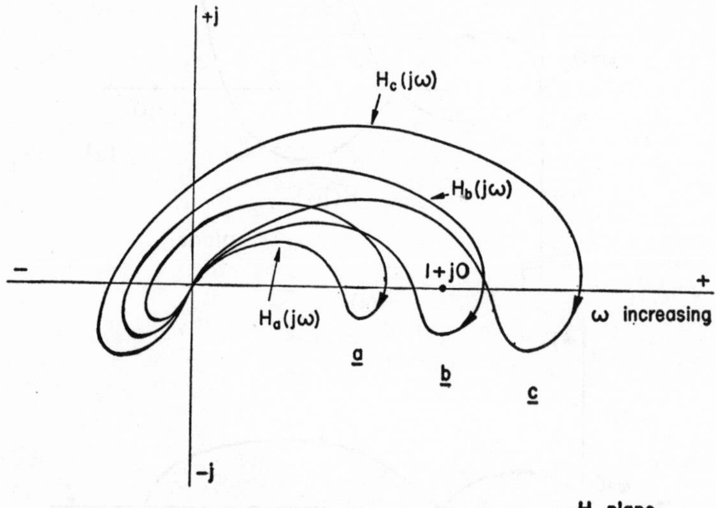

FIG. 12-16. Nyquist diagrams of a system for different values of gain, illustrating a case in which encircling the point $1 + j0$ in a clockwise direction is necessary for instability. (After Peterson, Kreer and Ware, *Proc. I.R.E.*, Oct., 1934.)

(d) **An Example of the Use of Nyquist's Criterion.** To illustrate the use of Nyquist's criterion, let us investigate the stability of the

[16] *Proc. I.R.E.*, Oct. (1934), p. 1191.

[17] For the sake of simplicity, only the loops for positive ω are shown in Fig. 12-16.

circuit in Fig. 12-17(a). Let

$$\left.\begin{aligned} E_p &= \text{plate voltage} \\ E_g &= \text{grid voltage} \end{aligned}\right\} \text{complex steady-state values}$$

$$\begin{aligned} \mu &= \text{amplification factor of tube} \\ r_p &= \text{plate resistance of tube} \\ Z(j\omega) &= \text{impedance of high-}Q\text{, tuned circuit.} \end{aligned}$$

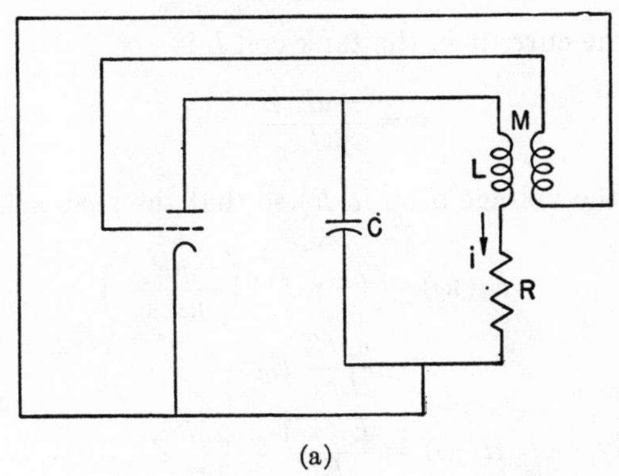

(a)

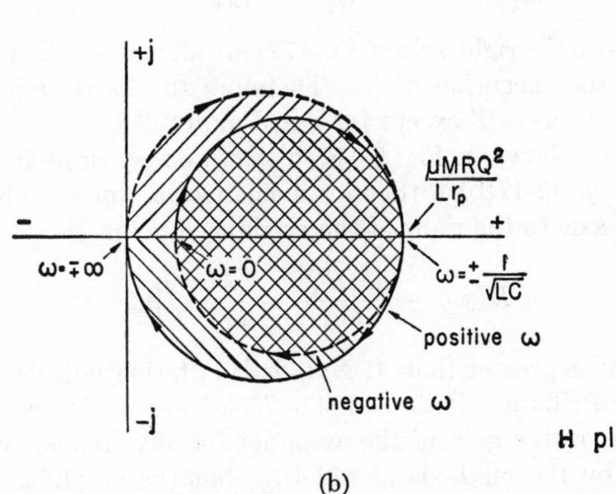

(b)

FIG. 12-17. (a) A feedback amplifier. (b) Locus of $H(j\omega)$ of the feedback amplifier in (a). (This is not a scale drawing. The smaller circle should be essentially coincident with the larger one. They have been separated so that positive and negative frequencies can be distinguished. Near the origin there are additional inaccuracies because the high-Q approximations no longer hold.)

For the sake of simplicity, assume that the internal capacities of the tube are of negligible importance and that

$$r_p \gg Z \tag{73}$$

so that Z is negligible in comparison with r_p. Then we may write

$$E_p = -\mu E_g \frac{Z}{r_p} \text{ (approx.)} \tag{74}$$

Therefore, the current in the tank coil L is

$$i = \frac{-\mu E_g Z}{j\omega L r_p} \tag{75}$$

(neglecting the voltage drop in R) so that the feedback voltage is

$$\begin{aligned} E_f(j\omega) &= (-j\omega M)\left(\frac{-\mu E_g Z}{j\omega L r_p}\right) \\ &= \frac{\mu M Z}{L r_p} E_g \end{aligned} \tag{76}$$

Consequently, $$H(j\omega) = \frac{E_f(j\omega)}{E_g} = \frac{\mu M}{L r_p} Z \tag{77}$$

The factors on the right side of Eq. (77) are all real and independent of ω, with the exception of Z. Therefore the locus $H(j\omega)$ is the same as the locus of Z except for a real multiplier. Now the locus of Z has been shown in Fig. 6-11, so that we may draw it again as $H(j\omega)$ in Fig. 12-17(b) with only a change of units. The curve crosses the axis to the right of the origin at a point

$$H(j\omega) = \frac{\mu M R Q^2}{L r_p} = \frac{\mu M}{L r_p} \cdot \frac{L}{CR} \tag{78}$$

If this value is greater than 1, Nyquist's criterion tells us that the circuit will oscillate. If the value of $H(j\omega)$ in Eq. (78) is less than 1, the regenerative gain of the amplifier for any frequency can be calculated by the methods of §12.4(a), but the amplifier will not oscillate.

(e) Llewellyn's Criterion for Oscillation.[18] In certain types of work on the capability of oscillation of a circuit such as that shown

[18] F. B. Llewellyn, *Proc. I.R.E.*, Nov. (1933), p. 1532. En-Lung Chu, *Proc. I.R.E.*, Oct. (1944), p. 630.

in Fig. 12-17(a), it is not practicable to measure or calculate the amplitude and phase of the feedback voltage as a function of frequency, so that it is difficult to apply Nyquist's criterion. Suppose that in such a case we open up the output circuit, as shown at terminals 1-2 in Fig. 12-18 (a) and measure the apparent impedance

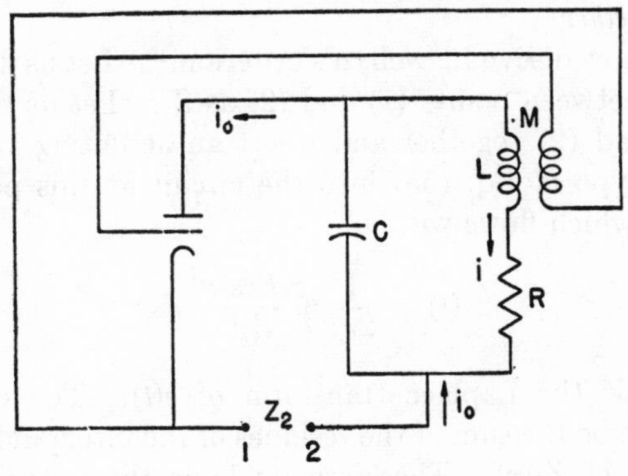

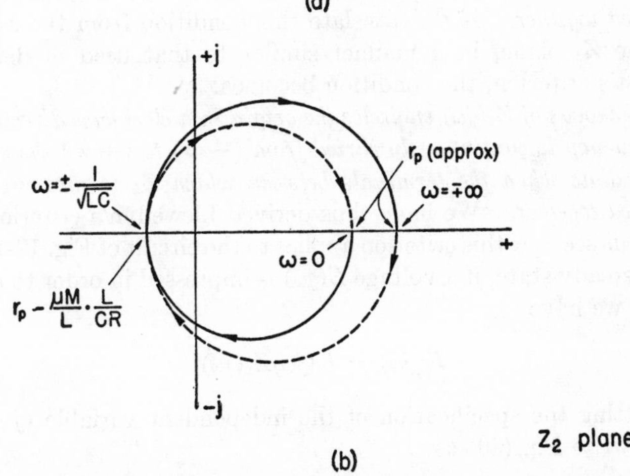

FIG. 12-18. (a) The impedance Z_2 between the terminals where the output circuit of a feedback amplifier has been opened. (b) The locus of $Z_2(j\omega)$ of the schematic in (a). [This is also not a scale drawing. Similar remarks to those of Fig. 12-17(b) apply.]

between these terminals as a function of frequency. For such cases, Llewellyn has stated the following criterion:

If the locus of the impedance $Z(j\omega)$ measured between two points encircles the origin in a clockwise direction as the frequency is continuously varied from $(-\infty)$ to $(+\infty)$, *then the system will oscillate when the terminals between which the impedance is measured are connected together.*

We will now derive Llewellyn's criterion.[19] Let us designate the impedance between points (1) and (2) as Z_2. Let us then connect points (1) and (2) together and insert an actuating voltage pulse $e(t)$ of the type of Eq. (55) into the circuit at this point. Then the current which flows will be

$$i_0(t) = \frac{1}{2\pi j} \oint \frac{E(s)\epsilon^{st}}{Z_2(s)} ds \tag{79}$$

where $E(s)$ is the Laplace transform of $e(t)$. The current $i_0(t)$ will therefore be the sum of the residues of the integrand of Eq. (79) at the zeros of $Z_2(s)$. Therefore we have the following rule: *If $Z_2(s)$ has a zero for a value of s with a positive real part, then the system will oscillate when the terminals between which Z_2 is measured are connected together.* If we translate this condition from the s plane into the Z_2 plane, in a manner similar to that used in deriving Nyquist's criterion, the condition becomes:

If the locus of $Z_2(j\omega)$ encircles the origin in a clockwise direction as the frequency is continuously varied from $(-\infty)$ to $(+\infty)$ the system will oscillate when the terminals between which Z_2 is measured are connected together. We have thus derived Llewellyn's criterion.

Let us see how this criterion applies to the circuit of Fig. 12-18(a). In the steady state, if a voltage $E(j\omega)$ is impressed in order to measure Z_2, we have

$$E(j\omega) = I_0(j\omega)Z_2(j\omega) \tag{80}$$

or omitting the specification of the independent variable $(j\omega)$, we may rewrite Eq. (80) as

$$E = I_0Z_2 \tag{81}$$

[19] The following investigation is general, and is not restricted to the specific circuit of Fig. 12–18(a).

Then, neglecting the voltage drop across R,

$$I = \frac{-I_0 Z}{j\omega L} \tag{82}$$

and

$$E_g = -j\omega MI = \frac{-j\omega M}{-j\omega L} I_0 Z = \frac{M}{L} I_0 Z \tag{83}$$

where Z is the impedance of the parallel-tuned circuit.

Now the total effective voltage in the main circuit is $(\mu E_g + E)$, so that

$$I_0 = \frac{\mu E_g + E}{Z + r_p} = \frac{\mu E_g + E}{r_p} \quad \text{(approx.)}$$

$$= \frac{\mu \frac{M}{L} I_0 Z + I_0 Z_2}{r_p} \tag{84}$$

Solving Eq. (84), we obtain

$$Z_2 = r_p - \frac{\mu M Z}{L} \tag{85}$$

The form of Z is known from Fig. 6-11, so that we can draw the curve of Eq. (85) very easily. This is shown in Fig. 12-18(b).

Equation (85) in conjunction with Fig. 12-18(b) shows that the circuit in Fig. 12-18(a) will oscillate if

$$\frac{\mu M}{L} \cdot \frac{L}{CR} \geq r_p \tag{86}$$

This conclusion agrees with that drawn from Eq. (78).

The reader may question the value of measuring Z_2 in order to determine whether the system will oscillate, since the question can be answered very simply by connecting points (1) and (2) and seeing whether oscillation starts. But a picture of the Z_2 locus gives much more information for design purposes, since it shows what changes must be made in order to change the system from an oscillator to a nonoscillator, and vice versa.

(f) Some Remarks on the Frequency Stability of Oscillators. When a system has gone into oscillation, in the absence of externally applied voltage,

$$E_f(j\omega) = E_1(j\omega) \tag{87}$$

in magnitude and phase. The frequency of oscillation is the frequency at which the left side of Eq. (87) is equal to the right side. If the curve of

$$\frac{E_f(j\omega)}{E_1(j\omega)}$$

encircles the point $1 + j0$ in a clockwise direction but crosses the real axis far to the right of this point, then as the system goes into oscillation the effective gain of the feedback loop decreases, due to cutoff and saturation in tubes, until Eq. (87) is exactly satisfied.

In the use of a vacuum-tube oscillator to generate a signal of given frequency, it is often desirable to keep the frequency as nearly constant as possible. Change of the frequency of oscillation may be due to variation in the effective operating values of the tube or circuit constants or of the feedback adjustments. Changes in the operating voltages are especially likely to change the tube constants, while mechanical vibration or changes in temperature and humidity are most likely to affect the circuit constants or feedback adjustments. Now the frequency of oscillation is determined primarily by the phase of the feedback voltage, since the amplitude is ordinarily more than adequate for oscillation before it is reduced by nonlinearity in the system. Since the phases of tuned impedances change rapidly near resonance,[20] a tuned impedance in the feedback loop can compensate for a large amount of phase variation without allowing an appreciable shift in the frequency of oscillation. An effective means of maintaining the oscillating frequency within narrow limits is therefore to use a very high Q resonant impedance in the system and to take pains to hold the resonant frequency of this impedance as constant as possible. The latter may be done by using a fundamentally stable impedance, such as a tuned transmission line or a tuned magnetostriction rod as the resonant impedance. If extreme frequency stability is required, the resonant impedance can further be kept in a vibration-free chamber at constant temperature and humidity, as is done with the crystal oscillators of some broadcast stations.

(g) The Stability of Amplifiers Designed for Negative Feedback in a Specified Frequency Range. As is well known, negative feed-

[20] Fig. 6-11 shows that the phase of a simple tuned impedance changes 90° in a narrow frequency range of $(f_0/2Q)$ on either side of resonance.

back can be used to obtain marked improvements in the performance of an amplifier. In particular, it can be used to reduce distortion and to tend to keep the output at a desired level in spite of variations in the properties of amplifier tubes or of variations in the impedance of the load circuit. In the usual amplifier controlled by negative feedback, the feedback voltage $E_f(j\omega)$ is π

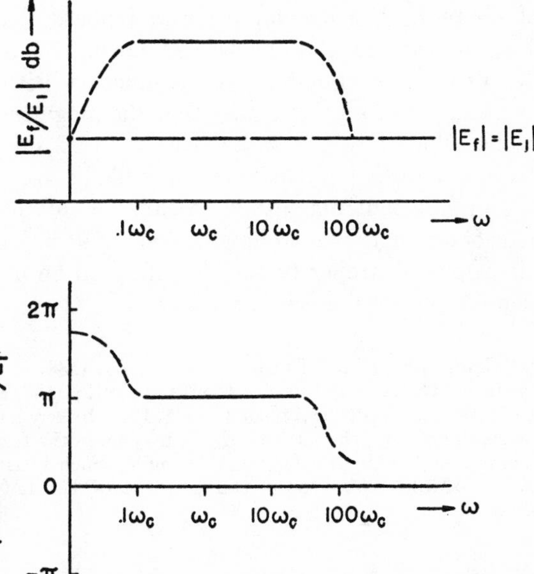

FIG. 12-19. Curves of the magnitude and phase of E_f/E_1 as a function of frequency in a typical case. (If the phase rises above 2π or falls below zero at a frequency for which $|E_f| > |E_1|$ the system is considered unstable for design purposes.)

radians (180°) out of phase with the total input voltage $E_1(j\omega)$ in the frequency region in which negative feedback is desired. Furthermore, in order to have good control, it is customary to have the feedback voltage much greater than the total input voltage; i.e.,

$$AB \gg 1 \tag{88}$$

in Eq. (38).

In Fig. 12-19 is a diagram of the amplitude and phase of the ratio of E_f/E_1 in a typical case. Suppose that it is desired to control the amplifier from, say, $0.1\omega_c$ to $10\omega_c$. In this frequency range, the magnitude of E_f/E_1 is kept at a large constant value and its phase is kept at π radians.[21] Outside this range, the values are generally unimportant except for stability considerations. Now the system will be stable unless the phase changes to zero or 2π before $|E_f|$ falls below $|E_1|$. The transfer immittance which controls the relation of E_f to E_1 has its amplitude and phase characteristics controlled by the various relations worked out in §7.9, in particular Eq. (133). From this equation, in conjunction with Nyquist's criterion, we can see in a general way that the magnitude of E_f/E_1 should not be allowed to decrease faster than 12 db per octave until $|E_f|$ is less than $|E_1|$. Otherwise E_f is likely to have the correct phase and sufficient magnitude to cause oscillation.[22] Practical methods of design for controlling the rate of decrease of $|E_f/E_1|$ and considerations of proper factors of safety to be used are discussed at length in books on servo theory.

---

[21] The "minimum phase" in this case, to which Eq. (133) or §7.9 applies, is zero radians rather than π radians. In order to apply Eq. (133) to Fig. 12-19, it is therefore necessary to reduce all phases in Fig. 12-19 by π radians.

[22] In an exceptional case, the locus of E_f/E_1 may cross the real axis to the right of the point $1 + j0$ without encircling this point. Such a case is shown in curve (c) of Fig. 12-16. This type of stability is, however, not reliable for design purposes.

APPENDIX A

Table of Integrals[1]

The following table includes a brief list of the elementary integrals, plus a number of definite integrals which are of special interest in connection with the present book. For a more extensive list, the reader should consult one of the standard tables of integrals. It may also be noted that the table of Laplace transforms in Appendix D is also a table of definite integrals.

1. $\displaystyle \int au\,dx = a\int u\,dx$

2. $\displaystyle \int (u+v)\,dx = \int u\,dx + \int v\,dx$

3. $\displaystyle \int (u-v)\,dx = \int u\,dx - \int v\,dx$

4. $\displaystyle \int \frac{dz}{dy}\frac{dy}{dx}\,dx = z + C$

5. $\displaystyle \int u\frac{dv}{dx}\,dx = uv - \int v\frac{du}{dx}\,dx$

6. $\displaystyle \int x^n\,dx = \frac{x^{n+1}}{n+1} + C$

7. $\displaystyle \int \epsilon^{bx}\,dx = \frac{\epsilon^{bx}}{b} + C$

8. $\displaystyle \int a^{bx}\,dx = \frac{a^{bx}}{b\log_\epsilon a} + C$

9. $\displaystyle \int \frac{dx}{x} = \log_\epsilon x + C = \log_\epsilon kx$

10. $\displaystyle \int \sin x\,dx = -\cos x + C$

11. $\displaystyle \int \cos x\,dx = \sin x + C$

[1] All logarithms in this table have the base ϵ.

12. $\int \tan x\,dx = -\log \cos x + C$

13. $\int \cot x\,dx = \log \sin x + C$

14. $\int \sec^2 x\,dx = \tan x + C$

15. $\int \csc^2 x\,dx = -\cot x + C$

16. $\int \tan x \sec x\,dx = \sec x + C$

17. $\int \cot x \csc x\,dx = -\csc x + C$

18. $\int \frac{dx}{a^2 + x^2} = \frac{1}{a} \tan^{-1}\left(\frac{x}{a}\right) + C = -\frac{1}{a} \cot^{-1}\left(\frac{x}{a}\right) + C'$

where $C' = C + \frac{\pi}{2}$

19. $\int \frac{dx}{\sqrt{a^2 - x^2}} = \sin^{-1}\left(\frac{x}{a}\right) + C = -\cos^{-1}\left(\frac{x}{a}\right) + C'$

20. $\int \frac{dx}{x\sqrt{x^2 - a^2}} = \frac{1}{a} \sec^{-1}\left(\frac{x}{a}\right) + C = -\frac{1}{a} \csc^{-1}\left(\frac{x}{a}\right) + C'$

21. $\int \sinh x\,dx = \cosh x + C$

22. $\int \cosh x\,dx = \sinh x + C$

23. $\int \frac{dx}{\sqrt{x^2 + a^2}} = \sinh^{-1}\left(\frac{x}{a}\right) + C = \log_\epsilon (x + \sqrt{x^2 + a^2}) + C$

24. $\int \frac{dx}{\sqrt{x^2 - a^2}} = \cosh^{-1}\left(\frac{x}{a}\right) + C = \log_\epsilon (x + \sqrt{x^2 - a^2}) + C$

25. $\int \frac{dx}{a^2 - x^2} = \frac{1}{a} \tanh^{-1}\left(\frac{x}{a}\right) + C = \frac{1}{2a} \log_\epsilon \left(\frac{a + x}{a - x}\right) + C$

26. $\int \frac{dx}{x^2 - a^2} = -\frac{1}{a} \coth^{-1}\left(\frac{x}{a}\right) + C = \frac{1}{2a} \log_\epsilon \left(\frac{x - a}{x + a}\right) + C$

27. $$\int \frac{dx}{x\sqrt{a^2 - x^2}} = \frac{-1}{a}\operatorname{sech}^{-1}\left(\frac{x}{a}\right) + C$$
$$= \frac{-1}{a}\log_\epsilon\left(\frac{a + \sqrt{a^2 - x^2}}{x}\right) + C$$

28. $$\int \frac{dx}{x\sqrt{a^2 + x^2}} = -\frac{1}{a}\operatorname{csch}^{-1}\left(\frac{x}{a}\right) + C$$
$$= \frac{1}{a}\log_\epsilon\left(\frac{a + \sqrt{a^2 + x^2}}{x}\right) + C$$

29. $$\int \sin^2 x\,dx = \frac{x}{2} - \frac{1}{2}\cos x \sin x + C = \frac{x}{2} - \frac{1}{4}\sin 2x + C$$

30. $$\int \cos^2 x\,dx = \frac{x}{2} + \frac{1}{2}\cos x \sin x + C = \frac{x}{2} + \frac{1}{4}\sin 2x + C$$

31. $$\int \sin mx \sin nx\,dx = \frac{\sin[(m-n)x]}{2(m-n)} - \frac{\sin[(m+n)x]}{2(m+n)} + C \qquad (m^2 \neq n^2)$$

32. $$\int \cos mx \cos nx\,dx = \frac{\sin[(m-n)x]}{2(m-n)} + \frac{\sin[(m+n)x]}{2(m+n)} + C \qquad (m^2 \neq n^2)$$

33. $$\int \sin mx \cos nx\,dx = -\frac{\cos[(m-n)x]}{2(m-n)} - \frac{\cos[(m+n)x]}{2(m+n)} + C$$

34. $$\int x \sin x\,dx = \sin x - x\cos x + C$$

35. $$\int x \cos x\,dx = \cos x + x\sin x + C$$

36. $$\int \epsilon^{ax}\sin bx\,dx = \frac{\epsilon^{ax}(a\sin bx - b\cos bx)}{a^2 + b^2} + C$$

37. $$\int \epsilon^{ax}\cos bx\,dx = \frac{\epsilon^{ax}(a\cos bx + b\sin bx)}{a^2 + b^2} + C$$

38. $$\int \epsilon^{ax}x^m\,dx = \frac{x^m\epsilon^{ax}}{a} - \frac{m}{a}\int \epsilon^{ax}x^{m-1}\,dx$$

39. $$\int_0^x \frac{\sin x}{x}\,dx = Si(x)$$

40. $$\int_x^\infty \frac{\cos x}{x}\,dx = -Ci(x)$$

41. $\int_0^\infty x^{n-1}\epsilon^{-x}\,dx = \Gamma(n) = (n-1)!$ (if n is an integer)

42. $\int_0^\infty \epsilon^{-ax^2}\,dx = \frac{1}{2}\sqrt{\frac{\pi}{a}}$

43. $\int_0^x \epsilon^{-x^2}\,dx = \frac{\sqrt{\pi}}{2}\,\mathrm{erf}\,(x)$

44. $\int_x^\infty \epsilon^{-x^2}\,dx = \frac{\sqrt{\pi}}{2}\,\mathrm{erfc}\,(x)$

45. $\frac{1}{\pi}\int_0^\pi \cos\,(n\phi - x\sin\phi)\,d\phi = J_n(x)$ (where n is any positive integer, including zero)

46. $\frac{1}{\pi}\int_0^\pi \sin\,(x\sin\phi)\sin n\phi\,d\phi$

$$= \begin{cases} J_n(x) & \text{(if } n \text{ is an odd positive integer)} \\ 0 & \text{(if } n \text{ is an even positive integer)} \end{cases}$$

47. $\frac{1}{\pi}\int_0^\pi \cos\,(x\sin\phi)\cos n\phi\,d\phi$

$$= \begin{cases} J_n(x) & \text{(if } n \text{ is an even positive integer)} \\ 0 & \text{(if } n \text{ is an odd positive integer)} \end{cases}$$

48. $\frac{1}{\pi}\int_0^\pi \cos\,(x\sin\phi)\,d\phi = J_0(x)$

49. $\int_0^\infty \frac{\sin mx}{x}\,dx = \frac{\pi}{2}$ (if m is positive)

50. $\int_0^\infty \frac{\cos bx}{1+x^2}\,dx = \begin{cases} \frac{\pi}{2}\epsilon^{-b} & \text{(if } b \text{ is a positive integer)} \\ \frac{\pi}{2}\epsilon^{b} & \text{(if } b \text{ is a negative integer)} \end{cases}$

51. $\int_0^\infty \frac{\tan x}{x}\,dx = \frac{\pi}{2}$

52. $\int_0^\infty \log\left(\frac{\epsilon^x+1}{\epsilon^x-1}\right)dx = \int_0^\infty \log\coth\frac{x}{2}\,dx = \frac{\pi^2}{4}$

53. $\int_{-\infty}^{+\infty} \epsilon^{-j2\pi ft}\,\frac{k}{\sqrt{\pi}}\,\epsilon^{-k^2t^2}\,dt = \epsilon^{-\frac{\pi^2f^2}{k^2}}$

54. $\int_0^\infty \frac{\sin^2 x}{x^2}\,dx = \frac{\pi}{2}$

APPENDIX B

Table of Identities Involving Hyperbolic Functions

1. $\sinh x = \dfrac{\epsilon^x - \epsilon^{-x}}{2}$

2. $\cosh x = \dfrac{\epsilon^x + \epsilon^{-x}}{2}$

3. $\tanh x = \dfrac{\sinh x}{\cosh x} = \dfrac{\epsilon^x - \epsilon^{-x}}{\epsilon^x + \epsilon^{-x}}$

4. $\coth x = \dfrac{\cosh x}{\sinh x} = \dfrac{\epsilon^x + \epsilon^{-x}}{\epsilon^x - \epsilon^{-x}}$

5. $\operatorname{sech} x = \dfrac{1}{\cosh x} = \dfrac{2}{\epsilon^x + \epsilon^{-x}}$

6. $\operatorname{csch} x = \dfrac{1}{\sinh x} = \dfrac{2}{\epsilon^x - \epsilon^{-x}}$

7. $\epsilon^x = \cosh x + \sinh x$

8. $\epsilon^{-x} = \cosh x - \sinh x$

9. $\cosh^2 x - \sinh^2 x = 1$

10. $\tanh^2 x + \operatorname{sech}^2 x = 1$

11. $\coth^2 x - \operatorname{csch}^2 x = 1$

12. $\sinh (-x) = -\sinh x$

13. $\cosh (-x) = \cosh x$

14. $\tanh (-x) = -\tanh x$

15. $\sinh (x + y) = \sinh x \cosh y + \cosh x \sinh y$

16. $\sinh (x - y) = \sinh x \cosh y - \cosh x \sinh y$

17. $\cosh (x + y) = \cosh x \cosh y + \sinh x \sinh y$

18. $\cosh (x - y) = \cosh x \cosh y - \sinh x \sinh y$

19. $\tanh (x + y) = \dfrac{\tanh x + \tanh y}{1 + \tanh x \tanh y}$

20. $\tanh (x - y) = \dfrac{\tanh x - \tanh y}{1 - \tanh x \tanh y}$

21. $\sinh 2x = 2 \sinh x \cosh x$

22. $\cosh 2x = \cosh^2 x + \sinh^2 x$

23. $\tanh 2x = \dfrac{2 \tanh x}{1 + \tanh^2 x}$

24. $\sinh\left(\dfrac{x}{2}\right) = \pm\sqrt{\dfrac{\cosh x - 1}{2}}$

25. $\cosh\left(\dfrac{x}{2}\right) = +\sqrt{\dfrac{\cosh x + 1}{2}}$

26. $\sinh (jx) = j \sin x$

27. $\cosh (jx) = \cos x$

28. $\tanh jx = j \tan x$

29. $\coth jx = -j \cot x$

30. $\cosh (\alpha + j\beta)x = \cosh \alpha x \cos \beta x + j \sinh \alpha x \sin \beta x$

31. $\sinh (\alpha + j\beta)x = \sinh \alpha x \cos \beta x + j \cosh \alpha x \sin \beta x$

32. $\sinh^{-1} x = \log_\epsilon (x + \sqrt{x^2 + 1})$ for any value of x

33. $\cosh^{-1} x = \log_\epsilon (x \pm \sqrt{x^2 - 1})$ provided $x > 1$

34. $\tanh^{-1} x = \dfrac{1}{2} \log_\epsilon \left(\dfrac{1 + x}{1 - x}\right)$ provided $x^2 < 1$

35. $\coth^{-1} x = \dfrac{1}{2} \log_\epsilon \left(\dfrac{x + 1}{x - 1}\right)$ provided $x^2 > 1$

36. $\operatorname{sech}^{-1} x = \log_\epsilon \left(\dfrac{1}{x} \pm \sqrt{\dfrac{1}{x^2} - 1}\right)$ provided $x < 1$

37. $\operatorname{csch}^{-1} x = \log_\epsilon \left(\dfrac{1}{x} + \sqrt{\dfrac{1}{x^2} + 1}\right)$ for any value of x

38. $\dfrac{d}{dx} (\sinh u) = \cosh u \dfrac{du}{dx}$

39. $\dfrac{d}{dx} (\cosh u) = \sinh u \dfrac{du}{dx}$

40. $\dfrac{d}{dx} (\tanh u) = \operatorname{sech}^2 u \dfrac{du}{dx}$

41. $\dfrac{d}{dx} (\coth u) = -\operatorname{csch}^2 u \dfrac{du}{dx}$

42. $\dfrac{d}{dx} (\operatorname{sech} u) = -\operatorname{sech} u \tanh u \dfrac{du}{dx}$

43. $\frac{d}{dx}(\operatorname{csch} u) = -\operatorname{csch} u \coth u \frac{du}{dx}$

44. $\frac{d}{dx}(\sinh^{-1} u) = \frac{\frac{du}{dx}}{\sqrt{u^2 + 1}}$

45. $\frac{d}{dx}(\cosh^{-1} u) = \frac{\pm \frac{du}{dx}}{\sqrt{u^2 - 1}}$

46. $\frac{d}{dx}(\tanh^{-1} u) = \frac{\frac{du}{dx}}{1 - u^2}$

47. $\frac{d}{dx}(\coth^{-1} u) = \frac{\frac{du}{dx}}{1 - u^2}$

48. $\frac{d}{dx}(\operatorname{sech}^{-1} u) = \frac{\pm \frac{du}{dx}}{u\sqrt{1 - u^2}}$

49. $\frac{d}{dx}(\operatorname{csch}^{-1} u) = \frac{\frac{du}{dx}}{-u\sqrt{u^2 + 1}}$

50. $\sinh x = x + \frac{x^3}{3!} + \frac{x^5}{5!} + \frac{x^7}{7!} + \cdots$

51. $\cosh x = 1 + \frac{x^2}{2!} + \frac{x^4}{4!} + \frac{x^6}{6!} + \cdots$

APPENDIX C

Basic Theory of Transmission Lines in the Steady State

C.1. Derivation of the fundamental equations

In this appendix we wish briefly to develop the principles of dealing with uniform transmission lines having distributed constants.[1] We will here limit the discussion to the development of the formulas which govern the steady-state operation of such lines. Methods of dealing with the transient state are developed in Chap. 10 and Chap. 11.

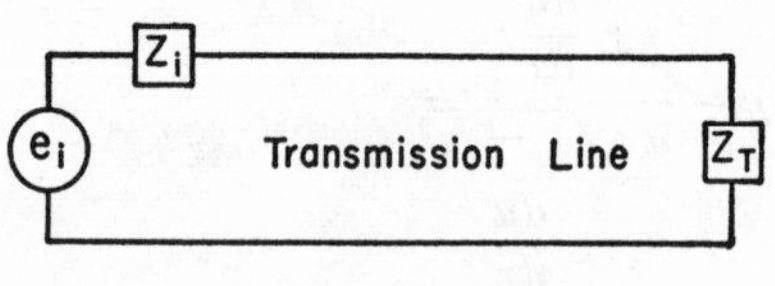

FIG. C-1.

A general example of a transmission line is shown in Fig. C-1. This may be pictured as two conductors which carry the electric power to a terminal impedance Z_T from a source, the latter having a voltage e_i and internal impedance Z_i. For direct current and very low frequencies, this line acts merely to add the resistance of the conductors as an element in series with the source and terminal impedances. However, as the frequency is increased, the distributed capacitance and inductance of the line become important quantities in the impedance of the system. Finally, at very high frequencies, the importance of the distributed capacitance and inductance becomes paramount and the line can better be described as a trans-

[1] There are also uniform transmission lines having lumped constants which have properties fundamentally similar to those of lines with distributed constants. These are described elsewhere (for example, in Chap. I of J. C. Slater's *Microwave Transmission*). However, since our interest in transmission lines is primarily as an illustration of the solution of partial differential equations by the methods of transformation calculus, we will not consider the lumped-constant lines.

mission path for traveling electric waves than it can as a pair of conducting elements between a source and a terminal impedance. It will now be our purpose to develop the fundamental equations which govern the behavior of transmission lines at high frequencies.

We will confine our considerations to what in electromagnetic theory is called the principal wave along the line. Under those circumstances, we can analyze the behavior of the line in terms of ordinary circuit theory with the aid of a few limiting processes. We will represent the transmission line as shown in Fig. C-2.

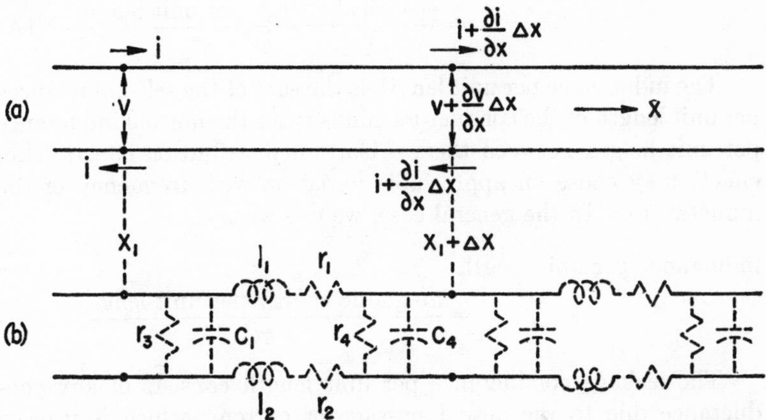

Fig. C-2. Representation of the elementary conditions in a transmission line.

Let x be the coordinate of length along the line and let x_1 be a particular location along the line. Let the voltage between the conductors at x_1 be v, and let the current along the line in the direction of the arrows be i. Then at the neighboring point $x_1 \times \Delta x$, the corresponding values are approximately

$$v + \frac{\partial v}{\partial x}\Delta x \qquad \text{and} \qquad i + \frac{\partial i}{\partial x}\Delta x$$

Next let

R = resistance per unit length of line
L = inductance per unit length
C = capacitance per unit length
G = leakage conductance per unit length

The resistance per unit length of the line is the ordinary resistance of the current-carrying conductors, also taking account of skin effect. The capacitance per unit length is the electrostatic capacitance between the conductors for most practical purposes. If, however, there are peculiarities in the potential distribution due to electromagnetic effects at close spacing and high frequency, the capacitance per unit length is more accurately determined by the equation

$$\text{capacitance per unit length} = \frac{\text{electrical energy per unit length}}{\frac{1}{2}v^2} \tag{1A}$$

The inductance per unit length is the sum of the self-inductances per unit length of the conductors minus twice the mutual inductance per unit length between them. Current distribution effects (skin effect) may cause an appreciable variation with frequency of the inductances. In the general case, we can write

$$\text{inductance per unit length} = \frac{\text{magnetic energy per unit length}}{\frac{1}{2}i^2} \tag{1B}$$

The leakage conductance per unit length consists of any conductance due to the actual passage of current, which is usually negligible, plus the dielectric loss per unit length divided by the square of the voltage.

With the foregoing interpretation, the equivalent impedance elements of the section of line between x_1 and $x_1 + \Delta x$ may then be represented as shown in Fig. C-2(b), where

$$r_1 + r_2 = \text{resistance of an elementary section of line of length } \Delta x = R\,\Delta x \tag{2}$$

$$l_1 + l_2 = \text{inductance of an elementary section of line of length } \Delta x = L\,\Delta x \tag{3}$$

$$\frac{1}{r_3} + \frac{1}{r_4} = \text{leakage conductance of an elementary section of line of length } \Delta x = G\,\Delta x \tag{4}$$

$$c_1 + c_2 = \text{capacitance of an elementary section of line of length } \Delta x = C\,\Delta x \tag{5}$$

If we express the voltage drop in the element Δx in terms of the line characteristics, we have, by the methods of Chap. 2,

$$-\frac{\partial v}{\partial x}\,\Delta x = \text{voltage drop in } \Delta x = Ri\,\Delta x + L\,\frac{\partial i}{\partial t}\,\Delta x \tag{6}$$

In a similar manner, we have for the decrease in current

$$\begin{aligned}-\frac{\partial i}{\partial x}\,\Delta x &= \text{decrease in line current in length } \Delta x\\ &= Gv\,\Delta x + \frac{\partial}{\partial t}\,(vC\,\Delta x) = Gv\,\Delta x + C\,\frac{\partial v}{\partial t}\,\Delta x\end{aligned} \tag{7}$$

Dividing Δx out of Eqs. (6) and (7), we obtain

$$-\frac{\partial v}{\partial x} = Ri + L\,\frac{\partial i}{\partial t} \tag{8}$$

$$-\frac{\partial i}{\partial x} = Gv + C\,\frac{\partial v}{\partial t} \tag{9}$$

Equations (8) and (9) are the fundamental equations of transmission-line theory. In the remainder of this appendix we will use them to derive the formulas which govern the behavior of transmission lines in steady-state operation. In Chap. 10 they are used in studying the transient behavior of lines.

C.2. The basic equations of transmission lines in steady-state operation

Let us now consider the steady-state operation of a transmission line, and suppose that the applied voltage is a simple harmonic function of time. Then, since there are no nonlinear elements in the line, so that Eqs. (8) and (9) are linear and have constant coefficients, the current and voltage at every point along the line will likewise be harmonic functions of time of the same frequency. If, then, we express the voltage and current as the complex exponentials[2]

$$v = V\epsilon^{j\omega t} \tag{10}$$

and

$$i = I\epsilon^{j\omega t} \tag{11}$$

[2] V and I are complex quantities, whose magnitudes represent the peak values of v and i and whose phases represent the phases of v and i with respect to some standard values. V and I are each functions of x but not of t.

Eqs. (8) and (9) become, after dividing through by $\epsilon^{j\omega t}$,

$$-\frac{\partial V}{\partial x} = (R + j\omega L)I \tag{12}$$

$$-\frac{\partial I}{\partial x} = (G + j\omega C)V \tag{13}$$

Differentiating Eq. (12) with respect to x and substituting it in Eq. (13), we obtain

$$\frac{\partial^2 V}{\partial x^2} = -(R + j\omega L)\frac{\partial I}{\partial x} = (R + j\omega L)(G + j\omega C)V \tag{14}$$

If we then let

$$n = \{(R + j\omega L)(G + j\omega C)\}^{\frac{1}{2}} = \alpha + j\beta \tag{15}$$

Eq. (14) becomes

$$\frac{\partial^2 V}{\partial x^2} = n^2 V \tag{16}$$

In a similar manner, we could obtain

$$\frac{\partial^2 I}{\partial x^2} = n^2 I \tag{17}$$

The quantity n is called the *propagation constant* of the line. Its significance, as well as that of α and β, will be explained very soon.

Since V and I are functions of x alone, Eqs. (16) and (17) can be solved by the methods of solving linear differential equations with constant coefficients. Their solutions are accordingly

$$V = a\epsilon^{nx} + b\epsilon^{-nx} \tag{18}$$

and

$$I = c\epsilon^{nx} + d\epsilon^{-nx} \tag{19}$$

The four constants a, b, c, and d are not all independent, but are related through Eqs. (12) and (13). If we substitute Eqs. (18) and (19) into Eq. (12), we obtain

$$-na\epsilon^{nx} + nb\epsilon^{-nx} = (R + j\omega L)(c\epsilon^{nx} + d\epsilon^{-nx}) \tag{20}$$

Since Eq. (20) holds for all values of x, and not just at isolated points, the coefficients of ϵ^{nx} and ϵ^{-nx} on opposite sides of the equation must be equal. Therefore.

$$c = \frac{-na}{R + j\omega L} = -\sqrt{\frac{G + j\omega C}{R + j\omega L}}\, a = \frac{-a}{Z_0} \tag{21}$$

and
$$d = \frac{nb}{R + j\omega L} = \sqrt{\frac{G + j\omega C}{R + j\omega L}}\, b = \frac{b}{Z_0} \tag{22}$$

where the quantity
$$Z_0 = \sqrt{\frac{R + j\omega L}{G + j\omega C}} \tag{23}$$

is called the *surge impedance*[3] of the transmission line.

If we substituted Eqs. (18) and (19) into Eq. (13), we would again get Eqs. (21) and (22). No new information is obtained, because Eqs. (12) and (13) were used together in deriving Eqs. (16) and (17).

We next substitute Eqs. (21) and (22) into Eq. (19) and obtain

$$I = \frac{-a\epsilon^{nx} + b\epsilon^{-nx}}{Z_0} \tag{24}$$

Equations (18) and (24) are the solutions of Eqs. (12) and (13) and hence are the formal solutions of our problem. The constants

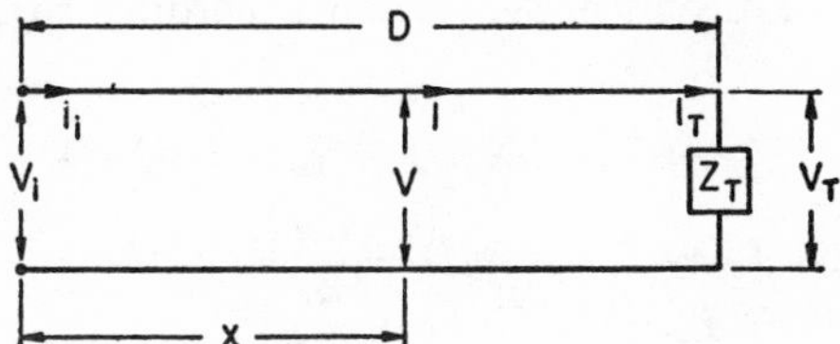

FIG. C-3. The specification of currents and voltages at various points along a transmission line.

a and b can be determined by specifying the boundary conditions. For example, suppose we specify the input of the line as the origin of x and let $V = V_i$ and $I = I_i$ at the input of the line. (See Fig. C-3.) Then we have, from Eq. (18),

[3] In the case of a line of uniform cross section, Z_0 is also called the characteristic impedance. [See Eqs. (88) and (89).] Since we are here discussing uniform lines, we may use the terms *surge impedance* and *characteristic impedance* interchangeably.

$$V_i = a + b \tag{25}$$

and from Eq. (24)
$$I_i = \frac{-a + b}{Z_0} \tag{26}$$

Therefore,
$$b = \frac{V_i + I_i Z_0}{2} \tag{27}$$

$$a = \frac{V_i - I_i Z_0}{2} \tag{28}$$

Thus Eqs. (18) and (24) become[4]

$$\begin{aligned} V &= \tfrac{1}{2}\{V_i(\epsilon^{nx} + \epsilon^{-nx}) - I_i Z_0(\epsilon^{nx} - \epsilon^{-nx})\} \\ &= V_i \cosh nx - I_i Z_0 \sinh nx \end{aligned} \tag{29}$$

$$\begin{aligned} I &= \frac{1}{2}\left\{I_i(\epsilon^{nx} + \epsilon^{-nx}) - \frac{V_i}{Z_0}(\epsilon^{nx} - \epsilon^{-nx})\right\} \\ &= I_i \cosh nx - \frac{V_i}{Z_0}\sinh nx \end{aligned} \tag{30}$$

Equations (29) and (30) give the values of the voltage V and current I at any point x along the line in terms of the values of V_i and I_i. Now suppose that the line is of length D, and is terminated in an impedance Z_T. Then according to Eqs. (29) and (30),

$$V_T = V_i \cosh nD - I_i Z_0 \sinh nD \tag{31}$$

$$I_T = I_i \cosh nD - \frac{V_i}{Z_0}\sinh nD \tag{32}$$

We can then also solve Eqs. (31) and (32) as simultaneous equations to get

$$V_i = V_T \cosh nD + Z_0 I_T \sinh nD \tag{33}$$

and
$$I_i = I_T \cosh nD + \frac{V_T}{Z_0}\sinh nD \tag{34}$$

making use of the fact that

$$\cosh^2 nD - \sinh^2 nD = 1 \tag{35}$$

[4] Formulas for relations involving hyperbolic functions are given in Appendix B.

The foregoing equations give the relations between input and output (terminal) voltages and currents in terms of the line length and characteristic impedance. These are very important practical formulas. Another formula of great practical importance is that for the input impedance of the line Z_i. This is obtained by dividing Eq. (33) by Eq. (34). Thus

$$Z_i = \frac{V_i}{I_i} = \frac{V_T \cosh nD + Z_0 I_T \sinh nD}{I_T \cosh nD + \dfrac{V_T}{Z_0} \sinh nD}$$

$$= Z_0 \left[\frac{Z_T \cosh nD + Z_0 \sinh nD}{Z_0 \cosh nD + Z_T \sinh nD} \right] \tag{36}$$

in which we have made use of the fact that

$$Z_T = \frac{V_T}{I_T} \tag{37}$$

From Eq. (33) we also obtain the driving impedance for output current with respect to input voltage

$$Z_{iT} = \frac{V_i}{I_T} = Z_T \cosh nD + Z_0 \sinh nD \tag{38}$$

The foregoing equations give a rather complete set of fundamental formulas for dealing with transmission lines. However, they do not yet give a clear physical picture of what is going on. For the intelligent use of these formulas and for facility in dealing with practical transmission-line problems, a good physical grasp of the situation is necessary. We therefore turn now to look into the physical meaning of some of the equations we have derived. As a preliminary, however, we will first briefly study the mathematical properties of traveling waves.

C.3. Traveling waves

A function of the form

$$A \cos \left(\omega t - \frac{2\pi x}{\lambda} + \phi \right) \tag{39}$$

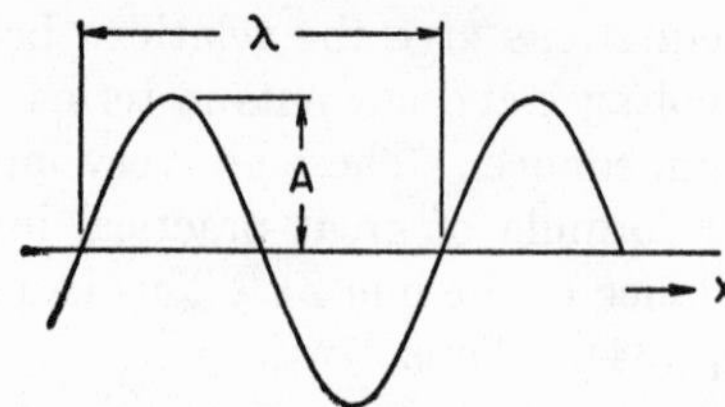

FIG. C-4. A cosine wave, showing its amplitude and wavelength.

may be called a pure traveling cosine wave. In the expression (39) the constants are (see Fig. C-4)

$A \equiv$ wave amplitude (peak value)
$\omega \equiv 2\pi$ times frequency
$\lambda \equiv$ wave length
$\phi \equiv$ phase constant

and the variables are

$t \equiv$ time
$x \equiv$ length (in the direction of propagation)

This expression is called a pure traveling cosine wave for the following combination of reasons:

1. At any point x_1, the function is

$$A \cos [\omega t + \theta_1] \tag{40}$$

as a function of time, where θ_1 is the phase constant

$$\theta_1 = \phi - \frac{2\pi x_1}{\lambda} \tag{41}$$

Thus Eq. (40) is a pure cosine wave as a function of time.

2. At any instant of time t_1, the function is

$$A \cos \left(\omega t_1 - \frac{2\pi x}{\lambda} + \phi\right) = A \cos \left(\frac{2\pi x}{\lambda} + \theta_2\right) \tag{42}$$

as a function of x, where θ_2 is the phase constant

$$\theta_2 = -\omega t_1 - \phi \tag{43}$$

Thus Eq. (42) is a pure cosine wave as a function of length.

3. The value of the function at location x_1 and time t_1 is

$$A \cos\left(\omega t_1 - \frac{2\pi x_1}{\lambda} + \phi\right)$$

The function (39) has the same value at location x_2 and time t_2 if

$$\omega t_1 - \frac{2\pi x_1}{\lambda} + \phi = \omega t_2 - \frac{2\pi x_2}{\lambda} + \phi \tag{44}$$

i.e., if

$$x_2 - x_1 = \frac{\omega\lambda}{2\pi}(t_2 - t_1) \tag{45}$$

Any value of the function may therefore be considered as traveling in the direction x with a velocity S, where

$$S = \frac{\omega\lambda}{2\pi} = f\lambda \tag{46}$$

and

$$f = \frac{\omega}{2\pi} = \text{frequency} \tag{47}$$

S is called the *wave velocity* or *phase velocity.*

The expression (39) may be transformed into a number of other forms, each of which is useful at times. Thus

$$\begin{aligned} A \cos\left(\omega t - \frac{2\pi x}{\lambda} + \phi\right) &= A \cos\left[\omega\left(t - \frac{x}{S}\right) + \phi\right] \\ &= A \cos\left[\frac{2\pi}{\lambda}(St - x) + \phi\right] \\ &= A \cos(\omega t - \beta x + \phi) \qquad (48) \end{aligned}$$

The symbol β in the last expression is called the *phase-shift constant.* A comparison of the expressions in Eq. (48) shows that

$$\beta = \frac{2\pi}{\lambda} = \frac{\omega}{S} \tag{49}$$

Any of the expressions in Eq. (48) may be used to represent a cosine wave traveling with a velocity S in the x direction, as shown in Fig. C-4. The traveling cosine waves in Eq. (48) may be changed to traveling sine waves by adding $\pi/2$ to the phase constant. Thus it follows from trigonometry that

$$A \cos\left(\omega t - \frac{2\pi x}{\lambda} + \phi\right) = A \sin\left(\omega t - \frac{2\pi x}{\lambda} + \phi + \frac{\pi}{2}\right) \quad (50)$$

The expressions in Eq. (48) represent a cosine wave traveling in the x direction without change of waveform or amplitude. In actual physical systems, it is not uncommon for signals to travel practically without change of waveform, but they usually undergo a gradual loss in amplitude. In many physical systems,[5] a given length of travel, say 100 ft, will attenuate the signal amplitude by the same ratio, regardless of the amplitude of the signal or of where in the path the particular 100 ft in question is chosen. The reader can show as an exercise that, in such a case, the amplitude of a signal may then be expressed as[6]

$$A = A_0\epsilon^{-\alpha x} \quad (51)$$

where A_0 is the amplitude of the wave at $x = 0$ and α is a constant. It is customary to call α the *attenuation constant* of the system. A pure cosine wave traveling through an attenuating system may therefore be expressed as

$$A_0\epsilon^{-\alpha x} \cos\left(\omega t - \frac{2\pi x}{\lambda} + \phi\right) \quad (52)$$

For many purposes, it is convenient to have an expression for (52) in complex exponential form, in which (52) is the real part of the complex expression. Thus we can write

$$A_0\epsilon^{-\alpha x} \cos\left(\omega t - \frac{2\pi x}{\lambda} + \phi\right) = Re\{A_0\epsilon^{-\alpha x + j\left[\omega t - \frac{2\pi x}{\lambda} + \phi\right]}\} \quad (53)$$

Actually, complex expressions of a somewhat more general form than Eq. (53) may represent attenuated cosine waves. For example, if B is the complex quantity

$$B = B_1\epsilon^{j\phi_1} \quad (54)$$

---

[5] In the next section, we will show that a transmission line is such a system.

[6] In this case,

$$\text{db loss per unit length} = 20\ (\log_{10} \epsilon)\alpha = 8.686\alpha$$

where B_1 and ϕ_1 are real, then

$$Re\{B\epsilon^{-\alpha x+b+j\left[\omega t-\frac{2\pi x}{\lambda}+\phi_0\right]}\} = (B_1\epsilon^b)\epsilon^{-\alpha x}\cos\left(\omega t - \frac{2\pi x}{\lambda} + \phi_0 + \phi_1\right) \tag{55}$$

is also an attenuated cosine wave. In the next section, we will meet expressions of the type of Eq. (55).

With the foregoing background on the subject of traveling waves, we are now ready to proceed with our study of the physical interpretation of transmission-line formulas.

C.4. The physical picture of transmission-line phenomena—propagation and reflection—characteristic impedance

In order to get a good physical picture of what is going on when a transmission line is in steady-state operation, we start with Eqs. (29) and (30) for the voltage and current variation along the line. We will find it more instructive to express these equations in terms of the terminal values of V and I rather than of the input values. Therefore, let us substitute Eqs. (33) and (34) into Eq. (29). Thus Eq. (29) becomes

$$\begin{aligned} V &= V_i \cosh nx - I_i Z_0 \sinh nx \\ &= [V_T \cosh nD + Z_0 I_T \sinh nD] \cosh nx \\ &\quad - Z_0\left[I_T \cosh nD + \frac{V_T}{Z_0}\sinh nD\right]\sinh nx \\ &= V_T \cosh nD \cosh nx + Z_0 I_T \sinh nD \cosh nx \\ &\quad - Z_0 I_T \cosh nD \sinh nx - V_T \sinh nD \sinh nx \\ &= V_T \cosh [n(D - x)] + Z_0 I_T \sinh [n(D - x)] \end{aligned} \tag{56}$$

In the foregoing manipulations, we have used Eqs. (16) and (18) of Appendix B.

In an entirely similar manner, if we start from Eq. (30), we can derive the equation

$$I = I_T \cosh [n(D - x)] + \frac{V_T}{Z_0}\sinh [n(D - x)] \tag{57}$$

According to Eqs. (10) and (11), the instantaneous current or voltage at any point x along the line is the real part of $I\epsilon^{j\omega t}$ or $V\epsilon^{j\omega t}$, respectively. From Eqs. (10) and (56) we therefore have, for the instantaneous complex voltage,

$$v = V\epsilon^{j\omega t} = \{V_T \cosh [n(D - x)] + Z_0 I_T \sinh [n(D - x)]\}\epsilon^{j\omega t}$$

$$= \left\{ V_T \frac{\epsilon^{n(D-x)} + \epsilon^{-n(D-x)}}{2} + Z_0 I_T \frac{\epsilon^{n(D-x)} - \epsilon^{-n(D-x)}}{2} \right\} \epsilon^{j\omega t}$$

$$= \left\{ V_T \frac{\epsilon^{(\alpha+j\beta)(D-x)} + \epsilon^{-(\alpha+j\beta)(D-x)}}{2} \right.$$

$$\left. + \frac{Z_0 V_T}{Z_T} \frac{\epsilon^{(\alpha+j\beta)(D-x)} - \epsilon^{-(\alpha+j\beta)(D-x)}}{2} \right\} \epsilon^{j\omega t}$$

$$= \frac{V_T}{2} \left\{ \left(1 + \frac{Z_0}{Z_T}\right) \epsilon^{\alpha(D-x)} \epsilon^{j[\omega t+\beta(D-x)]} \right.$$

$$\left. + \left(1 - \frac{Z_0}{Z_T}\right) \epsilon^{-\alpha(D-x)} \epsilon^{j[\omega t+\beta(D-x)]} \right\} \tag{58}$$

and from Eqs. (11) and (57) we have, after similar manipulations,

$$i = I\epsilon^{j\omega t} = \frac{I_T}{2} \left\{ \left(1 + \frac{Z_T}{Z_0}\right) \epsilon^{\alpha(D-x)} \epsilon^{j[\omega t+\beta(D-x)]} \right.$$

$$\left. + \left(1 - \frac{Z_T}{Z_0}\right) \epsilon^{-\alpha(D-x)} \epsilon^{j[\omega t-\beta(D-x)]} \right\} \tag{59}$$

In Eqs. (58) and (59) for the current and voltage in a transmission line, we finally have expressions of a form suitable for physical interpretation. Comparing Eq. (58) with (55) and (52) we see that Eq. (58) consists of the superposition of two traveling attenuated cosine waves

$$\frac{V_T}{2} \left(1 + \frac{Z_0}{Z_T}\right) \epsilon^{\alpha(D-x)} \epsilon^{j[\omega t+\beta(D-x)]} \tag{60}$$

and

$$\frac{V_T}{2} \left(1 - \frac{Z_0}{Z_T}\right) \epsilon^{-\alpha(D-x)} \epsilon^{j[\omega t-\beta(D-x)]} \tag{61}$$

Of these, (60) is traveling in the direction of $+x$ (i.e., toward the terminal impedance Z_T); and the term $\epsilon^{\alpha(D-x)}$ shows that it is attenuated at the rate of 20 $(\log_{10} \epsilon)\alpha$ db per unit length as it travels *toward* Z_T. On the other hand, (61) is traveling in the direction of $-x$ (i.e., away from Z_T); and the term $\epsilon^{-\alpha(D-x)}$ shows that it is attenuated at the rate of $20(\log_{10} \epsilon)\alpha$ db per unit length as it travels *away from* Z_T. Since the system is in the steady state, there is no attenuation with time. The expression (61) thus represents the reflected wave produced when the wave (60) is reflected at the terminal impedance. Comparison of expressions (60) and (61) shows that the coefficient of reflection at Z_T is

$$\frac{\left(1 - \frac{Z_0}{Z_T}\right)}{\left(1 + \frac{Z_0}{Z_T}\right)} = \frac{Z_T - Z_0}{Z_T + Z_0} \tag{62}$$

This means that at Z_T the reflected wave has an amplitude of

$$\left|\frac{Z_T - Z_0}{Z_T + Z_0}\right| \tag{63}$$

times the amplitude of the incident wave, and furthermore there is a phase change at reflection of the amount of the phase of the complex quantity

$$\frac{Z_T - Z_0}{Z_T + Z_0} \tag{64}$$

In an entirely similar manner, we can show that Eq. (59) represents a traveling cosine wave of current

$$\frac{I_T}{2}\left(1 + \frac{Z_T}{Z_0}\right) \epsilon^{\alpha(D-x)} \epsilon^{j[\omega t + \beta(D-x)]} \tag{65}$$

traveling toward Z_T, and the wave caused by its reflection at Z_T, namely

$$\frac{I_T}{2}\left(1 - \frac{Z_T}{Z_0}\right) \epsilon^{-\alpha(D-x)} \epsilon^{j[\omega t - \beta(D-x)]} \tag{66}$$

For the current wave, however, the coefficient of reflection is

$$\frac{\left(1 - \frac{Z_T}{Z_0}\right)}{\left(1 + \frac{Z_T}{Z_0}\right)} = \frac{Z_0 - Z_T}{Z_0 + Z_T} \tag{67}$$

This has the same magnitude as Eq. (62) but there is a phase difference[7] between them of 180°. (See Fig. C-5.)

We have now shown that the current and voltage in a transmission line each consists of the superposition of a wave traveling toward Z_T and the wave in the opposite direction produced by its reflection at Z_T. To complete the picture we will now investigate the significance of Z_0 by letting

$$Z_T = Z_0 \tag{68}$$

in Eqs. (58) and (59). When we do this, we see that the reflected wave is eliminated. Thus anywhere along the actual line, it is impossible to tell whether the line is infinitely long or whether it is

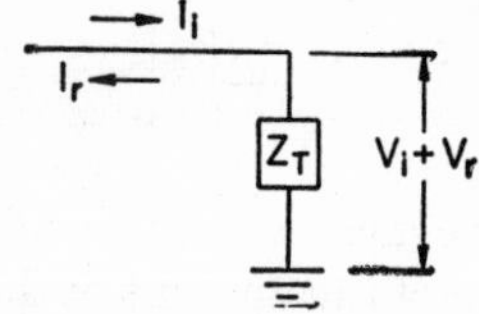

FIG. C-5.

terminated in its surge impedance. It thus appears that *an infinitely long line of surge impedance Z_0 looks, to its input terminals, like a fixed impedance Z_0 when we limit our consideration to the steady state.* This fact can be derived independently from Eq. (36), if we assume that the line has a finite attenuation constant α, regardless of how small α may be. In that case, Eq. (36) becomes

$$\lim_{D\to\infty} Z_i = \frac{V_T(\epsilon^{nD} + \epsilon^{-nD}) + Z_0 I_T(\epsilon^{nD} - \epsilon^{-nD})}{I_T(\epsilon^{nD} + \epsilon^{-nD}) + \dfrac{V_T}{Z_0}(\epsilon^{nD} - \epsilon^{-nD})}$$

$$= \frac{(V_T + Z_0 I_T)\epsilon^{nD}}{\left(I_T + \dfrac{V_T}{Z_0}\right)\epsilon^{nD}} = Z_0 \tag{69}$$

since $$\lim_{D\to\infty} \epsilon^{-nD} = \lim_{D\to\infty} \epsilon^{-(\alpha+j\beta)D} = 0 \tag{70}$$

Furthermore, regardless of the value of D or α, if $Z_T = Z_0$ in Eq. (36) then $Z_i = Z_0$. Thus, *a line terminated in its surge imped-*

[7] Figure C-5 shows in a general way why the incident and reflected current waves will have 180° more phase shift between them than the corresponding voltage waves.

ance has the same input impedance as an infinitely long line. This is not surprising, since, according to Eqs. (62) and (67), a line terminated in its surge impedance has no reflected wave.

C.5. Analysis in terms of multiple reflections

It is possible to derive alternative forms for Eqs. (58) and (59), which give, perhaps, an even clearer physical picture of what is really going on in a transmission line. Consider the system shown in Fig. C-6 in which a generator of terminal voltage E cos ωt, in

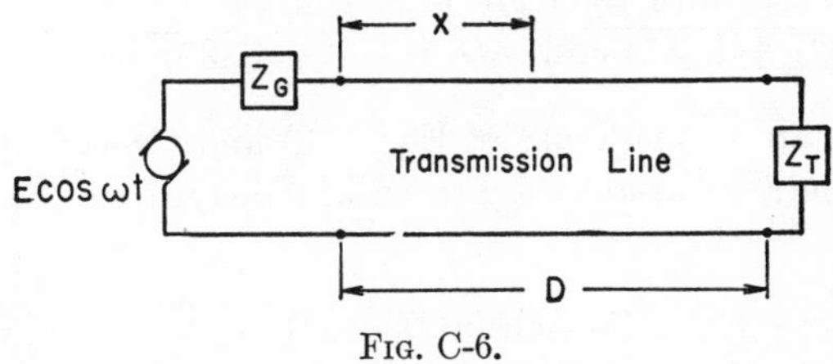

FIG. C-6.

series with an impedance Z_G, is attached to a transmission line of characteristic impedance Z_0, terminated in an impedance Z_T. Then the current entering the line is

$$I_i = \frac{E}{Z_G + Z_i} \tag{71}$$

where Z_i is the input impedance of the line given by Eq. (36). Substituting the value of Z_i from Eq. (36) into Eq. (71), we obtain

$$\begin{aligned} I_i &= \frac{E}{Z_G + Z_0\left[\dfrac{Z_T \cosh nD + Z_0 \sinh nD}{Z_0 \cosh nD + Z_T \sinh nD}\right]} \\ &= \frac{E(Z_0 \cosh nD + Z_T \sinh nD)}{(Z_0 Z_G + Z_0 Z_T) \cosh nD + (Z_0^2 + Z_G Z_T) \sinh nD} \end{aligned} \tag{72}$$

For the input voltage V_i across the line, we have

$$\begin{aligned} V_i = \frac{EZ_i}{Z_i + Z_G} &= \frac{EZ_0\left[\dfrac{Z_T \cosh nD + Z_0 \sinh nD}{Z_0 \cosh nD + Z_T \sinh nD}\right]}{Z_0\left[\dfrac{Z_T \cosh nD + Z_0 \sinh nD}{Z_0 \cosh nD + Z_T \sinh nD}\right] + Z_G} \\ &= \frac{EZ_0(Z_T \cosh nD + Z_0 \sinh nD)}{(Z_0 Z_T + Z_0 Z_G) \cosh nD + (Z_0^2 + Z_G Z_T) \sinh nD} \end{aligned} \tag{73}$$

Now the current at any point x is, according to Eq. (30),

$$I = I_i \cosh nx - \frac{V_i}{Z_0} \sinh nx \tag{74}$$

Substituting Eqs. (72) and (73) into Eq. (74), we obtain

$$I = \frac{E[(Z_0 \cosh nD + Z_T \sinh nD) \cosh nx - (Z_T \cosh nD + Z_0 \sinh nD) \sinh nx]}{(Z_0 Z_T + Z_0 Z_G) \cosh nD + (Z_0^2 + Z_G Z_T) \sinh nD}$$

$$= E \left\{ \frac{Z_0 \cosh [n(D - x)] + Z_T \sinh [n(D - x)]}{(Z_0 Z_T + Z_0 Z_G) \cosh nD + (Z_0^2 + Z_G Z_T) \sinh nD} \right\} \tag{75}$$

In the last step we made use of Eqs. (16) and (18) of Appendix B.

The numerator inside the braces in Eq. (75) can be put in the form

$$Z_0 \cosh [n(D - x)] + Z_T \sinh [n(D - x)] = \frac{Z_0(\epsilon^{nD-nx} + \epsilon^{-nD+nx}) + Z_T(\epsilon^{nD-nx} - \epsilon^{-nD+nx})}{2}$$

$$= \frac{\epsilon^{nD}}{2} [\epsilon^{-nx}(Z_0 + Z_T) + \epsilon^{-2nD+nx}(Z_0 - Z_T)] \tag{76}$$

The denominator of Eq. (75) can be put in the form

$$(Z_0 Z_T + Z_0 Z_G) \cosh nD + (Z_0^2 + Z_G Z_T) \sinh nD$$
$$= (Z_0 Z_T + Z_0 Z_G + Z_0^2 + Z_G Z_T) \frac{\epsilon^{nD}}{2} + (Z_0 Z_T + Z_0 Z_G - Z_0^2 - Z_G Z_T) \frac{\epsilon^{-nD}}{2}$$
$$= (Z_0 + Z_G)(Z_0 + Z_T) \frac{\epsilon^{nD}}{2} - (Z_0 - Z_G)(Z_0 - Z_T) \frac{\epsilon^{-nD}}{2}$$
$$= \frac{\epsilon^{nD}}{2} (Z_0 + Z_G)(Z_0 + Z_T) \left[1 - \frac{(Z_0 + Z_G)(Z_0 - Z_T)}{(Z_0 + Z_G)(Z_0 + Z_T)} \epsilon^{-2nD} \right] \tag{77}$$

Let us use the abbreviations

$$M = \frac{Z_0 - Z_G}{Z_0 + Z_G} \tag{78}$$

and

$$N = \frac{Z_0 - Z_T}{Z_0 + Z_T} \tag{79}$$

Then, substituting Eqs. (76) and (77) into Eq. (75), we have

$$I = E\,\frac{\dfrac{\epsilon^{nD}}{2}\,[(Z_0 + Z_T)\epsilon^{-nx} + (Z_0 - Z_T)\epsilon^{nx-2nD}]}{\dfrac{\epsilon^{nD}}{2}\,(Z_0 + Z_G)(Z_0 + Z_T)(1 - MN\epsilon^{-2nD})}$$

$$= \frac{E}{Z_0 + Z_G}\,\frac{\epsilon^{-nx} + N\epsilon^{nx-2nD}}{1 - MN\epsilon^{-2nD}} \qquad (80)$$

Now if the absolute value of y is less than 1, the quantity $\left(\dfrac{1}{1-y}\right)$ can be expanded into a convergent power series of the form

$$\frac{1}{1-y} = 1 + y + y^2 + y^3 + \cdots + y^n + \cdots \qquad (81)$$

Furthermore, in all physical transmission lines, the absolute value of $MN\epsilon^{-2nD}$ is actually less than 1. Therefore Eq. (80) can be expanded into the form

$$I = \frac{E}{Z_0 + Z_G}\,(\epsilon^{-nx} + N\epsilon^{nx-2nD})$$
$$(1 + MN\epsilon^{-2nD} + M^2N^2\epsilon^{-4nD} + \cdots) \qquad (82)$$

Substituting Eq. (82) into Eq. (11), and using the equation

$$n = \alpha + j\beta \qquad (83)$$

we have for the instantaneous complex current

$$i = \frac{E}{Z_0 + Z_G}\,\{\epsilon^{-\alpha x}\epsilon^{j(\omega t - \beta x)} + N\epsilon^{-\alpha(2D-x)}\epsilon^{j[\omega t - \beta(2D-x)]}$$
$$+ MN\epsilon^{-\alpha(2D+x)}\epsilon^{j[\omega t - \beta(2D+x)]} + MN^2\epsilon^{-\alpha(4D-x)}\epsilon^{j[\omega t - \beta(4D-x)]}$$
$$+ M^2N^2\epsilon^{-\alpha(4D+x)}\epsilon^{j[\omega t - \beta(4D+x)]} + M^2N^3\epsilon^{-\alpha(6D-x)}\epsilon^{j[\omega t - \beta(6D-x)]}$$
$$+ \cdots\} \qquad (84)$$

In a similar manner we could derive the equation for the instantaneous complex voltage

$$v = E\,\frac{Z_0}{Z_0 + Z_G}\,\{\epsilon^{-\alpha x}\epsilon^{j(\omega t - \beta x)} - N\epsilon^{-\alpha(2D-x)}\epsilon^{j[\omega t - \beta(2D-x)]}$$
$$+ MN\epsilon^{-\alpha(2D+x)}\epsilon^{j[\omega t - \beta(2D+x)]} - MN^2\epsilon^{-\alpha(4D-x)}\epsilon^{j[\omega t - \beta(4D-x)]}$$
$$+ M^2N^2\epsilon^{-\alpha(4D+x)}\epsilon^{j[\omega t - \beta(4D+x)]} - M^2N^3\epsilon^{-\alpha(6D-x)}\epsilon^{j[\omega t - \beta(6D-x)]}$$
$$+ \cdots\} \qquad (85)$$

Equations (84) and (85) have great physical significance. They tell us that, for example, the total current at any point along the line is the superposition of a wave

$$\frac{E}{Z_0 + Z_G} \epsilon^{-\alpha x} \epsilon^{j(\omega t - \beta x)}$$

which enters the line plus its reflection from Z_T, namely

$$\frac{E_0}{Z_0 + Z_G} N \epsilon^{-\alpha(2D-x)} \epsilon^{j[\omega t - \beta(2D-x)]}$$

plus the reflection of this wave at the generator end, plus multiple reflections back and forth from the ends of the line as long as there is any amplitude left. *The coefficient of reflection for current waves at Z_T and Z_G are N and M respectively, while the coefficients of reflection for voltage waves are $(-N)$ and $(-M)$.*

The foregoing analysis gives a clearer picture of the physical processes occurring in transmission lines than does the earlier analysis[8] of §C.4. The results are very important in practice. For example, we know from Eq. (78) that there is no reflection from the generator end of the line if

$$Z_G = Z_0 \tag{86}$$

Consequently, in this case, we have for the complete solution for the current

$$i = \frac{E}{Z_0 + Z_G} \{\epsilon^{-\alpha x} \epsilon^{j(\omega t - \beta x)} + N \epsilon^{-\alpha(2D-x)} \epsilon^{j[\omega t - \beta(2D-x)]}\} \tag{87}$$

with a corresponding equation for voltage.

A comparison of Eqs. (84) and (85) shows that, for forward-traveling waves (i.e., waves traveling toward Z_T),

$$\frac{V_f}{I_f} = Z_0 \tag{88}$$

[8] Equations (84) and (85) must, of course, actually give the same values of current and voltage as Eqs. (58) and (59). However, Eqs. (58) and (59) express the current and voltage in terms of terminal voltage and impedance instead of the generator voltage and impedance as done by Eqs. (84) and (85). Furthermore, the latter actually analyze the system into the individual multiple reflections. Each method of expression has its own field of application.

where V_f and I_f are the voltage and current of the particular wave. For backward-traveling waves (i.e., waves traveling toward Z_G),

$$\frac{V_b}{I_b} = -Z_0 \tag{89}$$

The ratio of voltage to current in a line for a wave of one frequency in the steady state is called the *characteristic impedance* of a line. For lines of uniform cross section, to which our analysis has been confined, Eqs. (88) and (89) tell us that the characteristic impedance, for all frequencies and in both directions, is equal to the surge impedance.[9]

Equations (88) and (89) are of special value in dealing with boundary conditions at a discontinuity in a line.

---

[9] The difference between Eqs. (88) and (89) is due to our sign conventions, and is not due to any real difference in the behavior of the line for waves traveling in opposite directions. Our sign conventions are based upon our definitions of V and I. Thus the voltage V at any point along the line is the difference of potential between the two conductors of the line at that point. One of these conductors, usually taken as the lower one in any figure, may be considered to be at standard (which is frequently ground) potential, and the sign of V is positive or negative depending upon whether the voltage of the second conductor is above or below that of the standard conductor. Likewise, by convention, the direction of current in the line is taken as positive if the current in the second conductor is in the direction toward Z_T.

It should be realized that the direction of motion of the traveling current wave is independent of the sign of I. Even though the wave is traveling toward Z_T, the actual current is traveling away from Z_T at all points where the phase of the current wave is between $n\pi$ and $(n + 1)\pi$, if n is an odd integer. The direction of the wave is the direction in which the instantaneous phase is traveling, and need not be the direction in which the current is traveling.

APPENDIX D

Table of Laplace Transforms

Laplace transforms are a pair of functions related by two fundamental equations: (1) *the Laplace transformation*

$$F(s) = \int_0^\infty f(t)\epsilon^{-st}\,dt$$

and (2) *the inversion theorem:*

for $t \geq 0$

$$f(t) = \frac{1}{2\pi j}\int_{\gamma-j\infty}^{\gamma+j\infty} F(s)\epsilon^{st}\,ds = \frac{1}{2\pi j}\oint F(s)\epsilon^{st}\,ds \text{ (usually)}$$

$= \text{sum of residues of } F(s)\epsilon^{st}$ with respect to its singular points (usually)

In the foregoing equations, t is limited to real values, while s may be complex. The closed contour in the integral above encloses all the singular points of the integrand. A pair of functions $F(s)$ and $f(t)$ related by the above equations are called Laplace transforms. The inverse transformation is a solution to the Laplace transformation, and vice versa, so that functions related by one of the above equations are of necessity related by the other also. In the following table are listed some of the most important Laplace transforms used in radio engineering. Additional forms may be found in the references listed.[1]

[1] Gardner and Barnes, *Transients in Linear Systems*, Appendix A (Wiley). R. V. Churchill, *Modern Operational Mathematics in Engineering*, Appendix III (McGraw-Hill). Campbell and Foster, "Fourier Integrals for Practical Applications, *Bell Telephone Monograph B-584*. N. W. McLachlan and P. Humbert, "Formulaire pour le Calcul Symbolique," (*Memorial des Sci. Mathematiques*, v. 100) Paris, 1941. J. Cossar and A. Erdélyi, *Dictionary of Laplace Transforms*, Admiralty Computing Service, Dept. of Scientific Research and Experiment, London.

General Functions

In this list, $f(t)$ and $F(s)$ are Laplace transforms, as are also $g(t)$ and $G(s)$

$F(s)$	$f(t)$ for $t \geq 0$
(a) $AF(s) + BG(s)$	$Af(t) + Bg(t)$
(b) $sF(s) - f(0+)$	$f'(t) \equiv \frac{d}{dt}[f(t)]$
(c) $s^nF(s) - s^{n-1}f(0+)$ $-s^{n-2}f'(0+)$ $--- -f^{(n-1)}(0+)$	$f^{(n)}(t) \equiv \frac{d^n}{dt^n}[f(t)]$
(d) $\frac{1}{s}F(s)$	$\int_0^t f(\tau)\,d\tau$
(e) $\frac{1}{s^2}F(s)$	$\int_0^t \int_0^\tau f(\lambda)\,d\lambda\,d\tau$
(f) $F(s) \cdot G(s)$	$\int_0^t f(t-\tau) \cdot g(\tau)\,d\tau$
(g) $\frac{d}{ds}F(s) = F'(s)$	$-tf(t)$
(h) $\int_s^\infty f(x)\,dx$	$\frac{1}{t}f(t)$
(i) $F(s+a)$	$\epsilon^{-at}f(t)$
(j) $\epsilon^{-bs}F(s)$	$f(t-b)U(t-b)$
(k) $F(cs)$	$\frac{1}{c}f\left(\frac{t}{c}\right)$

where c is a positive quantity independent of t and s.

(l) $\frac{\partial}{\partial a}F(s,a)$	$\frac{\partial}{\partial a}f(t,a)$

where a is a variable independent of t and s.

(m) $\int_{a_0}^a F(s,a)\,da$	$\int_{a_0}^a f(t,a)\,da$

where a is a variable independent of t and s.

Specific Functions

$F(s)$	$f(t)$ for $t \geq 0$
(1) 1	$\delta(t) = $ unit impulse at $t = 0$
(2) $\frac{1}{s}$	$1 = U(t) = $ unit step at $t = 0$
(3) $\frac{1}{s^2}$	t
(4) $\frac{1}{s^n}\ (n = 1,2, ---)$	$\frac{t^{n-1}}{(n-1)!}$
(5) $\frac{1}{s^k}$ ($k > 0$ but not necessarily integral)	$\frac{t^{k-1}}{\Gamma(k)}$
(6) s	$\delta'(t) = $ doublet impulse at $t = 0$
(7) $s^n (n = 1,2, ---)$	$\delta^{(n)}(t) = $ impulse of $(n + 1)$th order at $t = 0$
(8) $\frac{1}{\sqrt{s}}$	$\frac{1}{\sqrt{\pi t}}$
(9) $s^{-\frac{3}{2}}$	$2\sqrt{\frac{t}{\pi}}$
(10) $\frac{1}{s + \alpha}$	$\epsilon^{-\alpha t}$
(11) $\frac{1}{(s + \alpha)(s + \gamma)}$	$\frac{\epsilon^{-\alpha t} - \epsilon^{-\gamma t}}{\gamma - \alpha}$
(12) $\frac{s + a_0}{(s + \alpha)(s + \gamma)}$	$\frac{(a_0 - \alpha)\epsilon^{-\alpha t} - (a_0 - \gamma)\epsilon^{-\gamma t}}{\gamma - \alpha}$
(13) $\frac{1}{(s + \alpha)(s + \beta)(s + \gamma)}$	$\frac{\epsilon^{-\alpha t}}{(\beta - \alpha)(\gamma - \alpha)} + \frac{\epsilon^{-\beta t}}{(\alpha - \beta)(\gamma - \beta)} + \frac{\epsilon^{-\gamma t}}{(\alpha - \gamma)(\beta - \gamma)}$

	$F(s)$	$f(t)$ for $t \geq 0$
(14)	$\dfrac{s + a_0}{(s + \alpha)(s + \beta)(s + \gamma)}$	$\dfrac{(a_0 - \alpha)\epsilon^{-\alpha t}}{(\beta - \alpha)(\gamma - \alpha)} + \dfrac{(a_0 - \beta)\epsilon^{-\beta t}}{(\alpha - \beta)(\gamma - \beta)} + \dfrac{(a_0 - \gamma)\epsilon^{-\gamma t}}{(\alpha - \gamma)(\beta - \gamma)}$
(15)	$\dfrac{s^2 + a_1 s + a_0}{(s + \alpha)(s + \beta)(s + \gamma)}$	$\dfrac{(\alpha^2 - a_1\alpha + a_0)\,\epsilon^{-\alpha t}}{(\beta - \alpha)(\gamma - \alpha)} + \dfrac{(\beta^2 - a_1\beta + a_0)\epsilon^{-\beta t}}{(\alpha - \beta)(\gamma - \beta)} + \dfrac{(\gamma^2 - a_1\gamma + a_0)\epsilon^{-\gamma t}}{(\alpha - \gamma)(\beta - \gamma)}$
(16)	$\dfrac{1}{s^2 + \beta^2}$	$\dfrac{1}{\beta} \sin \beta t$
(17)	$\dfrac{1}{s^2 - \beta^2}$	$\dfrac{1}{\beta} \sinh \beta t$
(18)	$\dfrac{s}{s^2 + \beta^2}$	$\cos \beta t$
(19)	$\dfrac{s}{s^2 - \beta^2}$	$\cosh \beta t$
(20)	$\dfrac{1}{(s + \alpha)^2 + \beta^2}$	$\dfrac{1}{\beta} \epsilon^{-\alpha t} \sin \beta t$

	$F(s)$	$f(t)$ for $t \geq 0$
(21)	$\dfrac{s + a_0}{(s+\alpha)^2 + \beta^2}$	$\epsilon^{-\alpha t}\left[\cos \beta t + \dfrac{a_0 - \alpha}{\beta} \sin \beta t\right] = \dfrac{1}{\beta}[(a_0 - \alpha)^2 + \beta^2]^{\frac{1}{2}} \epsilon^{-\alpha t} \sin (\beta t + \psi)$ where $\psi = \tan^{-1} \dfrac{\beta}{a_0 - \alpha}$
(22)	$\dfrac{1}{(s+\gamma)[(s+\alpha)^2 + \beta^2]}$	$\dfrac{\epsilon^{-\gamma t}}{(\gamma - \alpha)^2 + \beta^2} - \dfrac{\epsilon^{-\alpha t} \cos \beta t}{(\gamma - \alpha)^2 + \beta^2} + \left(\dfrac{\gamma - \alpha}{\beta}\right) \dfrac{\epsilon^{-\alpha t} \sin \beta t}{(\gamma - \alpha)^2 + \beta^2}$ $= \dfrac{\epsilon^{-\gamma t}}{(\gamma - \alpha)^2 + \beta^2} + \dfrac{\epsilon^{-\alpha t} \sin (\beta t - \psi)}{\beta[(\gamma - \alpha)^2 + \beta^2]^{\frac{1}{2}}}$ where $\psi = \tan^{-1} \dfrac{\beta}{\gamma - \alpha}$
(23)	$\dfrac{s + a_0}{(s+\gamma)[(s+\alpha)^2 + \beta^2]}$	$\dfrac{(a_0 - \gamma)\epsilon^{-\gamma t}}{(\alpha - \gamma)^2 + \beta^2} + \dfrac{(\gamma - a_0)\epsilon^{-\alpha t} \cos \beta t}{(\alpha - \gamma)^2 + \beta^2} + \dfrac{[(\gamma - \alpha)(a_0 - \alpha) + \beta^2]\epsilon^{-\alpha t} \sin \beta t}{\beta[(\alpha - \gamma)^2 + \beta^2]}$ $= \dfrac{(a_0 - \gamma)\epsilon^{-\gamma t}}{(\alpha - \gamma)^2 + \beta^2} + \dfrac{1}{\beta}\left[\dfrac{(a_0 - \alpha)^2 + \beta^2}{(\gamma - \alpha)^2 + \beta^2}\right]^{\frac{1}{2}} \epsilon^{-\alpha t} \sin (\beta t + \psi)$ where $\psi = \tan^{-1} \dfrac{\beta}{a_0 - \alpha} - \tan^{-1} \dfrac{\beta}{\gamma - \alpha}$

	$F(s)$	$f(t)$ for $t \geq 0$
(24)	$\dfrac{s^2 + a_1 s + a_0}{(s+\gamma)[(s+\alpha)^2 + \beta^2]}$	$\dfrac{\gamma^2 - a_1\gamma + a_0}{(\alpha - \gamma)^2 + \beta^2}\epsilon^{-\gamma t} + \dfrac{[\alpha^2 + \beta^2 + a_1\gamma - 2\alpha\gamma - a_0]}{(\gamma - \alpha)^2 + \beta^2}\epsilon^{-\alpha t}\cos\beta t$ $+ \dfrac{(\gamma - \alpha)(\alpha^2 - \beta^2 - a_1\alpha + a_0) + \beta^2(a_1 - 2\alpha)}{\beta[(\gamma - \alpha)^2 + \beta^2]}\epsilon^{-\alpha t}\sin\beta t$ $= \dfrac{\gamma^2 - a_1\gamma + a_0}{(\alpha - \gamma)^2 + \beta^2}\epsilon^{-\gamma t} + \dfrac{1}{\beta}\left[\dfrac{(\alpha^2 - \beta^2 - a_1\alpha + a_0)^2 + \beta^2(a_1 - 2\alpha)^2}{(\gamma - \alpha)^2 + \beta^2}\right]^{\frac{1}{2}} \epsilon^{-\alpha t}\sin(\beta t + \psi)$ where $\psi = \tan^{-1}\dfrac{\beta(a_1 - 2\alpha)}{\alpha^2 - \beta^2 - a_1\alpha + a_0} - \tan^{-1}\dfrac{\beta}{\gamma - \alpha}$
(25)	$\dfrac{1}{(s^2 + \lambda^2)[(s+\alpha)^2 + \beta^2]}$	$\dfrac{1}{[(\alpha^2 + \beta^2 - \lambda^2)^2 + 4\alpha^2\lambda^2]^{\frac{1}{2}}}\left\{\dfrac{1}{\lambda}\sin(\lambda t - \psi_1) + \dfrac{1}{\beta}\epsilon^{-\alpha t}\sin(\beta t - \psi_2)\right\}$ where $\psi_1 = \tan^{-1}\dfrac{2\alpha\lambda}{\alpha^2 + \beta^2 - \lambda^2}$ and $\psi_2 = \tan^{-1}\dfrac{-2\alpha\beta}{a^2 - \beta^2 + \lambda^2}$

	$F(s)$	$f(t)$ for $t \geq 0$
(26)	$\dfrac{s + a_0}{(s^2 + \lambda^2)[(s + \alpha)^2 + \beta^2]}$	$\dfrac{1}{\lambda}\left\{\dfrac{a_0^2 + \lambda^2}{(\alpha^2 + \beta^2 - \lambda^2)^2 + 4\alpha^2\lambda^2}\right\}^{\frac{1}{2}} \sin(\lambda t + \psi_1) + \dfrac{1}{\beta}\left\{\dfrac{(a_0 - \alpha)^2 + \beta^2}{(\alpha^2 + \beta^2 - \lambda^2)^2 + 4\alpha^2\lambda^2}\right\}^{\frac{1}{2}} \epsilon^{-\alpha t} \sin(\beta t + \psi_2)$ where $\psi_1 = \tan^{-1}\dfrac{\lambda}{a_0} - \tan^{-1}\dfrac{2\alpha\lambda}{\alpha^2 + \beta^2 - \lambda^2}$ and $\psi_2 = \tan^{-1}\dfrac{\beta}{a_0 - \alpha} - \tan^{-1}\dfrac{-2\alpha\beta}{\alpha^2 - \beta^2 + \lambda^2}$
(27)	$\dfrac{s^2 + a_1 s + a_0}{(s^2 + \lambda^2)[(s + \alpha)^2 + \beta^2]}$	$\dfrac{1}{\lambda}\left\{\dfrac{(a_0 - \lambda^2)^2 + a_1^2\lambda^2}{(\alpha^2 + \beta^2 - \lambda^2)^2 + 4\alpha^2\lambda^2}\right\}^{\frac{1}{2}} \sin(\lambda t + \psi_1) +$ $\dfrac{1}{\beta}\left\{\dfrac{(\alpha^2 - \beta^2 - a_1\alpha + a_0)^2 + \beta^2(a_1 - 2\alpha)^2}{(\alpha^2 + \beta^2 - \lambda^2)^2 + 4\alpha^2\lambda^2}\right\}^{\frac{1}{2}} \epsilon^{-\alpha t} \sin(\beta t + \psi_2)$ where $\psi_1 = \tan^{-1}\dfrac{a_1\lambda}{a_0 - \lambda^2} - \tan^{-1}\dfrac{2\alpha\lambda}{\alpha^2 + \beta^2 - \lambda^2}$ and $\psi_2 = \tan^{-1}\dfrac{\beta(a_1 - 2\alpha)}{\alpha^2 - \beta^2 - a_1\alpha + a_0} - \tan^{-1}\dfrac{-2\alpha\beta}{\alpha^2 - \beta^2 + \lambda^2}$

	$F(s)$	$f(t)$ for $t \geq 0$
(28)	$\frac{1}{s}\,\epsilon^{-k/s}$	$J_0(2\sqrt{kt})$
(29)	$\frac{1}{\sqrt{s}}\,\epsilon^{-k/s}$	$\frac{1}{\sqrt{\pi t}}\cos(2\sqrt{kt})$
(30)	$\frac{1}{\sqrt{s}}\,\epsilon^{k/s}$	$\frac{1}{\sqrt{\pi t}}\cosh(2\sqrt{kt})$
(31)	$\frac{1}{s^{\frac{3}{2}}}\,\epsilon^{-k/s}$	$\frac{1}{\sqrt{\pi k}}\sin(2\sqrt{kt})$
(32)	$\frac{1}{s^{\frac{3}{2}}}\,\epsilon^{k/s}$	$\frac{1}{\sqrt{\pi k}}\sinh(2\sqrt{kt})$
(33)	$\epsilon^{-k\sqrt{s}}$ where $k > 0$	$\frac{k}{2\sqrt{\pi t^3}}\,\epsilon^{-k^2/4t}$
(34)	$\frac{1}{s}\,\epsilon^{-k\sqrt{s}}$ where $k \geqq 0$	$\operatorname{erfc}\left(\frac{k}{2\sqrt{t}}\right)$
(35)	$\frac{1}{\sqrt{s}}\,\epsilon^{-k\sqrt{s}}$ where $k \geqq 0$	$\frac{1}{\sqrt{\pi t}}\,\epsilon^{-k^2/4t}$
(36)	$\frac{1}{\sqrt{s^2 + a^2}}$	$J_0(at)$
(37)	$\frac{(\sqrt{s^2 + a^2} - s)^\nu}{\sqrt{s^2 + a^2}}$ where $\nu > -1$	$a^\nu J_\nu(at)$
(38)	$\frac{(s - \sqrt{s^2 - a^2})^\nu}{\sqrt{s^2 - a^2}}$ where $\nu > -1$	$a^\nu I_\nu(at)$
(39)	$\epsilon^{-ks} - \epsilon^{-k\sqrt{s^2+a^2}}$	$\frac{ak}{\sqrt{t^2 - k^2}}\,J_1(a\sqrt{t^2 - k^2})U(t - k)$
(40)	$\epsilon^{-k\sqrt{s^2-a^2}} - \epsilon^{-ks}$	$\frac{ak}{\sqrt{t^2 - k^2}}\,I_1(a\sqrt{t^2 - k^2})U(t - k)$
(41)	$\frac{1}{s}\log(s^2 + a^2)$ where $a > 0$	$2\log a - 2\operatorname{Ci}(at)$
(42)	$\frac{1}{s}\tan^{-1}\left(\frac{k}{s}\right)$	$\operatorname{Si}(kt)$

APPENDIX E
Fourier Integral Analysis[1]

E.1. Introduction

For the student who is unacquainted with Fourier analysis, particularly Fourier integral analysis, this appendix will outline those parts of the subject which are most closely related to the foregoing chapters. In Chap. 4, it was found advantageous to express a function of time $e(t)$ as a superposition of impulse functions by means of the integral

$$e(t) = \int_{-\infty}^{+\infty} e(\tau)\delta(t - \tau)\,d\tau \tag{1}$$

or as a superposition of step functions by means of the integral

$$e(t) = \int_{-\infty}^{+\infty} \left\{\frac{\partial e(\tau)}{\partial \tau}\right\} U(t - \tau)\,d\tau \tag{2}$$

These superposition processes are depicted in Figs. 4-8 and 4-6, respectively. This superposition is useful because the responses of systems to unit-step functions and unit-impulse functions are often known. The response to $e(t)$ can then be expressed as a superposition integral.

The responses of systems to another type of elementary function, the cosine (or sine), are also well known. It would therefore be useful if an arbitrary function such as $e(t)$ could be expressed as the superposition of cosine functions. Fortunately, this can be done. The integral that does this is called a Fourier integral. Its form is

$$\begin{aligned} e(t) &= \frac{1}{\pi}\int_{0}^{+\infty} S(\omega)\cos\,[\omega t + \phi(\omega)]\,d\omega \\ &= \int_{0}^{\infty} a(\omega)\cos\omega t\,d\omega + \int_{0}^{\infty} b(\omega)\sin\omega t\,d\omega \end{aligned} \tag{3}$$

where

$$S(\omega) = \sqrt{\left[\int_{-\infty}^{+\infty} e(t)\cos\omega t\,dt\right]^2 + \left[\int_{-\infty}^{+\infty} e(t)\sin\omega t\,dt\right]^2} \tag{4}$$

[1] An extensive discussion of this topic is given in the author's *Frequency Analysis, Modulation and Noise.*

$$a(\omega) = \frac{1}{\pi} \int_{-\infty}^{+\infty} e(t) \cos \omega t \, dt \tag{5}$$

and

$$b(\omega) = \frac{1}{\pi} \int_{-\infty}^{+\infty} e(t) \sin \omega t \, dt \tag{6}$$

The Fourier integral can be put into a more compact form with the aid of complex exponents. Thus

$$e(t) = \frac{1}{2\pi} \int_{-\infty}^{+\infty} \epsilon^{j\omega t} \Omega(\omega) \, d\omega \tag{7}$$

where

$$\Omega(\omega) = \int_{-\infty}^{+\infty} \epsilon^{-j\omega t} e(t) \, dt \tag{8}$$

Equation (3) or its equivalent, Eq. (7), is the expression of $e(t)$ as the superposition of cosine waves. The functions $S(\omega)$ and $\phi(\omega)$, or their equivalent $\Omega(\omega)$, give the magnitudes and phases of the cosine components. Whereas, however, the different elementary pulses and steps in Eqs. (1) and (2) differ in their time of occurrence, the different elementary cosine waves in Eq. (3) extend from $(-\infty)$ to $(+\infty)$ in time but differ correspondingly in frequency and phase.

It is very difficult to give a pictorial presentation of the superposition of a continuous distribution of frequencies. In order to understand the situation better, let us first consider a Fourier series. If a function $f(t)$ is defined in the interval from $T_1 \leq t \leq T_2$, the function can be expressed in the familiar Fourier series

$$\begin{aligned} f(t) &= \frac{a_0}{2} + \left(a_1 \cos \frac{2\pi t}{T_2 - T_1} + a_2 \cos \frac{4\pi t}{T_2 - T_1} + \cdots \right. \\ &\quad \left. + a_n \cos \frac{2\pi n t}{T_2 - T_1} + \cdots \right) + \left(b_1 \sin \frac{2\pi t}{T_2 - T_1} \right. \\ &\quad \left. + b_2 \sin \frac{4\pi t}{T_2 - T_1} + \cdots + b_n \sin \frac{2\pi n t}{T_2 - T_1} + \cdots \right) \\ &= \frac{a_0}{2} + \sum_{n=1}^{\infty} \left(a_n \cos \frac{2\pi n t}{T_2 - T_1} + b_n \sin \frac{2\pi n t}{T_2 - T_1}\right) \\ &= \sum_{n=-\infty}^{+\infty} C_n \epsilon^{j\frac{2\pi n t}{T_2 - T_1}} \end{aligned} \tag{9}$$

where
$$a_0 = \frac{2}{T_2 - T_1}\int_{T_1}^{T_2} f(t)\,dt \tag{10}$$
$$a_n = \frac{2}{T_2 - T_1}\int_{T_1}^{T_2} f(t)\cos\frac{2\pi nt}{T_2 - T_1}\,dt \tag{11}$$
$$b_n = \frac{2}{T_2 - T_1}\int_{T_1}^{T_2} f(t)\sin\frac{2\pi nt}{T_2 - T_1}\,dt \tag{12}$$
$$C_n = \frac{1}{T_2 - T_1}\int_{T_1}^{T_2} f(t)\epsilon^{-j\frac{2\pi nt}{T_2 - T_1}}\,dt \tag{13}$$

In Fig. E-1 is shown such a function $f(t)$ together with its Fourier components. These consists of an average or direct

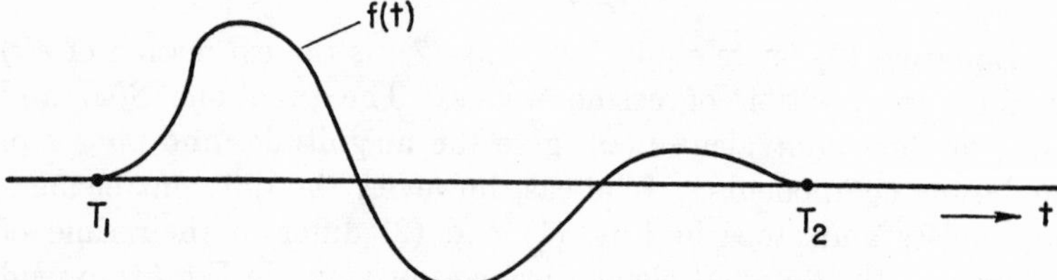

FIG. E-1. A function of t extending from T_1 to T_2.

component $a_0/2$, a fundamental
$$\left(a_1 \cos\frac{2\pi t}{T_2 - T_1} + b_1 \sin\frac{2\pi t}{T_2 - T_1}\right)$$
of period $(T_2 - T_1)$, and harmonics whose periods are integral submultiples of the fundamental; i.e.,
$$\frac{T_2 - T_1}{2}, \frac{T_2 - T_1}{3}, \text{ etc.}$$

In Fig. E-2(a) we have plotted the magnitudes of the Fourier components, using "reciprocal period" as abscissa. If now we let T_1 proceed to $(-\infty)$ and T_2 to $(+\infty)$, the reciprocal periods get closer and closer together as $(T_2 - T_1)$ increases. When $(T_2 - T_1)$ becomes infinite, the reciprocal periods form a continuous distribution as shown in Fig. E-2(b) and (c). Furthermore, for an infinite interval $(T_2 - T_1)$, the harmonic wave trains are infinitely long, so that they represent true frequency components. Thus, for an infinite interval of expansion $(T_2 - T_1)$, the Fourier series of Eq. (9) becomes the Fourier integral of Eq. (3) or Eq. (7). At the same

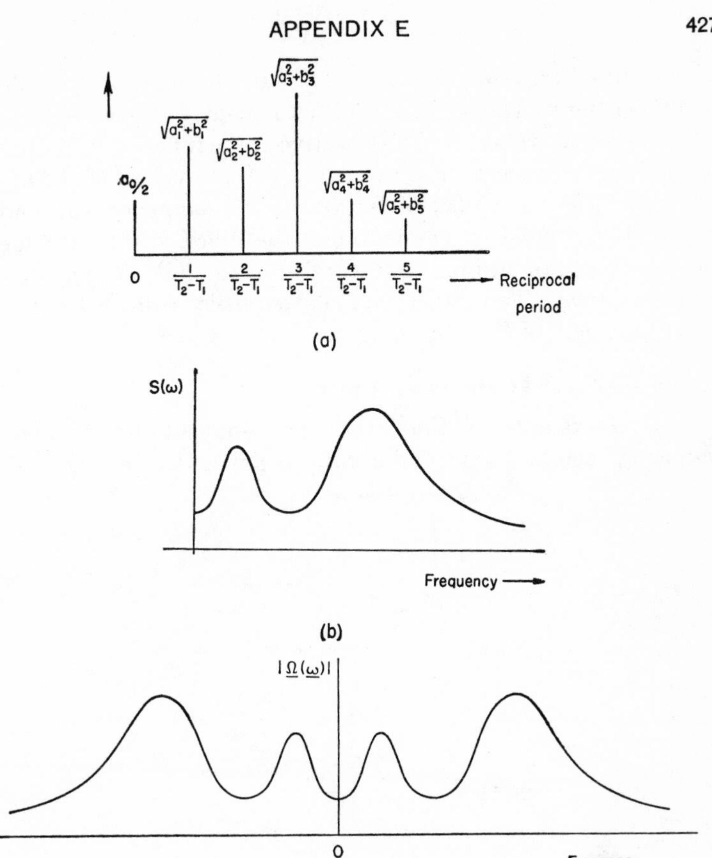

FIG. E-2. (a) Magnitudes of the Fourier-series components of the function in Fig. E-1. (b) The spectral distribution (magnitude of the Fourier frequency composition) of the function in Fig. E-1 as $T_2 - T_1$ becomes infinite. (c) The magnitude of the complex frequency composition of the function in Fig. E-1 as $T_2 - T_1$ becomes infinite.

time, the formulas, Eqs. (10) through (13), for the Fourier coefficients become the formulas, Eqs. (5), (6), and (8), for the frequency composition.[2]

In the case of the superposition integral involving the unit impulse, the magnitudes of the impulses are the same as the values

[2] The derivation of the various formulas involved in Fourier analysis will be found in H. S. Carlaw's *Fourier Series and Integrals.*

of the function itself [see Eq. (1)]. In the case of the integral involving the unit step [see Eq. (2)], the magnitudes of the steps are the same as the values of the derivative of the function. In the case of the Fourier integral, Eq. (3) or Eq. (7), the values of the magnitudes $a(\omega)$, $b(\omega)$, or $\Omega(\omega)$ of the frequency components are not so simple, but depend on the values of the function for all values of time and require an infinite integral, Eq. (5), (6), or (8), for their determination. The evaluation of frequency compositions is an important part of Fourier analysis.

E.2. Examples of Fourier-integral analysis

As an example of Fourier-integral analysis, let us find the frequency composition of the rectangular pulse in Fig. E-3(a).

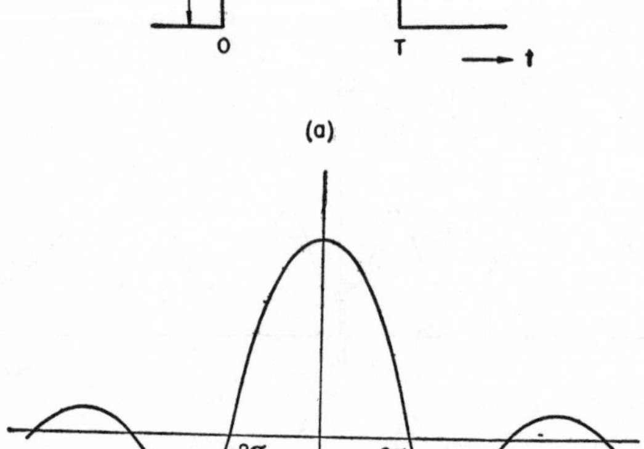

FIG. E-3. (a) A rectangular pulse. (b) Magnitude of the complex frequency composition of the pulse in (a).

Using Eq. (8), we have

$$\Omega(\omega) = \int_{-\infty}^{+\infty} \epsilon^{-j\omega t} e(t)\, dt = \int_0^T \epsilon^{-j\omega t} K\, dt$$

$$= K\left[\frac{\epsilon^{-j\omega T} - 1}{-j\omega}\right] = \left[\frac{2K}{\omega} \sin\frac{\omega T}{2}\right] \epsilon^{-j\omega\frac{T}{2}} \qquad (14)$$

The magnitude of $\Omega(\omega)$ is plotted in Fig. E-3(b). This shows that the principal energy of the pulse lies in the frequency range

$$\left(-\frac{1}{T} < f < \frac{1}{T}\right)$$

where $f = \omega/2\pi$.

Let us next find the output when a pulse such as that of Fig. E-3(a) passes through a low-pass filter having no attenuation up to the frequency $\omega_0/2\pi$ and having complete attenuation above that frequency. Using the superposition integral, Eq. (7), and also making use of Eq. (14), we have for the output

$$\begin{aligned} e_1(t) &= \frac{1}{2\pi}\int_{-\omega_0}^{+\omega_0} \epsilon^{j\omega t}\,\frac{K}{-j\omega}\,[\epsilon^{-j\omega T} - 1]\,d\omega \\ &= \frac{K}{2\pi}\int_{-\omega_0}^{+\omega_0} \frac{\epsilon^{j\omega(t-T)} - \epsilon^{j\omega t}}{-j\omega}\,d\omega \\ &= \frac{jK}{2\pi}\int_{-\omega_0}^{+\omega_0}\left\{\left[\frac{\cos\omega(t-T)}{\omega} - \frac{\cos\omega t}{\omega}\right]\right. \\ &\qquad\qquad \left. + j\left[\frac{\sin\omega(t-T)}{\omega} - \frac{\sin\omega t}{\omega}\right]\right\} d\omega \qquad (15) \end{aligned}$$

We now note that if A is any quantity independent of ω,

$$\int_{-\omega_0}^{0} \frac{\cos\omega A}{\omega}\,d\omega = -\int_{0}^{\omega_0} \frac{\cos\omega A}{\omega}\,d\omega \qquad (16)$$

and

$$\int_{-\omega_0}^{0} \frac{\sin\omega A}{\omega}\,d\omega = \int_{0}^{\omega} \frac{\sin\omega A}{\omega}\,d\omega \qquad (17)$$

In view of Eqs. (16) and (17), Eq. (15) reduces to

$$\begin{aligned} e_1(t) &= \frac{-K}{\pi}\int_0^{\omega_0}\left[\frac{\sin\omega(t-T)}{\omega} - \frac{\sin\omega t}{\omega}\right] d\omega \\ &= \frac{K}{\pi}\left\{\int_0^{\omega_0 t}\frac{\sin x}{x}\,dx - \int_0^{\omega_0(t-T)}\frac{\sin x}{x}\,dx\right\} \\ &= \frac{K}{\pi}\,\{Si(\omega_0 t) - Si[\omega_0(t-T)]\} \qquad (18) \end{aligned}$$

where

$$Si(y) = \int_0^y \frac{\sin y}{y}\,dy \qquad (19)$$

is the sine integral function of y for which tables of values are available.[3] A plot of Eq. (18) is shown in Fig. E-4.

With the aid of the foregoing we can readily express the unit step and the unit impulse as the superposition of frequency com-

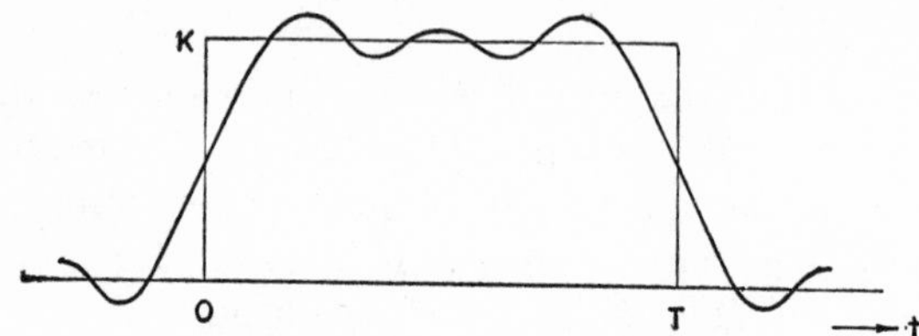

FIG. E-4. The output when a rectangular pulse passes through a low-pass filter.

ponents. Thus for the unit step going through a low-pass filter we have, from Eq. (18),

$$U_1(t) = \frac{1}{\pi}\left\{\int_0^{\omega_0 t} \frac{\sin x}{x}\,dx - \int_0^{\omega_0(t-\infty)} \frac{\sin x}{x}\,dx\right\} \tag{20}$$

Now

$$\int_0^{\omega_0(t-\infty)} \frac{\sin x}{x}\,dx = \int_0^{-\infty} \frac{\sin x}{x}\,dx = -\frac{\pi}{2} \tag{21}$$

Therefore

$$U_1(t) = \frac{1}{2} + \frac{1}{\pi}\int_0^{\omega_0 t} \frac{\sin x}{x}\,dx = \frac{1}{2} + \frac{1}{\pi}\int_0^{\omega_0} \frac{\sin \omega t}{\omega}\,d\omega \tag{22}$$

If next we let $\omega_0 \to \infty$, we obtain the expression for unit step itself, namely

$$U(t) = \frac{1}{2} + \frac{1}{\pi}\int_0^{\infty} \frac{\sin \omega t}{\omega}\,d\omega \tag{23}$$

In order to express the unit impulse as the superposition of frequency components, we start from Eq. (15) and write

$$\delta(t) = \lim_{\substack{\omega_0\to\infty \\ T\to 0 \\ KT\to 1}} \frac{1}{2\pi}\int_{-\omega_0}^{+\omega_0} \epsilon^{j\omega t}\,\frac{K[\epsilon^{-j\omega T} - 1]}{-j\omega}\,d\omega \tag{24}$$

[3] See, for example, p. 76 of the author's *Frequency Analysis, Modulation and Noise.*

Now

$$\lim_{\substack{T\to 0\\ KT\to 1}} \{K[\epsilon^{-j\omega T} - 1]\}$$

$$= \lim_{\substack{T\to 0\\ KT\to 1}} K\left\{\left[1 + (-j\omega T) + \frac{(-j\omega T)^2}{2!} + \cdots\right] - 1\right\}$$

$$= \lim_{\substack{T\to 0\\ KT\to 1}} K(-j\omega T) = -j\omega \tag{25}$$

Thus Eq. (24) reduces to

$$\delta(t) = \frac{1}{2\pi}\int_{-\infty}^{+\infty} \epsilon^{-j\omega t}\, d\omega = \frac{1}{\pi}\int_0^{\infty} \cos \omega t\, d\omega \tag{26}$$

Equations (23) and (26) have been used in § 4.10 of the foregoing book. An insight into their physical significance will be obtained below with the aid of the Fourier-integral energy theorem.

E.3. The Fourier-integral energy theorem

Equations (3) and (7) express an arbitrary function of time as the superposition of its frequency components. It is also possible to express the energy (quadratic content) of a function of time as the sum of the energies of its frequency components. This is done by means of the following equation, called the Fourier-integral energy theorem

$$\int_{-\infty}^{+\infty} [e(t)]^2\, dt = \frac{1}{2\pi}\int_{-\infty}^{+\infty} \Omega(\omega)\cdot\Omega^*(\omega)\, d\omega = \frac{1}{\pi}\int_0^{\infty} [S(\omega)]^2\, d\omega \tag{27}$$

Let us use Eq. (27) to find the energy of the pulse in Fig. E-3(a) and the energy of its frequency components in Fig. E-3(b). Thus

$$\int_{-\infty}^{+\infty} [e(t)]^2\, dt = \int_0^{T} K^2\, dt = K^2T \tag{28}$$

Using Eq. (14) we have also

$$\frac{1}{2\pi}\int_{-\infty}^{+\infty} \Omega(\omega)\cdot\Omega^*(\omega)\, d\omega = \frac{1}{2\pi}\int_{-\infty}^{+\infty} \left(\frac{2K}{\omega}\right)^2 \sin^2\left(\frac{\omega T}{2}\right) d\omega$$

$$= \frac{4K^2}{2\pi}\cdot\frac{T}{2}\int_{-\infty}^{+\infty} \frac{\sin^2 x}{x^2}\, dx = K^2T \tag{29}$$

since
$$\int_{-\infty}^{+\infty} \frac{\sin^2 x}{x^2}\, dx = \pi \tag{30}$$

We see by comparing Eqs. (28) and (29) that the energy of the pulse can be calculated either by considering the pulse directly or by integrating the energies of its frequency components. This was, of course, to be expected.

It is often interesting to consider the frequency distribution of the energy of a time function. Thus for the unit impulse, according to Eq. (26),
$$S(\omega) = 1 \tag{31}$$
Thus,
$$\frac{1}{\pi}\int_0^\infty [S(\omega)]^2\, d\omega = \frac{1}{\pi}\int_0^\infty d\omega = \infty \tag{32}$$

A theoretically perfect unit impulse thus has infinite energy, the infinite energy being contained in the extremely high frequencies. Theoretically perfect unit impulses can, of course, not be made, both because infinite amplitude and because infinite energy are not realizable. Eq. (14), however, shows that if
$$\omega \ll \frac{1}{T}$$
the frequency composition $S(\omega)$ of the pulse in Fig. E-3(a) is constant with respect to frequency. Thus a pulse of duration T may be considered an impulse insofar as frequencies which are small in comparison with $1/T$ are concerned.

Next consider the unit step. Equation (23) tells us that the unit step consists of a steady term of magnitude, $\frac{1}{2}$, shown in Fig. E-5(a), plus the variational term
$$\frac{1}{\pi}\int_0^\infty \frac{\sin \omega t}{\omega}\, d\omega$$
For the variational term,
$$S(\omega) = \frac{1}{\omega}$$
so that in the frequency band from ω_1 to ω_2
$$\frac{1}{\pi}\int_{\omega_1}^{\omega_2} [S(\omega)]^2\, d\omega = \frac{1}{\pi}\int_{\omega_1}^{\omega_2} \frac{d\omega}{\omega^2} = \frac{1}{\pi}\left(\frac{1}{\omega_1} - \frac{1}{\omega_2}\right) \tag{33}$$

We note that the total energy for all frequencies above some frequency $(\omega_0/2\pi)$ is proportional to $1/\omega_0$. On the other hand, the total energy in the frequency range below $(\omega_0/2\pi)$ is infinite. The energy of a step function is thus concentrated at the extremely low frequencies. The fact that the total energy in a unit step is infinite is also obvious from the fact that a unit step is an infinitely long signal.

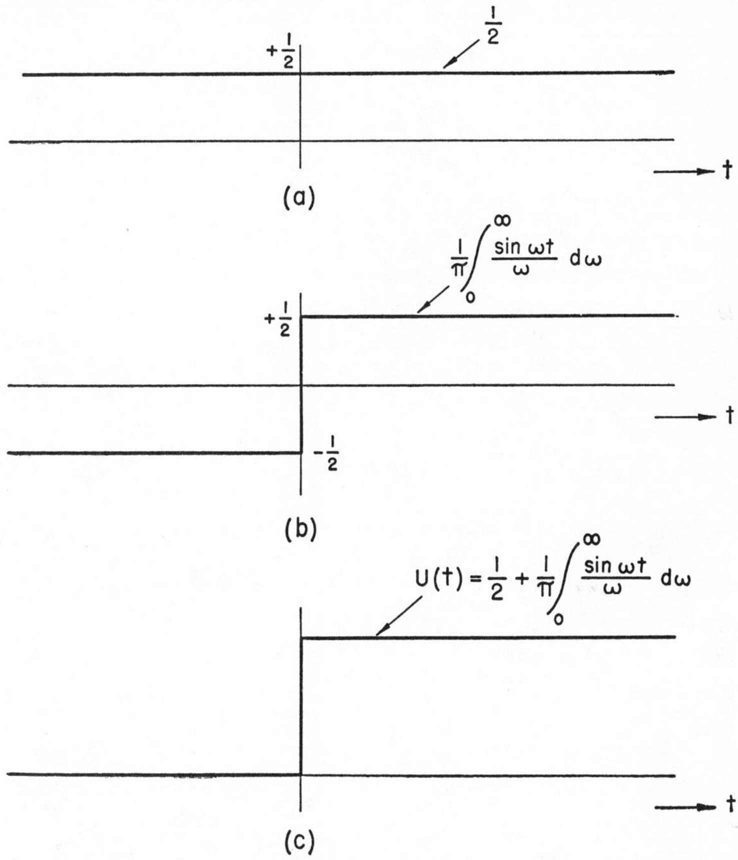

FIG. E-5. The unit-step function and its components.

Since the energy of any realizable signal $e(t)$ must be finite, the Fourier-integral energy theorem shows that $S(\omega)$ must vanish to a higher order than $1/\sqrt{\omega}$ as $\omega \to \infty$ for all realizable signals. It is most likely, however, that in all cases $S(\omega)$ actually vanishes much more rapidly at infinity than is indicated by the above condition. Thus, it appears from quantum theory that $S(\omega)$ must vanish exponentially as ω approaches infinity.

Index

CATALOGUE OF DOVER BOOKS

MATHEMATICS, ELEMENTARY TO INTERMEDIATE

HOW TO CALCULATE QUICKLY, Henry Sticker. This handy volume offers a tried and true method for helping you in the basic mathematics of daily life—addition, subtraction, multiplication, division, fractions, etc. It is designed to awaken your "number sense" or the ability to see relationships between numbers as whole quantities. It is not a collection of tricks working only on special numbers, but a serious course of over 9,000 problems and their solutions, teaching special techniques not taught in schools: left-to-right multiplication, new fast ways of division, etc. 5 or 10 minutes daily use will double or triple your calculation speed. Excellent for the scientific worker who is at home in higher math, but is not satisfied with his speed and accuracy in lower mathematics. 256pp. 5 x 7¼. T295 Paperbound **$1.00**

TEACH YOURSELF books. For adult self-study, for refresher and supplementary study.

The most effective series of home study mathematics books on the market! With absolutely no outside help, they will teach you as much as any similar college or high-school course, or will helpfully supplement any such course. Each step leads directly to the next, each question is anticipated. Numerous lucid examples and carefully-wrought practice problems illustrate meanings. Not skimpy outlines, not surveys, not usual classroom texts, these 204- to 380-page books are packed with the finest instruction you'll find anywhere for adult self-study.

TEACH YOURSELF ALGEBRA, P. Abbott. Formulas, coordinates, factors, graphs of quadratic functions, quadratic equations, logarithms, ratio, irrational numbers, arithmetical, geometrical series, much more. 1241 problems, solutions. Tables. 52 illus. 307pp. 6⅞ x 4¼. Clothbound **$2.00**

TEACH YOURSELF GEOMETRY, P. Abbott. Solids, lines, points, surfaces, angle measurement, triangles, theorem of Pythagoras, polygons, loci, the circle, tangents, symmetry, solid geometry, prisms, pyramids, solids of revolution, etc. 343 problems, solutions. 268 illus. 334pp. 6⅞ x 4¼. Clothbound **$2.00**

TEACH YOURSELF TRIGONOMETRY, P. Abbott. Geometrical foundations, indices, logarithms, trigonometrical ratios, relations between sides, angles of triangle, circular measure, trig. ratios of angles of any magnitude, much more. Requires elementary algebra, geometry. 465 problems, solutions. Tables. 102 illus. 204pp. 6⅞ x 4¼. Clothbound **$2.00**

TEACH YOURSELF THE CALCULUS, P. Abbott. Variations in functions, differentiation, solids of revolution, series, elementary differential equations, areas by integral calculus, much more. Requires algebra, trigonometry. 970 problems, solutions. Tables. 89 illus. 380pp. 6⅞ x 4¼. Clothbound **$2.00**

TEACH YOURSELF THE SLIDE RULE, B. Snodgrass. Fractions, decimals, A-D scales, log-log scales, trigonometrical scales, indices, logarithms. Commercial, precision, electrical, dualistic, Brighton rules. 80 problems, solutions. 10 illus. 207pp. 6⅞ x 4¼. Clothbound **$2.00**

ARITHMETICAL EXCURSIONS: AN ENRICHMENT OF ELEMENTARY MATHEMATICS, H. Bowers and J. Bowers. For students who want unusual methods of arithmetic never taught in school; for adults who want to increase their number sense. Little known facts about the most simple numbers, arithmetical entertainments and puzzles, figurate numbers, number chains, mysteries and folklore of numbers, the "Hin-dog-abic" number system, etc. First publication. Index. 529 numbered problems and diversions, all with answers. Bibliography. 50 figures. xiv + 320pp. 5⅜ x 8. T770 Paperbound **$1.65**

HOW DO YOU USE A SLIDE RULE? by A. A. Merrill. Not a manual for mathematicians and engineers, but a lucid step-by-step explanation that presents the fundamental rules clearly enough to be understood by anyone who could benefit by the use of a slide rule in his work or business. This work concentrates on the 2 most important operations: multiplication and division. 10 easy lessons, each with a clear drawing, will save you countless hours in your banking, business, statistical, and other work. First publication. Index. 2 Appendixes. 10 illustrations. 78 problems, all with answers. vi + 36pp. 6⅛ x 9¼. T62 Paperbound **60¢**

THE THEORY AND OPERATION OF THE SLIDE RULE, J. P. Ellis. Not a skimpy "instruction manual", but an exhaustive treatment that will save you hours throughout your career. Supplies full understanding of every scale on the Log Log Duplex Decitrig type of slide rule. Shows the most time-saving methods, and provides practice useful in the widest variety of actual engineering situations. Each operation introduced in terms of underlying logarithmic theory. Summary of prerequisite math. First publication. Index. 198 figures. Over 450 problems with answers. Bibliography. 12 Appendices. ix + 289pp. 5⅜ x 8. S727 Paperbound **$1.50**

COLLEGE ALGEBRA, H. B. Fine. Standard college text that gives a systematic and deductive structure to algebra; comprehensive, connected, with emphasis on theory. Discusses the commutative, associative, and distributive laws of number in unusual detail, and goes on with undetermined coefficients, quadratic equations, progressions, logarithms, permutations, probability, power series, and much more. Still most valuable elementary-intermediate text on the science and structure of algebra. Index. 1560 problems, all with answers. x + 631pp. 5⅜ x 8. T211 Paperbound **$2.50**

COORDINATE GEOMETRY, L. P. Eisenhart. Thorough, unified introduction. Unusual for advancing in dimension within each topic (treats together circle, sphere; polar coordinates, 3-dimensional coordinate systems; conic sections, quadric surfaces), affording exceptional insight into subject. Extensive use made of determinants, though no previous knowledge of them is assumed. Algebraic equations of 1st degree, 2 and 3 unknowns, carried further than usual in algebra courses. Over 500 exercises. Introduction. Appendix. Index. Bibliography. 43 illustrations. 310pp. 5⅜ x 8. S600 Paperbound **$1.65**

A TREATISE ON PLANE AND ADVANCED TRIGONOMETRY, E. W. Hobson. Extraordinarily wide coverage, going beyond usual college level trig, one of the few works covering advanced trig in full detail. By a great expositor with unerring anticipation and lucid clarification of potentially difficult points. Includes circular functions; expansion of functions of multiple angle; trig tables; relations between sides and angles of triangle; complex numbers; etc. Many problems solved completely. "The best work on the subject." Nature. Formerly entitled "A Treatise on Plane Trigonometry." 689 examples. 6 figures. xvi + 383pp. 5⅜ x 8. S353 Paperbound **$2.25**

FAMOUS PROBLEMS OF ELEMENTARY GEOMETRY, Felix Klein. Expanded version of the 1894 Easter lectures at Göttingen. 3 problems of classical geometry, in an excellent mathematical treatment by a famous mathematician: squaring the circle, trisecting angle, doubling cube. Considered with full modern implications: transcendental numbers, pi, etc. Notes by R. Archibald. 16 figures. xi + 92pp. 5⅜ x 8. T298 Paperbound **$1.00**

MONOGRAPHS ON TOPICS OF MODERN MATHEMATICS, edited by **J. W. A. Young.** Advanced mathematics for persons who haven't gone beyond or have forgotten high school algebra. 9 monographs on foundation of geometry, modern pure geometry, non-Euclidean geometry, fundamental propositions of algebra, algebraic equations, functions, calculus, theory of numbers, etc. Each monograph gives proofs of important results, and descriptions of leading methods, to provide wide coverage. New introduction by Prof. M. Kline, N. Y. University. 100 diagrams. xvi + 416pp. 6⅛ x 9¼. S289 Paperbound **$2.00**

HIGHER MATHEMATICS FOR STUDENTS OF CHEMISTRY AND PHYSICS, J. W. Mellor. Not abstract, but practical, building its problems out of familiar laboratory material, this covers differential calculus, coordinate, analytical geometry, functions, integral calculus, infinite series, numerical equations, differential equations, Fourier's theorem, probability, theory of errors, calculus of variations, determinants. "If the reader is not familiar with this book, it will repay him to examine it," CHEM. & ENGINEERING NEWS. 800 problems. 189 figures. Bibliography. xxi + 641pp. 5⅜ x 8. S193 Paperbound **$2.50**

TRIGONOMETRY REFRESHER FOR TECHNICAL MEN, A. Albert Klaf. 913 detailed questions and answers cover the most important aspects of plane and spherical trigonometry. They will help you to brush up or to clear up difficulties in special areas. The first portion of this book covers plane trigonometry, including angles, quadrants, trigonometrical functions, graphical representation, interpolation, equations, logarithms, solution of triangle, use of the slide rule and similar topics. 188 pages then discuss application of plane trigonometry to special problems in navigation, surveying, elasticity, architecture, and various fields of engineering. Small angles, periodic functions, vectors, polar coordinates, de Moivre's theorem are fully examined. The third section of the book then discusses spherical trigonometry and the solution of spherical triangles, with their applications to terrestrial and astronomical problems. Methods of saving time with numerical calculations, simplification of principal functions of angle, much practical information make this a most useful book. 913 questions answered. 1738 problems, answers to odd numbers. 494 figures. 24 pages of useful formulae, functions. Index. x + 629pp. 5⅜ x 8. T371 Paperbound **$2.00**

TEXTBOOK OF ALGEBRA, G. Chrystal. One of the great mathematical textbooks, still about the best source for complete treatments of the topics of elementary algebra; a chief reference work for teachers and students of algebra in advanced high school and university courses, or for the mathematician working on problems of elementary algebra or looking for a background to more advanced topics. Ranges from basic laws and processes to extensive examination of such topics as limits, infinite series, general properties of integral numbers, and probability theory. Emphasis is on algebraic form, the foundation of analytical geometry and the key to modern developments in algebra. Prior course in algebra is desirable, but not absolutely necessary. Includes theory of quotients, distribution of products, arithmetical theory of surds, theory of interest, permutations and combinations, general expansion theorems, recurring fractions, and much, much more. Two volume set. Index in each volume. Over 1500 exercises, approximately half with answers. Total of xlviii + 1187pp. 5⅜ x 8.
S750 Vol I Paperbound **$2.35**
S751 Vol II Paperbound **$2.35**
The set **$4.70**

MATHEMATICS—INTERMEDIATE TO ADVANCED

General

INTRODUCTION TO APPLIED MATHEMATICS, Francis D. Murnaghan. A practical and thoroughly sound introduction to a number of advanced branches of higher mathematics. Among the selected topics covered in detail are: vector and matrix analysis, partial and differential equations, integral equations, calculus of variations, Laplace transform theory, the vector triple product, linear vector functions, quadratic and bilinear forms, Fourier series, spherical harmonics, Bessel functions, the Heaviside expansion formula, and many others. Extremely useful book for graduate students in physics, engineering, chemistry, and mathematics. Index. 111 study exercises with answers. 41 illustrations. ix + 389pp. 5⅜ x 8½.
S1042 Paperbound **$2.00**

OPERATIONAL METHODS IN APPLIED MATHEMATICS, H. S. Carslaw and J. C. Jaeger. Explanation of the application of the Laplace Transformation to differential equations, a simple and effective substitute for more difficult and obscure operational methods. Of great practical value to engineers and to all workers in applied mathematics. Chapters on: Ordinary Linear Differential Equations with Constant Coefficients;; Electric Circuit Theory; Dynamical Applications; The Inversion Theorem for the Laplace Transformation; Conduction of Heat; Vibrations of Continuous Mechanical Systems; Hydrodynamics; Impulsive Functions; Chains of Differential Equations; and other related matters. 3 appendices. 153 problems, many with answers. 22 figures. xvi + 359pp. 5⅜ x 8½. S1011 Paperbound **$2.25**

APPLIED MATHEMATICS FOR RADIO AND COMMUNICATIONS ENGINEERS, C. E. Smith. No extraneous material here!—only the theories, equations, and operations essential and immediately useful for radio work. Can be used as refresher, as handbook of applications and tables, or as full home-study course. Ranges from simplest arithmetic through calculus, series, and wave forms, hyperbolic trigonometry, simultaneous equations in mesh circuits, etc. Supplies applications right along with each math topic discussed. 22 useful tables of functions, formulas, logs, etc. Index. 166 exercises, 140 examples, all with answers. 95 diagrams. Bibliography. x + 336pp. 5⅜ x 8. S141 Paperbound **$1.75**

Algebra, group theory, determinants, sets, matrix theory

ALGEBRAS AND THEIR ARITHMETICS, L. E. Dickson. Provides the foundation and background necessary to any advanced undergraduate or graduate student studying abstract algebra. Begins with elementary introduction to linear transformations, matrices, field of complex numbers; proceeds to order, basal units, modulus, quaternions, etc.; develops calculus of linears sets, describes various examples of algebras including invariant, difference, nilpotent, semi-simple. "Makes the reader marvel at his genius for clear and profound analysis," Amer. Mathematical Monthly. Index. xii + 241pp. 5⅜ x 8. S616 Paperbound **$1.50**

THE THEORY OF EQUATIONS WITH AN INTRODUCTION TO THE THEORY OF BINARY ALGEBRAIC FORMS, W. S. Burnside and A. W. Panton. Extremely thorough and concrete discussion of the theory of equations, with extensive detailed treatment of many topics curtailed in later texts. Covers theory of algebraic equations, properties of polynomials, symmetric functions, derived functions, Horner's process, complex numbers and the complex variable, determinants and methods of elimination, invariant theory (nearly 100 pages), transformations, introduction to Galois theory, Abelian equations, and much more. Invaluable supplementary work for modern students and teachers. 759 examples and exercises. Index in each volume. Two volume set. Total of xxiv + 604pp. 5⅜ x 8.
S714 Vol I Paperbound **$1.85**
S715 Vol II Paperbound **$1.85**
The set **$3.70**

COMPUTATIONAL METHODS OF LINEAR ALGEBRA, V. N. Faddeeva, translated by **C. D. Benster.** First English translation of a unique and valuable work, the only work in English presenting a systematic exposition of the most important methods of linear algebra—classical and contemporary. Shows in detail how to derive numerical solutions of problems in mathematical physics which are frequently connected with those of linear algebra. Theory as well as individual practice. Part I surveys the mathematical background that is indispensable to what follows. Parts II and III, the conclusion, set forth the most important methods of solution, for both exact and iterative groups. One of the most outstanding and valuable features of this work is the 23 tables, double and triple checked for accuracy. These tables will not be found elsewhere. Author's preface. Translator's note. New bibliography and index. x + 252pp. 5⅜ x 8. S424 Paperbound **$1.95**

ALGEBRAIC EQUATIONS, E. Dehn. Careful and complete presentation of Galois' theory of algebraic equations; theories of Lagrange and Galois developed in logical rather than historical form, with a more thorough exposition than in most modern books. Many concrete applications and fully-worked-out examples. Discusses basic theory (very clear exposition of the symmetric group); isomorphic, transitive, and Abelian groups; applications of Lagrange's and Galois' theories; and much more. Newly revised by the author. Index. List of Theorems. xi + 208pp. 5⅜ x 8. S697 Paperbound **$1.45**

ALGEBRAIC THEORIES, L. E. Dickson. Best thorough introduction to classical topics in higher algebra develops theories centering around matrices, invariants, groups. Higher algebra, Galois theory, finite linear groups, Klein's icosahedron, algebraic invariants, linear transformations, elementary divisors, invariant factors; quadratic, bi-linear, Hermitian forms, singly and in pairs. Proofs rigorous, detailed; topics developed lucidly, in close connection with their most frequent mathematical applications. Formerly "Modern Algebraic Theories." 155 problems. Bibliography. 2 indexes. 285pp. 5⅜ x 8. S547 Paperbound **$1.50**

LECTURES ON THE ICOSAHEDRON AND THE SOLUTION OF EQUATIONS OF THE FIFTH DEGREE, Felix Klein. The solution of quintics in terms of rotation of a regular icosahedron around its axes of symmetry. A classic & indispensable source for those interested in higher algebra, geometry, crystallography. Considerable explanatory material included. 230 footnotes, mostly bibliographic. 2nd edition, xvi + 289pp. 5⅜ x 8. S314 Paperbound **$2.25**

LINEAR GROUPS, WITH AN EXPOSITION OF THE GALOIS FIELD THEORY, L. E. Dickson. The classic exposition of the theory of groups, well within the range of the graduate student. Part I contains the most extensive and thorough presentation of the theory of Galois Fields available, with a wealth of examples and theorems. Part II is a full discussion of linear groups of finite order. Much material in this work is based on Dickson's own contributions. Also includes expositions of Jordan, Lie, Abel, Betti-Mathieu, Hermite, etc. "A milestone in the development of modern algebra," W. Magnus, in his historical introduction to this edition. Index. xv + 312pp. 5⅜ x 8. S482 Paperbound **$1.95**

INTRODUCTION TO THE THEORY OF GROUPS OF FINITE ORDER, R. Carmichael. Examines fundamental theorems and their application. Beginning with sets, systems, permutations, etc., it progresses in easy stages through important types of groups: Abelian, prime power, permutation, etc. Except 1 chapter where matrices are desirable, no higher math needed. 783 exercises, problems. Index. xvi + 447pp. 5⅜ x 8. S300 Paperbound **$2.25**

THEORY OF GROUPS OF FINITE ORDER, W. Burnside. First published some 40 years ago, this is still one of the clearest introductory texts. Partial contents: permutations, groups independent of representation, composition series of a group, isomorphism of a group with itself, Abelian groups, prime power groups, permutation groups, invariants of groups of linear substitution, graphical representation, etc. 45pp. of notes. Indexes. xxiv + 512pp. 5⅜ x 8. S38 Paperbound **$2.75**

CONTINUOUS GROUPS OF TRANSFORMATIONS, L. P. Eisenhart. Intensive study of the theory and geometrical applications of continuous groups of transformations; a standard work on the subject, called forth by the revolution in physics in the 1920's. Covers tensor analysis, Riemannian geometry, canonical parameters, transitivity, imprimitivity, differential invariants, the algebra of constants of structure, differential geometry, contact transformations, etc. "Likely to remain one of the standard works on the subject for many years . . . principal theorems are proved clearly and concisely, and the arrangement of the whole is coherent," MATHEMATICAL GAZETTE. Index. 72-item bibliography. 185 exercises. ix + 301pp. 5⅜ x 8. S781 Paperbound **$2.00**

THE THEORY OF GROUPS AND QUANTUM MECHANICS, H. Weyl. Discussions of Schroedinger's wave equation, de Broglie's waves of a particle, Jordan-Hoelder theorem, Lie's continuous groups of transformations, Pauli exclusion principle, quantization of Maxwell-Dirac field equations, etc. Unitary geometry, quantum theory, groups, application of groups to quantum mechanics, symmetry permutation group, algebra of symmetric transformation, etc. 2nd revised edition. Bibliography. Index. xxii + 422pp. 5⅜ x 8. S269 Paperbound **$2.35**

APPLIED GROUP-THEORETIC AND MATRIX METHODS, Bryan Higman. The first systematic treatment of group and matrix theory for the physical scientist. Contains a comprehensive, easily-followed exposition of the basic ideas of group theory (realized through matrices) and its applications in the various areas of physics and chemistry: tensor analysis, relativity, quantum theory, molecular structure and spectra, and Eddington's quantum relativity. Includes rigorous proofs available only in works of a far more advanced character. 34 figures, numerous tables. Bibliography. Index. xiii + 454pp. 5⅜ x 8⅜. S1147 Paperbound **$2.50**

THE THEORY OF GROUP REPRESENTATIONS, Francis D. Murnaghan. A comprehensive introduction to the theory of group representations. Particular attention is devoted to those groups—mainly the symmetric and rotation groups—which have proved to be of fundamental significance for quantum mechanics (esp. nuclear physics). Also a valuable contribution to the literature on matrices, since the usual representations of groups are groups of matrices. Covers the theory of group integration (as developed by Schur and Weyl), the theory of 2-valued or spin representations, the representations of the symmetric group, the crystallographic groups, the Lorentz group, reducibility (Schur's lemma, Burnside's Theorem, etc.), the alternating group, linear groups, the orthogonal group, etc. Index. List of references. xi + 369pp. 5⅜ x 8½. S1112 Paperbound **$2.35**

THEORY OF SETS, E. Kamke. Clearest, amplest introduction in English, well suited for independent study. Subdivision of main theory, such as theory of sets of points, are discussed, but emphasis is on general theory. Partial contents: rudiments of set theory, arbitrary sets and their cardinal numbers, ordered sets and their order types, well-ordered sets and their cardinal numbers. Bibliography. Key to symbols. Index. vii + 144pp. 5⅜ x 8. S141 Paperbound **$1.35**

THEORY AND APPLICATIONS OF FINITE GROUPS, G. A. Miller, H. F. Blichfeldt, L. E. Dickson. Unusually accurate and authoritative work, each section prepared by a leading specialist: Miller on substitution and abstract groups, Blichfeldt on finite groups of linear homogeneous transformations, Dickson on applications of finite groups. Unlike more modern works, this gives the concrete basis from which abstract group theory arose. Includes Abelian groups, prime-power groups, isomorphisms, matrix forms of linear transformations, Sylow groups, Galois' theory of algebraic equations, duplication of a cube, trisection of an angle, etc. 2 Indexes. 267 problems. xvii + 390pp. 5⅜ x 8. S216 Paperbound **$2.00**

THE THEORY OF DETERMINANTS, MATRICES, AND INVARIANTS, H. W. Turnbull. Important study includes all salient features and major theories. 7 chapters on determinants and matrices cover fundamental properties, Laplace identities, multiplication, linear equations, rank and differentiation, etc. Sections on invariants gives general properties, symbolic and direct methods of reduction, binary and polar forms, general linear transformation, first fundamental theorem, multilinear forms. Following chapters study development and proof of Hilbert's Basis Theorem, Gordan-Hilbert Finiteness Theorem, Clebsch's Theorem, and include discussions of apolarity, canonical forms, geometrical interpretations of algebraic forms, complete system of the general quadric, etc. New preface and appendix. Bibliography. xviii + 374pp. 5⅜ x 8. S699 Paperbound **$2.25**

AN INTRODUCTION TO THE THEORY OF CANONICAL MATRICES, H. W. Turnbull and A. C. Aitken. All principal aspects of the theory of canonical matrices, from definitions and fundamental properties of matrices to the practical applications of their reduction to canonical form. Beginning with matrix multiplications, reciprocals, and partitioned matrices, the authors go on to elementary transformations and bilinear and quadratic forms. Also covers such topics as a rational canonical form for the collineatory group, congruent and conjunctive transformation for quadratic and hermitian forms, unitary and orthogonal transformations, canonical reduction of pencils of matrices, etc. Index. Appendix. Historical notes at chapter ends. Bibliographies. 275 problems. xiv + 200pp. 5⅜ x 8. S177 Paperbound **$1.55**

A TREATISE ON THE THEORY OF DETERMINANTS, T. Muir. Unequalled as an exhaustive compilation of nearly all the known facts about determinants up to the early 1930's. Covers notation and general properties, row and column transformation, symmetry, compound determinants, adjugates, rectangular arrays and matrices, linear dependence, gradients, Jacobians, Hessians, Wronskians, and much more. Invaluable for libraries of industrial and research organizations as well as for student, teacher, and mathematician; very useful in the field of computing machines. Revised and enlarged by W. H. Metzler. Index. 485 problems and scores of numerical examples. iv + 766pp. 5⅜ x 8. S670 Paperbound **$3.00**

THEORY OF DETERMINANTS IN THE HISTORICAL ORDER OF DEVELOPMENT, Sir Thomas Muir. Unabridged reprinting of this complete study of 1,859 papers on determinant theory written between 1693 and 1900. Most important and original sections reproduced, valuable commentary on each. No other work is necessary for determinant research: all types are covered—each subdivision of the theory treated separately; all papers dealing with each type are covered; you are told exactly what each paper is about and how important its contribution is. Each result, theory, extension, or modification is assigned its own identifying numeral so that the full history may be more easily followed. Includes papers on determinants in general, determinants and linear equations, symmetric determinants, alternants, recurrents, determinants having invariant factors, and all other major types. "A model of what such histories ought to be," NATURE. "Mathematicians must ever be grateful to Sir Thomas for his monumental work," AMERICAN MATH MONTHLY. Four volumes bound as two. Indices. Bibliographies. Total of lxxxiv + 1977pp. 5⅜ x 8. S672-3 The set, Clothbound **$12.50**

Calculus and function theory, Fourier theory, infinite series, calculus of variations, real and complex functions

FIVE VOLUME "THEORY OF FUNCTIONS' SET BY KONRAD KNOPP

This five-volume set, prepared by Konrad Knopp, provides a complete and readily followed account of theory of functions. Proofs are given concisely, yet without sacrifice of completeness or rigor. These volumes are used as texts by such universities as M.I.T., University of Chicago, N. Y. City College, and many others. "Excellent introduction . . . remarkably readable, concise, clear, rigorous," JOURNAL OF THE AMERICAN STATISTICAL ASSOCIATION.

ELEMENTS OF THE THEORY OF FUNCTIONS, Konrad Knopp. This book provides the student with background for further volumes in this set, or texts on a similar level. Partial contents: foundations, system of complex numbers and the Gaussian plane of numbers, Riemann sphere of numbers, mapping by linear functions, normal forms, the logarithm, the cyclometric functions and binomial series. "Not only for the young student, but also for the student who knows all about what is in it," MATHEMATICAL JOURNAL. Bibliography. Index. 140pp. 5⅜ x 8. S154 Paperbound **$1.35**

THEORY OF FUNCTIONS, PART I, Konrad Knopp. With volume II, this book provides coverage of basic concepts and theorems. Partial contents: numbers and points, functions of a complex variable, integral of a continuous function, Cauchy's integral theorem, Cauchy's integral formulae, series with variable terms, expansion of analytic functions in power series, analytic continuation and complete definition of analytic functions, entire transcendental functions, Laurent expansion, types of singularities. Bibliography. Index. vii + 146pp. 5⅜ x 8. S156 Paperbound **$1.35**

THEORY OF FUNCTIONS, PART II, Konrad Knopp. Application and further development of general theory, special topics. Single valued functions, entire, Weierstrass, Meromorphic functions. Riemann surfaces. Algebraic functions. Analytical configuration, Riemann surface. Bibliography. Index. x + 150pp. 5⅜ x 8. S157 Paperbound **$1.35**

PROBLEM BOOK IN THE THEORY OF FUNCTIONS, VOLUME 1, Konrad Knopp. Problems in elementary theory, for use with Knopp's THEORY OF FUNCTIONS, or any other text, arranged according to increasing difficulty. Fundamental concepts, sequences of numbers and infinite series, complex variable, integral theorems, development in series, conformal mapping. 182 problems. Answers. viii + 126pp. 5⅜ x 8. S158 Paperbound **$1.35**

PROBLEM BOOK IN THE THEORY OF FUNCTIONS, VOLUME 2, Konrad Knopp. Advanced theory of functions, to be used either with Knopp's THEORY OF FUNCTIONS, or any other comparable text. Singularities, entire & meromorphic functions, periodic, analytic, continuation, multiple-valued functions, Riemann surfaces, conformal mapping. Includes a section of additional elementary problems. "The difficult task of selecting from the immense material of the modern theory of functions the problems just within the reach of the beginner is here masterfully accomplished," AM. MATH. SOC. Answers. 138pp. 5⅜ x 8. S159 Paperbound **$1.35**

A COURSE IN MATHEMATICAL ANALYSIS, Edouard Goursat. Trans. by E. R. Hedrick, O. Dunkel. Classic study of fundamental material thoroughly treated. Exceptionally lucid exposition of wide range of subject matter for student with 1 year of calculus. Vol. 1: Derivatives and Differentials, Definite Integrals, Expansion in Series, Applications to Geometry. Problems. Index. 52 illus. 556pp. Vol. 2, Part I: Functions of a Complex Variable, Conformal Representations, Doubly Periodic Functions, Natural Boundaries, etc. Problems. Index. 38 illus. 269pp. Vol. 2, Part 2: Differential Equations, Cauchy-Lipschitz Method, Non-linear Differential Equations, Simultaneous Equations, etc. Problems. Index. 308pp. 5⅜ x 8.
Vol. 1 S554 Paperbound **$2.50**
Vol. 2 part 1 S555 Paperbound **$1.85**
Vol. 2 part 2 S556 Paperbound **$1.85**
3 vol. set **$6.20**

MODERN THEORIES OF INTEGRATION, H. Kestelman. Connected and concrete coverage, with fully-worked-out proofs for every step. Ranges from elementary definitions through theory of aggregates, sets of points, Riemann and Lebesgue integration, and much more. This new revised and enlarged edition contains a new chapter on Riemann-Stieltjes integration, as well as a supplementary section of 186 exercises. Ideal for the mathematician, student, teacher, or self-studier. Index of Definitions and Symbols. General Index. Bibliography. x + 310pp. 5⅝ x 8⅜. S572 Paperbound **$2.25**

THEORY OF MAXIMA AND MINIMA, H. Hancock. Fullest treatment ever written; only work in English with extended discussion of maxima and minima for functions of 1, 2, or n variables, problems with subsidiary constraints, and relevant quadratic forms. Detailed proof of each important theorem. Covers the Scheeffer and von Dantscher theories, homogeneous quadratic forms, reversion of series, fallacious establishment of maxima and minima, etc. Unsurpassed treatise for advanced students of calculus, mathematicians, economists, statisticians. Index. 24 diagrams. 39 problems, many examples. 193pp. 5⅜ x 8. S665 Paperbound **$1.50**

AN ELEMENTARY TREATISE ON ELLIPTIC FUNCTIONS, A. Cayley. Still the fullest and clearest text on the theories of Jacobi and Legendre for the advanced student (and an excellent supplement for the beginner). A masterpiece of exposition by the great 19th century British mathematician (creator of the theory of matrices and abstract geometry), it covers the addition-theory, Landen's theorem, the 3 kinds of elliptic integrals, transformations, the q-functions, reduction of a differential expression, and much more. Index. xii + 386pp. 5⅜ x 8. S728 Paperbound **$2.00**

THE APPLICATIONS OF ELLIPTIC FUNCTIONS, A. G. Greenhill. Modern books forego detail for sake of brevity—this book offers complete exposition necessary for proper understanding, use of elliptic integrals. Formulas developed from definite physical, geometric problems; examples representative enough to offer basic information in widely useable form. Elliptic integrals, addition theorem, algebraical form of addition theorem, elliptic integrals of 2nd, 3rd kind, double periodicity, resolution into factors, series, transformation, etc. Introduction. Index. 25 illus. xi + 357pp. 5⅜ x 8. S603 Paperbound **$1.75**

THE THEORY OF FUNCTIONS OF REAL VARIABLES, James Pierpont. A 2-volume authoritative exposition, by one of the foremost mathematicians of his time. Each theorem stated with all conditions, then followed by proof. No need to go through complicated reasoning to discover conditions added without specific mention. Includes a particularly complete, rigorous presentation of theory of measure; and Pierpont's own work on a theory of Lebesgue integrals, and treatment of area of a curved surface. Partial contents, Vol. 1: rational numbers, exponentials, logarithms, point aggregates, maxima, minima, proper integrals, improper integrals, multiple proper integrals, continuity, discontinuity, indeterminate forms. Vol. 2: point sets, proper integrals, series, power series, aggregates, ordinal numbers, discontinuous functions, sub-, infra-uniform convergence, much more. Index. 95 illustrations. 1229pp. 5⅜ x 8. S558-9, 2 volume set, paperbound **$5.20**

FUNCTIONS OF A COMPLEX VARIABLE, James Pierpont. Long one of best in the field. A thorough treatment of fundamental elements, concepts, theorems. A complete study, rigorous, detailed, with carefully selected problems worked out to illustrate each topic. Partial contents: arithmetical operations, real term series, positive term series, exponential functions, integration, analytic functions, asymptotic expansions, functions of Weierstrass, Legendre, etc. Index. List of symbols. 122 illus. 597pp. 5⅜ x 8. S560 Paperbound **$2.45**

MODERN OPERATIONAL CALCULUS: WITH APPLICATIONS IN TECHNICAL MATHEMATICS, N. W. McLachlan. An introduction to modern operational calculus based upon the Laplace transform, applying it to the solution of ordinary and partial differential equations. For physicists, engineers, and applied mathematicians. Partial contents: Laplace transform, theorems or rules of the operational calculus, solution of ordinary and partial linear differential equations with constant coefficients, evaluation of integrals and establishment of mathematical relationships, derivation of Laplace transforms of various functions, etc. Six appendices deal with Heaviside's unit function, etc. Revised edition. Index. Bibliography. xiv + 218pp. 5⅜ x 8½. S192 Paperbound **$1.75**

ADVANCED CALCULUS, E. B. Wilson. An unabridged reprinting of the work which continues to be recognized as one of the most comprehensive and useful texts in the field. It contains an immense amount of well-presented, fundamental material, including chapters on vector functions, ordinary differential equations, special functions, calculus of variations, etc., which are excellent introductions to these areas. For students with only one year of calculus, more than 1300 exercises cover both pure math and applications to engineering and physical problems. For engineers, physicists, etc., this work, with its 54 page introductory review, is the ideal reference and refresher. Index. ix + 566pp. 5⅜ x 8. S504 Paperbound **$2.45**

ASYMPTOTIC EXPANSIONS, A. Erdélyi. The only modern work available in English, this is an unabridged reproduction of a monograph prepared for the Office of Naval Research. It discusses various procedures for asymptotic evaluation of integrals containing a large parameter and solutions of ordinary linear differential equations. Bibliography of 71 items. vi + 108pp. 5⅜ x 8. S318 Paperbound **$1.35**

INTRODUCTION TO ELLIPTIC FUNCTIONS: with applications, F. Bowman. Concise, practical introduction to elliptic integrals and functions. Beginning with the familiar trigonometric functions, it requires nothing more from the reader than a knowledge of basic principles of differentiation and integration. Discussion confined to the Jacobian functions. Enlarged bibliography. Index. 173 problems and examples. 56 figures, 4 tables. 115pp. 5⅜ x 8. S922 Paperbound **$1.25**

ON RIEMANN'S THEORY OF ALGEBRAIC FUNCTIONS AND THEIR INTEGRALS: A SUPPLEMENT TO THE USUAL TREATISES, Felix Klein. Klein demonstrates how the mathematical ideas in Riemann's work on Abelian integrals can be arrived at by thinking in terms of the flow of electric current on surfaces. Intuitive explanations, not detailed proofs given in an extremely clear exposition, concentrating on the kinds of functions which can be defined on Riemann surfaces. Also useful as an introduction to the origins of topological problems. Complete and unabridged. Approved translation by Frances Hardcastle. New introduction. 43 figures. Glossary. xii + 76pp. 5⅜ x 8½. S1072 Paperbound **$1.25**

COLLECTED WORKS OF BERNHARD RIEMANN. This important source book is the first to contain the complete text of both 1892 Werke and the 1902 supplement, unabridged. It contains 31 monographs, 3 complete lecture courses, 15 miscellaneous papers, which have been of enormous importance in relativity, topology, theory of complex variables, and other areas of mathematics. Edited by R. Dedekind, H. Weber, M. Noether, W. Wirtinger. German text. English introduction by Hans Lewy. 690pp. 5⅜ x 8. S226 Paperbound **$3.75**

THE TAYLOR SERIES, AN INTRODUCTION TO THE THEORY OF FUNCTIONS OF A COMPLEX VARIABLE, P. Dienes. This book investigates the entire realm of analytic functions. Only ordinary calculus is needed, except in the last two chapters. Starting with an introduction to real variables and complex algebra, the properties of infinite series, elementary functions, complex differentiation and integration are carefully derived. Also biuniform mapping, a thorough two part discussion of representation and singularities of analytic functions, overconvergence and gap theorems, divergent series, Taylor series on its circle of convergence, divergence and singularities, etc. Unabridged, corrected reissue of first edition. Preface and index. 186 examples, many fully worked out. 67 figures. xii + 555pp. 5⅜ x 8. S391 Paperbound **$2.75**

INTRODUCTION TO BESSEL FUNCTIONS, Frank Bowman. A rigorous self-contained exposition providing all necessary material during the development, which requires only some knowledge of calculus and acquaintance with differential equations. A balanced presentation including applications and practical use. Discusses Bessel Functions of Zero Order, of Any Real Order; Modified Bessel Functions of Zero Order; Definite Integrals; Asymptotic Expansions; Bessel's Solution to Kepler's Problem; Circular Membranes; much more. "Clear and straightforward . . . useful not only to students of physics and engineering, but to mathematical students in general," Nature. 226 problems. Short tables of Bessel functions. 27 figures. Index. x + 135pp. 5⅜ x 8. S462 Paperbound **$1.35**

ELEMENTS OF THE THEORY OF REAL FUNCTIONS, J. E. Littlewood. Based on lectures given at Trinity College, Cambridge, this book has proved to be extremely successful in introducing graduate students to the modern theory of functions. It offers a full and concise coverage of classes and cardinal numbers, well-ordered series, other types of series, and elements of the theory of sets of points. 3rd revised edition. vii + 71pp. 5⅜ x 8.
S171 Clothbound **$2.85**
S172 Paperbound **$1.25**

TRANSCENDENTAL AND ALGEBRAIC NUMBERS, A. O. Gelfond. First English translation of work by leading Soviet mathematician. Thue-Siegel theorem, its p-adic analogue, on approximation of algebraic numbers by numbers in fixed algebraic field; Hermite-Lindemann theorem on transcendency of Bessel functions, solutions of other differential equations; Gelfond-Schneider theorem on transcendency of alpha to power beta; Schneider's work on elliptic functions, with method developed by Gelfond. Translated by L. F. Boron. Index. Bibliography. 200pp. 5⅜ x 8. S615 Paperbound **$1.75**

ELLIPTIC INTEGRALS, H. Hancock. Invaluable in work involving differential equations containing cubics or quartics under the root sign, where elementary calculus methods are inadequate. Practical solutions to problems that occur in mathematics, engineering, physics: differential equations requiring integration of Lamé's, Briot's, or Bouquet's equations; determination of arc of ellipse, hyperbola, lemniscate; solutions of problems in elastica; motion of a projectile under resistance varying as the cube of the velocity; pendulums; many others. Exposition is in accordance with Legendre-Jacobi theory and includes rigorous discussion of Legendre transformations. 20 figures. 5 place table. Index. 104pp. 5⅛ x 8.
S484 Paperbound **$1.25**

LECTURES ON THE THEORY OF ELLIPTIC FUNCTIONS, H. Hancock. Reissue of the only book in English with so extensive a coverage, especially of Abel, Jacobi, Legendre, Weierstrasse, Hermite, Liouville, and Riemann. Unusual fullness of treatment, plus applications as well as theory, in discussing elliptic function (the universe of elliptic integrals originating in works of Abel and Jacobi), their existence, and ultimate meaning. Use is made of Riemann to provide the most general theory. 40 page table of formulas. 76 figures. xxiii + 498pp.
S483 Paperbound **$2.55**

THE THEORY AND FUNCTIONS OF A REAL VARIABLE AND THE THEORY OF FOURIER'S SERIES, E. W. Hobson. One of the best introductions to set theory and various aspects of functions and Fourier's series. Requires only a good background in calculus. Provides an exhaustive coverage of: metric and descriptive properties of sets of points; transfinite numbers and order types; functions of a real variable; the Riemann and Lebesgue integrals; sequences and series of numbers; power-series; functions representable by series sequences of continuous functions; trigonometrical series; representation of functions by Fourier's series; complete exposition (200pp.) on set theory; and much more. "The best possible guide," Nature. Vol. I: 88 detailed examples, 10 figures. Index. xv + 736pp. Vol. II: 117 detailed examples, 13 figures. Index. x + 780pp. 6⅛ x 9¼. Vol. I: S387 Paperbound **$3.00**
Vol. II: S388 Paperbound **$3.00**

ALMOST PERIODIC FUNCTIONS, A. S. Besicovitch. This unique and important summary by a well-known mathematician covers in detail the two stages of development in Bohr's theory of almost periodic functions: (1) as a generalization of pure periodicity, with results and proofs; (2) the work done by Stepanoff, Wiener, Weyl, and Bohr in generalizing the theory. Bibliography. xi + 180pp. 5⅜ x 8. S18 Paperbound **$1.75**

THE ANALYTICAL THEORY OF HEAT, Joseph Fourier. This book, which revolutionized mathematical physics, is listed in the Great Books program, and many other listings of great books. It has been used with profit by generations of mathematicians and physicists who are interested in either heat or in the application of the Fourier integral. Covers cause and reflection of rays of heat, radiant heating, heating of closed spaces, use of trigonometric series in the theory of heat, Fourier integral, etc. Translated by Alexander Freeman. 20 figures. xxii + 466pp. 5⅜ x 8. S93 Paperbound **$2.50**

AN INTRODUCTION TO FOURIER METHODS AND THE LAPLACE TRANSFORMATION, Philip Franklin. Concentrates upon essentials, enabling the reader with only a working knowledge of calculus to gain an understanding of Fourier methods in a broad sense, suitable for most applications. This work covers complex qualities with methods of computing elementary functions for complex values of the argument and finding approximations by the use of charts; Fourier series and integrals with half-range and complex Fourier series; harmonic analysis; Fourier and Laplace transformations, etc.; partial differential equations with applications to transmission of electricity; etc. The methods developed are related to physical problems of heat flow, vibrations, electrical transmission, electromagnetic radiation, etc. 828 problems with answers. Formerly entitled "Fourier Methods." Bibliography. Index. x + 289pp. 5⅜ x 8.
S452 Paperbound **$2.00**

THE FOURIER INTEGRAL AND CERTAIN OF ITS APPLICATIONS, Norbert Wiener. The only book-length study of the Fourier integral as link between pure and applied math. An expansion of lectures given at Cambridge. Partial contents: Plancherel's theorem, general Tauberian theorem, special Tauberian theorems, generalized harmonic analysis. Bibliography. viii + 201pp. 5⅜ x 8. S272 Paperbound **$1.50**

Differential equations, ordinary and partial; integral equations

INTRODUCTION TO THE DIFFERENTIAL EQUATIONS OF PHYSICS, L. Hopf. Especially valuable to the engineer with no math beyond elementary calculus. Emphasizing intuitive rather than formal aspects of concepts, the author covers an extensive territory. Partial contents: Law of causality, energy theorem, damped oscillations, coupling by friction, cylindrical and spherical coordinates, heat source, etc. Index. 48 figures. 160pp. 5⅜ x 8.
S120 Paperbound **$1.25**

INTRODUCTION TO THE THEORY OF LINEAR DIFFERENTIAL EQUATIONS, E. G. Poole. Authoritative discussions of important topics, with methods of solution more detailed than usual, for students with background of elementary course in differential equations. Studies existence theorems, linearly independent solutions; equations with constant coefficients; with uniform analytic coefficients; regular singularities; the hypergeometric equation; conformal representation; etc. Exercises. Index. 210pp. 5⅜ x 8. S629 Paperbound **$1.65**

DIFFERENTIAL EQUATIONS FOR ENGINEERS, P. Franklin. Outgrowth of a course given 10 years at M. I. T. Makes most useful branch of pure math accessible for practical work. Theoretical basis of D.E.'s; solution of ordinary D.E.'s and partial derivatives arising from heat flow, steady-state temperature of a plate, wave equations; analytic functions; convergence of Fourier Series. 400 problems on electricity, vibratory systems, other topics. Formerly "Differential Equations for Electrical Engineers." Index 41 illus. 307pp. 5⅜ x 8.
S601 Paperbound **$1.65**

DIFFERENTIAL EQUATIONS, F. R. Moulton. A detailed, rigorous exposition of all the non-elementary processes of solving ordinary differential equations. Several chapters devoted to the treatment of practical problems, especially those of a physical nature, which are far more advanced than problems usually given as illustrations. Includes analytic differential equations; variations of a parameter; integrals of differential equations; analytic implicit functions; problems of elliptic motion; sine-amplitude functions; deviation of formal bodies; Cauchy-Lipschitz process; linear differential equations with periodic coefficients; differential equations in infinitely many variations; much more. Historical notes. 10 figures. 222 problems. Index. xv + 395pp. 5⅜ x 8. S451 Paperbound **$2.00**

DIFFERENTIAL AND INTEGRAL EQUATIONS OF MECHANICS AND PHYSICS (DIE DIFFERENTIAL- UND INTEGRALGLEICHUNGEN DER MECHANIK UND PHYSIK), edited by P. Frank and R. von Mises. Most comprehensive and authoritative work on the mathematics of mathematical physics available today in the United States: the standard, definitive reference for teachers, physicists, engineers, and mathematicians—now published (in the original German) at a relatively inexpensive price for the first time! Every chapter in this 2,000-page set is by an expert in his field: Carathéodory, Courant, Frank, Mises, and a dozen others. Vol I, on mathematics, gives concise but complete coverages of advanced calculus, differential equations, integral equations, and potential, and partial differential equations. Index. xxiii + 916pp. Vol. II (physics): classical mechanics, optics, continuous mechanics, heat conduction and diffusion, the stationary and quasi-stationary electromagnetic field, electromagnetic oscillations, and wave mechanics. Index. xxiv + 1106pp. Two volume set. Each volume available separately. 5⅝ x 8⅜. S787 Vol I Clothbound **$7.50**
S788 Vol II Clothbound **$7.50**
The set **$15.00**

LECTURES ON CAUCHY'S PROBLEM, J. Hadamard. Based on lectures given at Columbia, Rome, this discusses work of Riemann, Kirchhoff, Volterra, and the author's own research on the hyperbolic case in linear partial differential equations. It extends spherical and cylindrical waves to apply to all (normal) hyperbolic equations. Partial contents: Cauchy's problem, fundamental formula, equations with odd number, with even number of independent variables; method of descent. 32 figures. Index. iii + 316pp. 5⅜ x 8. S105 Paperbound **$1.75**

THEORY OF DIFFERENTIAL EQUATIONS, A. R. Forsyth. Out of print for over a decade, the complete 6 volumes (now bound as 3) of this monumental work represent the most comprehensive treatment of differential equations ever written. Historical presentation includes in 2500 pages every substantial development. Vol. 1, 2: EXACT EQUATIONS, PFAFF'S PROBLEM; ORDINARY EQUATIONS, NOT LINEAR: methods of Grassmann, Clebsch, Lie, Darboux; Cauchy's theorem; branch points; etc. Vol. 3, 4: ORDINARY EQUATIONS, NOT LINEAR; ORDINARY LINEAR EQUATIONS: Zeta Fuchsian functions, general theorems on algebraic integrals, Brun's theorem, equations with uniform periodic coffiecients, etc. Vol. 4, 5: PARTIAL DIFFERENTIAL EQUATIONS: 2 existence-theorems, equations of theoretical dynamics, Laplace transformations, general transformation of equations of the 2nd order, much more. Indexes. Total of 2766pp. 5⅜ x 8. S576-7-8 Clothbound: the set **$15.00**

PARTIAL DIFFERENTIAL EQUATIONS OF MATHEMATICAL PHYSICS, A. G. Webster. A keystone work in the library of every mature physicist, engineer, researcher. Valuable sections on elasticity, compression theory, potential theory, theory of sound, heat conduction, wave propagation, vibration theory. Contents include: deduction of differential equations, vibrations, normal functions, Fourier's series, Cauchy's method, boundary problems, method of Riemann-Volterra. Spherical, cylindrical, ellipsoidal harmonics, applications, etc. 97 figures. vii + 440pp. 5⅜ x 8. S263 Paperbound **$2.00**

ORDINARY DIFFERENTIAL EQUATIONS, E. L. Ince. A most compendious analysis in real and complex domains. Existence and nature of solutions, continuous transformation groups, solutions in an infinite form, definite integrals, algebraic theory, Sturmian theory, boundary problems, existence theorems, 1st order, higher order, etc. "Deserves the highest praise, a notable addition to mathematical literature," BULLETIN, AM. MATH. SOC. Historical appendix. Bibliography. 18 figures. viii + 558pp. 5⅜ x 8. S349 Paperbound **$2.75**

INTRODUCTION TO NONLINEAR DIFFERENTIAL AND INTEGRAL EQUATIONS, Harold T. Davis. A thorough introduction to this important area, of increasing interest to mathematicians and scientists. First published by the United States Atomic Energy Commission, it includes chapters on the differential equation of the first order, the Riccati equation (as a bridge between linear and nonlinear equations), existence theorems, second order equations, elliptic integrals, elliptic functions, and theta functions, second order differential equations of polynomial class, continuous analytic continuation, the phase plane and its phenomena, nonlinear mechanics, the calculus of variations, etc. Appendices on Painlevé transcendents and Van der Pol and Volterra equations. Bibliography of 350 items. 137 problems. Index. xv + 566pp. 5⅜ x 8½. S971 Paperbound **$2.00**

THEORY OF FUNCTIONALS AND OF INTEGRAL AND INTEGRO-DIFFERENTIAL EQUATIONS, Vito Volterra. Unabridged republication of the only English translation. An exposition of the general theory of the functions depending on a continuous set of values of another function, based on the author's fundamental notion of the transition from a finite number of variables to a continually infinite number. Though dealing primarily with integral equations, much material on calculus of variations is included. The work makes no assumption of previous knowledge on the part of the reader. It begins with fundamental material and proceeds to Generalization of Analytic Functions, Integro-Differential Equations, Functional Derivative Equations, Applications, Other Directions of Theory of Functionals, etc. New introduction by G. C. Evans. Bibliography and criticism of Volterra's work by E. Whittaker. Bibliography. Index of authors cited. Index of subjects. xxxx + 226pp. 5⅜ x 8. S502 Paperbound **$1.75**

LINEAR INTEGRAL EQUATIONS, W. V. Lovitt. Systematic survey of general theory, with some application to differential equations, calculus of variations, problems of math, physics. Partial contents: integral equation of 2nd kind by successive substitutions; Fredholm's equation as ratio of 2 integral series in lambda, applications of the Fredholm theory, Hilbert-Schmidt theory of symmetric kernels, application, etc. Neumann, Dirichlet, vibratory problems. Index. ix + 253pp. 5⅜ x 8. S176 Paperbound **$1.60**

Foundations of mathematics

THE CONTINUUM AND OTHER TYPES OF SERIAL ORDER, E. V. Huntington. This famous book gives a systematic elementary account of the modern theory of the continuum as a type of serial order. Based on the Cantor-Dedekind ordinal theory, which requires no technical knowledge of higher mathematics, it offers an easily followed analysis of ordered classes, discrete and dense series, continuous series, Cantor's transfinite numbers. 2nd edition. Index. viii + 82pp. 5⅜ x 8. S130 Paperbound **$1.00**

CONTRIBUTIONS TO THE FOUNDING OF THE THEORY OF TRANSFINITE NUMBERS, Georg Cantor. These papers founded a new branch of mathematics. The famous articles of 1895-7 are translated, with an 82-page introduction by P. E. B. Jourdain dealing with Cantor, the background of his discoveries, their results, future possibilities. Bibliography. Index. Notes. ix + 211 pp. 5⅜ x 8. S45 Paperbound **$1.35**

ELEMENTARY MATHEMATICS FROM AN ADVANCED STANDPOINT, Felix Klein.

This classic text is an outgrowth of Klein's famous integration and survey course at Göttingen. Using one field of mathematics to interpret, adjust, illuminate another, it covers basic topics in each area, illustrating its discussion with extensive analysis. It is especially valuable in considering areas of modern mathematics. "Makes the reader feel the inspiration of . . . a great mathematician, inspiring teacher . . . with deep insight into the foundations and interrelations," BULLETIN, AMERICAN MATHEMATICAL SOCIETY.

Vol. 1. ARITHMETIC, ALGEBRA, ANALYSIS. Introducing the concept of function immediately, it enlivens abstract discussion with graphical and geometrically perceptual methods. Partial contents: natural numbers, extension of the notion of number, special properties, complex numbers. Real equations with real unknowns, complex quantities. Logarithmic, exponential functions, goniometric functions, infinitesimal calculus. Transcendence of e and pi, theory of assemblages. Index. 125 figures. ix + 274pp . 5⅜ x 8. S150 Paperbound **$1.85**

Vol. 2. GEOMETRY. A comprehensive view which accompanies the space perception inherent in geometry with analytic formulas which facilitate precise formulation. Partial contents: Simplest geometric manifolds: line segment, Grassmann determinant principles, classification of configurations of space, derivative manifolds. Geometric transformations: affine transformations, projective, higher point transformations, theory of the imaginary. Systematic discussion of geometry and its foundations. Indexes. 141 illustrations. ix + 214pp. 5⅜ x 8. S151 Paperbound **$1.75**

ESSAYS ON THE THEORY OF NUMBERS: 1. CONTINUITY AND IRRATIONAL NUMBERS; 2. THE NATURE AND MEANING OF NUMBERS, Richard Dedekind. The two most important essays on the logical foundations of the number system by the famous German mathematician. The first provides a purely arithmetic and perfectly rigorous foundation for irrational numbers and thereby a rigorous meaning to continuity in analysis. The second essay is an attempt to give a logical basis for transfinite numbers and properties of the natural numbers. Discusses the logical validity of mathematical induction. Authorized English translations by W. W. Deman of "Stetigkeit und irrationale Zahlen" and "Was sind und was sollen die Zahlen?" vii + 115pp. 5⅜ x 8. T1010 Paperbound **$1.00**

Geometry

THE FOUNDATIONS OF EUCLIDEAN GEOMETRY, H. G. Forder. The first rigorous account of Euclidean geometry, establishing propositions without recourse to empiricism, and without multiplying hypotheses. Corrects many traditional weaknesses of Euclidean proofs, and investigates the problems imposed on the axiom system by the discoveries of Bolyai and Lobachevsky. Some topics discussed are Classes and Relations; Axioms for Magnitudes; Congruence and Similarity; Algebra of Points; Hessenberg's Theorem; Continuity; Existence of Parallels; Reflections; Rotations; Isometries; etc. Invaluable for the light it throws on foundations of math. Lists: Axioms employed, Symbols, Constructions. 295pp. 5⅜ x 8. S481 Paperbound **$2.00**

ADVANCED EUCLIDEAN GEOMETRY, R. A. Johnson. For years the standard textbook on advanced Euclidean geometry, requires only high school geometry and trigonometry. Explores in unusual detail and gives proofs of hundreds of relatively recent theorems and corollaries, many formerly available only in widely scattered journals. Covers tangent circles, the theorem of Miquel, symmedian point, pedal triangles and circles, the Brocard configuration, and much more. Formerly "Modern Geometry." Index. 107 diagrams. xiii + 319pp. 5⅜ x 8. S669 Paperbound **$1.65**

HIGHER GEOMETRY: AN INTRODUCTION TO ADVANCED METHODS IN ANALYTIC GEOMETRY, F. S. Woods. Exceptionally thorough study of concepts and methods of advanced algebraic geometry (as distinguished from differential geometry). Exhaustive treatment of 1-, 2-, 3-, and 4-dimensional coordinate systems, leading to n-dimensional geometry in an abstract sense. Covers projectivity, tetracyclical coordinates, contact transformation, pentaspherical coordinates, much more. Based on M.I.T. lectures, requires sound preparation in analytic geometry and some knowledge of determinants. Index. Over 350 exercises. References. 60 figures. x + 423pp. 5⅜ x 8. S737 Paperbound **$2.00**

CONTEMPORARY GEOMETRY, André Delachet. Translated by Howard G. Bergmann. The recent developments in geometry covered in uncomplicated fashion. Clear discussions of modern thinking about the theory of groups, the concept of abstract geometry, projective geometry, algebraic geometry, vector spaces, new kinds of metric spaces, developments in differential geometry, etc. A large part of the book is devoted to problems, developments, and applications of topology. For advanced undergraduates and graduate students as well as mathematicians in other fields who want a brief introduction to current work in geometry. 39 figures. Index. xix + 94pp. 5⅜ x 8½. S988 Paperbound **$1.00**

ELEMENTS OF PROJECTIVE GEOMETRY, L. Cremona. Outstanding complete treatment of projective geometry by one of the foremost 19th century geometers. Detailed proofs of all fundamental principles, stress placed on the constructive aspects. Covers homology, law of duality, anharmonic ratios, theorems of Pascal and Brianchon, foci, polar reciprocal figures, etc. Only ordinary geometry necessary to understand this honored classic. Index. Over 150 fully worked out examples and problems. 252 diagrams. xx + 302pp. 5⅜ x 8. S668 Paperbound **$1.75**

AN INTRODUCTION TO PROJECTIVE GEOMETRY, R. M. Winger. One of the best introductory texts to an important area in modern mathematics. Contains full development of elementary concepts often omitted in other books. Employing the analytic method to capitalize on the student's collegiate training in algebra, analytic geometry and calculus, the author deals with such topics as Essential Constants, Duality, The Line at Infinity, Projective Properties and Double Ratio, Projective Coordinates, The Conic, Collineations and Involutions in One Dimension, Binary Forms, Algebraic Invariants, Analytic Treatment of the Conic, Collineations in the Plane, Cubic Involutions and the Rational Cubic Curve, and a clear discussion of Non-Euclidean Geometry. For senior-college students and graduates. "An excellent textbook . . . very clearly written . . . propositions stated concisely," A. Emch, Am. Math. Monthly. Corrected reprinting. 928 problems. Index. 116 figures. xii + 443pp. 5⅜ x 8. S949 Paperbound **$2.00**

ALGEBRAIC CURVES, Robert J. Walker, Professor of Mathematics, Cornell University. Fine introduction to algebraic geometry. Presents some of the recently developed algebraic methods of handling problems in algebraic geometry, shows how these methods are related to the older analytic and geometric problems, and applies them to those same geometric problems. Limited to the theory of curves, concentrating on birational transformations. Contents: Algebraic Preliminaries, Projective Spaces, Plane Algebraic Curves, Formal Power Series, Transformations of a Curve, Linear Series. 25 illustrations. Numerous exercises at ends of sections. Index. x + 201pp. 5⅜ x 8½. S336 Paperbound **$1.60**

THE ADVANCED GEOMETRY OF PLANE CURVES AND THEIR APPLICATIONS, C. Zwikker. An unusual study of many important curves, their geometrical properties and their applications, including discussions of many less well-known curves not often treated in textbooks on synthetic and analytic Euclidean geometry. Includes both algebraic and transcendental curves such as the conic sections, kinked curves, spirals, lemniscates, cycloids, etc. and curves generated as involutes, evolutes, anticaustics, pedals, envelopes and orthogonal trajectories. Dr. Zwikker represents the points of the curves by complex numbers instead of two real Cartesian coordinates, allowing direct and even elegant proofs. Formerly: "Advanced Plane Geometry." 273 figures. xii + 299pp. 5⅜ x 8½. S1078 Paperbound **$2.00**

A TREATISE ON THE DIFFERENTIAL GEOMETRY OF CURVES AND SURFACES, L. P. Eisenhart. Introductory treatise especially for the graduate student, for years a highly successful textbook. More detailed and concrete in approach than most more recent books. Covers space curves, osculating planes, moving axes, Gauss' method, the moving trihedral, geodesics, conformal representation, etc. Last section deals with deformation of surfaces, rectilinear congruences, cyclic systems, etc. Index. 683 problems. 30 diagrams. xii + 474pp. 5⅜ x 8. S667 Paperbound **$2.75**

A TREATISE ON ALGEBRAIC PLANE CURVES, J. L. Coolidge. Unabridged reprinting of one of few full coverages in English, offering detailed introduction to theory of algebraic plane curves and their relations to geometry and analysis. Treats topological properties, Riemann-Roch theorem, all aspects of wide variety of curves including real, covariant, polar, containing series of a given sort, elliptic, polygonal, rational, the pencil, two parameter nets, etc. This volume will enable the reader to appreciate the symbolic notation of Aronhold and Clebsch. Bibliography. Index. 17 illustrations. xxiv + 513pp. 5⅜ x 8. S543 Paperbound **$2.75**

AN INTRODUCTION TO THE GEOMETRY OF N DIMENSIONS, D. M. Y. Sommerville. An introduction presupposing no prior knowledge of the field, the only book in English devoted exclusively to higher dimensional geometry. Discusses fundamental ideas of incidence, parallelism, perpendicularity, angles between linear space; enumerative geometry; analytical geometry from projective and metric points of view; polytopes; elementary ideas in analysis situs; content of hyper-spacial figures. Bibliography. Index. 60 diagrams. 196pp. 5⅜ x 8. S494 Paperbound **$1.50**

GEOMETRY OF FOUR DIMENSIONS, H. P. Manning. Unique in English as a clear, concise introduction. Treatment is synthetic, and mostly Euclidean, although in hyperplanes and hyperspheres at infinity, non-Euclidean geometry is used. Historical introduction. Foundations of 4-dimensional geometry. Perpendicularity, simple angles. Angles of planes, higher order. Symmetry, order, motion; hyperpyramids, hypercones, hyperspheres; figures with parallel elements; volume, hypervolume in space; regular polyhedroids. Glossary. 78 figures. ix + 348pp. 5⅜ x 8. S182 Paperbound **$2.00**

CONVEX FIGURES AND POLYHEDRA, L. A. Lyusternik. An excellent elementary discussion by a leading Russian mathematician. Beginning with the basic concepts of convex figures and bodies and their supporting lines and planes, the author covers such matters as centrally symmetric convex figures, theorems of Euler, Cauchy, Steinitz and Alexandrov on convex polyhedra, linear systems of convex bodies, planar sections of convex bodies, the Brunn-Minkowski inequality and its consequences, and many other related topics. No more than a high school background in mathematics needed for complete understanding. First English translation by T. J. Smith. 182 illustrations. Index. x + 176pp. 5⅜ x 8½. S1021 Paperbound **$1.50**

NON-EUCLIDEAN GEOMETRY, Roberto Bonola. The standard coverage of non-Euclidean geometry. It examines from both a historical and mathematical point of view the geometries which have arisen from a study of Euclid's 5th postulate upon parallel lines. Also included are complete texts, translated, of Bolyai's SCIENCE OF ABSOLUTE SPACE. Lobachevsky's THEORY OF PARALLELS. 180 diagrams. 431pp. 5⅜ x 8. S27 Paperbound **$2.00**

ELEMENTS OF NON-EUCLIDEAN GEOMETRY, D. M. Y. Sommerville. Unique in proceeding step-by-step, in the manner of traditional geometry. Enables the student with only a good knowledge of high school algebra and geometry to grasp elementary hyperbolic, elliptic, analytic non-Euclidean geometries; space curvature and its philosophical implications; theory of radical axes; homothetic centres and systems of circles; parataxy and parallelism; absolute measure; Gauss' proof of the defect area theorem; geodesic representation; much more, all with exceptional clarity. 126 problems at chapter endings provide progressive practice and familiarity. 133 figures. Index. xvi + 274pp. 5⅜ x 8. S460 Paperbound **$1.50**

INTRODUCTORY NON-EUCLIDEAN GEOMETRY, H. P. Manning. Sound elementary introduction to non-Euclidean geometry. The first two thirds (Pangeometry and the Hyperbolic Geometry) require a grasp of plane and solid geometry and trigonometry. The last sections (the Elliptic Geometry and Analytic Non-Euclidean Geometry) necessitate also basic college calculus for understanding the text. The book does not propose to investigate the foundations of geometry, but rather begins with the theorems common to Euclidean and non-Euclidean geometry and then takes up the specific differences between them. A simple and direct account of the bases of this important branch of mathematics for teachers and students. 94 figures. vii + 95pp. 5⅜ x 8. S310 Paperbound **$1.00**

ELEMENTARY CONCEPTS OF TOPOLOGY, P. Alexandroff. First English translation of the famous brief introduction to topology for the beginner or for the mathematician not undertaking extensive study. This unusually useful intuitive approach deals primarily with the concepts of complex, cycle, and homology, and is wholly consistent with current investigations. Ranges from basic concepts of set-theoretic topology to the concept of Betti groups. "Glowing example of harmony between intuition and thought," David Hilbert. Translated by A. E. Farley. Introduction by D. Hilbert. Index. 25 figures. 73pp. 5⅜ x 8. S747 Paperbound **$1.00**

Number theory

INTRODUCTION TO THE THEORY OF NUMBERS, L. E. Dickson. Thorough, comprehensive approach with adequate coverage of classical literature, an introductory volume beginners can follow. Chapters on divisibility, congruences, quadratic residues & reciprocity, Diophantine equations, etc. Full treatment of binary quadratic forms without usual restriction to integral coefficients. Covers infinitude of primes, least residues, Fermat's theorem, Euler's phi function, Legendre's symbol, Gauss's lemma, automorphs, reduced forms, recent theorems of Thue & Siegel, many more. Much material not readily available elsewhere. 239 problems. Index. I figure. viii + 183pp. 5⅜ x 8. S342 Paperbound **$1.65**

ELEMENTS OF NUMBER THEORY, I. M. Vinogradov. Detailed 1st course for persons without advanced mathematics; 95% of this book can be understood by readers who have gone no farther than high school algebra. Partial contents: divisibility theory, important number theoretical functions, congruences, primitive roots and indices, etc. Solutions to both problems and exercises. Tables of primes, indices, etc. Covers almost every essential formula in elementary number theory! Translated from Russian. 233 problems, 104 exercises. viii + 227pp. 5⅜ x 8. S259 Paperbound **$1.60**

THEORY OF NUMBERS and DIOPHANTINE ANALYSIS, R. D. Carmichael. These two complete works in one volume form one of the most lucid introductions to number theory, requiring only a firm foundation in high school mathematics. "Theory of Numbers," partial contents: Eratosthenes' sieve, Euclid's fundamental theorem, G.C.F. and L.C.M. of two or more integers, linear congruences, etc "Diophantine Analysis": rational triangles, Pythagorean triangles, equations of third, fourth, higher degrees, method of functional equations, much more. "Theory of Numbers": 76 problems. Index. 94pp. "Diophantine Analysis": 222 problems. Index. 118pp. 5⅜ x 8. S529 Paperbound **$1.35**

Numerical analysis, tables

MATHEMATICAL TABLES AND FORMULAS, Compiled by Robert D. Carmichael and Edwin R. Smith. Valuable collection for students, etc. Contains all tables necessary in college algebra and trigonometry, such as five-place common logarithms, logarithmic sines and tangents of small angles, logarithmic trigonometric functions, natural trigonometric functions, four-place antilogarithms, tables for changing from sexagesimal to circular and from circular to sexagesimal measure of angles, etc. Also many tables and formulas not ordinarily accessible, including powers, roots, and reciprocals, exponential and hyperbolic functions, ten-place logarithms of prime numbers, and formulas and theorems from analytical and elementary geometry and from calculus. Explanatory introduction. viii + 269pp. 5⅜ x 8½. S111 Paperbound **$1.00**

MATHEMATICAL TABLES, H. B. Dwight. Unique for its coverage in one volume of almost every function of importance in applied mathematics, engineering, and the physical sciences. Three extremely fine tables of the three trig functions and their inverse functions to thousandths of radians; natural and common logarithms; squares, cubes; hyperbolic functions and the inverse hyperbolic functions; $(a^2 + b^2)$ exp. ½a; complete elliptic integrals of the 1st and 2nd kind; sine and cosine integrals; exponential integrals Ei(x) and Ei(−x); binomial coefficients; factorials to 250; surface zonal harmonics and first derivatives; Bernoulli and Euler numbers and their logs to base of 10; Gamma function; normal probability integral; over 60 pages of Bessel functions; the Riemann Zeta function. Each table with formulae generally used, sources of more extensive tables, interpolation data, etc. Over half have columns of differences, to facilitate interpolation. Introduction. Index. viii + 231pp. 5⅜ x 8. S445 Paperbound **$1.75**

TABLES OF FUNCTIONS WITH FORMULAE AND CURVES, E. Jahnke & F. Emde. The world's most comprehensive 1-volume English-text collection of tables, formulae, curves of transcendent functions. 4th corrected edition, new 76-page section giving tables, formulae for elementary functions—not in other English editions. Partial contents: sine, cosine, logarithmic integral; factorial function; error integral; theta functions; elliptic integrals, functions; Legendre, Bessel, Riemann, Mathieu, hypergeometric functions, etc. Supplementary books. Bibliography. Indexed. "Out of the way functions for which we know no other source," SCIENTIFIC COMPUTING SERVICE, Ltd. 212 figures. 400pp. 5⅜ x 8. S133 Paperbound **$2.00**

JACOBIAN ELLIPTIC FUNCTION TABLES, L. M. Milne-Thomson. An easy to follow, practical book which gives not only useful numerical tables, but also a complete elementary sketch of the application of elliptic functions. It covers Jacobian elliptic functions and a description of their principal properties; complete elliptic integrals; Fourier series and power series expansions; periods, zeros, poles, residues, formulas for special values of the argument; transformations, approximations, elliptic integrals, conformal mapping, factorization of cubic and quartic polynomials; application to the pendulum problem; etc. Tables and graphs form the body of the book: Graph, 5 figure table of the elliptic function sn (u m); cn (u m); dn (u m). 8 figure table of complete elliptic integrals K, K′, E, E′, and the nome q. 7 figure table of the Jacobian zeta-function Z(u). 3 figures. xi + 123pp. 5⅜ x 8.
S194 Paperbound **$1.35**

TABLES OF INDEFINITE INTEGRALS, G. Petit Bois. Comprehensive and accurate, this orderly grouping of over 2500 of the most useful indefinite integrals will save you hours of laborious mathematical groundwork. After a list of 49 common transformations of integral expressions, with a wide variety of examples, the book takes up algebraic functions, irrational monomials, products and quotients of binomials, transcendental functions, natural logs, etc. You will rarely or never encounter an integral of an algebraic or transcendental function not included here; any more comprehensive set of tables costs at least $12 or $15. Index. 2544 integrals. xii + 154pp. 6⅛ x 9¼.
S225 Paperbound **$2.00**

SUMMATION OF SERIES, Collected by L. B. W. Jolley. Over 1100 common series collected, summed, and grouped for easy reference—for mathematicians, physicists, computer technicians, engineers, and students. Arranged for convenience into categories, such as arithmetical and geometrical progressions, powers and products of natural numbers, figurate and polygonal numbers, inverse natural numbers, exponential and logarithmic series, binomial expansions, simple inverse products, factorials, and trigonometric and hyperbolic expansions. Also included are series representing various Bessel functions, elliptic integrals; discussions of special series involving Legendre polynomials, the zeta function, Bernoulli's function, and similar expressions. Revised, enlarged second edition. New preface. xii + 251pp. 5⅜ x 8½.
S23 Paperbound **$2.25**

A TABLE OF THE INCOMPLETE ELLIPTIC INTEGRAL OF THE THIRD KIND, R. G. Selfridge, J. E. Maxfield. The first complete 6-place tables of values of the incomplete integral of the third kind, prepared under the auspices of the Research Department of the U.S. Naval Ordnance Test Station. Calculated on an IBM type 704 calculator and thoroughly verified by echo-checking and a check integral at the completion of each value of **a.** Of inestimable value in problems where the surface area of geometrical bodies can only be expressed in terms of the incomplete integral of the third and lower kinds; problems in aero-, fluid-, and thermodynamics involving processes where nonsymmetrical repetitive volumes must be determined; various types of seismological problems; problems of magnetic potentials due to circular current; etc. Foreword. Acknowledgment. Introduction. Use of table. xiv + 805pp. 5⅝ x 8⅜.
S501 Clothbound **$7.50**

PRACTICAL ANALYSIS, GRAPHICAL AND NUMERICAL METHODS, F. A. Willers. Translated by R. T. Beyer. Immensely practical handbook for engineers, showing how to interpolate, use various methods of numerical differentiation and integration, determine the roots of a single algebraic equation, system of linear equations, use empirical formulas, integrate differential equations, etc. Hundreds of shortcuts for arriving at numerical solutions. Special section on American calculating machines, by T. W. Simpson. 132 illustrations. 422pp. 5⅜ x 8.
S273 Paperbound **$2.00**

NUMERICAL INTEGRATION OF DIFFERENTIAL EQUATIONS, A. A. Bennett, W. E. Milne, H. Bateman. Republication of original monograph prepared for National Research Council. New methods of integration of differential equations developed by 3 leading mathematicians: THE INTERPOLATIONAL POLYNOMIAL and SUCCESSIVE APPROXIMATIONS by A. A. Bennett; STEP-BY-STEP METHODS OF INTEGRATION by W. W. Milne; METHODS FOR PARTIAL DIFFERENTIAL EQUATIONS by H. Bateman. Methods for partial differential equations, transition from difference equations to differential equations, solution of differential equations to non-integral values of a parameter will interest mathematicians and physicists. 288 footnotes, mostly bibliographic; 235-item classified bibliography. 108pp. 5⅜ x 8. S305 Paperbound **$1.35**

INTRODUCTION TO RELAXATION METHODS, F. S. Shaw. Fluid mechanics, design of electrical networks, forces in structural frameworks, stress distribution, buckling, etc. Solve linear simultaneous equations, linear ordinary differential equations, partial differential equations, Eigen-value problems by relaxation methods. Detailed examples throughout. Special tables for dealing with awkwardly-shaped boundaries. Indexes. 253 diagrams. 72 tables. 400pp. 5⅜ x 8.
S244 Paperbound **$2.45**

NUMERICAL SOLUTIONS OF DIFFERENTIAL EQUATIONS, H. Levy & E. A. Baggott. Comprehensive collection of methods for solving ordinary differential equations of first and higher order. All must pass 2 requirements: easy to grasp and practical, more rapid than school methods. Partial contents: graphical integration of differential equations, graphical methods for detailed solution. Numerical solution. Simultaneous equations and equations of 2nd and higher orders. "Should be in the hands of all in research in applied mathematics, teaching," NATURE. 21 figures. viii + 238pp. 5⅜ x 8.
S168 Paperbound **$1.75**

Probability theory and information theory

AN ELEMENTARY INTRODUCTION TO THE THEORY OF PROBABILITY, B. V. Gnedenko and A. Ya. Khinchin. Translated by Leo F. Boron. A clear, compact introduction designed to equip the reader with a fundamental grasp of the theory of probability. It is thorough and authoritative within its purposely restricted range, yet the layman with a background in elementary mathematics will be able to follow it without difficulty. Covers such topics as the processes involved in the calculation of probabilities, conditional probabilities and the multiplication rule, Bayes's formula, Bernoulli's scheme and theorem, random variables and distribution laws, and dispersion and mean deviations. New translation of fifth (revised) Russian edition (1960)—the only translation checked and corrected by Gnedenko. New preface for Dover edition by B. V. Gnedenko. Index. Bibliography. Appendix: Table of values of function $\phi(a)$. xii + 130pp. 5⅜ x 8½. T155 Paperbound **$1.50**

AN INTRODUCTION TO MATHEMATICAL PROBABILITY, Julian Lowell Coolidge. A thorough introduction which presents the mathematical foundation of the theory of probability. A substantial body of material, yet can be understood with a knowledge of only elementary calculus. Contains: The Scope and Meaning of Mathematical Probability; Elementary Principles of Probability; Bernoulli's Theorem; Mean Value and Dispersion; Geometrical Probability; Probability of Causes; Errors of Observation; Errors in Many Variables; Indirect Observations; The Statistical Theory of Gases; and The Principles of Life Insurance. Six pages of logarithm tables. 4 diagrams. Subject and author indices. xii + 214pp. 5⅜ x 8½. S258 Paperbound **$1.35**

A GUIDE TO OPERATIONS RESEARCH, W. E. Duckworth. A brief nontechnical exposition of techniques and theories of operational research. A good introduction for the layman; also can provide the initiate with new understandings. No mathematical training needed, yet not an oversimplification. Covers game theory, mathematical analysis, information theory, linear programming, cybernetics, decision theory, etc. Also includes a discussion of the actual organization of an operational research program and an account of the uses of such programs in the oil, chemical, paper, and metallurgical industries, etc. Bibliographies at chapter ends. Appendices. 36 figures. 145pp. 5¼ x 8½. T1129 Clothbound **$3.50**

MATHEMATICAL FOUNDATIONS OF INFORMATION THEORY, A. I. Khinchin. For the first time mathematicians, statisticians, physicists, cyberneticists, and communications engineers are offered a complete and exact introduction to this relatively new field. Entropy as a measure of a finite scheme, applications to coding theory, study of sources, channels and codes, detailed proofs of both Shannon theorems for any ergodic source and any stationary channel with finite memory, and much more are covered. Bibliography. vii + 120pp. 5⅜ x 8. S434 Paperbound **$1.35**

SELECTED PAPERS ON NOISE AND STOCHASTIC PROCESS, edited by **Prof. Nelson Wax,** U. of Illinois. 6 basic papers for newcomers in the field, for those whose work involves noise characteristics. Chandrasekhar, Uhlenbeck & Ornstein, Uhlenbeck & Ming, Rice, Doob. Included is Kac's Chauvenet-Prize winning Random Walk. Extensive bibliography lists 200 articles, up through 1953. 21 figures. 337pp. 6⅛ x 9¼. S262 Paperbound **$2.50**

THEORY OF PROBABILITY, William Burnside. Synthesis, expansion of individual papers presents numerous problems in classical probability, offering many original views succinctly, effectively. Game theory, cards, selections from groups; geometrical probability in such areas as suppositions as to probability of position of point on a line, points on surface of sphere, etc. Includes methods of approximation, theory of errors, direct calculation of probabilities, etc. Index. 136pp. 5⅜ x 8. S567 Paperbound **$1.00**

Statistics

ELEMENTARY STATISTICS, WITH APPLICATIONS IN MEDICINE AND THE BIOLOGICAL SCIENCES, F. E. Croxton. A sound introduction to statistics for anyone in the physical sciences, assuming no prior acquaintance and requiring only a modest knowledge of math. All basic formulas carefully explained and illustrated; all necessary reference tables included. From basic terms and concepts, the study proceeds to frequency distribution, linear, non-linear, and multiple correlation, skewness, kurtosis, etc. A large section deals with reliability and significance of statistical methods. Containing concrete examples from medicine and biology, this book will prove unusually helpful to workers in those fields who increasingly must evaluate, check, and interpret statistics. Formerly titled "Elementary Statistics with Applications in Medicine." 101 charts. 57 tables. 14 appendices. Index. iv + 376pp. 5⅜ x 8. S506 Paperbound **$2.00**

ANALYSIS & DESIGN OF EXPERIMENTS, H. B. Mann. Offers a method for grasping the analysis of variance and variance design within a short time. Partial contents: Chi-square distribution and analysis of variance distribution, matrices, quadratic forms, likelihood ration tests and tests of linear hypotheses, power of analysis, Galois fields, non-orthogonal data, interblock estimates, etc. 15pp. of useful tables. x + 195pp. 5 x 7⅜. S180 Paperbound **$1.45**

METHODS OF STATISTICS, L. H. C. Tippett. A classic in its field, this unusually complete systematic introduction to statistical methods begins at beginner's level and progresses to advanced levels for experimenters and poll-takers in all fields of statistical research. Supplies fundamental knowledge of virtually all elementary methods in use today by sociologists, psychologists, biologists, engineers, mathematicians, etc. Explains logical and mathematical basis of each method described, with examples for each section. Covers frequency distributions and measures, inference from random samples, errors in large samples, simple analysis of variance, multiple and partial regression and correlation, etc. 4th revised (1952) edition. 16 charts. 5 significance tables. 152-item bibliography. 96 tables. 22 figures. 395pp. 6 x 9.
S228 Clothbound **$7.50**

STATISTICS MANUAL, E. L. Crow, F. A. Davis, M. W. Maxfield. Comprehensive collection of classical, modern statistics methods, prepared under auspices of U. S. Naval Ordnance Test Station, China Lake, Calif. Many examples from ordnance will be valuable to workers in all fields. Emphasis is on use, with information on fiducial limits, sign tests, Chi-square runs, sensitivity, quality control, much more. "Well written . . . excellent reference work," Operations Research. Corrected edition of NAVORD Report 3360 NOTS 948. Introduction. Appendix of 32 tables, charts. Index. Bibliography. 95 illustrations. 306pp. 5⅜ x 8.
S599 Paperbound **$1.75**

Symbolic logic

AN INTRODUCTION TO SYMBOLIC LOGIC, Susanne K. Langer. Probably the clearest book ever written on symbolic logic for the philosopher, general scientist and layman. It will be particularly appreciated by those who have been rebuffed by other introductory works because of insufficient mathematical training. No special knowledge of mathematics is required. Starting with the simplest symbols and conventions, you are led to a remarkable grasp of the Boole-Schroeder and Russell-Whitehead systems clearly and quickly. PARTIAL CONTENTS: Study of forms, Essentials of logical structure, Generalization, Classes, The deductive system of classes, The algebra of logic, Abstraction of interpretation, Calculus of propositions, Assumptions of PRINCIPIA MATHEMATICA, Logistics, Logic of the syllogism, Proofs of theorems. "One of the clearest and simplest introductions to a subject which is very much alive. The style is easy, symbolism is introduced gradually, and the intelligent non-mathematician should have no difficulty in following the argument," MATHEMATICS GAZETTE. Revised, expanded second edition. Truth-value tables. 368pp. 5⅜ x 8.
S164 Paperbound **$1.85**

A SURVEY OF SYMBOLIC LOGIC: THE CLASSIC ALGEBRA OF LOGIC, C. I. Lewis. Classic survey of the field, comprehensive and thorough. Indicates content of major systems, alternative methods of procedure, and relation of these to the Boole-Schroeder algebra and to one another. Contains historical summary, as well as full proofs and applications of the classic, or Boole-Schroeder, algebra of logic. Discusses diagrams for the logical relations of classes, the two-valued algebra, propositional functions of two or more variables, etc. Chapters 5 and 6 of the original edition, which contained material not directly pertinent, have been omitted in this edition at the author's request. Appendix. Bibliography. Index. viii + 352pp. 5⅝ x 8⅜.
S643 Paperbound **$2.00**

INTRODUCTION TO SYMBOLIC LOGIC AND ITS APPLICATIONS, R. Carnap. One of the clearest, most comprehensive, and rigorous introductions to modern symbolic logic by perhaps its greatest living master. Symbolic languages are analyzed and one constructed. Applications to math (symbolic representation of axiom systems for set theory, natural numbers, real numbers, topology, Dedekind and Cantor explanations of continuity), physics (the general analysis of concepts of determination, causality, space-time-topology, based on Einstein), biology (symbolic representation of an axiom system for basic concepts). "A masterpiece," Zentralblatt für Mathematik und ihre Grenzgebiete. Over 300 exercises. 5 figures. Bibliography. Index. xvi + 241pp. 5⅜ x 8.
S453 Paperbound **$1.85**
Clothbound **$4.00**

SYMBOLIC LOGIC, C. I. Lewis, C. H. Langford. Probably the most cited book in symbolic logic, this is one of the fullest treatments of paradoxes. A wide coverage of the entire field of symbolic logic, plus considerable material that has not appeared elsewhere. Basic to the entire volume is the distinction between the logic of extensions and of intensions. Considerable emphasis is placed on converse substitution, while the matrix system presents the supposition of a variety of non-Aristotelian logics. It has especially valuable sections on strict limitations, existence of terms, 2-valued algebra and its extension to propositional functions, truth value systems, the matrix method, implication and deductibility, general theory of propositions, propositions of ordinary discourse, and similar topics. "Authoritative, most valuable," TIMES, London. Bibliography. 506pp. 5⅜ x 8. S170 Paperbound **$2.35**

THE ELEMENTS OF MATHEMATICAL LOGIC, Paul Rosenbloom. First publication in any language. This book is intended for readers who are mature mathematically, but have no previous training in symbolic logic. It does not limit itself to a single system, but covers the field as a whole. It is a development of lectures given at Lund University, Sweden, in 1948. Partial contents: Logic of classes, fundamental theorems, Boolean algebra, logic of propositions, logic of propositional functions, expressive languages, combinatory logics, development of mathematics within an object language, paradoxes, theorems of Post and Goedel, Church's theorem, and similar topics. iv + 214pp. 5⅜ x 8. S227 Paperbound **$1.45**

BOOKS EXPLAINING SCIENCE AND MATHEMATICS

General

WHAT IS SCIENCE?, Norman Campbell. This excellent introduction explains scientific method, role of mathematics, types of scientific laws. Contents: 2 aspects of science, science & nature, laws of science, discovery of laws, explanation of laws, measurement & numerical laws, applications of science. 192pp. 5⅜ x 8. S43 Paperbound **$1.25**

THE COMMON SENSE OF THE EXACT SCIENCES, W. K. Clifford. Introduction by James Newman, edited by Karl Pearson. For 70 years this has been a guide to classical scientific and mathematical thought. Explains with unusual clarity basic concepts, such as extension of meaning of symbols, characteristics of surface boundaries, properties of plane figures, vectors, Cartesian method of determining position, etc. Long preface by Bertrand Russell. Bibliography of Clifford. Corrected, 130 diagrams redrawn. 249pp. 5⅜ x 8. T61 Paperbound **$1.60**

SCIENCE THEORY AND MAN, Erwin Schrödinger. This is a complete and unabridged reissue of SCIENCE AND THE HUMAN TEMPERAMENT plus an additional essay: "What is an Elementary Particle?" Nobel laureate Schrödinger discusses such topics as nature of scientific method, the nature of science, chance and determinism, science and society, conceptual models for physical entities, elementary particles and wave mechanics. Presentation is popular and may be followed by most people with little or no scientific training. "Fine practical preparation for a time when laws of nature, human institutions . . . are undergoing a critical examination without parallel," Waldemar Kaempffert, N. Y. TIMES. 192pp. 5⅜ x 8. T428 Paperbound **$1.35**

FADS AND FALLACIES IN THE NAME OF SCIENCE, Martin Gardner. Examines various cults, quack systems, frauds, delusions which at various times have masqueraded as science. Accounts of hollow-earth fanatics like Symmes; Velikovsky and wandering planets; Hoerbiger; Bellamy and the theory of multiple moons; Charles Fort; dowsing, pseudoscientific methods for finding water, ores, oil. Sections on naturopathy, iridiagnosis, zone therapy, food fads, etc. Analytical accounts of Wilhelm Reich and orgone sex energy; L. Ron Hubbard and Dianetics; A. Korzybski and General Semantics; many others. Brought up to date to include Bridey Murphy, others. Not just a collection of anecdotes, but a fair, reasoned appraisal of eccentric theory. Formerly titled IN THE NAME OF SCIENCE. Preface. Index. x + 384pp. 5⅜ x 8. T394 Paperbound **$1.50**

A DOVER SCIENCE SAMPLER, edited by George Barkin. 64-page book, sturdily bound, containing excerpts from over 20 Dover books, explaining science. Edwin Hubble, George Sarton, Ernst Mach, A. d'Abro, Galileo, Newton, others, discussing island universes, scientific truth, biological phenomena, stability in bridges, etc. Copies limited; no more than 1 to a customer, FREE

POPULAR SCIENTIFIC LECTURES, Hermann von Helmholtz. Helmholtz was a superb expositor as well as a scientist of genius in many areas. The seven essays in this volume are models of clarity, and even today they rank among the best general descriptions of their subjects ever written. "The Physiological Causes of Harmony in Music" was the first significant physiological explanation of musical consonance and dissonance. Two essays, "On the Interaction of Natural Forces" and "On the Conservation of Force," were of great importance in the history of science, for they firmly established the principle of the conservation of energy. Other lectures include "On the Relation of Optics to Painting," "On Recent Progress in the Theory of Vision," "On Goethe's Scientific Researches," and "On the Origin and Significance of Geometrical Axioms." Selected and edited with an introduction by Professor Morris Kline. xii + 286pp. 5⅜ x 8½. T799 Paperbound **$1.45**

BOOKS EXPLAINING SCIENCE AND MATHEMATICS

Physics

CONCERNING THE NATURE OF THINGS, Sir William Bragg. Christmas lectures delivered at the Royal Society by Nobel laureate. Why a spinning ball travels in a curved track; how uranium is transmuted to lead, etc. Partial contents: atoms, gases, liquids, crystals, metals, etc. No scientific background needed; wonderful for intelligent child. 32pp. of photos, 57 figures. xii + 232pp. 5⅜ x 8. T31 Paperbound **$1.50**

THE RESTLESS UNIVERSE, Max Born. New enlarged version of this remarkably readable account by a Nobel laureate. Moving from sub-atomic particles to universe, the author explains in very simple terms the latest theories of wave mechanics. Partial contents: air and its relatives, electrons & ions, waves & particles, electronic structure of the atom, nuclear physics. Nearly 1000 illustrations, including 7 animated sequences. 325pp. 6 x 9. T412 Paperbound **$2.00**

TEACH YOURSELF MECHANICS, P. Abbott. The lever, centre of gravity, parallelogram of force, friction, acceleration, Newton's laws of motion, machines, specific gravity, gas, liquid pressure, much more. 280 problems, solutions. Tables. 163 illus. 271pp. 6⅞ x 4¼.
Clothbound **$2.00**

MATTER & MOTION, James Clerk Maxwell, This excellent exposition begins with simple particles and proceeds gradually to physical systems beyond complete analysis: motion, force, properties of centre of mass of material system, work, energy, gravitation, etc. Written with all Maxwell's original insights and clarity. Notes by E. Larmor. 17 diagrams. 178pp. 5⅜ x 8.
S188 Paperbound **$1.35**

SOAP BUBBLES, THEIR COLOURS AND THE FORCES WHICH MOULD THEM, C. V. Boys. Only complete edition, half again as much material as any other. Includes Boys' hints on performing his experiments, sources of supply. Dozens of lucid experiments show complexities of liquid films, surface tension, etc. Best treatment ever written. Introduction. 83 illustrations. Color plate. 202pp. 5⅜ x 8. T542 Paperbound **95¢**

MATTER & LIGHT, THE NEW PHYSICS, L. de Broglie. Non-technical papers by a Nobel laureate explain electromagnetic theory, relativity, matter, light and radiation, wave mechanics, quantum physics, philosophy of science. Einstein, Planck, Bohr, others explained so easily that no mathematical training is needed for all but 2 of the 21 chapters. Unabridged. Index. 300pp. 5⅜ x 8. T35 Paperbound **$1.85**

SPACE AND TIME, Emile Borel. An entirely non-technical introduction to relativity, by world-renowned mathematician, Sorbonne professor. (Notes on basic mathematics are included separately.) This book has never been surpassed for insight, and extraordinary clarity of thought, as it presents scores of examples, analogies, arguments, illustrations, which explain such topics as: difficulties due to motion; gravitation a force of inertia; geodesic lines; wave-length and difference of phase; x-rays and crystal structure; the special theory of relativity; and much more. Indexes. 4 appendixes. 15 figures. xvi + 243pp. 5⅜ x 8.
T592 Paperbound **$1.45**

BOOKS EXPLAINING SCIENCE AND MATHEMATICS

Astronomy

THE FRIENDLY STARS, Martha Evans Martin. This engaging survey of stellar lore and science is a well-known classic, which has introduced thousands to the fascinating world of stars and other celestial bodies. Descriptions of Capella, Sirius, Arcturus, Vega, Polaris, etc.—all the important stars, with informative discussions of rising and setting of stars, their number, names, brightness, distances, etc. in a non-technical, highly readable style. Also: double stars, constellations, clusters—concentrating on stars and formations visible to the naked eye. New edition, revised (1963) by D. H. Menzel, Director Harvard Observatory. 23 diagrams by Prof. Ching-Sung Yu. Foreword by D. H. Menzel and W. W. Morgan. 2 Star Charts. Index. xii + 147pp. 5⅜ x 8½. T1099 Paperbound **$1.00**

AN ELEMENTARY SURVEY OF CELESTIAL MECHANICS, Y. Ryabov. Elementary exposition of gravitational theory and celestial mechanics. Historical introduction and coverage of basic principles, including: the elliptic, the orbital plane, the 2- and 3-body problems, the discovery of Neptune, planetary rotation, the length of the day, the shapes of galaxies, satellites (detailed treatment of Sputnik I), etc. First American reprinting of successful Russian popular exposition. Elementary algebra and trigonometry helpful, but not necessary; presentation chiefly verbal. Appendix of theorem proofs. 58 figures. 165pp. 5⅜ x 8.
T756 Paperbound **$1.25**

THE SKY AND ITS MYSTERIES, E. A. Beet. One of most lucid books on mysteries of universe; deals with astronomy from earliest observations to latest theories of expansion of universe, source of stellar energy, birth of planets, origin of moon craters, possibility of life on other planets. Discusses effects of sunspots on weather; distances, ages of several stars; master plan of universe; methods and tools of astronomers; much more. "Eminently readable book," London Times. Extensive bibliography. Over 50 diagrams. 12 full-page plates, fold-out star map. Introduction. Index. 5¼ x 7½. T627 Clothbound **$3.50**

THE REALM OF THE NEBULAE, E. Hubble. One of the great astronomers of our time records his formulation of the concept of "island universes," and its impact on astronomy. Such topics are covered as the velocity-distance relation; classification, nature, distances, general field of nebulae; cosmological theories; nebulae in the neighborhood of the Milky Way. 39 photos of nebulae, nebulae clusters, spectra of nebulae, and velocity distance relations shown by spectrum comparison. "One of the most progressive lines of astronomical research," The Times (London). New introduction by A. Sandage. 55 illustrations. Index. iv + 201pp. 5⅜ x 8. S455 Paperbound **$1.50**

GEOLOGY, GEOGRAPHY, METEOROLOGY

PRINCIPLES OF STRATIGRAPHY, A. W. Grabau. Classic of 20th century geology, unmatched in scope and comprehensiveness. Nearly 600 pages cover the structure and origins of every kind of sedimentary, hydrogenic, oceanic, pyroclastic, atmoclastic, hydroclastic, marine hydroclastic, and bioclastic rock; metamorphism; erosion; etc. Includes also the constitution of the atmosphere; morphology of oceans, rivers, glaciers; volcanic activities; faults and earthquakes; and fundamental principles of paleontology (nearly 200 pages). New introduction by Prof. M. Kay, Columbia U. 1277 bibliographical entries. 264 diagrams. Tables, maps, etc. Two volume set. Total of xxxii + 1185pp. 5⅜ x 8.
S686 Vol I Paperbound **$2.50**
S687 Vol II Paperbound **$2.50**
The set **$5.00**

TREATISE ON SEDIMENTATION, William H. Twenhofel. A milestone in the history of geology, this two-volume work, prepared under the auspices of the United States Research Council, contains practically everything known about sedimentation up to 1932. Brings together all the findings of leading American and foreign geologists and geographers and has never been surpassed for completeness, thoroughness of description, or accuracy of detail. Vol. 1 discusses the sources and production of sediments, their transportation, deposition, diagenesis, and lithification. Also modification of sediments by organisms and topographical, climatic, etc. conditions which contribute to the alteration of sedimentary processes. 220 pages deal with products of sedimentation: minerals, limestones, dolomites, coals, etc. Vol. 2 continues the examination of products such as gypsum and saline residues, silica, strontium, manganese, etc. An extensive exposition of structures, textures and colors of sediments: stratification, cross-lamination, ripple mark, oolitic and pisolitic textures, etc. Chapters on environments or realms of sedimentation and field and laboratory techniques are also included. Indispensable to modern-day geologists and students. Index. List of authors cited. 1733-item bibliography. 121 diagrams. Total of xxxiii + 926pp. 5⅜ x 8½.
Vol. I: S950 Paperbound **$2.50**
Vol. II: S951 Paperbound **$2.50**
Two volume set Paperbound **$5.00**

THE EVOLUTION OF THE IGNEOUS ROCKS, N. L. Bowen. Invaluable serious introduction applies techniques of physics and chemistry to explain igneous rock diversity in terms of chemical composition and fractional crystallization. Discusses liquid immiscibility in silicate magmas, crystal sorting, liquid lines of descent, fractional resorption of complex minerals, petrogenesis, etc. Of prime importance to geologists & mining engineers, also to physicists, chemists working with high temperatures and pressures. "Most important," TIMES, London. 3 indexes. 263 bibliographic notes. 82 figures. xviii + 334pp. 5⅜ x 8. S311 Paperbound **$2.25**

INTERNAL CONSTITUTION OF THE EARTH, edited by **Beno Gutenberg.** Completely revised. Brought up-to-date, reset. Prepared for the National Research Council this is a complete & thorough coverage of such topics as earth origins, continent formation, nature & behavior of the earth's core, petrology of the crust, cooling forces in the core, seismic & earthquake material, gravity, elastic constants, strain characteristics and similar topics. "One is filled with admiration . . . a high standard . . . there is no reader who will not learn something from this book," London, Edinburgh, Dublin, Philosophic Magazine. Largest bibliography in print: 1127 classified items. Indexes. Tables of constants. 43 diagrams. 439pp. 6⅛ x 9¼.
S414 Paperbound **$3.00**

HYDROLOGY, edited by **Oscar E. Meinzer.** Prepared for the National Research Council. Detailed complete reference library on precipitation, evaporation, snow, snow surveying, glaciers, lakes, infiltration, soil moisture, ground water, runoff, drought, physical changes produced by water, hydrology of limestone terranes, etc. Practical in application, especially valuable for engineers. 24 experts have created "the most up-to-date, most complete treatment of the subject," AM. ASSOC. of PETROLEUM GEOLOGISTS. Bibliography. Index. 165 illustrations. xi + 712pp. 6⅛ x 9¼. S191 Paperbound **$3.50**

SNOW CRYSTALS, W. A. Bentley and W. J. Humphreys. Over 200 pages of Bentley's famous microphotographs of snow flakes—the product of painstaking, methodical work at his Jericho, Vermont studio. The pictures, which also include plates of frost, glaze and dew on vegetation, spider webs, windowpanes; sleet; graupel or soft hail, were chosen both for their scientific interest and their aesthetic qualities. The wonder of nature's diversity is exhibited in the intricate, beautiful patterns of the snow flakes. Introductory text by W. J. Humphreys. Selected bibliography. 2,453 illustrations. 224pp. 8 x 10¼. T287 Paperbound **$2.95**

PHYSICS OF THE AIR, W. J. Humphreys. A very thorough coverage of classical materials and theories in meteorology . . . written by one of this century's most highly respected physical meteorologists. Contains the standard account in English of atmospheric optics. 5 main sections: Mechanics and Thermodynamics of the Atmosphere, Atmospheric Electricity and Auroras, Meteorological Acoustics, Atmospheric Optics, and Factors of Climatic Control. Under these headings, topics covered are: theoretical relations between temperature, pressure, and volume in the atmosphere; composition, pressure, and density; circulation; evaporation and condensation; fog, clouds, thunderstorms, lightning; aurora polaris; principal ice-age theories; etc. New preface by Prof. Julius London. 226 illustrations. Index. xviii + 676pp. 5⅜ x 8½.
S1044 Paperbound **$3.00**